THE
Best Divisions
FOR
Knowledge
OF THE
Regions

The Center for Muslim Contribution to Civilization

THE
Best Divisions
FOR
Knowledge
OF THE
Regions

Aḥsan al-Taqāsīm fī Maʿrifat al-Aqālīm

Al-Muqaddasī

Translated by Professor Basil Collins

Reviewed by Dr Mohammad Hamid Alta'i

Garnet PUBLISHING

THE BEST DIVISIONS FOR KNOWLEDGE OF THE REGIONS

Published by
Garnet Publishing Limited
8 Southern Court
South Street
Reading
RG1 4QS
UK

Quotations from the Holy Qurʾān follow the text of *The Bounteous Koran:*
A Translation of Meaning and Commentary by Dr M.M. Khatib. Authorized by
Al-Ahzar 1984. London: Macmillan Press, 1986

The front endpapers show the title page and opening of Manuscript B; these illustrations and
maps I–XIX herein from MS. Sprenger 5 – Ahlwardt 6034 are reproduced by kind permission
of the Staatsbibliothek Preussischer Kulturbesitz, Berlin, Orientabteilung.

The back endpapers show the text of the poem that ends Manuscript C; this illustration and
map XX herein from Ayasofya, 2971 m. are reproduced by kind permission of T.C.
Basbakanlik, Kültür Müstesarligi, Süleymaniye Kütüphanesi Müdürlügü, Istanbul,
Turkey. Translation of the poem is on pp. 403–4 below.

ISBN 1 85964 136 9

First Edition 1994
First Paperback Edition 2001

British Library Cataloguing-in-Publication Data
A catalogue record for this book is available from the British Library

Jacket design by David Rose
Typeset by Samantha Barden

Printed in Lebanon

CONTENTS

List of Maps   vii
Foreword   ix
About this Series   xi
Center for Muslim Contribution to Civilization: Board of Trustees   xiii
Center for Muslim Contribution to Civilization: Board   xiv
Preface   xv
Introduction   xxi

THE BEST DIVISIONS FOR KNOWLEDGE OF THE REGIONS   1
   An Account of the Seas and Rivers   9
   An Account of Names and their Diversities   23
   An Account of the Distinctive Features of the Regions   30
   An Account of the Madhāhib [Schools of Islamic Law] and the
      Dhimma [Free Non-Muslim Subjects]   34

NARRATIVE OF MY ACTUAL EXPERIENCES   41
   Report of Places on which Accounts Differ   44
   Abridgement for the Use of Jurists   46
   An Account of the Climates of the World and the Position of the *Qibla*   53

THE EMPIRE OF AL-ISLĀM   59
   The Peninsula of the Arabs   63
   The Region of Al-ʿIrāq   95
   The Region of Aqūr (Al-Jazīra) [Upper Mesopotamia]   115
   The Region of Al-Shām (Syria)   128
   The Region of Misr (Egypt)   163
   The Region of the Maghrib (Northern Africa West of Egypt; Andalusia)   183
   An Account of the Desert of the Bedouin   207

AN ACCOUNT OF THE EIGHT REGIONS OF THE NON-ARAB PEOPLES   215
   The Region of Al-Mashriq (The Eastern Territories)   218
     The Province of Haytal (Right Bank of Jayhūn)   219
       An Account of the Jayhūn River and the Settlements on it   233
       An Account of the Crossing points and of the Distributaries of
         the River (Jayhūn)   239
     The Territory of the Khurāsān side of the River   239
   The Region of Al-Daylam (Lowlands and Highlands of Gīlān)   287
   The Region of Al-Rihāb (Ādharbayjān—Armenia)   303
   The Region of Al-Jibāl ("The Mountains": wide Mountain area
      WNW Irān—ENE ʿIrāq)   313

The Region of Khūzistān (Littoral Lowlands of Īrān at Head of Arabian Gulf)   329
The Region of Fārs (Southwest Īrān)   344
The Region of Kirmān (South Central Īrān)   372
The Region of Al-Sind (Plain of Lower Indus)   384
The Desert that Lies Among these Regions   394

Appendix: English keys to the Arabic maps   405
Index   425

MAPS

Map I: The Persian Sea   10
Map II: Bahr al-Rūm   14
Map III: Al-Kaʿba   54
Map IV: Arabia   65
Map V: Al-ʿIrāq   96
Map VI: Al-Jazīra   116
Map VII: Al-Shām   131
Map VIII: Misr   164
Map IX: Al-Maghrib   184
Map X: The Arabian Desert   208
Map XI: Mā warāʾa al-Nahr   220
Map XII: Khurāsān   242
Map XIII: Tabar Daylam   288
Map XIV: Ādharbayjān   304
Map XV: Jibāl Al-Daylam   314
Map XVI: Khūzistān   331
Map XVII: Fārs   345
Map XVIII: Kirmān   373
Map XIX: Al-Sind   385
Map XX: The Persian Desert   395
Appendix: English keys to the Arabic maps   405

In the Name of God, the Beneficent, the Merciful

FOREWORD

THE interrelationship and interaction of human cultures and civilizations has made the contributions of each the common heritage of men in all ages and all places. Early Muslim scholars were able to communicate with their Western counterparts through contacts made during the Crusades; at Muslim universities and centers of learning in Muslim Spain (al-Andalus, or Andalusia) and Sicily to which many European students went for education; and at the universities and centers of learning in Europe itself (such as Salerno, Padua, Montpellier, Paris, and Oxford), where Islamic works were taught in Latin translations. Among the Muslim scholars well-known in the centers of learning throughout the world were al-Rāzī (Rhazes), Ibn Sīnā (Avicenna), Ibn Rushd (Averroes), al Khwārizmī and Ibn Khaldūn. Muslim scholars such as these and others produced original works in many fields. Many of them possessed encyclopaedic knowledge and distinguished themselves in many disparate fields of knowledge.

In view of this, the Center for Muslim Contribution to Civilization was established in order to acquaint non-Muslims with the contributions Islam has given to human civilization as a whole. The Great Books of Islamic Civilization Project attempts to cover the first 800 years of Islam, or what may be called Islam's Classical Period. This project aims at making available in English a wide selection of works representative of Islamic civilization in all its diversity. It is made up of translations of original Arabic works that were produced in the formative centuries of Islam, and is meant to serve the needs of a potentially large readership. Not only the specialist and scholar, but the non-specialist with an interest in Islam and its cultural heritage will be able to benefit from the series. Together, the works should serve as a rich source for the study of the early periods of Islamic thought.

In selecting the books for the series, the Center took into account all major areas of Islamic intellectual pursuit that could be represented. Thus the series includes works not only on better-known subjects such as law, theology, jurisprudence, history and politics, but also on subjects such as literature, medicine, astronomy, optics and geography. The specific criteria, used to select individual books, were these: that a book should give a faithful and comprehensive account of its field; and that it should be an authoritative source. The reader thus has at his disposal virtually a whole library of informative and enlightening works.

Each book in the series has been translated by a qualified scholar and reviewed by another expert. While the style of one translation will naturally differ from another, the translators have endeavored, to the extent it was possible, to make the works accessible to the common reader. As a rule, the use of footnotes has been kept to a minimum, though a more extensive use of them was necessitated in some cases.

This series is presented in the hope that it will contribute to a greater under-standing in the West of the cultural and intellectual heritage of Islam and will therefore provide an important means towards greater understanding of today's world.

May God Help Us!

Muhammad bin Hamad Al-Thani
Chairman of the Board of Trustees

ABOUT THIS SERIES

THIS series of Arabic works, made available in English translation, represents an outstanding selection of important Islamic studies in a variety of fields of knowledge. The works selected for inclusion in this series meet specific criteria. They are recognized by Muslim scholars as being early and important in their fields, as works whose importance is broadly recognized by international scholars, and as having had a genuinely significant impact on the development of human culture.

Readers will therefore see that this series includes a variety of works in the purely Islamic sciences, such as Qur'ān, ḥadīth, theology, prophetic traditions (sunna), and jurisprudence (fiqh). Also represented will be books by Muslim scientists on medicine, astronomy, geography, physics, chemistry, horticulture, and other fields.

The work of translating these texts has been entrusted to a group of professors in the Islamic and Western worlds who are recognized authorities in their fields. It has been deemed appropriate, in order to ensure accuracy and fluency, that two persons, one with Arabic as his mother tongue and another with English as his mother tongue, should participate together in the translation and revision of each text.

This series is distinguished from other similar intercultural projects by its distinctive objectives and methodology. These works will fill a genuine gap in the library of human thought. They will prove extremely useful to all those with an interest in Islamic culture, its interaction with Western thought, and its impact on culture throughout the world. They will, it is hoped, fulfil an important rôle in enhancing world understanding at a time when there is such evident and urgent need for the development of peaceful coexistence.

This series is published by the Center for Muslim Contribution to Civilization, which serves as a research centre under the patronage of H.H. Sheikh Hamad bin Khalifa al-Thani, Amir of Qatar. It is directed by a Board of Trustees chaired by H.E. Sheikh Muhammad bin Hamad al-Thani, the former Minister of Education of Qatar. The Board is comprised of a group of prominent scholars. These include H.E. Dr Abul-Wafa al-Taftazani*, Deputy Rector of Cairo University, and Dr Yusuf al-Qaradhawi, Director of the Sira and Sunna Research Center. At its inception the Center was directed by the late Dr Muhammad Ibrahim Kazim, former Rector of Qatar University, who established its initial objectives.

The Center was until recently directed by Dr Kamal Nagi, the Foreign Cultural Relations Advisor of the Ministry of Education of Qatar. He was assisted by a Board comprising a number of academicians of Qatar University, in addition to

---

* Died 1994, may Allāh have mercy on him.

a consultative committee chaired by Dr Ezzeddin Ibrahim, former Rector of the University of the United Arab Emirates. A further committee acting on behalf of the Center has been the prominent university professors who act under the chairmanship of Dr Raji Rammuny, Professor of Arabic at the University of Michigan. This committee is charged with making known, in Europe and in America, the books selected for translation, and in selecting and enlisting properly qualified university professors, orientalists and students of Islamic studies to undertake the work of translation and revision, as well as overseeing the publication process.

PREFACE

The work that follows herein is a rendition into English of a geographical treatise written in Arabic in the tenth century of our era. The Arabic title of the treatise, *Ahsan al-Taqāsīm fī Maʿrifat al-Aqālīm*, may be rendered in English, *The Best Divisions for Knowledge of the Regions*; its author is Shams al-Dīn Abū ʿAbd Allāh Muhammad bin Ahmad bin Abī Bakr al-Bannāʾ al-Shāmī al-Muqaddasī al-maʿrūf bi [known as] al-Bashshārī, now usually referred to simply as al-Muqaddasī, that is, "the man from Jerusalem."

The manuscript source of this work consists of two important apographs in Arabic, of which one, MS. Sprenger 5 (Ahlwardt No. 6034)—herein called MS. B(erolinense)—resides in the Staatsbibliothek Preussischer Kulturbesitz, Orientabteilung, Berlin; the other, Aya Sofia No. 2971 *bis*—herein called MS. C(onstantinopolitanum) is in Süleymaniye Kütüphanesi, Istanbul. It is fitting that here, at the outset, I acknowledge the generous cooperation of the custodians of these two MSS, in their giving me access to their content; and in granting permission to reproduce herein some illustrative material, including the maps, from these MSS. A copy of MS. C made in the middle of the nineteenth century CE, is Cod. Or. 2063 in the Bibliotheek der Rijksuniversiteit in Leiden. MS. C was made in the year 1259 CE, which fairly well corresponds with the year 658 AH of the Muslim lunar calendar; this latter begins the era from the migration, or hijra, of the Prophet Muhammad from Makka to Madīna in the year 622 CE. In the text, years are given by the Muslim calendar; equivalents for the CE are added herein, in the pattern AH/CE. The copying of MS. B may be attributed to the end of the fifteenth century CE, and it lacks the last folio. From the two apographs B and C Michael Jan de Goeje derived a text, published in 1877 (revised 1906—pp. vii + 498) as the third volume of *Bibliotheca Geographorum Arabicorum* (Leiden: E.J. Brill). This published Arabic text (*BGA III*), on which the present rendition is primarily based, relies mainly on the content of MS. B; de Goeje supplies additional or variant readings from MS. C. In the preparation for the rendition given here, the reading of de Goeje's text on the one side was compared with those of the apographs, MS. B and MS. C, on the other, for some three-fourths of the printed text: the comparison attests the great fidelity of the text to the readings of the apographs. MS. B contains nineteen maps, MS. C, fifteen; de Goeje's text does not include any, from either MS.

The Berlin codex may represent a redaction attributable to the year 378 AH/988 CE; MS. C, though lacking some sections found in MS. B, has material not found in the latter, and offers a text completed, perhaps, in the year 375/985. Internal evidence strongly suggests the precedence of the version represented by MS. C; it remains, however, that both the priority of composition between these versions, and the suggested respective dates of their completion, are uncertain, but both certainly date from within the last two decades of the tenth century CE; de Goeje discusses the possibilities upon the possibilities of these questions in the 'Praefatio' to volume IV (1879) of the *Bibliotheca Geographorum Arabicorum*.

Some sections of al-Muqaddasī's work, based on de Goeje's text, have appeared in translation, as follows:

Gildemeister, J. *Beiträge zur Palästinakunde aus arabischen Quellen: Mukaddasī, ZDPV* (1884), pp. 143-172; 215-226—a German translation, somewhat inadequate, of the section on al-Shām (Syria), *BGA III*, pp. 151-192; followed (pp. 226-230) by some brief passages from other sections of the work.

Le Strange, Guy. *Description of Syria including Palestine, by Mukaddasi*. London, 1896—a well annotated translation into English of *BGA III*, pp. 151-192; with map and diagrams.

Ranking, G.S.A., and Azoo, R.F. *Ahsanu—T—Taqāsim Fi Ma'rifat—l Aqālim known as al-Muqaddasī*. Bibliotheca Indica, Fascicles I-IV. Calcutta: 1897, 1899, 1901, 1910—a translation into English, well annotated, of *BGA III*, pp. 1-202.

Pellat, Charles. *Description de l'Occident Musulman au IVe/Xe siècle, par al-Muqaddasī—Texte arabe et traduction française*: Bibliothèque arabe-francaise N⁰ IX. Alger, 1950—a well-annotated translation into French, with facing Arabic text, of *BGA III*, pp. 215-248.

Miquel, André. *Ahsan at-Taqāsim fi Ma'rifat al-Aqālim* (La meilleure répartition pour la connaissance des provinces). Damas, 1963.—a translation into French of *BGA III* pp. 1-24; 30-47; 57-66; 151-192—illustrated with maps and diagrams; extensively and minutely annotated; indexes and glossary.

Collins, Basil Anthony. *Al-Muqaddasī: The Man and His Work: With Selected Passages Translated from the Arabic*. Ann Arbor: The University of Michigan— Michigan Geographical Publication N⁰ 10, 1974. Passages comprise English translation of assorted representative geographic sections of *BGA III*.

One who works with medieval Muslim geographers almost inevitably becomes indebted, as am I, to Konrad Miller's *Mappae Arabicae: Arabische Welt-und Länderkarten des 9-13 Jahrhunderts*. 6 volumes. [Stuttgart: 1926-31]. (Auszugsweise herausgegeben von Heinz Gaube. 3 volumes [Wiesbaden: Dr. Ludwig Reichert Verlag, 1986]).

In the rendition into English that follows here, the numbers in the margins correspond to the pagination of de Goeje's Arabic text; the variation in the amounts of copy per page of de Goeje's text derives from the inclusion, at the foot of every page, of varying amounts of additional discourse, or of variant readings, from MS. C, together with certain readings, and other diplomatic and critical minutiae which are of purely scholarly interest. Except for the additional discourse from MS. C, this footnote material is deemed to be but of little use to the general reader, for whose perusal the series of "Great Books of Islamic Civilization" is intended; it accordingly is not included here except for the tacit incorporation into the English rendition of an occasional textual emendation, or a phrasal expression from MS. C. The additional extended discourse from MS. C has been included *in loco*.

The absence here of textual, historical, bibliographical and other addenda of the like, is deliberate, such sediment distracting the reader, should he notice it at all. Moreover, both the general reader and the specialist are now very well served by a great number of studies and volumes of reference, relevant to the work in hand. Preeminent among these is *The Encyclopedia of Islam: New Edition (EI²)* [Leiden: E.J. Brill, 1960—], now well advanced, and with an *Index* covering volumes I-VI. *An Historical Atlas of Islam*, edited by William C. Brice [Leiden: E.J. Brill, 1981], supplements *EI²*. The single-volume *Dictionary of Islam* (1885), by Thomas Patrick Hughes, is brimfull of material succinctly presented; recent reprints in Lahore, and in the U.S.A. An ever-flowing cornucopia of studies continues to enrich and challenge the understanding of western readers, prompted to inquire into the temporal, spiritual, and cultural world that is background of the subject of al-Muqaddasī's treatise.

It is not feasible to give here even a moderately brief listing of articles, books, and authors that could interest, inform, and even delight the reader; however, even though at risk of seeming invidiousness, the following are recommended:

Palestine under the Moslems [London: 1890]; and *The Lands of the Eastern Caliphate* [Cambridge University Press: 1905, and reprints], both by Guy Le Strange;

La géographie humaine du monde musulman jusqu'au milieu du IIᵉ siècle [Paris: 1967]; and *L'Islam et sa civilisation VIIᵉ-XXᵉ siècle* [Paris: 1968], both by André Miquel;

A History of the Arab Peoples, by Albert Hourani. [Harvard University Press: 1991];

Dictionnaire Détaillé des Noms de Vêtements chez les Arabes, by Reinhart Pieter Anne Dozy. [Amsterdam: 1845; reprint, Bayrūt: Librairie du Liban, 1969]; also the article "LIBĀS" in *EI²*, Vol. V;

La Civilisation de l'Islam Classique, par Dominique et Janine Sourdel. [Paris: Arthaud, 1968];

The Renaissance of Islam, by Adam Mez (translated from German). [Patna: 1937].

The Cambridge History of Islam: two volumes. P.M. Holt, Anne K.S. Lambton, Bernard Lewis, eds. [Cambridge: At The University Press, 1970].

The History of Cartography: Volume Two, Book One—Cartography in the Traditional Islamic and South Asian Societies. J.B. Harley, David Woodward, *et al.*, eds. [Chicago: The University of Chicago Press, 1992].

The following three works provide many details of circumstance and environment that bring to life the culture and physical milieu within which al-Muqaddasī moved, about eight hundred years before they were written; apart from this relevance to our author, they are all notable and rewarding in their own right:

An Account of the Manners and Customs of the Modern Egyptians, by Edward William Lane. [London: 1846, and many reprints];
Personal Narrative of a Pilgrimage to al-Madinah and Meccah, by Richard R. Burton. [London: 1893; reprint New York: Dover Publications, Inc.: 1964].
Travels in Arabia Deserta, by Charles M. Doughty. [London: third ed., Jonathan Cape Ltd., 1936; reprint New York: Dover Publications, Inc., 1979].

The following few works may be of special interest to the reader:

The Hajj Today: A Survey of the Contemporary Makkah Pilgrimage, by David Edwin Long. [Albany, N.Y.: State University of New York Press, 1979].
Lost in the Crowd, by Jalāl āl-ē-Ahmad. [Washington D.C.: Three Continents Press, 1985].
Islamische Masse und Gewichte, by Walter Hinz. [Leiden: E.J. Brill, 1955].
The Northern Hijaz in the writings of the Arab Geographes: 800-1150. by Abdallah al-Wohaibi. [Beirut: Al-Risalah Ets., 1973]

For the transliteration of the Arabic into Roman characters, no one system has general acceptance. The system used here recognizes that many of the letters of the Arabic alphabet have appropriate counterparts in the Roman, as sounded in English usage. However, Arabic phonology differentiates among members of a few small groups of sounds that enter the untrained ear as much the same sound. In representing some of these groups here, it seemed unnecessary, and indeed undesirable, to add differentiating diacritical marks to the Roman letters, in an attempt to indicate the presence of differences elusive to the unaccustomed ear; hence one Roman letter serves here to represent each such group. Except for the use of this expedient, the present rendition mostly uses the transliteration of proper names, and of some other words, following the practice of *EI*[2]. Remarkably, toponymic orthography, in Brice's *Historical Atlas of Islam*, in a number of instances is not uniform within the *Atlas* itself, and, in some cases, not in accord with the usage of *EI*[2]. In a number of instances, too, al-Muqaddasī gives place-names two or three slightly variant forms; just one spelling has been attempted in the text herewith for each such instance.

The following rendition is indebted in different ways to the works mentioned above, and to many more; and the acknowledgement evokes for me the pleasant recollection of my reading the Arabic text of al-Muqaddasī, from time to time with good friends. I read the text first, in its entirety, with Dr. Burhān M. al-ʿAjouz, of Bayrūt; later with Dr. ʿĀdil M. al-Aseer of Palestine. I read much of it, too, with Walīd ʿAbd al-Rahmān Krōnful, of Bayrūt, and ʿIsa ʿAlī of Kuwayt. Protocol for the preparation for publication of the "Great Books of Islamic Civilization" requires the reading by a reviewer of the English translations of the texts being made ready for publication, to ensure the sense of the Arabic text is, in fact, translated. In this I had the cooperation of Dr. Muhammad Hamīd al-Tā'i of Baghdād; he had all but completed his review of the material from MS. B in the de Goeje Arabic text, when the invasions in the Middle East occurred in the Fall of 1990, making ordinary postal exchange between here and there extremely difficult. Dr. Nadīm Bītār of Lebanon agreed to review with me the readings from MS. C.

The personnel of the Division of Interlibrary Loans here have been, throughout, unstinting in their cooperation in gaining me access to much rare material to be consulted in the preparation of the following work.

I gratefully acknowledge, also, the remarkable expertise of Ms. Theresa Bach in her typing of all the many drafts of this demanding MS; and I am indebted, too, to my Department which put space and other facilities at my disposal during the work in process.

Basil A. Collins
The Department of Geography and Planning
The University of Toledo, Ohio
January 1995

INTRODUCTION

Muhammad, the Prophet of al-Islām, the human vessel, the last through whom God communicated the divine will to man, died in the year 11/632. Within two decades of his death his followers, the Muslims, had carried Islām, the expression of the divine revelation given to him through the Holy *Qur'ān*, throughout the length and breadth of the Arabian Peninsula, along the north coast of Africa to beyond Khalīj Surt (Gulf of Sirte), northward along the east coast of Bahr Buntus (the Black Sea) and part of the west shore of Bahr al-Khazar (the Caspian Sea), eastward to Kabul and to the Sulaymān Range. Within eighty years of the Prophet's death they had, in al-Andalus (the Iberian Peninsula), reached north beyond the mouth of Wādī Tajū (River Tagus), triumphed as far as Wādī Duwayro (Duero), and the Wādī Ibruh (Ebro) to the neighborhood of Saraqusta (Saragossa). By the year 93/711 the realm of Islām stretched from the Iberian Peninsula in the West to beyond the left bank of the Indus River in the East, and into Central Asia. Over the three and one half centuries between the Prophet's death, and the latter half of the IV/X century when the geographer al-Muqaddasī traveled and wrote, the peoples of this realm, of different traditions, languages, environments, had achieved a factionally diversified unity under the faith of Islām. In this period the seat of governance of the Islamic community had been moved from al-Madīna to Dimashq (Damascus), thence to Baghdād, and, by the time of al-Muqaddasī, the political realm stretching from the Atlantic east to beyond the Indus River had dissolved into a number of independent local dynasties that pursued military, political, and economic fates and fortunes of their own. Yet the Faith remained to identify a realm, distinct thus from the non-Muslim portion of the world, inspiring intellects to explore and examine its contents and conditions, and express themselves in the methods and manners of various disciplines, including the geographic.

The diffusion of Islamic culture and administration over so widespread a population had a reciprocal effect on the actors in the process, so that infusion blended in the diffusion in many places and in many directions, with the result that the cross-insemination especially from Greek sources, themselves fertilized directly or indirectly from Hindu and Pahlevi intermediaries, brought the knowledge, technologies, and philosophies of the sciences of the older traditions to blend progressively and to varying extents into the dominant culture. In pace with the redistribution of political power new cosmological perspectives emerged. By the ninth century of the Common Era, Arab geographical sensibility had acquired a way of looking at the earth and the heavens, derived in method and nomenclature mainly from the work of Greek predecessors; and by the early part of the IV/X century, a considerable body of astronomical, mathematical, cartographical, and philosophical work, some of it dealing with the earth and man's relation to it—that is to say, with the essence of the geographical exercise—already existed in the Arabic language. At times, this literature had utilitarian purposes, and individual works had appeared under a title which may be extended to a whole class—*Al-Masālik wal-Mamālik* [*The Routes and the Realms*]: the earliest surviving book with this title is that of Ibn Khurradādhbih datable to about a century before the birth of al-Muqaddasī. In this class of writing, the perspective of the world as a whole was discussed, then the Islamic realm in greater detail; especial attention was given to the road system and pilgrimage routes, the interconnecting system of the realm, with distances between stopping places, and using the location of Baghdād as a central point. These works served secular purposes also, providing information on the mathematics and astronomy, with topography and human occupancy, all relevant to the geographic exercise. This early literature included tables of coordinates of latitude and longitude of some places and the positions of some stars, together with lists of names of towns, islands, mountains, and other geographic features. In some instances the authors were officials or administrators of the ʿAbbāsids ruling from Baghdād; and produced such works for administrative purposes to the beginning of the tenth century—mensuration, land distribution, taxation, way stations on the post roads, elevation of stars, tides, and some other systems in nature.

Early in the tenth century of the Common Era a new school of geographers formed, distinguished from the former by having a pre-determined Islamic framework for their perspective, though not designed to be less materially useful than the other. This school introduced a number of notions then new to Arabic geographic writing, perhaps the foremost innovation being the deliberate giving of exclusive attention to the extensive area of the surface of the earth under Muslim domination, clearly distinguished from that of the non-Muslims. Islām thus defined the region, which was in turn subdivisble in regions defined by the distribution of physical phenomena and political sovereignties. It is as representing this new school of geography that *Ahsan al-Taqāsīm fī Marʿrifat al-Aqālīm* of al-Muqaddasī, of which an English rendition follows herein, reaches the highest point attained in medieval geographic writing. The first version of the work appeared in the year 375/985, and is probably that represented in MS. C and in a derivative of the latter, an apograph, MS. L, residing in the Bibliotheek der Rijksuniversiteit in Leiden [Cod. Or. 2063]; the other version, probably the later, contained in MS. B, followed in 378/988. MS. C seems to recognize the ascendancy of the Sāmānids, though about to perish, MS. B that of the Fātimids. No other literary work is attributed to this author.

The dates of al-Muqaddasī's birth and death are not known, but may be fairly surmised; that he was born in or about the year 334/945 is a highly reasonable supposition; he may well have lived to the year 391/1000, for the latest datable information in his treatise pertains to the end of the IV/X century. The form of his name used herein, and the more widely used, means that he was from Jerusalem; al-Maqdisī is another form of the sobriquet, and so early Arab writers refer to him as al-Bashshārī. His paternal grandfather was Abū Bakr al-Bannā' ["the builder"], whom Ahmad Ibn Tūlūn, ruler of Egypt 254-270/868-883, appointed architect to build walls and fortifications at the port of ʿAkkā; his maternal grandfather, Abu al-Tayyib bin al-Shawā, had emigrated from Biyār in Qūmis, to Jerusalem. The inheritance from his close ancestors likely included some acquaintance with the Persian and other languages. He was an educated and well-read young man with a critical knowledge of the writings of his Islamic predecessors in geography, and he had read, at least in part, the work of al-Jāhiz (d. 256/869), one of the great litterateurs in Arabic. He was learned, too, in the Holy Qurʾān, and the modes of reciting it, and familiar with the tenets of the main religious schools in Islām.

By his own account, al-Muqaddasī was a pilgrim at Makka in 356/966, when he was about twenty years of age; he returned there in the years 367/977 and 377/987. He did not complete his geographical treatise until he was aged about forty. He may very well have begun his travels, which eventually extended over the area from Northwest Africa to the border of Sind, about the time of his first visit to Makka. What prompted him to travel so extensively, and for twenty years, he does not reveal, but it could very well, in the beginning at any rate, have been the pure disinterested spirit of learning: he was after all, well-educated, and, as he proved himself, conversable, intelligent, versatile, inquisitive. It has been suggested that he was a dāʿin, a propagandist missioner, for the Fātimid regime ruling in Egypt, and that in this role he had to keep on the move, enabled by exercise of the many skills he possessed. It must be supposed that he made notes as the circumstances of his travels permitted, and, at times, the concision of expression in Ahsan al-Taqāsīm suggests aide-memoire; certainly his writing is too well informed everywhere for reliance on memory only—"a pernicious practice for a traveller;" and "forgetting is the most vexatious thing in science!"

During the time of his traveling, al-Muqaddasī witnessed the profound changes in the shifting distributions of political power in the Islamic world. The greatness had departed from the ʿAbbāsids in Baghdād, and the power of the Fātimids in Egypt was ascendant. In such circumstances a man so hardy, well-informed, intelligent, daring, at times so provocative as to invite his murder, all in all with such an extraordinary range of endowment, may be easily seen inwardly compelled not to be merely a spectator, but to be a participant, whether to satisfy his interest, or save his life. As traveler and merchant he had a mind for the practical, and the pursuits that occupied his life, every activity except begging and grievous sin, indicate a manysidedness that is also reflected in his observations on the human being in his milieu: this single work bespeaks a product of Islamic civilization at its finest. It may be, too, that consciousness of his foreign origins may have prompted al-Muqaddasī to begin his travels: he journeyed to Biyār and stayed there for four months with his mother's relatives.

As to his aim in writing about his travels, al-Muqaddasī is explicit: a learned and a pious man, he would write a book that would ensure the survival of his own name. He wished to be known as having established a science that would give life to his memory, be of service to mankind, and give satisfaction to his Lord. This work would be necessary for travelers and profitable for merchants, would appeal to the virtuous and the godly; it was to serve kings, nobles, judges, jurists, delight both commoners and men of rank. The works of his Muslim predecessors he deemed to have fallen far short, in any of a number of ways, of what he believed they could be, and these deficiencies he would remedy. But beyond this, in the manner of some of the old Semitic prophets, he sensed the imposing of a task on him by the Deity: God had predestined that he travel over the great realm of Islām, and had inspired him to write an account of it for the benefit of all Muslims.

The writing of al-Muqaddasī's work in point of antecedence and succession represents the climax in quality and content of the geographical works produced by Muslim authors in the period from a century or so before his time to a few centuries after his death. About the middle of the II/VIII century the ʿAbbāsid khalifate established itself in Baghdād, and, following on this, Muslim authors began to produce in the Arabic language what became a considerable body of important literature which, borrowing from the Greeks they called *jūghrāfiya* (djūghrāfiya), in their own language *sūrat al-ardh* ("image of the earth"). In the period prior to that of al-Muqaddasī some geographers had written with, it is true, a personal stamp at times, but mainly to provide practical compendia of the routes, post-roads, and frontier conditions of the Islamic realm: these are the books of *Masālik wa-Mamālik* above mentioned, and once done well hardly need repeating. Others of these geographers, too, showed themselves heirs to the science of the Greeks of the Hellenistic period to the point of employing not only knowledge and concepts in their works, but even of adapting to their own use some of the vocabulary of the Greeks—for example, the word *aqālīm* (plural form of *iqlīm*), a key term in the present treatise, used by many Arab geographic writers to refer to a number of zones into which the earth is divided and running parallel to the equator, is but an Arabicized form of the Greek word *klima*. These latter works were sometimes political, or mathematical, sometimes anecdotal, sometimes works of literature. Then came the period of al-Muqaddasī and of the school of geographic writers of which he was the most eminent. After the period of al-Muqaddasī the epigonoi, characteristically, produced the dictionary and encyclopaedic type of work; later, too, came the genre of the *rihla*, the travels, so very well represented by works of Ibn Jubayr, 540/1145-614/1217, and Ibn

Battūta, 703/1304-779/1377. Between the prior and this last period al-Muqaddasī wrote his work which, alone among them all, constitutes a total science of geography, and puts the discipline on foundations he so picturesquely likens to the substructure of an edifice. While he recognizes the *masālik* (routes) as an important part of the landscape, he puts his accounts of them as appendages to his main discourse. He recognizes the interplay of the man-land relationship as constituting the monad of geography; and the spirit and picture of this relationship is evoked continually in the orderly components of his book. Basic to the framework of al-Muqaddasī's treatise is the concept of the region, still an essential in the methodology of geographic enquiry. The unit, the greater region, with which al-Muqaddasī is concerned is that portion of the earth's surface perceived as the realm of Islām, distinct from the non-Muslim areas. This realm seen as a region in itself was defined by a culture, civilization, economy, code of religious law, giving it a homogeneity in its topographical, linguistic, climatic, ethnographic, and political diversity: al-Muqaddasī wrote for a public for which he could assume a ready recognition of this homogeneity. Acknowledging the diversity, al-Muqaddasī employed the concept of regions within the larger region, and these were identified by the occupancy and use of habitable areas of varying environmental possibilities available to the communities living in them: consider his milieu distinct from man and the geographic perspective is blinkered, so al-Muqaddasī does not view as regions the uninhabited seas and deserts, though he treats of them, in fact likening one to the other. His region, an abstract device, tends to be defined by political divisions, or, rather, in the absence of more precise boundaries, spheres of influence; for example, his region of al-Mashriq—the Eastern Territories—comprises Sijistān, Khurāsān, and Mā warā' al-Nahr, an independent geographical and historical entity under the strong dominance of the dynasty of Sāmān (page 260 text).

In the systematic discourse of his opening pages al-Muqaddasī aims to be the complete, as indeed he turns out to be the most original of the medieval Islamic geographers. In good literary manner he straightway sets forth what he intends to write about. He will, he says, give an account of the regions of the realm of al-Islām, including the cold and the hot areas, the deserts and seas with their places of danger; the rocky deserts, those of sand; saltpans, hills, plains, mountains, wooded areas, limestones, sandstones solid and friable, lakes and rivers; land division organization, taxation, capitals, noted towns, way stations, distances on the roads and highways; places of abundance, places of scarcity and infertility; agricultural products, quality of water, fields watered by rain; foods and drinks, pharmaceuticals, items of cargo and commerce, imports and exports, weights, measures, coinage. Of the populations he will recount their diversity in languages, complexion, manners and customs, doctrinal adherence, places of pious visitation; their glories and their shortcomings. Al-Muqaddasī does all of this in varying measure for different regions, and, indeed, for some regions gives much more, at times by expression of opinion, by anecdote, or mention of some exceptional resource, practice, or phenomenon.

Al-Muqaddasī's method of assembling, selecting, and presenting his material involves mention of the predecessors in his science; and the chronological and developmental context of his work in medieval Muslim geographic writing is given by S. Maqbul Ahmad in the article "Djughrāfiyā", *EI*². Al-Muqaddasī had read the literature, and was satisfied that the science of geography had been but inadequately and imperfectly presented by his predecessors.

Breaking new ground, then, he set the standards for his science. The primary epistemological guide for him is the *Qurʾān*, the word and will of God revealed to man ultimately through Muhammad, the Prophet; while leaning on this authority to help settle a point or two, he does not refrain from providing his own interpretation of some passages to further his argument. Proceeding against this background he evaluates the sources of his knowledge, giving first and preeminent importance to his autopsy, what he witnessed: this is what provides the major strength of *Ahsan al-Taqāsīm*.

The firsthand experiences of his twenty years of travel on land and sea were gained in the pursuit of an impressive range and variety of occupations, by which he made his living and was enabled to achieve the objectives of his travel; these occupations he lists, in their practice at times enjoying honors and distinctions, at times suffering ignominy, imprisonment, and the near presence of death. Except for two, which he is at pains to specify, he entered every one of the regions, enquired, interviewed, keenly observed, tasted foods and waters, earned a living and discovered the material he incorporated in his science: in his narrative he is factual, balanced, objective, and thus assures its coherence and credibility. He emphasizes his autopsy again and again, and, for him, it constitutes the solid props and pillars upon which he raised the structure of his work.

The next best source for al-Muqaddasī is the witness of persons who were possessors of firsthand knowledge, of good judgment and reliability, of areas he did not enter to examine for himself. What he was told he attempted to verify from the reports of others: what they agreed on he accepted, only. However, even with these precautions he is circumspect; a report he accepted, but for which he had but one attestation, he ascribes specifically to its source. Where he has no stronger testimony he cautiously says, "it is claimed that ...".

A lesser source, for al-Muqaddasī, is what he found in books, many of them consulted, as he himself specifies, in the royal libraries he visited. A clear blend of these sources and methods may be seen in his investigation of particulars about the "Sea of China" (pages 10-11 text). A further guide to his reasoning is the *Sharīʿa*, or system of Islamic jurisprudence of which the *hadīth*, a recounting of the deeds and sayings of the Prophet and his Companions, constitute a source second only to the *Qurʾān*. The next source in order of importance is *ijmāʿ*, that is, the consensus of the religious scholars on matters not provided for in the higher sources. This latter is the equivalent of what is generally known and accepted, the local common knowledge, and has its own validity. A further source, *qiyās*, analogical reasoning, is also employed by al-Muqaddasī in making a point or reaching a conclusion; and this, suggestive of a conclusion though it may be, can be set aside by the exercise of *istihsān*, that is, the application of discretion in a legal decision, where common sense dictates a resort to expediency. A body of law is supposed to represent a distillation of common sense, and the use by al-Muqaddasī of the framework and mechanism of the *Sharīʿa* gives a methodical orderliness to the composition of his work. As scientists often do, al-Muqaddasī makes terms technical by defining them; and in his discourse on every region he proceeds from a general overview of it to a consideration of the parts, returning at the end to some aspect of the whole.

Every one of the manuscripts, MS. B and MSS. C and L, contains maps adjunct to al-Muqaddasī's text; they represent some general features of medieval Islamic cartography, which, distinct from the Western tradition, usually though not invariably presents the north-south axis rotated through one hundred eighty degrees, so that south is at the top of the map. In and of themselves the maps here generally add little to the text, and are, moreover, usually imitative of, or derivative from maps that had accompanied the geographical works of predecessors in the school of geographers in which al-Muqaddasī is included. Assessment of the cartography of this school, and the problems of ascription of authorship—and these are many—are discussed and examined in some detail, and illustrated, by Gerald R. Tibbetts in Harley and Woodward's *The History of Cartography, Volume Two, Book One*. MS. B contains nineteen maps, five of them without counterparts in MS. C, which has one without a counterpart in MS. B. In execution as distinct from amount of content, the maps in MS. C are more carefully drawn and lettered than in the other, seeming to represent a finished product. Several of these show more place-names and detail than those in MS. B, and even some decorative features. The manuscript at Leiden matches MS. C map for map, with hardly a whit of difference between any pair. In the amount of content the maps of MS. B usually have more detail and place-names than the other; in point of execution, however, they suggest preliminary sketches made with straightedge and ships curves, with considerable freehand, all, perhaps a guide for the draughtsman. Overall, the maps that accompany al-Muqaddasī's text, whoever made them, do not at all exhibit the advances in cartography that were part and parcel of the legacy of the map-making of Claudius Ptolemy, geographer and astronomer at Alexandria in the second century of the Common Era; Ptolemy showed on a flat surface the knowledge of the round world the Romans had in his time, using parallels of latitude from the equator north, and meridians converging toward the North Pole. This grid, a conic projection, was within the knowledge of the Muslims before al-Muqaddasī's time; and, in fact, the construction of another grid, rectangular, with maps on it, based on a cylindrical projection, is described in detail in *Kitāb ʿAjā'ib al-Aqālīm al-Sabʿa* (Book of the Wonders of the Seven Climates) written by Suhrāb Ibn Sarābiyūn during approximately the decade before al-Muqaddasī was born. In invoking the Ptolemaic tradition it is well to bear in mind that the tradition itself was indebted to the Iranian and Hindu, and perhaps others: of course, at any stage of the process of diffusion and cross-fertilization of ideas and technology, the provenance and direction of flow of the genetic components in the mix may be ultimately undeterminable. In any event, the maps in MSS. B and C are abstracts of the layout of the areas they purport to portray, distributions are generalized, little is owed to scale, and nothing to the projections of the Ptolemaic tradition, in which the providing of maps as central to a geographic text is a basic element. Yet it would appear that al-Muqaddasī intended that his maps represent to some extent the matter of his text; he recounts the efforts he made to determine the outlines of what he calls the "Sea of China" [in fact, the sea that washes the circuit of the Arabian Peninsula, and includes the Red Sea, Arabian Gulf, Indian Ocean, and western Pacific]; he examined maps made by predecessors, voyaged around the Arabian Peninsula himself, consulted pilots and their manuals of navigation, interviewed shipmasters, commercial agents, coast guards, and others, eventually accepting only that information on which there was no disagreement among them (text pp. 10-11). Moreover, he intends that his maps should speak to the viewer, hence he chooses red to depict the major roads, yellow for the golden sands, green for the salt seas, blue for the great rivers, dust colour for famous mountains (text p. 9). Again, in the text he gives at least a limited notion of scale by the use of dots variously placed over a term applied to a measure of time-distance that corresponds to a differentiating range of units of surface distance (text p. 106).

Ahsan al-Taqāsīm is, first and foremost, a geographical treatise, the most original of its genre in medieval Islamic literature. Its freshness, for its time, appears in the systematic treatment of topics in the opening chapters; moreover, the method and terminology used in, for example, the classification and ranking of settlements from metropoles to villages, by function, intensively and extensively, bespeaks the approach of the scientist, and is, in itself, remarkably modern. (Of many of the lesser settlements mentioned no evident remains now exist.) The classification which is characteristic of the author's approach, throughout, is fortified in this latter case by an analogy which represents the *amsār* (metropoles) as kings, the *qasabāt* (fortified provincial capitals) as chamberlains, the *madā'in* (provincial towns) as armies, the *qurā* (villages) as footsoldiers. The author refines his definition of metropole further, differentiating among the definitions of others and his own (p. 47 text). Nor does he adduce analogy as proof, only as clarification, and, as remarked above, he readily modifies his use of it as circumstances delimit (see *e.g.*, p. 156 text). Such efforts at exposition of his meaning confirm that man in his milieu entails for al-Muqaddasī, as it does still, the complete range of vision of the geographic perspective.

The reliability and objectivity of al-Muqaddasī's insistence on his eyewitness, and other personal testing, including the precautions he takes in his sifting and verification of reported information is shown, in relief, in contrast with the possibility of error when he derives material, though with precautionary disclaimer, from the writings of others. The account of the climates, and the position of the *Qibla* (pp. 59 & *seqq.*, text) has a number of mistakes, contradictions, and absurdities, that one may suppose he would have avoided had he subjected the material to the tests which he usually required: but he did not, and it is well for his reputation that he acknowledges the borrowed nature of the material. Again, the boast supposedly made by the khalif to the Romaean ruler (p. 64 text) seems to be without point.

Besides being a strong, comprehensive, and illustrative work in the science of geography, *Ahsan al-Taqāsīm* may be classed as *adab*, or belles-lettres. Apart from where the discourse is necessarily enumerative, the style used is frequently eloquent, noble, and exalted: this may be seen in many of the passages introductory to the individual sections or regions, and again in a number of logical analyses, debating at a high level one side and another of some questions of preference or interpretation. Use of metaphor, too, is common, and apt. The attitude struck is generally amiable—polite and broad-mindedly charitable. Stories, folklore, proverbs, verses, wonders and marvels are introduced here and there, somewhat after the manner of Herodotus, to provide some diversion for the reader. Indeed, al-Muqaddasī maintains a consistently high level of discourse throughout virtually all of his writing; he perpetrates, however, an egregious exception in the inanity and turgidity of a purple patch, drawing the exasperation of an offended reader sufficiently to indite on page 187 of MS. B a bitter protest, invoking divine wrath on the author: see text pp. 386 *et seqq.* Apart from this lapse, however, and except for passages that are deliberately eloquent, the writing throughout tends to be lean, concise, elliptical, classical, and, indeed, sometimes difficult. Frequently the author indulges in *saj*ᶜ, a rhetorical practice in which words occurring at the end of short phrases are selected for rhyme, though the effect is by no means poetic. Though used effectively in the older verses of the *Qurᵓān*, this device of rhyme had descended to a rather graceless vogue, tending to bedevil writing at every level, so that the sense is often sacrificed for the rhyme. While in the English rendition of *Ahsan al-Taqāsīm* herewith effort has been generally made to parallel, where feasible, the syntax of the Arabic original, no attempt has been made to parallel in English the effect of the *saj*ᶜ. Even if the entire exordium is written in *saj'* without any strain on the sense, the remarks introductory to the account of each region sometimes fall into contradiction because sound predisposed to take precedence over sense.

Embodied in the good classical laconic style that is generally characteristic of *Ahsan al-Taqāsīm* is the finest production of medieval Arab geographic writing, yet quite fresh and modern, at times humanly personal and revealing, though never familiar. It gives a wealth of information on religious ideas of the time, and on the geography of religion, with a humane perspective, generous and brotherly. It preserves important details of persons and places, economic, social, ethnographic, linguistic, architectural features of the greatest interest; and is a major source of the knowledge of weights and measures of the medieval Muslim world.

THE BEST DIVISIONS FOR
KNOWLEDGE OF THE REGIONS

IN THE NAME OF GOD THE MOST BENIGNANT, THE MERCIFUL: FACILITATE
MY TASK, AND HELP ME BY YOUR GRACIOUSNESS, O MUNIFICENT LORD!

Praise be to God who created the world: He foreordained it, then moulded
its shape, bringing to perfection the work of creation (*Qurʾān*, sūra 25, v. 2),
without a counselor to help Him. He arranged it without a helper, and to what
perfection unaided, He brought it! He established it firmly without assistance
from anyone. He pegged the world down with towering mountains so that it
should not be moved (*Qurʾān*, sūra 16, v. 15; sūra 78, v. 7); and He surrounded
it with the sea so that its waters might not rise up and overwhelm it. He scattered
His servants over it so He could see how they would conduct themselves: some
of them believed, and took the correct way, but some did not believe, and turned
away. May God abundantly put His blessing on the best of the creation, and the
most noble of men, Muhammad, and on his family and his Companions, and
may He grant them salvation!

Abū ʿAbd Allāh Muhammad bin Ahmad al-Muqaddasī has said: "The
scholars have always desired to compose works so that their traces may not
vanish from this earth, and their fame not pass away." It has been my wish to
follow their established practices, to walk in their footsteps, and put in order a
science which will give life to my memory, and which will be of service to
mankind, so that I may be pleasing to my Lord. Now, I have found that the
scholars who formerly dealt with the sciences wrote the initial works: then their
successors in turn commented on and summarized their works. Accordingly, it
occurred to me to direct my attention to a science which they had neglected, and
to specialize in a branch of learning they had not dealt with, except defectively—I
mean an account of the Islamic regions, with the deserts and the seas in them;
the lakes and rivers there; a description of their famous metropoles, and noted
settlements: the way stations that are well used and the roads that are frequented.
I will state in my account the ingredients of their medicaments and drugs, the
sources and cargoes of commerce; the diversity of the peoples of the countries in
their expressions, intonations, languages, complexions; their doctrinal schools,
their measures, their weights, their coins, large and small; with particulars of
their food and drink, their fruits and waters; a recounting of what is to their
credit and discredit; their trade in export and import. Mention is also made
of the places of danger in the deserts, and the number of way stations in the
intervals between settlements. There will be mention of the saltpans, the rocky
deserts, and those of sand; the hills, the plains, the mountains; the limestones

and the red sandstones: the soils rich and poor; the lands of profusion and fertility: the places of scarcity and barrenness. There will be mention of the places of veneration, and of the watchposts, the specialties of the countries, the usages of the inhabitants: the countries, the boundaries, the cold areas, and the hot areas; the Yamanī land divisions, Kurdish land divisions, areas surveyed for the assessment of taxes, and the frontiers; the handiworks and the learned pursuits; the fields watered solely by rain, also the wooded areas; the places of sacrifice and ceremonies of the Pilgrimage.

I realized that this is a work travelers and merchants cannot do without, and that it is indispensable for devout and upright people; it has been desired by kings and nobility; judges and jurists have sought it: commoners and elite delight in it: every traveler may use it to advantage, and every merchant may profit by it.

I could not complete the compilation of it until after my travels throughout the countries, and my visiting the regions of Islām; until after I had met the learned, and been of service to princes, had meetings with the Qādhīs, and studied under the jurists; had frequented the society of men of letters, the Readers of the Qurʾān, and writers of the traditions; had associated with ascetics and the Sūfīs; been present at the assemblies of the tellers of stories, and of public preachers, all this while engaging in trade everywhere, and associating with all the people I encountered.

I paid careful attention to the elements of my science until I was familiar with them, and to the measurements of the regions in *farsakhs* [originally a measure of distance over time: 4 km./hr. on foot, 6 km. for cavalry; now 6 km. See herein *Muq.* pp. 58, 59, 65, 66] so that I determined them with precision. I traveled around the frontiers so that I could define them, and traversed the military districts so that I knew them. I made inquiry about the religious sects so that I became familiar with them; and arrived at a knowledge of the languages and complexions of the peoples so that I could classify them. I paid close attention to the districts so as to categorize them, and I researched the taxes on land so that I could calculate their amounts; I tasted the air, and I evaluated the water. With all this, I suffered severe privation, and spent lots of money. I sought to practice what is lawful, and avoid what is sinful, while dealing honestly with Muslims so as to please God.

In patience I bore my humble condition and absence from home, and I have p. 3 been mindful of God and apprehensive of Him: all this after I had awakened in my soul a desire to earn some recompence from God, and filled it with the desire for a good reputation, and dread of misdeeds. I have avoided falsehoods and excesses; by arguments I have guarded myself against censure. I did not set down anything so that its meaning would extend beyond what is proper, nor anything inconsistent, listening only to the reports of trustworthy people.

May God grant us His help in what we have aspired to do: may He move us to success in what He desires and approves; for it is He whom we worship, and it is to Him that we return.

Preliminary and Prerequisite Observations

Know that I have built this book on firm foundations and supported it with powerful pillars. I have striven for accuracy with all my might, and have sought the help of the understanding of men of intelligence; and I have besought God—glorious is His name—to have me avoid error and oversight, to enable me to achieve my expectation and my hope, to raise up the pillars of this work, and to firmly join its structure with the use of what I have witnessed and understood, learned and noted. Thus have I raised the building, and established its columns and pillars. Among its supports and pillars, moreover, in the establishing of which I sought assistance, was my putting questions to men of intelligence whom I knew to be neither careless nor confused, about the districts and the areas in the border territories distant from me, which it was not possible for me to reach. For that on which they agreed, I accepted as authentic: that on which they differed, I rejected. Whenever it was necessary that I myself should go to a place and make inquiries there, I did so; whatever I found unsatisfactory, and that my reasoning would not accept I have ascribed to the person who related it, or I have simply written, "it has been asserted." I have supplemented my work, too, with materials I came across in the royal archives.

No predecessor of mine in this subject has adopted the method of procedure that I have, or sought out the useful information that I aimed at. First of all, there was Abū ʿAbd Allāh al-Jayhānī; he was minister to the *Amīr* of Khurāsān, and he cultivated the pursuits of philosophy, astrology, and astronomy. He assembled around himself some foreigners and questioned them about the countries and p. 4 their revenues, the condition of the roads thither, the elevation of the stars above the horizons there, and the length of the meridian shadow cast by the sun. His design was by these means to achieve conquest of the territories, and to acquire knowledge of the resources of countries. He would also perfect for himself his knowledge of the stars and the revolution of the celestial spheres. Do you not see how he divided the world into seven regions, assigning to each region its particular planet? At times he would talk about the stars and mathematics; then he would move to a discussion of something that is of no interest to the people at large. Now he is describing the idols of al-Hind, now the wonders of al-Sind; then he gives details of the taxes and revenues. I have found him mention stations that are otherwise unknown, and traveling stages that have been abandoned. At the same time, he has not subdivided the districts, nor classified the military districts; neither has he described the cities, or enumerated them. Rather, he just mentions the routes to the east, the west, the north and the south, with an outline of the plains, the mountains, the valleys, the hills, the woods and the rivers that are there. Thus his book was drawn out to a great length, while he neglected to mention most of the routes of the military districts, and to describe the important cities.

Addition/version MS. C.

I saw his work, in seven volumes, in the libraries of ʿAdhud al-Dawla, though not ascribed to him. Indeed some ascribe the authorship to Ibn Khurradādhbih. I have seen, moreover, in Naysābūr, two succinct works of which one was ascribed to al-Jayhānī, the other bearing the name of Ibn Khurradādhbih as author. They agreed with each other in substance, except that al-Jayhānī had provided some additional matter.

For his part, Abū Zayd al-Balkhī aimed at providing in his book some sketches and a map of the world. He accordingly divided the earth into twenty parts; then he commented on every sketch and was very concise. He did not, however, mention the interesting particulars nor did he give any useful information in his classification and organization. In fact, he left many of the metropoles without mention of them; nor did he travel in and become familiar with the countries, nor did he visit the provinces. This is why when the *Amīr* of Khurāsān invited him to his court to be his adviser, having reached the Jayhūn [Oxus] River, he wrote to the *Amīr* as follows: "If you have summoned me to you on the strength of what you have heard about the soundness of my judgment, well my judgment now dissuades me from crossing this river." When the *Amīr* read this he ordered him to depart for Balkh.

As for Ibn al-Faqīh al-Hamadhānī, he too has followed a different method. He mentions only the largest towns, and does not classify areas or military districts. Moreover, he includes in his book matters that have no relevance to the sciences—at one time he is urging one to renounce the world, at another time he is exciting one's desire for it; then at one turn he excites tears, at another he amuses and provokes laughter. There are also al-Jāhiz and Ibn Khurradādhbih: p. 5 their works are very much abridged, and nothing of much utility is to be derived from them.

Addition/version MS. C.

I saw, moreover, a book in the library of al-Sāhib, the authorship ascribed to Abū Zayd al-Balkhī, and with maps. I also saw a copy of exactly the same book in Naysābūr, transcribed from the work in the possession of al-Raʾīs Abū Muhammad al-Mīkālī; however, the name of the author was not given, though some credit its authorship to Ibn al-Marzubān al-Karkhī. I have seen a copy of the same work in Bukhārā, the authorship ascribed to Ibrāhīm bin Muhammad al-Fārisī. This latter ascription is the most correct, for I have met with a number of persons who had met him, and had in fact seen him in the act of composing it; among these was al-Hākim Abū Hāmid al-Hamdānī and al-Hākim Abū Nasr al-Harbī. This is a book of which the maps are indeed well done; however, the author has erred in many places in the work, has far from excelled in his presentation; and has not divided the regions into districts. I have seen, too, a work written by Ibn al-Faqīh al-Hamadhānī, consisting of five volumes, and in this he follows a different course. He mentioned only the larger towns, and introduces a variety of material; at one time he is urging one to renounce this world, then again he is exciting one's desire for it. At times he excites to tears, at times amuses, and provokes laughter. The *Kitāb al-Amsār* (*The Book of Capital Cities*) of al-Jāhiz is a small work, and the book of Ibn al-Faqīh is along the same lines as it, though containing more trifling matter and stories. They excuse themselves for this by claiming that what they have introduced into their books they have done, so that the reader may find some relief, should he be bored. I have once in a while looked at the book of Ibn al-Faqīh, and have encountered storytelling and literary artifice regardless of what country I read of. This I do not approve of; even so, I have included some stories and discussions as fitted to the subject at hand, but not so as to distract from the matter under consideration. Indeed I have used rhyming prose in some parts to entertain the ordinary reader; for while the cultured classes prefer prose to verse, the commonalty like rhymes and rhyming prose.

These are the only works on this subject that I have found after searching, enquiring, and examining libraries and collections of books. I have endeavored p. 6 not to repeat anything they reported, nor to relate any matter that they mentioned, except where it is necessary to do so, so as not to detract from any credit due them or plagiarize their works.

Addition/version MS. C.
For the scope of this science is, in our opinion, so wide that we need not repeat, copy from a book, or purloin the work of another, excepting only where the nature of the matter compels, or some difficulty makes such action imperative; this is what we have done in the account of the region of al-Sind and in the account of al-Sadd (the Rampart). Indeed, only he will recognize the superiority of our book who examines their books, or who travels over the various countries, and who is a person of understanding and perspicacity. As for the maps in which we have portrayed the countries, we made every effort to ensure their correctness, having carefully studied a number of drawings. Of these, one drawing I found in the library of the ruler of al-Mashriq, done on a sheet of paper in the form of a square, though on this I did not depend. Another drawing I came across, done on a piece of linen, was in the possession of Abu al-Qāsim bin al-Anmātī, also at Naysābūr, and square in shape. I saw, too, the drawings which Ibrāhīm al-Fārisī made, and these, coming closer to the facts, may be relied upon, even though he shows confusion, and errs in many places. I saw an old man in Sarakhs who had made detailed drawings and maps of the countries of both the infidel and those of al-Islām: everything in them was wrong, with little exception! I asked him if he had ever travelled. Said he: "I have never been away from Sarakhs." "Well," said I, "I have heard of some who described the regions from hearsay, and of course the result was confusion; but I have never seen anyone who mapped the regions from hearsay, other than you."

Indeed, only he can appreciate the excellence of my present work who has examined the works of these others, or who has himself traversed the countries with comprehension, and is of the persons of education and intelligence. Of course I do not acquit myself of error, nor my book of defect; neither do I submit it to be free of redundance and deficiency, nor that it is above criticism in every respect.

Moreover, my reporting on those elements which I specified in my introduction will vary in completeness from one region to another, and will be uneven in its scope; for I relate only what I know absolutely. This science is not such that proceeds by analogy, or is always uniform; rather it may be fully attained only by observation and enquiry.

In this book of ours, elliptical expressions are used to indicate precise p. 7 meanings. For instance, our saying of something that it is "nonpareil" implies that there is absolutely nothing else like it whatsoever: for example, the elongated quinces of Jerusalem, the *nayda* (a pastry) of Egypt, the citrus of al-Basra—no equal of these is to be found, though there are varieties of them. If we say "superlative", it means in excellence among the varieties; for example, the ᶜUmarī plum of Shīrāz, the Damascene fig in al-Ramla, the ᶜAslūnī apricot, and the Rībās currant in Naysābūr. When we say "good" the existence of a better kind is implied, [lacuna in MS.] for instance [the raisins] of al-Tāʾif; as for the indigo of Arīhā (Jericho), the Zabīdī variety is better, and as for the peach of Makka, the Dāriqī variety is more excellent. Sometimes we make a summary statement, of which an elaboration is to be understood; for example, when we speak about al-Ahwāz we say that its mosque lacks reverence. We say this because it is continually thronging with scoundrels, blackguards, and reprobates, who resort thither and congregate, so that there are always rascals sitting around while the faithful are saying their prayers; it is truly a haunt of beggars and a center of the profligate. Similarly, when we say that there are no people more respectable than those of Jerusalem, we mean that you will not see anyone bilking, or giving short measure, there; you see no one drinking in broad daylight, nor even a drunkard, there; there, you find no brothel, either secret or public. But you will see their godliness and sincere devotion, so much that when the inhabitants learned that their governor was carousing, they scaled the walls of his house and routed his social gathering. Again, when we say about Shīrāz that no distinction attaches to those there who wear the *taylasān* [a garment of black wool, rounded or semi-circular, and worn, shawl-like, and usually by persons of distinction], we say it because it is the raiment of the noble and of the plebeian, of the learned and of the ignorant. How many drunks have I not seen there with their *taylasāns* in disarray, trailing them on the ground! In fact, whenever I asked for an audience with the Wazīr, wearing the *taylasān*, I would be debarred, unless I was recognized; but when I came dressed in the *durrāᶜa* [narrow-sleeved woollen tunic, slit in front], I would be admitted.

Sometimes we have used both the masculine and feminine genders in mentioning one town or other; the masculine is ascribed to the designation of the town as *misr* [a metropolis], and the feminine to its function as *qasaba* [an administrative centre], or *madīna* [inner city]. Litterateurs have authorized this usage in referring to inanimate objects. The word *balad* is used to denote a metropolis, an administrative center, a rural area, a district, a territory. When we describe the capital city in its area, we mention it by its proper name: for instance al-Fustāt, Numūjkath, al-Yahūdiyya. Otherwise, when we mention the capitals we refer to them by the names by which they are generally known to people; and so we say Misr, Bukhārā, Isbahān. When we use the term al-Mashriq (Orient) we mean specifically the territories of the Sāmānids; while when we say al-Sharq (East) we include also Fārs, Kirmān and al-Sind. Similarly when we say al-Maghrib (Occident), that refers to the region, while when we say al-Gharb (West), that includes Egypt and al-Shām (Syria).

p. 8

We have included in our work some obscure phrases and rhetorical flourishes, so that the writing will have an enhanced and an elliptical quality. We have included proofs in authentication of what we say, and narratives by way of confirmation. We use rhythmic rhymed prose for embellishment, and sacred narratives so as to merit a blessing. The greater portion of the work, however, we have written in a easy style, so that people in general may understand it, if they but study it. We have arranged the material after the manner of legal works, so that it will find favor in the eyes of the learned if they will reflect on it. We have pointed out differences of opinion in great detail, and given numerous instances by way of precaution. We have extended the work by describing cities from various aspects; and we have given accounts of important characteristics because of their obvious usefulness. We have given a clear account of the routes because of the absolute need for this; and have shown on maps the regions so as to facilitate one's perception of them; and we have enumerated the settlements, as seemed the most expedient thing to do. We have asked God—may He be exalted—for guidance before entering on the compilation of our work, and requested of Him success and assistance. We have, too, taken counsel with our foremost contemporaries and leaders. We showed our draft notes to the chief Qādhī, savant of Khurāsān, and the most respected of the judges of his time; everyone approved it, praised it, and encouraged its publication. Indeed, we have asserted what we have seen, and recounted what we have heard; and the truth of that which we established for ourselves by observation and successive corroboration we have set down without reservation. Anything, however, that we doubted or that was derived from one individual source only, we have ascribed to him from whom we heard it. We do not mention in our book other than the person of distinction, a renowned scholar, or an exalted ruler, except where it is necessary, or in the course of a citation, or as a matter of respect; when we do mention a man in this way we mention his status, lest his name be thought to be included in the category of persons of distinction.

You should know that notwithstanding these safeguards and preconditions, I did not publish my work until I had reached the age of forty years, had traversed all the regions, and had been in the service of men of science and religion. The completion of it in the metropolis of Fārs coincided with the suzerainty of the Commander of the Faithful, Abū Bakr ʿAbd al-Karīm al-Tāʾiʿ

p. 9

lillāh and in the western regions that of Abū Mansūr Nazār al-ʿAzīz billāh, Commander of the Faithful, in the year 375 AH/985 CE.

Addition/version MS. C.

. . . and in the days of the overlord al-Amīr Abu al-Qāsim Nūh bin Mansūr, Client of Amīr al-Muʾminīn (Commander of the Faithful).

We have written here only about the realm of Islam; we do not bother ourselves with the countries of the unbelievers, because we did not enter them, and we see no use whatever in describing them: of course we mention those areas among them where Muslims are settled. We have divided the realm into fourteen regions, treating separately the regions of the non-Arabs as distinct from those of the Arabs.

Then we classified the districts of each region, assigned the metropoles, mentioned its primary cities, listed in order its towns and military districts, after we had depicted in a map their frontiers and boundary lines. In the maps we coloured the well-known roads red, the golden sands yellow, the salt seas green, the well-known rivers blue, the principal mountains in dust colour: thus the descriptions may be more readily perceptible to the understanding, and accessible to the specialist and layman alike.

The Arabian regions are Jazīrat al-ʿArab (the Peninsula of the Arabs); al-ʿIrāq; Aqūr (Mesopotamia); al-Shām (Syria); Misr (Egypt); and al-Maghrib. p. 10 The regions of the non-Arabs are, in order, al-Mashriq; al-Daylam; al-Rihāb; al-Jibāl; Khūzistān; Fārs; Kirmān; and al-Sind. Among the regions of the Arabs is a steppe and amidst the regions of the non-Arabs is a desert, both of which we must treat of separately and describe in full detail, because this is absolutely necessary, considering the number of routes crossing them. As for the seas and rivers, we have given a separate and sufficient chapter to these, because of the great necessity for this, and because of the general uncertainty on the subject.

An Account of the Seas and Rivers

Know that we have not seen in the realm of Islām more than two seas. One of the two issues from the direction of the south-east and lies between the country of China and the country of the Blacks. Where it touches the realm of Islām it rounds the Peninsula of the Arabs, just as we have drawn it on the map. It has many gulfs and numerous inlets. There is a difference of account among those who have described it, and among those who have mapped it are differences in its delineation. Among them some have shown it in the form of a *taylasān* that at one end touches the country of China, at the other that of the Abyssinians, with one arm in al-Qulzum, another in ʿAbbādān. Abū Zayd, for his part, has given it the form of a bird with its beak at al-Qulzum—but he does not notice the gulf of Wayla [ʿAqaba]—its neck in al-ʿIrāq, its tail between Abyssinia and China. I have also seen a representation of it, on paper, in the library of the *Amīr* of Khurāsān; and another on a piece of cotton cloth in the possession of Abu al-Qāsim ibn al-Anmātī, in Naysābūr; also in the library of ʿAdhud al-Dawla, and in that of Al-Sāhib [ibn ʿAbbād]. Well, each representation differed from the others, and in some of them were gulfs and inlets unknown to me. Now I, myself, have traveled over it a distance of about two thousand *farsakhs*, and have gone around the entire Peninsula from al-Qulzum to ʿAbbādān; and, in addition, to wherever the ships changed course to the islands and depths of this sea. Thus I became acquainted with men of standing who were born and bred there—shipmasters, cargo masters, coastguards, commercial agents, and merchants—and I considered them among the most discerning of people about this sea, and its anchorages, its winds, and its islands. I questioned them about it, about the conditions on it, and about its limits. I noticed, too, in their
p. 11 possession navigation instructions which they study carefully together and on which they rely completely, proceeding according to what is in them. From these sources I took copious notes of essential information, after I had studied them and evaluated them; and this I compared with the maps I have referred to. Now one day, as I was sitting with Abū ʿAlī bin Hāzim and looking at the sea—we were on the shore at ʿAdan—said he to me: "What is it with which you seem to me to be so preoccupied?" Said I: "God support the Shaykh! My mind is perplexed concerning this sea, so great is the number of conflicting accounts of it. The Shaykh now is the most knowledgeable of men about it, because he is chief of the merchants, and his ships are continually traveling to the furthermost parts of it. Should he be willing to give me a description of it I can rely on, and relieve me of doubt about it, perhaps he will do so." Said he: "You have encountered an expert in the matter!" He smoothed the sand with the palm of his hand and drew a figure of the sea on it. [Map I] It was neither a *taylasān*, nor a bird. But he showed it having gulfs, tongues, and numerous bays. Then said he: "This is a representation of this sea—

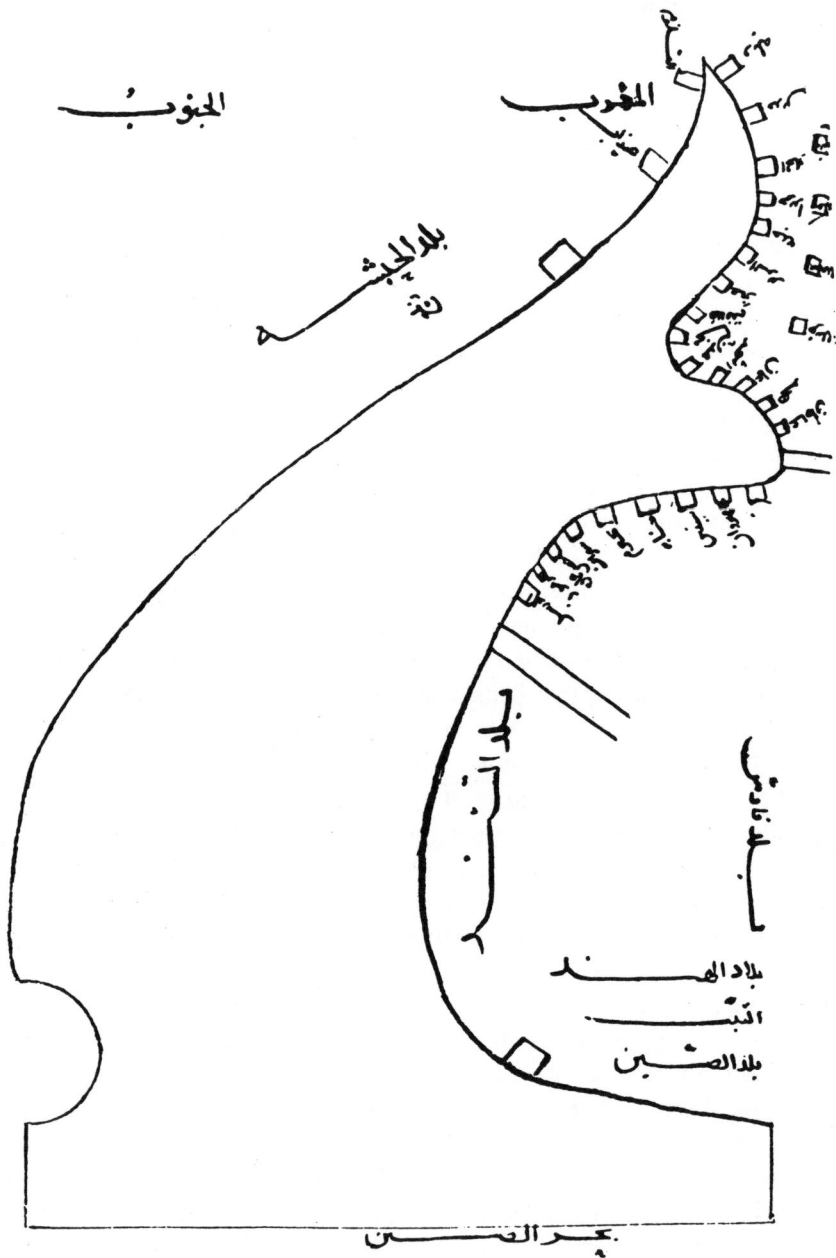

Map I: The Persian Sea (see p. 405).
From MS. Sprenger 5—Ahlwardt 6034 by kind permission of the Staatsbibliothek
Preussischer Kulturbesitz, Berlin, Orientabteilung.

Addition/version MS. C.
. . . and, in a word, there is no doubt that it has two arms, one of which extends to Wayla, the other to al-Qulzum, and a gulf extending from the other side to ʿAbbādān . . .

it has no other form but this." I shall draw a rather general map of it, however, and omit the gulfs and bays, ⋅except for the gulf of Wayla, because it is important, and because of the great need for intelligence of it, and the frequency of voyages over it. I omit anything on which there is disagreement, and include only that on which there is complete accord. Now there is absolutely no doubt that this sea flows around three quarters of the Peninsula of the Arabs, and that it has two tongues, as we mentioned, on the side towards Egypt. These diverge at the extremity of al-Hijāz at a place called Fārān (Tārān). This sea is most vast and forbidding between ʿAdan and ʿUmān, attaining a width here of some six hundred *farsakhs*; thence a tongue stretches to ʿAbbādān.

The perilous passages of it in the realm of Islām are: Jubaylān, the place of the drowning of Pharaoh; it is the fathomless deep of al-Qulzum, and here ships must travel athwart, so as to return from the desolate side to the civilized and cultivated side. Next is Fārān, a place where the winds blow from the direction both of Egypt and of Syria to form an overpowering whirl, so there is utter destruction of ships there. A practice of theirs is to send a party of men to observe the wind; if the winds abate, or if that one prevails which blows from their side, they proceed; otherwise they have to stay a long time until the arrival of the hour of relief. Next is the port of al-Hawra', abounding in rocks, so that ships are taken by surprise on attempting to enter it. In fact reaching from al-Qulzum as far as al-Jār are dangerous rocks on account of which ships do not proceed except by day. The captain takes his position in the crow's nest, and is completely absorbed in observing the sea. If a rock should be sighted he cries out: "To the right!" or, "To the left!" Two cabin boys are so stationed to repeat the cry. The helmsman has two ropes in hand which he pulls right or left, according to the directions. If they are negligent about this, the ship may strike the rocks, and be wrecked. Next, off the island of al-Silāb is a strait hazardous to ships, and a source of apprehension; one steers to the left of it to be out on the open sea. Next there is Jābir (Jāʾiz), truly a place of calamity, where one may see the bottom of the sea; in this shallow many a ship has been wrecked. At the entrance to Kamarān is fearfulness and calamity. Al-Mandam (Mandab), too, is a difficult strait, not to be negotiated except with the force of a freshening wind. From here the sea becomes a vast deep until ʿUmān; and here are seen, as God has mentioned, waves like towering and immovable mountains (*Qurʾān*, sūra 11, v. 42). It is entirely safe for outbound vessels, but perilous for those inbound, because of the danger of both shipwreck and drowning. Every ship passing through here needs to carry armed men, and personnel to throw Greek fire. Then there is the port of ʿUmān, bad and destructive. Further on is Fam al-Sabʿ (Fam al-Asad) [the lion's mouth], a fearsome strait; thereafter are al-Khashabāt (the wooden piles) pertaining to al-Basra. This, of course, is the most over-whelmingly disastrous feature, a narrow and a shallow combined. Here into the bottom of the sea trunks of palm trees have been driven, and on them huts built in which people are stationed who keep fires lighted by night, that ships may steer well away from them, and avoid the shallow places. In this connection, I have heard an old man say: "Distress really overtook us there. The ship hit bottom ten times—over this place forty ships travel, and one returns." However, I do not wish to enlarge on this topic, otherwise I would need to mention the anchorages of this sea, and the routes over it.

p. 13   The waters of this Sea of China rise about the middle and the end of each month, and twice in every day and night. From this circumstance come the ebb and flow of the tide at al-Basra; when the tide rises, it pushes back the waters of the Dijla (Tigris), which then flow into the mouths of the channels that irrigate the agricultural estates there. When it falls, the waters recede. People differ on the cause of this phenomenon: some say that an angel plunges his finger into the water every day and hence the tide flows; when he removes his finger, the ebb ensues. According to Kaʿb al-Ahbār, al-Khidhr [a popular storied gifted person in the service of God. See *Qurʾān*, sūra 18, vv. 60 & *seqq.*] met an angel, and asked to be informed about the flow and the ebb. The angel explained that the whale breathes in so the water flows into its nostrils, and that is the ebb; then the whale breathes out so that it expels the water from its nostrils, and that is the flow. Another explanation of the matter was told us, which I shall mention in the account of the region of al-'Irāq.

Addition/version MS. C.
The astronomers give another explanation for this, to be found in the work of Abū Maʿshar al-Balkhī, the astronomer.

In this sea also are narrows and deeps, the narrowest place being between Ra's al-Jumjuma and al-Daybul. Beyond this is a sea the depth of which is unknown, in it innumerable islands. Some of these islands are ruled by an Arab king, and others to the number of one thousand seven hundred, it is said, are under the rule of a woman. Those who have entered her kingdom assert that she sits before her subjects, naked, on a couch, wearing a crown; around her stand four thousand maids of honour, naked. Further on is the Sea of Harkand (Bay of Bengal), vast as an ocean, in which is situated Sarandīb (Island of Ceylon): this island is eighty *farsakhs* in length, and has a like width. In it is situated the mountain on which Adam was thrown: it is called al-Rahūn (Adam's Peak), and may be seen from a distance of a journey of several days.

On it is the impress of a foot sunk to a depth of about seventy cubits; the other footprint is distant the journey of a day and a night, and is in the floor of the sea. A light is seen on it every night. Here also are found rubies, the best p. 14 ones being those that the wind causes to roll. Here too is an aromatic plant, resembling musk. On this island are three kings. Also here is the camphor tree than which none grows higher. The trunk is of white wood, and one tree will give shade to more than two hundred men. The lower portion of the tree is bored and the camphor flows out on it like a gum, after which the tree withers. Close by is the island of al-Kalb (Nicobar) in which are mines of gold. The coconut is the food of the inhabitants, who are fair, nude, and handsome. Close to this is the island called al-Ramī (Sumatra). Here the tree called Baqqam (a red-wood) flourishes, being propagated by offsets; its fruit resembles that of the locust, and tastes bitter. Its roots provide an antidote for even a very quick poison. The island of Usqūtra (Socotra) is like a tower in the dark sea; it marks the limit of the Indian pirates, the terror of ships hereabouts, nor do they cease to fear them until they have cleared the island. This is the more favored of the two seas, the more highly regarded.

The other sea issues from the furthest west between al-Sūs al-Aqsā and al-Andalus. It is broad where it emerges from the ocean, thereafter it narrows, then widens again as far as the confines of Syria. [Map II] I heard one of the learned men of the Maghrib interpret the verse, "Lord of the two easts and Lord of the two wests" (Qurʾān, sūra 55, v. 17) as follows: the two wests are the two sides of this sea, the sundown of summer being on the right side and the sundown of winter on the left of it.

Addition/version MS. C.
I have heard the people of Tanja say that in some places it has a width of some few *farsakhs*, and at the passes of al-Andalus a journey of six days. It is said that its length from east to west is two thousand ...

I heard some from there say, too, that the sea is so narrow in the vicinity of Tanja that it. ... [lacuna in MS.], and they agreed that at the passes of al-Andalus one who sees one shore may have the other in view also. Ibn al-Faqīh points out that the length of this western Romaean sea is two thousand five hundred p. 15 *farsakhs*, measured from Antākiya to Jazāʾir al-Saʿāda (the Fortunate Isles), and its width in one place is five hundred *farsakhs*, and in another two hundred *farsakhs*. All the shoreland on the south side from Tarsūs to Dimyāt, and thence to al-Sūs is held by the Muslims; all of the other side, meaning the left of the sea, is held by Christians.

Addition/version MS. C.
The sum total of the islands is one hundred sixty-two. These were in a flourishing condition until the Muslims invaded them and ravaged them, excepting three large ones—Qubrus (Cyprus), situated opposite Dimashq (Damascus), and with a circuit of one hundred thirteen *farsakhs*; Iqrītish (Crete), over against Barqa, with a circuit of one hundred *farsakhs*; and the island of Isqiliyya (Sicily), which we will thoroughly examine in our account of the region of al-Maghrib.

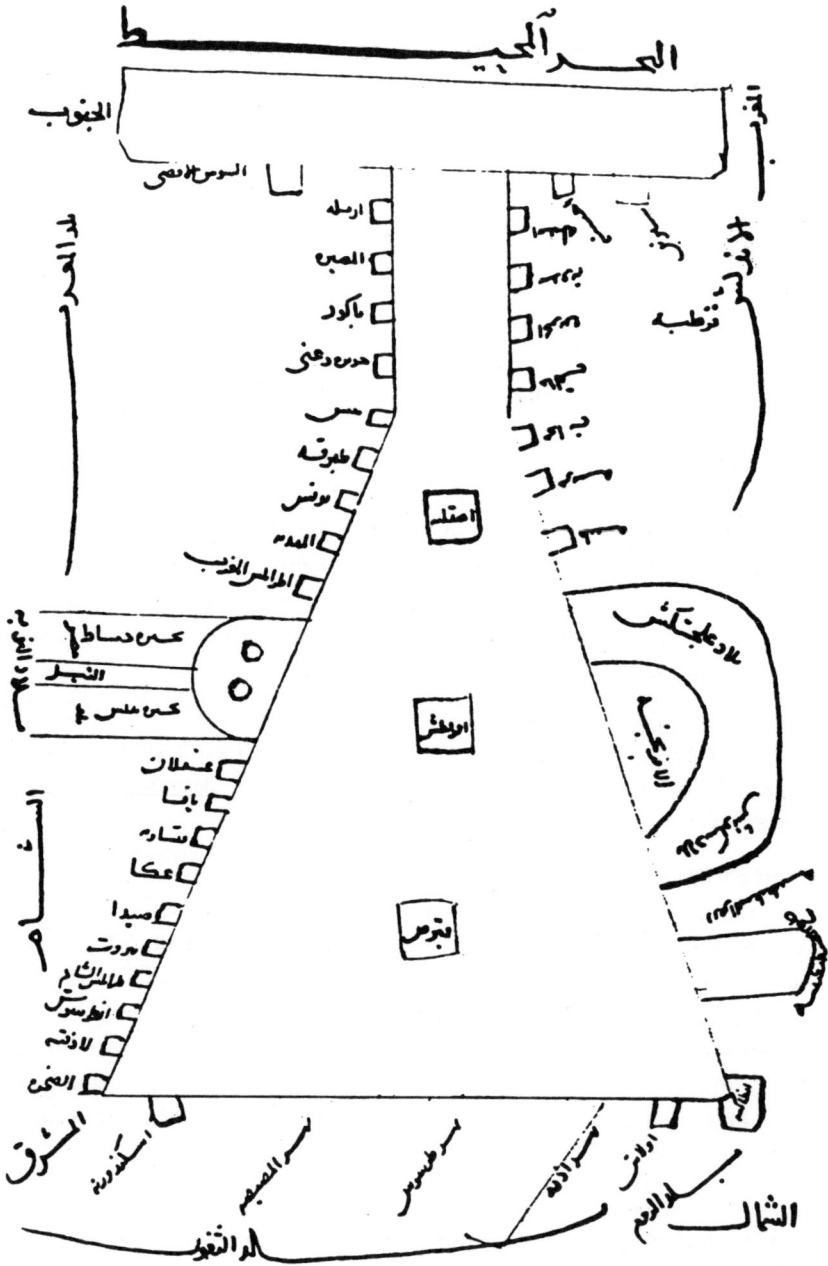

Map II: Bahr al-Rūm (see p. 406).
From MS. Sprenger 5—Ahlwardt 6034 by kind permission of the Staatsbibliothek
Preussischer Kulturbesitz, Berlin, Orientabteilung.

In this sea are three flourishing and populous islands—Isqiliyya (Sicily) facing al-Maghrib, Iqrītish (Crete) opposite Egypt, and Qubrus (Cyprus) over against Syria. It has a number of well-known gulfs. On its shore are many towns, important frontier posts and military stations. Part of the sea borders the territory of the Romaeans to the borders of al-Andalus. The Romaeans are the masters here and very much dreaded; and they and the inhabitants of Sicily and al-Andalus are the most familiar with this sea, its confines and its gulfs, because they constantly journey over it, raiding the lands on the opposite side. Their routes, too, to Egypt and Syria are across this sea. I have been on board ship there with them for a long time, always asking them about it and about its characteristics; I would repeat to them what I had learned about it from hearsay, but rarely did I find them differing over it. It is a difficult and stormy sea, its booming always audible especially on Thursday nights. [The nychthemeron that includes the day of Friday begins at sundown on Thursday.]

I was informed of the following tradition by the jurist Abu al-Tayyib ʿAbd Allāh bin Muhammad al-Jalāl, at al-Rayy, who had it from Ahmad bin Muhammad bin Yazīd al-Astarābādhī, who had it from ʿAbbās bin Muhammad, who had it from Abū Salama, who had it from Saʿīd bin Zayd, who had it from Ibn Yasār reporting it from ʿAbd Allāh bin ʿAmr. The tradition relates that when God created the Sea of al-Shām, he uttered this inspiration to it: "I have created thee and designed thee as a carrier for some of my servants, who seek my bounty, praising me, worshipping me, magnifying me, and glorifying me; so how wilt thou act towards them?" Said the sea: "My Lord, then I shall drown them." Said the Lord: "Begone, for I curse thee, and will diminish thy worth and thy fish." Then the Lord inspired into the sea of al-ʿIrāq (the Indian Ocean) the selfsame words, and it said: "My Lord, in that case I shall carry them on my back; when they praise Thee I praise Thee with them, and when they worship Thee I worship Thee with them, when they magnify Thee I magnify Thee with them." Said the Lord: "Go, for I have blessed thee, and will increase thy bounty and thy fish." Here then is proof that there are but two seas.

p. 16

Now I do not know whether these two seas empty into the ocean or proceed from it. I have read in some books that they both proceed from it; but that they pour into it is more probable.

Addition/version MS. C.
Sāhib al-Zīj ("the keeper of the astronomical tables"), and Qudāma al-Kātib, and al-Jayhānī have made the seas five in number, adding the Encircling Ocean, the Gulf [of Qustantīniyya, Constantinople], and the lake of Tabaristān. As for Ibrāhīm [al-Fārisī al-Istakhrī], he makes the number of seas three, including the Encircling Ocean. As for us, we do not go beyond what God—may He be praised and exalted—says in His Book ...

Indeed, if a person goes out from Farghāna he does not cease to descend until he arrives at Egypt, and from there, again, to the remotest part of al-Maghrib.

Moreover, the people of al-ʿIrāq call the Persians the people of the upper ground, and the people of al-Maghrib the people of the lower ground. This supports the views we have expressed, and indicates that the seas are rivers that combine and pour into the ocean—but God knows best. Abū Zayd made the seas three in number, by the addition of the ocean, but we ourselves do not include it in our reckoning, because it, as is said, encircles the world as with a ring—having neither bound nor limit. As for al-Jayhānī, he makes the seas five in number, by the addition of the Sea of the Khazars (Caspian), and of the Gulf of Constantinople (Sea of Marmara). For our part we have limited ourselves to the number God made known in His Book where it says: "He let forth the two seas to meet together, between them a barrier they cannot surpass. Come forth from them are the pearl and the coral" (Qurʾān, sūra 55, vv. 19, 20, 22). The barrier is the land from al-Faramā to al-Qulzum, a distance of three days' journey. But if it were to be argued that God—may He be exalted—wished by the expression "the two seas" (Qurʾān, sūra 25, v. 53), to refer only to the one of fresh water and one of salt water, since they do not mingle, as the verse says: "It is He who has made to flow the two seas," we reply that the pearl and the coral are not found in fresh water, whereas God says "from them both;" and there is no disagreement among the learned that the pearl is taken from the Sea of China, and the coral from the Romaean Sea. Therefore we are certain the reference is to

p. 17 these two seas only. Again, suppose it were to be argued that the seas are seven in number, since God—may He be exalted and glorified—has said: "Were all the trees on earth to become pens, and the sea, ink, and the sea increased again with seven other seas. ..." (Qurʾān, sūra 31, v. 27), and the addition be made of al-Maqlūba (Dead Sea) and the Sea of Khwārazm (Aral Sea); the reply is that God—may He be exalted—did not say "the seas are seven in number," but rather He mentions only the Sea of the Arabs, and suggests that if there should be seven seas like it and they, too, were to be made into ink; this is the same sense in which He said: "Were the iniquitous to have all that is in the earth all together and the like of it with it ..." (Qurʾān, sūra 39, v. 47) In fact, on the basis of this claim the seas would have to be reckoned eight in number, so let us raise this supposition now as a question and deal with it thoroughly. For suppose we allow that the sea is the Sea of al-Hijāz, and the seven are the sea of al-Qulzum, the Sea of al-Yaman, the Sea of ʿUmān, the Sea of Makrān, the Sea of Kirmān, the Sea of Fārs, and the Sea of Hajar—and that makes eight, just as the verse says. Indeed it may be urged further that you must, according to this interpretation, allow the existence of even more than ten seas, seeing that you have omitted the Sea of China, the Sea of India, and the Sea of al-Zanj (Blacks). The answer to this is twofold. In the first place, God—may He be exalted—spoke to the Arabs about what they knew and could see with their own eyes, so as to impress the argument on them with greater force. Now their voyages were solely in these seas, and, as you realize, this is the sea that, under various names, surrounds the realm of the Arabs from al-Qulzum (Red Sea) to

ʿAbbādān. Our second point is, that, supposing we do not deny that the seas might be many, and that God—may He be exalted—in this verse referred to eight of them only. Suppose we were to allow all this, then you may say that the argument comes back on me, and that I have to admit that the seas may be seven, and God mentioned in that verse only two of them. Now my answer is that the one position does not correspond with the other. You see, God—may He be exalted—said in that verse, "He let forth the two seas to meet together;" in this He refers to two particular seas, using the "a" and the "l" ["al"="the"], not to refer to just the class in general, but rather to specify the individual. When He said in this verse that "if He were to add seven seas to it," He did not insert the definite article; and of course there is the possibility that He could mean by that "seven out of a number," just as He said, "He compelled it against them seven nights and eight days, grueling," (*Qurʾ ān*, sūra 69, v. 7)—and the days of God are many. However, He has said in another verse, "as for the three who lagged behind ..." (*Qurʾ ān*, sūra 9, v. 118); it is not possible to say that the men were more than three in number.

If it were to be argued that, since there is a disagreement about the interpretation of this verse, and we know that the Sea of China does not meet that of the Romaeans, the argument based upon the verse then collapses, and that the other verse is clearly established so that the seas must be seven: my
p. 18   answer to that is that the disagreement is removed by God's saying, "Come forth from them are the pearl and the coral;" and as to their meeting, a number of the elders of Egypt have told me that the Nile used to flow into the Sea of China up to recently.

If it were to be said here, "Your interpretation necessarily entails a contradiction, because according to it the two seas meet; but between them, as you have already said, there is a distance of three days' journey—and the Book of God is exempt from contradiction: so our interpretation is in order, the meeting of the two is the flowing of the fresh over the salt water, and the barrier is the prevention of their mixing with each other;" we reply that our explanation is also in order and we have given to every expression its proper meaning; for we have said that the meeting is what we mentioned in respect of the flow of the Nile into the Sea of China; and as part of the Nile today debouches into the Romaean Sea, it is in the Nile that the meeting of the two seas takes place. In fact it is said that the mother of Mūsā—on him be peace—cast the cradle in which he lay into the sea of al-Qulzum and it floated on the Nile to the capital. Moreover, the meeting of things is not necessarily a mingling, because there may be a separation and a distance between things that meet; but what they mean should be called mingling, and not meeting.

If someone should say: "Why did you include the seas of the Persians among the seven, seeing you had said that God spoke to the Arabs only about what they were familiar with?" The answer to this has two parts. In the first place, the Arabs had frequently traveled to Fārs. You know that ʿUmar bin al-Khattāb—may he be pleasing to God—said, "I learned justice from Kisrā;" and he mentions the apprehension of God of that monarch, and his conduct of government. Moreover, anyone who makes a journey to Hajar and ʿAbbādān must have a knowledge of the seas of Fārs, Kirmān, and Tīz Makrān; and do you not know that many people refer to the part of this sea as far as the coast of al-Yaman as the Sea of Fārs; or that most of the ship-builders and mariners are Persians? In addition, this sea that stretches from ʿUmān to ʿAbbādān is not very wide, so that a voyager cannot be unfamiliar with its coasts.

If it were then said: "Why, then, did you not say the same in respect of the sea of al-Qulzum to the place where it grows wide?" We answer that we have already said that from al-Qulzum to ʿAydhāb, and beyond, is desert and void. p. 19 It has not been understood that any part of this region has given its name to this sea. Besides, we have resolved this question in our previous answers.

If it is asked how we can consider one sea as if it were eight separate seas—the answer is that this is well known to everyone who sails the sea. You see how God referred to the Sea of the Romaeans as "two seas," as He says: "And when Moses said to his page, 'I shall keep on walking until I reach the confluence of the two seas, though for ages I continue roaming.' And when they reached the meeting-point of both, ..." (Qurʾān, sūra 18, vv. 60–61). Now, all this took place on the coast of Syria, and the traces of it, plainly to be seen, including Sakhrat Mūsā (the Rock of Moses), are there in evidence. But now, of course, it may be asked, "Why have you not interpreted God's utterance, 'He set loose the two seas,' as meaning but one sea?" We reply that this is inadmissible, because God—the most exalted—said "between the two is a barrier," and the barrier is a partition.

In any case, we say to the one who controverts the matter with us: "If the matter is as you assert, then show us eight seas in the realm of Islām!" If he wants to include the encircling ocean we say that that is on the boundary of the world, with no known limits. Should he want to include the Gulf of Constantinople, we should say that it is but a gulf of the Romaean Sea that goes out beyond Sicily—for are they not constantly setting out on raids over it? If he were to suggest the Sea of the Khazars (Caspian Sea), we would say that it is a lake: do not most people call it the Lake of Tabaristān, and of course you must know how close its shores are to each other? If he were to mention al-Maqlūba (Dead Sea), and the Lake of Khwārazm (Aral Sea), we should say that whoever considers these two part of the total number of seas must similarly consider the lakes of al-Riḥāb, Fārs, and Turkistān, so that the number then would exceed twenty. So if our disputant is fair, he will simply accept our argument—but God knows best.

The rivers that have an abundant flow in the realm, and that are the most distinguished in my opinion, are twelve in number: Dijla (Tigris), al-Furāt (Euphrates), al-Nīl (Nile), Jayhūn (Oxus), Nahr al-Shāsh (Jaxartes), Sayhān, Jayhān, Baradān, Mihrān (Indus), Nahr al-Rass (Araxes), Nahr al-Malik, Nahr al-Ahwāz (Kārūn), all of which are navigable. Of lesser importance are another fifteen: Nahr al-Marwayn, Nahr Harāt (Harī Rūd), the river of Sijistān (Hilmand), the river of Balkh, Nahr al-Sughd, Tayfūrī, Zandarūd, Nahr al-ʿAbbās, Baradā, Nahr al-Urdunn (Jordan), al-Maqlūb (Orontes), the river of Antākiya (Orontes, p. 20 lower course), the river of Arrajān (Tāb), the river Shīrīn, and the river of Samandar.

Less important waterways than these are small, and some of them we shall mention in our accounts of the different regions, such as the river Tāb, al-Nahrawān [canal in al-ʿIrāq], al-Zāb, and the like.

The Tigris takes its origin from a spring which emerges from below the fortress of Dhu al-Qarnayn near Bāb al-Zulmāt (Gate of the Dark Regions), in the region of Aqūr (Mesopotamia) above al-Mawṣil,

Addition/version MS. C.
between two mountains near Āmid. There, a river joins it coming from the direction of the town of Balad, and again it falls between two mountains.

Lower down it is joined by a number of streams, among them al-Zāb, and continues until it is met by the Euphrates, and the branches of al-Nahrawān, close to Baghdād.

Addition/version MS. C.
Its length as far as ʿAbbādān is about eight hundred miles.

The Euphrates comes out of the territory of the Romaeans,

Addition/version MS. C.
between Malatya and Shimshāt.

then makes a circuit

Addition/version MS. C.
... in a southerly direction.

around the region of Aqūr; it receives its tributary, the Khābūr, then enters al-ʿIrāq. Here it spreads out widely to form the marshes beyond al-Kūfa; then joins with the Tigris in four branches.

Addition/version MS. C.
It then divides into two branches, one taking its course towards the west until it reaches al-Kūfa, the other taking a direct course, and so waters the cultivated area around Baghdād. A part of it then spreads out to form marshes, and a part meets the Tigris at Wāsit, after a number of streams have branched off from it below al-Anbār, to join the Tigris in the district of Baghdād. From its source in upper Aqūr to where it ends at the other side of Wāsit is one hundred thirty-five miles.

With respect to the Nile, it comes forth from the country of the Nubians,

Addition/version MS. C.

[The outlet of the Nile is from the country of the Nubians] in the district of the Upper Saʿīd, and it flows to the city of Uswān. It then turns away and follows a sinuous course between the mountains called Balūqiyā, returning to Maqadūniya, passing close by al-Fustāt, afterwards dividing into seven branches. Of these, one branch flows to Alexandria, then, after dividing into two channels, flows westward and falls into the sea. The remaining six branches flow in a direct course towards two lagoons, where Tinnīs and Dimyāt are situated, to pour into the Romaean Sea. I have heard some of the people there say that a branch of it used to flow to the Sea of China, debouching into it above al-Qulzum, and indeed they pointed the place out to me. From its source at the extremity of the region to its debouchment is a distance of two thousand miles.

then cuts through the region of Egypt. It forms branches below al-Fustāt, one flowing into the sea at al-Iskandariyya (Alexandria), the other at Dimyāt (Damietta). According to al-Jayhānī it has its origin in the Mountain of the Moon, discharges into two lakes beyond the equator, thence makes its course through the land of the Nubians. Others have said that its origin is not known, and that no one knows where it comes from.

p. 21   We have received a tradition from Abu al-Hasan al-Khalīl bin al-Hasan al-Sarakhsī in Naysābūr, following Abu al-Hasan ʿAlī bin Muhammad al-Qantarī, following al-Maʾmūn bin Ahmad al-Salmī, following Muhammad bin Khalaf, following Abū Sālih, secretary of al-Layth bin Saʿad, who heard it from al-Layth himself. It has been recounted—but God alone knows the truth of the matter—that there was among the descendants of al-ʿĪs [Esau] a man named Hāʾidh bin-Abī Shālūm bin al-ʿĪs, who, fleeing for refuge from one of their kings, entered the land of Egypt, where he remained for a number of years. However, when he saw the wonders of its Nile, and the products it brings forth there he vowed to God that he would not leave its banks until he reached the extremity of it, where it has its origin, unless he should die in the meantime. He accordingly journeyed until he reached a green sea, and beheld the Nile cutting its course through this sea—Muqaddasī says that this sea is the encircling ocean. He walked along the sea-shore, and came upon a man standing in prayer under an apple tree; and when he saw him, he was cordial towards him and greeted him. Then enquired the man: "Who art thou?" Said he: "I am Hāʾidh the son of Abu' Shālūm, the son of al-ʿĪs, the son of Ishāq—God's peace and blessings be upon him—and who art thou?" Said he: "I am ʿImrān the son of al-ʿĪs, the son of Ishāq—may peace be upon him." "And what has caused thee to come here, O ʿImrān?" "What brought me hither is what brought thee; and when I had arrived at this place, God—may He be exalted—instructed me: 'Remain in this place until you receive my instruction.'" Said the other: "O ʿImrān, inform me about the Nile." Said he: "I will not tell thee unless thou doest what I ask thee." Said he: "And what is that?" Said ʿImrān, "If on thy return to me, and I am still living, thou shalt remain with me until God will reveal to me what to do in the matter; or if God should take me, then thou shalt inter me." Said Hā'idh, "I accept these conditions." Said ʿImrān to him: "Continue thy journey along the shore of this sea, and thou wilt come to where there is a riding animal that is confronting the sun, at which, on its rising, it rushes to devour it. Do not allow this to frighten thee; rather, mount it, and it will take thee to the other shore of the sea; travel along the shore and return until thou endest up at the Nile. Travel along its course and thou shalt reach a land of iron, where the mountains and the trees and the plains are [all of iron. Proceed until thou shalt reach an area of

p. 22 silver, where the mountains and the trees, and all other objects are of silver. Do thou go on until thou shalt come to an area of gold, in which everything is (text supplied from *Muʿjām al-Buldān* of Yāqūt)] of gold. Thou shalt finally come upon a dome of gold, in which knowledge of the Nile will be given to thee."

He accordingly pursued his course until he came to the dome, and lo! water was flowing down the wall into the dome. Here it divided and flowed through the four doors. However, three of the streamlets sank into the ground, but there was one that flowed on the surface of the earth—and this is the Nile—so he drank from its waters and rested. He then advanced to the wall and aspired to climb it, when an angel appeared and said to him: "O Hā'idh, stay where thou art for thou hast achieved knowledge of the Nile, and this is Paradise." The narrator recounted this story at full length.

The Jayhūn (Oxus) has its origin in the country of Wakhkhān, flows toward al-Khuttal, where it widens and increases with six tributaries flowing into it—the rivers Hulbuk, then the river Barbān, then the river of Fārghar, next is the river of Andījārāgh, then the river Wakhshāb, and this is the deepest one of them. Then the river of al-Quwādiyān [Qubādhiyān] joins it; then the rivers of al-Saghāniyān. All these are from the Haytal side of the river. Then enlarged like a lake it drops down to Khwārazm, and flows into a marsh of briny water, having already irrigated a number of cities, among them all those of Khwārazm, east and west.

The river al-Shāsh (Syr Daryā) emerges from on the right of the country of the Turks (Turkistān), and flows also into the lake of Khwārazm (Aral Sea). It approaches the Jayhūn River in volume, but it appears, as it were, without life.

Addition/version MS. C.
Then a channel runs from it into the area lying between Usrūshana and Ghujanda. From the beginning to the end of this river is a distance of one hundred forty *farsakhs*.

As for the Sayhān, the Jayhān, and the Baradān, these are the rivers of Tarsūs, Adhana and al-Massīsa. They emerge from the land of the Romaeans, then they flow into the sea, as do the other rivers of Syria with the exception of the Baradā and al-Urdunn (the Jordan); both of these flow into the Dead Sea. The Baradā debouches from the mountains above Damascus, flows through the capital, and irrigates the district. The remaining waters divide themselves, one portion forming an evaporative fen at the extremity of the district, the other part flowing down towards the Jordan.

The river Mihrān (Indus) emerges from al-Hind, then pours into the Sea of p. 23 China after receiving a number of tributaries in its course through the regions. In the taste of its water, in its color, in its rise, together with the presence of crocodiles in it, it resembles the Nile.

The rivers al-Rass, al-Malik, and al-Kurr all emerge from the domains of the Romaeans, and irrigate the region of al-Rihāb; they then fall into the lake of the Khazars (Caspian).

The rivers of al-Ahwāz consist of a number of streams that descend over the region from the mountains, then unite by Hisn Mahdī, and empty themselves into the Sea of China near ʿAbbādān. I have come across the following in a book in al-Basra: "Four rivers from Paradise are in this world—the Nile, Jayhūn, the Euphrates, and al-Rass; four are from the rivers of hell—al-Zabadānī, al-Kurr, Sanja, and al-Samm."

The rivers of al-Marwayn, Harāt, Sijistān, and Balkh emerge from the four sides of the country of al-Ghūr, then flow down into their respective districts and irrigate them.

The Tayfūrī descends from the mountains of Jurjān and waters the district; the river of al-Rayy emerges above the town in what is like a bubbling fountain; it then divides itself into branches and descends to the district. The Zandarūd comes down from the mountains of Isfahān, enters into al-Yahūdiyya, and p. 24 irrigates the district. As for the rivers of Fārs, they flow into five lakes in the region. The river Tāb comes from al-Burj beyond Sumayram, then flows by the frontiers of Fārs, to pour into the Sea of China near Sīnīz. The river of Arrajān gushes out from the mountains of Fārs; some briny water flows into it below al-ʿAqaba (the mountain pass) and it irrigates the district by individual allotments.

An Account of Names and their Diversities

You should know that in the realm of Islām are towns and districts and villages that have similar names, but are in different locations. This circumstance itself is a difficulty for people in general, as is the matter of people who are named after those places. We accordingly decided to provide this chapter, and devote it to those names. We shall likewise give the names of things that peoples of the regions name differently, as this will undoubtedly be of use to people visiting those regions.

Al-Sūs—a district in the furthest extremity of al-Maghrib; a town in the beginning of it; another in Haytal; a district in Khūzistān. In al-Maghrib also is *Sūsa*.

Atrābulus (Tripoli)—a town on the coast of (the district of) Dimashq; another on the coast of Barqa.

Bayrūt—a town in (the district of) Dimashq; a town in Khūzistān.

ʿAsqalān—a town on the coast of Filastīn; [a town with] a *minbar* (pulpit, mosque) in Balkh.

Ramāda—a town in al-Maghrib; a village in Balkh; another in Naysābūr; another in al-Ramla.

Tabarān—a city on the border of Qūmis; the *rustāq* (outlying rural district with towns and villages) of Sarakhs. *Tābarān*, the capital of Tūs; *Tabaristān* a district; *Tabariyya*, the capital of al-Urdunn; *Tuwārān*, a district in al-Sind; *Tabarak*, a place in al-Rayy.

Qūhistān—a district in Khurāsān; a town in Kirmān.

Tabas al-Tamr (of the dates) and *Tabas al-ʿUnnāb* (of the jujube), two towns in Qūhistān.

Dihistān—a town in Kirmān; an area in Jurjān; an area in Bādhghīs.

Nasā—a town in Khurāsān; another in Fārs; another in Kirmān.

Al-Baydhāʾ—is also Nasā of Fārs; a district in al-Maghrib; a town in the area of al-Khazar.

p. 25 *Al-Basra*—in al-ʿIrāq; a town in al-Maghrib.

Al-Hīra—a town that at one time existed in the district of al-Kūfa; a village in Fārs; a way station in Sijistān; a quarter in the city of Naysābūr.

Al-Jūr—a town in Fārs; and al-Jūr, a quarter in the city of Naysābūr.

Hulwān—a district in al-ʿIrāq; a town in Misr; a village in Naysābūr; another in Qūhistān.

Karkh—a town in the district of Sāmarrā; a quarter in the city of Baghdād; a [place with a] mosque (*minbar*) in al-Rihāb; a village in the district of Baghdād: and

Karkha—a town in Khūzistān; *Karūkh* a town in Harāt.

Al-Shāsh—a district in Haytal; a village in al-Rayy.

Astarābādh—a town in Jurjān; a village in Nasā of Khurāsān.

Karaj—townland and town in Hamadhān; a village in al-Rayy.

Dastajird—a town in al-Saghāniyān; some villages in al-Rayy and Naysābur; the town of Dastajird in Kirmān.

Mughūn—a town in Qūmis; another in Kirmān.

Bāsand—a town in al-Saghāniyān; another in al-Sind.

Āwa—two towns in al-Jibāl.

Al-Ahwāz—the metropolis of Khūzistān; a village in al-Rayy.

Al-Raqqa—in Athūr; a town in Qūhistān.

Khwār—a town in the district of al-Rayy; another on the borders of Qūmis; and there is *Khūr* in Balkh and *Khūr* in Qūhistān.

Nūqān—a town in Tūs; a village in Naysābūr; *Mūqān*—a town in al-Rihāb; and *Manūqān*—a town in Kirmān.

Al-Kūfa—in al-ʿIrāq; Kūfā, a town in Bādhghīs; and *Kūfan*—the caravanserai of Abīward.

Khāniqīn—a town in Hulwān of al-ʿIrāq; al-Khāniqīn in the district of al-Kūfa; and

Khānūqa—in the district of Athūr; al-Khāniqa, the conventicle of the Karrāmiyya sect in Īliyā (Jerusalem).

Al-Hadītha—a town on the Tigris and another on the Euphrates in Aqūr; and *al-Hadath*—a town in the district of Qinnasrīn; and *al-Muhdatha*, a stopping-place in the open country of Taymāʾ.

p. 26

Al-Nabk and *alʿAwnīd*—two towns in al-Hijāz; two stopping-places in the open country of Taymāʾ.

Al-Zarqāʾ—a village on the road to al-Rayy; a place on the road to Dimashq.

ʿAkkā—a town on the coast in the district of al-Urdunn; and ʿAkk is a tribe in al-Yaman.

Al-Yahūdiyya—the capital of the district of Isfahān; the capital of Jūzjān.

Al-Anbār—a town in the district of Baghdād; *Anbār*—a town in Jūzjān.

Isfahān—a district; and the village of *Isfahānak* is on the road thereto; and *al-Isbahānāt*—a town in Fārs.

Madīna—the City of the Prophet—God's peace and blessings be upon him; the *Madīna* of al-Rayy; the *Madīna* of Isfahān; also *Madīnat al-Salām* [Baghdād]; also *al-Madāʾin* in al-ʿIrāq.

Kūtā Rabbā and *Kūtā* al-Tarīq—a town and a village in al-ʿIrāq.

Al-Daskara—in Khūzistān; and *Daskara* in al-ʿIrāq.

Bārāb—a country district in Isbījāb; and *Fāryāb* in Jūzjān.

Al-Tālaqān—a town in al-Daylam; also Tālaqān in Jūzjān.

Abshīn—the royal city of the Shār; also a town in Ghaznīn.

Harāt—of Khurāsān; a town of Istakhr.

Baghlān—Upper, and Lower: two towns in Tukhāristān.

Asadāwādh—a town in al-Jibāl; a village in Naysābūr.

Biyār—a townlike settlement in Qūmis; a village in Nasā of Khurāsān.

Widhār—a *rustāq* of Samarqand.

p. 27 *Jurjān*—a district in al-Daylam; and *Jurjāniyya*, a town in Khwārazm.

Balkh; and *Balkhān*—a town beyond Abīward.

Qazwīn—a town in the district of al-Rayy; and *Qazwīnak* a village in al-Dīnawar.

Filastīn—of al-Shām; also, a village in al-ʿIrāq.

Al-Ramla—the capital of Filastīn; a village in al-ʿIrāq;

Qaryat al-Raml—a town in Khūzistān.

Firabr—a town on the Jayhūn; *Farah*—a town of Sijistān; *Afrāwa*—the caravanserai of Nasā.

Āmul—a town on the Jayhūn; the capital of Tabaristān; *Itil*—the capital of al-Khazar.

Bakrābādh—a townlike settlement in Jurjān; a way station in Sijistān.

Al-Nil—the river of Misr; a town in al-ʿIrāq.

Jabala—a town associated with Hims; *Jubayl*—on the littoral of Dimashq.

Qubā—a town in Farghānā; a village in Yathrib; a way station in the desert.

Qūmis—a district in al-Daylam; Qūmisa—a village in Isfahan.

Al-Shāmāt—the townships of al-Shām; a town in Kirmān; a quarter in the suburbs of Naysābūr.

Jurash—a town in al-Yaman; *Jabal Jarash* in al-Urdunn.

Sanjān—a town in the district of al-Rihāb; another in Marw; a village in Naysābur; *Sinjār*—a town in Athūr; *Zanjān*—a town in the district of al-Rayy.

There are *Marw* al-Shāhijān, and *Marw* al-Rūdh.

Suqyā Yazīd—a town and a stopping place in al-Hijāz; *Suqyā Banī Ghifār*.

Hadhramawt—a town in al-Ahqāf; a quarter in the town of al-Mawsil.

Al-Rusāfa—a quarter in Baghdād; a village in Arrajān.

Nīnawā—al-Qadīma (ancient) and al-Hadītha (modern), in al-Mawsil.

ʿAskar Abī Jaʿfar—to the eastern side of Baghdād; a village in al-Basra; *ʿAskar Mukram*—a district of Khūzistān;

ʿAskar Banjahīr—an area in Balkh; al-ʿAskar—a quarter in the city of al-Ramla, another in Naysābūr; a village in Bukhārā.

Al-Dawraq—a district, town, and village in Khūzistān.

Al-Zubaydiyya—a way station in al-Jibāl; one in al-Baṭāʾih; a water hole in the desert; *al-Zabadānī*—a town in [the district of] Dimashq.

p. 28 *Al-Haddāda*—a village in Qūmis; al-Haddādiyya—a village in al- Baṭāʾih.

Naysābūr, Sābūr, Jundaysābūr—three towns which Sābur built, he built besides, in Arrajān, the town Balāsābur, and in Istakhr, *Arsābur*.

Kirmān—a region; *Karmān Shāhān*—a town in al-Jibāl; *Karmīniya*—a town in Bukhārā; *Bayt Karmā*—a village in Īliyā (Jerusalem).

ʿUmān—a district in al-Jazīra; *ʿAmmān*—a town in Filastīn.

Al-Zāb—an area in al-Maghrib; a river in Aqūr.

Iskāf—Upper, and Lower, in Baghdād.

Jīlān—in al-Daylam, commonly called Gīlān; *al-Jīl*—a town in al-ʿIrāq.

Jazīrat al-ʿArab [the Peninsula of the Arabs]—a region; *Jazīrat ibn ʿUmar* in Aqūr; *Jazīrat Banī Zaghannāya*, and *Jazīrat Abī Sharīk* in Ifrīqiya; *al-Jazīra*— a town near al-Fustāt; *Jazīrat Banī Haddān* in the sea of al-Qulzum.

Qalʿat al-Sirāt, Qalʿat al-Qawārib, Qalʿat Burjuma, Qalʿat al-Nusūr, Qalʿat Shamīt, Qalʿat Ibn al-Harab, Qalʿat Abī Thawr, Qalʿat al-Ballūt—all in al-Maghrib, and there is *al-Qalʿa* in al-Rihāb—all of these are towns.

Hisn Mahdī—a town in al-Ahwāz; *Hisn al-Sūdān, Hisn al-Barār, Hisn Ibn Sālih*, towns in the district of *Sijilmāsa; Hisn Bulkūna*—a town in al-Andalus; *Hisn al-Khawābī* in al-Shām; *Hisn Mansūr* in al-Thugūr [collective: The Frontier Towns].

Qasr Ibn Hubayra, Qasr al-Jiss in al-ʿIrāq; *Qasr al-Fulūs*, a town in the district of Tāhart; *Qasr al-Ifrīqī, Madīnat al-Qusūr* (Taqiyūs) in Ifrīqiya; *Qasr al-Rīh*— a way station in Naysābūr; *Qasr al-Lusūs*—a way station in al-Jibāl.

p. 29 *Tāhart*—the Upper, a district, the Lower, a town; in al-Maghrib.

Sūq Ibn Khalaf in Ifrīqiya; *Sūq Ibn Habla, Sūq Karā, Sūq Ibn Mablūl, Sūq Ibrāhīm*—towns in the district of Tāhart. There are market towns [*sūq* = market] named after the days of the week in Khūzistān; some towns in Tukhāristān are named according to the markets.

Al-Ahsāʾ—a district; also a way station in al-Hijāz.

Al-Qādisiyya—a town in the district of al-Kūfa; a way station in Sāmarrā.

Ghazza in Filastīn; *al-Ghuzza* in Tāhart.

Bathāʾ of Makka; *al-Bathāʾ*—a town in Tāhart.

Harān—a village in Isfahān; *Wahrān*—a town in Tāhart.

Tabrīz—in al-Rihāb; *Tabrīn* in Tāhart.

Tāwīlt Abī Maghūl, and another (Tāwīlt) two towns in Tāhart.

ʿAyn al-Mughattā—in Isqiliyya (Sicily);

ʿAyn Zarba—in al-Thugūr; *Raʾs al-ʿAyn*, in Athūr: towns and villages; *Yanbuʿ* in al-Hijāz; *ʿAinūnā*—a town of Wayla; *Bayt ʿAynūn*—a village in Īliyā.

Sabra—a city in Ifrīqiya; another in Barqa. *Marsā al-Kharaz; Marsā al-Hajjāmīn; Marsā al-Hajar; Marsa al-Dajāj*—towns in al-Maghrib.

Kharrāra—a village in Fārs; a town in Tāhart.

p. 30 *Kūl*—towns in Ifrīqiya, al-Mashriq, and Fārs.

Juwaym Abī Ahmad—a town, and the village *Juwaym*—in Fārs.

Qustantīniyya, Qusantīniya, Qastīliya—towns in al-Maghrib; *al-Qastal*, a village on the borders of al-Shām.

Maʿarrat al-Nuʿmān, and *Maʿarrat Qinnasrīn*, two towns in al-Shām.

Al-Lajjūn—two towns of this name in al-Shām.

There is Thaghr (The Frontier Town) of *Tarsūs*; and on the coast of al-Shām, *Antarsūs* (Antartūs).

Dār al-Balāt—in the metropolis of the Romaeans; *Balāt Marwān*—a town in al-Andalus; Īliyā is also called *al-Balāt*.

Wādi al-Qurā in al-Hijāz; *Wādi al-Rummān* in al-Andalus, as is also *Wādi ʾl-Hijāra*.

Bāniyās—a town, and *Bānās*, a river near Dimashq; *Baysān*—a town in al-Urdunn.

Al-Ruhā—a town in Athūr; *Wādī 'l-Ruhā*—a town in Ifrīqiya.

Some towns have more than one name: for example,

Makka, Bakka;

al-Madīna, Yathrib, Tayba, Tāba, Jābira, Miskīna, Mahbūra, Yandar, al-Dār, Dār al-Hijra;

Bayt al-Maqdis, Īliyā, al-Quds, al-Balāt;

ʿUmān, Suhār, Mazūn;

ʿAdan, Samarān, al-Sarra, al-Hays;

al-Bahrayn, Hajar;

Jur, Fīrūzābādh;

Nasā, al-Baydhāʾ.

Three capital cities are called Shahrastān—Jurjān, Sābūr, and Kāth. There are capitals called by the names of their districts, and have names other than these also, for example, Bukhārā, Naysābūr, and Misr.

Some referents are variously named among the inhabitants of the regions; for example:

lahhām, jazzār, qassāb, a butcher;

kursuf, ʿutb, qutn, cotton;

qattān, hallāj, a cleaner or spinner of cotton;

al-bazzāzīn, al-karābīsiyyīn, al-rahādina, the linen drapers;

p. 31   *jabbān, tabbākh, baqqāl, fāmī, tājir*, a food vendor;

mīzāb; mirzāb, mizrāb, mathʿab, a drainpipe;

bāqillān, fūl, beans;

qidr, burma, an earthenware pot;

mawqida, athāfī, fireplace;

zinbīl, miktal, quffa, a basket;

sifl, mirkan, ijjāna, taghār, a washbasin;

qintār, buhār, a (varying) weight;

mann, ratl, a (varying) weight;

habba, tassūj, a grain weight;

khādim, qayyim, mufarrik, ballān, a bathhouse attendant;

shamshak, sandal, a sandal;

hisn, qalʿa, quhandiz, kalāt, a fortress;

sāhib rabʿ, sāhib maslaha, sāhib maslaha, sāhib al-tarīq, a tax-collector;

ʿashshār, makkās, marsadī, a collector of customs;

mukhāsim, khasīm, a litigant;

hākim, qādhī, a judge;

wakīl, jarī, a deputy;

shayraj, salīt, oil of sesame;

zajjāj, qawārīrī, a glassmaker;

safᶜ, sakk, striking on the neck;

buqᶜa, mawdhiᶜ, a place;

qitta, sinnawr, dimma, hirra, a cat;

muᶜallim, khādim, ustādh, shaykh, khasī, an eunuch;

dabbāgh, sarrām, adamī, sikhtiyānī, julūdī, a tanner;

faᶜil, rūzkārī, a labourer;

qarayātī, rustāqī, sawādī, a rustic;

zarrāᶜ, fallāh, harrāth, a farmer;

funduq, khān, tīm, dār al-tujjār, an inn;

mirzaba, akla, a mattock;

habl, qals, a rope;

watad, kanūrā, a stake;

haddanahā, karkarahā, he dispersed them;

liss, mashūshā, robber;

janahat, walajat, it bent under the burden;

unqidha, zawira, to collapse;

qif, halā, whoa!

hayārā, jamāᶜa, a company, community;

lakīshā, kathīr, much;

zarnūq, dūlāb, hannāna, a waterwheel;

dāliya, karma, a grapevine;

mishāt, mijrafa, a spade;

miᶜwal, faᶜs, a hatchet;

sāᶜidan, ziqāfan, upstream;

munhadiran, shibālan, downstream;

tārūs, shartah, a favourable wind;

sukkān, rijl, a rudder;

rubbān, raᶜs, a captain of a ship;

mallāh, nūtī, a sailor;

sāhil, shatt, a shore;

ruqᶜa, bitāqa, a letter, document;

rawha, nafasa, a breeze;

safīna, jāsūs, zawraq, raqqiyya, talawwā, ᶜirdās, tayyār, zabzab, kārawāniyya, muthallatha, wāsitiyya, malqūta, shankūliyya, burākiyya, khaytiyya, shamūt,
p. 32 *musabbahiyya, jabaliyya, makkiyya, zabarbādhiyya, barka, sūqiyya, maᶜbar, walajiyya, tayra, barᶜānī, shabūq, markab, shadhān, burma, qārib, dūnij, hamāma, shīnī, shalandī, bīraja,* boats [of different kinds, sizes, functions].

Similar instances are abundant, and were we to include them all our book would be unreasonably lengthened. However, we will speak, for every region, in the dialect of its inhabitants, debate them on their own terms, quote some of their proverbs, so that their language, and the particular methods of their jurisprudents may become generally known. Whenever we are treating of matters other than the regions themselves, as for instance in these chapters, we use the language of al-Shām [Syria], because it is my native region, and I was reared in it; and I dispute according to the system of al-Qādhī Abu al-Husayn al-Qazwīnī, because he was the first Imām under whom I studied. You will notice the elegance of our style in treating of the region of al-Mashriq, since they of all people use the purest Arabic, having earnestly studied the language in acquiring it from others. Then again look at the pallid style of our language when we treat of al-Misr and al-Maghrib, and the wretchedness of it in our dealing with al-Batāʾih, for it is the speech of the people. Indeed we have aimed in this book only at giving information and definition, not to express emulation or rivalry. You should know, moreover, that I have decided the questions arising from this science in terms of accepted and approved usage, and with full discretion, just as jurists apply the rules in the treatise on *al-Mukātib* [negotiated self-enfranchisement of a slave], and that on Oaths. We have, moreover, arranged the work according to the methods of the schools of the people of al-ʿIrāq, because it is those I have studied and those I prefer. I have also used reasoning by analogy where it seemed good and fitting—but by God is all success granted!

An Account of the Distinctive Features
of the Regions

The fairest of the regions is al-ʿIrāq. The climate is most cheering to the heart,
p. 33 invigorating to the mind. There, the heart feels better, the mind clearer—as long
as one has a sufficiency of means. The most sublime of the regions, that most
abundant in fruits, the most prolific in learned men and illustrious persons,
the most noted for the coldness of its climate, is al-Mashriq.

The richest in wool, silk, and revenue in proportion to its size is al-Daylam.
The region that is best for milk and honey, has the most delicious bread, the
strongest saffron, is al-Jibāl. The region that is the most abundant in fruits
and meats, the cheapest in prices, and with the dullest people, is al-Rihāb. The
most wretched people, the vilest, from top to bottom, are those of Khūzistān.
The sweetest dates, the most abject people are those of Kirmān. The area
most abundant in sugar candy, rice, musk, and unbelievers [camphor?] is
al-Sind. The region with the smartest people, and traders, but the most sinful is
Fārs. The place with the most heat, drought, date palms is the Peninsula of the
Arabs. The region endowed with most blessings, upright people, ascetics, and
shrines is al-Shām. The region most abounding in worshippers, Readers of the
Qurʾān, with resources, trade, special products, and grains, is Misr. The region
with the most dreaded roads, the finest horses, the most generous people,
is Aqūr. The region with the coarsest, most lumpish, most fraudulent people,
and which has the largest number of towns, and the most extensive area, is
al-Maghrib.

ʿAbd al-Rahmān, son of the brother of al-Asmaʿī narrates: "I went to see
al-Jāhiz and said, 'Give me some useful insights into cities.' Said he: 'The
endowments of the capitals are ten: chivalry in Baghdād, eloquence in al-Kūfa,
manufacture in al-Basra, commerce in Misr, treachery in al-Rayy, harshness
in Naysābūr, avarice in Marw, boasting in Balkh, and craftsmanship in
Samarqand.'" And upon my life, he told the truth! However, in Naysābūr, as
well, there are skilled craftsmen, commerce in al-Basra, eloquence in Makka,
ingenuity in Marw. Sanʿāʾ has an agreeable climate, Bayt al-Maqdis is well
constructed; while Sughar and Jurjān are places of pestilence. Damascus has
many streams, Sughd extensive woods, al-Ramla delicious fruits, Tabaristān
persistent rains, Farghānā has low prices; al-Marwa and al-Juhfa, the home
of the licentious. Al-Raqqa is a place of dangers; Hamadhān and Tinnīs, the
p. 34 abode of the well-born. Al-Shām is the region of the best people, and Samarqand
the place of assembly of merchants. Naysābūr is the city of the noble people, and
al-Fustāt the most populous of the capitals. Blessed are the people of al-Gharj in
the justice of their Shār (ruler); the people of Isfahān with their climate, their
dress, and their earthenware. The customs in Shīrāz are a blemish on Islām;
ʿAdan is the vestibule of al-Sīn, also Suhār. In al-Saghāniyān are pasturage,

fruits, and birds; and Bukhārā would be splendid were it not for its water and frequent conflagrations. Balkh is the treasury of jurisprudence, having also spaciousness and prosperity; Īliyā suits both those who are religious, and those who care for the things of this world. The people of Baghdād are short-lived, while Sanʿāʾ and Naysābūr are the reverse of this.

Nowhere are the popular preachers in greater number, or more degraded than in Naysābūr; nor are any people more avaricious than the people of Makka, no poorer people than the people of Yathrib, none more virtuous than the people of Bayt al-Maqdis. There are none more civil than the people of Harāt and Biyār, none more intelligent than those of al-Rayy, none more proficient than the people of Sijistān; no people are more fraudulent than the people of ʿUmān, nor any more ignorant than the people of ʿAmmān. No people have more correct weights and measures than are used by the inhabitants of al-Kūfa and ʿAskar Mukram. None are more handsome than the people of Hims and Bukhārā, none uglier than the people of Khwārazm, and no better looking beards are there than those of the men of al-Daylam. No greater tipplers of wine are there than the people of Baʿlabakk and Misr, no more wanton than the people of Sīrāf; nor are any more rebellious than the people of Sijistān and Damascus, nor any more riotous than the people of Samarqand and al-Shāsh. None are more docile than the people of Misr, none more obtuse than those of al-Bahrayn, none more foolish than the people of Hims. None are more refined than the people of Fasā, Nābulus, then of al-Rayy, and above all Baghdād. None have fairer speech than the people of Baghdād, none ruder than that of Saydā and Harāt. No speech is more correct than that of Khurāsān, no Persian speech more beautiful than that of the people of Balkh and al-Shāsh. No speech is more incorrect than that of the people of al-Batā'ih. None are more pure of heart than the people of Haytal, none more gracious than those of Gharj al-Shār.

Now, suppose someone asked: "Which town is the best?" Such a question may be answered thus. Should he be one seeking the advantages of both worlds, he should be told, Bayt al-Maqdis. If he were virtuous, and free of covetousness, he should be told, Makka.

p. 35

Addition/version MS. C.

[A reader's notation in the margin at this passage reads]:

The author's statement that Makka is to be recommended to one who is free of ambition, and his previous statement that none are more covetous than the inhabitants of Makka, do not necessarily involve a contradiction. What he says here is copying from others, whereas what he says above is his own opinion. The true statement is in that which he copied, for what he said before has the appearance of falsehood, and indeed that is exactly what it is. Of course, judgments change with times, individuals, temperaments, and perceptions.

Were he one who seeks pleasures and possessions, low prices and fruits, he should be told, "Every town will serve you.

Addition/version MS. C.

Should his interest be fixed on this world, and the accumulation of wealth, then Misr, or ʿAdan, or ʿUmān may be recommended. If his quest is after waters and fruits, then every place the name of which ends in "-ān" may be recommended to him.

Otherwise, you may choose from among five major cities—Dimashq, al-Basra, al-Rayy, Bukhārā, and Balkh; or from among five cities—Qaysāriyya, Bāʿaynāthā, Khujanda, al-Dīnawar, and Nūqān; or from among five districts—al-Sughd, al-Saghāniyān, Nihāwand, Jazīrat Ibn ʿUmar, and Sābūr. Choose whichever you wish from among them, for they are the pleasure gardens of Islām." As for al-Andalus, it is said to be a paradise; however, the bountiful gardens of this world are four: Ghūta Dimashq, the river of al-Ubulla, the meadows of al-Sughd, and Shiʿb (valley) of Bawwān. One interested in commerce has a choice among ʿAdan, ʿUmān, Misr.

Whenever we mention some of the faults attributable to the inhabitants of different countries, the scholars, litterateurs, and especially the jurisprudents are excepted from our remarks, for I have seen their excellent qualities for myself.

You should know that in the case of every town in the name of which the
p. 36 letter *sād* occurs, the inhabitants are stupid, with the exception of al-Basra.

Addition/version MS. C.

[A reader's rubric in the margin at this passage reads]:
Influence of the spelling of the names on the temperaments of the natives of the places named.

If two letters *sād* occur together, as in al-Massīsa or Sarsar, then may God preserve us! For any town the name of which is used in attribution to a person born there, and the letters *zāy* and *yā* occur together in the attributed name, the person thus named will be subtle; for example, the person from al-Rayy (Rāzī), the person from Marw (Marwazī), the person from Sijistān (Sijizī). Every town the name of which ends in ān has some special quality or excellence, for instance Jurjān, Mūqān, Arrajān. In every country in which the cold is severe the people are inclined to be more fat and stout, are more handsome and have thicker beards, for example Farghānā, Khwārazm, and Armīniyya. Every town that is on the seacoast or by a river seethes with fornication and pederasty, such as Sīrāf, Bukhārā, and ʿAdan. Every town that lies among rivers has turbulence and unrest in its population, such as Dimashq, Samarqand, al-Salīq. Every town that is extensive and opulent offers limited means of livelihood, excepting Balkh.

You should know that Baghdād was formerly a splendid city, but is now falling into ruin and disorder, its splendour departed. I did not find it agreeable, nor anything to admire in it; if I have praised it, it is only in conventional terms.

Fustāt of Misr is today as Baghdād was of old; and I do not know in Islām a town more splendid than it. As for the region of al-Mashriq, because of the spread of tyranny there, it has declined from what it was, though it is still better than the others. The non-Arab regions are not to the liking of the people who live lower down; but if al-Ramla had but a stream of running water we should consider it, without exception, the most pleasant town in Islām. It is a delightful place, and lively, set in the midst of holy ground and fortresses, between low-lying land and the sea. The climate is equable, the fruits delicious, the people high-minded, though uninformed. It is the storehouse of Misr, the entrepôt of the two seas, and, in all, a comfortable and prosperous place.

Addition/version MS. C.

... and in short, the best places are those in which there is an abundance of good things, even should such a place be but a village.

An Account of the Madhāhib
[Schools of Islamic Law] and the Dhimma
[Free Non-Muslim Subjects]

You should know that the *madhāhib* (doctrinal schools—sing. *madhhab*) recognized in the realm of Islām at present, that have private and public places of assembly, or are missionary, or are congregational in character are twenty-eight in number. Of these, four deal with jurisprudence, four with theology, four with the correlations between these two, four that have fallen into desuetude, four concerned with Tradition (hadīth), four have been taken over by another four, and four are present in rural areas.

Schools of Jurisprudence: al-Hanafiyya, al-Mālikiyya, al-Shafaʿwiyya, al-Dāwūdiyya.
Schools of Theology: al-Muʿtazila, al-Najjāriyya, al-Kullābiyya, and al-Sālimiyya.
Schools Having Both Fiqh (Jurisprudence) and Kalām (Theology): al-Shīʿa, al-Khwārij (The Revolters), al-Karrāmiyya, and al-Bāṭiniyya.
Schools of Adherents to Tradition: al-Hanbaliyya, al-Rāhwiyya, al-Awzāʿiyya, and al-Mundhiriyya.
Schools Fallen Into Desuetude: al-ʿAtāʾiyya, al-Thawriyya, al-Ibādhiyya, and al-Tāqiyya.
Schools Only in Rural Areas: al-Zaʿfarāniyya, al-Khurramdīniyya, al-Abyadhiyya, al-Sarakhsiyya.
Schools Taken Over by Four Analogous to Them: al-Kullābiyya by al-Ashʿariyya, al-Qarmatiyya by al-Bāṭiniyya, al-Qadariyya by al-Muʿtazila, al-Zaydiyya by al-Shīʿa, al-Najjāriyya by al-Jahmiyya.

This is the entire number of the doctrinal schools that are recognized in Islām at present, but they have branched into innumerable sects. Those schools we have mentioned are known by other names and designations, which would merely be repetitions of them without increasing the number of them that we have given: this fact is well known to scholars.

Four schools have an *agnomen*; four, a *laudatory appellation*; four, a designation of *disavowal*; four are *variously defined*. Four names are given in reproach to those concerned with tradition; four are identical in meaning; and four there are among which only the well-versed can differentiate.

Agnomen: al-Rawāfidh (Rejecters), al-Mujbira (Predestinators), al-Murjiʾa (Procrastinators), al-Shukkāk (Doubters).

Laudatory: Ahl al-ʿSunna wal-Jamāʿa, followers of the precedents and communal authority; Ahl al-ʿAdl wal-Tawhīd, those who profess the justice and unity of God; al-Muʾminūn, the believing; and Ashāb al-Hudā, the rightly guided.

Disavowal: al-Kullābiyya, who disavow divine constraint on man; al-Hanbaliyya, disavowed for their hatred of ʿAlī; those who do not recognize the attributes of God, and are disavowed because of their anthropomorphism; and those who disavow all the attributes of God.

Variously Defined: According to al-Karrāmiyya, *al-Jabr* (compulsion) implies the identification of the capacity to act with the doing of the act itself; while according to al-Muʿtazila evil is foreordained by the power of God—may He be exalted—and the actions of men are said to be the creations of God. As for al-Murjiʾa, they are those, according to Ahl al-Hadīth [those who claimed that formal traditions of the Prophet Muhammad superseded other current community traditions], who consider works as secondary to faith; while according to al-Karrāmiyya, they are those who deny the statutory obligation of works. Again, according to al-Maʾmūniyya, they are those who waver in their position on the faith; while according to Ashāb al-Kalām, they are those who are indeterminate in their position on those who commit grievous sins, and do not admit of an intermediate position. As for al-Shukkāk (the Doubters), they are those who, according to Ashāb al-Kalām, waver in respect of the *Qurʾān*, while according to al-Karrāmiyya, they are those who qualify the declaration of faith. Then al-Rawāfidh (the Rejecters) are those who, according to al-Shīʿa, put the *Khilāfā* [office or rule of khalif] of ʿAlī lower in order of occurrence; while according to all others, they are those who deny the *Khilāfa* of Abū Bakr, and of ʿUmar.

The four schools that are the same in meaning are al-Zaʿfarāniyya, al-Wāqifiyya, al-Shukkāk, and al-Rustāqiyya.

The four names given in reproach to Ahl al-Hadīth are: al-Hashwiyya [accepting some anthropomorphic traditions], al-Shukkāk, al-Nawāsib [detesters of ʿAlī, dogmatically], and al-Mujbira [deniers of free will in man].

Those that are differentiated by the well-versed only are Ahl al-Hadīth as distinct from al-Shafʿawiyya, al-Thawriyya from al-Hanafiyya, al-Najjāriyya from al-Jahmiyya, and al-Qadariyya from al-Muʿtazila.

You should know that all the schools of the Muslims have branched from an original four, al-Shīʿa, al-Khawārij, al-Murjiʾa, and al-Muʿtazila: the basis of their disunion was the murder of ʿUthmān. They further ramified and will continue in disunion until the emergence of al-Mahdī [a ruler who shall in the last days appear upon the earth—Hughes, *Dict. Islam*]. In this context, the *Irjā* (deferral) is the refusal to take a position on those who have grievously sinned, and the Ahl al-Raʾy [people of subjective opinion—followers of the *madhhab* of Abū Hanīfa] and the Ahl al-Hadīth [followers of tradition—the *madhāhib* of Mālik, al-Shāfiʿī, and Ibn Hanbal] also share in this position. The Muʿtazila say that every *Mujtahid* [a doctor of law who exerts himself to the full in reaching an opinion on a legal question] is correct in the applied *fiqh* (jurisprudence) only; and their assertion derives from some people who were uncertain about the position of the *Qibla* [direction—towards the Kaʿba—in which Muslims turn in prayer], in the time of the Prophet—God's peace and blessings be upon him—and of whom each turned in prayer in a different direction. He did not command those who were in error to repeat their prayers, but rather put them on the same footing as those who had been correct. And this point pleases me very much, for, do you not see, the Companions of the Prophet—God's peace and blessings be upon him—have differed among themselves, but he said that their differences were an act of divine providence, for, said he: "Whichever one among them you follow, you will be rightly guided." Moreover, Sufyān bin ʿUyayna has said: "Almighty God does not punish anyone for anything over which the learned disagree." Do you not see that, after all, it is as when a judge has given a verdict in a case, it is not in the power of another to set that verdict aside, even if he should consider it to be in error. However, a segment of the Karrāmiyya say that every *Mujtahid* is correct in both *al-Usūl* (the fundamentals) and *al-Furūʾ* (the derivatives), except for the freethinkers. The originator of this opinion, which is the opinion of a group of the Murjiʾa, justifies it by a saying ascribed to the Prophet—God's peace and blessings be upon him: "My community will be divided into seventy-three sects, seventy-two will be in Paradise and one in Hell." However, all the other authorities maintain that "only those are correct who conform with righteousness, and these constitute one category of men, only." They base their argument on the other tradition, which has "seventy-two in Hell and but one to be saved." Of course, this later tradition is more generally known, although the first one rests on a more correct chain of tradition; but God knows best. In any case, if the first version is correct, then the damned sect are the Bātiniyya; if the second version is the truth, then those to be saved will be the great majority of the people. For my part, I have never considered the great majority to be other than those following the four schools: the adherents of Abū Hanīfa in al-Mashriq, the adherents of Mālik in al-Maghrib, the adherents of al-Shāfiʿī in al-Shāsh and the libraries of Naysābūr, and the traditionists in al-Shām, Aqūr, and al-Rihāb. As for the other regions, they represent an intermixture, and I have made this clear in the account of the regions as shown in this book.

As for the modes of reading [the *Qurʾān*] in use at the present time, these are four in number: the system of the people of al-Hijāz, comprising, in turn, four: the reading of Nāfiʿ, that of Ibn Kathīr, that of Shayba, and that of Abū Jaʿfar; the system of the people of al-ʿIrāq, containing, likewise, four: the reading of ʿĀsim, that of Hamza, that of al-Kisāʾī, and that of Abū ʿAmr. The reading used by the people of al-Shām is that of ʿAbd Allāh bin ʿĀmir. Then there are the systems of individuals, being four in number: the reading of Yaʿqūb al-Hadhramī, the Selection of Abū ʿUbayd, the Selection of Abū Hātim, and the reading of al-Aʿmash. The majority of the doctors agree that all of these are in the right. For my part, of the schools, I have chosen to follow that of Abū Hanīfa, may God have mercy on him, for the characteristics which I mention in the account of the region of al-ʿIrāq; and of the systems of reading the *Qurʾān*, I prefer that of Abū ʿImrān ʿAbd-Allāh bin ʿĀmir al-Yahsabī, for the reasons I give in the account of the region of Aqūr.

You should know that some people have deviated from the teaching of Abū Hanīfa on four points: on the prayers of the two festivals [the Festival of the Breaking of the Fast, after the end of the month of Ramadhān, and the Feast of Immolation on the tenth day of the month of Dhu al-Hijja], except in Zabīd and Biyār; on the alms tax levied on horses; the orientation [towards the *Qibla*] of the body of a person at the time of death; and the obligation of sacrifice, except p. 40 in Bukhārā and al-Rayy. Some have deviated from the rules of Mālik on four points also: praying in front of the Imām except in al-Maghrib, and on Fridays in Misr, and the prayers at funerals in al-Shām; eating the flesh of dogs, save in two cities in al-Maghrib where the sale is an overt practice, and its inclusion, secretly, in the making of *harīsa* [pottage of meat and burghul] in Misr and Yathrib; finishing prayers with just one *taslīma* [saying the benediction, "*al-salāmu ʿalaykum wa rahmat Allāh*: peace be with you, and the mercy of God"], except in certain areas of al-Maghrib; and in the permissiveness in the laudations of God during the bows and prostrations of prayer, except among the ignorant. Some have deviated from the rule of al-Shāfiʿī in four matters: the pronouncing in a loud voice of the invocation of the name of God [*bismillāh*], except in al-Mashriq in the mosques of the adherents to al-Shāfiʿī; in respect of the *qunūt* [prayer of supplication, uttered standing], in the morning prayer; the expression of the *nīya* [declaration of the right intention in one's heart] together with the *takbīra* ["*Allāhu akbar*—God is most great"], at the beginning of prayer; and in the omission of the supplication in *witr* ["odd number"—prayers to be said in odd numbers, three, five, or seven], in other than the latter half of Ramadhān, except in Nasā. Some have departed from the school of Dāwūd in four matters: the marrying more than four wives; bestowing on two daughters half of the estate; that the prayers of one who lives in the neighborhood of a *masjid* (mosque) may not be recited except in the *masjid*; and in the question of *al-ʿAwl* [proportional reductions in some bequests]. Some departed from the school of the traditionists in four points: the *mutʿa* [the relaxation of restrictions allowed in the *ʿUmra* or Minor Pilgrimage] during the *Hajj* (Pilgrimage); drawing the hand over the turban [as a gesture to substitute for wetting the head in the ceremonial purification]; not allowing the *tayammum* [the ceremony of ablutions with dust or sand where the use of water is not feasible] with sand; and the nulling of the efficacy of the ablution if done during laughter. However, four groups have agreed with those, on one or other of these four matters: on the matter of the laughter, Abū Hanīfa—may God show him mercy; regarding the *mutʿa*, the Shīʿa; on the ablution with sand, al-Shāfiʿī; and on the drawing the hand over the turban, the Karrāmiyya. Some have differed from the doctrine of the Shīʿa in four respects: the *mutʿa*; the efficacy of the triple repudiation in the act of divorce; the rubbing the feet; and the *hayʿala* [in the utterance *Hayya ʿalā khayr al-ʿamal*—"come to the best of works"] in the call to prayer. Some have differed from the school of the Karrāmiyya on four points: the remission of the declaration of intention accompanying each obligatory devotion; the saying of the obligatory prayers while on a riding animal; the presumption of having properly observed the fast in the case of one who has eaten after sunrise but is unaware of it; and the validity of the prayers of one on whom the sun rises while he is saying them. However, the mass of the people differ from all the schools in four points: the *takbīr* in the days of the *tashrīq* [the 11th, 12th, and 13th p. 41 days of the month of Pilgrimage]; the prayer preceding the two festivals; the abandoning of the practice of returning [to Makka] from Minā at the end of the day, before sunset; and the washing of the foot three times in the ablution.

Few indeed are the jurists of the school of Abū Ḥanīfa—may God show him mercy—that I have ever seen wanting in four aspects: high office discharged with decorum, committal to memory of the *Qurʾān*, fear of God, and piety. As for the followers of Mālik, their four characteristics are crudeness, stupidity, religion, and following of custom. As for the followers of al-Shāfiʿī, their four characteristics are insight, disorderliness, manliness, and abusiveness. As for the followers of Dāwūd, their four marks are aggrandizement, excitability, garrulity, and affluence. The Muʿtazilites similarly have four marks: elegance, wisdom, lewdness, and mockery. Of the Shīʿa the four marks are hatred, rebelliousness, prosperity, and renown. The adherents to Tradition have four: setting example, active zeal, charity, and success. The four marks of the Karrāmiyya are piety, fanaticism, baseness, and beggary. For the men of letters four points: sprightliness, self-conceit, confident demeanour, and elegance of dress. The four marks of the Readers: greed, pederasty, hypocrisy, and pomp.

The religions of those who are *dhimma* [non-Muslims under the protection of the law], are four: the Jews, the Christians, the Magians (Zoroastrians), and the Sabians.

For our part, we will report the predominance of every one of the groups we have mentioned, without partiality or prejudice, if God so wills, in their respective places, and we shall describe their merits and their defects. Now, supposing it should be said: "Most of what you set down is false, and at variance with what people generally know; and you have contravened the fundamental rules by your making quaternary groupings and you have rejected septenary groupings, you who know very well that God—let His name be exalted—created the heavens and the earth seven and seven, and made the days and the nights seven and seven, that the provisions of man are of seven kinds; that the *Qurʾān* was sent down in seven wordings, and that the *masājid* [the parts of the body that touch the ground in prayerful prostration] are seven;"

Addition/version MS. C.

Moreover, the planets are seven in number; the principal joints are seven; the kinds of prayer are seven; the circumambulations [of the Kaʿba], the runnings [between al-Ṣafā and al-Marwa], and the pebbles cast [at the three pillars at Minā] are in every instance seven. Fasting is obligatory on one reaching the age of seven years; the nights and days of the week are each seven; the climates of the world are seven. Too, the principles to be followed in questions on the distribution of shares in bequests are seven;

and some things may be mentioned to which I will reply further. Well, the reply

p. 42 to that is that I have been on my guard in this by saying the "schools that are recognized", not "the sects of the Muslims." If the facts of the matter are at variance in some instances with what we have said, this is indeed rare, and, on the whole, matters are as we have stated them.

Addition/version MS. C.
The worshippers of idols in al-Sind are not included in the *Dhimma* [free non-Muslim subjects in Muslim countries], for as you see, they do not render the *jizya* (poll-tax). As for the *Majūs* (Mazdaeans), they are included among the *Dhimma* according to the command of ʿUmar that they be treated in the same way as the People of the Book (Jews and Christians). It should be understood that our referring to the adherents of one and the same doctrinal school by two names, one of praise and one of blame, does not at all imply an intent to commend or revile, or our part; rather, it is simply to show what others say about any doctrinal school, and the names they give them.

It's essential then, that anyone who reads this book of ours keep his wits about him and give careful consideration to what he reads so that he will be well aware of what our intent is; otherwise he will hold our work in contempt, and, in fact, throw discredit on us.

The Samaritans are a branch of the Jews, for, as you see, their prophet is Moses, peace be upon him.

Addition/version MS. C.
It is common knowledge that Abū Hanīfa avoided theological discussion; I have observed the same of the most illustrious doctors of our own time, as Abū Bakr al-Jassās, Abū Bakr bin al-Fadhl, al-Ismāʿīlī, al-Saʿwānī, and al-ʿAqīlī. I myself have heard Abu al-Husayn al-Qazwīnī point out that while Abū Hanīfa was undoubtedly of the Murjiʾa, the majority of those of his followers who professed to the study of theology are Muʿtazila. If then the matter is as we say, we cannot attribute the practice of both jurisprudence and theology to Abū Hanīfa; all we can say is that of his followers, some studied theology, and some of those studying theology also studied jurisprudence.

As for the quaternary groupings, they occur naturally, and are not anything I deliberately intended. But even so, they have their parallels in the fundamental principles; for as you know the sacred Books are four [the *Old Testament*, the *New Testament*, the *Book of Psalms*, the *Qurʾān*] and the nature of man is of four parts,

Addition/version MS. C.
From among the birds Abraham took four classes, every one of which he divided in four, and placed four of them on every one of four separate mountains.

(*Qurʾān*, sūra 2, v. 259). The great regional rivers are four, the mountains, the battlefields are each four. The towns of paradise are four, the corners of the Kaʿba are four, the sacred months are four; the days and the nights are divided into four kinds; the winds are four, the pillars of Islām, next to the declaration of faith, are four, the ritual ablution is on four members of the body; the number of witnesses required for a charge of adultery is four, *sillim* [immediate payment against remote delivery] contracts are lawful in only four kinds of wares, and a Muslim may not take wives more than four. The gardens of the world are four, the *takbīrs* [saying *Allāhu akbar*] in the burial service are four, the rightly-guided Khalīfas are four, and four things there are relating to four categories that are of an obligatory nature.

the elements are four, the seasons four, the rivers four [*i.e.* of paradise: Nile, Euphrates, Sayhān, Jayhūn], the corners of the Kaʿba four, and the sacred months are four [al-Muharram, Rajab, Dhu al-Qaʿda, Dhu al-Hijja—respectively first, seventh, eleventh and twelfth months of the Islamic year]. We have received a tradition from Abū Bakr Ahmad bin ʿAbdān, of al-Ahwāz, who had it from Muhammad bin Muʿāwiya ai-Ansārī, who had it from Ismāʿīl bin Sabīh, who p. 43 had it from Sufyān al-Harīrī, who had it from ʿAbd al Muʾmin, who had it from Zakariyya, the father of Yahyā, who had it from al-Asbagh bin Nabāta, that the last-named heard ʿAlī—may God be pleased with him—say: "The *Qurʾān* came down, a fourth of it pertaining to us, a fourth concerning our enemies, a fourth containing histories and parables, and a fourth prescriptions and laws." So these also are fundamental principles which are not to be set aside.

NARRATIVE OF MY ACTUAL
EXPERIENCES

You should know that many men of learning and ministers of state have written on this subject, even though rather deficiently, but most of them, let me say rather all of them, have done so from hearsay. However, for my part, there is not a single region I have not visited, and but few subjects with which I have not made myself acquainted. Along with this, I have not neglected making exhaustive scrutiny, observation, and enquiry, regarding matters obscure. This book of ours, then, falls into three parts: first, what I myself have witnessed; second, what I have heard from persons worthy of confidence; and third, what I have found in books devoted to this subject, and other than this. No royal library remained without my persistent examination of it, no literary works of any sect that I have not scrutinized, no people with whose opinions I have not acquainted myself; there is no group of ascetics with which I did not mingle, no preachers anywhere whose convocations I have not attended. In this way I attained to the soundness of the knowledge I strove for in this science. I have been given thirty-six names, by which I have been called and addressed; such as Muqaddasī (Jerusalemite), Filastīnī (Palestinian), Misrī (Egyptian), Maghribī (from al-Maghrib), Khurāsānī (from Khurāsān), Silmī (from Salamiyya), Muqriʾ (reciter of the *Qurʾān*), Faqīh (jurist), Sūfī (mystic), Walī (holy man), Ābid (servant of God), Zāhid (ascetic), Sayyāh (pilgrim), Warrāq (copyist), Mujallid (bookbinder), Tājir (merchant), Mudhakkir (reciter), Imām, Muʾadhdhin (the one who calls to prayer), Khatīb (preacher), Gharīb (foreigner), ʿIrāqī, Baghdādī, Shāmī (Syrian), Hanīfī (adherent to school of Abū Hanīfa), Mutaʾaddib (scholar), Karī (employer), Mutafaqqih (jurisconsult), Mutaʿallim (learner), Farāʾidhī (notary), Ustādh (master), Dānishūmand (sage), Shaykh (master), Nishāstah (schoolman), Rākib (rider), and Rasūl (messenger): all this on account of the various countries in which I have lived, and the many places I visited. Nothing remains of what befalls travellers that did not fall to my lot, barring only begging, and the commission of grievous sin. I studied law and letters; practiced asceticism and devoutness; lectured on law and letters; preached from pulpits; made the call to prayer from minarets; officiated as Imām in the *masājid* (mosques); delivered the sermons in *jawāmiʿ* (congregational mosques); frequented the schools. I said the prayers in convocation, spoke in councils; consumed *harīsa* with the Sūfīs, *tharīd* (broth) with the cenobites, and *ʿasīda* [flour, butter, and honey pudding] with seamen. I was ejected in the night from mosques, have wandered in the steppes, gone astray in the deserts; at times I have been scrupulously abstinent, while again, at other times, have openly eaten forbidden foods. I have associated with the devotees of Jabal Lubnān (Mount Lebanon), also been on intimate terms with those in power. I have owned slaves,

p. 44

but have had to carry baskets on my head. A number of times I was close to drowning, and our caravans have been robbed on the highway. I have been in the service of judges and persons of distinction, have conversed with rulers and ministers. I have kept company on the road with the licentious, and sold goods in the marketplaces. I have been confined in prison, and accused as a spy; I have myself witnessed the warring of the Romaeans in warships, and the striking of bells in the night [at Christian meetings]. I have bound books for profit, bought water at high prices; have traveled in litters and on horseback; trudged in the hot sandstorms, and the snows; have frequented royal courts among noblemen, and lived among the ignorant in the weavers' quarters. To what power and rank I have attained! Yet my murder has been plotted more than once. I have made the Pilgrimage, and lived in the dependency of the mosque; I have fought in raids, when doing service at frontier posts. At Makka I have drunk *sawīq* (ptisan) from the public fountain, have eaten bread and chickpeas in the monasteries, been fed at the hospice of Abraham, the Friend of God, and have eaten the fruit of the wild sycamore of ʿAsqalān. I have been invested with robes of honour by kings, and they have ordered that rich gifts be given me. I have been naked and necessitous many times. Yet distinguished people have corresponded with me, and the illustrious have reprimanded me. I have been given the responsibility of administering religious endowments, and have had to submit to blackguards. Heresy has been imputed to me, and I have been accused of covetousness. Princes and Qādhīs have elevated me to positions of trust, my name has been entered into bequests, and I have been made an executor. I have had dire experience of pickpockets, and seen firsthand the artifices of scoundrels. Miscreants have hounded me, the envious opposed me, I have been slandered before the rulers. I have entered the baths of Tabariyya and the fortresses of Persia; I have witnessed the Festival of al-Fawwāra (the Fountain) and the Feast of Barbārah [celebrated December 4th], also visited the Well of Budhāʿah, the castle of Jacob, and his villages.

p. 45

Experiences of this kind are abundant, and I have mentioned as many as I have, that the reader of my book may perceive that I did not compile it haphazardly, nor arrange it in random fashion; he will thus be able to distinguish it above others, for, after all, what a difference there is between one who has personally undergone all these experiences, and one who has compiled his book at his ease, merely basing it on the reports of others. I have spent in these journeyings of mine more than ten thousand *dirhams*, without taking into the reckoning my shortcomings in the observance of my religious obligations. For there is not a license permitted by any school of which I did not take advantage; thus, I have simply rubbed over the feet, have fulfilled my prayers by saying *mudhāmmatāni* (*Qurʾān*, sūra 55, v. 64), have departed [from Minā for Makka] before the going down of the sun, have said the obligatory prayers while in the saddle, and while having foul filth on my clothes. There has been omission of the *tasbīh* (glorification of God) in the *rukūʾ* (bowing) and the *sujūd* (prostration), and I made the prostrations of inadvertence [as a penance] before the salutation. I have joined a number of prayers together at the same time, and have fallen short in my devotions even when not traveling. Even so, I did not depart from the canons of the leading jurisprudents, and I never at any time deferred a prayer to a time beyond that appointed for it. In fact, whenever I was traveling on the highway, and there remained a distance of ten *farsakhs* or less between me and a town, I would leave the caravan and make my way thither, that I might see it before the others. Indeed sometimes I employed some men to accompany me, making any journey at night so as to get back to my companions, and this at a cost to me of money and tribulation.

You should know that in the realm of Islām are places and shrines the locations of which have not been exactly established, so there is no agreement on them. It is necessary to devote a separate chapter to them so that the reality [of other sites] may be distinguished; we will thus avoid the topic when we mention the places in the accounts of the various regions.

In Kāzarūn is a dome beside the pass, which the Magians assert is the middle of the world; a festival in its honour is celebrated every year.

Outside Yanbuʿ, towards the sea, is a sacred spot said to be the tongue of the earth, in its uttering, "We come willingly." (*Qurʾān*, sūra 41, v. 11).

At al-Jashsh is a place where, it is said, was the chain of David, used for establishing the certitude of evidence.

Some have said that the grave of Adam is near by the minaret of the mosque of al-Khayf, others have said that it is near the grave of Abraham; others again that it is in al-Hind, others yet that it is in the desert; a man in Īliyā asserts that he saw in a dream that it is behind Jabal Zaytā (Mount Olivet).

The People of the Book [Jews and Christians] say that the grave of David is in Sihyawn (Zion); some have said that the cities of Lot were between Kirmān and Khurāsān; some have maintained that the fire of Abraham was at Jarmaq. According to some, the platform at al-Gharī is the tomb of Nūh (Noah).

ʿAlī is entombed in the *mihrāb* [niche in the center of wall, marking the direction of Makka] of the great mosque of al-Kūfa, but, according to others, beside the leaning tower. According to some, Fātima is buried as is the Prophet— God's peace and blessings be upon him—in the Hujra (chamber), or, some say in al-Baqīʿ [a cemetery in al-Madīna].

Outside Marw, and towards Sarakhs, is a hospice wherein is a small tomb said to be that of the head of al-Husayn, the son of ʿAlī. In Farghānā is said to be the tomb of Ayyūb (Job). On the summit of Mount Sīnā [Sinai] is an olive tree said to be the one "neither of the east, nor of the west." (*Qurʾān*, sūra 24, v. 35); on Mount Zaytā is another of which the same is said.

According to some the Rock of Moses is in Sharwān; they say that the sea is the Lake of Tabaristān (Caspian); that the village of Bājarwān and the killing of the youth occurred in a place near the village of Khazarān. (*Qurʾān*, sūra 18, vv. 60–81).

Some say the rampart of Yājūj and Mājūj (Gog and Magog) is beyond al-Andalus; others say it is at the mountain pass of Khazarān, and that Gog and Magog are the Khazars. (*Qurʾān*, sūra, 18, vv. 92–98).

I have heard Abū ʿAlī al-Hasan, son of Abū Bakr al-Bannāʾ say: "The tomb of Joseph is a mound, also said to be the grave of al-Asbāt [a tribe of Israel]. However, a man came from Khurāsān who said it had been told him in a dream: ʿGo to Bayt al-Maqdis (Jerusalem) and tell them there it is, is the tomb of Joseph the Righteous.'" He continued: "The governor ordered my father to leave for the place, and I went with him. As the workers continued digging they eventually came on the wood of a bier, which, however, was found to have disintegrated." I still find that some of our old people preserve pieces of that wood by means of which they seek a cure for ophthalmia.

Abridgement for the Use of Jurists

This chapter is assigned especially to the use of those who wish to learn the metropoles of the Muslims, and the districts of the regions, and to be acquainted with the number of the capitals and their towns, but who have not the leisure to study what we have written in detail, and do not need a copy of our entire treatise; at the same time requiring a summary that is easy to carry in traveling, and to retain, because of its brevity. How many times I have been asked for this extract, this chapter desired of me! I have accordingly introduced it here before entering on an account of the realm of Islām; I have used conciseness of expression, avoiding prolixity and obscure language. He who can will understand it; and otherwise the information is in the text.

You understand that we represent the metropoles as kings, the capitals as chamberlains, the towns as armies, the villages as foot soldiers. There is a difference of opinion about the meaning of metropolis: the jurisprudents define "metropole" as any town with a large population, in which legal punishments are administered, having a resident governor, its revenue sufficient for its expenses, and administratively associated with its rural district, for example: ʿAthr, Nābulus, Zūzan. The linguists define as a metropole every city that lies close to the boundary between two countries, such as al-Basra, al-Raqqa, Arrajān. In popular speech metropole means any large and important town such as al-Rayy, al-Mawsil, and al-Ramla. For our part we use the term metropole in the sense of any town which is the seat of the highest authority, where the governmental bureaux are assembled, to which is assigned the functions of administration, and which, for the towns of the entire region constitutes a central place, for example: Dimashq, al-Qayrawān, and Shīrāz.

A metropole or a capital may have districts, which have, themselves, towns, for example Tukhāristān in relation to Balkh; al-Baṭāʾih (the Swamps) of Wāsit; and al-Zāb of Ifrīqiya.

The regions are fourteen in number. Six of them are Arabian: the Peninsula of the Arabs, al-ʿIrāq, Aqūr, al-Shām, Misr, and al-Maghrib. Eight are non-Arabian: al-Mashriq, al-Daylam, al-Rihāb, al-Jibāl, Khūzistān, Fārs, Kirmān, and al-Sind.

Every region must have districts, every district a capital, every capital a number of towns: exceptions occur in the Peninsula of the Arabs, al-Mashriq, and al-Maghrib, for every one of these has two metropoles. The metropole is the capital of its district, but every capital is not necessarily a metropole. The names of the metropoles are also the names of their districts, except for the first four, al-Mansūra, and the last three.

We shall begin our list from al-Mashriq, and carry on through to al-Maghrib.

The metropoles are,—Samarqand, Īranshahr, Shahrastān, Ardabīl, Hamadhān, al-Ahwāz, Shīrāz, al-Sīrjān, al-Mansūra, Zabīd, Makka, Baghdād, al-Mawsil, Dimashq, al-Fustāt, al-Qayrawān and Qurtuba. The remaining capitals of districts are seventy-seven:—Bunjikath, Numūjkath, Balkh, Ghaznīn, Bust, Zaranj, Harāt, Qāyin, Marw, al-Yahūdiyya, al-Dāmghān, Āmul, Barwān, Itil, Marāgha, Dabīl, al-Rayy, al-Yahūdiyya, al-Sūs, Jundaysābūr, Tustar, al-ʿAskar, al-Dawraq, Rāmhurmuz, Arrajān, Sīrāf, Darābjird, Shahrastān, Istakhr, Ardashīr, Narmāsīr, Bamm, Jīruft, Bannajbūr, Quzdār, Wayhind, Qannawj, al-Multān, Sanʿāʾ, al-Basra, al-Kūfa, Wāsit, Hulwān, Sāmarrā, Āmid, al-Raqqa, Halab, Hims, Tabariyya, al-Ramla, Sughar, al-Faramā, Bilbays, al-ʿAbbāsiyya, Iskandariyya, Uswān, Barqa, Balarm, Tāhart, Fās, Sijilmāsa and Tarfāna.

We shall now mention the towns that surround their capitals, naming first the chamberlain [capital] and following up with its troops [towns]. Anyone having difficulty in understanding anything here may research it in its proper region.

Akhsīkat,—Nasrābādh, Ranjad, Zārākan, Khayralām, Washabshān, (Bishabishān), Ushtīqān, Zarandarāmish, Ūzkand, Ūsh, Qubā, Birink, Marghīnān, Rishtān, Bāb, Jārak, Usht, Tūbakār, Uwāl, Dakarkard, Nawqād, Muskān, Bīkān, Ashkhīkhān (?), Jidghil, Shāwadān, Khujanda. Isbījāb has: Khawralūgh, Jamshalāghū, Usbānīkat, Bārāb, Shāwaghar, Sawrān, Turār Zarākh, Shaghlajān, Bālāj, Barūkat, Barūkh, Yakānkath, Adhakhkath, Dih-Nūjīkat, Tarāz, Bāluwā, Jikil, Barskhān, Utlukh, Jamūkat, Shiljī, Kūl, Sūs, Takābkath, Balāsakun, Labān, Shūy, Abāligh, Mādānkath, Barsiyān, Balgh, Jikarkān, Yagh, Yakāligh, Rawānjam, Katāk, Shūr Jashmah, Dil Awās, Jarkard. Binkath has: Nukkath, p. 49 Jīnānjakath, Najākath, Binākath, Kharashkath, Gharjand, Ghannāj, Jamūzan (Jabūzan), Warduk, Kabarna, Namadwānak, Nūjkath, Ghazak, Anūdhkath, Bishkat, Barkūsh, Khātūnkath, Jīghūkath, Farankad, Kadāk, Nakālak, Tall Awsh, Ghuzkard, Zarānkath, Darwā, Faradkath, Ajakh. Among its districts are: Īlāq, the capital of which is Tūnkath, with the towns of Shāwakath, Bānjkhāsh, Nūkath, Bālāyān, Arbilakh, Namūdhlagh, Khumrak, Sīkath, Kuhsīm, Adakhkath, Khās, Khujākath, Gharjand, Sāmsīrak, Biskath. Bunjikath has: Arsubānīkath, Kurdakath, Ghazaq, Sābāt, Zāmīn, Dīzak, Nūjkath, Qatawān-Dizah Kharaqāna, Khisht, Marsmanda. Numūjkath has: Baykand, al-Tawāwīs, Zandana, Bamijkath, Khudīmankan, ʿUrwān, Bakhsūn, Sīkath, Aryāmīthan, Warakhshā, Zarmīthan, Kamajkath, Fagharsīn, Kashafghan, Nawīdak, Warkā. Its district of Kish includes the towns of Nawqad-Quraysh, Sūnaj, and Iskīfghan. Nasaf, also a district, has the towns Kasba, Bazda, and Sīrakath. Samarqand has Bunjikath, Waraghsar, Abghar, Kushāniya, Ishtīkhan, Dabūsiya, Karmīniya, Rabinjan, Qatawāna.

On the Jayhūn are:—the district of Khuttal; its chief city is Hulbuk, and the towns are Marand, Andījārāgh, Halāward, Lāwakand, Kārbank, Tamliyāt, Iskandara, Munk, Fārghar, and Bank: also the towns Tirmidh, Kālif, Zamm, Nawīdah, Āmul, and Firabr. The district of al-Saghāniyān has the towns Dārzanjī, Bāsand, Sankardah, Bahām, Zīnwar, Rīkdasht, al-Shūmān, Quwādiyān, Andiyān, Dastajird (Wāshjird), and Hanbān. The capital of Khwārazm on the Haytal side is Kāth, and its towns are Ghardamān, Wāyikhān, Ardhakhīwa, Nawkafāgh, Kardar, Mazdākhqān, Jashīra, Sadūr, Zardūkh, Qaryat-Barātakīn and Madkamīniyya.

The capital of Khwārazm on the side of Khurāsān is al-Jurjāniyya, and the towns are Nuzwār, Zamakhshar, Rūzawand, Wazārmand (Awzārmand), Daskākhān-Khās, Khushmīthan, Madāmīthan, Khīwa, Kardarānkhās, Hazār-asf (Hazārasp), Jiqarwand, Sadfar, Jurjāniyya, Jāz, Darghān and Jīt.

Balkh has Ushfūrqān, Salīm, Karkū, Jāh, Madhr, Barwāz. The district of Tukhāristān has the towns Walwālij, al-Tāliqān, Khulm, Gharbank, Siminjān, Iskalkand, Rūb, Baghlān al-ʿUlyā (the upper) Baghlān al-Suflā (the lower), p. 50 Askīmasht, Rāwan, Ārhan, Andarāb and Sarā-ʿAsim. The district of al-Bāmiyān has towns: Basghūrfand, Saqāwand, Lakhrāb, Badhakhshān, Banjahīr, Jārbāyah, Barwān. Ghaznīn has Kardīz, Sakāwand, Nawah, Bardan, Damrākhī, Hashsh-Bārah, Farmul, Sarhūn, Lajrā, Khuwāsht-Ghurāb, Zāwah, Kāwīl, Kābul, Lamghān, Būdan, Lahūkar. It has the district of Wālishtān; its towns are Afshīn, Asbīdajah, Mastank, Shāl, Sakīra, Sīwah. Bust has Jālāqān, Bān, Qarma, Būzād, Dāwar, Sarwistān, Qaryat al-Jawz, Rakhūd, Bakrāwādh, Banjawāy, Tālaqān. Zaranj has Kuwayn, Zanbūk, Farah, Darhind, Qarnīn, Kawārabwādh. Bāranwādh, Kizah, Sinj, Bāb al-Taʿām, Karwādikan, Nih, al-Tāq. Harāt has Karūkh, Awbah, Mālin al-Safalqāt, Khaysār, Astarabyān, Mārābādh. Its districts are: Būshanj, which has the towns Kharkard, Faljard, Kūsūy and Karah; Bādhghīs, with towns Dihistān, Kūghanābādh, Kūfā, Busht, Jadhāwā, Kābrūn, Kālwūn, and Jabal al-Fidhdha; Kanj Rustāq, has the towns Baban, Kīf and Bagh; Asfuzār has the towns Kuwāshān, Kuwārān, Kūshk and Adraskar. Of the district of Gharjistān the capital is Abshīn; it has the towns Shūrmīn, Balīkān and Astabūn (?). Al-Yahūdiyya has Anbār, Barzūr, Fāryāb, Kalān, al-Jurzuwān. Marw has Kharaq, Hurmuzfarrah, Bāshān, Sanjān, Sawsqān, Sahba, Kīrank, Sink-ʿAbbādī, Dandānaqān. Its district is Marw al-Rūdh, having the towns Qasr Ahnaf and Tālaqān, also the town of Sarakhs. Qāyin has Tūn, Khwāst, Khūr, Kurī, Tabas (al-ʿUnnāb), al-Raqqa, Yunābidh, Sanāwadh, Tabas as-Suflā, p. 51 (the lower). Īrānshahr has Būzjān, Zūzan, Turthīth, Sābzawār, Khusrūjird, Azādhwār, Khūjān, Rīwand, Māzul, Mālin, Jājarm. Its entrepôts are: *Tūs*, with its capital al-Tābarān, and towns al-Nūqān, al-Rādakān, Junābid, Ustūrqān, Turūghbadh; *Nasā* has towns Isfīnaqān, al-Sarmaqān, Afrāwa, Shahristānah; and *Abīward* has towns Mahana, Kūfan.

Al-Dāmghān has Bistām, Mughūn, Simnān, Zaghna, Biyār. Shahristān has Ābaskūn, Alham, Astarābādh, Ākhur, al-Ribāt, Amul, Sālūs, Sāriya, Mīla, Māmatīr, Turunjā (Barjī), Tamīs, Harī, Būd, Mamtīr, Nāmiya, Tamīsa. Barwān has Walāmir, Shakīraz, Tārum, Khashm. Its district, al-Jīl; and its towns, Dūlāb, Baylaman, Shahr, Kuhan-Rūdh. Itil has Bulghār, Samandar, Suwār, Baghand, Qayshawā, al-Baydhāʾ, Khamlīj, Balanjar.

Bardhaʿa has Tiflīs, al-Qalʿa, Khunān, Shamkūr, Janza, Bardīj, al-Shamākhiya, Shirwān, Bākūh, al-Shābarān, Bāb al-Abwāb, al-Abkhāz, Qabala, Shakkī, Malāzkird, Tablā. Dabīl has Bidlīs, Khilāt, Arjīsh, Barkarī, Khūy, Salamās, Urmiya, Dākharraqān, Marāgha, Ahr, Marand, Sanjān, Qālīqalā. Ardabīl has Rasba, Tabrīz, Jābirwān, al-Miyānij, al-Sarāt, Warthān, Mūqān, Mīmadh, Barzand.

Al-Rayy has Qumm, Āwah, Sāwa, Āwa, Qazwīn, Abhar, Zanjān, Shalanba, Wayma. Hamadhān has Asadāwādh, Tazar, Qarmāsīn, Būstah, Rāman, Wabah, Sīrāwand. It has a number of great districts, without towns, such as, Nihāwand, with the town of Rūdhrāwar; Karaj-Abī- Dulaf, with another Ḳaraj; Marj; Barūjird; al-Saymara, without towns; al-Dīnawar, without towns; and Shahrazūr [lacuna in MS]. Al-Yahūdiyya has al-Madīna, Khālanjān, al-Ribāt, Lūrdakān, Sumayram, Yazd, Nāyin, Niyāstānah, Ardistān, Qāshān.

Al-Sūs has al-Bidhān, Basinnā, Bayrūt, Qaryat al-Raml, Karkha. Jun-daysābūr has al-Diz, al-Rūnāsh, Bāyūh, Qādhibīn, al-Lūr. In Tustar I have seen no town whatever. Al-ʿAskar has Jūbak, Zaydān, Sūq al-Thalāthāʾ (Tuesday market), Hubk-dhū Qurtum. Al-Ahwāz has Nahr Tīrā, Jūzdak, Bīrūh, Sūq al-Arbaʿāʾ (Wednesday market), Hisn Mahdī, Bāsiyān, Shūrāb, Bandam, Dawraq, Khān Tawq, Sana, Manādhir al-Sughrā. Al-Dawraq has Azam (Ajam), Bakhsābādh, al-Diz, Andabār, Āzar, Jubbā, Mīrāqiyān, Mīrāthiyān. Rāmhurmuz has Sanbīl, Īdhaj, Tīram, Bāzank, Lādh, Gharwa, Bāfaj, Kūzūk.

Arrajān has Qūstān, Dāryān, Mahrūbān, Jannāba, Sīnīz, Balāsābūr, Hinduwān. Sīrāf has Jūr, Maymand, Nāband, al-Sīmakān, Khabr, Khawaristān, al-Ghundijān, Kurān, Samīrān, Zīrabādh, Najīram, Nāband-Dūn (the lower), Sūrā, Raʾs Kishm. Dārābjird has Tabastān, al-Kurdibān, Kurram, Yaz-dikhwāst, Rustāq al-Rustāq, Burk, Azbarāh, Sinān, Juwaym-Abī-Ahmad, al-Isbahānāt. Shīrāz has al-Baydhāʾ, Fasā, al-Mass, Kūl, Jūr, Kārazīn, Dasht-Bārīn, Jamm, Jūbak, Jamkān, Kūrd, Bajjah, Hazār, (Azār Sābūr), Abak. Shahrastān has Darīz, Kāzarūn, Khurrah, al-Nawbandijān, Kāriyān, Kundurān, Tawwaz, Ramm (Zamm) al-Akrād, Junbad, Khasht. Istakhr has Harāt, Maybudh, Māʾīn, al-Fahraj, al-Hīra, Sarwistān, Usbānjān, Bawwān, Shahr-Bātiq, Ūrd, al-Rūn, Dih Ushturān, Khurrama, Tarkanīshān, Sāhah (Sāhak).

Bardasīr has Māhān, Kūghūn, Zarand, Janzarūdh, Kūh-Binān, Qawāf, Zāwar, Unās, Khūnāwab, Ghubayrā, Kārishtān. Its district is Khabīs; its towns, Nashk, Kashīd, Kūk, Kathrawā. Some of the isolated towns are Janzarūdh, Firzīn, Nājat, Khīr, Marzuqān, al-Sūraqān, Maghūn, Jayrūqān. Al-Sīrjān has Bīmand, al-Shāmāt, Wājib, Bazūrak, Khūr, Dasht-Barīn, Kashīstān. Narmāsīr has Bāhar, Karak, Rīkān, Nasā, Dārjīn. Bamm has Dārzhīn, Tūshtān, Awārak, Mihrikird, Rāyin, Māʾīn, Raʾīn. Jīruft has Bās, Jakīn, Manūqān, Darahqān, Juwī-Sulaymān, Kūh-Bārjān, Qūhistān, Maghūn, Jawā-wan, Walāshjird, Rūdhkān, Darfānī.

Bannajbūr has Mashka, Kīj, Sarī-Shahr, Barbūr, Khwāsh, Damandān, Jālak, Dazak, Dasht-ʿAlī, al-Tīz, Kabartūn, Rāsak, Bih, Band, Qasr-Qand, Asfiqa, Fahal-Fahrah, Qanbalā, Armaʾīl. Wayhind has Qāmuhul, Kanbāya, Sūbāra [lacuna in MS], Ūriha, Zahū, Har, Barhīrawā. Quzdār has Qandābīl, Bajathrad, Jathrad (Kathrad), Bakānān, Khūzī, Rustākuhan, Mūrdān, Rūdh, Māsakān, Kaharkūr, Mahālī, Kīzkānān, Sūra (Shūra), Quzdār. Al-Mansūra has Daybul, Zandarīj, Kadar, Māyil, Tanbalī, Bīrūn, Qāllarī, Annarī, Ballarī, al-Maswāhī, al-Bahrāj, Bāniya, Manhātarī (Manjābarī), al-Rūr (Arūr), Sūbāra, Kīnās, Saymūr.

Zabīd has Maʿqir, Kadra, Mahjam, Mawr, ʿAtana, al-Sharja, Ghalāfiqa, Mukhā, al-Hirda, al-Jurayb, al-Lasʿa, Sharma, al-ʿAshīra, Ranqa, al-Khasūf, as-Sāʿid, al-Jarada, al-Hamidha. The district of ʿAthr has towns, Baysh, al-Jurayb, Haly, as-Sirrayn. Sanʿāʾ has Saʿda, Najrān, Jurash, al-ʿUrf, Jublān, al-Janad, Dhamār, Nasafān, Yahsib, as-Suhūl, al-Mudhaykhira, Khawlān. Makka has Minā, Amaj, al-Juhfa, al-Furʿ, Jabala, Mahāyiʿ, Hādha, al-Tāʾif, Balda. The district of Yathrib has towns, Badr, al-Jār, Yanbuʿ, al-ʿUshayra, al-Hawrāʾ, al-Marwa, Suqyā-Yazīd, Khaybar. The district of Qurh: its capital is Wādī ʾl-Qurā; its towns, al-Hijr, al-ʿAwnīd, Badā Yaʿqūb, Dhabba, an-Nabk. Suhār has Nazwa, al-Sirr, Dhank, Hafīt, Dabā, Salūt, Jullafār, Samad, Lasyā, Milah. The district of Mahra: its towns are al-Shihr [lacuna in MS]. The district of al-Ahqāf; chief town, Hadhramawt. The district of Sabā; the district of al-Yamāma. Al-Ahsāʾ has al-Zarqāʾ, Sābūn, Uwāl, al-ʿUqayr.

Al-Basra has al-Ubulla, Nahr al-Dayr, Matārā, Madhār, Nahr Zabān, Badrān, Bayān, Nahr al-Amīr, Nahr al-Qadīm, ʿAbbādān, Abu al-Khasīb, Nahr-Dubbā, al-Muttawwiʿa, al-Qindal, al-Maftah, al-Jaʿfariyya. Al-Kūfa has Hammām ʿUmar, al-Jāmiʿayn, Sūrā, al-Nīl, al-Qādisiyya, ʿAyn al-Tamr. Baghdād has Baradān, al-Nahrawān, Kāra, al-Daskara, Tarāstān, Hārūniyya, Jalūlā, Bājisrā, Bāquba, Buwahriz, Kalwādhā, Darzījān, al-Madāʾin, Asbānbur, Gīl, Sīb, Dayr al-ʿAqūl, al-Nuʿmāniyya, Jabbul, ʿAbartā, Bābil, Qasr Hubayra, ʿAbdas, Nahrawā. Wāsit has Fam al-Silh, Nahr Sābus, Darmakān, Bādhibīn, Qurāquba, Siyāda, al-Sikr, Qurqūb, al-Tīb, Lahbān, al-Basāmiya, Ūdisa. The district of al-Batāʾih has capital, al-Salīq, and towns, Jāmida, Hurār, al-Haddādiyya, al-Zubaydiyya. Hulwān has Khāniqīn, Zabūjān, al-Marj, Shalā-shilān, al-Jāmid, al-Hurr, al-Sīrawān, Bandanījān. Sāmarrā has al-Karkh, ʿUkbarā, al-Dūr, al-Jāmiʿayn, Batt, Rādhānāt, Qasr al-Jass, Harī, Aywānā, Barīqā, Sindiyya, Rāqafrūba, Dimimmā, al-Anbār, Hīt, Takrīt, al-Sinn.

Al-Mawsil has Nūnawā, al-Haditha, Maʿlathāya, al-Hasaniyya, Tall Aʿfar, Sinjār, al-Jibāl, Balad, Adhrama, Barqaʿīd, Nasībīn, Dārā, Kafartūthā, Raʾs al-ʿAyn, Thamānīn. Āmid has Mayyāfāriqīn, Tall Fāfān, Hisn Kayfā, al-Fār, Hādhiya. Al-Raqqa has al-Muhtariqa, al-Rāfiqa, Khānūqa, al-Harīsh, Tall Mahrā, Bājarwān, Hisn Maslama, Tarʿūz, Harrān, al-Ruhā. Some of the districts: Jazīrat-Ibn-ʿUmar; towns: Fayshābūr, Bāʿaynāthā, al-Mughītha, al-Zawazān. The district of Sarūj has towns, Kafarzāb, Kafarsīrīn. The district of al-Furāt: chief city, Qarqīsiyā; towns, al-Rahba, al-Dāliya, ʿAna, al-Hadītha. The district of al-Khābūr: chief city, ʿArābān; towns, al-Husayn, al-Shamsīniyya, Maykasīn, Sukayr al-ʿAbbās, al-Khaysha, al-Sakīniyya, al-Tunānīr.

Halab has Antākiya, Bālis, Sumaysāt, al-Maʿarratayn, Manbij, Bayyās, al-Tināt, Qinnasrīn, al-Suwaydiyya. Hims has Salamiyya, Tadmur, al-Khunāsira, Kafartāb, al-Lādhiqiyya, Jabala, Jubayl, Antarsūs (Antartūs), Bulunyās, Hisn al-Khawābī, Lajjūn, Rafaniyya, Jūsiya, Hamāt, Shayzar, Wādī Butnān. Dimashq has Dārayyā, Bāniyās, Saydā, Bayrūt, ʿArqa, Atrābulus, al-Zabadānī. The district of al-Biqāʿ: chief city, Baʿlabakk: towns, Kāmid, ʿArjamūsh. Tabariyya has

Baysān, Adhriᶜāt, Qadas, Kābul, al-Lajjūn, ᶜAkkā, Sūr, al-Farādhiya. Al-Ramla has Bayt al-Maqdis, Bayt-Jibrīl, Ghazza, ᶜAsqalān, Yāfā, Arsūf, Qaysāriyya, Nābulus, Arīḥā, ᶜAmmān. Sughar has Wayla, ᶜAynūnā, Madyan, Tabūk, Adhruh, Maᵓāb, Muᶜān.

Al-Faramā has al-Baqqāra, al-Warrāda, al-ᶜArīsh, Tinnīs, Dimyāt, Shatā, Dabqū. Al-ᶜAbbāsiyya has Shubrū-wāzah, Damanhūr, Sanhūr, Banhā al-ᶜAsal,
p. 55　Shatnūf, Malīj, Damīra, Būra, Daqahla, Sanhūr, Barīs (?), Sandafā, and seven other towns each named *Mahalla*. Bilbays has Mashtūl, Fāqūs, Jurjīr, Sandafā, Banhā alᶜAsal, Damīrā, Tūkh, and Tantathanā also known as Dayr Natāy. Al-Iskandariyya has al-Rashīd, Mahallat-Ḥafs, Dhāt al-Humām, Burullus. Al-Fustāt has al-Jazīra, al-Jīza, al-Qāhira, al-ᶜAzīziyya, ᶜAyn Shams, Bahnā, al-Mahalla, Sandafā, Damanhūr, Hulwān, al-Qulzum. Uswān has Qūs, Akhmīm, Bulyanā, Tahā, Sumustā, Būsīr, Ushmūnayn, Ajmaᶜ. Also the district of al-Fayyūm.

Barqa has Ramāda, Atrābulus, Ajdābiya, al-Sūs, Sabra, Qābis, Ghāfiq. Balarm has al-Khālisa, Atrābunush, Māzar, ᶜAyn al-Mughattā, Qalᶜat al-Ballūt, Jirjant, Buthīra, Saraqūsa, Lantīnī, Qatāniya, Alyāj, Fatarnuwā (Batarnuwā), Tabarmīn, Mīqush, Massīna, Rimta, Damannash, Jārās, Qalᶜat al-Qawārib, Qalᶜat al-Sirāt, Qalᶜat Abī-Thawr, Batarliya, Thirma, Būrqād, Qurliyūn, Qarīnash, Bartinīq, Akhyās, Balja, Bartanna. Al-Qayrawān has Sabra, Asfāqus, al-Mahdiyya, Sūsa, Tūnis, Banzart, Tabarqa, Marsā al-Kharaz, Būna, Bāja,
p. 56　Lurbus, Qarna, Marnīsa, Mas, Banjad, Marmājanna, Sabība, Qamūda, Qafsa, Qastīliya, Nafzāwa, Lāfis, Awdha, Qalānus, Qabīsha, Rusfa, Banūnush, Lajam, Jazīrat Abī Sharīk, Bāghāy, Sūq-Ibn-Khalaf, Dūfāna, al-Masīla, Ashīr, Sūq Hamza, Jazīrat Bani-Zaghannāya, Mattīja, Tanas, Dār, Sūq Ibrāhīm, al-Ghuzza, Qalᶜat Burjuma, Bāghir, Yalal, Jabal Tūjān, Wahrān, Jurāwa, Arzkūl, Malīla, Nakūr, Sabta, Kalzāwa, Jabal Zālāgh, Asfāqus, Munastīr, Marsā al-Hajjāmīn, Banzart, Tabarqa, Hayyāja, Lurbus, Marsā al-Hajar, Jamūnas al-Sābūn, Taras, Qastīliya, Nafta, Taqiyūs known as Madīnat al-Qusūr, Miskiyāna, Bāghay, Dūfāna, ᶜAyn al-ᶜAsāfir, Dār Maluwwal, Tubna, Maqqara, Tījis, Madīnat al-Mahriyyīn, Tāmasnat, Dakkamā, Qasr al-Ifrīqī, Rakwā, al-Qustantīniyya, Mīla, Jījil, Tābarrīt, Satīf, Īkijā, Marsā al-Dajāj, Ashīr. Tāhart has Yammama, Tāghalīsiya, Qalᶜat Ibn al-Harab, Hazāra, al-Jaᶜba, Ghadīr al-Durūᶜ, Lamāya, Mindās, Sūq Ibn Habla, Matmāta, Jabal Tujān, Wahrān, Shalif, Tīr, al-Ghuzza, Sūq Ibrāhīm, Rahbāya, al-Batha, al-Zaytūna, Tamammā, Yaᶜūd, al-Khadhrāᵓ, Wārīfan, Tanas, Qasr al- Fulūs, Bahriyya, Sūq Karā, Manjasa, Ūzikī, Tabrīn, Sūq Ibn Mablūl, Rubā, Tāwīlt Abī-Maghūl Tāmazzīt, another Tāwīlt (Laghwā), Fakkān.

Sijilmāsa has Darᶜa, Tādanqūst, Athar, Aylā, Wīlmīs, Hisn Ibn Sālih,
p. 57　al-Nahhāsīn, Hisn al-Sūdān, Hilāl, Imsalā, Dār al-Amīr, Hisn Barāra, al-Khiyāmāt, Tāzrūt. Fās has al-Basra, Zalūl, al-Jāhid, Sūq al-Kutāmī, Wargha, Sabū, Sanhāja, Hawwāra, Tīzā, Matmāta, Kazannāya, Salā, Madīnat Banī Qarbās, Mazhāhiyya, Azīlā, Sabta, Balad Ghumār, Qalᶜat al-Nusūr, Nakūr, Balash,

Marnīsa, Tābarīdā, Sāʿ, another town, Miknāsa, Qalʿat Shamīt, Madāʾin, Burjan Ūzikī, Tayūnū, Maksīn, Amlīl, Amlāh Abi al-Hasan, Qastīna, Nafzāwa, Niqāwus, Biskra, Qabīsha. Its districts: Al-Zāb: its capital, al-Masīla; towns, Maqqara, Tubna, Biskra, Bādis, Tahūdhā, Tawlaqā, Jamīlā, Bantiyūs, Adna, Ashīr. Tanja: its towns, Walīla, Madraka, Matrūka, Zaffūn, Ghuzza, Ghumīra, al-Hājir, Tājarājarā, al-Baydhāʾ, al-Khadhrāʾ. Tarfāna has Āghmāt Waylā [=Aylān], [Āghmāt] Warīka, Tandalī, Māssa, Zaffūn, Ghuzza, Ghumīra, al-Hājir, Qaytūn, al-Khadhrāʾ. Among the noted towns of Qurtuba are: Tulaytula, Lārida, Tutīla, Saraqusta (Saraqūsa), Turtūsha, Balansiya, Mursiya, Bajjāna, Mālaqa, Istija, Rayya, Jayyān, Shantara, Ghāfiq, Turjāla, Qūriya, Mārida, Bāja, Shantarīn, Ukhshunuba, Ishbīliya, Sadūna (Shadhūna), Jabal Tāriq, Qarmūna, Mawrūr, al-Jazīra.

Had I entered al-Andalus I should have divided it into districts, considering the great number of towns, provinces, and districts there; for al-Andalus is comparable with Haytal, but is more important. Indeed there remain other cities of Islām we did not mention through our lack of acquaintance with them. Al-Andalus resembles the African side of this province, or nearly so.

Ibn Khurradādhbih mentions that there are forty cities there, and these are those listed above.

An Account of the Climates of the World and the Position of the Qibla

p. 58 You should know that everyone who has written on this subject has fixed the number of climates at fourteen—seven distinctly manifest and habitable and seven uninhabitable. I have heard one astronomer say that all created beings live in the west, and that no one lives in the east, because of the heat; but I have heard another say because of the cold. It has been estimated that from the remotest part of al-Maghrib to these habitable lands at the limits of the territory of the Turks, is [two thousand] six hundred *farsakhs*, as the crow flies. It is on this basis that the authors we have mentioned have written their works on this subject; and from them, and from the eminent astronomers we have met, we have derived the material for this section. Certainly this knowledge is required in determining the direction of the *Qibla*, and the situation of the climates relative thereto. For my part, I myself have encountered people who have changed the *Qibla*, and differed on its direction. Had they known the basic principles herein they would not have been at variance about its position, nor would they have changed what the ancient authorities established. [Map III]

The earth resembles a sphere somewhat. It is situated within the celestial sphere, as the yolk is within the egg. The air surrounds the earth, and attracts it from every point on earth in the direction of the celestial sphere. The equilibrium of the condition of creatures on the earth is because the atmosphere attracts the lightness that is in them, and the earth the heaviness that is in them, for the earth is comparable to the stone that attracts iron. Some have made a comparison between the celestial sphere and a turner's rotating a hollowed out object having a walnut inside it: when he turns the hollow object the walnut stays in the middle.

The earth is divided into two equal parts defined by the equator, which extends from east to west, and represents the longitude of the earth; it is the longest line on the terrestrial sphere, just as the zone of the zodiac represents the greatest length in the celestial sphere. The latitude of the earth is from the south pole, round which Suhayl (Canopus) turns, to the north pole, round which turn Banāt Naʿsh (Ursa Major and Ursa Minor). The circumference of the earth at the equator is three hundred sixty degrees; as a degree is twenty-five *farsakhs*, the circumference is nine thousand *farsakhs*. From the equator to each of the poles is ninety degrees. The circumference of the earth latitudinally is the same as at the equator. However, the inhabited portion of the earth, beyond the equator is twenty four degrees, the rest being submerged beneath the sea. Humankind inhabits the northern quarter of the earth, the southern quarter being uninhabitable; the hemisphere that is beneath us has no inhabitants. The two quarters of which we have knowledge constitute the fourteen regions mentioned above.

Map III: Al-KaᶜBa (see p. 407).
From MS. Sprenger 5—Ahlwardt 6034 by kind permission of the Staatsbibliothek
Preussischer Kulturbesitz, Berlin, Orientabteilung.

The *First Climate* is thirty-eight thousand five hundred *farsakhs* in length, and in latitude is one thousand nine hundred ninety-five *farsakhs*. [In this *Account of the Climates ...*, derived from others, al-Muqaddasī, as right here, is many times inconsistent and extravagant in his figures]. It begins where, when the day is equal to the night, the shadow at noon is a foot and a half plus a tenth and a sixth of a tenth of a foot; it ends where, at this same time, it is two and three fifths feet. The distance of latitude between the two extremities is about three hundred ninety miles, a mile being the equivalent of four thousand cubits. Its middle lies close to the position of Sanʿāʾ, ʿAdan, and al-Ahqāf; the extremity which is close to Syria lies in Tihāma, near Makka. Among the primary settlements it contains are Sanʿāʾ, ʿAdan, Hadhramawt, Najrān, Jurash, Jayshān, Saʿda, Tabāla, ʿUmān, al-Bahrayn, the furthermost portions of the country of the Sūdān [Blacks], on to al-Maghrib, some portions of al-Hind (India) and China that adjoin the seashore. All places that have the same latitude as these, both to the east and to the west, are likewise within this climate.

The *Second Climate* begins where, when the day and night are equal, the shadow at noon, as already said, is two and three fifths feet. The distance between the two extremities is three hundred fifty miles, in a straight line. The middle of it lies about Yathrib, the southernmost portion beyond Makka; the other extremity towards the north is close to al-Thaʿlabiyya, Makka and al-Thaʿlabiyya being between two climates. Some towns in this climate are: Makka, Yathrib, al-Rabadha, Fayd, al-Thaʿlabiyya, Uswān of Misr, thence to the border of Nubia, also al-Mansūra, al-Yamāma, and portions of the territories of al-Sind and al-Hind. All places in the latitude of these, to the east and to the west, are in this climate.

The *Third Climate* begins where the shadow, at midday, is three feet plus half a foot, plus one tenth and one sixth of a tenth of a foot. It ends where the shadow at the equinox at midday is four feet and a half of a foot, plus a third of a tenth of a foot. The day attains, in the middle of this climate, a length of fourteen hours, its middle lying near Madyan Shuʾayb on the Syrian side, and near Wāqisa on the side of al-ʿIrāq. The breadth of this zone is about three hundred miles and a half ["and a half" should probably read "and upwards" by a plausible amendment of the Arabic text], as the crow flies. Al-Thaʿlabiyya, and every place on that latitude, to the east and to the west, are on the furthermost extremity of this climate to the south; Baghdād, Fārs, Qandahār of al-Hind, al-Urdunn, Bayrūt are on the extremity closest to Syria; and similarly for all places on the same latitude, to the east and to the west. Wāqisa, and every place on its parallel, to the east and to the west are thus between two climates. Of the towns within this climate are: al-Kūfa, al-Basra, Wāsit, Misr, al-Iskandariyya, al-Ramla, al-Urdunn, Dimashq, ʿAsqalān, the Holy Land, Qandahār of al-Hind, the coasts of Kirmān, Sijistān, al-Qayrawān, Kaskar, and al-Madāʾin. Similarly, all places on the same parallel as these, to the east and to the west, are within this climate.

The *Fourth Climate* has its beginning where the shadow, at the time we have specified, is four feet and three fifths, and a third of a fifth of a foot. Its breadth is somewhat upwards of two hundred sixty miles as the crow flies. Its middle part lies close to Aqūr, Manbij, ʿArqa, Salamiyya and Qūmis, on the side towards al-Rayy. Its lower extremity, which is towards al-ʿIrāq, is close to Baghdād, and the places on that parallel, to the east and to the west. Its upper extremity is towards al-Shām, close to Qālīqalā and the shores of Tabaristān, on to Ardabīl, Jurjān, and all places on this parallel. Of the notable towns in this climate are: Nasībīn, Dārā, al-Raqqa, Qinnasrīn, Halab, Harrān, Sumaysāt, the frontier towns of al-Shām, al-Mawsil, Sāmarrā, Hulwān, Shahrazūr, Māsabadhān, al-Dīnawar, Nihāwand, Hamadhān, Isbahān, al-Marāgha, Zanjān, Qazwīn, Tūs, Balkh, and all places coming near these towns in latitude.

p. 61

The *Fifth Climate* begins where the shadow is five feet, plus three fifths, and a sixth of a fifth of a foot: the distance, in width, between one extremity and the other, is about two hundred thirty miles as the crow flies. Its middlepoint is close to the area of Tiflīs in al-Rihāb, to Marw in Khurāsān, and to the country of Jurjān, and all towns in this zone, to the east and to the west. Its upper extremity towards the north is close to Dabīl. Within it some towns are: Qālīqalā, Tabaristān, Malatya, Rūmiyya, Daylamān, Jīlān, ʿAmmūriyya, Sarakhs, Nasā, Abīward, Kish, al-Andalus, and places close to Rūmiyya, and Antāliya.

The *Sixth Climate* begins where the shadow is six feet plus six tenths and a sixth of a tenth of a foot; its shadow at the extremity differs from that at the beginning by just one foot. Its breadth is somewhat more than two hundred miles, as the crow flies. Its lower extremity towards the south coincides with the upper northern border of the adjacent fifth climate; and that is the latitude of Dabīl, to the east and to the west. Its uppermost limit towards the north lies close to the land of Khwārazm and what is beyond it, and to Isbījāb beside the territory of the Turks. Its middle part lies close to al-Qustantīniyya, Āmul in Khurāsān, Farghānā, and places on this latitude, to the east and to the west. In it lie Samarqand, Bardhaʿa, Qabala, al-Khazar, al-Jīl, the parts of al-Andalus which are towards the north, and the southernmost territories of the Saqāliba (Slavs).

The *Seventh Climate* has its beginning where the shadow there is seven feet plus a half plus a tenth plus a sixth of one tenth of a foot, as at the end of the sixth; in fact the end of the sixth is the beginning of the seventh. Its southernmost limit corresponds with the northernmost limit of the climate adjacent to it, which is the sixth. That is the latitude of Khwārazm and Turārband, to the east and to the west. Its furthermost extremity towards the north lies in the remotest parts of the land of the Saqāliba, and on the territories of the Turks, which adjoin Khwārazm on the north. Its middle portion lies in the country of al-Lān, without any well- known towns.

ʿAbd Allāh the son of ʿAmr asserts: the earth extends for a journey of five hundred years, four hundred years desolate, and one hundred inhabited. Of this, the territory of the Muslims constitutes one year. According to Abu al-Jald the extent of the earth is twenty-four thousand *farsakhs*, al-Sūdān accounting for twelve thousand, (the land of) the Romaeans eight thousand, Fārs, three thousand, and (the lands of) the Arabs one thousand *farsakhs*.

THE EMPIRE OF AL-ISLĀM

You should know that the empire of al-Islām—may God, most exalted, watch over it!—is not uniform so as to make it possible to describe it as a quadrangle, or as having length and breadth. It is, in fact, quite irregular, as anyone realizes who pays careful attention to the points of the rising and setting of the sun, who has traversed the countries, has become acquainted with its routes, and measured its regions in *farsakhs*. We shall do our best to give as close a description of it as is possible, and represent it to the minds of people of intelligence and understanding, should God—may He be exalted—so will.

The sun sets at the extremity of al-Maghrib, where one may see it descending into the Encircling Ocean; similarly, the people of al-Shām see it disappear into the Sea of the Romaeans [Mediterranean].

The region of Misr (Egypt) begins at the Sea of the Romaeans, and extends its length to the country of the Nubians; it lies between the Sea of al-Qulzum (Red Sea) and the borders of al-Maghrib. Al-Maghrib extends from the borders of Misr to the Encircling Ocean, as a strip compressed between the Sea of the Romaeans on the north, and the countries of the Blacks to the south.

p. 63   The region of al-Shām extends from the border of Misr northwards to the country of the Romaeans, and lies between the Romaean Sea and the Desert of the Arabs. The desert, and part of al-Shām adjoin the Peninsula of the Arabs; while the Sea of China encloses the Peninsula from Misr to ʿAbbādān. The country of al-ʿIrāq borders on the desert and a part of the Peninsula. The northern limits of al-ʿIrāq are bordered by the region of Aqūr, which extends to the country of the Romaeans, while the Euphrates encircles it towards the west. Beyond the Euphrates lies the remaining portion of the desert, and an area of al-Shām. These are the regions of the Arabs.

Khūzistān and al-Jibāl lie along the eastern frontiers of al-ʿIrāq; parts of al-Jibāl and the region of al-Rihāb are on the border of Aqūr to the east. Fārs, Kirmān, and al-Sind lie beyond Khūzistān, aligned in a single row: the sea is to the south, the desert and Khurāsān to the north. Al-Sind and Khurāsān to the east adjoin the countries of the Infidels; while al-Rihāb borders the country of the Romaeans to the west and north. The region of al-Daylam lies between al-Rihāb, al-Jibāl, the desert, and Khurāsān.

This is, then, the empire of al-Islām: study it carefully. There are variations in direction and altitude for anyone who traverses it from east to west. You see that if you go from the Encircling Ocean to Misr you are on a direct course, which then, however, slants slightly towards al-ʿIrāq; then the line goes circuitously in the non-Arab regions to Khurāsān, tending towards the north. Do you not see that the sun rises to the right of Bukhārā, from the direction of Isbījāb?

Following are the dimensions of the empire we have described.

From the Encircling Ocean to al-Qayrawān, 120 stages;
thence to the Nile, 60 stages;
thence to the Tigris, 50 stages;
thence to the Jayhūn, 60 stages;
thence to Tūnkath, 15 days journey;
thence to Tarāz, 15 days journey.

If you turn towards Farghānā, then from the Jayhūn to Ūzkand is 30 stages.
p. 64 If you turn towards Kāshghar, the distance is 40 stages.

By another course you may go from the coasts of al-Yaman to al-Basra, 50 days journey;
thence to Isfahān, 138 *farsakhs*;
thence to Naysābūr, 30 stages;
thence to the Jayhūn, 20 stages;
thence to Tarāz, 30 stages.

All these distances are as the crow flies, the regions of Misr, al-Maghrib, and al-Shām being omitted.

In terms of breadth there is considerable variation, for while the region of al-Maghrib is of little width, and likewise Misr, yet if you follow on a parallel in this direction towards al-Shām, the empire increases in breadth, and continues to be enlarged beyond the Jayhūn to the country of al-Sind, where its breadth is about a three months' journey.

Abū Zayd determines the width to extend from Malatya to the Peninsula, al-ʿIrāq, Fārs, and Kirmān, to the territory of al-Mansūra. He does not mention the stages, saying only that it is a journey of about four months less ten days. What we have said is clearer and more sound: from the easternmost confines at Kāshghar to remotest Sūs is a journey of about ten months.

In the year 232/847 an estimate was made by order of the khalif of the amount of revenue raised from land-taxes, legal alms taxes, but omitting patronage and imposts, for the entire realm. It amounted to two million, three hundred twenty thousand, two hundred sixty four and one half *dinārs*. The land tax of the Romaeans one time was calculated by order of al-Muʿtasim, and it amounted to five hundred *qintārs* [a *qintār* equalled six thousand *dinārs*], and some more *qintārs*, the equivalent of less than three million *dinārs*. So he wrote to the king of the Romaeans: "The least of the territories ruled by the least of my subjects provides a revenue larger than your whole dominion." [The inconsistency of the figures given by al-Muqaddasī makes pointless the boast of al-Muʿtasim].

Addition / version MS. C.
Bear in mind that my book deals with matters only as I found them at the time

of my being present; but circumstances change. Do you not know that on my visiting the city of Sarakhs in the year 374/984, I found the governor there a man of unsound mind, and their preacher grievous to the spirit? And indeed it may well be that we have inadvertently omitted the mention or description of some towns, well-known though they may be, and which we in fact have visited; let not the people of such towns reproach us, since error and forgetting are part of the human condition. Again, let no person be distressed when we mention the shortcomings of his country, for such mention does not by any means add to its defamation; any more than mention of its merits adds to its commendation. Indeed, this is a science that is founded on integrity and accuracy, and the mention of both the good and the bad; and were I to have concealed the shortcomings of any town I should have concealed the faults of my own native town, because of its great distinction and holiness in the sight of God, may He be exalted, and of His creatures! Again, it may happen that one looks into our book and supposes he finds contradictions therein: let him persevere in his consideration of it, and he will come to realize what we are getting at. After all, have not some people courted eternal damnation for themselves through their holding the opinion that the Book of God, that august and noble work of which it is written, "Mendacity comes not to it from before it, nor from behind it," (*Qurʾān*, sūra 41, v. 41) contradicts itself? How then with the words of a weak and worthless creature?

You should realize, too, that we do not concern ourselves with the honorific titles of those whose names we mention in our book, such as "illustrious", "learned", for these are of the style of letter-writing, not of literary composition. I have noticed that the writers who preceded me are of two sorts: one will inaugurate a series of lectures to be given over an extended period of time thus drawing to himself students from abroad, and those eager to be trained as disciples. In this way his name is spread abroad and known to all people. As soon as he fulfills his hope and his reputation grows, he writes a book, and his work meets with acceptance.

People of understanding are receptive to his wisdom,
And thus did Kaʿbī and Karkhī proceed.
Some dedicate their books to an important ruler,
Or to an eminent leader,
So as to give distinction to their works;
And this is the course followed by Ibn Qutayba and (?);
This is the route I have taken, whither I went, and which I chose.
And so I carefully considered the kings, and the princes, the notable, and the
    ministers.
And I thought about the most worthy person to whom I should dedicate my
    book,
And publicly associate it with him;
So I had my riding camel kneel at his door,
One who has surpassed all praises,
Supplies needs, bestows favors:
A man of wise judgment and decisive resolve,

One whom you see at all times elevating the pure,
Honouring the pious, loving what is best;
The virtuous constantly crowding around his door;
Who does not tire from giving and praying
And from extoling God, may He be exalted, in the state of His sovereignty.
One whose renown is great among men,
And whom ʿAmīd al-Dawla selected and appointed minister;
Whom the King of the Orient privileged and aided;
Whose virtues are manifest, his opinions mature,
His magnanimity evident, his title distinguished,
His lineage lofty, his country honourable,
His character pure:
The learned Shaykh, the chieftain Abu al-Hasan ʿAlī bin al-Hasan.
That God—may He be exalted in His glory—may grant length and approval
   to his life.
And make felicitous his life hereafter, with continuance of the blessings of
   his life here.
May he make inalienable what He has bestowed on him, and granted him,
And especially this, a science possessed alone of ministers and of those who
   love it;
Of those who write it and those who elevate it.
This we have already mentioned to you in the prefatory material of our book.
However, I have made this compendium general, while the dedicated part is
specific, and I have titled it *The Book of Distances and Governments*, and this
because important and influential people have a predilection for what is written
concisely and effectively.

p. 65 The length of the empire, as we have shown, is two thousand six hundred
farsakhs; one hundred *farsakh*s being the equivalent of one million two hundred
thousand cubits, the *farsakh* thus equals twelve thousand cubits. The cubit is
p. 66 equal to twenty-four fingers, a finger equalling the breadth of six grains of barley
put side by side. A mile is one third of a *farsakhs*; however, there is variation in
the length of a *barīd* (post stage): in the desert and in al-ʿIrāq it is twelve miles,
in al-Shām and Khurāsān it is six. You see that in Khurāsān, a station has been
built every two *farsakhs*, with facilities for the officials of the post route: this
latter distance, accordingly, is the measure we adopt [for the *barīd*].

The Peninsula of the Arabs

We have begun with the Peninsula of the Arabs because in it is situated the Sacred House of God, as also the City of the Prophet—blessing and peace be on him!—and from here the religion of Islām was disseminated. Here, moreover, lived the rightly-guided Khalīfas [Abū Bakr, ʿUmar, ʿUthmā, and ʿAlī, immediately succeeding the Prophet], as well as the *Ansār* [Helpers of the Prophet at al-Madīna], and the *Muhājirūn* [the Emigrants—those who joined the Prophet in his emigration from Makka to Yathrib]. The flags of the Muslims stood together there, the interests of religion strengthened. Moreover, here are the places of ritual and ceremony for the appointed time on the Pilgrimage. Also, as it is a country with a tithing system, so the doctors of the laws have recorded it in their registers; and teachers of the law need a thorough knowledge of it for their commentaries. From this country also the earth was stretched out (*Qurʾān*, sūra 79, v. 30), and from here Abraham—on him be peace!—addressed the human race. Along with this, the Peninsula comprises within it important divisions, some large districts, some valuable acreages. As you see, it contains al-Hijāz in its entirety, as well as the whole of al-Yaman, the area of Sabā, al-Ahqāf (*Qurʾān*, sūra 46, v. 21), al-Yamāma, al-Ashhār, Hajar, ʿUmān, al-Tāʾif, Najrān, Hunayn, al-Mikhlāf, Hijr Sālih (*Qurʾān*, sūra 7, vv. 73-79), the lands of ʿĀd and Thamūd, the Abandoned Well and the Lofty Palace (*Qurʾān*, sūra 22, v. 45); it is the site of Iram of the pillars (*Qurʾān*, sūra 89, v. 7), the place of the "Makers of the Pit" (*Qurʾān*, sūra 85, v. 4), the Prison of Shaddād, the Tomb of Hūd, the domain of Kinda, the twin mountains of Tayyiʾ, Buyūt al-Fārihīn [the dwellings of those who enjoyed their lives in the valley] (*Qurʾān*, sūra 26, vv. 146 & seqq.), the mountain of Sīnā, Madyan of Shuʿayb, ʿUyūn [the wells of] Mūsā. It is the greatest of the regions in extent, the broadest in area, the most excellent in soil, the most exalted in sacredness. Its towns are the most famous: here is Sanʿāʾ which surpasses all other cities, and ʿAdan to which the travelers flock. Here are the land divisions which are a glory to al-Islām, and delightful Yaman and al-Hijāz.

Now, should someone say, "Why have you made al-Yaman, al-Mashriq, and al-Maghrib each to consist of two sides?" I should say to him that as for al-Yaman, the Prophet—God's peace and blessings be upon him—made it the rendezvous point for those going to the sacred places.

Addition/version MS. C.

If it were said that the words of the Prophet meant that the people of Najd, not the people of al-Yaman, should begin the Pilgrimage at Qarn, my reply is that there is no disagreement that the people of Sanʿāʾ are among those who begin the Pilgrimage at Qarn, and there is no doubt that Sanʿāʾ is of al-Yaman. The meaning is, therefore, that the people of al-Yaman should begin the Pilgrimage from Yalamlam, with the exception only of the people of Najd; this is just as if a man were to say to his servant: "Pay to the *Ashrāf* [descendants of the family of the Prophet] one thousand each, and to the descendants of ʿAlī two thousand each." Analogies to this are to be found in the Book and in the Laws.

As for Khurāsān, Abū Zayd considered it two regions, and he was an authority in this science, especially concerning his own region; accordingly, it is no criticism of us if we have made it two sides [of one province]. Should someone say, "Then why do you differ from him, having acknowledged him as an authority, by making Khurāsān one region", I should reply "We have two answers to this. The first is that we would not wish to divide the domain of the House of Sāmān; and it is widely recognized in the realm of al-Islām that they are the rulers of Khurāsān, but that the seat of their government is at Haytal". The second answer is that Abū ʿAbd Allāh al-Jayhānī, also an authority in this science, has not separated Khurāsān. What we have said, then, is in agreement with one or other of these two on one point, and disagrees on the other.

Addition/version MS. C.
Moreover, Ibn Khurradādhbih and Ibn al-Faqīh were also authorities in this science, and no one of them made a division of the region of al-Mashriq. I have, therefore, accepted the writing of al-Fārisī that it consists of *two sides*, and the statements of the others we mentioned to mean that it is *one region*. Do you not see that it is just as when some related of the Prophet—God's peace and blessings be upon him—that in lifting his hands in prayer he reached the height of his shoulders, others say he reached the height of the ears; so, our doctors of the laws sanction the raising of the hands so as to combine the essence of both situations as differently reported. Now should it be said: "The method you have devised differs from the methods of all those whom you have mentioned"; I should reply "I have differed from them only in my setting forth clearly some topics in which they made erroneous statements." And indeed, were their books satisfactory and all of their statements correct, and had there been a profit to the man in the street from their compilations, I should not have taken on myself the burden I did. However, I did not see them going beyond distances and kingdoms and maps, and somewhat of curiosities, and the science of the stars. As for the region of al-Maghrib, we divided it on the pattern of the region of al-Mashriq, the similarity between the two residing in that each of them represents a boundary of the realm of al-Islām in its longitudinal extent, and the point of rising and setting of the luminary of the earth.

This is the form of the Peninsula of the Arabs. [Map IV]
We have divided this region into four extensive provinces, and four large districts. The provinces are al-Ḥijāz, al-Yaman, ʿUmān, Hajar; the districts al-Aḥqāf, al-Ashḥār, al-Yamāma, Qurḥ.

p. 69   The capital of al-Ḥijāz is Makka; among its towns are Yathrib, Yanbuʿ, Qurḥ, Khaybar, al-Marwa, al-Hawrāʾ, Judda, al-Ṭāʾif, al-Jār, al-Suqyā (Yazīd), al-ʿAwnīd, al-Juḥfa, and al-ʿUshayra: these are the larger towns. Lesser towns are Badr, Khulays, Amaj, al-Ḥijr, Badā Yaʿqūb, al-Suwāriqiyya, al-Furʿ, al-Sayra, Jabala, Maḥāyiʿ, Hādha.

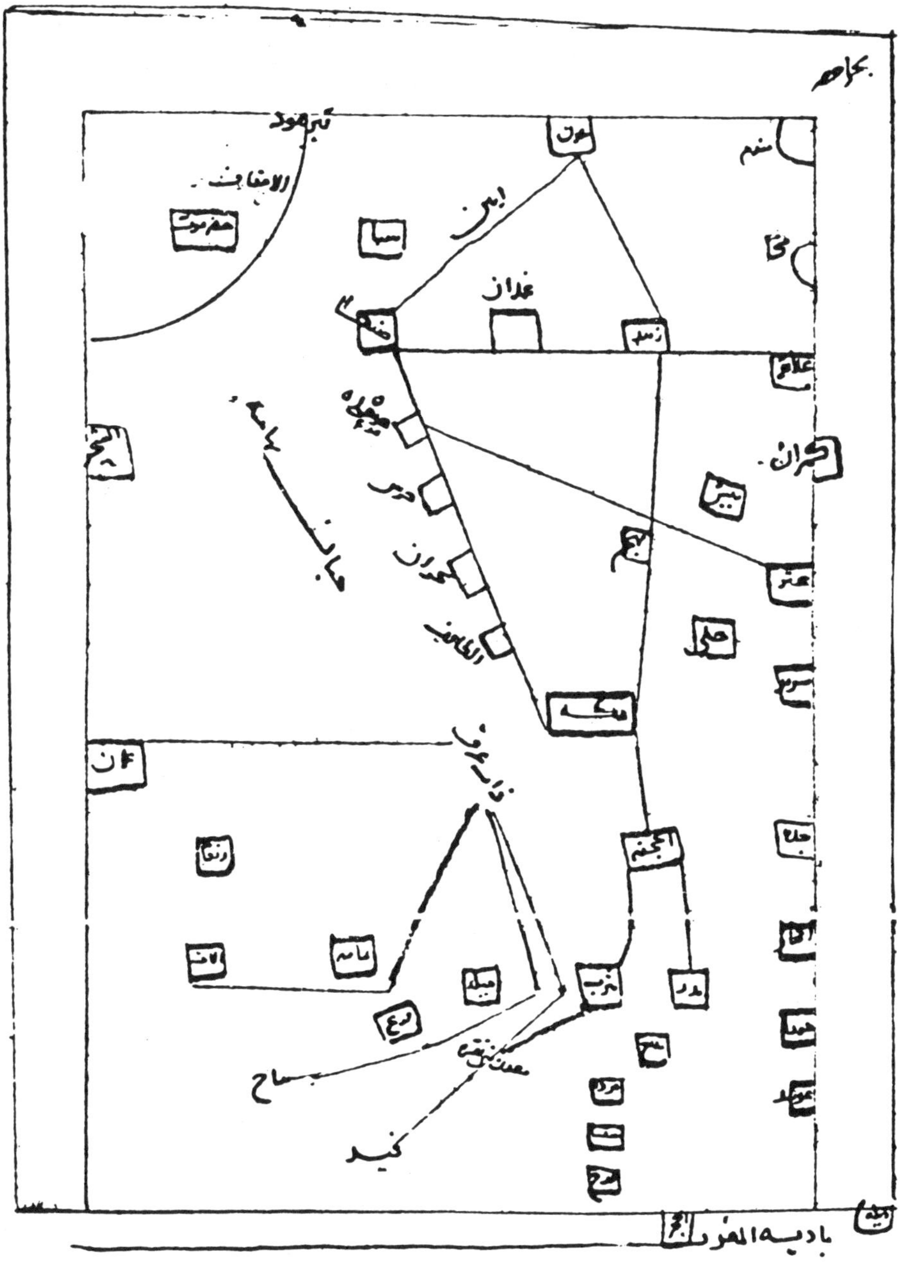

Map IV: Arabia (see p. 408).
(see p. 408)
From MS. Sprenger 5—Ahlwardt 6034 by kind permission of the Staatsbibliothek
Preussischer Kulturbesitz, Berlin, Orientabteilung.

Al-Yaman is in two divisions, one towards the sea, lowlying, and named Tihāma. Its capital is Zabīd, and its towns include the following: Maʿqir, Kadra, Mawr, ʿAtana, al-Sharja, Duwayma, al-Hamidha, Ghalāfiqa, Mukhā, Kamarān, al-Hirda, al-Lasʿa, Sharma, al-ʿAshīra, Ranqa, al-Khasūf, al-Sāʿid, al-Mahjam, and there are others. Here is the district of Abyan with towns ʿAdan and Lahj; the district of ʿAthr with towns Baysh, Haly, Sirrayn; also the district of al-Sarawāt. The part of al-Yaman towards the mountains is a cold area called Najd. Its capital is Sanʿāʾ and of its towns are Saʿda, Najrān, Jurash, al-ʿUrf, Jublān, al-Janad, Dhamār, Nasafān, Yahsib, al-Suhūl, al-Mudhaykhira, Khawlān. Here also is the district of al-Ahqāf with just one town, Hadhramawt. Another district is Mahra, with chief town al-Shihr; there is also the district of Sabaʾ.

The capital of ʿUmān is Suhār. Its towns are: Nazwa, al-Sirr, Dhank, Hafīt, Dabā, Salūt, Jullafār, Samad, Lasyā, Milah. The capital of Hajar is al-Ahsāʾ; its towns Sābūn, al-Zarqāʾ, Uwāl, al-ʿUqayr. The district here is al-Yamāma. Most of the towns of this Peninsula are small, yet have the full reputation of towns. I now turn to a description of the towns of the provinces, as far as is possible, and omit whatever is of no profit.

Makka, the metropolis of this region, is laid out around the Kaʿba, and is situated in a mountain valley. I have seen three other towns situated like this—ʿAmmān in al-Shām, Istakhr in Fārs, and Qaryat al-Hamrāʾ in Khurāsān. The buildings of Makka are of black smooth stone and some white stone; the upper parts are of baked brick. The houses commonly have projecting windows of teakwood, and are multistoreyed, whitewashed, and clean. It is hot in the summer, but the nights are pleasant; in any case God has lifted from them the trouble of heating their houses, and has relieved them of the cost of keeping themselves warm. The area that slopes down from al-Masjid al-Harām is known as al-Masfala (the lower quarter), what is higher is called al-Maʿalāt (the upper). The width of the town is the width of the valley in which it lies. The Masjid, longer than it is wide, is situated two-thirds of the way towards the Masfala quarter; the Kaʿba stands in its middle. The door of the Kaʿba is raised above the ground about six feet; it consists of two leaves overlaid with silver, chased with gold. The door faces east. The length of the Masjid is three hundred seventy cubits, its width three hundred fifteen cubits. The Kaʿba measures twenty-four cubits and a span by twenty-three cubits and a span. The measurement around al-Hijr (enclosure) is twenty-five cubits; the distance of the *tawāf* [seven-fold circumambulations of the Kaʿba during the Pilgrimage] is one hundred seven cubits. The height of the Kaʿba is twenty-seven cubits. The Hijr is on the side towards al-Shām; it is like a barn, and the *mīzāb* (drainpipe) discharges onto it. Its walls, which are waist-high, as well as its floor, are faced with white marble; it is also called al-Hatīm. The *tawāf* passes from behind it, and it is not lawful to pray facing it. Should someone then maintain that as the *tawāf* can be performed around this place only, it follows that it is lawful to say prayers facing it, I should

p. 70
p. 71
p. 72

say that this is a matter that may not be simply comprehended, as there is an ambiguity here [whether or not the Hijr forms part of the Kaʿba]; so that it is necessary to be cautious here with respect to both aspects of the matter.

Al-Hajar al-Aswad (The Black Stone) is in the east corner of the Kaʿba, close to the door, and set into the point of the corner itself. It is shaped like a man's head, and a person kissing it must bend slightly. The domed structure over the well of Zamzam is opposite to the door of the Kaʿba, and the course of the *tawāf* runs between the two. Behind Zamzam is Qubbat al-Sharāb (the Dome of Drink) where is a reservoir in which *sawīq* (a porridge) and wine were provided in former times.

The *Maqām* [standing stone of Abraham] is immediately in front of the middle of the wall of the house in which is the door; it is closer to the Kaʿba than Zamzam, so is included in the course of the *tawāf* during the days of the Pilgrimage. A great iron chest is over it, fixed firmly in the ground, its height greater than the height of a man. This is covered with a cloth. Every year the *Maqām* is lifted into the house, and when it is returned to its place a wooden housing is put over it, with a door which is opened when prayers are said. As the Imām ends the prayers he touches the stone, and the door is then closed. The *Maqām* bears the mark of the feet of Abraham, with the positions of the right and the left transposed. It is black, and is bigger than the Black Stone.

The ground of the *tawāf* is strewn with sand, and that of the mosque with gravel. Around the courtyard are three porticoes on pillars of white marble, which al-Mahdī brought there from Alexandria, by sea, to Judda. The mosque is of his building. The walls of the porticoes on the outside are decorated with mosaic, for which artisans were brought from al-Shām and Miṣr; you may still see their names on it.

The mosque has nineteen gates: the gate of Banū Shayba, the gate of the Prophet, the gate of Banū Hāshim, the gate of the Oil-merchants, the gate of the Cloth-merchants, the gate of the Fullers, the gate of Banū Makhzūm, the gate of al-Ṣafā, the gate of Zuqāq al-Shatawī, the gate of the Date-sellers, the gate of Dār al-Wazīr, the gate of Jiyād, the gate of al-Hazwara, the gate of Ibrāhīm, the gate of Banū Sahm, the gate of Banū Jumaḥ, the gate of al-ʿAjala, the gate of al-Nadwa, the gate of al-Bishāra. The market places of the town are on the east and south sides, and the buildings and the lodging houses for the Egyptians are on the west. The course of *al-saʿy* [the ceremony, during the Pilgrimage, of come-and-go seven times] between al-Ṣafā and al-Marwa runs through the eastern market, the dash being from the corner of the mosque to the gate of Banū Hāshim. Here are green pillars. Behind these two markets are two other markets which carry to the end of the *Maʿalāt* (upper quarter) with passageways between them. A pilgrim entering from the way of al-ʿIrāq seeking the gate of the Banū Shayba needs to turn to the right, proceeding through Sūq (the market of) Raʾs al-Radam, not by way of Sūq al-Layl. On the other hand, Egyptians making for this gate, as soon as they arrive at al-Jarrāhiyya, outside the

p. 73

town, have to turn towards the left to the Thaniyya, then descend to the
p. 74 cemeteries to reach the entrance of those coming from al-ʿIrāq. The town is
entered from three sides, one gate on the Minā side towards al-ʿIrāq, where are
two roads; another is on the road of al-ʿUmra; the third is the road of al Yaman
in *al-Masfala*. All these gates are covered with iron plates, for the town is
well-fortified. Mount Abū Qubays overlooks the mosque; one ascends to it from
al-Safā by a flight of steps. The area of the *tawāf* is surrounded by pillars of
bronze and wooden posts, from which candelabra are suspended for wax tapers
lighted in the name of the rulers of Misr, al-Yaman, and the Shār, the ruler of
Gharjistān. In Makka are three reservoirs filled from a canal which Zubayda
caused to be cut from Bustān Banī ʿĀmir; there are also wells of rather middling
water. Their houses are their only sources of revenue to the people here.

. Abū Bakr bin ʿAbdān al-Shīrāzī told me that he had it from ʿAlī bin
al-Husayn ibn Maʿdān that he had it from Muhammad bin Sulaymān Luwayn
al-Massīsī that he had it from Abu al-Ahūs on the authority of al-ʿAshʿath bin
Salīm on the authority of al-Aswad bin Yazīd, to the effect that ʿĀʾisha—God be
pleased with her—recounted: "I once asked the Prophet—God's peace and
blessings be upon him—whether the Hijr is part of the Sacred House. He
answered, 'Yes.' I then asked him: 'Then why have they not included it in the
House?' He said that the people fell short of funds for the cost. I also asked him
concerning the door of the House, why it is raised above the ground. He replied:
'Your people did so that they might admit whom they willed to enter, and deny
whom they willed. And indeed, were it not that your people had only recently
been in contact with paganism, so that I feared that their hearts would be
changed, I should certainly have considered including the Hijr in the House,
and fixing the door on a level with the ground.'"

Ibn al-Zubayr is said to have brought in ten of the chief Companions of
the Prophet to hear this from ʿĀʾisha herself. He then ordered the Kaʿba to be
pulled down. The people gathered against him and protested this action, but he
rejected their representations that he not demolish it. The people fled a *farsakh*
away, in dread of the enormity of the deed and the descent of punishment on
themselves. However, nothing but good came of it, and he rebuilt it in accord
with what ʿĀʾisha had told him, and the people returned.

When al-Hajjāj invested the city [72/692], Ibn al-Zubayr sought the
sanctuary of the Kaʿba. Al-Hajjāj positioned the catapult on the Hill of Abū
p. 75 Qubays, and said: "Destroy the additions which this presumptuous heretic has
made." So they bombarded the site of al-Hatīm; and he had Ibn al-Zubayr taken
out and crucified. He restored the wall to what it had been formerly. Moreover,
he took of the stones that were left over, closed up the western door with them,
and paved the House with the remainder, so that they would not be lost.

I heard the following from one of the elders of al-Qayrawān. Said he: "When
al-Mansūr went on the Pilgrimage, he was struck by the smallness of the Holy
Sanctuary, its state of disrepair, and the scant recognition of its sanctity. In fact,

he saw the Bedouin doing the rounds of the *tawāf* on camel or dromedary. This grieved him, so he decided on buying the houses around there, adding them to it, making it grander, and plastering it. He accordingly assembled the owners of the houses and tempted them with the offer of a considerable sum of money for them. They, however, declined and would not sell the houses, unwilling to give up their proximity to the sacred house of God. This distressed al-Mansūr, but he would not usurp ownership of the houses. He accordingly did not show himself to anyone for three days, and this caused much comment. Now it happened that Abū Hanīfa was on the Pilgrimage that year, while as yet not become well-known, nor had people become acquainted with his learning, or the soundness of his opinions. He went straight to the camp of al-Mansūr, which was in al-Abtah, and enquired about the Commander of the Faithful, and the reason he had concealed himself. When the facts were related to him, he said: "This is an easy matter to resolve, and should I meet him I will show him how." This was told to al-Mansūr, who bade Abū Hanīfa come before him. When he enquired of him on the matter, Abū Hanīfa said: "May the Commander of the Faithful have them brought to his presence, and let him ask: 'Did this Kaʿba descend to you, or did you descend on it' Were they to say: 'It descended on us'; that could be refuted, because it is from here that all the earth was stretched out. Were they to say: 'It is we, ourselves, who have settled down around it,' they should be told in answer that 'the number of visitors has become so great and the area around it so limited, the greater right attaches to the surrounding space, so you must vacate it.'" Having assembled them and asked them the question, their spokesman, a man of the tribe of Hāshim said: "We ourselves came down on it." "Then," said he, "restore its space, for its visitors have grown many, and there is need for it." They were completely confounded, and agreed to the sale. This narrative confirms one of the two opinions attributed to Abū Hanīfa, in his aversion to selling the houses of Makka, or the acceptance of rent for them; but perhaps there is another explanation.

p. 76   The town of Minā, a *farsakh* from Makka, is part of the holy territory, and is two miles long. It is peopled in the season of the Pilgrimage, but devoid of inhabitants the rest of the year, except for those who have the safekeeping of it. Abu al-Hasan al-Karkhī used to allege in vindication of Abū Hanīfa the legality of saying the Friday prayers there, on the grounds that Minā and Makka are like one metropolis. When, however, Abū Bakr al-Jassās went on the Pilgrimage, and perceived the distance between the two places, he considered the argument deficient. He said that it is, indeed, one of the metropoles of the Muslims, populous at one season, empty at another, its evacuation not excluding it from the category of metropoles. The Qādhī Abu al-Hasan al-Qazwīnī maintains the same view. He asked me one day how many people lived there throughout the year. "Twenty or thirty men," said I, "and there is hardly a campsite there in which you do not find a woman taking care of it." Said he, "Abū Bakr is right, and was quite correct in what he taught you about this." In my meeting the jurist, Abū Hāmid al-Baghūlanī, in Naysābūr, I told him the foregoing, and he said: "The argument lies with what Abu al-Hasan stipulates. Do you not consider the saying of God - glory to His name: 'Then the sacrifice shall take place at the ancient House,' (Qur'ān, sūra 22, v. 33), and also: 'An offering to reach the Ka'ba?' (Qur'ān, sūra 5, v. 95) And in fact the sacrifice occurs at Minā."

Few are the towns of any importance in Islām that do not have a campsite there for their inhabitants. At the entrance of the town, to the side towards Makka, is a pass ('Aqaba), on which the pebbles are cast on Yawn al-Nahr [the Day of Sacrifice—tenth day of the month of Pilgrimage], as well as the three following days: the first (heap of pebbles) is near Masjid al-Khayf (Mosque of the Slope), the middle one between the first heap and that of al-'Aqaba. Minā consists of two valleys, each with its own pathways. The Masjid (al-Khayf) is on the right-hand road, and the Masjid al-Kabsh [the ram sacrificed by Abraham] close to the pass.

In Minā are wells, water tanks, commercial houses, stores. The town is well-built, being of stone and teakwood, and is situated between two mountains that overlook it.

Al-Muzdalifa is distant a *farsakh* from Minā. It has an oratory, a public
p. 77 fountain, a minaret, and a number of ponds of water. It lies towards the mountain of Thabīr, of which Arabs used to say: "Shine, O Thabīr, that we may move." But there are variants on this. Al-Muzdalifa is also called Jam' [place where people collect themselves], and al-Mash'ar [place for performance of religious ceremonies] al-Harām.

'Arafa is a village in which are planted fields, vegetable gardens, and melon patches; here are substantial houses belonging to the people of Makka which they occupy on the Day of 'Arafa. The place of standing is within shouting distance of it, near a low, flat mountain; here are public fountains, reservoirs, and a flowing canal. A guidepost has been erected here behind which the Imām stands making the invocation, the people around him standing on the hillocks nearby. The Musallā [place of prayer] is on the edge of the valley of 'Urana on the outskirts of 'Arafa. Standing in the valley itself is not permitted, and should anyone go out to it before the setting of the sun, he is obliged to atone by a blood sacrifice. On the boundary of 'Arafa are white pillars, and in the place of prayer is a pulpit of baked brick, behind that a large pond. Two miles ahead of that is al-Ma'zimayn (the two straits), the limit of al-Haram. Batn Muhassir is a valley between Minā and al-Muzdalifa, forming the boundary of al-Muzdalifa.

Al-Tan'īm is a place in which a number of mosques stand around Masjid 'Ā'isha, also drinking fountains. It is on the road to al-Madīna. From here the Makkans go in their *ihrām* [two seamless sheets, of wool or linen, usually white] during the ceremonies of the 'Umra. White pillars surround the Haram (sacred precinct) which stretches three miles to the west on the road to al-Tan'īm; on the road of al-'Irāq nine miles, on the road of al-Yaman, seven miles, on the road of al-Tā'if, eleven miles, and on the main highway, ten miles.

Dhu al-Hulayfa is a village near Yathrib, having a good mosque, with wells close by; but you see no one around here. Al-Juhfa is a thriving city inhabited by the Banū Jaʿfar; it is protected with a fortress having two gates. There are some wells here; and two miles away is a spring. It has a large reservoir, though sometimes the water runs scarce. Fevers are quite common. I was informed of the following tradition by Shāfiʿ bin Muhammad who had it from ʿAlī bin al-Rajāʾ, who had it from Abū ʿUtba, who had it from Muhammad bin Yūsuf, who had it from Sufyān on the authority of Hishām bin ʿUrwa, who had it on the authority of his father, who had it from ʿĀʾisha. Said she: "The Messenger of God—God's peace and blessings be upon him—said: 'O God! Endear al-Madīna to us as you have endeared Makka, and even more so; and transfer its fevers to al-Juhfa'".

Qarn is a small town beyond al-Ṭāʾif, on the road to Sanʿāʾ. Yalamlam is a way station on the road to Zabīd; thriving. Dhāt ʿIrq, a village with some wells from which water is easily drawn; it is an arid, gloomy place two stages away from Makka.

Ibrāhīm bin ʿAbd Allāh al-Isbahānī related to me a tradition, saying that he had it from Muhammad bin Ishāq al-Sarrāj, who had it from Qutayba bin Saʿīd, who had it from al-Layth bin Saʿd, who had it from Nāfiʿ the Mawla of ibn ʿUmar, on the authority of ʿAbd Allāh bin ʿUmar: A man stood up in the Masjid and said: "O Messenger of God, from what place do you direct us to begin the Pilgrimage?" Said the Messenger of God—God's peace and blessings be upon him—in reply: "The people of al-Madīna begin at Dhu al-Hulayfa, the people of al-Shām at al-Juhfa, the people of Najd at Qarn." Ibn ʿUmar says, moreover, that there are those who assert that the Messenger of God—God's peace and blessings be upon him—said also, on another occasion: "The people of al-Yaman begin at Yalamlam, the people of al-ʿIrāq at Dhāt ʿIrq."

Al-Dhabīb is the *mīqāt* (rendezvous) for pilgrims coming from the west; it is a mountain on the sea coast across from al-Juhfa; Shiqqān, the rendezvous for the people of al-Yaman, is on the sea and faces Yalamlam. ʿAydhāb is a town across from Judda, and anyone coming on the Pilgrimage from this direction, here assumes the *ihrām*. These, then, are the points of rendezvous for the provinces; should anyone pass beyond them on his way to Makka and then return, and if he had uttered his call of *Labbayka* [God, here I am at your service!], the requirement of a blood sacrifice from him is annulled. Some say, however, that it is not annulled; some others maintain that it is annulled even if the *talbiya* [a prayer of obedience recited during the Pilgrimage] was not said. A pilgrim from the provinces may not pass beyond a rendezvous without having assumed the *ihrām*. This is true even if it is not his assigned rendezvous, as if, for example, a Syrian passes through Dhu al-Hulayfa. The rendezvous of the Makkans on pilgrimage is, of course, the city itself.

Al-Jiʿrāna is distant one stage from Makka; people have to go out to it to assume the *ihrām* for the ʿUmra [a pilgrimage at Makka lesser than the Hajj].

p. 79   These, then, are the ceremonial places of ritual for the Pilgrimage. In all, the
rituals performed there comprise: three *Farā'idh* [sing. *Farīdha*—duty enjoined
in the *Qur'ān* or in a tradition], six *Wājibāt* [sing. *Wājiba*—obligation, though
possibly not enjoined in the *Qur'ān* or tradition], and five *Sunan* [sing. *Sunna*—
that which was said or done by the Prophet]. The *Farā'idh* are: al-Ihrām, the
Wuqūf (standing) at 'Arafa, and the *Tawāf* (circumambulations) *lil-Ziyāra*. The
Wājibāt are: assuming the ritual garb from the rendezvous point, the *sa'y* or the
to-and-fro between al-Safā and al-Marwa, and descent from 'Arafāt after sunset.
The *Sunan* are the *tawāf* on arrival, making three circumambulations at a trot,
the to-and-fro in the *sa'y* between the two pillars, the descent from al-Muzdalifa
before dawn, and staying at Minā during the special days known as the days
of Minā. Some maintain that the *sa'y* is a *Fardh* (duty), some that the *tawāf* of
arrival is a *Wājib*, and that the *tawāf* at dawn is a *Sunna*.

We now return to a description of the towns of this area, and its districts,
in order.

Al-Tā'if is a small town, Syrian in climate and in the coolness of its water.
Most of the fruits of Makka are from here. Pomegranates abound here, raisins,
excellent grapes, superb fruits. It is situated on the back of Jabal Ghazwān, so the
water freezes here at times. Tanneries are the commonest places of work here.
When the elite of Makka find the heat unbearable they come to this town.

Judda is a city on the seashore, from which circumstance it derives its
name. A fortified, well-developed, populous place, its people are merchants, and
well-to-do; it is the granary of Makka, the entrepôt of al-Yaman and Misr. Here
is a distinguished mosque. However, the people here suffer great inconvenience
from deficiency of water, though the town has many reservoirs; water has to
be brought from some distance away. The Persians are the predominant class
there, where they have splendid mansions. Its streets are straight, the situation
excellent, but the heat is excessive.

Amaj is a small town with five forts, two of stone and three of clay;
the mosque is right on the side of the road. Khulays adjoins it, and here are
a reservoir, a canal, varieties of dates, vegetable gardens, and cultivated fields.
Al-Suwāriqiyya has many forts, and many gardens, cultivated fields, and livestock.
Al-Fur' and al-Sayra are two forts in each one of which is a moque. Jabala is a
large town, with many commercial establishments; over it stands an impregnable
fortress called al-Muhd, the mosque standing outside it. Mahāyi' compares with
p. 80   Jabala, and both stand above the valleys of Sāya. Hadha is a beautiful town peopled
by descendants of Abū Bakr; it has a number of forts, and a large mosque.

Yathrib (al-Madīna)—this is the City of the Prophet—God's peace and
blessings be upon him. We treat it here as a district because it is surrounded by
important towns and has access to well-known maritime amenities. It is less
than half the size of Makka. For most of its environs, gardens, groves of palm
trees, and villages surround it. There are a few cultivated fields, and water of but
middling quality. There are cisterns here into which some ducts spill, situated

near the gates of the city, and reached by a set of steps. ʿUmar, God be pleased with him, had a canal constructed leading to the gate of the mosque, but it has fallen into disuse. The marketplaces are close to the mosque. The town is bright and splendid. The people are, for the most part, descendants of Husayn, the son of ʿAlī, God be pleased with them both. The buildings here are of clay, the soil is rather saline, the population scant. The mosque is situated two thirds of the way through the town towards Baqīʿ al-Gharqad; it is on the model of the mosque of Damascus, and not large. This, and the mosque of Damascus were built by Walīd, son of ʿAbd al-Malik; however, the ʿAbbāsids have added to it. The Prophet himself—God's peace and blessings be upon him—said: "Even if this mosque were extended as far as Sanʿāʾ, it would still be my mosque."

The first person to enlarge it was ʿUmar, God be pleased with him, extending it from the pillars which face the *maqsūra* [enclosed place set apart in mosque, usually occupied during prayers by ruler] at the present time, to the southern wall. Next ʿUthmān, God be pleased with him, added to it from near the place of the *Qibla* to its present location. After that al-Walīd extended it, but he did not extend it for the glory of God, but on account of the house of al-Hasan the son of al-Hasan bin ʿAlī, God be pleased with him; the door of this was within the mosque, so he could emerge from it during the prayer. It was built of pointed stone and mosaic. ʿUmar bin ʿAbd al-ʿAzīz, God be pleased with him, supervised the building of it; and when he was about to pull down the *mihrāb*, he called to p. 81 the elders of the Muhājirūn and the Ansār and said to them: "Be present at the building of your *Qibla*, so that you do not say, 'ʿUmar changed it.'"

The extension made by al-Walīd ran from the east to the west, comprising six pillars; and he extended it in the direction of al-Shām, beginning with the square pillar in the necropolis, fourteen pillars, of which ten are in the courtyard and four in the porticoes. Then when al-Mahdī made the Pilgrimage in the year 160/776, he added to the mosque one hundred cubits in the direction of al-Shām, an extent of ten pillars. Accordingly, its length today is one hundred fifty-four cubits, its width one hundred sixty-three cubits. The length of the courtyard is one hundred sixty-five cubits, its width, one hundred sixty-five cubits.

It is said that al-Walīd wrote to the king of the Romaeans: "We desire to restore the great mosque of our Prophet; so help me in this with artisans and mosaic work." He accordingly sent him a number of loads, and more than twenty craftsmen, among them ten whose services were the equivalent of one hundred eighty thousand *dīnārs*. It is said that on an occasion these men were alone in the mosque, and one of them stood and said: "I will piss on the grave of their Prophet," but when he released his drawers he was dry.

Men are not in agreement about the respective positions of the graves of the Prophet—God's peace and blessings be upon him—and of his two companions. This is one account: the Prophet, behind him Abū Bakr, then behind him, ʿUmar. According to the account of Mālik ibn Anas, the Prophet is to the western side of the house, opposite him is a vacant space; behind the Prophet is Abū Bakr, and beyond the vacant space, ʿUmar. The vacant space was that mentioned to ʿUmar bin ʿAbd al-ʿAzīz, but he did not consider himself worthy of it. It is said that here ʿĪsa, peace be upon him, will be buried.

I have been told the following tradition by Abū Bakr Muhammad bin ʿAlī al-Faqīh, in Sāwa, who had it from Muhammad bin Hilāl al-Shāshī, who had it from Muhammad bin Ishāq, who had it from Yūnus, who had it from Muhammad bin Ismāʿīl bin Abū Fudayk, on the authority of ʿAmr bin ʿUthmā, on the authority of Qāsim: "I went to ʿĀʾisha and said, ʿOh Mother, disclose to us the grave of the Messenger of God—God's peace and blessings be upon him—and of his two companions,' and she pointed out three graves to me, neither raised, nor lowered, but just level with the ground of al-ʿArsa al-Hamrāʾ (the red courtyard). And I saw the grave of the Prophet—God's peace and blessings be upon him—in front, Abū Bakr was near his head, his feet between the shoulders of the Prophet; while ʿUmar had his head at the feet of the Prophet—God's peace and blessings be upon him!"

p. 82

The pulpit is in the middle of the roofed part of the mosque; it forms a covering for the pulpit of the Prophet—God's peace and blessings be upon him—placed in a garden paved with marble. This storied garden is beside a red pillar, between the pulpit and the grave. I read in the records of al-Madīna that Muʿāwiya ordered the pulpit taken to the side of the *mihrāb*, just as all pulpits are; but when they set about moving it the town itself quaked, and bolts of lightning appeared nearby; so he said: "Leave it as it is," and ordered the making of the present pulpit over it. This latter has five steps, the first one but three. The mosque has twenty gates. The city itself has really splendid gates, four in number: the gate of al-Baqīʿ, the gate of al-Thaniyya, the gate of Juhayna, and the gate of al-Khandaq. Al-Khandaq, (the fosse) is on the Makkan side. Al-Madīna is splendidly provided with a towering fortress.

Al-Baqīʿ is to the east of al-Madīna. The soil around here is salty. Here is the grave of Ibrāhīm, son of the Prophet—God's peace and blessings be upon him—and the graves of al-Hasan, and of a number of the Companions. The grave of ʿUthmān is at the remote end.

Qubā is a village two miles away, on the left side of the road to Makka; it has many buildings of stone. It has the Masjid al-Taqwā [Mosque of Veneration— *Qurʾān*, sūra 9, v. 108]: this is a well-built mosque, in front of it a paved court and an open area. It has many places associated with the Prophet. The water here is fresh. Here also is Masjid al-Dhirār [Mosque of Mischief—*Qurʾān*, sūra 9, v. 107] in the pulling down of which the people performed a pious deed.

Uhud is a hill three miles distant [from al-Madīna]. By it is the grave of Hamza situated in a mosque, before which is a well, beside it an enclosure containing the graves of the Martyrs [killed in the battle at Uhud]. On this hill is a place wherein the Prophet—God's peace and blessings be upon him—once concealed himself. It is the hill nearest to al-Madīna.

Al-ʿAqīq is a thriving village two miles distant, in the direction of Makka, and here the governor resides. Its water is fresh. All the area between the two ridges of al-Madīna is a precinct as sacred as the sacred precinct of Makka itself.

p. 83   Badr is a small town situated towards the coast; the dates here are excellent. Here are found ʿAyn al-Nabī (the spring of the Prophet)—God's peace and blessings be upon him—and the site of the battle [fought 19 Ramadhān A.H. 2/C.E. 15 March 624] and a number of mosques which the rulers of Egypt founded.

Al-Jār is on the seacoast. It is fortified on three sides by a wall, the quarter facing the sea being open. It has lofty dwellings and a thriving market. It is the granary of al-Madīna and its towns. Water is carried thither from Badr, grain from Egypt. The mosque is without a courtyard.

Al-ʿUshayra is a small town on the coast, opposite to Yanbuʿ. It has some date palms and an incomparable caravanserai.

Yanbuʿ is a large splendid town, well fortified by a wall. It has an abundant supply of water. It is more flourishing than Yathrib, and has more groves of date palms. The fortress is well-built, the markets bustling. It has two gates, close to one of which stands the mosque. Predominant here are the descendants of al-Hasan. Raʾs al-ʿAyn is twelve miles distant.

Al-Marwa is a fortified town with an abundance of palm trees and excellent dates. The drinking water is derived from a canal that flows abundantly. Around it is a ditch, and the gates are iron. It is a source of the doom palm, and of an excellent variety of dates known as *burdī*. It is hot here in the summer. The Banū Jaʿfar predominate here.

Al-Hawrāʾ is the port of Khaybar; it has a fortress, and the suburbs are densely inhabited; the market here is on the side towards the sea.

Khaybar is a fortified town, somewhat resembling al-Marwa. It has a very good mosque. Nearby is the gate which the Prince of the Faithful snatched up [ʿAlī, on dropping his shield in the attack]. This town and al-Marwa and al-Hawrāʾ are the towns of the district of Khaybar.

The district of Qurh is also called Wādī 'l-Qurā. There is not in al-Hijāz today, aside from Makka, a town more important, more thriving, more populous, with more commerce, wealth, and natural products, than this town [Qurh]. It is

p. 84   protected by an impregnable stronghold from one corner of which a castle rises. Villages surround it, and palms shelter it round about. Dates here are cheap, breads excellent, its waters abundant, its residences delightful. The markets bustle with people. A ditch surrounds the town, and it has three gates with iron plates affixed. The mosque stands facing on some alleys, and in its *mihrāb* is a bone said to be that which spoke to the Prophet—God's peace and blessings upon him—saying: "Do not eat me, for I am poisoned." This town is, indeed, Syrian, Egyptian, ʿIrāqī, and Hijāzī all together in one. However, its water is indigestible, its dates of middling quality. The public bath is outside the town. Most of the people there are Jews.

Al-Hijr is a small fortified town with many wells and cultivated fields. The mosque of Sālih is close by on an eminence; it is as if a gallery had been excavated from the rock. Here are to be found the wonders of Thamūd and their dwelling places. Suqyā Yazīd is the finest town in this area; palm groves and orchards join it in a continuous line with Qurh. The mosque is outside the town. Badā Yaʿqūb is on the main road to Egypt, thriving and populous. Al-ʿAwnīd is the port of Qurh: a thriving town, producing plenty of honey, and having a fine anchorage.

Zabīd, the capital of Tihāma, is one of its two metropoles, this being the residence of the kings of al-Yaman. It is a splendid, well-built town, and popularly called "the Baghdād of al-Yaman." The inhabitants are reasonably polite, and among them are merchants, nobles, scholars, litterateurs. It is a profitable place for one who visits it, a blessed place for one who lives there. Their wells are sweet, their baths clean. Over it is a fortress built of clay, and it has four gates: Bāb Ghalāfiqa, Bāb ʿAdan, Bāb Hishām (Sihām), and Bāb Shabāriq. Around it are villages and cultivated fields. It is more populous than Makka, bigger, and more prosperous. Their buildings are mostly of brick, their residences spacious and in good condition. The mosque, which is some distance from the markets, is clean, and the floor is cemented. Beneath the pulpit is a
p. 85 hollow, so that the rows of worshippers will be continuous. Ibn Ziyād had a channel led to the town. It is an attractive town, without equal in al-Yaman. However, the markets are cramped, prices are high, fruits scarce. Their food for the most part consists of millet and sorghum.

Maʿqir is on the road to ʿAdan, as are ʿAbra, Ghāra, and al-Makhnaq: these are all small towns.

ʿAdan is a splendid, flourishing, populous town, fortified, and with a pleasant climate. It is the corridor of al-Sīn, the seaport of al-Yaman, the granary of al-Maghrib, an entrepôt of various kinds of merchandise. There are many mansions in it. It is a source of good fortune to those who visit it, a source of prosperity to those who settle in it. The mosques are excellent, the means of earning a livelihood abundant. The mode of life is pure, prosperity evident on all sides. Indeed, the Prophet—God's peace and blessings be upon him—gave his blessing to the markets of Minā and ʿAdan. The town is shaped like a sheepfold, the mountains surrounding it altogether, encircling it down to the sea. An inlet of the sea passes behind this mountain, so that it is approached only by crossing this inlet, and thus arriving at the mountain. A pass, truly remarkable, has been cut in the rock, at its adit an iron gate. On the side towards the sea, a wall, pierced by five gates, extends from one extremity of the mountain to the other. The mosque is distant from the markets. The water in the wells is somewhat salty, so recourse is had to a number of cisterns. It is said that in olden times this place was the prisonhouse of Shaddād, the son of ʿĀd. However, it is a barren, gloomy place, without cultivation or stockfarming, without trees, fruits, water, grazing. Conflagrations and shipwrecks are frequent here; the mosque is neglected, in disorder, and filthy, the baths in disarray. Water is carried thither from a distance of one stage.

Abyan is older than ʿAdan, ʿAdan being in close relation with it, because the inhabitants of ʿAdan derive their wheat, fruits and vegetables from there, as there are many villages and cultivated fields around it. Such also is Lahj. Mandam (Mandab) is a crowded town on the sea. Sailing ships are detained here by the wind. It is a rather squalid town.

Mukhā is a flourishing town depending on Zabīd; it produces a large quantity of sesame oil. The inhabitants derive their drinking water from a spring outside the town. The mosque is on the outskirts of the town towards the shore.

p. 86

Ghalāfiqa is the port of Zabīd; a mosque here is right on the shore; this they hold in special respect, and attend assiduously to pray. It is a flourishing populous town, having palm plantations, coconut groves, and wells of fresh water. However, the climate is pestilential, and fatal to foreigners.

Al-Sharja, and al-Hirda, and ʿAtana are towns on the coast: here are the granaries for the sorghum exported to ʿAdan and Judda. While it is a land of milk, water must be brought to it from a distance. The mosques here are on the seashore.

The province of ʿAthr: this is an important district governed by an independent ruler, and having prosperous towns. ʿAthr is a large, fine town and very well-known, being the capital of the area, and the port of Sanʿāʾ and Saʿda. It has a fine market, a well-built mosque. Water has to be brought to the town from a distance, and the public bath is filthy. Baysh has a better climate than ʿAthr and purer water. Here the ruler resides, his house standing beside the mosque. Al-Jurayb is a town known for its bananas; it is the most prosperous town of the area, and, it seemed to me, the most remarkable.

Haly is a coastal town, flourishing, prosperous, and well endowed. Al-Sirrayn is a small town with a fort within which stands the mosque. At the gate of the town is a reservoir for storing rain-water. It is the port of al-Sarawāt. Al-Sarawāt is the source of grain, abounding in good things, having some inferior varieties of dates, and much honey. I do not know whether these places are towns or just villages, because I did not enter them.

Sanʿāʾ is the capital of Najd al-Yaman. It used to be more important than Zabīd, more prosperous, and the prestige attached to it. However, now it has greatly deteriorated, though there are still in it learned men whose likes I have not seen in all of al-Yaman, in bearing and intellect. This is a spacious city with abundance of fruits; prices are low, bread is good, and it has profitable merchandise. It is larger than Zabīd; and do not even ask about the excellence of the climate, because it is superb! Along with this, it is a friendly, kindly place.

p. 87

Saʿda is smaller than Sanʿāʾ, a flourishing town in the mountains. Here are made the finest leather water bottles, excellent leather mats, and the best tanned skins are exported from here. It is the city of the ʿAlawiyya, and their seat of government.

Jurash is of medium size, with date palms, though al-Yaman is not a country of palms. Najrān is about the size of Jurash, and each one of them is smaller than Saʿda. Most of the leathers you see come from these towns.

Al-Himyarī, that is, the city of Qahtān [ancestor of the Himyarites], is between Zabīd and Sanʿāʾ, and has many villages. The climate is bad and noxious, but the traders do well here. Al-Maʿāfir is a spacious district, with cultivated fields, villages, and natural advantages.

Sabaʾ is a district beyond these areas. The town itself is flourishing, but the area around is desolate.

Hadhramawt is the capital of al-Ahqāf, built in the sands at some distance from the shore. It is a flourishing and populous place, the inhabitants inclined to learning and philanthropy; yet, they lean to heresy. The colour of their skin is quite dark.

Al-Shihr is a town on the sea, an important centre for enormous fishes, which are exported to ʿUmān and ʿAdan, thence to al-Basra, and to the towns of al-Yaman. Here are trees of which the resin is frankincense.

The site of Iram of the Columns betrays no trace of its remains; from Lahj to it is a distance of two *farsakhs*, over level ground. You may see it glimmering from a long way off, but as you approach it you see not a thing. The water of ʿAdan is brought from here.

p. 88   Sakhīn is a town belonging to a tribe of the Quraysh known as Banū Sāma; I have heard that they number four thousand archers. Al-Shuqra consists of the dwellings of Khathʿam [a tribe]; palm trees and villages surround it.

You should realize that al-Yaman is an extensive country, in which I spent one whole year visiting those towns I have described. However, much of it is not personally known to me, but I will recount what I heard about it from those who are well-informed. I give an exhaustive list of its *mikhlāfs* (districts), though I have not visited them all, for it is a country distinguished by its *mikhlāfs*. I shall also give an account of the position and form of the Peninsula of the Arabs, along with a description of it that everyone will be able to understand, if it is the will of God, the Most High.

The *makhālif* (districts) of al-Yaman are:

The *mikhlāf* of Sanʿāʾ; al-Khashab; Ruhāba; Marmal;
the *mikhlāf* of al-Bawn; the *mikhlāf* of Khaywān.
To the right of Sanʿāʾ, *mikhlāf* Shākir; Wādiʿa; Yām; Arhab.
In the direction of al-Tāʾif, the *mikhlāf* of Najrān; Turaba; al-Hujayra; Kuthba; Jurash; al-Sarāt.

In Tihāma the *mikhlāf* of Dhankān; ʿAsham; Bīsha; ʿAkk. The *mikhlāf* of
p. 89 al-Hirda; the *mikhlāf* of Hamdān; the *mikhlāf* of Jawf Hamdān; the *mikhlāf* of Jawf Murād; the *mikhlāf* of Shanūʾa; Sudāʿ; Juʿfi; the *mikhlāf* of al-Jasra; the *mikhlāf* of al-Mashriq; Būshān; Ghudar; the *mikhlāf* of Aʿlā and Anʿum;

al-Masna°tayn; Banī Ghutayf; Qaryat Ma°rib; the *mikhlāf* of Hadhramawt; the *mikhlāf* of Khawlān Rudā°; the *mikhlāf* of Ahwar; the *mikhlāf* of al-Haql; Dhimār; the *mikhlāf* of Ibn °Āmir; Thāt; Radā°; the *mikhlāf* of Dathīna; the *mikhlāf* of al-Sharaf; the *mikhlāf* of Ru°ayn; Nasafān; Kahlān; the *mikhlāf*

p. 90 Dhankān; Dhubhān; the *mikhlāf* of Nāfi°; Mashā; the *mikhlāf* of Hujr and Badr; Akhalla; al-Suhayb; the *mikhlāf* of al-Thujja; al-Mazra°; *mikhlāf* Dhī Makārim; al-Umlūk; the *mikhlāf* of al-Salif; al-Adam; the *mikhlāf* of Najlān; Nahb; the

p. 91 *mikhlāf* of al-Janad; the *mikhlāf* of al-Sakāsik. Towards al-Ma°āfir: the *mikhlāf* of al-Ziyādī; the *mikhlāf* of al-Ma°āfir; *mikhlāf* Banī Majīd; the *mikhlāf* of al-Rakb; the *mikhlāf* of Saqf; the *mikhlāf* of al-Mudhaykhira; the *mikhlāf* of Hamul; Shar°ab; the *mikhlāf* of °Unna; °Unnāba. On the other side, the *mikhlāf* of Wuhādha; the *mikhlāf* of Sifl-Yahsib; the *mikhlāf* of al-Qufā°a; al-Wazīra; al-Hujr. The *mikhlāf* of Zabīd, opposite to which is the coast of Ghalāfiqa and the coast of al-Mandab; the *mikhlāf* of Rima°; the *mikhlāf* of Muqrā; the *mikhlāf* of Alhān; the *mikhlāf* of Jublān; the *mikhlāf* Dhī Jura; the *mikhlāf* of al- Maytam (al-Batam); the *mikhlāf* of al-Yamm(?) On the farther side of San°ā°: the *mikhlāf* of Khawlān; the *mikhlāf* of Mīsāri°; the *mikhlāf* of Harāz and Hawzan; the

p. 92 *mikhlāf* of al-Ukhrūj; the *mikhlāf* of Majnah; the *mikhlāf* of Hadhūr; the *mikhlāf* of Mājin; the *mikhlāf* of Wadhi°; al- Ma°lal; al- °Usba; the *mikhlāf* of Khunās (Hiyādh); Milhān; Hakam and Jāzān; Marsā 'l-Sharja; the *mikhlāf* of Hajūr; the *mikhlāf* of Qudum; and opposite it the village of Mahjara; the *mikhlāf* of Hayya and al- Kawdan; the *mikhlāf* of Maskh; the *mikhlāf* of Kinda and al-Sakūn; the *mikhlāf* of al-Sadif.

Suhār is the capital of °Umān, and there is not on the Sea of China today a more important town than it. It is a flourishing, populous, beautiful, pleasant, and delightful place. It has prosperity, and a merchant class, and is blessed with fruits and natural resources. It is more distinguished than Zabīd and San°ā°. It has remarkable markets; and this charming town is stretched along the shore of the sea. Its houses, towering and elegant, are built of baked brick and teakwood. The mosque here is on the seashore, and situated at the extreme end of the markets, with a beautiful high minaret. There are wells of middling water, a canal of fresh water, and an abundance of goods of all kinds. It is the gateway to China, the storehouse of the East and of al-°Irāq, and the promptuary of al-Yaman. Persians predominate here. The open place appointed for prayer is in the midst of date palms.

Masjid Suhār is a half *farsakh* away; there it was knelt the camel of the

p. 93 Messenger of God—God's peace and blessings be upon him. Its construction is of the very finest style; and the climate here is superior to that of the capital. The *mihrāb* of the mosque turns on a gudgeon, now seen yellow, now green, now red. Nazwa is a large town close to the mountains; the buildings here are of mud. The mosque is in the middle of the marketplace, and when the river overflows in winter it floods it. The drinking water here is from streams and wells. Al-Sirr is smaller than Nazwa; the mosque is in the market. The drinking water here is from streams and wells. It is completely surrounded with date palms. Dhank is a small town in the midst of palms. Authority here is always firm, as the inhabitants are heretical and refractory. Hafit abounds in palm trees; it lies in the direction of Hajar, and the mosque is in the markets. Salūt is a large town to the left of Nazwa. Dabā and Jullafār, both in the direction of Hajar, are close to the sea. Samad is a town of Nazwa. Lasyā, Milah, Barzam, al-Qalaʿ, and Dhankān are other towns. Al-Masqat is the first place ships from al-Yaman encounter; I have seen it myself, a delightful place, with abundance of fruits. Tuʾām has been dominated by a branch of the Quraysh; they are men of fortitude and forcefulness. ʿUmān is an important territory, measuring some eighty *farsakhs* in length as well as in breadth; it is virtually covered with date palms and gardens. Generally, the irrigation water is drawn from wells, the water of which is close to the surface; cattle draw it. Most of the wells are in the mountains. The people of these towns we have mentioned are heretical Arabs.

Al-Ahsāʾ is the capital of Hajar, which is also called al-Bahrayn. It is large, and abounding in date palms, flourishing, and populous. It is a place of heat and aridity. Situated at a distance of one stage from the sea, for the people there it is, p. 94 as it were, a cornucopia of merchandise! Nearby are some islands. This town is the place of residence of the Qarāmita, partisans of Abū Saʿīd. Good government and justice prevail here; however, the mosque is in disuse. Close by is the treasury of al-Mahdī, and they have other treasuries besides. Part of the wealth is kept in that, the remainder in their own treasuries. Al-Zarqāʾ and Sābūn are among their treasuries, as is also Uwāl. The remaining towns are on the sea, or close to it. Al-Yamāma is a district, the capital, al-Hajar. This is a large town, producing excellent dates. It is surrounded by forts and towns, one of which is al-Falaj.

You should know that the form of this Peninsula is that of a hall longer than it is wide, in which a couch has been placed from its front side to its door; between it and each of the two walls, to the right and left, is an empty space. The couch consists of two pieces: the inner piece represents Najd al-Yaman, a mountainous area in which lie Sanʿāʾ, Saʿda, Jurash, Najrān, and the City of Qahtān. ʿAdan is at the front of the hall at the end of the Sarawāt uplands, for the three walls are the Sea of China itself. These uplands are highly cultivated, producing grapes and corn. The open space on the right of the couch is Tihāma in which is Zabīd, with its towns. The open space on the left is called Najd al-Yaman, and here are al-Ahqāf, and Mahra, up to the borders of al-Yamāma; some include this latter with ʿUmān in this layout. This piece of the couch with the open spaces is al-Yaman. The piece of couch closest to the door of the hall is called al-Harra, extending from the borders of al-Yaman to Qurh: this is a range of mountains entirely arid, nothing growing there except a little grazing for cattle, brambles, and panic grass. Here are situated al-Haram, al-ʿUmaq, and Maʿdin al-Naqira, and there are some barren areas. The open space on the right is called al-Hijāb. Al-Hijāz [Al-Hijāb?] is small in area; it contains Yanbuʿ, al-Marwa, and al-ʿAmīs; also the coastal areas which are inhabited, and produce date palms. The open space on the left is called Najd al-Hijāz; in it are p. 95 al-Yamāma, and Fayd, and the halting places that are on the main road. This piece of the couch, with its spaces, is al-Hijāz, and Hajar is included in this; opposite to the door of the hall lies the desert. All this I have surveyed myself, and sectioned—and God knows best!

A Summary Account of Conditions in this Region

This is an intensely hot region, except for the realm of the Sarawāt hills, where the climate is equable—indeed it has been related to me that a man in Sanʿāʾ cooked a pot of meat, after which he departed to go on the Pilgrimage; on his return he found the food altogether unchanged. The clothing used here for the winter and for the summer is the same. The nights in Makka in summer are agreeable, but oppressive in Tihāma. In ʿUmān there falls during the night a type of date honey, while in the Haram the heat is severe, a killing wind blows, the number of flies beyond reckoning. Fruit is scarce in this region except in the Sarawāt hills. There is not a date palm in al-Yaman, waters are not abundant, and the shores are sterile, devoid altogether of water, except for Ghalāfiqa. People have inhabited those towns solely because of the sea. There is not in the entire region a lake, nor is there a river navigable for ships.

Jurisprudents are few here, as are preachers and readers, and Jews are more numerous than Christians. Apart from these there are no other tributary subjects. I did not encounter a single case of elephantiasis there.

Abu al-Fadhl bin Nahāma of Shīrāz has informed me of the following tradition. He asserted he had it from Abū Saʿīd Khalaf bin al-Fadhl, who had it from Abu al-Hasan Muhammad bin Hamdān, who had it from ʿAmr bin ʿAlī bin Yahyā bin Kathīr, who had it from ʿĀmir bin Ibrāhīm al-Isbahānī, who had it from Khattāb bin Jaʿfar, who had it from his father, who had it on the authority of Saʿīd bin Jubayr, who had it on the authority of Ibn ʿAbbās. He explains that the utterance, "the winter and summer journey," (Qurʾān, sūra 106, v. 2), refers to the people spending the winter in Makka and the summer in al-Tāʾif. Moreover, by the saying, "and has given them security from fear," (ibid, v. 4) the fear of elephantiasis is meant. White leprosy occurs there; and there are many p. 96 Blacks. The majority of the people are tan in colour, generally slight and lean of figure. Their clothing is made chiefly of cotton, and they go shod. They do not use raincloaks, experiencing neither snow nor freezing. No fruits have they in winter, nor any jerked meat, except what has been dried of the sacrificial meat at Minā.

Religious Sects. In Makka, Tihāma, Sanʿāʾ and Qurh they are Sunnī; the rural population around Sanʿāʾ and its adjacent districts, as also the country people of

ʿUmān, are fanatical heretics, the remainder of al-Hijāz are Ahl al-Ray [people of subjective judgment, followers of Abū Hanīfa]. In ʿUmān, Hajar and Saʿda, the people are Shīʿa; the Shīʿa of ʿUmān, Saʿda and the people of the Sarawāt hills and of the coasts of al-Haramayn, are Muʿtazilites, even those of ʿUmān. Predominant in Sanʿāʾ and Saʿda are the followers of Abū Hanīfa, the mosques being in their hands. In al-Maʿāfir the teaching of Ibn al-Mundhir is followed, and in the districts of Najd al-Yaman that of Sufyān. The *adhān* [the summons to public prayers] in Tihāma and in Makka is repeated [in a low voice, then in a raised voice], and if you pay attention to it for a moment you realize it is done in accord with the school of Mālik. In Zabīd, the *takbīr* is said on the days of the two festivals, according to the teaching of Ibn Masʿūd; this practice was instituted by al-Qādhī Abū ʿAbd Allāh al-Saʿwānī, during my stay there. The practice in al-Hajar is according to the tenets of the Qarāmita. In ʿUmān are some Dāwūdiyya, where they have an academy.

The **language** of the people of this region is Arabic, except in Suhār, where they call out to one another and speak in Persian. The majority of the people of ʿAdan and Judda are Persian, yet their language is Arabic. On the borders of al-Himyarī is a tribe of Arabs whose dialect is incomprehensible. The people of ʿAdan say for "rijlayhi," "rijlaynah" (his two feet); for "yadayhi" they say "yadaynah" (his two hands), and so forth. For the sound of the letter "jīm" they pronounce the "kāf", thus for "rajab" (the month Rajab) they say "rakab", and for "rajul" (a man) they say "rakul."

In fact it is related concerning the Prophet—God's peace and blessings be upon him—that a piece of dung was brought him in connection with a ceremony of purification, and this he threw from him saying, "it is 'riks'" [instead of "rijs" (filth)]. This has left the jurisprudents in a quandary. It may well be that their interpretation of it is admissible; of course it may be, too, that he was employing this dialect. All the dialects spoken by the Arabs are found in the deserts of this peninsula; however, the purest is the dialect of Hudhayl, then that of the two Najds, then that spoken in the rest of al-Hijāz. Al-Ahqāf is an exception—their speech is uncouth.

p. 97

Systems of Reading. In Makka they employ the system of Ibn Kathīr, in al-Yaman, the reading of ʿĀsim; however, the reading of Abū ʿAmr is used throughout the rest of the region. I have heard a preeminent reader in Makka say: "We have neither ourselves witnessed nor have we heard that any Imām led the prayer from behind this *maqām*, using other than the system of Ibn Kathīr, except at the present day."

Commerce in this region is truly profitable, for here are the two ports of the world, as well as the market of Minā, and here is the sea that reaches to China. Here, too, are Judda and al-Jār, the two granaries of Egypt; Wādī 'l-Qurā, the entrepôt of al-Shām and al-ʿIrāq; al-Yaman that produces scarves, carnelians, pelts, slaves. To ʿUmān are exported pharmaceutical goods, perfumery of all kinds even including musk; also saffron, brazilwood, teakwood, sāsam (a wood), ivory, pearls, silk brocade, onyx, sapphire, ebony, coconuts, camphor, sandarax resin, aloe, iron, lead, bamboos, clay for chinaware, sandalwood, glass, pepper, and other commodities.

ʿAdan receives ambergris, *shurūb* (fine linens), shields, Abyssinian slaves, eunuchs, tiger skins, and indeed so much more that were I to enumerate all in detail the book would be unnecessarily prolonged. In connection with the goods of China they have coined proverbial expressions, such as their saying, "they came to you to trade with you or to rule you."

Once, as I had embarked on the sea of al-Yaman, it so happened that I encountered Abū ʿAlī al-Hāfidh al-Marwazī on board ship. When we had become well acquainted with each other he said to me, "In truth you have made me concerned about you." Said I, "In what way?" Said he, "I see in you a man who walks in the path of goodness. You love virtue and those who practice it, and you aspire after the acquisition of knowledge. You are now bound for a country that has beguiled many people, and diverted them from the way of piety and contentment. And I am afraid that when you will have entered ʿAdan, and heard of one man departing with a thousand *dirhams*, and returning with a thousand p. 98 *dinārs*; of another coming with a hundred, and returning with five hundred; of yet another going out with frankincense and returning with a like quantity of camphor—that you will become inclined to emulate them." Said I, "I pray God that He preserve me!" However, when I did enter it, and heard even more than what he had told me, by heavens I hungered after the same thing as the others, and prepared to go to the lands of the Zanj (Negroes). So I brought whatever it was necessary for me to buy, and put it in the hands of shipping agents. But God—exalted be His name—caused my interest in the venture to cool, with the death of my partner. I had made a contract with him, but my spirit was shattered at the remembrance of death, and what comes after that. And you may as well realize—may you be guided aright—that for every gain we have mentioned there is a hazard; profits are always attended with dangers; so the wise man must not be deluded in this respect. And indeed he should be aware that God, may He be exalted, will give His servant, for two prostrations in prayer, offered sincerely to Him, more than the world lock, stock and barrel. And indeed, what boots prosperity, with death in its wake, and the accumulation of wealth which one inescapably must leave behind?

Among the **specialties** of the districts of this region are: the leather of Zabīd, and its indigo, incomparable because it is azure, the *shurūb* (fine linens) of ʿAdan preferred over the soft linens of Egypt, the fibers of al-Mahjara called *līf* (bast), the *burūd* (striped cloths) of Suhūlā and Jurayb, the leather mats and water bottles of Saʿda, the superb cloth of Sanʿāʾ known as *saʿīdī*, and its carnelian; the carboys of ʿAthr, the drinking cups of Haly, whetstones of Yanbuʿ, and its henna; the *ben* tree of Yathrib with its clusters of *sayhānī* dates; the excellent *burdī* dates of al-Marwa and its bdellium trees; the frankincense of Mahra and its fish, the *wars* (yellow dye) of ʿAdan, and the dried peaches of Qurh; the senna of Makka, the aloes of Usqūtra, and the superb *masīn* dates of ʿUmān.

The **measures** of this region are: the *sāʿ*, the *mudd*, and the *makkūk*; the *mudd* is a fourth of the *sāʿ*, the *sāʿ* a third of the *makkūk*—this is in al-Hijāz, but there are varying capacities in this [the *sāʿ*]. The standard generally used has a weight of five and one third *ratls*. I have heard the jurisprudent Abū ʿAbd Allāh at Damascus say that when Abū Yūsuf went on the Pilgrimage, and had visited al-Madīna, he revoked two matters in favor of their practice, the first, the admissibility of the *adhān* before daybreak, the second, the calculation of the *sāʿ*. For the *sāʿ* that ʿUmar assessed in the presence of the Companions, and which he used in expiating his vows was the equivalent of eight *ratls*; however, Saʿīd bin al-ʿĀsī restored it to five and one third, witness the quotation of the versifier:

p. 99

> So to us, to famish us, came Saʿīd,
> diminishing the *sāʿ* not enlarging it.

On board ship they employ two *sāʿs*, by one of which they measure the rations of the crew; they transact business using the larger one.

Their **weights**. In Makka the standard is the *mann* which is well-known in all the countries of Islām; however, they call it a *ratl*. The *ratl* of Yathrib as far as Qurh is two hundred *dirhams*; the *ratl* of al-Yaman is the same as that of Baghdād. In ʿUmān the *mann* is the standard, in the rest of the region the standard is that of Baghdād. In use, also, is the *buhār*, an equivalent of three hundred *ratls*.

There is variation in their **coinages**: the people of Makka have the *mutawwaqa* which, like the *ʿAthariyya* are each two thirds of a *mithqāl* [a gold coin equaling in weight one and one-third of the *dirham*, a silver coin]; they are counted out by number like the *dirhams* of al-Yaman. They are higher than the *ʿAthariyya*, and in fact there may between the two be a difference of something just under a *dirham*. The *dīnār* [a gold coin, the basic monetary unit in Islamic territory] of ʿAdan is of a value of seven *dirhams*, which is two thirds of the *baghawī*: they are weighed, not counted. The *dīnār* of ʿUmān is of thirty *dirhams*, but it is weighed. The *dirhams* current in the region are called in Makka *al-Muhammadiyya*; the natives of Makka also have the *muzabbaq*, twenty-four to a *mutawwaq*, or a double *akhtamī*. These are withdrawn from currency from the sixth day of Dhu al-Hijja until the end of the season [of Pilgrimage]. The people of al-Yaman have the coinage called *ʿAlawiyya* which varies in value in different places, though it may not be current in some places there at all. Its worth is four of them to a *dirham*, its weight about that of the *dānaq* [the sixth part of a *dirham*]. They also have the *qurūdh*, which sometimes goes up in value so that three may equal a *dānaq*; at other times it would be four. Among the natives of ʿUmān the *tasūh* [one twenty-fourth part of a *dirham*] circulates.

p. 100   It is the mode in this region to dress in the *wizr* (small tunic), and the *izār* (wraparound apron) without shirt, except for a small minority. In Mukhā they deride anyone who wears drawers, for it may be only the *izār*, a single garment, in which one wraps oneself.

In Ramadhān they read the entire *Qu'rān* in prayer; they then invoke God's blessing and perform prostrations. I led the congregation in the *tarāwīh* [the prayers recited at night during the month of Ramadhān] at ʿAdan on one occasion, and I invoked the blessing after the *salām*; this surprised them greatly. Thereafter Ibn Hāzim and Ibn Jābir bade me attend their mosques so I would do the same thing there.

They usually light their lamps with a *sayfa*, which is fish oil, imported from Mahra. Their lime is black, like black pitch.

In al-Yaman they paste papers together and line the inside covers of their books with starch. On an occasion the *amīr* of ʿAdan sent me a copy of the *Qur'ān* to bind, so I asked for the glue from the druggists, but they did not know what that was. They referred me, however, to the *muhtasib* [inspector of markets, and weights and measures], suggesting him as one who might know of it. When I enquired of him about it, said he, "Where are you from?" Said I, "From Palestine." Said he, "You are from the country of abundance. If they had glue here they would eat it! Use the starch!" They admire fine binding, and will offer a handsome price for it. At times I was given two *dīnārs* for binding one copy of the *Qur'ān*.

At ʿAdan they decorate the roofs of the houses two days before Ramadhān, and they beat drums on them. When Ramadhān begins, a group gathers and goes about at early dawn, reciting poems until the night is over. As the festival nears they levy a sum of money from the people. On Nayrūz (New Year's day) they construct canopies which they carry, with their drums, around to the people who are exchanging greetings on the festival. This way they collect a considerable sum of money.

In Makka pavilions are erected on the eve of the breaking of the Fast, and they decorate the market between al-Safā and al-Marwa; then they beat the drums until morning. When the morning prayer is over, the young girls, festively dressed and with fans in their hands, circumambulate the House. They appoint five Imāms to lead the *tarāwīh* prayers. As they say each *tarwīha* they go around the Kaʿba seven times; at the same time the muezzins proclaim *Allāhū akbar* (God is most great), and exclaim *Lā ilāha ill-allāh* (there is no god but God). Then they crack the thongs, as is done at prayer, whereupon the next

Imām advances. They say the night prayer when one-third of the night has
passed, and finish with one third yet remaining. Then the time of the *sahūr* [last
meal before daybreak] is announced from Abū Qubays. No more attractive
raiment is to be seen than that of the people of Makka as they go out for the
Pilgrimage, for every single one of them in this respect is as well-dressed as
an ʿIrāqī!

The **waters** of this region vary in quality. The water at ʿAdan, the canal in
Makka, and the water of Zabīd and Yathrib are potable; the water at Ghalāfiqa
is deadly. The water of Qurh and Yanbuʿ is unhealthy. Water elsewhere in the
region is acceptable. I went on the Pilgrimage in the year 356/966 and I found
the water of Zamzam distasteful; when I went back in the year 367/978 I
found it quite agreeable. Most of the water on the coasts is somewhat brackish,
but acceptable. Should someone say, "Whence do you derive this 'acceptability,'
and 'distastefulness' of water?", I should reply that there are four considerations.
First, all water that cools quickly is wholesome, and I have not seen water quicker
to cool than that of Taymāʾ and Arīhā. These two are the most wholesome waters
in the realm of al-Islām, and it was from here I derived this consideration, which
I have since verified through abundant experience. Second, acceptable water
is slow to be discharged from the body, while one who drinks unacceptable
water has to urinate quickly. Third, good water whets the appetite for food, and
promotes digestion. Fourth, should you want to assess the water of a place, visit
their clothmakers and druggists, and scrutinize their faces. If you see water in
them, you may know that the excellence of the water is in proportion to the
freshness of countenance; if they appear to you like the faces of the dead, and
you see their heads are drooping, make a hasty retreat from there!

Noxious products: At Makka is a type of eggplant that causes illness. In
al-Madīna are leeks from the effect of which the guinea-worm is generated.

Mines: Pearls are found in this region on the coasts of Hajar. They are obtained
by diving into the sea for them opposite Uwāl and the island of Khārak. It was
from there that the "incomparable darra" (pearl) was fished out. Men hired for the
purpose dive and bring out the seashell, the pearl within it. The greatest hazard
for them is a large fish that darts at their eyes; but the profit from this activity is
very evident. One who seeks carnelian buys a piece of land at a place near Sanʿāʾ,
where he digs for it. He may find a piece as large as a rock or smaller, sometimes
he finds nothing. Between Yanbuʿ and al-Marwa are mines of gold. Ambergris is
tossed on to the seashore from ʿAdan to Mukhā, and in the direction of Zaylaʿ also.
Anyone who finds any of it, little or much, takes it to the deputy of the governor,
who pays him for it, giving him in return a piece of canvas and a *dīnār*. The
ambergris is not found except when the south wind blows; incidentally, I have never
found out what ambergris actually is. Dragon's blood is found opposite al-Juhfa.

Sectarian factionalism arises at Makka between the tailors, who are Shīʿa, and the butchers, who are Sunna—factionalism and fighting. Enmity and brawls arise at ʿAdan between the Jamājimiyyīn and the sailors, as also between the Sunna and the Shīʿa in Yanbuʿ. Among the Baja, the Abyssinians, and the Nubians at Zabīd, a strange state of affairs exists; also between the butchers and the Bedouin at al-Yamāma. In fact, it is said that they divided the mosque between themselves, and would say to the stranger, "Belong to either side of us as you will, or else get out!"

Places of Veneration: At Makka, *Mawlid al-Nabī*, [the birthplace of the Prophet—God's peace and blessings be upon him] in the quarter of the Mahāmiliyyīn, [where the camel litters are made]; the House of the Forty in the cloth merchants' quarter; the House of Khadīja behind the druggists' quarter; Ghār (Cave of) Thawr one *farsakh* below Makka; and (Mount) Hirāʾ towards Minā. There is another cave behind the hill of Abū Qubays. The Hill of Quʿayqiʿān, opposite Abū Qubays, and in al-Haram, the sacred precinct. The grave of Maymūna on the road to Judda. In al-Thaniyya the graves of al-Fudhayl, of Sufyān bin ʿUyayna, and Wuhayb bin al-Ward. Between the two Masjids [Makka and al-Madīna] is a number of holy places associated with the names of the Prophet and ʿAlī. Masjid al-Shajara (the Mosque of the Tree) at Dhu al-Hulayfa; there is also a tree at Qubā, where is also Hajar Fātima. The grave of Hūd—peace be on him—at al-Ahqāf, on the coast. The place whence fire issues at ʿAdan is a mountain in the sea; and behind the town is the mosque of Abān. The *mikhlāf* of Muʿādh is behind Mukhā. Too, the mosque of the Abandoned Well and the Lofty Palace (*Qurʾān*, sūra 22, v. 45) in the *mikhlāf* of al-Bawn. In the *mikhlāf* Marmal, one of the provinces of Sanʿāʾ, came forth the fire which burned the garden of the oath-mongers (*Qurʾān*, sūra 68, v. 20). The well of ʿUthmā on the road to Syria. Near al-ʿArj is a hill through which, it is said, Gabriel split open for the Prophet— God's peace and blessings be upon him—on the occasion of his emigration, a way to al-Madīna. There fell down a fire between al-Marwa and al-Hawrāʾ, and it burned as burns the coal. The houses of al-Fārihīn (*Qurʾān*, sūra 26, v. 148) in al-Hijr are remarkable for their doors, arched, and decorated in arabesques. Al-Tāghiya, a town in ruins. Behind Khaym Umm Maʿbad in the Sarawāt hills are remarkable strongholds. Kamarān, an island in the sea, has in it a town with fresh water; it is called al-ʿAql, and here are the prisons of the ruler of al-Yaman.

p. 103

Among the **characteristics** of the people of Makka is arrogance; the people of al-Yaman lack elegance. The people of ʿUmān give short measure, cheat, and fornicate. Adultery in ʿAdan is overt. The people of al-Ahqāf are fanatics, not speaking good Arabic. Al-Hijāz is a country, poor and barren.

The Tribes: As one goes from the Sarawāt hills in the direction of Syria, one is in the territory of al-Agharr bin Haytham; thence one departs to the dwellings of

Ya'lā bin Abī Ya'lā; thence to Surdud; thence to the dwellings of 'Anz Wā'il in the territory of Banī Ghaziyya; after that one is in the habitations of Jurash,

p. 104 al-'Atl, and Julājil. From there one goes to the territories of al-Shuqra where live the Khat'am; he then reaches the territory of the Hārith, where the chief town is called Dhanūb, the name of its coast al-Shārā; thence to the territory of Shākir and 'Āmir; thence to Bajīla; thence to Fahm; thence to among the Banī 'Āsim; thence to 'Adwān; thence to the Banī Salūl; thence to Mutār, where is a quarry providing stone from which cooking pots are made; thence to the territory of Birma in which are situated al-Abraqa and Hisn al-Mahyā. Thereupon, you are at al-Falaj.

Jurisdiction over this region is divided. Al-Hijāz has always been under the control of the rulers of Egypt, because it is the source of its supplies. Al-Yaman is under the Āl (Family of) Ziyād dynasty, whose roots are from Hamdān. Ibn Taraf controls 'Athr, and over San'ā' is a ruler; however Ibn Ziyād pays him money so that he delivers the *khutba* [sermon at the midday prayers in the mosque on Fridays] in his name. Sometimes 'Adan is seized from their hands. The Āl Qahtān are in the mountains, they are the oldest dynasty of al-Yaman. The 'Alawiyya are over Sa'da, and read the *khutba* in the name of Āl Ziyād—they are the most just of people. 'Umān belongs to al-Daylam, and Hajar to the Qarāmita. Over al-Ahqāf is a native ruler.

Taxes and tolls: At Judda is exacted on every load of wheat half a *dīnār*, and a *kayl* (gallon) on each half of a camel load; on a bundle of *Shatawī* fine linen cloth, three *dīnārs*, on a bundle of *Dabīqū* cloth, two *dīnārs*; on a bale of wool two *dīnārs*. At 'Athr on every load one *dīnār*, and on every basket of saffron, one *dīnār*, similarly per head on slaves: this is taken from those leaving the town, and the same levy is imposed at al-Sirrayn on anyone passing through, also at Kamarān. At 'Adan, merchandise is appraised in terms of Zakāwī *dīnārs*, then one tenth of the value is exacted in 'Atharī *dīnārs*. It is estimated that one

p. 105 third of the wealth of the merchants reaches the treasury of the ruler, for here the inspection is strict. The levies at places on the coast are light, except at Ghalāfiqa. Tolls are levied by land: on the caravans going between Judda and Makka, at al-Qarīn, and Batn Marr—at each place half of a *dīnār*. At the gate of Zabīd one *dīnār* on a load of musk, half a *dīnār* on a bale of linen. At the other tollbooths, payment is made in 'Alawī *dirhams*. The ruler of Sa'da does not levy a tax on anybody, except that he takes the quarter of the tithe from the merchants.

The Peninsula is tithed. In 'Umān a *dirham* is levied on every date palm tree. I have found it in the work of Ibn Khurradādhbih that the revenue of al-Yaman is six hundred thousand *dīnārs*; I do not know what he means by this, because I did not see it in *Kitāb al-Kharāj (The Book of Tribute)*. In fact, rather, it is well-known that the Peninsula of the Arabs is on a tithing system. The province of al-Yaman formerly was divided into three departments, a governor over al-Janad and its districts, another over San^ca[>] and its districts, and a third over Hadhramawt and its districts. Qudāma bin Ja^cfar al-Kātib has noted that the revenue of al-Haramayn [the two Sacred Cities] is one hundred thousand *dīnārs*, of al-Yaman six hundred thousand *dīnārs*, of al-Yamāma and al-Bahrayn five hundred ten thousand *dīnārs*, and of ^cUmān three hundred thousand *dīnārs*.

The inhabitants of this region are people of contentment, and slender of figure. They are nourished on plain food, and make do with scant attire. God, may He be exalted, has bestowed on them the best of fruits, and the mistress of trees, dates and the palm.

The following tradition was related to me by Abū ^cAbd Allāh Muhammad bin Ahmad in the city of Arrajān. He said he had had it from al-Qādhī al-Hasan bin ^cAbd al-Rahmān bin Khallād, who had it from Mūsā bin al-Husayn, who had it from Shaybān bin Farrūkh, who had it from Masrūr bin Sufyān al-Tamīmī, from al-Awzā^cī, from ^cUrwa bin Ruwaym, from ^cAlī bin Abī Tālib—God be pleased with him. He said that the Messenger of God—God's peace and blessings be upon him—said on one occasion: "Honour your father's sister, the palm tree, for it was created of the clay of which Adam was created. Of the trees none are pollinated other than it. Feed your women, at the time of their bringing forth, the sweetened ripe date; if there are no sweetened ripe dates, give them those freshly dried."

With regard to **distances**, let it be observed that the word *waw* (and) is connective, that the word *thumma* (then—thence) refers to places in their order; and the word *aw* (or) indicates an alternative. For example, when we say to "such and such a place *and* such and such a place," then these two places are in the one locality, such as, Khulays and Amaj, Mazīnān and Bahman Abādh. When we say *thumma* we mean it to be taken in conjunction with what precedes it, as when we say "to Batn Marr, *then* to ^cUsfān," "to Ghazza *then* to Rafh." If we say *aw* (or), then we go back to the word before this last one, as when we say, from al-Ramla to Īliyā *or* to ^cAsqalān, from Shīrāz to Juwaym *or* to Sāhah. We have reckoned the *marhala* (stage) at six *farsakhs* or seven; should it exceed this we place two dots over the letter *hā[>]* [in the word for "stage"]; should it exceed ten *farsakhs* we point it with two dots under the letter *lām* [in the word for "stage"]; if it is less than six *farsakhs*, we put one dot over the letter [>]*hā[>]*.

You travel from Makka to Batn Marr, one stage;
    thence to ^cUsfān one stage;
    thence to Khulays and Amaj one stage;
    thence to al-Khaym one stage;
    thence to al-Juhfa one stage;
    thence to al-Abwā[>] one stage;
    thence to Suqyā Banī Ghifār one stage;

p. 106

thence to al-ʿArj one stage;
thence to al-Rawhāʾ one stage;
thence to Ruwaytha one stage;
thence to Yathrib one stage.

You travel from Makka to Yalamlam, one stage;
thence to Qarn, one stage;
thence to al-Sirrayn, one stage.

You travel from Makka to Bustān Banī ʿĀmir, one stage
thence to Dhāt ʿIrq, one stage;
thence to al-Ghamra, one stage.

You travel from Makka to Qarīn, one stage;
thence to Judda, one stage.

p. 107 From Batn Marr to Judda it is one stage.

You travel from al-Juhfa to Badr, one stage;
thence to al-Safrāʾ and al-Maʿlāt, one stage;
thence to al-Rawhāʾ, one stage.

You travel from Badr to Yanbuʿ, two stages;
thence to Raʾs al-ʿAyn, one stage;
thence to al-Maʿdin (the mine), one stage;
thence to al-Marwa, two stages.

You travel from Badr to al-Jār, one stage;
thence to al-Juhfa or Yanbuʿ, two stages either way.

You travel from Judda to al-Jār or al-Sirrayn, four stages, either way.

You travel from Yathrib to al-Suwaydiyya or to Batn al-Nakhl, two stages, either way;
from al-Suwaydiyya to al-Marwa, the same number of stages; and from Batn al-Nakhl to Maʿdin al-Naqira likewise.

If you wish to take the high road to Egypt, travel from al-Marwa to al-Suqyā;
thence to Badā Yaʿqūb, three stages;
thence to al-ʿAwnīd, one stage.

If you wish to go to Syria travel from al-Suqyā (Yazīd) to Wādī ʾl-Qurā, one stage; thence to al-Hijr, one stage; thence to Taymāʾ, three stages.

If you wish to travel to Makka by the Kūfa road, take it from Zubāla, which is
inhabited and has abundance of water, to al-Shuqūq, twenty-one miles;
    thence to al-Bitān, twenty-nine miles;
    thence to al-Tha'labiyya, twenty-nine miles;
this place marks one-third of the way. It is inhabited, has a large number of tanks
p. 108   and some wells of brackish but drinkable water.

    Thence to al-Khuzaymiyya, thirty-two miles;
    thence to Ajfur, twenty-four miles;
    thence to Fayd, thirty-six miles:

this is a flourishing town with two forts and abundance of water.
    Thence to Tawwaz, which is half way, thirty-one miles;
    thence to Samīrā', twenty miles.

It has many tanks, an abundant supply of water and cultivated fields; the water
is brackish but drinkable;
    thence to Hājir, thirty-three miles;
    thence to Ma'din al-Naqira, thirty-four miles.

It has a fort; the water supply is poor and the place desolate.
    Thence to al-Mughītha, thirty-three miles;
    thence to al-Rabadha, twenty-four miles: the water is bitter and the place in
    ruins.
    Thence to Ma'din Banī Sulaym, twenty-four miles;
    thence to al-Salīla, twenty-six miles;
    thence to al-'Umaq, twenty-one miles. Al-'Umaq has remarkable wells, but
    the water is not abundant.
    Thence to al-Ufay'iya, thirty-two miles;
    thence to al-Mislah, thirty-four miles: here are tanks, and water is abundant.
    Thence to Ghamra, eighteen miles: water is abundant here.

p. 109   If you wish to get to it (Makka) from al-Basra, go from al-Basra to al-Hufayr,
eighteen miles;
    thence to al-Ruhayl, twenty-eight miles;
    thence to al-Shajī, twenty-seven miles;
    thence to Hafr Abī Mūsā, twenty-six;
    thence to Māwiyya, thirty-two;
    thence to Dhāt al-'Ushar, twenty-nine;
    thence to al-Yansū'a, twenty-three;
    thence to al-Sumayna, twenty-nine;
    thence to al-Qaryatayn, twenty-two;
    thence to al-Nibāj, twenty-three;

thence to al-ʿAwsaja, twenty-nine;
thence to to Rāma ...;
thence to Immara, twenty-seven;
thence to Tikhfa, twenty-six;
thence to Dhariyya, eighteen;
thence to Jadīla, thirty-two;
thence to Mulha, thirty-five;
thence to al-Dathīna, twenty-six;
thence to Qubā, twenty-seven;
thence to al-Shubayka (Sunbula), twenty-seven;
thence to Wajra, forty;
thence to Dhāt ʿIrq, twenty-seven.
The whole distance is seven hundred miles.

Now as for the road of the West: you travel from Wayla to Sharaf Dhi al-Naml, one stage;
thence to Madyan, one stage;
p. 110   thence to al-Aʿrā', one stage;
thence to a halting-place, one stage;
thence to al-Kulāya (al-Kilāba), one stage;
thence to Shaghb, one stage;
thence to Badā, one stage;
thence to al-Sarhatayn;
thence to al-Baydhā';
thence to Wādī 'I-Qurā.

The route now in use is as follows: from Sharaf Dhi al-Naml to al-Salā;
thence to al-Nabk;
thence to Dhabba;
thence to al-ʿAwnīd;
thence to al-Ruhba;
thence to Munkhūs;
thence to al-Buhayra;
thence to al-Ahsā';
thence to al-ʿUshayra;
thence to al-Jār;
thence to Badr.

If you desire to go there (Makka) from ʿUmān, go from Suhār to Nazwa;
thence to ʿAjla, thirty miles;
thence to ʿAdhwa, which is a fortress, twenty-four miles;
thence to Biʾr al-Silāh, thirty miles;
p. 111   thence to Makka, twenty-one days;

on this route four stations have wells, while eight stages pass through a desert of sand.

If you travel to it from Hajar, go from al-Ahsāʾ to [lacuna in MS].

If one wishes to start from Sanʿāʾ one travels first to al- Rayda, one stage;
thence to Athāfit;
thence to Khaywān;
thence to al-Aʿmashiyya;
thence to Saʿda;
thence to Gharfa;
thence to al-Mahjara;
thence to Sharūrāh;
thence to al-Thujja;
thence to Kuthba;
thence to Yabanbam, which is at a distance of eight miles from Jurash;
thence to Banāt Jarm, one stage;
thence to Jasadāʾ;
p. 112   thence to Bīsha;
thence to Tabāla;
thence to Ranya;
thence to Kudayy;
thence to Safr;
thence to Turaba;
thence to al-Futuq;
thence to al-Judad;
thence to al-Ghamra.

The direct route is by way of al-Tāʾif, although I have not traveled on this route. From Makka to al-Tāʾif there are two routes. You go to Biʾr Ibn al-Murtafiʿ, one stage;
thence to Qarn, one stage;
thence to al-Tāʾif, one stage.

The other route is by way of ʿArafāt, two stages over the hill.

For one who wishes to go there (Makka) starting from Wayla, and this is the route of all pilgrims from the west, there is a number of ways. The route along the coast you take from Wayla to Sharaf al-Baʿl, one stage;
thence to al-Salā, one stage;
thence to al-Nabk, one stage;
thence to Dhabba, one stage;
thence to ʿAwnīd, one stage;

thence to al-Ruhba, one stage;
thence to Munkhūs, one stage;
thence to al-Buhayra, one stage;
thence to al-Ashā᾽, one stage [lacuna in MS]
thence to al-Aʿrā᾽, one stage;
thence to al-Kilāba, one stage;
thence to Shaghb, one stage;
thence to Badā, one stage;
thence to al-Sarhatayn, one stage;
thence to al-Baydhā᾽, one stage;
thence to Qurh, one stage;
thence to Suqyā Yazīd, one stage.

As for the system in al-Yaman, I am not about to render a precise computation of the stages of the routes here as in the case of other districts; I will, however, state what I have known, and summarize what I have heard.

From Sanʿā᾽ to Sudā᾽, forty-two *farsakhs*.
From Sanʿā᾽ to Hadhramawt, seventy-four *farsakhs*.
From Sanʿā᾽ to Dhamār, sixteen *farsakhs*;
    thence to Nasafān and Kahlān, one stage;
    thence to Hujr and Badr, twenty *farsakhs*;
    thence to ʿAdan, twenty-four *farsakhs*.
From Dhamār to Yahsib, one stage; [Map V]
    thence to al-Suhūl, one stage;
p. 113   thence to al-Thujja, the same distance;
    thence to al-Janad, the same.
From Sanʿā᾽ to al-Janad, forty-eight *farsakhs*.
From Sanʿā᾽ to al-ʿUrf, one stage;
    thence to Alhān, ten *farsakhs*;
    thence to Jublān, fourteen;
    thence to Zabīd, twelve.
From Sanʿā᾽ to Shibām, one stage.
From Sanʿā᾽ to ʿAthr, ten stages.
From ʿAdan to Abyan, three *farsakhs*.

The Region of Al-ʿIrāq

This is the region of men of refinement, the fountainhead of scholars. The water is delightful, the air marvelous; it is the chosen place of the khalifs. It produced Abū Ḥanīfa, the jurist of jurisprudents; and Sufyān, the best of the Quranic Readers. From here came Abū ʿUbayda, and al-Farraʾ; and Abū ʿAmr, author of a system of Quranic reading. It is the birthplace of Ḥamza, and al-Kisāʾī: of virtually every jurist, Reader, and litterateur; of notables, sages, thinkers, ascetics, distinguished people; of charming and quick-witted people. Here is the birthplace of Abraham, the Companion of God, thither journeyed many noble Companions of the Prophet. Is not al-Basra there, which can be compared to the entire world? and Baghdād, praised by all mankind? sublime al-Kūfa and Sāmarrā? Its river most certainly is of Paradise; and the dates of al-Basra cannot be forgotten. Its excellences are many and beyond count. The Sea of China touches its furthermost extremity, and the desert stretches along the edge of it, as you see. The Euphrates debouches within its limits.

Yet it is the home of dissension and high prices, and every day it retrogresses; from injustice and taxes there is trouble, and distress. Its fruits are few, its vices many, and the oppression on the people is heavy.

This is the map and representation of it, but God is more knowing, and wiser. [Map V]

p. 114 We have made al-ʿIrāq six districts and a section. The districts in olden times were different from these, except for Hulwān; but we always treat the matter according to what is now generally accepted. We have included the old districts and capitals in the military districts, the districts bearing the same name as the capitals.

The first of these, starting from the Peninsula of the Arabs, is al-Kūfa, next al-Basra; then Wāsit, Baghdād; Hulwān, then Sāmarrā.

Al-Kūfa—among its towns are: Ḥammām Ibn ʿUmar; al-Jāmiʿayn; Sūrā; al-Nīl; al-Qādisiyya; ʿAyn al-Tamr.

Al-Basra—among its towns are: al-Ubulla; Shiqq ʿUthmān; Zabān; Badrān; Bayān; Nahr al-Malik; Dubbā; Nahr al-Amīr; Abu al-Khaṣīb; Sulaymānān; ʿAbbādān; al-Muṭawwiʿa; al-Qindal; al-Maftaḥ; al-Jaʿfariyya.

Wāsit—among its towns are: Fam al-Silḥ; Darmakān; Qurāquba; Siyāda; Bādhibīn; al-Sikr; al-Ṭīb; Qurqūb; Qaryat al-Raml; Nahr Tīrā; Lahbān; Basāmiya; Ūdisa.

Baghdād—among its towns are: al-Nahrawān; Baradān; Kāra; al-Daskara; p. 115 Tarāstān; Hārūniyya; Jalūlā; Bājisrā; Bāquba; Iskāf; Buwahriz; Kalwādhā; Darzījān; al-Madāʾin; Kīl(Gīl); Sīb; Dayr al-ʿĀqūl; al-Nuʿmāniyya; Jarjarāyā; Jabbul; Nahr Sābus; ʿAbartā; Bābil; ʿAbdas; Qaṣr Ibn Hubayra.

Hulwān—among its towns are: Khāniqīn; Zabūjān; Shalāshilān; al-Jāmid; al-Ḥurr; al-Sīrawān; Bandanījān.

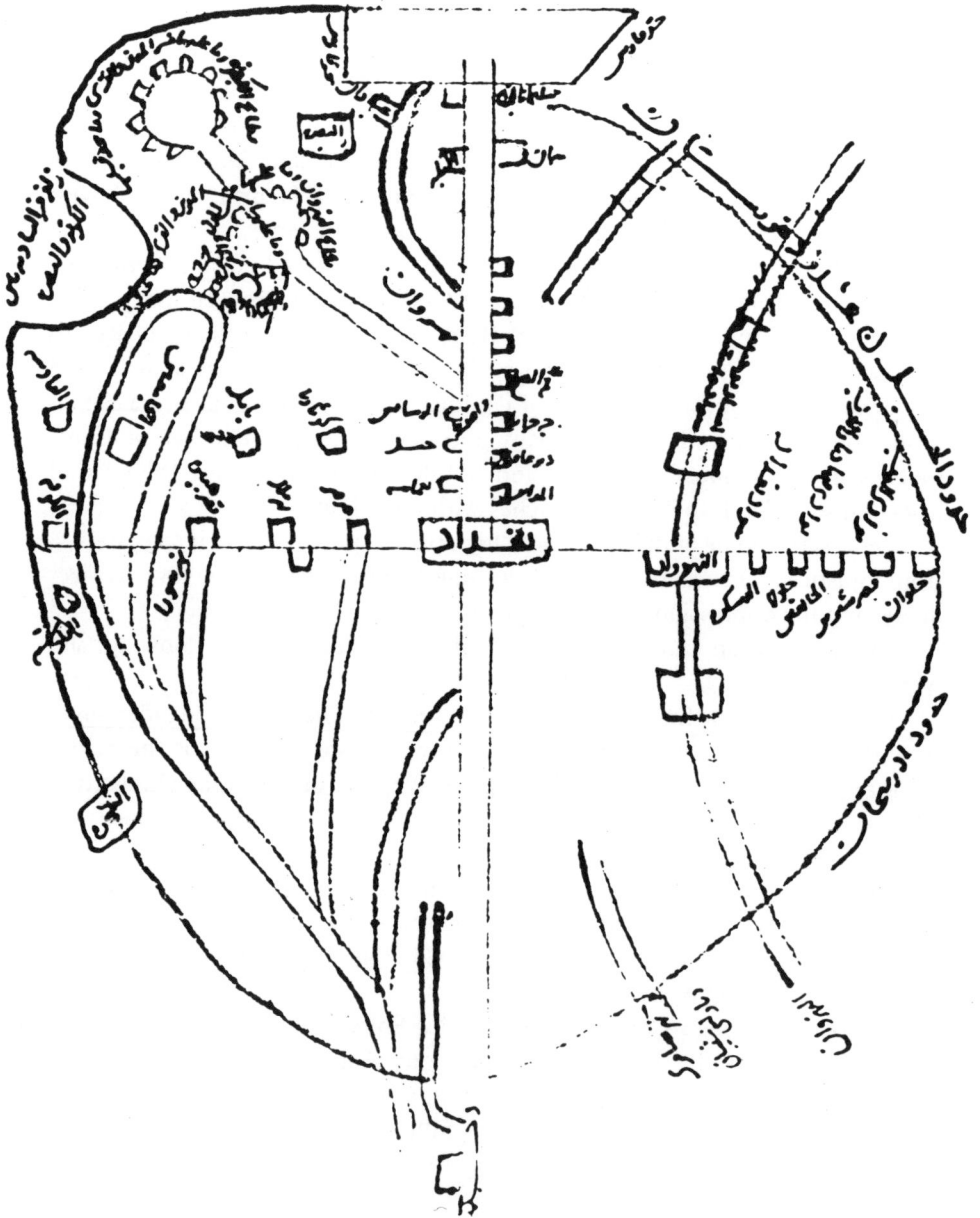

Map V: Al-ʿIrāq (see p. 409).
From MS. Sprenger 5—Ahlwardt 6034 by kind permission of the Staatsbibliothek
Preussischer Kulturbesitz, Berlin, Orientabteilung.

Sāmarrā—among its towns are: al-Karkh; ʿUkbarā; al-Dūr; al-Jāmiʿayn (the two Mosques); Batt; Rādhānāt; Qasr al-Jass; Harī; Aywānā; Barīqā; Sindiyya; Rāqafrūba; Dimimmā; al-Anbār; Hīt; Takrīt; al-Sinn.

Now someone may say: "Why did you consider Bābil to be a district town, seeing that the whole region around was named after it in olden times? Did not al-Jayhānī begin his work by mentioning these districts, calling the area by the name of Bābil? Wahb named it similarly in his *Mubtadaʾ* (*First Principles*), as did other scholars besides him": I reply that we have protected ourselves against this and similar questions in the treatment of our subject, by dealing with the matter according to general usage, and as is the case in the matter of Oaths. Do you not see that if a man should swear that he would not eat heads, and then would eat
p. 116 of the heads of oxen or sheep, he would thus break his oath; but Abū Yūsuf and Muhammad [ibn al-Hasan al-Shaybānī] say that he would not thereby break his oath? Now, I have heard our leading doctors say that they do not consider that there is any discrepancy between the two positions. Because, you see, in the time of Abū Hanīfa these heads used to be sold and eaten; but that practice ceased in their time. Now, we have journeyed over the length and breadth of the realm of Islām, and have not heard anyone say other than that this is the region of al-ʿIrāq—in fact, the vast majority of people do not know where Bābil is. Moreover, consider the answer of Abū Bakr to ʿUmar, when the latter asked him to send his troops to this area. Said he: "That God may conquer by my hands one span of the Holy Land would be more pleasing to me than one entire district of the districts of al-ʿIrāq." He did not say, "of the districts of Bābil." If someone were to adduce the saying of God—may He be exalted—"And what was sent down to the two angels in Bābil" (*Qurʾān*, sura 2, v. 102), as proof of what we have said, then I would say that it may very well be that this name may include both the region and the town. Now, with regard to the name being applied to the town there is absolute agreement, for no one disputes with another about its name: that the name is applied to the region is controversial. The burden of proof is, then, on the one who so applies it.

Al-Kūfa is a splendid, charming, and beautiful metropolis, with lofty buildings, very fine markets, and an abundance of supplies: it is a well-populated, prosperous place. Saʿad bin Abī Waqqās founded it in the days of ʿUmar. Any tract where sand is mixed with pebbles is called 'kūfa': do you not notice the nature of the ground here? The town that was formerly here was al-Hīra, but it fell into ruins. The first of the Companions to settle here [in al-Kūfa] was ʿAlī bin Abī Tālib, under whose authority were ʿAbd Allāh bin Masʿūd and Abu al-Dardā; the others who followed neglected it.

The mosque is in the eastern quarter, built on tall jointed pillars of stone;
p. 117 it is handsome and perfectly constructed. The river flows on that side of the city that is towards Baghdād. The wells are of brackish water, but drinkable, and all around it are palm groves and gardens. Here also are reservoirs and underground conduits. The district called al-Kunāsa is toward the desert. The

town has deteriorated and its suburbs are in ruin: at one time it was as great as Baghdād.

Al-Qādisiyya is a town situated on the edge of the desert, flourishing during the season of the Pilgrimage, when all kinds of good things are carried thither. It has two gates, and a fortress of clay. A canal has been carried from the Euphrates to a reservoir at the Baghdād Gate. There are springs of tolerable water there too, and another watercourse which they cause to flow around to the gate on the desert side, at the season of the Pilgrimage. The town consists of one marketplace, the mosque standing in it.

Sūrā is a town with an abundance of fruits and grapes; it is populous. The other towns here are small and populous. ʿAyn al-Tamr is a fortified place, its people covetous.

Al-Basra is a distinguished capital; the Muslims founded it in the time of ʿUmar. He wrote to his Commander: "Build for the Muslims a city central to Fārs and the country of the Arabs, towards the border of al-ʿIrāq, on the Sea of China." So they agreed on the site of al-Basra, and the Arabs settled there. Do you not see, even today, how it is laid out in quarters? Then ʿUtba bin Ghazwān made it a metropolis. It is in the shape of a *taylasān*. From the Tigris two canals have been led thither—Nahr al-Ubulla and Nahr Maʿqil: after they come together they flow by the city. Several canals branch off from it from the side of ʿAbbādān and al-Madhār. The city stretches lengthwise along the river, and its houses, on the landside, extend to the desert: on this side is one gate, between which and the canal is a distance of about three miles. Three mosques stand in this city. One, a splendid one, is in the markets, an important mosque, well-built and well attended; there is nothing else like it in al-ʿIrāq. It is built on white pillars. Another mosque, the oldest of them, is near Bāb al-Bādiya (the Gate of the Desert); the remaining one is at the edge of the town. The markets are in three sections: Al-Kallāʾ ("a mooring for ships") which is along the canal, the Great Market, and the Bāb al-Jāmiʿ market. All these markets are quite good. For me, this town is superior to Baghdād, because of the prosperity here and the great number of pious people. Once I was present in an assembly that included many of the jurisprudents of Baghdād, and its scholars. They were conversing p. 118 about Baghdād and al-Basra; and they concluded that if the inhabited areas of Baghdād were to be brought together, and the ruined parts removed, it would be no bigger than al-Basra: although by then the desert side of al-Basra had fallen into ruins. The name of this city is derived from the black stones which the ships of al-Yaman used to use as ballast, and then would throw out here. Some, however, say, not so; that it is derived from a soft whitish rock. And Qutrub says that the name is derived from the rugged ground.

The baths here are excellent. Fish and dates are here aplenty, besides meat, vegetables, grains, dairy products; the sciences and commerce flourish. Yet, good water is scarce, the air is constantly changing and baneful, and the people are amazingly given to riot.

Al-Ubulla is on the Tigris at the mouth of the canal of al-Basra, on the north side; the mosque is toward the farther side of it. It is a large and well-populated village, with better services than al-Basra, and more spacious.

Shiqq ꜤUthmān is exactly opposite to it on the south bank. The mosque, which is very fine, is at the extreme end of the canal. The other towns are on canals on both sides of the Tigris, both to the right and left, and to the south and north. They are all large and important towns.

ꜤAbbādān is a town situated on an island lying between the Tigris of al-ꜤIrāq and the river of Khūzistān; it is on the coast. There is no town beyond it, no village—nothing but sea. There are defense posts here, and virtuous and upright people, most of them makers of mats from the reeds. However, fresh water here is scarce, the sea surrounding it entirely.

Addition / version MS. C.

The Prophet—God's peace and blessings be upon him—said: "Should any one of you reach ꜤAbbādān, let him take up his position there, for it is clay of the clay of Jerusalem which the flood took to there in the time of Noah, and which will return to its original place on the Day of the Resurrection."

Wāsit is a large capital in two sections, with two mosques, and a bridge between them. It is a place of plenty, and abounds in fish. The mosque of al-Hajjāj, and his dome, are towards the west, on the edge of the markets, far from the riverbank. It has fallen into ruin somewhat, but is crowded with reciters of the *Qurān*. Al-Hajjāj planned the construction of it, and it was named Wāsit, because of its situation between the chief cities of al-ꜤIrāq and the city of al-Ahwāz. It is a well-supplied place, the air is healthy, the water sweet. The markets are excellent, with an extensive rural area nearby. At each end of the bridge is a place for the passage of ships. The inhabitants are people of refinement.

p. 119 The other towns of Wāsit are small and in poor condition, the more substantial of them being al-Tīb and Qurqūb; the district is prosperous, however.

Al-Salīq is a city on the shore of a lake that measures forty *farsakhs* in length. Its domain reaches the outskirts of al-Kūfa. The heat is intense, the air depressing and the place is filthy. The housebugs are murderous, and life is miserable! With their bread the inhabitants eat fish, their drinking water is hot, their nights are torture. Their intellects are weak, their language is corrupt, and there is but little esprit. Great is their distress! However, it is a source of flour, and government there is mild; and both water and fish are abundant. The town has a great name, and every man there is both steadfast in war, and skilled on the river. They have a beautiful situation, resembling the canal at al-Ubulla. Al-Jāmida is closest to it in size: both towns are some distance from the Tigris. The remaining towns are inferior to these two. The wide flats of this area with pools and shallows, known as al-Batāʾih, have cultivated areas, also, and al-ꜤIrāq derives considerable provisions from them.

Baghdād is the metropolis of Islām, and within it is Madīnat al-Salām [the City of Peace]. Its people have distinctive characteristics of wittiness, charm, refinement, and correct scholarship. The climate is mild, and all that is good and beautiful is to be found there. Every skillful person comes from there, and every refinement is found there. Every heart yearns for it; every battle is fought over it, and every hand is raised to defend it. It is too renowned to need description, more glorious than we could possibly portray it, and is indeed beyond praise.

Abu al-ʿAbbās al-Saffāh founded it, then al-Mansūr built in it the City of Peace, and the khalifs after him added to it. When he determined to build the City of Peace he inquired about its winter, its summer, the season of rains, the gnats, and the climate. He ordered certain men to live there through all the seasons of the year, so that they should learn all these particulars. He then consulted the judicious from among its inhabitants, who said to him: "We deem it advisable that you settle in the midst of the four districts, on the east Būq and Kalwādhā, and on the west Qutrabbul and Bādūraya. Thus you will be surrounded by palms and be close to water. If, then, one of the districts should suffer from drought, or its cultivation be delayed, another would relieve the situation. Moreover, you are on the banks of al-Sarāt, so that supplies can come to you by the vessels plying on the Euphrates; the caravans from Egypt and Syria will come across the desert, goods of all different kinds from China will reach you by sea, and from the Romaeans and al-Mawsil by the Tigris. Again, you are in a place between rivers so that the enemy cannot reach you except by ship, or by bridge, by way of the Tigris or the Euphrates."

p. 120

Accordingly, he built the city in four sections, the City of Peace, Bādūraya, al-Rusāfa, and the quarter where the palace of the khalif stands today. It used to be the most beautiful possession of the Muslims, a most splendid city, far exceeding our description of it.

However, the authority of the khalifs declined, the city deteriorated, and the population dwindled. The City of Peace is now desolate: the Mosque alone is frequented on Fridays, and otherwise the whole place is deserted. The most populous areas there now are Qatīʿat al-Rabīʿ, and al-Karkh on the western side, and on the east Bāb al-Tāq and the neighbourhood of the palace of the *Amīr*. The public buildings and the markets for the most part are in the western quarter. The bridge is near Bāb al-Tāq and close by is a hospital, founded by ʿAdhud al-Dawla. There is in each of the districts we have mentioned a congregational mosque. Day by day the town is going from bad to worse: truly, I fear it will become like Sāmarrā, what with the corruption, the ignorance and immorality, and the outrageous oppression of the ruler.

Abū Bakr al-Ismāʿīlī told us, at Jurjān, that he had it from Ibn Nājiya, who had it from Ibrāhīm al-Tarjumānī, who had it from Sayf bin Muhammad, who had it from ʿĀsim al-Ahwal, that Abū ʿUthmān al-Nahdī recounted the following: "I was one time in the company of Jarīr bin ʿAbd Allāh and he asked those present: 'By what name is this river called?' And they said, 'Tigris.' Said he: 'And this other stream?' They said, 'Dujayl' (Little Tigris). 'And this river?' They said 'Sarāt'. Said he: 'And this stand of palms?' They said, 'Qutrabbul.' Thereupon, he rode his steed hastily away, saying: 'I once heard the Messenger of God—God's peace and blessings be upon him—say: "A city will be built between the Tigris, Dujayl, Qutrabbul and al-Sarāt, to which will be gathered the treasures of the earth in tribute. And the people in their arrogance will be brought low, and their descent into the earth will be faster than the sinking of an iron spike in soft ground"'."

The canals from the Euphrates flow into the Tigris south of the city; but to the front of the city and to the north of it only the Tigris flows. Vessels sail on these branches of the Euphrates as far as al-Kūfa, on the Tigris as far as al-Mawsil.

p.121   Al-Shimshātī mentions in his *History* that when al-Mansūr purposed to build the City of Peace he brought together before him the most famous people in legal practice, and jurisprudence, possessed of impartiality and integrity, and a knowledge of engineering. Among these were Abū Hanīfa al-Naʿmān ibn Thābit, and al-Hajjāj bin Artāt. He assembled the craftsmen and the workers from Syria, al-Mawsil, al-Jabal, and his other provinces. He ordered the lines of the city to be plotted, and the foundations dug in the year 145/762, and it was finished in the year 149/766. He ordered the thickness of the wall at the base to be fifty cubits, and he provided the city with eight gates, four small inner gates, and four large outer gates. These were the Basra Gate, the Syria Gate, the Khurāsān Gate, and the Kūfa Gate. He placed the great mosque and the palace in the center of the city. The *Qibla* of the great mosque of al-Rusāfa is more correct than that of the mosque here. I learned from a book I found in one of the libraries of the khalifs that al-Mansūr spent in building the City of Peace four million and eight hundred and thirty-three *dirhams*: the wages of an *ustādh* (overseer) was a *qīrāt*, that of a labourer, two *habbas* (grains).

Al-Nahrawān is a town situated on both banks of the canal, the eastern side being the more populous, spacious, and well developed. Between the two quarters is a bridge. The mosque is on the eastern side, and on this bank the pilgrims halt to rest on their way.

Al-Daskara is a small town having a single long market, at the lower end of which stands the mosque: the air in the building is sultry and the light deficient. It has a long arched portico.

Jalūlā, surrounded by trees, is not well fortified. These towns and Khāniqīn are on the main road to Hulwān; they are of little importance, and are hardly worthy of Baghdād.

Sarsar also is like a village of Palestine; the canal flows beside it; similarly Nahr al-Malik and al-Sarāt are mere villages.

Qasr Ibn Hubayra, on the other hand, is a large town with excellent markets. Water is brought to it from the Euphrates. Weavers and Jews are there in great numbers. The mosque stands beside the marketplace.

Bābil is a small place remote from the road; the high road runs over a bridge nearby. The other towns around here are of the same description, for instance al-Nīl, and ʿAbdas, and Kūtā.

p. 122 Kūtā Rabbā is the native town of Abraham, and here are some mounds said to be the ashes of the fire of Nimrūd. Close to Kūtā al-Tarīq is a structure resembling a tower, and the inhabitants have a tradition about it.

There is not on the Tigris, in the direction of Wāsit, a town more splendid than Dayr al-ʿĀqūl. It is large, prosperous, and populous, with its great mosque away from the marketplace. The markets, which are excellent, have branches throughout the city; in fact it very much resembles the towns in Palestine.

Next to this town in size is Jabbul, a thriving and populous place. The mosque, which is graceful, stands beside the marketplace. Next to this is al-Nuʿmāniyya, a small town, with its mosque in the marketplace. Next is Jarjarāyā: it used to be a great town, but today it is in disorder, and its buildings are isolated. The mosque, which is close to the river bank, is in splendid condition. A canal flows around part of the town. These towns we have mentioned lie on the western side of the Tigris. The remaining towns are small in size.

In the direction of Sāmarrā lies the town of ʿUkbarā, large and prosperous, abounding in fruits, producing superb grapes: all-in-all, a distinguished town.

As regards al-Madāʾin, it is in the direction of Wāsit; it is a populous town, its buildings of baked brick; the mosque is in the marketplace. Towards the east lies Asbānbur, in which is the tomb of Salmān, also the Palace of the Kisrā.

So these are the towns of Baghdād; at the same time, in Khurāsān are many villages more important than most of these towns.

Sāmarrā was formerly a great metropolis, the abode of the khalifs. Al-Muʿtasim established it, and after him al-Mutawakkil increased its circuit to about a whole day's journey. It was a remarkably beautiful city, so that it used to be called *Surūr man Raʾā*, "the Delight of the Beholder." This name was abridged to Surmarā. The city has a large mosque which used to be considered superior to the mosque at Damascus. Its walls had been coated with enamel, pillars of marble were erected within it, and it was paved with marble. The mosque has a tall minaret, and all its other features are in keeping with this. Sāmarrā was indeed a considerable town, but is now gone to ruin, so a man may walk for two or three miles and not come upon an inhabited place. The town is on the east bank of the river, while on the west bank are extensive gardens. Al-Muʿtasim also erected there a building resembling the Kaʿba, and laid out a walk for circumambulation.

p. 123 He also set up places to resemble Minā and ʿArafāt, thereby imposing on some Amīrs [Turkish guards] in his service, when they asked permission to go on the Pilgrimage, and he feared they might quit his service. When the town fell into ruin, and into the condition as we have described it, it came to be called *Sāʾa man raʾā*—"he is grieved who sees it". That name was shortened, and became Sāmarrā.

Al-Karkh, a town that adjoins it toward al-Mawsil, is in better condition. I once heard the Qādhī Abu al-Husayn al-Qazwīnī say: "Baghdād has never produced any jurist whatsoever, except Abū Mūsā al-Dharīr." "And," said I, "what about Abu al-Hasan al-Karkhī?" Said he: "He was not from Karkh of Baghdād at all, he was from Karkh near Sāmarrā."

Al-Anbār is a large city, and here al-Mansūr first resided; his palace is there, but the town has become unimportant.

Hīt is a large town enclosed by a wall, situated on the Euphrates, and close to the desert.

Takrīt is a large town, producing sesame; woolworkers are there. Here the Christians have a convent to which they make pilgrimage.

ʿAlth is a large town connected by canal to the Tigris. It has wells of easily accessible fresh water, not deep, but copious. The town is populous, with many persons of distinction.

Al-Sinn is a large town situated on the Tigris; to the east of it flows the River Zāb. Its mosque stands among the markets. The buildings are of stone. The mountains are close by the town, which is on the borders of Aqūr.

The towns of the district of Sāmarrā are more splendid than the towns of the district of Baghdād.

Hulwān is a small capital city, partly on the plains and partly in the hills. It is surrounded by gardens, grape vines, and fig trees, and is situated close to the mountains. It has a long market, and an ancient fortress, and nearby is a small stream. It has a *quhandiz* [ancient town fortress] within which stands the mosque. Eight roads lead to the town: the road of Khurāsān, the road of al-Bāqāt, the road of al-Musallā (the Oratory), the road of the Jews, the road of Baghdād, the road of Barqīt, the road of the Jewess, and the road of Mājakān. The Jews have a temple there which they hold in great reverence; it is outside the town, built of gypsum and stone. However, the city of Bayt al-Maqdis (Jerusalem) is bigger, more splendid, more flourishing, more elegant than this city, besides having more doctors of the law and scholars attached to it. The towns of this district are small, in ruin, and not worth mention.

p. 124   As for the Tigris, its water may be described as feminine, pleasant and excellent, favorable to jurists; Abū Bakr al-Jassās used to order his water brought to him from a place above the canal of al-Sarāt, before the Euphrates reaches it. This river, the Tigris, emerges from Aqūr, and we shall mention its origins when we treat of that area. Then in this region a number of streams join it. In the district of Baghdād four canals from the Euphrates flow down into it —al-Sarāt, Nahr ʿĪsā, Nahr Sarsar, and Nahr al-Malik. Moreover, it receives from the east side, below Baghdād, the waters of the Nahrawānāt canals. Then when it passes Wāsit the river spreads out, so that its navigation is difficult as far as the environs of al-Basra. Boats are continually sailed up and down stream, and with considerable skill. At Baghdād the people come and go, and cross the river by these vessels: there is constant bustle and stir. Indeed, two-thirds of the charm of Baghdād derives from this river.

The Euphrates, on the other hand, is a masculine river: it has a hardness about it. Its origin is in the country of the Romaeans and it flows in a curve around a portion of this region. It arrives at al-Kūfa, after forming a number of branches. It then flows down to the west of Wāsit. There it sprawls out into an extensive surface of water surrounded by flourishing villages, from which the river does not emerge again. Boats from as far up as al-Raqqa may navigate this river.

One should be aware that al-ʿIrāq is not a land of abundance, but it has become important and populous because of these two rivers, and what is transported on them; and because of the Sea of China, which is adjacent to it. Baghdād is distinguished over all others in the excellence of its climate, the like of which is never seen elsewhere; and in speaking of al-Basra, it is not possible to say too much about its waters, its storage cisterns, and the ebb and flow of the tides there.

Abu al-Hasan Mutahhar bin Muhammad related to me, in Rāma-Hurmuz, that he had it from Ahmad bin ʿAmr bin Zakariyyāʾ, who had it from al-Hasan bin ʿAlī bin Bahr, who had it from Abū Shuʿayb al-Qaysī, who had it from Ashras, who said: "I once asked Ibn ʿAbbās about the ebb and flow of the tides. He told me: 'An angel is charged with the responsibility over the great depths of the ocean: when he puts down his foot, the water flows, and when he lifts his foot, it ebbs.'"

p. 125 The flow and reflow of the tides is a source of constant wonder to the people of al-Basra, and a boon besides, as the water visits them twice in every day and night: it enters the canals, waters the gardens, and carries the boats to the villages. The tide is useful also in its ebb, because it works mills situated at the mouths of the canals: as the water goes out, it turns them. The flood tide reaches as far as al-Batāʿih (the swamps). The tides have definite seasons which recur with those of the moon.

A Summary Account of Conditions in this Region

The **climate** of this region is varied. For example, Baghdād and Wāsit and the area in between have a gentle climate, but it is quick to change: sometimes in the summer it is white-hot and unbearable here, when suddenly a change sets in.

At al-Kūfa conditions are in contrast with this. At al-Basra the heat is oppressive, except when the north wind blows: then the weather becomes pleasant there. In an account of al-Basra I read the following: "Our life in al-Basra is remarkable: when the north wind blows, we are in a planted countryside; however, when the south wind blows, we are in a sewer." Indeed, I have noticed them in a most depressed mood with the south wind blowing, and a man would meet his friend and say, "Do you not see the condition we are in now?" and the other would answer: "We implore God for relief." Sometimes there descends on them at night moisture resembling the thick syrup of ripe dates.

Hulwān, on the other hand, has an equable climate; but as for al-Baṭāʾih, heaven help us! Anyone who visits this place in summer has some remarkable experiences to endure. In fact, they sleep within curtains, because there is an insect there with a stinging organ like a needle, consisting of the insect's entire forepart.

p. 126 In these cities are many doctors of the law, readers of the *Qurʾān*, litterateurs, eminent professional people, and kingly personages, especially in Baghdād and al-Basra. Preachers here are held in low estimation. Ice is brought hither from afar. The weather is cold in winter: sometimes water freezes at al-Basra, but commonly at Baghdād. The people of al-Kūfa and al-Basra are tawny of skin.

There are many Magians in this region, and *dhimmī*, both Christians and Jews. A number of Islamic *sects* are here, the preponderants in Baghdād being Hanbalites and Shīʿa. The pre-eminence of the jurisprudents of the two ʿIrāqs [the cities of al-Kūfa and al-Basra] has been recognized for ages. Also in this region are Mālikites, Ashʿarites, Muʿtazilites, Najjārites; in al-Kūfa the people are Shīʿa, except in the quarter of al-Kunāsa, where they are Sunnī. At al-Basra are institutes and public sessions of the Sālimites, a group that claims to study theology and practice asceticism: most of the preachers here are from this group. They do not proclaim themselves a school of jurisprudence, those of them who study jurisprudence following the teaching of Mālik. They maintain however, that their founder, Ibn Sālim, learned his law from Abū Hanīfa—Sālim had been a slave of Sahl bin ʿAbd Allāh al-Tustarī. To me they seemed to be an upright group of people, endowed with great grace; however, they are excessive in the laudation of their leader. I frequented their company for a long time, knew their secrets, and won a place in their hearts; for I am a man who loves ascetic people, inclining towards those who practice self-denial, whoever they may be. There is a graciousness in their speech and their writings, their assemblies are uplifting, and contention is far removed from them.

Most of the people of al-Basra are Qadarites and Shīʿa; next in number are the Hanbalites. In Baghdād is a sect of fanatics, who go beyond all bounds in their love of Muʿāwiya; here are also the Mushabbites (anthropomorphists), and the Barbahārites.

Addition/version MS. C.
The Hanbalites of al-ʿIrāq are fanatic anthropomorphites. They exceed all bounds in their attachment to Muʿāwiya; and they relate in this respect some abominable stories, especially the Barbahāriyya.

One day I was in the mosque in Wāsit, when I saw a man there around whom a crowd of people had gathered. I approached the group and heard him declare: "So and so has related to us that he learned from so and so that the Prophet—God's peace and blessings be upon him—said that God would draw Muʿāwiya close to him on the Day of the Resurrection, and would seat him by

His side. He would anoint him with His own hands, and display him to mankind as He would a bride." So said I to him: "Why should that be? Is it because he waged war with ʿAlī? May God be pleased with Muʿāwiya, but you are a liar, you misguided one." At this the man exclaimed: "Seize this unbeliever." The crowd moved towards me, but one of the learned men there recognized me, and restrained them.

p. 127   The majority of the jurisprudents and the judges of this region are followers of Abū Ḥanīfa. One day I was in the assembly of Abū Muḥammad al-Sīrāfī, and said he to me: "You are a Syrian, and the people of your region are adherents of Tradition, and follow the law in the interpretation of al-Shāfiʿī; so why have you expressed an interpretation in accord with Abū Ḥanīfa?" Said I: "There are three reasons, may God preserve the Faqīh!" Said he: "And what are they?" Said I: "First, I have noticed his reliance on the authority of ʿAlī, may God be pleased with him. Now the Prophet has said, 'I am the city of learning, and ʿAlī is its gate.' He has also said: 'The most skilled jurist among you is ʿAlī, meaning in the application of the *fiqh* (jurisprudence)'. I have also observed his reliance on the authority of ʿAbd Allāh bin Masʿūd, of whom the Prophet—peace be upon him—has said: "I approve for my community whatever the son of Umm ʿAbd approves." He said, moreover: "A purse filled with learning"; he said also: "Take ye two-thirds of your religion from the son of Umm ʿAbd." Unquestionably, the learning of the people of al-Kūfa is derived from these two men.

"The second point is that I deem him the earliest of the leading authorities in the law, and the closest of them to the age of the Companions, as well as being the most profound in faith, and the most devout. Now, the Prophet—God's peace and blessings be upon him—also said: 'Cleave to that which is old.' He said, moreover: 'The best of you are those living in the age in which I am, then those who are next to them, and then those in turn who immediately follow them. Then will falsehood spread about.' He lived in the age of truth, and of the people who spoke the truth.

"The third point is this: I have observed that all the learned differ from him on a question in which he is clearly in the right, and they are wrong." Said he: "And what is it?" I replied: "The learned professor is aware that it is a point of doctrine with him that the acceptance of a fee for the performance of any righteous deed or work on behalf of another person is not lawful. Now I have noticed that a person who goes on the Pilgrimage for hire undergoes a degradation of spirit; and if he repeats the deed his decadence increases and his piousness diminishes to the extent of his accepting recompense as a surrogate on two or even three Pilgrimages at the same time. However, I have never known such people to enjoy any blessing or gain any wealth thereby. The same is true in the case of the *Imāms* [the Imām is an exemplary person who leads the community in prayer], the *mu'adhdhins* (who call to the prayers), and of those like them, who having merited their recompense from God have taken it from His creatures." On this, he said: "You have examined the matter closely, O

Muqaddasī, and you have dealt with it with circumspection." Now, should someone say: "Abū Hanīfa has been deprecated by some," it may be said in reply: "Know that all men may be divided into three classes: a class for which there is complete agreement on their uprightness, a class for which there is complete agreement on their iniquity, and a class of those who are praised by some and disparaged by others. These last are the best of the three, and you may take as an instance of these the case of the Companions. The praised among them are Ibn Masʿūd, Muʿādh, and Zayd; the censured, ʿAbd Allāh bin Ubayy. The best of them, however, are the four khalifs. Yet you know what the Khārijites and the ignorant among the Shīʿa say about them. Similarly, in relation to Abū Hanīfa, even though there is a minority of stupid people who disparage him, there is a population of the righteous who invoke his authority and extol him. Along with this, consider how God enlightened his heart so that he organized the sacred law into a system and relieved mankind of their burden. Moreover, consider his preference of accepting flogging and imprisonment rather than the office of Qādhī." The like of Abū Hanīfa is not to be seen anywhere!

p. 128

The **seven systems of reading** the *Qurʾān* are employed in this region. Formerly in Baghdād the system of Hamza was the fashion; and that of Yaʿqūb al-Hadhramī was followed in al-Basra. I observed Abū Bakr al-Jartakī in leading the prayer reading according to this latter usage, in the mosque there; he said that it was the usage of the elders.

There is a variety of **dialects** in use, the most correct being that spoken at al-Kūfa; this is because of their closeness to the desert and their remoteness from the Nabataeans. Apart from that the language of the region is pleasant to hear, but most ungrammatical, especially in Baghdād. However in al-Bataʾih are the Nabataeans, a people having neither language nor brains.

The production of articles of **commerce** here is considerable. Have you not heard of the silks and linens of al-Basra, of the rare and exquisite articles produced there, and of its galbanum? It is a mine of pearls and gems, a port on the sea and an emporium on the land. Here are produced antimony, cinnabar, verdigris, and litharge of silver. Dates are exported from here to places far away, as well as henna, silk, essence of violet, and rosewater. At al-Ubulla, also, linen cloths of exquisite fineness are made, embroidered. In al-Kūfa are made turbans of silk, and essence of violet the most excellent. In the City of Peace elegant and varied apparel is made, and cloths of silk, and other materials. From this region come the excellent ʿAbbādānī mats, and the finest *sāmān* rush mats.

Among the **specialties** of this region are the essence of violet, and *azādh* dates of al-Kūfa: the *muhkam* (strong cloth) and other uncommon things of

Baghdād, the superb *ma'qilī* dates of al-Basra, the figs of Hulwān, the *shim* and *bunnī* fishes of Wāsit. In Nu'māniyya are made superb garments and cloths of wool the colour of honey, and at Baghdād shawls and turbans of special *yakānakī* fabrics. There are, too, the kerchiefs of fabrics made in al-Qasr and al-Buwayb,

p. 129 along with the woolen cloth of Takrīt, and the draperies of Wāsit.

Their Measures of Capacity

The *qafīz* is the equivalent of thirty *mana*,
the *makkūk*, five *mana*,
the *kaylaja*, two *mana*,
their *ratl* is one half of a *mann*.

The Coinage of al-'Irāq. Their coins are calculated by weight; however, their standard of weight is heavier than that of Khurāsān.

Some Customs of the People of al-'Irāq. The people here like to dress well, and wear the *taylasān*. They usually wear sandals, dress up their turbans so that they are tall, and clothe themselves in fine calico. Seldom do they wear the *taylasān* with a scalloped edge.

At the time of transport of new dates to Wāsit, a watch is kept for the first boat to arrive, and the merchant who owns it decorates the riverbank as far as his shop with carpets and draperies.

Over the biers of women they build tall, rather crude canopies.

Those who cook *harīsa* have places above their shops in which are mats, and tables with pickles. Here are servants with washbasins, pitchers, and potash [for soap], and when a person leaves the place he pays a single *dānaq*.

At the beginning of the season of violets they go the rounds of the markets with violets, dressed handsomely for the occasion.

By the doors of the mosques are washbasins for ablution, for the use of which payment must be made.

The *khatībs* [who preach on Friday], wear their outer garment with full-length sleeves and girdle. They do not chant in reciting the call to prayer, and have a goodly number of other excellent practices.

Their **waters** are chiefly from the river Tigris, from the Euphrates, from the Zāb, and from the Nahrawānāt canals, and from these, also, they irrigate their fields. Water at al-Basra is scarce, for it must be brought by boat from al-Ubulla, as the water nearby is not so sweet, nor pleasant to taste. In fact there is the saying that the water of al-Basra is one third seawater, one third tidewater, and one third sewage. This is because at ebb tide the canal banks are laid bare and people relieve their bowels there: then the tide coming in carries the excrement with it. When the south wind blows the water becomes warm.

The most grievous **sectarian quarrels** arise in al-Basra between the Rubaʿyyīn,
p. 130 who are Shīʿa, and the Saʿdiyyīn, who are Sunnī; the people of the countryside
take part in these too. Indeed few are the towns in which there are not violent
contentions for other than religious reasons.

The **holy places** in this region are many. At Kūtā, Abraham was born, and
his fire lighted (*Qurʾān*, sūra 21, v. 69). At al-Kūfa, Noah built his ark, and the
fountains on the surface of the earth bubbled over. (*Qurʾān*, sūra 11, v. 40). The
monuments of ʿAlī are there, with his grave, as well as the grave of al-Husayn,
and the place of his killing. At al-Basra are the graves of Talha, Zubayr, the
Prophet's brother, al-Hasan al-Basrī, Anas bin Mālik, ʿImrān bin Husayn, Sufyān
al-Thawrī, Mālik bin Dīnār, ʿUtba the Slave, Muhammad bin Wāsiʿ, Sālih
al-Murrī, Ayyūb al-Sikhtiyānī, Sahl al-Tustarī, and Rābiʿa al-ʿAdawiyya; there
also is the grave of Ibn Sālim. At Baghdād is the grave of Abū Hanīfa over which
Abū Jaʿfar al-Zammām has built a mausoleum. Beside it, behind the Market
of Yahyā is a grave. The grave of Abū Yūsuf is in the cemetery of the Quraysh.
There also are the graves of Ahmad ibn Hanbal, Maʿrūf al-Karkhī, Bishr al-Hāfī,
and others. The grave of Salmān is at al-Madāʾin. Moreover, at al-Kūfa is the
grave of a prophet whom I believe to be Yūnus, peace be on him.

As for their **dispositions**, the people are gentle in nature, and show a ready
wit. Nevertheless, when the vagabonds of Baghdād bestir themselves they work
havoc there: depravity is rife. At al-Basra, however, are people who are upright,
ascetic, pious, and chaste. They delay the performance of the noon prayer, but
are beforehand with afternoon prayer. They linger in the Mosque for the arrival
of people from the outlying areas. The *Imām* preaches every morning and prays
in supplication. It is said that this practice derives from Ibn ʿAbbās, God be
pleased with him.

Addition/version MS. C.
At al-Basra are to be found nine and forty varieties of dates: al-Dhabbī; al-
Harthī; al-Khayshūm; al-Sahrī; al-Sukkar; al-Bashkar; al-Thabarzad; al-Ahmar;
al-Asfar; al-Khastawānī; al-Maʿqibī; al-Azādh; al-Hilyāth; al-Karāmī; al Qathriyya
[al-Qathawiyya?]; al-Qarīthī [al-Qurayzī?]; al-Hayrūm; al-Badālī; al-Rīfī;
al-ʿArūsī; al-Bādhanjānī; al-Ibrahīmī; al-Zunbūrī; al-Yaʿdhūdh [al Taʿdhūdh?];
al-Burnāj; al-Mahdar; al-Bīrūnī; al-Shuwayqī; al-Jaysuwān; al-ʿAmrī; al-Qurashī;
al-Yamānī; al-Barnī; al-Suhrīz; al-Hazkā; al-Hābīrān al-Asfar; al-Muhkarm;
al-Qasab; al-Jinānī; al-Mahdahraj; al-Gharānī; al-Sharqī; al-Khwārazmī; al-Fahl;
al-Māburī; Baydh al-Baghl; al-Fāwasān. To be included also is Sayhānī, which
Abū Ahmed al-Mūsāʿī transplanted from al-Madīna; but the ripe dates of this
variety at al-Basra are lopped of only every two months.

Addition/version MS. C.
At al-Basra are to be found, also, twenty-four varieties of fish in the Tigris river:

al-Shīm; al-Zajr; al-Bunnī; al-Jirrī; al-Shilq; al-Zunjūr; al-Bimmī; al-Sāh
[al-Saj?]; al-Shā'im; al-Kartak; al-Shilānī [al-Shilābī]; al-Dabaqāh; al-Ramā'īm;
al-Baydhāwī; al-Irbiyān; al-Birāk; al-Barasūh [al-Barashtūj?]; al-Isbūl; al-Harrāq
[al-Jawwāf]; al-Rabaltī [al-Rubaythā?]; al-ʿAyn [al-ʿAyr?]; al-Zajar; al-Sahadān
[al-Shahadhān?]; al-Mārimāhī.

p. 131 **The Government.** This region is the place of residence of the khalifs of
the House of ʿAbbās, God be pleased with him. It used to be always that their
word was law; however, they declined and the Daylamites overcame them; now,
no one heeds them, or pays any attention to their opinions.

The first ruler of the line was Abu al-ʿAbbās ʿAbd Allāh bin Muhammad
bin ʿAlī bin al-ʿAbbās: to him allegiance was pledged as sovereign leader in the
year 132/769; he died in the year 136/756 at al-Anbār. His Qādhī [chief justice]
was Yahyā bin Saʿīd al-Ansārī. He was succeeded by al-Mansūr Abū Jaʿfar
ʿAbdallāh bin Muhammad, to whom the people pledged allegiance in the year
136/754; he died in the year 158/775. His Qādhīs were ʿUbayd Allāh bin
Safwān, Sharīk, and al-Hasan bin ʿUmāra. After him al-Mahdī Abū ʿAbd Allāh,
son of al-Mansūr ascended the throne in the year 158/775. His Qādhīs were
Muhammad bin ʿAbd Allāh bin ʿAlāqa, and ʿĀfiya ibn Yazīd. He died in the year
169/785. Thereupon, al-Hādī Abū Muhammad Mūsā, son of al-Mahdī, received
the allegiance of the people. His Qādis were Abū Yūsuf, and Saʿīd bin ʿAbd
al-Rahmān. He died in the year 170/786, to be succeeded in authority by
al-Rashīd Abū Jaʿfar Hārūn, son of al-Mahdī, on the night before Friday, the
fourteenth day of Rabīʿ I [third month of Muslin year], the year being 170/786.
His Qādhīs were al-Husayn bin al-Hasan al-Sūfī, then ʿAwn bin ʿAbd Allāh
al-Masʿūdī, and Hafs bin Ghiyāth. He died at Tūs in the year 193/809. On
this, his son, al-Amīn Muhammad was made khalif after seven days of the month
of Jumādā II [sixth month of Muslim year] had passed, in the year 193/809.
His brother al-Maʾmūm rose up against him and killed him, and was, in turn
recognized as khalif in the year 198/813. The Qādhīs of al-Maʾmūm were
al-Wāqidī, Muhammad bin ʿAbd al-Rahmān al-Makhzūmī, after him Bishr bin
al-Walīd, and Yahyā bin Aktham.

He died in the year 218/833 at Tarsūs. Then Abū Ishāq Muhammad bin
p. 132 al-Rashīd, al-Muʿtasim, succeeded, whose Qādhī was Ahmad bin Abī Duʾād.
Al-Muʿtasim died in the year 227/842, and his son, al-Wāthiq Abū Jaʿfar Hārūn
was acknowledged khalif, and his Qādhī was Ahmad bin Abī Duʾād. He died in
232/847, and was succeeded by his brother Abu al-Fadhl Jaʿfar al-Mutawakkil;
his Qādhī was Jaʿfar bin ʿAbd al-Wāhid al-Hāshimī. He died in 247/862 and his
son, al-Muntasir Abū Jaʿfar Muhammad was proclaimed khalif, and his Qādhī
was Jaʿfar bin ʿAbd al-Wāhid. He died in the year 248/862, and was succeeded
by his son Abu al-ʿAbbās Ahmad al-Mustaʿīn, whose Qādhī was Jaʿfar bin
Muhammad ibn ʿAmmār. He abdicated after three years and eight months,
and was succeeded by al-Muʿtazz, son of al-Mutawakkil; his Qādhī was al-Hasan
bin Muhammad bin Abi al-Shawārib. After him, al-Muʿtamid Abu al-ʿAbbās

Ahmad, son of al-Mutawakkil, received allegiance as khalif in 256/870; his Qāḍhī was Ibn Abi al-Shawārib. He died in 279/892, and was succeeded by his son, Abu al-ʿAbbās Ahmad bin Abī Ahmad, al-Muʿtadhid; his Qāḍhīs were Ismāʿīl bin Ishāq, Yūsuf bin Yaʿqūb, and Ibn Abi al-Shawārib. He died in 289/902. His son Abū Muhammad ʿAlī al-Muktafī was proclaimed khalif, and his Qāḍhīs were Yūsuf bin Yaʿqūb and Muhammad his son. He died in the year 295/908. Then Abu al-Fadhl Jaʿfar al-Muqtadir bi-Allāh, also son of al-Muʿtadhid, succeeded him. His Qāḍhīs were Muhammad bin Yūsuf bin Yaʿqūb, the latter's son Yūsuf, and Yaʿqūb Abū ʿAmr. This khalif was killed in the year 320/932. Al-Qāhir succeeded him for a year and six months; after him, al-Rāḍhī ruled for seven years and ten days; then al-Muttaqī for three years and eleven months as khalif. After him, al-Mustakfī became khalif in the year 333/944; his Qāḍhī was Abū ʿAbd Allāh ibn Abī Mūsā al-Dharīr. He was blinded in the year 334/946, and al-Mutīʿ Abu al-Qāsim al-Fadhl was placed on the throne: all of these were descendants of al-Muʿtadhid. Al-Mutīʿ remained in power until the year 363/974, when he abdicated and placed on the throne his son ʿAbd al-Karīm Abū Bakr al-Ṭāʾiʿ, whose Qāḍhī is Abū Muhammad ʿUbayd Allāh bin Ahmad bin Maʿrūf.

p. 133 The first of the Daylamites to seize power over the area was [Muʿizz al-Dawla] Abu al-Hasan [in fact: Abu al-Husayn] ibn Buwayh, and his son, Bakhtiyār succeeded him. ʿAdhud al-Dawla came next in succession, and after him his son, Balkārzār; later, his elder son, Abu al-Fawāris succeeded.

The Land-Taxes. The cultivable land of this region amounts to thirty six million *jarīb* [*jarīb*, land measure sixty cubits square; see p. 451 text]. On an acre of wheat there is a tax of four *dirhams*; on an acre of barley, two *dirhams*; and on an acre of palm trees, eight *dirhams*. This assessment was fixed by ʿUmar himself. He also imposed a poll tax on five hundred thousand *dhimmī*. So the revenue of the Sawād [the rural area of ʿIrāq] amounted to one hundred twenty-eight million *dirhams*. ʿUmar bin ʿAbd al-ʿAzīz collected taxes to the extent of one hundred twenty-four million *dirhams*. Al-Hajjāj collected taxes to the extent of eighteen million, that is, without the one hundred million. Al-Basra and al-Kūfa are taxed by tithes. I read in a book in the library of ʿAdhud al-Dawla that the value of all the crops of the Sawād amounts to eighty-six millon seven hundred eighty thousand *dirhams*; and from other sources of revenue in the Sawād four million eight thousand *dirhams* are realized. The revenue from the District of the Tigris is eight million five hundred thousand *dirhams*.

Al-ʿIrāq is divided into *tassūj* (townships) to the number of sixty:

In the district of Hulwān, five;

in Shādh Qubādh, eight;

in Barmāsiyān, three;

in Upper Bih Qubādh, six;

in Middle (Bih Qubādh), four;

in Ardashīr-Bābakān, five;
in Shādh Sābūr, four;
in Shādh Bahman, four;
in Astān al-ʿAl, four;
in Lower Bih Qubādh five;
in Shādh Hurmuz, seven;
in Nahrawānāt, five.

As for **imposts**, they are heavy and manifold, and of recent imposition. They are imposed on commerce on the river and on land, entailing rigorous inspection and rather severe exactions at al-Basra; it is likewise at al-Bataʾih, where the arrangement and assessment of goods are conducted. The Qarāmita have a tollhouse at the gate of al-Basra, the Daylamites have a similar one, so that on a single sheep up to four *dirhams* are collected. The gate is not open except for one p. 134 hour a day. When people return from the Pilgrimage, taxes are collected both on the loads of hides and on the Arabian camels; similarly at al-Kūfa and Baghdād. On a camelborne litter sixty *dirhams* are levied on the pilgrims; on a howdah, or on a load of linen, one hundred *dirhams*; and on the smaller howdah fifty *dirhams*, and one hundred at al-Basra and al-Kūfa.

The **area** of al-ʿIrāq: its length from the sea to al-Sinn is one hundred twenty-five *farsakhs*; its breadth from al-ʿUdhayb to ʿAqabat Hulwān is eighty *farsakhs*. So if you calculate it accordingly, the area amounts to ten thousand *farsakhs*.

The **distances on main roads**: You take the road from Baghdād to Nahr al-Malik, one stage;
thence to al-Qasr, one stage;
thence to Hammān Ibn ʿUmar one stage;
thence to al-Kūfa, one stage;
thence to al-Qādisiyya, one stage.

From Baghdād to al-Madaʾin, one stage;
thence to al-Sīb, one stage;
thence to Dayr al-ʿĀqūl, one stage;
thence to Jarjarāyā, one stage;
thence to al-Nuʿmāniyya, one stage;
thence to Jabbul, one stage;
thence to Nahr Sābus, one stage;
thence to Matāra, two *barīds* [*barīd* equals six miles];
thence to al-Jazīra, the same;
thence to al-Ishāqiyya, one stage;
thence to al-Mihrāqa, two *barīds*;
thence to al-Haddādiyya, the same;
thence to Turumāna, one stage;
thence to Wāsit, one stage.

You may also go from al-Haddādiyya to al-Zubaydiyya, one stage;
thence to Wāsit, two *barīds*.

From al-Mihrāqa to al-Jāmida, two *barīds*; and from al-Haddādiyya to al-Salīq,
two *barīds*.

From al-Basra to al-Ubulla, two *barīds*; thence to Bayān, one stage;
thence to ʿAbbādān, one stage.

From Baghdād to al-Saylahīn, two *barīds*;
thence to al-Anbār, one stage;
thence to al-Rabb, one stage;
thence to Hīt, two stages.

You may go from Baghdād to al-Baradān, two *barīds*;
thence to ʿUkbarā, one stage;
thence to Bāhamshā, half a stage;
thence to al-Qādisiyya, one stage;
thence to al-Karkh, one stage;
thence to Jabiltā, one stage;
thence to al-Sūdaqāniya, the same;
thence to Bārimmā, the same;
thence to al-Sinn, the same.

From Baghdād to al-Nahrawān, two *barīds*;
thence to Dayr Bārimmā, the same;
thence to al-Daskara, one stage;
thence to Jalūlā, one stage;
thence to Khāniqīn, one stage.

From Hīt to al-Nā'ūsa, one stage;
thence to ʿĀna, one stage;
thence to Alūsa, one stage;
thence to al-Fuhayma, one stage;
thence to al-Hadītha, one stage;
thence to al-Nahiyya (al-Nahba), one stage.

You go from Hulwān to Mādharwāstān, two *barīds*;
thence to al-Marj, one stage;
thence to Qasr Yazīd, two *barīds*;
thence to al-Zubaydiyya, one stage;
thence to Qasr ʿAmr, one stage;
thence to Qarmāsīn, half a stage.

p. 135

From Hulwān to Qasr Shīrīn, one stage;
    thence to Khāniqīn, one stage.

From al-Ubulla to al-Khūziyya, one stage by water;
    from al-Ubulla to Nahr Dubbā, one stage;
    thence to Fam al-ʿAdhudī [the mouth of the ʿAdhudī Canal], one stage.

ʿAskar Abī Jaʿfar lies opposite al-Ubulla, and there is a ferry here.
    Wāsit (central) was so named because the distance from it to each of the following: Baghdād, al-Kūfa, al-Basra, Hulwān, and al-Ahwāz, is, in every instance, fifty *farsakhs*. It is not at the centre of al-ʿIrāq, for the town there is Dayr al-ʿĀqūl. There is also a route from al-Kūfa.

The Region of Aqūr (Al-Jazīra)
[Upper Mesopotamia]

This also is an important region, one of superiority, for here are the shrines of prophets, the abodes of holy men. Here the ark of Noah came to rest on al-Jūdī; here settled his associates, and built the town of Thamānīn. God restored the people of Jonas to his grace here, and caused the spring of water to gush forth. Here also is the entryway of Dhu al-Qarnayn (*Qurʾān*, sūra 18, v. 83) to the Realm of Darkness. Here also occurred the remarkable events of Jirjīs with Dādhiyāna. God caused to sprout there for Jonas the gourd (*Qurʾān*, sūra 37, v. 146); from it goes out the blessed river of our holy community, the renowned Tigris. Is not the mosque of Jonas there at Tall Tawba (Hill of Repentance), seven visits to which are said to be the equivalent of going on a pilgrimage; and numerous shrines and many excellences? It is a frontier area of the Muslims, a stronghold of their strongholds; for at present, Āmid is the base of their campaign, Mawsil one of their greatest resources, and Jazīrat ibn ʿUmar one of their most delightful parks. Along with this, it lies between al-ʿIrāq and Syria, and the way stations for the Arabs in the practice of Islam. This region is the source of the best horses, and of most of the provisions of al-ʿIrāq. Prices are low, fruits excellent. It is the country of upright men.

We have been informed of a tradition by al-Hākim Abū Nasr Mansūr bin Muhammad al-Harbī, *muhtasib* of Bukhārā, who had it from al-Haytham bin Kulayb, who had it from Abū Yaʿlā al-Hasan bin Ismāʿīl and Abū Sulaymān Muhammad bin Mansūr al-Faqīh, who both had it from Ismāʿīl, that is Ibn Abī Uways, who had it from Kathīr bin ʿAbd Allāh, who had it from his (Kathīr) father, who had it from his (Kathīr) grandfather, who related that the Messenger of God—God's peace and blessings be upon him—said: "Four mountains there are which are of the mountains of Paradise, four rivers of the rivers of Paradise, four bloody battles of the battles of Paradise." It was asked of him which are the mountains. Said he, "Uhud, it loves us and we love it; and Majanna, a mountain of the mountains of Paradise; and al-Tūr (Sinai), a mountain of the mountains of Paradise. The rivers are the Nile, the Euphrates, Sayhān, and Jayhān; the bloody battles are Badr, Uhud, al-Khandaq, and Hunayn."

The Euphrates, which has this dignification, curves around this region, and the Tigris, a river of renown, rises from here. The region is favored with blessings, sacred shrines, frontier fortresses, and mosques; yet it is the abode of highwaymen, the roads through it are difficult, and the Romaeans have devastated its frontiers.

This is the form and representation of it. [Map VI]

We have made our divisions of this region to correspond with the tribes of the Arabs there, so that the areas they occupy may be known and distinguished from one another. We have designated three districts, according to the number

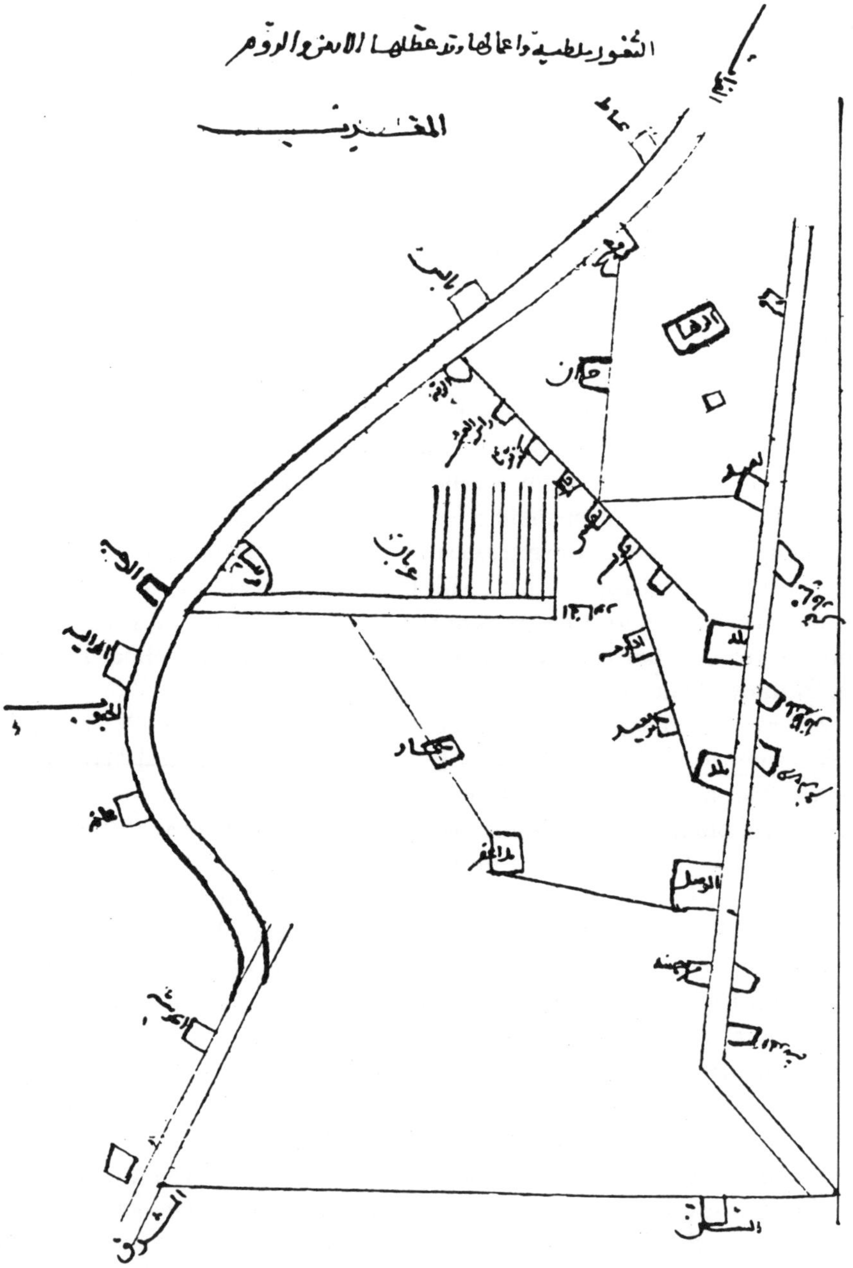

Map VI: Al-Jazīra (see p. 410).
From MS. Sprenger 5—Ahlwardt 6034 by kind permission of the Staatsbibliothek
Preussischer Kulturbesitz, Berlin, Orientabteilung.

of their tribes. The first from the side of al-ʿIrāq is Diyār Rabīʿa; then Diyār Mudhar, then Diyār Bakr; in it also are four related areas.

Diyār Rabīʿa of which the capital is al-Mawsil; among its towns are al-Hadītha, Maʿlathāya, al-Hasaniyya, Tall ʿAfar, Sinjār, al-Jibāl, Balad, Adhrama, Barqaʿid, Nasībīn, Dārā, Kafartūthā, Raʾs al-ʿAyn, Thamānīn. Its related area is Jazīrat Ibn ʿUmar: its towns, Fayshābūr, Bāʿaynāthā, al-Mughītha, al-Zawazān.

Of Diyār Mudhar, the capital is al-Raqqa; some of its towns are al-Muhtariqa, al-Rāfiqa, Khānūqa, al-Harīsh, Tall Mahrā, Bājarwān, Hisn Maslama, Tarʿūz, Harrān, al-Ruhā. The related area: Sarūj, Kafarzāb, Kafarsīrīn.

Of Diyār Bakr, the capital is Āmid; among its towns are Mayyāfāriqīn, Tall Fāfān, Hisn Kayfā, al-Fār, Hādhiya; and there are others.

p. 138

Of the towns of al-Furātiyya (the Euphrates district) the largest is Rahbat Ibn Tawq; then Qarqīsiyā, ʿĀna, al-Dāliya, al-Hadītha.

The capital of the Khābūr area is ʿArābān; of its towns are: al-Husayn, al-Shamsīniyya, Maykasīn, Sukayr al-ʿAbbās, al-Khaysha, al-Sakīniyya, al-Tunānīr.

Al-Mawsil (Mosul) is the metropolis of this region. It is a splendid city, beautifully built; the climate is pleasant, the water healthy. Highly renowned, and of great antiquity, it is possessed of excellent markets and inns, and is inhabited by many personages of account, and learned men; nor does it lack a high authority in the Traditions, or a celebrated doctor of the law. From here come provisions for Baghdād, and thither go the caravans of al-Rihāb. It has, besides, parks, specialties, excellent fruits, very fine baths, magnificent houses, and good meats: all in all the town is thriving. However, the gardens are remote from the city, the south wind is noxious, and the level of the water is far from the surface of the ground, so as to make the drawing of it difficult. The town is in the form of a *taylasān* just as is al-Basra, and is not large in size. Along one-third of its boundary is a building like a fortress, called al-Murabbaʿa (the Square). It lies on the river Zubayda, and is known as Sūq al-Arbaʿaʾ (the Wednesday Market). Within is an expansive area in which the hired people and the harvesters congregate, and at each corner of the area stands an inn. Between the mosque and the riverbank is the distance of a bow shot; it is built on higher ground, and is approached by steps from the side towards the river: fewer steps are on the market side. It is entirely surrounded by arched galleries of *bānāt* (a soft marble) stone. The front of the roofed part of the mosque is without any doors. Most of the markets are roofed. The wells are saline; drinking water is derived from the Tigris, and from the Zubayda river.

Names of some of the main roads here are Dayr al-Aʿlā, Bāslūt, al-Jassāsīn, (the sellers of gypsum), Banī Mayda, al-Jassāsa (the gypsum quarry), the road of the Millstone of the Amīr al-Muʾminīn, of al-Dabbāghīn (the tanners), and the road of Jamīl.

The city lies along the bank of the river, while the palace of the khalif is distant half a *farsakh* from the other side of the river, near ancient Nūnawā. The

p. 139 name of al-Mawsil used to be Khawlān, but when the Arabs extended their abodes to this place, and appointed it their centre, it was named al-Mawsil. Nūnawā (Nineveh) is near al-Mawsil; it is the city of Yūnus, son of Matta. It was guarded by a fortress which the wind has thrown down. Now it consists of cultivated fields, beside which flows the river al-Khūsar. Mar Juhayna is situated on the Tigris, towards al-Mawsil and towards al-ʿIrāq; it has many dovecotes, and a fortress built of gypsum and stone. The mosque stands in the centre of the town.

Al-Hadītha is also on the Tigris, situated on an acclivity so that steps lead up to it. The mosque is close to the riverbank, and is shaped like a *taylasān* [semi-circular in form]. The buildings are of clay, with the exception of the mosque. This town is on the east bank of the river.

Maʿlathāyā is towards Āmid; it is small, has many gardens, and is situated along the banks of a stream. The buildings are of clay, and the mosque is on a hill.

Al-Hasaniyya is on a river that approaches from Urmiya: this is the river over which stands the [masonry] Bridge of Sanja. The mosque is in the middle of the town, and the river flows beside it.

Thamānīn, a town situated on a copious stream which flows from Armenia, at the foot of Mount al-Jūdī. Abū Saʿīd bin Hamdān related to me that he had the following tradition from Abū Hāmid al-Julūdī, who had it from Abū Hāniʾ, who said his father told him he had it from ʿAbd al-Munʿim bin Idrīs, who had it from his father, who had it from Wahb bin Munabbih: when Noah came out of the ark, he built a town and named it Thamānīn ("eighty"); this was the first town after the Flood, and Noah built it according to their number, a house for every one of those who were with him; moreover, it is the first town ever built in al-Jazīra.

Jazīrat Ibn ʿUmar: a large town around which water flows on three sides, the Tigris flowing between it and the mountain. It is a very fine, pleasant place, its buildings are of stone, and it is situated on the east bank of the Tigris. It is muddy in winter.

Bāʿaynāthā is a delightful and pleasant place. It is divided into twenty-five quarters, with gardens and streams interpenetrating. There is not the like of it in al-ʿIrāq: it is a place of plenty, and low prices.

p. 140   Balad is on the Tigris, which here has an abundant flow; in it are many castles. It is well-built of gypsum and stone. The markets are spacious, the mosque in the center of the town.

Adhrama is a small town in the steppe; the inhabitants get their drinking water from wells; their buildings are dome-shaped.

Barqaʿīd is somewhat the same, except that it is larger.

Nasībīn is more delightful, smaller, but broader than al-Mawsil. It has an abundance of fruits, excellent baths and lofty palaces. The people are prosperous and refined. The market extends from gate to gate, and a citadel of stone and cement stands over the town; the mosque is in the middle of the town. But may God protect us from the scorpions of this place!

Dārā is small and pleasant. An aqueduct distributes water throughout the town; it is carried over the housetops, and after gushing out at the mosque it drops into a low-lying area. The buildings are of black stone and cement.

Sinjār is in a waterless desert: palm trees are there in abundance. Shoemakers are here in great numbers, and the mosque is in their quarter. The people's drinking water is from a stream of passably good water, and from numerous springs.

Ra's al-ʿAyn is on a plain, where the lower portion has many holes made by the water, which gushes forth in springs. Here is a small lake in which the water is to a depth of about two fathoms, so clear that a *dirham* thrown into it could be seen on the bottom. Their buildings are of stone and gypsum. They have gardens and cultivated fields. Three hundred sixty springs combine their fresh waters here to form a stream that flows to al-Raqqa. [In fact to Qarqīsiya]

Āmid is a well fortified town with beautiful and remarkable buildings. It resembles Antākiya, having an encircling outer wall shaped somewhat like a chair, with gates and parapets. Between the walls and the fortress is an extensive open space. The town is smaller than Antākiya, and is built of hard black stone, as are also the foundations of the houses. It has a number of springs to the west of the Tigris, and is spacious and attractive. It is a frontier town for the Muslims, and an inexpugnable fortress. The mosque is in the centre of the town. The town has five gates: the Water Gate, the Mountain Gate, the Gate of the Romaeans, the Hill Gate, and the Gate of Anas [also named Bāb al-Sirr, "the Secret Gate"]. The last named gate is small, and is required in time of war. The fortress is built partly on the mountain. Some of the forts are on a hill; I know of no town that the Muslims have today that is better fortified, or an outpost more important than Āmid.

Mayyāfāriqīn is a pleasant, well-fortified town, with battlements, an encircling stone wall, and a ditch; however, there is a poverty of learning, and of gardens. Drinking water is from springs and a stream. It is muddy in winter, a filthy place, and truly the sewer of the region.

p. 141 Al-Jibāl (al-Janāb?)is a secure town having a fortress and suburbs. A mosque stands at the edge of the town. The drinking water of the inhabitants is from canals of middling water, their buildings are of stone and clay. The town wall is by no means well fortified.

Tall Fāfān lies in the direction of the mountain between the Tigris and the Razm. It is surrounded by gardens, and prices there are low. The markets are roofed, and their buildings are of clay.

Hisn Kayfā is a place of abundance. A strong citadel is there, and many churches. The drinking water of the inhabitants is from the Tigris. Al-Fār and Hādhiya are smaller towns.

This then is all we know about the towns of this district. With regard to Bidlīs, different opinions are expressed, which we mention in the region of al-Rihāb.

Al-Raqqa is the capital of Diyār Mudhar, on the Euphrates. It is fortified by a broad wall, on top of which two horsemen can ride abreast. It is not a large town and has two gates, yet it is a pleasant restful place. It was platted long ago, and has good markets and many villages and gardens. The land is bounteous, and yields the finest soap, and olives. It has a remarkable mosque and very good baths. Its markets are roofed and shaded, its palaces highly decorated. The name of the town is well known in both provinces: Syria is on its border, and the Euphrates is on its side. Learning flourishes there. However, the Arabs surround it on all sides, and the roads to it are difficult. Al-Raqqa al-Muhtariqa (Raqqa, the Burnt) is close to it, but it is abandoned and in ruin. Al-Rāfiqa is the suburb of al-Raqqa; its mosque stands in the Goldsmiths' quarter, while the mosque of al-Raqqa is in the Drapers' quarter. In this latter mosque are two jujube trees and a mulberry. Close by is a mosque supported by a single column.

Harrān is a most pleasant city, over which stands a fortress of stone. It is somewhat like Jerusalem in the beauty of its architectural style. There is a channel here the source of which is not known. The mosque is at the edge of the town. The fields are irrigated from wells. It produces most excellent cotton. The integrity of the weights and measures here is proverbial.

Al-Ruhā is on the design of al-Tīb, and is fortified. The mosque, somewhat run down, is at the edge of the town. Here is a remarkable church with vaulted galleries decorated with mosaic: it is one of the wonders of the world.

'Arābān is the capital of the district of al-Khābur, on a high hill, and
p. 142 surrounded by gardens. Prices there are low, and there are many cultivated fields. The other towns are more spacious. Of the district of the Euphrates the most important city is al-Rahba, a large town on the desert side. It is in the shape of a *taylasān* [semi-circular], and has a fortress and a suburb. The remaining towns all lie towards the desert, and are flourishing.

A Summary Account of Conditions in this Region

The **climate** and the **customs** of the region of Aqūr approximate those of Syria, and are somewhat similar to those of al-'Irāq. There are hot areas here in which are date palms, such as Sinjār and the towns of the Euphrates. The district of Āmid is cold because of its proximity to the mountains; of its towns, the healthiest climate is that of al-Mawsil (Mosul). Most of the buildings are of stone. I am not aware of any bad water here, pestilential river valley, or food that is not appetizing. There are no Magians at all here; Sabians are found in al-Ruhā and Harrān only, in the entire realm. Here is no lake, nor does the country border on the sea. Its preachers are of little repute, and there is no mart for matters of the spirit.

With regard to their **religious sects**, they are followers of tradition and corporate authority, except in ʿĀna, where Muʿtazilites abound. Of the rationalists you find only the schools of Abū Hanīfa and al-Shāfiʿī. Some Hanbalites are there, and a manifest faction of Shīʿa. There is no temptation to heresy to divide the hearts of the people, for their jurists do not exchange views on scholastic theology. They prefer the system of reading of ʿAbd Allāh ibn ʿĀmir.

The contention between the Bajāt and the Abyssinians occurred while I was at Zabīd, and the Qādhī deputed me to lead them in the sunset and night prayers. One day he said to me: "The congregation is certainly thankful to you, but I have a rebuke for you." Said I, "On what ground? May God strengthen the Qādhī!" Said he, "You are a man who has devoted himself to the study of the law according to the practice of the people of al-Kūfa. Why then do you not read according to their system, and what is it that has inclined you to reading according to the system of Ibn ʿĀmir?" Said I, "There are four reasons." Said he, "What are they?" Said I, "The first reason is this: Ibn Mujāhid has related three traditions about Ibn ʿĀmir. The first of these is that he read the *Qurʾān* under the discipline of ʿUthmān bin ʿAffān; the second is that he heard the *Qurʾān* from ʿUthmān when he was a boy; the third is that he read it under a person who had himself read under ʿUthmān. Now this can not be said of any other master of recitation. In fact, between every one of them and ʿAlī, ʿAbd Allāh, Ubayy or Ibn ʿAbbās, there are two men or three. So the one, then, between whom and ʿUthmān—on whose version of the *Qurʾān* the Muslims have decided unanimously, and agreed, without exception, on its compilation, and used it with one another time after time—such a man, I say, is more worthy to be followed in reading than another between whom and one whose compilation is not used anyway, and on whose version of the *Qurʾān* there is no agreement, there are two men or three. Furthermore, I looked at the old copies of the *Qurʾān* in Syria, Egypt and al-Hijāz that are attributed to ʿUthmān, and they are not at variance with the reading of Ibn ʿĀmir one whit.

p. 143

"The second reason: I have noticed the system of Ibn ʿĀmir to be consistent. If he uses the 't' or makes a difficult pronunciation in one case he employs it in all similar instances; whereas others say, 'in such-and-such a *sūra* it is "t" and in such-and-such a *sūra* it is "y"', and read in one place *saddan*, in another place *suddan*; and again *kharājan* and *kharjan*, *kurhan* and *karhan*, and similar instances of this are many. Now, as a man who has always exerted himself in the study of the law, I deemed the system of Ibn ʿĀmir more admissible as far as I am concerned, and closer to the methods of jurisprudence.

"The third reason is that I have found that the other readers have from three to thirty different readings being attributed as derived from them; however, Ibn ʿĀmir has no one except Yahyā through whom he transmitted the reading. Anyway the differences in his readings are as heard from Yahyā, because both Ibn Dhakwān and Hishām bin ʿAmmār were readers under the discipline of Yahyā, so I was satisfied that he had a sound knowledge and certainty of his reading.

"The fourth reason is that I am a man from Syria, and even though I had separated myself from the school of law there, nevertheless I do not wish to separate myself from them in a style of reading the superiority of which is unquestionable as far as I am concerned." Then said the Qāḍhī: "How capable you are, O Abū ʿAbd Allāh, and how splendid your affirmation. In fact this reading now has risen in my esteem after it had been one of those I had no particular use for." Now, should a disputant say: "And has not Ibn ʿĀmir been inconsistent in a number of places," I should answer: "Had he not been inconsistent I should make no use of his reading, and we would indeed have been uncertain about it, because reading should not be learned according to analogy. But when he was inconsistent with us we knew that he was in fact adhering to an authority and deriving from him; and his transmission is entirely consistent with the rules". If such a one should say: "But did not our predecessors challenge him, and find fault in some words," I answer: "No one of the authorities in reading was exempted from attack. Do you not see how they attacked ʿĀsim and Hamza in the word *dhaʿf* (*Qurʾān*, sūra 8, v. 66), and Abū ʿAmr in *nansaʾhā* and in *hādhayni*? But the distinguished scholars vindicated them to the public at large, and pronounced their views correct. In any case, no one attacks the acknowledged authorities but an ignoramus." If he should say that Ibn ʿĀmir is relatively unknown, and his reading undistinguished, I should reply to him: "Had Ibn ʿĀmir been in al-Ḥijāz or al-ʿIrāq he would not have been unknown, nor would his reading have been exceptional. But since he was in Egypt, in a remote part of the realm, few sought him out to learn from him, and few transmitted his style of reading. Do you not see that al-Awzāʿī was one of the great scholars in jurisprudence, and his system has fallen into disuse for this same reason? However, if these two men had been on the route of the pilgrims, people from the east and from the west would have disseminated their systems." Now if this person should continue and say, "Are you not one of those who have met the masters of knowledge and piety, and do not most of them forbid exceptionally private systems of reading, and prefer that in general usage?" I should reply, "Yes! but while I have traveled about, meeting the master readers, I liked to read before them, and thus benefit from them. So when I would read according to the generally accepted system they would belittle me and assign me to their disciples; but when I read after an individual system, they took personal interest in me."

The **waters** of this region are plentiful, most of them deriving from the Tigris, the Euphrates, and the Khābūr, this last a river that comes from springs the waters of which collect and flow into the Euphrates. As for the source of the Tigris of al-ʿIrāq, it emerges from under Kahf al-Zulamāt (the Cave of the Dark Regions), its water green. It is later joined by a number of streams, on its way to where the Zāb joins it. Where it starts the Tigris cannot turn more than one mill wheel. The first river to join it is the River Dhīb, next is the river al-Rams,

p. 144

p. 145 then al-Masūliyāt. Below this it crosses al-Kārūkha. Further on it receives the Sarbat, then the spring of Tall Fāfān; then the river al-Rizb, then the Zāb, after which you are in al-ʿIrāq. There is a saying that the Euphrates is blessed, the Tigris accursed.

A number of articles of **commerce** are produced in this region. From Mosul come grains, honey, *namaksūd* (dried meat), coal, fats, cheese, honeydew, sumac, pomegranate seeds, pitch, iron, metal buckets, knives, arrows, most excellent salted fish, and chains. From Sinjār come the kernels of almonds, pomegranate seeds, reeds, and sumac. From Nasībīn: chestnuts—a nut somewhat bigger and more delicious than the hazelnut, and not round; also dried fruits, balances, inkstands, and beating rods for fulling. From al-Raqqa: soap, olive oil, reed pens; from Harrān: *qubbayt* [preserves of locust fruit and nuts], honey of bees in earthen wine jars, cotton, and balances. From al-Jazīra: walnuts, almonds, clarified butter, and the very finest horses; from al-Hasaniyya: cheese, partridge, chickens, cheeses of the Shīrāz variety, dried fruit, and raisins. From Maʿlathāyā, dairy products, coal, grapes, fresh fruit, cannabis seed, hemp, and dried meat. From Balad, biestings in jars, carried by boat: a jar fetched five *dānaqs*, and contains five *manas* [*mana* equals two pounds]. From al-Rahba quinces of the most surpassing excellence; from Āmid, woolen cloths and Romaean linens of the type made in Sicily.

The **specialties** of this region are horses, soap, chains, leather straps; and the *qubbayt*, cotton, and balances of Harrān.

Dry measures: these are the *mudd*, the *makkūk*, the *qafīz*, and the *kāra*. The *makkūk* equals fifteen *ratls*, and the *mudd* a fourth of this. The *kāra* is two p. 146 hundred forty *ratls*, the *qafīz* a fourth of this. The *makkūk* is a fourth of a *qafīz*. The *ratls* of this region are the same as those of Baghdād; and their *farq*, also the same as that of Baghdād, equals thirty-six *ratls*.

The **vernacular** is standard and refined, and more correct than that of Syria, since the people here are Arabs. The best language is that of Mosul, where the people also are the most handsome of face. This town also is more healthy in climate than the rest of the region. The city contains people from most of the tribes, but the greatest number among them are the Hārithī.

There are **sacred places** here: in the countryside near Mosul are the Mosque of Jonas, and other places associated with his name. Close to Ancient Nūnawā is a place known as Tall Tawba (Hill of Repentance) atop which is a mosque, and residences for the devout. It was built by Jamīla, daughter of Nāsir al-Dawla, and she settled a considerable bequest on it. It is said that seven visits to it equal a Pilgrimage to Makka; it is visited on Thursday nights. It is the place whither the people of Jonas went when they were convinced of impending chastisement. Half a *farsakh* from this place is ʿAyn Yūnus (the Spring of Jonas). Outside the town of Balad is a spring out of which it is claimed Jonas emerged: healing of leprosy is sought in its waters. Here is a mosque in his name, and also the place of the gourd plant. (*Qurʾān*, sūra 37, v. 146).

A *farsakh* distant from Mayyāfāriqīn is Dayr Tūmā (Monastery of St. Thomas), in which is a body, desiccated, standing erect, and claimed to be that of one of the apostles of Jesus Christ. The Fortress of Dhu al-Qarnayn is on the way to al-Rihāb; it is strong and well equipped. Below it is the Cave of Darkness which Dhu al-Qarnayn entered. Maslama, son of ʿAbd al-Malik was bent on entering it, procuring torches and candles; but they were extinguished and he returned.

Among the **marvels** of this region: at Nasībīn is a spring from which flows white lime, and it is used as lime in baths and houses. In the area of Mosul is Dayr al-Kalab [the Monastery of Hydrophobia] whither is carried one bitten by a rabid dog; if the person remains with the monks of this monastery for fifty days, he is made to recover by the grace of God, the Most High. In this district also is a spring, and whoso drinks from it dies after three days. A *barīd* [two leagues] distant from Mosul is the village of Bāʿashīqā, where a plant grows that whoso plucks it, should he be suffering from haemorrhoids or scrofula, his disabilities fall away from him. Indeed, were a person suffering these two p. 147 afflictions to send a man with a *dirham* and a large needle to a community there who inherit the capability, and were any one of them to carry the needle to where this plant grows, and pluck it in the name of the afflicted one, this one is cured, though he were in al-Shāsh; the other man may use the *dirham* for himself.

It used to be said that the wonders of the world are three: the Lighthouse of Alexandria, the [masonry] Bridge of Sanja, and the Church of al-Ruhā; however, when the Masjid al-Aqsā was built it was substituted for the church. When the earthquake demolished the Masjid, the Mosque of Damascus, in turn, was substituted for it. This Bridge of Sanja is distant five *farsakhs* from Mount al-Jūdī; it is a large, overtowering bridge and goes as far as the mountain. It is constructed on intersticed stone, and when the water overflows it, it sways.

We must certainly give an account of al-Qustantīniyya (Constantinople), seeing that the Muslims have a house there in which they gather and profess their religion. There have been many conflicting reports and false statements about this place, and about the city itself, its dimensions and its architecture, so I thought I should portray it to the eye, and clarify it to the mind. I should, too, mention the routes thither, as the Muslims are in need of this when they purpose to ransom prisoners, send dispatches, invade, or conduct trade.

Know that when Maslama, son of ʿAbd al-Malik, invaded the country of the Romaeans and entered this metropolis, he imposed as a condition on the Romaean Dog [*i.e.* the Emperor of Constantinople] that he build a house opposite his palace on the race course, in which notables and persons of rank could reside if taken prisoner: in this way they would be under his protection and care. He consented, and built Dār al-Balāt [Palatium; Royal Court]. The Balāt itself is situated beyond the race course, and here the royal silk brocade is manufactured.

Constantinople is about the size of al-Basra, perhaps smaller; its buildings are of stone. It is fortified as other cities are, but protected by one fortress alone. The sea touches one side of it, and the racecourse is on its shore. Dār al-Balāt and the royal palace are in a line, with the racecourse between the two buildings, their doors facing each other. In the middle of the racecourse is a platform with p. 148 steps going up to it. None of the Muslims may reside in Dār al-Balāt except notables, and these are officially privileged, and may promenade. The rest of the prisoners from the commonalty of the Muslims they enslave, and engage them in productive tasks. The discreet man, therefore, is he who, when asked about his craft, does not reveal it. Sometimes the prisoners may trade with one another and profit themselves. This people does not compel any one of their prisoners to eat the flesh of swine, neither do they pierce the nose or slit the tongue.

From the palace of the [Romaean] Dog to Dār al-Balāt a midway stretches, and on it stands the image of a horse in bronze. At times appointed the inhabitants meet for sporting contests; in these contests the name of the king is "Waynatwā" and the name of the chief minister is "Brāsiyāna." [see Edward Gibbon, *The History of the Decline and Fall of the Roman Empire, cap.* XL-ii] If they want to make a prediction from their games they form two groups, and race horses around the platform. If the horses of the party of the [Romaean] Dog come first they say that the Romaeans will have the victory, and they shout, "Waynatwā, Waynatwā." If the horses of the minister's party should win, they say that the victory will be to the Muslims, and shout, "Brāsiyānā, Brāsiyānā," and they go to the Muslims, and give them robes of honour; but they are jealous of them, because theirs is the victory.

The city has very fine markets, prices are low, and fruits plentiful.

There are Muslims also in the towns of al-Tibn, as well as Maʿdin al-Nuhās, also in Atrābazund (Trebizond).

The most direct route to al-Qustantīniyya is through this region, and because of this we have described it in it. The frontier town of this region was Malatya and its communities, but the enemy has laid them waste.

Distances Along the High Roads In This Region

From Mosul to Mar Juhayna
    or to Balad
    or to al-Mahlabiyya
    or to Mazāriʿī
    in every case one stage:

p. 149 Then from Marjuhayna to al-Hadītha one stage;
    thence to al-Buqayʿa one stage;

thence to al-Sinn one stage;
from Balad to Barqaʿid one stage;
thence to Adhrama one stage;
thence to al-Mūnisa one stage;
thence to al-Nasībīn one stage;
thence to Dārā one stage.

Then from al-Mahlabiyya to al-Shahhājiyya one stage;
thence to Tall Aʿfar one stage;
thence to Sinjār one stage.

Then from Mazāriʿi to Maʿlathāyā one stage;
thence to al-Hasaniyya one stage;
thence to Thamanīn one stage;
thence to Jazīrat Ibn ʿUmar one stage;
thence to Tall Fāfān one stage.

From Mosul to Shahrazūr sixty *farsakhs*.

From Āmid to Mayyāfāriqīn one stage;
thence to Arzan one stage;
thence to Masjid Uways one stage;
thence to al-Maʿdin one stage;
thence to Bidlīs one stage.

From Āmid to Shimshāt one stage;
thence to Tall Hūm one stage;
thence to Jarnān one stage;
thence to Bāmaqrā one stage;
thence to Jullāb one stage;
thence to al-Ruhā two *barīds*;
thence to Harrān the same;
thence to Bājarwān one stage;
thence to al-Raqqa half a stage.

From al-Rahba to Qarqīsiyā one stage;
thence to al-Dāliya or to Bīrā one stage.

p. 150 From Qarqīsiyā to Fudayn one stage;
thence to al-Sukayr one stage.

From Āmid to Tall Hawr one stage;
thence to Malatīn one stage;

thence to Tabūs one stage;

thence to Shimshāt one stage;

thence to al-Faʿūniya one stage;

thence to Hisn Ziyād one stage;

thence to Malatīn one stage;

thence to ʿArqa one stage;

thence to al-Safsāf one stage;

thence to al-Rummāna one stage;

thence to Samandū two stages;

thence to Marj Qaysāriyya one stage;

thence to Anqira four hard stages;

thence to Jasr Shāghir in the country of Ibn al-Malātī three stages;

thence to al-Niqumūdhiyya one stage;

thence to Malʿab al-Malik (the King's Theatre), one stage;

thence to Hārifa one stage;

thence to al-Qustantīniyya one stage.

As desired, one may go from Mayyāfāriqīn to Mūsh four stages; thence to Qunb one stage;

thence to Sinn Nuhās one stage: this is at the crossing of the roads of Qālīqalā, Malāzkird, Mūsh, and al-Khālidāt, from which it is distant two stages.

Thence to Samūqamūsh a like distance;

thence to Qalūniyat al-ʿAwfī two stages;

thence to Nafshāriya four stages;

thence to Martyrs' Pass [ʿAqabat al-Shuhadāʾ] one stage;

thence to al-Aflāghūniya (Paphlagonia) one stage;

thence to al-Sūnisha one stage;

thence to Namūlisa one stage;

thence to Balad Ibn al-Suwānītī one stage;

thence to Dūsaniya one stage;

thence to Bāhū-riya(?) one stage;

thence to Qatābūlī, where Muslim troops are stationed, one stage;

p. 151   thence to Balad Ibn al-Malātī two stages, and this place provides a hospitable reception for Muslims.

Thence to al-Buhayrat al-Hulwa (the Fresh Water Lake) one stage;

thence to Hisn Sāʿis one stage.

The Region of Al-Shām (Syria)

The region of Syria is splendid! Syria the abode of the Prophets, the habitation of the righteous, the home of the successors of the Prophets. It is the destination sought by the upright. It contains the First *Qibla* [*i.e.* Jerusalem], the scene of the Day of Resurrection, and of the Night Journey of the Prophet; the Holy Land, caravanserais most excellent, frontier posts most commanding, mountains eminent. Here are the places to which Abraham migrated, also his grave. Here too are the habitations of Job, and his well; the oratory of David, and his gate; the wonders of Solomon, and his cities; the tomb of Isaac and his mother; the birthplace of the Messiah, and his cradle; similarly the village of Tālūt (Saul), and his river; the place of the slaying of Jālūt (Goliath), and also his fortress; the cistern of Jeremiah, and his prison; the place of prayer of Uriah, and his house; the dome of Muhammad, and his gate; the Rock of Moses; Rabwa ʿIsā (the hill of Jesus); the oratory of Zakariyyā, and the battleground of John; the shrines of the prophets; the villages of Job, and the habitations of Jacob. The Masjid al-Aqsā (Further Mosque) is there; Jabal Zaytā (Olivet); the city of ʿAkkā; the Shrine of Siddīqā; the grave of Moses; the resting place of Abraham and his grave; the city of ʿAsqalān; the spring of Sulwān (Siloam); the home of Luqmān (*Qurʾān*, sūra 31, v. 12); the Valley of Kanʿān; the cities of Lot; and the place of the Gardens; ʿUmar's mosques and ʿUthmān's *waqf* (endowment); the gate named by the two men (*Qurʾān*, sūra 5, v. 23); also the chamber to which were brought the two disputants (*Qurʾān*, sūra 50, v. 41); the wall that will separate those punished and those pardoned (*Qurʾān*, sūra 57, v. 13); the Near Place [Dome of the Rock]; the Shrine of Baysān; the gate of Hitta great and glorious; the Gate of al-Sūr (the Trumpet); and the Place of Certain Truth; the tombs of both Mary and Rachel; the meeting place of the two seas (*Qurʾān*, sūra 18, v. 60), and the dividing place between the two worlds (*Qurʾān*, sūra 57, v. 13); the Gate of al-Sakīna (the Divine Presence), and Qubbat al-Silsila (the Dome of the Chain); the station place of the Kaʿba, together with shrines, too numerous to count, and excellences that cannot be hidden; fruits and abundant prosperity, trees and water. This land provides for the needs of this world and the next; for here the heart is cheered and worshippers extend their bodies in prayer. Then of course there is Damascus, the paradise of this earth, and Sughar which is like a miniature Basra; beautiful Ramla, with its white bread, and Īliyā (Jerusalem) p. 152 the splendid, without tribulation; Hims is famous for low prices and excellent air; the mountain of Busrā with its vineyards should not be forgotten; nor Tiberias, renowned for its crops and its villages.

The [Romaean] sea extends along the west side of this region, with freight coming and going on it constantly; too, the Sea of China [Indian Ocean] touches it on the further side. Here are plains, mountains, low valleys, and other features; and the desert lying on its borders is a corridor from it to Taymāʾ. Here are quarries of marble, and the ingredients to compound every medicine. People of wealth, and of commerce, and of refinement, as well as jurisprudents, scribes, artisans, physicians, all live here. However, the people live in dread of the Romaeans, as if they were in a foreign land, for their frontiers have been ravaged, and their border defenses shattered.

Neither are the people here the equals of the Persians in science, religion, and intelligence. Some have apostasized, while others pay tribute, putting obedience to created man before obedience to the Lord of Heaven. The general public is ignorant and churlish, showing no zeal for the holy strife, no rancour towards enemies.

It has been said that Syria has been called al-Shām because it is to the left of the Ka'ba; others say it is because one goes to the left, or north, in traveling thither. Others say that it is so called for the beauty spots—like moles on the skin—there, red, white, and black.

The learned of al-'Irāq call all the territory that, from their side, is beyond the Euphrates, al-Shām (Syria), and it is in this sense that Muhammad bin al-Hasan uses the term in his works. However, as a matter of fact, none of the land beyond the Euphrates pertains to Syria, excepting the district of Qinnasrīn only; the rest is the Desert of the Arabs, and Syria is what lies beyond that again. Of course Muhammad wishes to use the expression only in general terms, and according to accepted usage, just as Khurāsān is called al-Mashriq (the East), even though, properly speaking, the East is the territory beyond that again. It can be said that al-Shām is that portion of country opposite to al-Yaman, with al-Hijāz lying between the two. But supposing someone were to say: "There is no denying that the extreme edge of the desert even to the borders of al-'Irāq pertains, in fact, to Syria, for this agrees with what the learned of al-'Irāq have said," we would reply that we have apportioned the regions and defined the boundaries, and we must not assign to one region what pertains to another. And if someone should say: "What is your authority for saying that it was not part of it in ancient times?" then we should say that jurists and geographers have never disagreed that this land here under dispute pertains to the Peninsula of the Arabs. If anyone considers this area part of Syria, and is not speaking in general terms, we simply say to him that the boundaries of Syria are as we have drawn them, and that this is generally accepted. Moreover, we say, the tract you are adding is in dispute, and on whoever makes the claim for this addition must lie the burden of proof.

p. 153   We have omitted altogether the description of Tarsūs and its district inasmuch as it is in the hands of the Romaeans. However, as for the Cave [of the Seven Sleepers], the city to which it belongs is, in fact, Tarsūs, and here also is the tomb of Daqyānūs. [Decius, *Lat.* Decianus, Roman Emperor 249-251 C.E.] In its countryside is a hill on which is a mosque, said to be built over the Cave. The jurisprudent Abū 'Abd Allāh Muhammad bin 'Umar al-Bukhārī has told us a tradition which he received from Abū Tālib al-Yamānī, who had it from al-Hasan bin Yahyā, who had it from his father, who had it from Muhammad bin Sahl al-Khurāsānī, who told him that he had attended the lectures of Hishām bin Muhammad, to whom Mujāhid bin Yazīd related the following: "I went forth with Khālid al-Barīdī [Royal Courier] when he was sent on an embassy to the Romaean despot in the year 102/720; nor was there a third Muslim with us. Having visited Constantinople, we set out to return by ʿAmmūriya, whence after traveling four nights we arrived at Lādhiqiyya al-Muhtariqa ["the Burnt"]. We finally arrived at al-Hawiyya, lying in a depression in the mountains. Here we were told that there were some dead bodies, their identities unknown, but with guards over them.

"The people had us enter an underground passage, some fifty cubits long and two cubits broad. We had lamps with us, and behold, in the middle of the tunnel was an iron door, this being a hiding place for their families during the incursions of the Arabs on them. There were considerable ruins here, in the midst of which was a pit, full of water, about fifteen cubits across, and from here the sky was visible. The cavern from here entered the interior of the mountain, and we were led to a hollow right in the bowels of al-Hawiyya, about twenty cubits in length. Behold, here were thirteen men, lying on their backs, on each one of them a cloak, I know not whether of wool or of camel's hair, but they were dust coloured, also a garment, dust coloured, which crackled as crackles the parchment. The face of each one, and the rest of his body, were covered by the garment, which was fringed, on some were boots halfway up the leg, some had sandals, and some had shoes: everything looked new. I uncovered the face of one of them, and lo, there was the hair of his head, and that of his beard altogether unchanged; the skin of his face was radiant, and the blood in his cheeks evident, as if they had lain down but just a moment before. Their limbs were lithe as the limbs of a living man. All were youths, except for some whom age had turned gray. Now, one had been decapitated, and on an enquiry to some people about it they replied, saying: 'The Arabs overwhelmed us and took posession of al-Hawiyya. We related the story of these men, but they would not believe us, and one of them struck off the head of this one.'

p. 154   "The men of al-Hawiyya further asserted that at the beginning of each year, on the feast day devoted to these men, they assemble here and raise the bodies up, man by man, so that they put them into an upright position. Then they wipe them and shake the dust from their clothes, and smooth out their garments, while the bodies do not fall or totter; they just lay them down on the ground again. Moreover, they trim their nails three times a year, for these continue to grow. We then asked for an account of these people and their origins, but they declared that they knew absolutely nothing about the matter, saying only: 'We call them the prophets.'" Mujāhid and Khālid themselves are of the opinion that these are the Companions of the Cave—but God knows best.

The form of the region, and representation of it are on the next page. [Map VII]

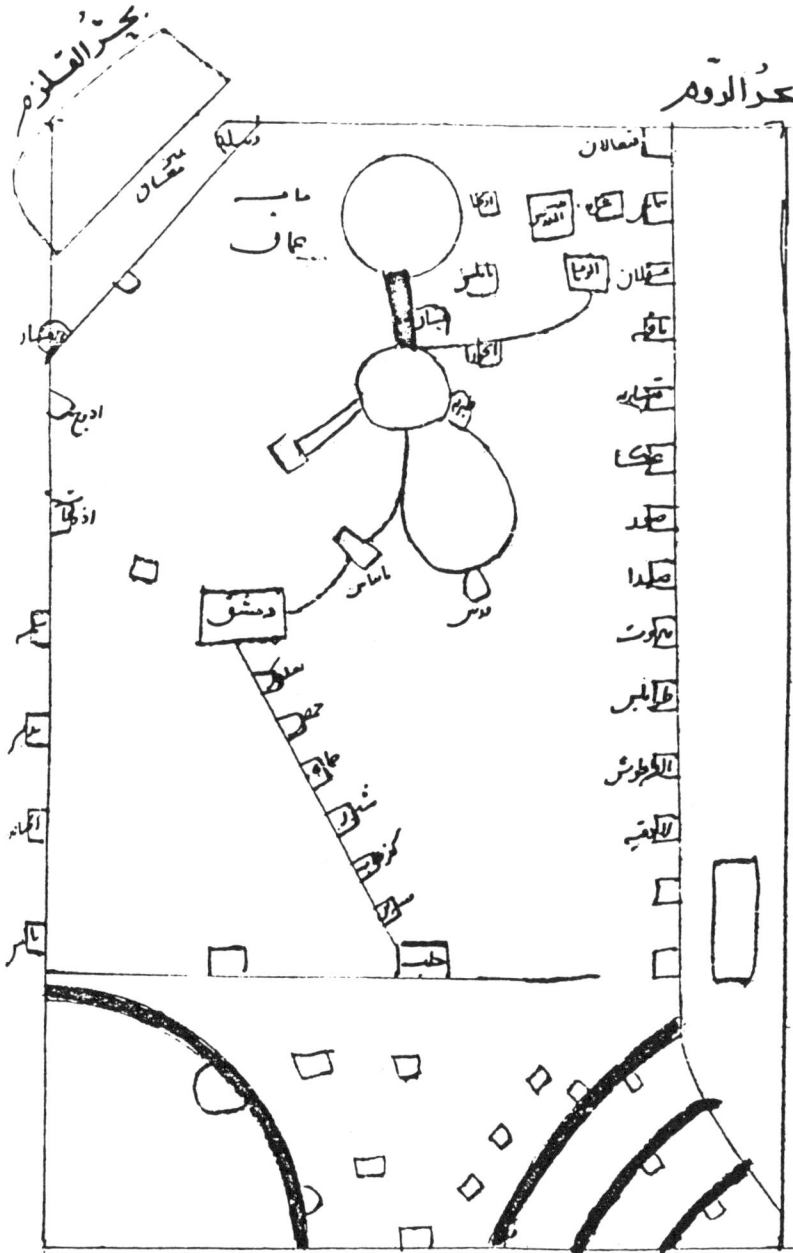

Map VII: Al-Shām (see p. 411).
From MS. Sprenger 5—Ahlwardt 6034 by kind permission of the Staatsbibliothek
Preussischer Kulturbesitz, Berlin, Orientabteilung.

We have divided this region into six districts. The first as you go from Aqūr (Mesopotamia) is Qinnasrīn; then Hims; then Dimashq (Damascus); al-Urdunn (Jordan); Filastīn (Palestine); then al-Sharāt.

The District of Qinnasrīn. Its capital is Halab (Aleppo), and among its cities are Antākiya (Antioch), Bālis, al-Suwaydiyya, Sumaysāt, Manbij, Bayyās, al-Tīnāt, Qinnasrīn, Marʿash, Iskandarūna (Alexandretta), Lajjūn, Rafaniyya, Jūsiya, Hamāt, Shayzar, Wādī Butnān, Maʿarrat al-Nuʿmān, Maʿarrat Qinnasrīn.

The District of Hims [Homs, Emesa]. Its capital bears the same name. Among its cities are: Salamiyya, Tadmur (Palmyra), al-Khunāsira, Kafartāb, al-Lādhiqiyya, Jabala, Antarsūs [Antartūs], Bulunyās, Hisn al-Khawābī.

The District of Dimashq (Damascus). Its capital is of the same name. Its cities are: Bāniyās, Saydā (Sidon), Bayrūt, Atrābulus (Tripoli), ʿArqa.

The territory of al-Biqāʿ. Chief city, Baʿlabakk; towns Kāmid, ʿArjamūsh, and al-Zabadānī.

p. 155 The District of Damascus includes six rural territories: al-Ghūta, Hawrān, al-Bathaniyya, al-Jawlān, al-Biqāʿ, and al-Hūla.

The District of al-Urdunn. Its capital is Tabariyya (Tiberias). Among its towns are: Qadas, Sūr (Tyre), ʿAkkā (Acre), al-Lajjūn, Kābul, Baysān, Adhriʿāt.

The District of Filastīn (Palestine). Its capital is al-Ramla. Its towns: Bayt al-Maqdis (Jerusalem), Bayt-Jibrīl, Ghazza (Gaza), Mīmās, ʿAsqalān (Ascalon), Yāfā (Jaffa), Arsūf, Qaysāriyya, Nābulus, Arīhā (Jericho), ʿAmmān.

The District of al-Sharāt: we consider Sughar its capital. Its chief towns are: Ma'āb (Moab), Muʿān, Tabūk, Adhruh, Wayla, Madyan.

In this region are villages more splendid and larger than many of the chief towns of the Peninsula, such as Dārayyā, Bayt-Lihyā, Kafar Sallām, and Kafar Sābā. However, as they have the characteristics of villages they are considered as such; for, as we have said, we use the designations employed in general usage.

Halab is a superb, delightful, fortified city, its inhabitants refined, prosperous, and gifted. The buildings are of stone and in excellent condition. In its midst stands a strong and spacious citadel, with its own water supply; and here also is the ruler's treasury. The great mosque stands in the town. The inhabitants derive their drinking water from the Quwayq River, which enters the town close to the Palace of Sayf-al-Dawla, through an iron grille. Though the town is not large, yet it is the seat of government. The city has seven gates: the Gate of Hims, the Gate of al-Raqqa, the Gate of Qinnasrīn, the Gate of the Jews, the Gate of al-ʿIrāq, the Gate of the Watermelon Market (Bāb Dār al-Bittīkh), and the Gate of Antākiya. The Gate of the Forty (Bāb al-Arbaʿīn) is now closed.

Bālis, situated on the extreme point of the boundary towards al-Raqqa is a flourishing place.

Qinnasrīn is a town of which the number of the inhabitants has dwindled. The worthy Shaykh Abū Saʿīd Ahmad bin Muhammad related to me at Naysābūr that he had it from Abū Bakr Muhammad bin Ishāq bin Khuzayma, that he had p. 156 it from Abū ʿAmmār bin Hurayth al-Marwazī, that he had it from al-Fadhl Abū

Mūsā, that he had it from ʿĪsā bin ʿUbayd, that he had it from Ghaylān bin ʿAbd Allāh al-ʿĀmirī, that he had it from Abū Zurʿa, that he had it from ʿAmr ibn Jarīr, who heard the Prophet—God's peace and blessings be upon him—say: "God, may He be exalted and glorified, spoke to me in a revelation, saying: 'At whichever of these three places you alight, that will be the abode of your migration—al-Madīna, Bahrayn, or Qinnasrīn'."

Now, if someone should say: "Why have you considered Halab the capital of the district, while here is a town bearing the same name?" I reply to him: "I have already stated that the capitals are compared with generals, and towns with troops. Hence it would not be right that we assign to Halab, with all its eminence, and its being the seat of government and the location of the government offices, or to Antākiya with all its excellence, or to Bālis, with its teeming population, the position of towns subordinate to a small and ruined city."

But should he say: "Why have you not employed similar reasoning in the instance of Shīrāz, associating with it Istakhr and its towns?" we reply that, as there are some towns around Istakhr at some distance from Istakhr itself, we have deemed it appropriate to deal with the matter just as we did. In fact expediency, in this science of ours, sometimes may supersede the rule, as we have pointed out in questions pertaining to *Mukātib* [negotiated enfranchisement of a slave]. Do you not see how postponement of payments by reason of Nayrūz (vernal equinox) and Mihrajān (autumnal equinox), although deemed irregular in other official matters is, nevertheless, admissible in *Kitāba* [installments payable on the bond of freedom in the matter of *Mukātib*] as a matter of expediency?

Hims—there is not in Syria a larger city than this. A citadel stands high above the town, which you may descry from afar. Most of the drinking water is from rainfall, and there is also a river. When the Muslims conquered this town they took over the church, and made half of it into a mosque. Nearby in the market place is a dome on the summit of which is the figure of a man wrought in brass, standing on a fish which the four winds cause to rotate. About it many stories are told, but not to be believed. This town has suffered violent disorders, and is falling into ruin. The people there are stupid.

The other towns here are also going to ruin. Prices are moderate all over, and those towns on the coast are well fortified.

Tadmur (Palmyra) is in similar condition and it is, as it were, built on an elevated throne. It is one of the cities of Solomon, the son of David. It has a fortress close to the desert, spacious and substantial.

Dimashq (Damascus) is the metropolis of Syria, the royal residence in the days of the House of Umayya. Here are their palaces, and their monuments. The houses here are of wood and mud-brick. The city is commanded by a fortress, which was being restored while I was there, built of clay. Most of the markets p. 157 are roofed, one of them, running the length of the town, being spacious and well built. It is a town crisscrossed by streams, and encircled by trees. There is an abundance of fruits there, and prices are moderate. Snow is to be had there, and every other conceivable kind of thing. No more magnificent hot baths than theirs are to be seen, nor more beautiful fountains, nor more worthy people. Such as I myself know of its gates are: the Jābiya gate, the gate al-Saghīr (Small), the gate al-Kabīr (Great), the gate al-Sharqī (Eastern), the gate of Tūmā (Thomas), the gate of al-Nahr (the River), the gate of Mahāmiliyyīn (those who make camel litters).

Though it is indeed a very fine city, yet the air is unpleasantly dry; the people are rowdy, the fruit is insipid, the meat tough, the houses are cramped, the alleys gloomy. The bread is of very poor quality, and a livelihood is difficult to make. The city is about half a *farsakh* in length and in breadth, and stands on a level plain.

The mosque is easily the finest the Muslims now have, and nowhere among them is a collection of wealth greater than here. Its foundation walls are of squared stones, accurately cut, fitting closely together, and of large size: topping them are splendid battlements. The columns supporting the roof are black polished pillars, in three rows, and set wide apart. In the center, fronting the *mihrāb*, is a great dome. Around the courtyard are lofty arcades set with smaller arches, and the whole area is paved with white marble. The walls, for a height of twelve feet, are faced with a variegated marble, and above this, even to the ceiling, are mosaics of various colours; in the gilded part are representations of trees and towns, together with inscriptions, all of the most remarkable beauty and delicacy and refinement of workmanship. Indeed, few are the kinds of tree, and few the well-known towns that are not represented on these walls. The capitals of the columns are overlaid with gold, and the vaulting above the arcades is everywhere adorned with mosaic. The columns around the court are all of white marble; while the walls that enclose it, the vaulted arcades, and the small arches above are adorned in mosaic with arabesque designs. The roofs are everywhere overlaid with sheets of lead, and the battlements on both sides are faced with mosaic work. To the right in the courtyard is a Treasure House, raised

p. 158   on eight columns; it is finely ornamented and the walls are covered with mosaic. Within the *mihrāb*, and surrounding it, are set carnelian and turquoise stones of the largest size. To the left of this is another *mihrāb*, inferior to it, for the special use of the ruler. The centre of this *mihrāb* had fallen somewhat into decay; but I learn that he has expended on it five hundred *dīnārs*, and restored it to its former condition. On the vertex of the cupola is a citron, above that a pomegranate, both in gold. But of the most remarkable of the sights here is the setting of the variegated marbles, every vein matched with the one beside it. Should an artist frequent this place over a year, he might discover every day some new pattern and some fresh design. It is said that al-Walīd assembled for its construction skilled artisans from Persia, India, Western Africa, and Byzantium, and spent thereon the revenue of Syria for seven years, together with eighteen shiploads of gold and silver that came from Qubrus (Cyprus); all this is beside what the Emperor of the Romaeans gave him in the matter of materials and mosaics.

Addition/version MS. C.

Mosaic work (*fusāfisā*) is a product made from glass in the shape of a two-*dirham* weight, yellow, dust-coloured, black, red, variegated, and gilded; gold is worked on to the front of the piece, and over that a thin glaze. Plaster is steeped in gum arabic, spread on the wall, and this *fusāfisā* is set into it. Images, inscriptions, and other patterns are formed in it, all of them gilt; and you perceive the entire wall gilded and sparkling.

The people enter the mosque by four gates. The first, Bāb al-Barīd [the gate of the postal mail] gives access to the right-hand side [of the courtyard]. It is of great size and has a postern to the right and to the left of it. Every one of these—the larger gate and the posterns—has double doors covered with plates of gilded copper. Over the main gate and the posterns are three porticoes, and each door opens into an arcade vaulted over, with the arches resting on marble pillars, the walls covered in the way we have already described. All the ceilings are embellished with the most exquisite designs. In these arcades is the place of the secretaries and the court of the deputy of the Qādhī. This gate is between the covered part of the mosque and the courtyard. Opposite to it, on the left-hand side is the second, Bāb Jayrūn, which is similarly appointed, except that its arcades are vaulted over in the breadth. You ascend to this gate by steps, and here sit astrologers and other such people. The third, Bāb al-Sāʿāt (the gate of the Hours), is in the eastern angle of the covered part of the mosque: its double doors are without embellishment. Over it are arcades under which are seated the notaries and the like. The fourth gate is the Bāb al-Farādīs (gate of the Gardens), also with double doors. It is opposite the *mihrāb*, and leads into the arcades between the two additions here, on the right and on the left. Above it rises a minaret, recently built and ornamented in the manner already described.

Beside every one of these gates is a pavilion for ablutions, tiled with marble, with closets within which the water runs; and fountains which flow into great basins of marble. From al-Khadhrā', the palace of the ruler, are gates leading to the *maqsūra*, plated with fine sheets of gold.

Now, talking to my father's brother one day said I: "O my uncle, surely it was not fitting for al-Walīd to expend the resources of the Muslims on the mosque at Damascus. Had he expended as much in building roads, or the water tanks, or in repairing the fortresses, it would have been more proper and more to his credit." Said he: "You simply do not understand, my dear son. Al-Walīd was absolutely right, and it was open to him to do a worthy work. For he saw that Syria was a country settled by the Christians, and he noted there their churches so handsome with their enchanting decorations, renowned far and wide, such as are the Qumāma, and the churches of Ludd (Lydda) and al-Ruhā. So he undertook for the Muslims the building of a mosque that would divert their attention from the churches, and make it one of the wonders of the world. Do you not realize how ʿAbd al-Malik, seeing the greatness of the dome of the Qumāma and its splendour, fearing lest it should beguile the hearts of the Muslims, hence erected, above the Rock, the dome you now see there?"

Addition / version MS. C.

The people enter the mosque via four doors—Bāb Jayrūn, Bāb al-Farādīs; Bāb al-Barīd; Bāb al-Sā'āt. Behind the mosque stands the ruler's residence, named al-Khadhrāʾ, from which doors lead to the *maqsūra*; all the doors are overlaid with gilded brass. At each door is a basin for the ritual ablution, paved with marble, containing a water fountain which flows over into cisterns of marble. Compartments paved in marble stand by the doors, in every compartment a basin of marble into which water ceaselessly flows. There is, too, in the mosque a spot where an opening is made once every year, so that the mosque is filled with water to the depth of about a cubit, and so the walls and the floor of the mosque are washed. Then another spot is opened so that all the water seeps away through it.

I have found it stated in a book in the library of 'Adhud al-Dawla that the two brides of the world are Damascus and al-Rayy; and Yahyā ibn Aktham says: "There are not on earth more delightful places than these three—the Valley of Samarqand, the Ghūta of Damascus, and the Ubulla Canal."

Damascus was founded by Dimashq, the son of Qānī, the son of Mālik, the son of Arfakhshadh, the son of Sām, five years before the birth of Abraham. Al-Asma'ī however says rather, that the name is to be derived from the word p. 160 "Damshaqūhā", that is, "they hurried it up." It is said that 'Umar bin 'Abd al-'Azīz wanted to diminish the resources of the mosque and devote the proceeds to the welfare of the Muslims, but they persuaded him to abandon the project. I have read in a book that there was expended on the building of the mosque no less than the value of eighteen mule loads of gold.

A satirist said of the people of Damascus:

O you who ask concerning our religion!
When you see the splendour of their doctors of the law,
And their mincing walk in public,
Their outward appearance does not reflect their inner secrets.
They have nothing to boast of save a mosque,
And by it have gone beyond their proper limits.
Should a neighbour come to them for a light from their fire
In an eternity they would not give him a live coal.
To their neighbours they are lions—but their enemies
In security strut haughtily in their homes.

This verse is false, however, because their enemies always go in dread of them.

The city of Bāniyās is on the border of al-Hūla, at the foot of the mountain. It is more comfortable and more prosperous than Damascus. Thither have gone most of the people of the frontiers since Tarsūs was taken; it was thus enlarged, and continues to grow every day. An extremely cold river, emerging from under the Mountain of Snow, gushes forth in the middle of the city. This city is the granary of Damascus. It is bounteous to its inhabitants, lying amidst splendid country districts. It must be said, however, that the drinking water there is bad.

Saydā (Sidon) and Bayrūt are two fortified towns on the coast: so too Atrābulus, (Tripoli), which is, however, greater. Baʿlabakk is an ancient city with remarkable ruins, and farms providing an abundance of grapes. The remaining cities of this province are in good condition, and spacious. In Hawrān and al-Bathaniyya are the villages of Job and his lands: the chief city here is Nawā, a source of abundant wheat and grain. Al-Hūla is a source of cotton and flowers: it is low lying and has many streams. The Ghūta [intensively irrigated, highly productive agricultural area, extending some nine miles towards the east and south of Damascus, to the steppe] is a day's journey across it each way, and is beyond description!

p. 161 Tabariyya (Tiberias) is the capital of Jordan and a city of Wādī (the Valley of) Kanʿan. It is situated between the mountain and the lake, cramped, with suffocating heat in summer, and unhealthy. Its length is about a *farsakh*, but it has virtually no breadth. Its marketplace extends from one gate to the other, with its cemetery on the hill. There are eight hot baths here needing no fuel, along with numerous basins of hot water. The mosque is large and fine, and stands in the marketplace; its floor is laid in pebbles, and the building rests on pillars of joined stone.

It is said of the people of Tiberias that for two months they dance, for two more months they glut; for two months they flail about, and for two more months they go naked; for two months they pipe, and for two more months they wallow. The explanation of this is that they dance from the number of fleas, then glut themselves with the lotus fruit; they slap about at the hornets with fly-swatters, to drive them from their meat and fruits; then they go naked from the intense heat; they suck the sugarcane; and then they must wade through their muddy streets. Beyond the lower end of the lake is a great bridge over which goes the road to Damascus. The drinking water is from the lake. All around the lake are villages and palm trees, and on its surface boats pass to and fro. Water from the baths and the hot springs flows into the lake so that its water is distasteful to strangers. Still the water teems with fish, and is easy to digest. The towering mountain overhangs the town.

Qadas is a small town at the foot of a hill, and is a place of plenty. The district of the town is Jabal ʿĀmila. Here are three springs from which the people drink, and they have one bath situated below the town. The mosque is in the market,

p. 162 and beside it is a palm tree. The place is scorching. A lake lies about a *farsakh* away, and the waters debouch into the Lake of Tiberias. Across the river a dam of remarkable construction has been raised, so the water has gathered to form the lake. Along the shore are thickets of the halfāʾ reed, which provides the people their livelihood, for very many of them weave mats and twist ropes therefrom.

In the lake are many kinds of fish including the *bunnī* (a carp), brought here from Wāsit. Many free non–Muslim subjects live here.

Jabal ʿĀmila has a number of delightful villages, and produces grapes and other fruits, olives, and plums. The rainfall waters their farms. The district overhangs the sea, and adjoins the mountain of Lebanon.

Addition / version MS. C.
All the area has important villages, growing olives and grapes. Below Qadas is a small lake beside which is a great stand of esparto, and all this is of much benefit to them: most of the inhabitants weave mats, plait ropes, and fish.

Adhriʿāt is a city close to the desert. It pertains to the country district of Jabal Jarash, which lies opposite to Jabal ʿĀmila. There are many villages here; and Tiberias has flourished because of these two districts called 'Jabal'.

Baysān lies on the river. It abounds in palm trees, and supplies the rice of Palestine and Jordan. Water is abundant everywhere, but it is rather difficult of digestion; [the stream cuts through the town. The mosque stands in the marketplace, and many men of piety live here.—MS. C].

Al-Lajjūn is a city at the start of the frontier of Palestine, in mountain country. Running water is found here; and it is a spacious and delightful place.

Kābul is a coastal town. Here are farms of sugarcane, and here is refined sugar the most excellent.

Al-Farādhiya is a large village having a pulpit in the mosque. Grapes are abundant here, and vineyards. Here water is plentiful, the site delightful.

ʿAkkā (Acre) is a fortified city on the sea; its mosque is very large, having a grove of olive trees in its court, providing sufficient oil for the lamps, with some to spare. It had not been so well fortified as it is now until Ibn Tūlūn visited it. He had seen Tyre, with its fortifications, and the encirclement with walls of its harbour: he wished to construct a like harbour at ʿAkkā. Accordingly, he convened the craftsmen of the province and laid the matter before them; but it was allowed that nobody then knew how to set a construction in water. Thereupon, mention was made to him of my grandfather, Abū Bakr, the architect, and it was asserted that if anyone should have the requisite knowledge, then it should be he. So Ibn Tūlūn wrote to his deputy in Jerusalem to have him send my grandfather to him: he arrived, and the matter was laid before him. Said my grandfather: "This is an easy matter; bring me split trunks of sycamore that are sturdy." He lined up the beams on the surface of the water according to the plan of a land fortress, and bound them one to the other; he left, however, a large opening towards the west. Upon these beams he raised a structure of stones and mortar; and whenever he had laid five courses of stone he would tie them to sturdy pillars, to strengthen the construction. As the beams became more and more weighted they began to sink; and eventually knowing they were resting on the sand, he left them there a full year so they would set solidly. Then he recommenced building from where he had left off; and as the structure reached

p. 163

the old wall he bonded both together and joined the beams. Over the opening he built a bridge, so that the ships every night enter the port and a chain is drawn across, just as at Tyre. It is said that my grandfather was paid for this work the sum of one thousand *dinārs*, besides robes of honour, riding animals, and other considerations, and that his name was inscribed on the work. Before that time the enemy used to make raids on the ships here.

Al-Jashsh is a village close in size to a capital city. It is in the centre of four rural districts close to the sea.

p. 164 Sūr (Tyre) is a fortified town on the sea, or rather in the sea. It is entered through one gate only, over a single causeway, and the sea is around it. The other portion is enclosed by three walls which rise out of the sea; the ships enter the harbour every night, and a chain is drawn across. All this is as described by Muhammad bin al-Hasan in his *Kitāb al-Ikrāh* (*Treatise on Constraints*). Water is brought to the town by an overhead aqueduct. Tyre is really a beautiful and delightful city. Many things are produced there, including specialties. Between Acre and Tyre is a sort of inlet of the sea, hence the saying: "Acre face-to-face with Tyre is found, but you still have to go the way around," that is, around the water.

Al-Ramla is the capital of Palestine. It is a delightful and well-built city. The water is good to drink and flows freely; fruits are abundant, and of every possible kind. It is situated in the midst of fertile rural areas, splendid cities, holy places, and pleasant villages. Trade here is profitable, and the means of livelihood easy. There is not in Islām a more splendid mosque than that here, no more delicious or excellent than its white bread. No lands more favoured, no fruits more delicious! It is situated in a productive countryside, with walled towns and pleasant suburbs. It possesses elegant hostelries and pleasant baths; superb food, and condiments in abundance; spacious houses, fine mosques, and broad streets. It is highly advantaged, being on a plain, yet near to mountain and sea. It has both fig trees and palms; its fields yield without irrigation—in fact it has many advantages and excellences. However, in the winter the place is a slough of mud; in summer a crater of powdery sand: no water flows nor is there anything green; the soil is not moist, nor is there snow. Fleas are everywhere. The wells are deep and salty, and the rainwater is held in closed cisterns; hence

p. 165 the poor go thirsty, and strangers are helpless and at a loss what to do. In the baths a fee must be paid so that the attendants will turn the water wheels. The city is a mile square, and its houses are of finely quarried stone and baked brick. Such as I know of its gates are: the Darb Biʾr al-ʿAskar (Gate of the Soldiers' Well), the Gate of the ʿAnnaba Mosque, the Gate of Jerusalem, the Gate of Baylaʿa, Darb Ludd (the Lydda Gate), Darb Yāfā (the Jaffa Gate), Darb Misr (the Egyptian Gate), and the Dājūn Gate. Close by is a town named Dājūn, with its mosque. The chief mosque of al-Ramla is in the market, more magnificent, more elegant than the mosque of Damascus. It is called al-Abyadh (the White Mosque), and in all Islām there is found no larger *mihrāb* than that here, and after the pulpit in Jerusalem there is no more beautiful pulpit than the one here; it also possesses a splendid minaret. The mosque was built by Hishām bin 'Abd al-Malik. I have heard my uncle say that when the khalif was about to build the mosque, it was reported to him that the Christians possessed columns of marble, then buried beneath the sand, which they had prepared for the church of Bāli'a. Thereupon, Hishām bin 'Abd al-Malik informed the Christians that they must either reveal them to him, or he would demolish the church at Lydda, so as to build this mosque using its columns. They revealed the columns to him, and they are, indeed, rugged, and tall, and beautiful. The floor of the covered area of the mosque is paved with marble, and the courtyard paved with stone tightly fitted together. The gates of the covered part are made of cypress wood and cedar, sculpted in relief, and very beautiful in appearance.

Bayt al-Maqdis (Jerusalem)—there is not among the towns of the provinces one bigger than it; and indeed many capitals are smaller, for example, Istakhr, and Qāyin, and al-Faramā. The cold here is not extreme, neither is the heat, and snow falls but rarely.

<p. 166>The Qādhī Abu al-Qāsim, son of the Qādhī of the two Holy Cities, enquired of me concerning the climate in Jerusalem. "Moderate," said I, "neither hot nor cold in excess." "That," said he, "is the very description of Paradise." The buildings are of stone, and you will not find finer or more solid construction anywhere. There is no more virtuous populace than that here, no better living conditions, no cleaner markets than theirs. Its mosque is of the largest, and nowhere are Holy Places more numerous. Its grapes are first-rate, and its quinces nonpareil. In Jerusalem are all manner of illuminati and physicians, and the hearts of the wise ever yearn towards it. Never for a day are its streets empty of strangers.

Now it happened that one day in al-Basra I sat in the assembly of al-Qādhī al-Mukhtār Abū Yahyā Ibn Bahrām, and the conversation turned on the city of Cairo and others, and it was asked of me what town is the most sublime. Said I, "My own native town." I was asked, "Which is the most delightful?" "My own," said I. It was asked, "Which is the most excellent?" "Mine," said I. It was asked, "Which is the most beautiful?" "My own city," said I. It was asked, "And which is most abundant in good things?" "My city," said I. It was asked, "Which is the most spacious?" "Mine," said I. The assembly were astonished at that and said to me, "You are a learned man, but you pretend to more than can be conceded to you. You may be likened only to the owner of the she-camel in his conversation with al-Hajjāj. He, however, came with his proof!" Said I: "Now, as to my saying that Jerusalem is the most sublime of cities, it is because it unites in itself the advantages of this world and of the next. He who is of the sons of this world and yet yearns after the things of the next, finds their market here; and he who would be of the children of the next world, and yet desire the amenities of this world, he finds them here also. Consider the pleasantness of the climate: the cold there does not injure, nor does the heat afflict. As to its being the finest city, nowhere are to be seen finer buildings, or cleaner than those there, or a mosque more beautiful. As for its being the most abundant in good things, God—may He be exalted—has gathered together there all the fruits of the lowlands, of the plains, and of the hill country, and of every conceivable kind, such as the citron, the almond, the date, the nut, the fig, and the banana, besides milk in plenty, and honey and sugar. As for the excellence of the city, is it not indeed to be the plain

p. 167 of the Resurrection, and the marshalling place on the day of judgment for the risen dead? Now it is true that Makka and al-Madīna are in the ascendant with the Kaʿba and the Prophet—God's peace and blessings be upon him—but truly, on the Day of Resurrection, they will both hasten to Jerusalem, and the excellence of all of them will be encompassed there together. As to its being the most spacious of cities, since all creation is to be assembled there, what place on earth is more extensive than it?" The company were delighted with what I said, and agreed with the truth of it.

However, Jerusalem has a number of disadvantages. Thus, it is said that it is written in the Torah: "Jerusalem is a golden basin filled with scorpions." You will not find any more filthy than its baths, any more highly priced provisions. Few are the learned there, many are the Christians, and these make themselves distasteful in the public places. In the hostelries taxes are heavy on anything that is sold, for there are guards at every gate, so it is not possible for anyone to sell anything on which one might make a profit, except in these places, and then with little gain. The oppressed here have no protectors; the blameless are aggrieved, the rich envied. The jurisprudent is in solitude, and the man of letters disregarded; schools are unattended, and there is no instruction. The Christians and the Jews are predominant here, and the mosque devoid of congregations and assemblies.

Jerusalem is smaller than Makka and larger than al-Madīna. Over the city is a castle, one side of which is against the hillside, the other defended by a fosse. The city has eight iron gates: Bāb Sihyawn (of Sion); Bāb al-Tīh (of the Wilderness); Bāb al-Ballāt (of the Palace); Bāb Jubb Irmiyā (of Jeremiah's Well); Bāb Sulwān (of Siloam); Bāb Arīhā (of Jericho); Bāb al-ʿAmūd (of the Column); Bāb Mihrāb Dāwūd (of David's Oratory).

There is water in Jerusalem in abundance. Hence there is a saying that "there is no place in Jerusalem but where one may get water, and hear the call to prayer." Indeed, few are the houses in which there are not one or more cisterns.

p. 168   Within the city are three great tanks: Birkat Banī Isrāʾīl, Birkat Sulaymān, and Birkat ʿIyādh, and close by are their baths. The water channels of the streets lead to the tanks. In the area of the mosque are twenty underground capacious cisterns, and there is hardly any quarter of the city without a public drinking fountain, even if the water is what drains from the streets. At a valley some six miles from the city two pools have been made, into which flow the torrents of the winter rains. Leading from these two pools, channels to the city carry water to the town in springtime so as to fill the cisterns in the mosque, and those in other places.

The Masjid al-Aqṣā (the Further Mosque) lies at the southeastern corner of the city. Its foundations were laid by David, the length of each stone being ten cubits or less. They are carefully draughted and faced, fitted well together, and are of the hardest material. On these ʿAbd al-Malik built, using small but well-shaped stones, and crenellated it. This mosque was even more beautiful than that of Damascus.

Addition / version MS. C.
... because it had to stand comparison with the great church belonging to the Christians, which was in Jerusalem; so they built the mosque more magnificent than that.

However, an earthquake occurred in the time of the ʿAbbāsids that threw down the covered portion, except the part around the *mihrāb*. When news of this reached the khalif, he was told that not even everything in the treasury of the Muslims would suffice to restore it to its former state. Accordingly, he wrote to the governors of the provinces, and to other commanders, that each one of them should undertake to build a colonnade. So they built it firmer though less elegant in structure than it had been before. That older portion remained, even like a beauty spot amid the new, and it extends as far as the limit of the marble columns. What extends beyond the concrete columns is the new portion.

The covered portion of the mosque has twenty-six doors, and that opposite the *mihrāb* is called Bāb al-Naḥās al-Aʿdham (the Great Brazen Gate). It is p. 169 overlaid with gilded brass, and only a man strong of shoulder and powerful of arm can move a leaf of it. To the right of this are seven large doors, the center one overlaid with gilt plates—and it is the same to the left. On the east side are eleven doors, unornamented. Over the fifteen doors mentioned above is a portico supported on marble columns, built at the instigation of ʿAbd Allāh bin Ṭāhir. In the courtyard of the mosque, on the right-hand side are porticoes supported on marble columns and pillars; on the further side are chambers arched in stone. Over the center of the covered portion of the mosque is a great peaked roof behind a magnificent dome. The ceilings everywhere, except on the further side, are covered with sheets of lead, those on the further side being regularly patterned with large mosaics.

The entire court is paved. In its center stands a platform, as in the mosque at Yathrib (al-Madīna), to which ascend from the four sides wide flights of steps. On the platform stand four domes—the Dome of the Chain, Qubbat al-Miʿrāj (the Dome of the Ascent), and Qubbat al-Nabī (the Dome of the Prophet)— God's peace and blessings be upon him; these three are small, sheathed in lead, and stand on marble columns, being without walls. And in the center stands Qubbat al-Sakhra (the Dome of the Rock), rising over an octagonal building with four gates, each gate facing one each of the flights of steps. These are the Qibla (Southern) Gate, the Gate of Isrāfil, the Gate al-Ṣūr (of the Trumpet), and the Gate of al-Nisāʾ (the Women), which last opens toward the west. All of them are decorated with gold, and closing each one of them is a handsome door of cedar wood, worked in fine bas-relief: these were made at the command of the mother of al-Muqtadir Billāh. At each gate is a vestibule of marble and cedar-wood, to which brass is fitted on the outside; and at these gates are doors also, but they are unornamented. Within the building are three concentric colonnades with columns of polished marble of incomparable splendour and magnificence, and over these a low vaulting. Within these again is another gallery over the Rock—

p. 170 circular and not octagonal, however—with polished pillars supporting round arches. Built above these is the drum of the Dome rising high in the air, with large openings in it: above this, the Dome. The Dome from its great base, and including its pinnacle which rises into the air, is in height a hundred cubits, and may be seen from afar. Atop it is the beautiful pinnacle with a height of that of a man, plus a cubit. The Dome, for all its great size, is entirely covered with plates of gilded brass, while the floor of the building itself, together with its walls, and the drum, from within and without, are ornamented with marble and mosaic, such as we have already described in our account of the mosque at Damascus. The cupola of the Dome is of three sections: the inner one is of ornamental panels, the second is of iron girders made into a truss, done so that the wind may not cause it to sway; and the third is of wood and on these are fixed the outer plates. Through the middle of the cupola is a means of access to the pinnacle by which a workman may ascend to inspect or repair it. As soon as the beams of the sun strike the cupola, and the drum radiates the light, then indeed is this marvelous to behold; in short, I have never seen in all Islām the like of it; nor have I ever heard that in all the realm of the idolaters is the like of this dome to be found. The mosque is entered through thirteen openings, closed by twenty gates: Bāb Hitta (the Gate of Indulgence), the two Gates of the Prophet—God's peace and blessings be upon him—the Gates of Mihrāb Maryam (Mary's Oratory), the two Gates al-Rahma (of Mercy), the Gate of the Birka (Pool) of Banī Isrāʿīl, the Gates al-Asbāt (of the Tribes), the Gates of the Hāshimites, the Gate of al-Walīd, the Gate of Ibrāhīm (Abraham), the Gate of Umm Khālid (the Mother of Khālid), and the Gate of Dāwūd (David).

Of the holy places within the Mosque are the Mihrāb Maryam (Oratory of Mary), Zakariyyāʾ, Yaʿqūb (of Jacob), and al-Khidhr; the Station of the Prophet, and of Jibrāʾīl (Gabriel), the Place of the Ants, and of the Light, and of the Kaʿba, also of al-Sirāt [Bridge over the fire of hell]. These shrines are scattered over the sacred area.

On the north side are no colonnades. The roofed building of the mosque does not extend to the eastern wall, hence it has been said "The queue

p. 171 of worshippers will not be complete here ever." Why this portion was left uncompleted two reasons are given. One is that ʿUmar commanded the people, "Build in the western part of this mosque a place of prayer for Muslims," so they left this portion unoccupied so as not to go counter to his injunction. The other reason given is that if they had extended the main building to the corner, the Rock would not lie opposite the *mihrāb*, and this was repugnant to them. But God knows best.

The length of the mosque is a thousand cubits, using the Hāshimite cubit, and its width is seven hundred. In its ceilings are four thousand wooden beams, seven hundred marble columns. On the roof are forty-five thousand sheets of lead. The dimensions of the Rock itself are thirty-three cubits by twenty-seven, and the cavern which is beneath it will hold sixty-nine persons. Its endowment provides monthly for one hundred *qists* [one *qist* equals two and one-tenth liters, approximately], of olive oil, and in the year they use eight hundred thousand cubits of matting. The attendants of the mosque are assigned to it, solely. Their service was established by ʿAbd al-Malik from the Imperial Fifth of the Prisoners of War, so they are called al-Akhmās (the Quintans). No one besides these may serve, and they take their vigil in turn.

Sulwān (Siloam) is a place on the outskirts of the city. Below the village is a spring with water of moderate quality which irrigates the large gardens bequeathed by ʿUthmān bin ʿAffān for the poor of the city. Lower down again is Biʾr Ayyūb (Job's Well), and it is said that the water of Zamzam visits the water of this well on the Night of ʿArafa [ninth day of the month of the Pilgrimage].

Wādī Jahannam runs from the angle of the sanctuary area to its furthest point, along the eastern side. In the wādī are gardens and vineyards, churches, caverns, chapels, tombs, and other remarkable features, also cultivated fields. In its midst stands a church over the sepulchre of Mary, and overlooking the p. 172 valley are tombs, among them those of Shaddād bin Aws al-Khazrajī, and ʿUbāda bin al-Sāmit.

Jabal Zaytā (the Mount of Olives) overlooks the mosque from the east side of this valley. On its summit is a mosque built in memory of ʿUmar, who stayed here for some days at the capitulation of the city. There is, too, a church here on the spot from which Jesus—peace be on him—ascended; also a place that is called al-Sāhira (the Plain); and I have been informed on the authority of Ibn ʿAbbās that al-Sāhira will be the scene of the resurrection. The ground is pure, never has blood been spilled on it.

Bayt Lahm (Bethlehem) is a village about a *farsakh* away, in the direction of Hebron. Jesus was born here, and here was the Palm Tree (*Qurʾān*, sūra 19, v. 23). Palms do not produce ripe dates in this district, but this happened by a miracle. Here also is a church, incomparable in the country around.

Habrā (Hebron) is the village of Abraham al-Khalīl (the Friend of God)— on him be peace. Within it is a strong fortress said to be of the building of the jinns, being of enormous squared stones. In the middle of this stands a dome of stone, built in Islamic times, over the sepulchre of Abraham. The tomb of Isaac lies forward, in the main building of the mosque, the tomb of Jacob to the rear; facing each prophet lies his wife. The enclosure has been converted into a mosque, and built round about it are rest houses for the pilgrims, so that they adjoin the main edifice on all sides. A small water conduit has been conducted to them. All the countryside around this town for about half a stage has villages in every direction, with vineyards and grounds producing grapes; and apples called Jabal Nadhra, the likes of which are not to be seen, being fruit of unsurpassed excellence. Sometimes here, apples of good quality will sell at a thousand for p. 173 a *dirham*, and indeed one apple alone may weigh one hundred *dirhams*. Much of this fruit is dried, and sent to Egypt.

In Hebron is a public guest house continuously open, with a cook, a baker, and servants in regular attendance. These offer a dish of lentils and olive oil to every poor person who arrives, and it is set before the rich, too, should they wish to partake. Most men express the opinion this is a continuation of the guest house of Abraham; however it is, in fact, from the bequest of Tamīm al-Dārī and others. In any case, it were better, to my mind, to avoid this guest house.

Addition/version MS. C.
Now, the Amīr of Khurāsān—may God, most exalted, confirm his dominion— had assigned to this charity one thousand *dirhams* yearly; moreover, al-Shār al-ʿĀdil bestowed on it a substantial bequest. At the present time I do not know in all the real of al-Islām any house of hospitality and charity more excellent than this one; for the hungry, and the wayfarers may have the best food here, and you find continued here the custom of Abraham; for he delighted during his lifetime in the giving of hospitality, and God—may He be exalted—has caused the custom to be kept going after his death.

A *farsakh* distant from Hebron is a small mountain overlooking the Lake of Sughar (Dead Sea) and the site of the cities of Lot. Here stands a mosque which Abū Bakr al-Sabāhī built; within it is the resting place of Abraham—peace be upon him—which has sunk below the surface of the dry ground about a cubit. It is related that when Abraham saw the cities of Lot in the air he fell prostrate there and said: "I now bear witness that this is in truth the time of Certainty [of death]." (See *Qurʾān*, sūra 74, v. 43-48 and sūra 15, v. 99).

The limit of the Holy City extends over the area around Jerusalem for forty miles, including the capital and dependent towns, twelve miles of the seashore, towns Sughar and Maʾāb, and five miles of desert. To the south it extends to beyond al-Kusayfa and the land parallel to this. To the north it reaches the limits of Nābulus. This land is "blessed," as God—may he be exalted—has declared; the hills are covered with trees, the plains are cultivated, needing neither irrigation nor the watering of rivers. As the two men reported to Moses the son of ʿImrān: "We came on a land flowing with milk and honey."

Addition/version MS. C.
At times I myself have seen in Jerusalem cheese selling at one *dānaq* [a sixth of a *dirham*] for a *ratl*, and sugar for a *dirham* per *ratl*, and for the same price one and one half *ratls* of olive oil, or four *ratls* of raisins.

p. 174   Bayt Jibrīl is a city partly in the plain and partly in the hill country. Its rural district is called al-Dārūm, and here are marble quarries. It is the granary of the capital, the storehouse for the district. It is a country of fruitfulness and abundance, with very fine estates. The population has, however, decreased in number, effeminacy is rife.

Ghazza (Gaza) is a large town on the main road to Egypt, and on the edge of the desert, yet close to the sea. There is here a beautiful mosque, also the monument of ʿUmar bin al-Khaṭṭāb. It is, too, the birth place of al-Shāfiʿī, and has the tomb of Hāshim bin ʿAbd Manāf.

Mīmās, on the sea, is a small fortified town pertaining to Gaza.

ʿAsqalān (Ascalon), on the sea, is a fine city strongly garrisoned. Fruit is abundant here, especially that of the sycamore tree. Its mosque stands in the Market of the Clothmerchants, and is paved with marble. It is a delightful, favoured, excellent, and well-fortified town. Its silk is renowned, its products are plentiful, and life there is delightful. Its markets are attractive, and the guardhouses are excellent. Yet, its harbour is unsafe, its water of middling quality, and its *dalam* (sand tick), noxious.

Yāfā (Jaffa) situated on the sea, is a small town, even though it is the entrepôt of Palestine and the port of al-Ramla. It is protected by a strong fortress, having gates covered with iron plate. The sea gate is wholly of iron. The mosque overlooks the sea, a pleasure to behold; the harbour is superb.

Arsūf is smaller than Yāfā, well fortified and populous. There is here a beautiful pulpit made in the first instance for al-Ramla, but being too small, taken to Arsūf.

Qaysāriyya (Caesarea)—there is not on the Romaean Sea a city more beautiful or with more bounty. It is a wellspring of prosperity, and useful products gush from it. The soil is excellent, the fruits delicious,

Addition/version MS. C.
... and the town is also a source of buffalo milk and white bread.

An impregnable fortress guards it, and well-populated suburbs are protected by the fortress. The drinking water of the inhabitants is from wells and cisterns. It has a beautiful mosque.

Nābulus is situated in the mountains. It has an abundance of olive trees, and it is even called "Little Damascus." It lies in a valley, shut in between two mountains. Its marketplace extends from gate to gate, and another to the centre of the town, while the mosque is in the midst of the town. The town is paved and clean, with a stream of running water through it; the buildings are of stone, and some remarkable mills may be seen here.

Arīḥā (Jericho): this is the City of the Giants, and herein is the gate of which p. 175 God spoke to the Children of Israel (*Qurʾān*, sūra 5, v. 23). It is an abundant source of indigo and has many palms. Its rural district is the Ghawr, where the fields are watered from the springs. The heat here is excessive, snakes and scorpions are numerous.

Addition/version MS. C.
This city is also the home of the theriacal serpents, and the excellence of the theriac of Jerusalem is owing to the use therein of the flesh of those serpents.

The people are tan and swarthy, and fleas abound. Even so, the water is the lightest on the digestion you will find in Islām; bananas are plentiful, as are fresh dates, and fragrant plants.

ʿAmmān, situated on the edge of the desert, has around it many villages and cultivated fields. Its rural district is al-Balqāʾ, rich in grain and flocks. Many streams flow through the town, on which are mills which the water turns. It has a fine mosque beside the marketplace, its courtyard tiled with mosaic. As we have remarked before, this town somewhat resembles Makka. The Castle of Goliath is on a hill overhanging the city. In the city is the tomb of Uriah, over which stands a mosque. Here also is the stadium of Solomon. Living costs are low, fruit is plentiful. On the other hand, the people there are uneducated, the roads thither difficult.

Al-Raqīm is a village lying about a *farsakh* from ʿAmmān, and on the border of the desert. In it is a cavern with two entrances, one small, one large: they say that anyone who enters by the larger is unable to leave by the smaller, without his having a guide. In the cavern are three tombs, concerning which Abu al-Fadhl Muhammad bin Mansūr related to me the following tradition, having had it from Abū Bakr bin Saʿīd, who had it from al-Fadhl bin Hammād, who had it from Ibn Abī Maryam, who had it from Ismāʿil bin Ibrāhīm bin ʿUqba, who had it from Nāfiʿ, who had it from ʿAbd Allāh ibn ʿUmar, who had it from the Messenger of God himself—God's peace and blessings be upon him! It seems that once, while a party of three men were walking, the rain overtook them, and compelled them to a cave in the mountain. But a boulder fell down from the mountain, blocking the mouth of their cave, and they were shut in. Then said one of them to the others: "Direct your attention to God—may He be exalted and glorified—of such good deeds as you have done, and beseech God that therefor perchance He will split open the boulder." Said one of them: "O God, do I not have my parents, venerable and advanced in years, and my little children besides? And I used to pasture sheep to provide for them, and when I would return to them and milk the ewes, would give of the milk to my parents
p. 176 to drink even before giving to my children. However, forced labour detained me one day, so I did not arrive until late in the evening, and behold my parents were sleeping. I did the milking as usual, and brought of the milk, and stood close to their heads, yet dreading lest I should awaken them from their sleep, while at the same time loth to give of it to the children before them, though they were sorely in need of it. Thus I remained until break of dawn. Since Thou knowest I did this to find favor before Thee, do Thou burst open a gap for us through which we may see the sky." So God—may He be exalted—rent open a gap for them through which they saw the sky.

Then said the second one: "O God, was there not the daughter of my uncle whom I loved as passionately as man can? And whenever I sought to possess her, she would refuse herself to me, saying I should bring her a hundred *dīnārs*. So I strove until I collected the hundred *dīnārs*, and brought them to her. But as I lay down between her legs she called out: 'O servant of God, fear God; and break not the seal except in lawfulness.' So I rose up from her. Now Thou knowest that I did that to find favor before Thee, so do Thou open further a gap for us." So God opened the gap further for them.

Said the third, "O God, I hired a serving man for the customary portion of rice, and when his work was finished said he: 'Give me my due.' So I presented to him his due, but he would not accept it, and spurned it. However, I continued to use it for sowing until I acquired from its produce cattle and a herdsman. He eventually came to me and said, "Fear God, and oppress me not, but give me my due." So I replied: "Go thou to those cattle and their herdsman and receive them." Said he: 'Fear God and mock me not.' Said I: 'I do not mock thee; take thou those cattle and their herd.' So he took them and went his way. And as Thou knowest I did that to find favour in Thine eyes; so do Thou split what remains of the rock." And God opened up the way before them.

In this district are large villages possessed of their own mosques, and these are more populous and more flourishing than most of the cities of the Arabian Peninsula. They are well-known places; however, since they have not attained the influence of cities or their splendour, nor are they of the insignificance of villages in their obscurity, but rather wavering in degree, as it were, between the two, it is incumbent on us to mention them specifically and describe their situations. Among these are: Ludd (Lydda), which lies about a mile from al-Ramla. There is here a great mosque wherein large numbers of people assemble from the capital, and from the villages around. Here too is a remarkable church, at the door of which Jesus will slay the Antichrist.

Kafar Sābā, a large place, with a mosque, and on the main road to Damascus.

ʿĀqir, a large village possessing a fine mosque. The people here are given to good works. Their bread is incomparable. It is on the main road to Makka.

Yubnā with its beautiful mosque: this is the source of the excellent fig known as "the Damascene."

ʿAmawās (Emmaus) is said to have been the capital in olden times; however, p. 177 the population moved towards the low-lying land, and towards the sea, on account of the wells, because these are on the edge of the hill country.

Kafar Sallām is one of the villages of Caesarea; it is large, well populated, and has a mosque. It lies on the high road.

This capital has *ribāt* (watch stations) along the sea coast where the men under arms assemble. The warships and the galleys of the Romaeans pull into them, bringing with them captives taken from the Muslims, for ransom at the rate of three for one hundred *dīnārs*. At each of these stations are men who know their language, since they have missions to them, and trade with them in provisions of all kinds. The alarm is sounded when the Romaean ships come into sight: if it be night a beacon is lighted at the station, and if it be by day they make a smoke. From each coastal station to the capital is a series of lofty towers in each of which is stationed a company of men. As soon as the beacon is lighted at the coastal station, it is then done at the next one, and then in turn at the others, so that it is scarcely an hour before the capital is under levy. Drums are beaten at the tower calling people to their respective watch stations. They move out in force, under arms, and the young men of the countryside assemble. Then the ransoming begins. They will exchange man for man, or offer money or jewelry until they ransom all the captives that have been brought. The watch stations in this district at which the ransoming occurs are: Ghazza, Mīmās, ʿAsqalān, Māhūz-(the Port of)Azdūd, Māhūz- (the Port of) Yubnā, Yāfā, and Arsūf.

p. 178   Sughar—the people of the two neighbouring districts call it Saqar ("Hell"); and a Jerusalemite here once addressed a letter to his friends from "Saqar al-Suflā ('Lower Hell') to the Upper Paradise." And indeed this is a country that is deadly to strangers, for the water here is vile; and he for whom the Angel of Death falters, let him travel thither, for I do not know in Islām a place like it in this respect. Indeed I have seen plague-ridden countries, but none the like of this. The people are swarthy and stocky. The waters are hot as hellfire. It is nevertheless a little Basra, and trade there is lucrative. The town stands on the shore of the Overturned Lake (Dead Sea), and is the remnant of the cities of Lot, being spared only because the inhabitants knew nothing of the abominations. The mountains rise up close by.

Maʾāb lies in the mountains. It has many villages, producing almonds and grapes. It is close to the desert. Muʾta is one of its villages, where is the tomb of Jaʿfar al-Tayyār, also that of ʿAbd Allāh bin Rawāha.

Adhruh is an outlying town on the borders of al-Hijāz and Syria. They keep here the mantle of the Messenger of God—God's peace and blessings be upon him—and a treaty from him written on parchment.

Wayla is a town on the edge of a branch of the Sea of China. It is a well-populated and beautiful city, producing palms and fish. It is the port of Palestine, and the entrepôt of al-Hijāz. The general populace call it, "Ayla", but in fact Ayla, now in ruins, is close by here. This is the place of which God—may He be exalted—said: "ask them of the township that was by the sea." (Qurʾān, sūra 7, v. 163).

Madyan is in fact within the borders of al-Hijāz, because the Peninsula of the
p. 179 Arabs includes all that is encircled by the sea, and Madyan is in this tract. Here is the rock which Moses—peace be upon him—removed when he gave water to the flocks of Shuʿayb. Water is here abundant. The weights and measures of this town, and their manners and customs, are those of Syria. About Wayla, the people of Syria, and those of al-Hijāz, and the Egyptians, dispute among themselves as to which province it belongs—just as is the case with regard to ʿAbbādān—but its inclusion in Syria is more reasonable, because the customs of

the people and their weights and measures are Syrian; and it is, too, the port of Palestine, from which the merchant barges sail.

Tabūk is a small town in which stands the mosque of the Prophet—God's peace and blessings be upon him.

A Summary Account of Conditions in this Region

The **climate** of Syria is temperate, except for that portion of the centre of the region from al-Sharāt to al-Hūlah: this area is hot, producing indigo, the banana, and the palm. One time when we were in Jericho, the physician Ghassān, said to me: "Do you see this valley?" Said I: "Yes, indeed." "Well," said he, "it extends from here to al-Hijāz, thence through to al-Yamāma and on to ʿUmān and Hajar; then it goes by Basra on to Baghdād, then up to the left (west) of al-Mawsil to al-Raqqa: it is indeed a wādī of heat and of palm trees."

The coldest place in this region is Baʿlabakk and the area around there. A popular saying here is that "it was asked of the cold, 'Where will we find you?' It said, 'In al-Balqā'. 'But if we find you not there?' it answered, 'Baʿlabakk is my home.' "

This is a blessed region, a land of low prices and of fruits; and of upright people. The area that is upwards towards where the Romaeans are abounds more in streams and fruits, and the climate is colder. The lower area is more favored and more pleasant, the fruits too are more delicious, and it is more abundant in palm trees. There is not in the province, however, a river that is navigable, except by ferries. Learned men are rare, non-Muslims are numerous, as are lepers. There is no respect for preachers. The Samaritans are to be met with there, all the way from Palestine to Tiberias, but you will not meet there either Magians or Sabaeans.

As to **affiliation with schools of theology**, the people of Syria are those rightly guided, upholders of authority and tradition. The people of Tiberias, however, and half the population of Nābulus and Qadas, and most of the people of ʿAmmān, are Shīʿa. The Muʿtazilites have but little presence here, and remain in concealment. At Jerusalem is a community of the Karrāmites who possess cloisters and houses of assembly. You do not meet a follower of the school of Mālik or of Dāwūd in this region. The adherents of al-Awzāʿī hold their assembly p. 180 in the mosque of Damascus. In ritual practice the people of Syria used to follow the role of the Traditionists. The jurisprudents are followers of al-Shāfiʿī. It is the rare city or town where you do not find disciples of Abū Hanīfa, and oftentimes the Qādhīs (judges) are of this school. Now if it should be asked of me: "Why do you not just say that the ritual practices of religion are carried out according to the school of al-Shāfiʿī, considering that the leading scholars there are all of this school?" I reply: "This is the utterance of one who cannot make a distinction. You see, it is the practice of the school of al-Shāfiʿī to recite out loud the 'Bismillāh' (in the name of God), and to recite the *qunūt* during the dawn prayer. But as for us, we do not recite the *qunūt* except in the days of the latter half of the month of Ramadhān, during the '*witr*'. And there are other practices that the people of Syria do not adopt, for they disapprove of them. Was it not seen how, when their ruler ordered the recitation of the 'Bismillāh' out loud in Tiberias, the people protested this iniquity to Kāfūr al-Ikhshīdī because they found his deed utterly repugnant?" Today the ritual is generally according to the practice of the Fātimites, and we shall refer to these, with other of their peculiar customs, in our account of the region of the western countries, if it please God, may He be exalted.

Of the systems of **Reading** the *Qurʾān*, by far the most prevalently followed is that of Abū ʿAmr, except only in Damascus, where none may lead the prayer in the mosque unless he read according to the system of Ibn ʿĀmir, for this is the best-known among the people, and is their choice. The system of reading of al-Kisāʾī has gained ground throughout the region; in any case, they make use of the seven systems of Readings, and strive earnestly to achieve perfection in observing them.

Commerce. The trade of Syria is profitable. From *Palestine* come olive-oil, quttayn (figs), raisins, and locust fruit; poplin, soap, and towels. From *Jerusalem* come cheeses, cotton, the famous raisins known as ʿAynūnī, and Dūrī; excellent apples, and bananas,

Addition/version MS. C.
The banana is a fruit in the form of a cucumber, covered with a skin which is peeled off from the fruit. It is soft like the water melon, though more delicious and sweeter.

the incomparable pine nuts called "Quraysh-Bite"; also mirrors, lamp-jars, and needles. From *Jericho*, indigo of the finest quality; from *Sughar* and *Baysān*, indigo and dates. From *ʿAmmān*, grain, lambs, honey; from *Tiberias*, carpet
p. 181 material, paper, and cloth; from *Qadas*, cloths called "munayyar" and "balʿisī"; also ropes. From *Tyre* come sugar, glass beads, and glass vessels both cut and elegantly formed; from *Maʾāb* the kernels of almonds; from *Baysān*, rice. From *Damascus* come olive oil fresh pressed, balʿisī cloth, silk brocade, essence of violet of an inferior quality, brass vessels, paper, nuts, figs, and raisins. From *Aleppo*, cotton, clothes, potash, and al-Maghra (red ochre); from *Baʿlabakk*, the fig sweetmeat called "Malban".

Unequalled are the quttayn figs, omphacine oil, white bread, the veils of *al-Ramla*; and nonpareil are the quinces, the pine nuts called "Quraysh-Bite", the ʿAynūnī and Dūrī raisins, the theriac, the calaminth, and the rosaries of *Jerusalem*. You should know, moreover, that gathered together in the province of Palestine are thirty-six products not to be found together in any other land. The first seven of these are found only in Palestine; the following seven are rarely found in other countries; and of the remaining two and twenty, though only found assembled together in Palestine, many are found variously associated elsewhere. The first seven are the pine nuts called "Quraysh-Bite", quince, ʿAynūnī and Dūrī raisins, the Kāfūrī plum, the Sibāʿī fig, and the Damascene fig. The next seven are the Colocasia water lily, the sycamore fruit, the locust fruit, the artichoke, the jujube, sugarcane, and the Syrian apple. The others are fresh dates and olives, citron, indigo, juniper, bitter orange, the mandrake, the lotus fruit, the nut, the almond, asparagus, bananas, sumac, cabbage, truffles, lupins, and the early black prune called "al-Tarī"; together with snow, buffalo milk, beeswax, the superb ʿĀsimī grape, and the date fig. There is the preserve called *al-qubbayt* [sweetmeat of carob, almonds, pistaschios]; certainly the like of it may be found elsewhere, but the flavour is different. You also see the lettuce, included usually among the vegetables, except at al-Ahwāz, where it is really of surpassing excellence. Incidentally, at al-Basra, also, it is considered distinct from the more common vegetables.

Measures of Capacity: The people of al-Ramla use the *qafīz*, the *wayba*, the *makkūk*, and the *kaylaja*.

The *kaylaja* equals about one and one half *sāʿ*s.

The *makkūk* equals three *kaylajas*.

The *wayba* equals two *makkūks*.

The *qafīz* is four *waybas*.

The people of Jerusalem are distinctive in that they use the *mudy* (*modius*), and it contains two-thirds of a *qafīz*; and they use the *qabb*, which is a fourth of the *mudy*. They do not use the *makkūk* except in official measurements.

In ʿAmmān the *mudy* is six *kaylajas*; their *qafīz* is half a *kaylaja*, and it is by this measure they sell their olives and *quttayn* figs.

In Tyre the *qafīz* is the same as the *mudy* of Jerusalem, and their *kaylaja* equals a *sāʿ*.

The *ghirāra* of Damascus equals one and one half Palestinian *qafīz*.

p. 182 **Measures of Weight.** Over the area from Hims to al-Jifār the *ratls* are of some six hundred (*dirhams* of weight), though there are variations. The heaviest is the *ratl* of Acre, the lightest that of Damascus.

The *ūqiyya* (ounce) varies from fifty down to forty and a few odd (*dirhams* of weight), and every *ratl* contains twelve *uqiyya*; except only at Qinnasrīn, where it is two thirds of this.

The standard weight of the coinage is approximately the same everywhere, and the *dirham* should weigh sixty grains, the grain being the grain of barleycorn. The *dānaq* should weigh ten grains, the *dīnār* twenty-four *qīrats*, and the *qīrat* is three and one half grains of barley.

Manners and Customs. In Syria their custom is to keep the lamps in their mosques always lighted, and suspend them by chains, as at Makka. In every provincial capital, in the great mosque is a treasury in a chamber resting on pillars. Between the covered portion of the mosque and the court are doors, except at Jericho; and you do not see paving of the court with pebbles, except at the mosque of Tiberias. The minarets are square, and the centres of the roofs of the covered portions of the mosques are ridged. Moreover, at the gates of the mosques, and in the market places, are places for the ablution.

It is customary to be seated between every two *taslīma* of the *tarāwīh*, and some persons recite but once the prayers enjoined to be said in series of uneven numbers (*witr*), though formerly they were said thrice. In my day Abū Ishāq of Marw issued an order as a result of which they made a distinction in this practice in Jerusalem. When the Imām rises to pray at each *tarwīha*, the crier calling the prayer adds the words, "God have mercy upon you"; in Jerusalem they pray six *tarwīhas*. The preachers are usually professional tellers of pious stories; however, the followers of Abū Hanīfa hold their assembly for preaching in the Masjid al-Aqsā, reading from a volume, just as also do the Karrāmites in their cloisters. It is the custom for the guards to proclaim aloud the profession of faith after the Friday prayers. The jurisprudents hold their assemblies between the two day prayers, and between the two evening prayers, and the reciters of the *Qurʾān* also hold their assemblies in the mosques.

Among the Christian feasts that the Muslims here acknowledge, and by which they determine the seasons of the year are: Easter, about the time of *Nayrūz* (the New Year); Whitsuntide, at the time of heat; and the Nativity, at the time of cold; the Feast of St. Barbāra at the time of the rains, and indeed there is a popular saying to this effect: "When the Feast of St. Barbāra comes round, the mason may pick up his flute," meaning that he may as well sit at p. 183 home. There is also the Feast of the Kalends (first day of January), and again one of their proverbs is, "When the Kalends come, sit close to the fire and stay in the house!"—the Feast of the Cross (mid-September) at the time of the grape harvest, and the Feast of Lydda (late April) at sowing time. The months in use here are those of the Romaeans: Tishrīn first and second (October and November), Kānūn first and second (December and January), Shubāt (February), Adhār (March), Naysān (April), Ayyār (May), Hazīrān (June), Tammūz (July), Āb (August), and Aylūl (September).

It is seldom you encounter a jurisprudent here who introduces heretical doctrines, or a Muslim who has a secretaryship; the exception is at Tiberias, which has always produced scribes. I must say that the scribes here, as in Egypt, are Christians, the Muslims simply depending on their knowledge of their language, they themselves not undertaking the literary discipline even as foreigners do. Whenever I was present at the assembly of the Chief of the Qādhīs in Baghdād I used to be embarrassed at how ungrammatical his use of Arabic was; this, however, is not considered a blemish.

Most of the assayers, the dyers, cambists, and tanners in this region are Jews; while the physicians and the scribes are generally Christians.

Let me state here that there are five feasts in five areas in the realm of Islām that have special splendour: Ramadhān [the month of fasting] at Makka; Laylat al-Khatma [the night of completion of the reading of the *Qurʾān*], in the Aqsā Mosque; the two Feasts [ʿId al-Fitr at end of Ramadhān, and ʿId al-Adhha beginning the tenth day of the month of Pilgrimage] in Isqiliyya (Sicily); the Day of ʿArafa [ninth day of the month of Pilgrimage] at Shīrāz; and Friday in Baghdād. In addition to these the middle night of the month of Shaʿban at Jerusalem; and the Day of the ʿĀshūrāʾ [tenth day of Muslim month of Muharram] at Makka are splendidly observed.

The Syrians dress well, both the scholar and the simple wearing the long loose outer *ridāʾ* (cloak). They do not go shod in summertime, except in the use of the single-soled sandal. Their graves are built up in mounds; the people walk behind the bier, and gently draw the corpse, head foremost, from the bier to the grave. In order to complete the reading of the *Qurʾān*, they go to the burial ground for the three days following a person's death.

The people here wear their raincloaks thrown open; and they do not scallop their *taylasāns*. In al-Ramla, the chief cloth merchants ride Egyptian asses, with saddles; it is only Amīrs or Chiefs who ride horses. It is only the villagers and the scribes who wear the *durrāʿa*. The clothing of the rustics in the country district around Jerusalem and Nābulus is the single *kisāʾ* [long shirt-like enveloping garment], and without drawers. Ovens are used here called *furn*; the countrypeople make ovens called *tābūn*, of baked brick, small, and in the ground. These they pave with pebbles, and ignite a fire of dried dung around and above. When the fire has become red–hot the loaves are thrown on the pebbles. There are also in this region cooks who specialize in lentil dishes and *baysār* [a dish containing Jew's mallow, beans, butter, and sometimes meat]. They also set to boil, in olive oil, beans that have sprouted, then fry them; these are sold to p. 184 be eaten with olives. Also, they salt lupine, and eat quite a lot of it. They make from the locust tree a sweetmeat which they call *qubbayt*; that which they make from sugar they call *nātif*. They make *zalābiya* (sweet cakes) in the winter, but they do not plait the dough. In the majority of the above customs they correspond to the people of Egypt; in some few customs the people of al-ʿIrāq and Aqūr resemble them.

Products. There are iron mines in the mountains above Bayrūt, and near Aleppo is the red mineral (*Maghra*), here of excellent quality, some inferior to it being at ʿAmmān. In this region of Syria occur reddish coloured mountains, the material of which is called *samaqa* (sandstone): it is easy to work. There are whitish mountains the material of which is called *hawwāra* (chalk), less hard than the *samaqa*, used to whitewash ceilings, and plaster the roofs of the terraces. In Palestine are quarries of white stone, and a quarry of marble is at Bayt Jibrīl. In the area of the Ghawr are mines of sulphur and other minerals; from the Dead Sea, salt in powder form is derived. The best honey is that from Jerusalem and from Jabal ʿĀmila, derived from the wild thyme. The best *murī* [fish or meat pickle] condiment is that made at Jericho.

Holy Places. We have mentioned most of these in the introductory to this region; were we to enumerate their locations our book would be over-long. However, I will just mention that the greater number of them are in the neighbourhood of Jerusalem, fewer throughout Palestine, and still fewer in Jordan.

Waters. The *waters* of this region are for the most part very good. However, the water at Bāniyās is purgative, that of Tyre, constipating. The water at Baysān is heavy and unhealthy, but God preserve us from that at Sughar! The water of Bayt al-Rām is very bad; however you do not find lighter, more digestible water than that at Jericho. The water of al-Ramla is easy of digestion; but that of Nābulus is rough. The waters at Damascus and Jerusalem are the least rough, for the climate is the least arid.

In this region is a number of *rivers* which flow into the Romaean Sea (Mediterranean), except for the Baradā, which cuts through below the city of Damascus and waters the district, after dividing into a number of branches. It curves around the northern portion of the city, then separates into two streams of which one flows towards the desert and into a fen, while the other descends to join the Jordan river. [The Jordan also is an exception.] The Jordan River flows down from above Bāniyās and forms a lake opposite Qadas; thence descending to Tiberias, it passes into the lake there, descending whence through the valleys of the Ghawr it falls into the Overturned Lake (Dead Sea): this is completely salty, wild, inverted, and stinking. It is set amid the mountains, and has but few waves.

The Romaean Sea bounds Syria on the west, and the Sea of China touches its southern coast. Opposite Tyre is the Island of Qubrus (Cyprus), said to be a journey of twelve days all around it. Here are populous cities, and for the Muslims here are advantages and prosperity, by reason of the abundance of goods coming from there, products including cloth stuffs, and manufactures. It is ruled by whatever power is dominant around there at the time. The distance thither by sea is the sailing of a day and a night; therefrom to the country of the Romaeans is a like distance.

p. 185 **The Remarkable Sights of the Region of Syria.** There is at Jerusalem on the outskirts of the city a cave of immense size. I have heard some of the learned say, and have read, besides, in books, that it leads to the people of Moses. (*Qurʾān*, sūra 28, vv. 76-81; sūra 29, v. 40) I am far from sure of this, for it seems to be but a stone quarry. It has passages throughout along which one may go with torches. Between Palestine and the Hijāz, that is, between al-Ramla and Wayla, are the stones with which the people of Lot were pelted. (*Qurʾān*, sūra 11, vv. 82-83) They lie along the Road of the Pilgrims, are striped, and both large and small.

Near Tiberias are boiling springs that supply most of the hot baths of the town. A conduit has been laid to each bath, so that the steam heats the rooms of the building, and thus there is no need for a fire. In the first compartment you enter, cold water is at hand which may be mingled with the hot in the amount to cleanse oneself, and there are lavatories for the Ablution with this same water. In this area are other hot springs called al-Hamma (hot waters); should one suffering from mange, ulcers, or tumours, or other such maladies bathe himself here for three days, and then bathe himself in another spring which is cold, he will be cured, if God wills it. I have heard the people of Tiberias relate that all around these springs there used to be bath houses, each house for the relief of a specific ailment; anyone with that disease who bathed there would be cured; these bath houses were there right down to the time of Aristotle. He, however, requested of the king of that time the demolition of these bath houses, lest people be able to dispense with the services of physicians. This account, indeed, may very well be true, seeing that on the arrival of every sick person, he is obliged to immerse himself completely in the water of each spring, so that he may attain the one that provides his cure.

The Lake of Sughar (the Dead Sea) is a remarkable place, for the River Jordan and the River of al-Sharāt both pour into it but do not change its condition. It is said that one does not sink easily in its waters; it is said, moreover, that if one has an enema from its waters it will cure him of many disorders. They hold a feast day in the month of Āb (August) when those with bad symptoms and ailments repair thither. In the mountains of al-Sharāt, too, are hot springs.

p. 186   In Palestine, every night in summer when the south wind blows, there falls a dew in such quantity that from it water flows in the drain pipes of the Masjid al-Aqsā.

The Abū Riyāh (wind vane) at Hims is a talisman made to protect against scorpions. If one takes clay and presses it thereon, he will obtain relief from the sting of the scorpion, by the grace of God—may He be exalted; the effect, of course, derives from the image, not from the clay. The cities of Solomon—peace on him—Baʿlabakk and Tadmur, are among the wonders here, as are the Dome of the Rock, the Mosque of Damascus, and the harbours of Tyre and Acre.

Addition/version MS. C.
Jerusalem has a talisman against the bite of serpents; and behind the pulpit in the mosque at Jerusalem is a marble slab bearing an inscription, rather faint, in the veining of the stone, saying: "Muhammad is the Messenger of God." Another slab bears the inscription: "In the name of God, the Most Benignant, the Merciful."

The **situation** of this region (of Syria) is delightful. It may be divided into four zones. The first zone is that which borders the Romaean Sea. It is a plains area, with frequent accumulations of sand and soils of varied qualities. Of the towns here are al-Ramla, and all the cities on the sea coast. The second zone is the mountain country, wooded, with villages, springs, and cultivated fields. Of the cities situated here are: Bayt Jibrīl, Jerusalem, Nābulus, al-Lajjūn, Kābul, Qadas, al-Biqāʿ, and Antākiya (Antioch). The third zone is that of the valleys of the Ghawr wherein are villages and streams, palm trees, cultivated fields, and indigo. Among the towns here are Wayla, Tabūk, Sughar, Arīhā, Baysān, Tiberias, and Bāniyās. The fourth zone is that bordering on the desert. Here, mountains are high and bleak; and though the climate is close to that of the desert, yet it has villages, and springs, and trees. Of the towns therein are Maʾāb, ʿAmmān, Adhriʿāt, Damascus, Hims, Tadmur, and Aleppo. The sacred mountains such as the Mount of Olives, the hills of Siddīqā, of the Lebanon, and of al-Lukkām, are in the second zone; the "Navel of the Holy Land" is in the mountains that overhang the coast.

One day I happened to be present at the assembly of Abū Muhammad al-Mīkālī, the chief doctor of law at Naysābūr, and the jurisprudents were in attendance for open discussion. Abu al-Haytham was asked whether he could provide proof of the acceptability of the *tayammum* with chalk. He advanced as argument the saying of the Prophet—God's peace and blessings be upon him— "Thou hast made the earth for me a place of prayer and a means of purification," extending the meaning to soil of all kinds. Responded the questioner, "Not at all! Only the soil of the plain is intended, and not that of the mountain." Then followed a lot of exchange and discussion, and they delighted in their own loquacity. Then said I, speaking to Abū Dharr bin Hamdān, one of the most disputatious: "We must disavow the speaker of such a faulty argument as this learned jurisprudent has advanced. For has not God—may He be exalted—said: 'Enter into the Holy Land' (*Qurʾān*, sūra 5, v. 21), and is not the same a mountainous country?" So he began to quibble and split hairs, alleging matters that did not at all refute our argument. Then another jurisprudent, Sahl bin al-Suʿlūkī remarked: "He absolutely said only: 'Enter the land'; and not 'Go ye up into the mountains.'" But the discussion was dropped. Now, should someone say to me why it may not be pointed out that the gate to the Holy Land being at Jericho, and God having commanded them to enter thereby; and since Jericho is in the Ghawr and not in the mountains, then that which the Imām, the son of the Imām, adduced was correct: then my refutation of this would be two-fold. First of all is the jurisprudential argument, to wit, that the Holy Land is a mountainous country, without doubt or question whatever, and Jericho is in the plains, and a dependency of it. Now the clear and literal meaning of the verse refers to al-Quds (the Holy City), which is Jerusalem, and which is, indeed, situated in the mountains; it does not refer to the dependencies of the plains or of the valleys of the Ghawr. But if it were maintained that the verse refers to the City of the Giants, that is Jericho, which they were commanded to enter, then the verse applies to both interpretations: entering into the Holy Land, and also into the aforementioned city (Jericho); however the application of the verse, according to your interpretation, is confined to the land alone, despite the fact

p. 187

that the more extended signification we can give a reading of the *Qurʾān*, the better. Further, it may be pointed out that God—exalted be His name—clearly meant the interpretations I have given, by His saying: "And We bequeathed upon the people who languished, all the east and the west of the land We had blessed." (*Qurʾān*, sūra 7, v. 137); without question both the plains of Palestine, and its mountains are intended in this verse. And their [*i.e.*, the Israelites] statement, "there are people in it, oppressors," (*Qurʾān*, sūra 5, v. 22), means "in the vicinity of that area."

The second point of my rebuttal is geographical. Since they [the Israelites] were bade to make their entry into al-Quds (the Holy City), while the "oppressors" were in Jericho, which same lies in the valley of the Ghawr, between the mountain country and the Dead Sea, and seeing that it is not possible for it to be argued that they were bade to go by sea, then the only remaining possibility is their entering the land through the mountains, as, in fact, they did; for they entered it from below al-Balqāʾ and crossed over the Jordan to Jericho. Furthermore, he who persists in the argument is faced with one of two p. 188 conclusions: either that they were commanded not to enter the mountains of the Holy City, or that the mountains of Jerusalem and of al-Balqāʾ are no part of the Holy Land. Whoever would insist on either of these two assertions, it were much better not to argue with him.

Now as for the jurisprudent Abū Dharr, when I urged these arguments on him, said he to me: "You evidently yourself have never entered the Holy City, for had you done so you would know it lies on the plain and not among the mountains." But the leader of the discussion, Abū Muḥammad said, "He comes from there!"

I have heard my maternal uncle, ʿAbd Allāh bin al-Shawā recount how some ruler or other had it in mind to take possession of Dayr Shamwīl, which is a village about a *farsakh* from Jerusalem; so said he to the owner thereof: "Describe your village to me." "My village", said he— "may God support you—

is close to the heavens,
far above the low plains;
in sweet grass is poor,
in acorns, rich;
hard is the labor,
the profit is low.
Weeds are all over,
almonds are bitter.
One bushel you sow,
one bushel you reap;
the seeds that you sow
excel what you reap!"

Said the ruler: "Begone! We have no need for your village."

Now, as for the **lofty mountains** of the region, they are: Jabal Zaytā (the Mount of Olives), which overhangs the Holy City, and of which we have already made mention. There is Jabal Siddīqā, lying between Tyre, Qadas, Bāniyās and Saydā. Here is the tomb of Siddīqā, with a mosque close by, in relation to which a festival is held on the middle day of the month of Shaᶜbān; great numbers of people gather there from the towns all around, and the deputy of the ruler is also present. It so happened that once, when I was staying in this area, and the middle day of Shaᶜbān fell on a Friday, the Qāḍhī Abu al-Qāsim bin al-ᶜAbbās invited me to preach. In my sermon I urged on them the restoration of this mosque, which they executed, and built a pulpit therein. I have heard them assert that a dog in pursuit of a wild animal, reaching the boundaries of this holy place, stops short; and there are other stories of a like kind.

Jabal Lubnān (Mount Lebanon) is a continuation of this mountain. It is well wooded and abounds in fruits that may be eaten communally. Here are a number of small springs, around which devotees have built for themselves huts of straw. They subsist on those communal fruits, and they earn money from cutting the Persian reeds and the myrtle, and other such things which they carry into the towns; all this is sufficient to support them.

Jabal al-Jawlān is over against this, towards Damascus, as we have stated. Here it was I met Abū Ishāq al-Ballūtī, with forty men dressed in garments of wool. These people have a mosque in which they assemble. I found him to be quite a learned jurisprudent, of the sect of Sufyān al-Thawrī. I learned that these people feed themselves on acorns—a fruit about the size of a date, but bitter. They split it, keep it until it turns sweet, then grind it; and here is also a wild barley which they mix with it.

p. 189 Jabal Lukkām is the most populous mountain area of Syria; it is also the largest in extent, and the richest in fruit trees. At present, however, it is in the hands of the Armenians. Tarsūs is beyond these mountains, Antioch on this side of them.

The **government** is in the hands of the ruler of Egypt. Sayf al-Dawla had some time ago gained control of the northern portion of the country.

Taxes in Syria are light, except for those levied on the caravanserais, in which case they are absolutely oppressive, as we mentioned in our account of the Holy City. The *himāyāt* (property taxes) are also heavy. From Qinnasrīn and al-ᶜAwāsim they amount to three hundred sixty thousand *dīnārs*; from al-Urdunn (Jordan), one hundred seventy thousand *dīnārs*; from Palestine two hundred fifty-nine thousand *dīnārs*; from the area of Damascus, upwards of four hundred thousand *dīnārs*. I have seen it said in the book of Ibn Khurradādhbih that the *kharāj* (land tax) of Qinnasrīn is four hundred thousand *dīnārs*, that of Hims three hundred forty thousand, that of Jordan three hundred fifty thousand, and that of Palestine five hundred thousand *dīnārs*.

Addition/version MS. C.

The length of Syria extends from Midyan Shuᶜayb up to the frontiers [with the

Romaeans], and is a journey of thirty-nine days. The width varies: that portion of Syria near al-Hijāz is rather narrow, while that portion towards the frontiers is wider.

p. 190 **Distances Along the Main Roads**
From Halab to Bālis, two days.
From Halab to Quinnasrīn, one day;
    likewise to al-Athārib.
From Halab to Manbij, two days.
From Halab to Antākiya, five days.
From Antākiya to al-Lādhiqiyya, three days.
From Manbij to the Euphrates, one stage.
From Hims to Jūsiya, one stage;
    thence to Ya'āth, one stage;
    thence to Ba'labakk, half a stage;
    thence to al-Zabadānī, one stage;
    thence to Damascus, one stage.
From Hims to Shamsī, one stage;
    thence to Qārā, one stage;
    thence to al-Nabk, one stage;
    thence to al-Qutayyifa, one stage;
    thence to Damascus, one stage.
From Hims to Salamiyya, one stage;
    thence to al-Qastal, two stages;
    thence to Darrā'a, the same;
    thence to al-Rusāfa, the same;
    thence to al-Raqqa, half a stage.
From Hims to Hamāt, one stage;
    thence to Shayzar, one stage;
    thence to Kafartāb, one stage;
    thence to Qinnasrīn, one stage;
    thence to Halab, one stage.

From Damascus to Ba'labakk, or to any of the following places is a two-day journey: Tarābulus, Bayrūt, Saydā, Bāniyās, Hawrān, al-Bathaniyya, and Adhri'āt.

From Damascus to the further limit of the Ghūta, or to Bayt Sar'a is, in either case, one stage.

From Damascus to al-Kuswa is two *barīds*;
    thence to Jāsim, one stage;
    thence to Fīq (Afīq), the same;
    thence to Tiberias, one post-stage (three miles).

From Bāniyās to Qadas or to Jubb Yūsuf (Joseph's Pit) is, in either case, two post stages.

From Bayrūt to Saydā, or to Atrābulus is, in either case, one stage.

p. 191   From Tiberias to al-Lajjūn, or to either Jubb Yūsuf, Baysān, ʿAqabat Afīq, al-Jashsh, or Kafarkīlā, is in every case, one stage.

From Tiberias to Adhriʿāt or to Qadas, one stage.

From ʿAqabat Afīq to Nawā, one stage;
    thence to Damascus, one stage.

From Jubb Yūsuf to Bāniyās, one stage.

From al-Lajjūn to Qalansuwa is one stage;
    thence to al-Ramla, one stage.

If you prefer you may go from al-Lajjūn to Kafar Sābā by the post road, one stage; thence to al-Ramla, one stage.

From Baysān to Taʿāsīr, two post stages;
    thence to Nābulus, the same;
    and thence to Jerusalem, one stage.

From Jubb Yūsuf to Qaryat al-ʿUyūn, two stages;
    thence to al-Qarʿūn, one stage;
    thence to ʿAyn al-Jarr, one stage;
    thence to Baʿlabakk, one stage; this route goes by the name of Tarīq al-Madārij (the Way of the Ladders).

From al-Jashsh to Sūr, one stage.

From Sūr to Saydā, one stage.

From Sūr to Qadas, or to Majdal Salim, is two post stages.

From Majdal Salim to Bāniyās, two post stages.

From Tiberias to ʿAkkā, two stages.

From Jabal Lubnān (Mountains of Lebanon) to Nābulus, or to Qadas, or to Saydā, or to Sūr, is, in every case, about one stage.

p. 192 From al-Ramla to either Jerusalem, or to Bayt Jibrīl, or to ʿAsqalān, or to al-Sukkariyya, or to Ghazza, or to Kafar Sābā, by the post road, is, in every case, one stage.

From al-Ramla to Nābulus, or to Kafar Sallām, or to Masjid Ibrāhīm, or to Arīhā is, in every case, one stage.

From al-Ramla to Yāfā, or to al-Māhūz, or to Arsūf, or to Azdūd, or to Rafh is, in every case, one stage.

From Jerusalem to Bayt Jibrīl, or to Masjid Ibrāhīm, or to the River Jordan is, in every instance, one stage.

From ʿAsqalān to Yāfā, or to Rafh, in each case, is one stage.

From Ghazza to Bayt Jibrīl, or to Azdūd, or to Rafh, is, in every instance, one stage.

From Masjid Ibrāhīm (Hebron) to Qāwūs is one stage; thence to Sughar is one stage.

From Kafar Sābā to Qalansuwa is one stage.

From the River Jordan to ʿAmmān is one stage.

From Nābulus to Arīhā, or to Kafar Sallām, or to Baysān, in every case is one stage.

From Arīhā to Bayt al-Rām is two post stages; thence to ʿAmmān is one stage.

From Sughar to Maʾāb is one stage, and from Sughar to Wayla is four stages.

From ʿAmmān either to Maʾāb or to al-Zurayqāʾ (al-Zarqāʾ) is, in every instance, one stage.

From al-Zurayqāʾ to Adhriʿāt is one stage; and from Adhriʿāt to Damascus is two stages.

From Qaysāriyya (Caesarea) to Kafar Sallām, or to Kafar Sābā, or to Arsūf, or to al-Kanīsa, every instance is one stage.

From Yāfā to ʿAsqalān is one stage.

The Region of Misr (Egypt)

This is the region in ruling which Pharaoh gloried over all mankind (*Qurʾān*, sūra 43, v. 51); and supplied at the hands of Joseph sufficient to feed the inhabitants of the world. There are to be found the vestiges of the Prophets, the Wilderness, and Mount Sinai; the monuments of Joseph, the scenes of the miracles of Moses. Thither fled Mary with Jesus. God has mentioned this region repeatedly in the *Qurʾān*, and has shown its preeminence to mankind. It is one of the two wings of the world; and the excellences of which it can boast are countless. Its metropolis is the dome of Islām, its river the most splendid of rivers. Through its natural prosperity is Hijāz populated, and by its populace the season of the Pilgrimage is enlivened. Its beneficence spreads to the East and to the West, for God placed it between the two seas, and has extolled its reputation in the areas of the sunrise and of the place of sunset. Let me tell you that Syria, with all its greatness, is just a rural district of it, and Hijāz, with its inhabitants, depends on it. It is said to be "the height of land" (al-Rabwa) (*Qurʾān*, sūra 23, v. 50), and its river flows with honey in Paradise. It has become again the abode of the Commander of the Faithful, and Baghdād has been superseded until the Day of Judgment; its metropole has now become the greatest glory of the Muslims. Even so, it has had drought for seven consecutive years; grapes and figs there are dear. The customs of the Copts prevail here, and calamities visit the people constantly.

Misr, the son of Hām, the son of Noah (on whom be peace) colonized the country.

Herewith is an outline and representation of it. [Map VIII]

We have divided the region of Egypt into seven districts, six of which are populated; it has, moreover, some extensive territories, with a number of large villages. Towns in Egypt are not numerous, because the majority of the people of the countryside are Copts; and in accordance with the terms of our science, a town is only so designated if it has a *minbar* [pulpit, i.e., as representing a mosque]. Coming from the direction of Syria, the districts are al-Jifār; al-Hawf; al-Rīf; Iskandariyya; Maqadūniya; al-Saʿīd; and the seventh, al-Wāhāt (the Oases).

Al-Jifār: Its capital is Al-Faramā. Its chief towns are: al-Baqqāra, al-Warrāda, al-ʿArīsh.

Al-Hawf: Its capital is Bilbays, and among its towns are: Mashtūl, Jurjīr, Fāqūs, Ghayfā, Dabqū, Tūna, Barrīm, al-Qulzum.

Al-Rīf: Its capital is al-ʿAbbāsiyya. Among its cities are: Shubrū, Damanhūr, Sanhūr, Banha al-ʿAsal, Shatnūf, Malīj, Mahallat Sidr, Mahallat Karmīn, al-Mahallat al-Kabīra, Sandafā, Damīra, Būra, Daqahla, Mahallat Zayd, Mahallat Hafs, Mahallat Ziyād, Sanhūr al-Sughrā, Barīs.

Al-Iskandariyya (Alexandria): Its capital is of the same name. Among its cities are: Al-Rashīd (Rosetta), Maryūt, Dhāt al-Humām, Burullus.

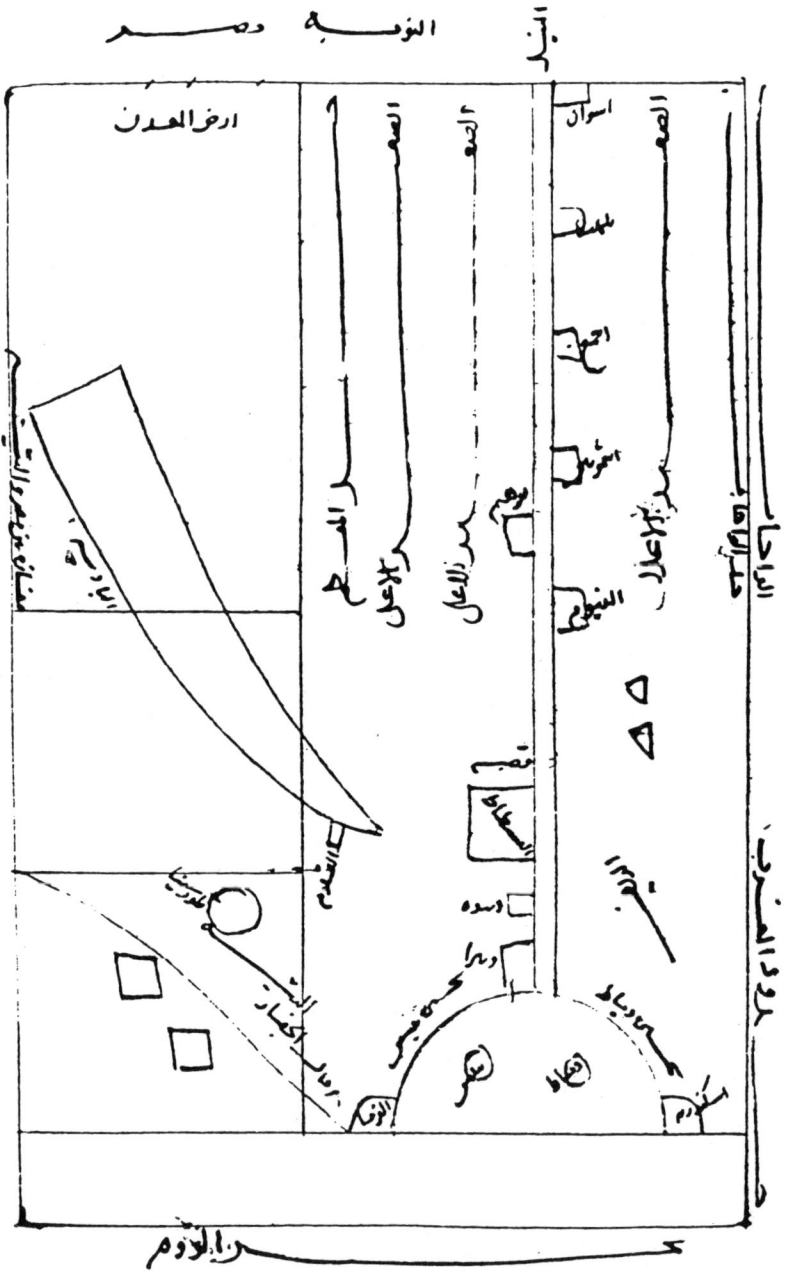

Map VIII: Misr (see p. 412).
From MS. Sprenger 5—Ahlwardt 6034 by kind permission of the Staatsbibliothek
Preussischer Kulturbesitz, Berlin, Orientabteilung.

Maqadūniya: Its capital is al-Fustāt, which is also the metropolis. Among its towns are: Al-ʿAzīziyya, al-Jīza, ʿAyn Shams.

Al-Saʿīd: Its capital is Uswān. Among its towns are: Hulwān, Qūs, Akhmīn, p. 195 Bulyanā, ʿAllāqī, Ajmaʿ, Būsīr, al-Fayyūm, Ushmūnayn, Sumustā, Tanda, Tahā, Bahnasa, Qays.

Close to al-Hawf are two islands in two lakes, on which are situated the towns Tinnīs and Dimyāt (Damietta).

Addition / version MS. C.

The island of Tinnīs and the island of Dimyāt are situated in two small bodies of water connected with the Romaean Sea and the Nile. In this region are villages that have become famous by reason of goods derived from them, for instance Shatā, Tahā, Bahnasa, Qays, Zufaytā, Zuftāf, Zuftatā, and indeed there remain many other towns I do not know about; however the more prominent ones are those I have mentioned. Over against the region, in the Romaean Sea, is the island of Iqrītish (Crete); it is a large island with cities and advantages. The Romaeans had achieved dominion over it; however, the Fātimids have seized it from them.

Al-Faramā on the shore of the Romaean Sea is the capital of al-Jifār, and lies about a *farsakh* from the sea. It is a flourishing populous town, over which stands a fortress, and it has fine markets. The town is situated in a salt marsh, so its water is brackish. The area around it provides hunting grounds for quail, and a source of the most excellent fish. A great variety of contrasting things is to be found here, and an abundance of agricultural products. Here, is the point of junction of well-known and well-traveled roads. However, its water is salty, and the flesh of the birds unhealthy to eat. This entire district of al-Jifār is covered with golden sands, and the towns we have mentioned lie here and there within it. The district is traversed by roads, provides dates, has wells, and at a distance of every six miles there is a mart for supplies. Still, the wind sometimes plays upon the sands, the road is covered, and travel in the area is rendered difficult.

Bilbays is the capital of al-Hawf. It is large and flourishing, with many villages around it, and cultivated fields. The buildings are of mud.

Al-Mashtūl has many mills, whence come most of the supplies of the Hijāz in the way of flour and biscuits. I took a count at one period of the year, and this trade amounted to three thousand camel loads every week, entirely of grains and flour.

p. 196 Al-Qulzum is an ancient town on the edge of the Sea of China. It is a dry barren place, having neither water nor pasture, neither tillage nor animal husbandry; no firewood, no trees, no grapes, no fruit. Water is carried thither in boats, also on camels, from a place some six miles away called Suways (Suez); it is drinkable, but of poor quality. A saying of theirs runs: "The provisions of the inhabitants of al-Qulzum come from Bilbays, their drinking water from Suways; they eat the meat of the billy goat, and for fire burn the rafters of their houses."

The place is, indeed, one of the cesspools of the world. The waters of its baths are of intense saltiness. The place is noisome and depressing, and to get there is difficult. Yet, the mosques here are well built, it has imposing public buildings, and thriving markets. It is the promptuary of Egypt, the seaport to al-Hijāz, a resort for relief to those on the Pilgrimage. One day I bought a *dirham's* worth of groats, to cook it required another *dirham's* worth of firewood! This district has nothing good about it, and I see no merit in mentioning the remainder of its towns.

Al-ʿAbbāsa is the capital of al-Rīf; it is a populous, pleasant, and ancient town. The people derive their drinking water from the Nile. It is a place of fertility and abundance. The buildings are more spacious than the buildings of Misr (the capital). A variety of contrasting products is brought here. It has a fine mosque built of brick—altogether delightful, and distinguished.

Al-Mahallat al-Kabīra has two sides [on the river], the name of the further side being Sandafā. On each of these sides is a mosque, that of al-Mahalla being in its centre, that of the other side pleasantly situated on the river bank. The side of al-Mahalla is more populous, and has a fine oil market. The people travel back and forth in boats, and it seemed to me to look very much like Wāsit.

Damīra extends along the river bank; it is populous, and produces a melon of outstanding quality.

p. 197 Al-Iskandariyya (Alexandria) is a delightful town on the shore of the Romaean Sea. Commanded by an impregnable fortress it is a distinguished city with a goodly meed of upright and devout people. The drinking water of the inhabitants is derived from the Nile, which reaches them in the season of its flood via an aqueduct, and fills their cisterns. It resembles Syria in climate and customs; rainfall is abundant; and every conceivable type of product is brought together there. The countryside round about is splendid, producing excellent fruits, and fine grapes. It is a clean town, and their buildings are of the kind of stone suited for maritime construction; it is also a source of marble. It has two mosques. On their cisterns are doors which are secured at night so that thieves may not make their way up through them. The remaining towns here are very well developed; and in the surrounding area grow locust, olives, and almonds, and their cultivated lands are watered by the rain. It is near here that the Nile debouches into the Romaean Sea. It is the city founded by Dhu al-Qarnayn (Alexander the Great), and has, indeed, a remarkable citadel.

Al-Fustāt is a metropolis in every sense of the word; here are together all the departments of government administration, and moreover, it is the seat of the Commander of the Faithful. It sets apart the Occident from the domain of the Arabs, is of wide extent, its inhabitants many. The region around it is well cultivated. Its name is renowned, its glory increased; for truly it is the capital city of Egypt. It has superseded Baghdād, and is the glory of Islām, and is the marketplace for all mankind. It is more sublime than the City of Peace [Baghdād]. It is the storehouse of the Occident, the entrepot of the Orient, and is crowded with people at the time of the Pilgrimage festival. Among the capitals there is none more populous than it, and it abounds in noble and learned men. Its goods of commerce and specialties are remarkable, its markets excellent as is its mode of life. Its baths are the peak of perfection, its bazaars splendid and handsome. Nowhere in the realm of Islām is there a mosque more crowded than here, nor people more handsomely adorned, no shore with a greater number of boats. It is more populous than Naysābūr, more splendid than al-Basra, larger than Damascus. Victuals here are most appetizing, their savories superb. Confectioneries are cheap, bananas plentiful, as are fresh dates; vegetables and firewood are abundant. The water is palatable, the air salubrious. It is a treasury of learned men; and the winter here is agreeable. The people are well-disposed, and well-to-do, marked by kindness and charity. Their intonation in reciting the

p. 198 Qurʾān is pleasant, and their delight in good deeds is evident; the devoutness of their worship is well-known throughout the world. They have rested secure from injurious rains, and safe from the tumult of evildoers. They are most discriminating in the selection of the preacher and of the leader in prayer; nor will they appoint anyone to lead them but the most worthy, regardless of expense to themselves. Their judge is always dignified, their *muhtasib* deferred to like a prince. They are never free from the supervision of the ruler and the minister. Indeed were it not that it has faults aplenty, this city would be without compare in the world.

The town stretches for about two-thirds of a *farsakh*, in tiers one above the other. It used to consist of two quarters, al-Fustāt and al-Jīza, but later on, one of the khalifs of the House of al-ʿAbbās had a canal cut around a portion of the town, and this portion became known as al-Jazīra (the island), because of its lying between the main course of the river and the canal. The canal itself was named the "Canal of the Commander of the Faithful," and from it the people draw their drinking water. Their buildings are of four storeys or five, just as are lighthouses; the light enters them from a central area. I have heard it said that about two hundred people live in one building. In fact, when al-Hasan bin Ahmad al-Qarmatī arrived there, the people came out to meet him; seeing them, as he considered, like a cloud of locusts, he was alarmed, and asked what this meant. The reply was: "These are the sightseers of Misr; those who did not come out are more numerous still."

I was one day walking on the bank of the river, and marveling at the great number of ships, both those riding at anchor, and those coming and going, when a man from the locality accosted me, saying: "Where do you hail from?" Said I, "From the Holy City." Said he, "It is a large city. But I tell you, good sir—may God hold you dear to Him—that of the vessels along this shore, and of those that set sail from here to the towns and the villages—if all these ships were to go to your native city they could carry away its people, with everything that appertains to it, and the stones thereof and the timber thereof, so that it would be said: 'At one time here stood a city.'"

I once heard it said that there pray in front of the Imān on Friday close to ten thousand people. I did not believe it until I went out with the foremost of those bustling to the Sūq al-Ṭayr (Bird Market), and saw for myself that the matter was just about as had been stated. And being late, one day, I was strenuously repairing to the Friday prayers, and I found the lines of people in the markets extending to more than a thousand cubits from the mosque. And I saw, moreover, that the mercantile establishments, and the places of worship, and the shops around the mosque were filled on every side with worshippers.

p. 199

This particular mosque is known as al-Suflānī (the lower). It was founded by ʿAmr bin al-ʿĀs, and within it stands his pulpit. The building is well constructed, with some mosaics set into its walls. It stands on pillars of marble, and is bigger than the mosque at Damascus, and the crowding in it is greater than that of any of the six other mosques here. The markets are all around it, except that between them and the mosque, on the side towards the *Qibla*, is the Dār al-Shatt, as well as storage places, and a place for performing the ablution. This district is the most flourishing in Misr; to its left is the Zuqāq al-Qanādīl (the Corridor of the Lamps)—but one can have no idea of what Zuqāq al-Qanādīl is like!

The Fawqānī (Upper) mosque was built by the House of Taylūn—it is larger and more magnificent than the Suflānī mosque. It is built on massive pillars adorned with stucco, its roofs are lofty. In its centre is a vaulted structure resembling that of Zamzam, and therein is a drinking fountain. The mosque overlooks both the mouth of the canal and some part of it. Some extensions have been added to it, while behind it are some handsome residences. Its minaret is of stone; it is small, and the steps to the top of it are on the outside.

In between the Lower and the Upper mosques stands the Mosque of ʿAbd Allāh, built to the dimensions of the Kaʿba.

Addition/version MS. C.

A mosque stands in al-Jazīra and another in al-Jīza; and in the area round about the town (al-Fustāt) stand quite a number of mosques, and attractive drinking places; also a group of servants of God, called al-Qarāfa, who have a handsome mosque, built by Umm al-Maghribī. On the edge of al-Jazīra is an area called al-Mukhtāra, wherein are situated the pleasure grounds of the kings of Egypt; here, too, is a mosque, and yet another in al-Qāhira (Cairo), this bringing the number to seven. Cairo used to be some distance from al-Fustāt, but now the extent of its development reaches to the latter, which thus, at the present day has grown bigger than Baghdād. Al-Qāhira is a city which al-Maghrabī [i.e. the Fātimids] built, when he conquered Egypt and defeated those who were there. His army is stationed there, and his palace is there; it is a large city, with forty public baths and beautiful marketplaces.

A full description of the qualities of its markets and its magnificence would extend to a great length. It is enough to say that it is the most important of the metropoles of the Muslims, their greatest pride, and the most populous of their towns. Yet notwithstanding this great aggregation of people, I have bought there the purest white bread—in fact they bake no other—at thirty *ratls* for a *dirham*, eggs at eight for a *dānaq*, the quince at seventy to the *dirham*; bananas and dates are cheap also. The fruits of Syria and the Maghrib are brought there in all seasons, and people travel thither from al-ʿIrāq and the countries of the East. The ships of the Peninsula (Arabia) and of the Romaean countries traverse

p. 200 the seas thither constantly. Its commerce is remarkable, its trades profitable, its wealth abundant. Nowhere will you find sweeter water, more agreeable people, finer linen, or a river more beneficent.

For all that, its dwellings are cramped and full of fleas, the rooms noisome and oppressive. Fruits are scarce, the water is muddy, the wells filthy, the houses are dirty, bugridden and stinking; mange is chronic. Meats are expensive, dogs numerous. The people use abominable oaths, their manners are vile. They are in constant fear of famine and the failure of the river, and are on the verge of compulsory exile—in fact they are constantly expecting calamity. Their elders do not abstain from the drinking of wine, nor their women from fornication. Thus, a woman has two husbands, and you will see the elder drunk. Even in their religion they have two factions; their countenances are dark, their language debased.

Al-Jazīra is lightly populated. The mosque and the Nilometer are at the end of it near the bridge, on the side towards the metropolis. Here are gardens and palms; and the promenade of the Commander of the Faithful is close to the canal, at a place called al-Mukhtāra.

Al-Jīza is a town beyond the other side of the main stream. The road thither from al-Jazīra used to go over a bridge there until the Fātimids removed it. The town has a mosque, and is more flourishing and larger than al-Jazīra. The high road departs from here to al-Maghrib. The canal joins the main stream below al-Jazīra, at al-Mukhtāra. Al-Qāhira (Cairo) is a town which Jawhar the Fātimid built after he had conquered Egypt, and subjugated its inhabitants. It is large and well-built, with a splendid mosque. The imperial palace stands in its centre. The town is well fortified, having iron-plated gates. It is on the main road to Syria, and no one may enter al-Fustāt except through here, as both places are situated between the mountain and the river. The *Musallā* (place of prayer), where public prayers in connection with the two festivals are said, is beyond the town, while the burial grounds are between the metropolis and the mountain.

Al-ʿAzīzīyya has become dilapidated, and altogether fallen into ruin. It was the capital in olden days, and here the Firʿawn (the Pharaoh) used to reside; his Qasr (palace) is still there, as well as the mosque of Jacob and Joseph.

ʿAyn Shams is a town on the main road to Syria, with widely cultivated fields; here is one of the dams of the Nile to hold the waters during its flood. The mosque stands in the marketplace.

Al-Mahalla is a town on the Alexandrian branch of the river. It has an elegant mosque, but not many markets. Otherwise, it is a well-developed place, having a pleasant riverbank and a delightful view of the river. Facing it is Sandafā with its mosque, and flourishing. The situation here seemed to me to resemble that at Wāsit, except that here no bridge connects the two towns, the people crossing in boats.

Hulwān is a town in the direction of al-Saʿīd, with caves and quarries, and remarkable things. It possesses a public bath, above which another bath is built. The remaining towns are on either the main stream of the Nile or one or other of its two branches.

p. 201

Uswān is the capital of al-Saʿīd (Upper Egypt), on the Nile. It is a large, flourishing town, possessing a tall minaret. Here are date palms in abundance, vineyards, natural resources, and it produces commercial products. It is, in fact, one of the major cities of Egypt.

Akhmīm, a town abounding in date palms, is situated on one of the branches of the Nile, possessing also vineyards, and cultivated fields. From here came Dhu al-Nūn, the Hermit. This area is the most elevated land in Egypt, and from within it the Nile issues forth.

Al-Fayyūm is an important place, with fields of the finest rice, and cotton of an inferior quality. It has a number of rich villages that are called al-Jawhariyyāt.

Al-ʿAllāqī is a town on the outskirts of the district, on the road to ʿAydhāb. With regard to al-Wāhāt (the Oases), they used to constitute a rich district, with trees and fields; and even today are found there varieties of fruits, and sheep and livestock, which have become wild. The Oases adjoin the territory of al-Sūdān, and touch also the boundary of the region of al-Maghrib, of which, in fact, some make it a part.

Tinnīs, situated between the Romaean Sea and the Nile, is a small island in a lake, the whole of which has been built as a city—and what a city! It is Baghdād in miniature! A mountain of gold! The emporium of the Orient and of the West! Markets are elegant, fish cheap. It is the goal of travelers, prosperity is evident, the shore delightful, the mosque exquisite, the palaces lofty. It is a town with resources, and well-populated, yet as it is situated on a narrow island, the water encircles it like a ring. It is, too, a boring, filthy place, where the water, kept in cisterns, is locked up. Most of its inhabitants are Copts. The refuse is thrown into the streets. Here are made coloured cloths and garments. Beside it is a place in which are piled up the dead of the unbelievers, one upon another, while the cemeteries of the Muslims are in the centre of the town.

Dimyāt (Damietta): you may travel in this lake for a day and a night, sometimes meeting with fresh water, and narrow straits, until reaching another town, which is better [than Tinnīs], more spacious, wider, more open, more frequented; with more fruits, better construction, more water, artisans more skillful, cloths finer, more finished workmanship, better baths, stronger walls, and fewer vexations. Over it stands a fortress built of stone. It has many gates, and a large number of well-garrisoned outposts. A festival is held here every year to which the members of the garrisons come from all around. The Romaean Sea is within shouting distance of it, and the houses of the Copts are on the shore. It is here that the Nile flows into the sea.

p. 202

Shatā, a village between these two towns, and situated on the lake, is inhabited by Copts, and to it that distinctive cloth *Shatawī* owes its name.

Tahā is a village in Upper Egypt in which woolen cloths of very high quality are made. From here came the jurist, al-Imām Abū Jaʿfar al-Azdī. At Bahnasa are made curtains and coverlets; while the finest quality flax is grown in Būsīr.

A Summary Account of Conditions in this Region

As for this region, when fortune smiles on it you need not ask about its fertility and low prices; but when it suffers drought, God save us from its famine, which once lasted seven years, so that the people were eating the dogs, and the most terrible epidemic afflicted them! The heat here is more intense than on the coasts of Syria, and in Tūba [5th month of Coptic calendar] the cold is unbearable. Date palms are here in abundance. Most of the *dhimmī* here are Christians, denominated Copts; Jews are few. Lepers are many, and mange is chronic, because the place is decayed and stinking. Their main fare is fish.

The [Muslim] people here adhere to the **schools** of the inhabitants of Syria, though most of their jurists belong to the Mālikite school of theology: as you observe, they pray in front of the Imām. Moreover, they raise dogs. The people of the upper part of the capital and those of Sandafā are Shīʿa, while all the other schools are openly represented in al-Fustāt. In this city is a separate quarter of the Karrāmites, and the Muʿtazilites are very much in evidence, as are the Hanbalites. Formal legal opinion at present is given according to the schools of the Fātimites, of which we treat in the account of the region of the Maghrib.

The seven systems of **reading** the Qurʾān are in use here, though that of Ibn ʿĀmir is the least used. On an occasion when I used the latter in reading to

p. 203 Abu al-Tayyib bin Ghalbūn said he, "Give up this reading, for it is outmoded." Said I, "We have been told, 'Keep the ancient tradition.'" Said he, "Very well, keep it." I then read to him according to the system of Abū ʿAmr, and he continued to bid me to trill the "r" in "Maryam," and in "al-Tūria." The most prevalent and preferred among them is the reading according to the system of Nāfiʿ, and in fact I heard a scholar in the Suflānī mosque say: "No Imām led the prayer before this *mihrāb*, ever, that did not interpret the law according to Mālik, and read according to the system of Nāfiʿ, except for this one," meaning Ibn al-Khayyāt. I asked him why that was. Said he, "We have found none better than he." He was a Shāfiʿite, and read in the system of Abū ʿAmr. Never have I witnessed in all Islām finer chanting than his.

Their **language** is Arabic, but incorrect and lax; the non-Muslims converse in Coptic.

Egypt is a country of **commerce**; it is an important source of very fine leather, resistant to water, sturdy, and pliant; leather of sheep and asses' skins, leggings, and cloth of three-ply yarn of camelshair and goats wool—all these are from the metropolis. From Upper Egypt come rice, wool, dates, vinegar, raisins. From Tinnīs, (but not from Dimyāt), cloth variegated in colour; from Dimyāt, sugar cane. From al-Fayyūm, rice, and a linen of inferior quality; from Būsīr, shrimp, and cotton of superior quality. From al-Faramā, fish, and, from the towns around it, large baskets, and ropes made of fiber of the finest quality. Here are produced white cloth of the greatest fineness, wraps, canvas, the mats of ʿAbbādānī style of very fine quality, grains, grass peas, oils of rape, and of jasmine, and of other plants besides these.

Their **specialties** include reedpens incomparable! and their vitriol, marble, vinegar, wool, canvas, cloth, linen, leathers, shoes, leggings, fibers from the palm tree, geese, plantains, wax, sugar candy, fine linen, dyes, apparel, spun yarn, waterskins, *harisa*, the sweet pastry called *nayda*, chick peas, lupine, clover, arum, mats, asses, cattle, girdles; their farms, rivers; their devoutness, the excellence of their chanting, the structure of their mosques; their special cheese, their confection [made of dates, butter and curds], their fish, their commercial establishments, their commerce, their tithing—all of these are of most surpassing merit. To be found here also from among the special products of Palestine is the Colocasia—it is somewhat about the size of the round radish; it has a skin on it, and is quite piquant. It is fried in oil, and tossed with *sikbāj* [a mixture of cut flesh-meat, flour, and vinegar]. The banana also—it is about the size of the cucumber; its thin skin is peeled off it, then the fruit is eaten; this has a sweetness and a pungency. The sycamore fig, also, which is smaller than the regular fig, and has a long pod. Also the fruit of the lupine, about the size of a fingernail; dry and bitter, it is sweetened and then salted. The lotus fruit, too; it is about the size of a medlar, and has a large pit: it is sweet, and is the fruit of the lotus tree. But they go beyond all of these in production of the *nayda*: this is a kind of marzipan, made in an interesting way, being spread over a piece of cane until it dries and hardens. Moreover, oil of balsam is derived from a plant that grows there.

p. 204

Addition/version MS. C.
We have already mentioned the banana, a fruit found in al-Basra, al-Hijāz, al-Yaman. Also the sycamore: this is a fruit about the size of a fig, with a long red appendage, a taste differing from that of the fig. The tree itself is enormous, and you will not see a thicker trunk than it; in fact, generally the doors of inns are made of this wood. The tree yields seven crops of fruit in the year, so no wonder it is cheap and everywhere available. The lupine has a seed about the size of a fingernail; it is sweetened and sold in the markets, then ground and fermented. Spices are added to it, and it is exported to Bukhārā, where the women buy it for cooking. ... There is also the *sidar* fruit, popularly called the lotus of paradise, because of its scarcity. The people here use *nayda* much more than do the people of Syria: this is a type of marzipan, made in an interesting

way. ... Oil of balsam is extracted from a plant here ... there is also the Colocasia ... which is fried in oil and tossed with *sikbāj*: it is a weeping plant. It is extremely useful in that one need only split up a root of it into date-size pieces, then plant them in the soil, and a plant like a banana tree will grow from each piece, with pretty leaves resembling the foliage of the banana tree.

The **coinage** of old here was the *mithqāl* (miskal) and the *dirham* (dirhem). They still use the silver *muzabbaqa*—fifty to the *dīnār*—and conduct many transactions using the *rādhī*, the Fātimids having changed the coinage but these two, abolishing the [brass] *qitʿ* and the miskals.

Measures: the *wayba* (whiba), the equivalent of fifteen *manns*, and the *irdab* (ardeb), six whibas. The *tillīs* is eight whibas, but is no longer in use.

p. 205 The **customs**: in the mosques of this region, when the Imām recites the morning prayer every day, he places before him a copy of the *Qurʾān* from which he reads a portion, while the people gather around him just as gather around the preachers. They also recite a call to prayer that is peculiar to themselves; it is like a wail, and is used the last third of the night, and pertaining to it is a story they are fond of telling. During the last two prayers of the day their mosque is filled with the chatter of the jurisprudents, the leaders in reading, the litterateurs, and the savants. I used to go in there with a group from Jerusalem, and we would sit and chat, and we would hear the summons from two sides: "Turn your attention to the assembly!" and we would look, and there we would be, sitting between two assemblies. It is like this in all the mosques, and I have counted in one, one hundred ten sessions. When they had performed the evening prayer, up to a third of the people would remain, and enliven the market as they returned from the mosque. You will never encounter better than the assemblies of the reciters of the *Qurʾān* here; here is also an assembly for the musicians. A custom of theirs consists of placing canopies outside their mosques at the time of the sermon, as at al-Basra. Their markets are empty on Fridays.

Seldom do they wear clothes that have been washed or sandals that have had the hair removed. They do not eat meat often. They make movements as they need to during the prayer, clearing their throats and their noses in the mosque, and voiding under the mats.

In the country districts the people at threshing time bake bread sufficient for their needs for the coming year; this they dry and store. They here use the winnowing machine resembling that of Syria. They are a people polite, sociable, and given to flattery. Their biggest oath is, "By God's head!" and the smallest is, "May ʿAlī confirm!" They enjoy eating fish heads, and it is said that if they see a Syrian who has bought a fish they will follow him so that when he discards the head they may retrieve it. They constantly eat the *dillīnis* (a shellfish), a most filthy thing; it is a creature between two small shells which they split open, then drink; it is like mucus.

Among their **blemishes:** the faintness of their hearts, the scarcity of their fruits. The Syrians constantly reproach them, and mocking them, say "the rain of the Egyptians is the dew, and their bird is the kite; their speech when they say 'yā sīdī' is languid like that of women. God love you! May you be always free from such things." Their food is the *dillīnis*, their tidbits are chickpeas, their cheese, *al-ḥālūm*, consists of dried curds, their confection is the *nayda*, their steaks are of the pig, their oaths blasphemous.

p. 206

Now, in respect of the **Nile**—I have never tasted, nor have I heard that in the entire world is there water sweeter than it, except for the river al-Mansūra (Mihrān). Its increase is from the month of Bawna to the month of Tūt, about the time of the Festival of the Cross. Two dams there are, one of the two at ʿAyn Shams, where the canal is dammed with esparto grass and mud before the increase of the river. When the water comes the dam retains it, and the water rises on the embankment to beyond the capital; thus those villages are irrigated, such as Bahtīt, al-Munyatayn, Shabrū, and Damanhūr. This dam is that of the canal of the Commander of the Faithful. When the day of the Festival of the Cross arrives, the time at the end of the sweetening of the grapes, the Ruler goes out to ʿAyn Shams, and orders the opening of this canal, because the people on the embankment have already dammed up the mouths of the streams, so that no water escapes from them. Accordingly supervisors are put in charge, so that the water descends to all the villages of al-Rīf.

The other canal is lower down than the first one, and bigger than it; however, the Ruler does not go there. Its being opened signifies the lowering of the Nile; this happens at Sardūs.

The Nilometer: a pond in the middle of which is a tall column whereon are the marks in cubits and fingers; in charge of it is a superintendent, and around it are doors that fit together tightly. A report is presented to the Ruler every day of the amount the water has risen, whereupon the herald proclaims, "God hath augmented today the blessed Nile by so much; its increase last year on this day was so much; and may God bring it to completeness!" The rise is not proclaimed until after it has reached twelve cubits, it is announced to the Ruler only, for at twelve cubits the water does not extend to the cultivated villages of the countryside. However, when the height of the water reaches fourteen cubits, the lower portion of the region is watered; but if it reaches sixteen cubits, there is a general rejoicing, for there will be a good year. Should it go above that there is fertility and abundance. When the water has gone down, the people begin ploughing and sowing. During the days of the flood of the river, Egypt is as if it were covered by the sea, so that it is not possible to go from one village to another in some areas except by rowboats.

p. 207

Connected with this occurrence was an evil custom in ancient times, as I have been told by Abū Yāsir, the guest of Ibn ʿAbd Allāh al-Ansārī. He heard it from Yūsuf bin ʿAlī, who had it from al-Maʾmūn, who had it from Muhammad bin Khalaf, who had it from Abū Ṣāliḥ, who had it from Ibn Lahī'a, who had it from Qays bin al-Ḥujjāj. It seems that when Egypt was conquered, its people came to 'Amr bin al-'Āṣ during the beginning of the month of Bawna and they said: "Oh, Prince, regarding this Nile of ours there is a practice embodied in tradition without which it will not flow. On the twelfth night of this month we select a virgin girl who is the firstborn to her parents, and we recompense them both. We dress her in jewelry and raiment the best there are, then we cast her into the river." Said 'Amr to them, "This will not come to pass, ever, because Islām supersedes what was there before it." So they waited that month, and the next month, and the following month, but the Nile flowed with not a little and not a lot. As a result, the people were on the point of emigrating, on seeing which 'Amr wrote to 'Umar bin al-Khaṭṭāb on the matter. He replied, "You acted correctly in what you did, for Islām supersedes whatever preceded it," and he sent a slip of paper within his letter, saying to 'Amr, "I have sent you a slip of paper, which you should throw into the Nile." When the letter arrived, 'Amr opened it and perceived what was on the slip of paper: "From the servant of God, 'Umar, Commander of the Faithful, to the Nile of Egypt, now then! If you flow by your own power alone, then flow not! If, however, it be the One God, the Conqueror, that causes you to flow then we ask Him—exalted be He—to make you flow." 'Amr threw the paper into the Nile before the Festival of the Cross, for the people had been preparing to emigrate. But when they arose on the morning of the Festival of the Cross, God had caused the river to flow so that it reached a height of sixteen cubits. God has thus prohibited that evil custom among them to this day.

The water of the river becomes muddy on the days of the flood, and the people throw crushed apricot stones into it so that it becomes limpid; moreover it becomes cold, and remains cold for about two months. I chanced one day to attend the session of al-Ḥalīmī in the mosque, when a jar of water was brought him and he drank from it. Then said he, "We are your equals, O Muqaddasī, in the excellence of the water." "Not at all," said I, "may God support the jurist. The cold of our water is constant, this condition of yours is just temporary."

They have a system on the bank by which they take water from the river by means of hydraulic equipment, taking it up for half a *dānaq*, and for every extra storey a *muzabbaqa*.

p. 208   When the north wind blows, the waves of the sea roll over each other, and push back the water of the Nile from the lake; when the south wind blows, it pushes back the water of the sea from the lake and the force of the flow of the Nile prevails. The people of Tinnīs during those four months fill their cisterns by means of the hydraulic equipment and water skins. I have heard a group in al-Faramā say that the Nile sometimes reaches to the minarets; the Nile also reaches the citadel of Alexandria, brought in by means of pipes made of iron, whereby they fill their cisterns: then it is stopped.

In the Nile is an animal called the crocodile; it resembles the lizard. Its head is one third of its body. Weapons are of no avail against it except under the axilla; its mouth will snatch a person. Most of those seen are in Upper Egypt and Sardūs, so that among the proverbs there is, "Beware of Sardūs, even if the water is merely a jarful," the jar meaning the small jug on a waterwheel. One day I was aboard a ship near Sardūs, and it scraped something, so I said, "Is it bottom we scraped?" I was told no, but rather the back of a crocodile.

The Nile used not reach to al-Fayyūm, so the people complained to Joseph—peace be on him—about it. He built a great dam in the river, and at the bottom of it he installed valves in ducts of glass. The dam retained the water, so that it rose until it reached the ground of al-Fayyūm, and irrigated it. At present it is the most watered area in Egypt—do you not see that there are the farms of rice, or do you not notice the burden of its land taxes, the greatness of its income? During its flood the water goes over the top of the dam; so sometimes they allow the boats to go over with the flow, and they glide down safely, though sometimes they capsize and turn upside down. When the people no longer need the water, the valves are opened and the water subsides.

All the wells that are close to the Nile are sweet, while those some distance away from it are disagreeable. The best baths are those by the shore. Entering through the town are canals from which they draw their water by means of water wheels. On the Nile itself also are numerous wheels which irrigate the gardens when the river is low. The water at al-Fayyūm is unhealthy because it flows over the rice farms.

A saying of theirs is to the effect that the kid goat as soon as it is born says, "Get out, foreigners." At Alexandria is found a striped fish called the *sharb* [stockfish]; whoever eats of it sees terrible dreams, unless he is of those who drink wine, in which case it will not hurt him. At al-Faramā is found a bird called *al-sumānī* (quail), of which whoever eats sickens, and suffers crampness in his joints. A person in al-Fustāt who continually eats fish is afflicted with a severe mange which does not leave him for seven years.

p. 209

In Egypt is a mountain wherein is a gold mine; they possess, too, sources of vitriol the like of which you do not see elsewhere, and a clay called *tafl* (fullers). In the Muqattam hills are quarries of very fine white stone which may be sawn as wood is sawn.

Places of veneration in this region. Some commentators say that "height of land, a sheltered place with a water spring" (*Qurʾān*, sūra 23, v. 50), is Egypt, and that Jesus and Mary were there for some time. Mount Sinai is near the Red Sea; one approaches it from a village called al-Amn (Elim). This is the place by which Moses and the children of Israel departed, and here are twelve springs of water of rather middling quality. The Mount is about two days journey from Elim. On it is a monastery belonging to the Christians, many farms, and an olive tree believed to be that of which God said, "it is neither of the east nor of the west"

(*Qurʾān*, sūra 24, v. 35): the olive oil from it is delivered to the rulers. In al-Fustāt is the spot in which Joseph—peace be upon him—was sold; in the hills of al-Muqattam are locations whither people like to repair, and places of retreat to which they betake themselves on Friday nights. Within shouting distance of al-Fustāt is a place called al-Qarāfa wherein is a mosque with handsome drinking fountains; here too is an assemblage of worshippers, also a place of seclusion—it is a market for those who seek the next world. There is, too, a very fine central mosque. The cemeteries here are the most beautiful possible architecturally—you see the town with its dusty colour, while the cemeteries are white. These stretch the length of the capital, and include the grave of al-Shāfiʿī between those of al-Maznī and Abū Ishāq al-Marwazī. There is too, by the Red Sea, the spot from which the children of Israel entered the sea. Close by Sardūs is the mosque of al-Khidhr, on whom be peace! As to Tīh Banī Isrāʾil [the wilderness associated with the children of Israel] about this there is controversy; however, it lies, in fact, between Egypt and Syria, stretches about forty *farsakhs*, and consists of sands, saltflats, and sandstone: however, some date palms and springs occur there. One boundary reaches al-Jifār, another Mount Sinai; the boundary of the desert is the countryside towards the Red Sea, while the boundary with Syria corresponds with their high road to Makka.

p. 210

Among the **remarkable things** in this region are al-Haramān (the two pyramids), which are one of the wonders of the world. Of stone, and resembling two edifices, they rise, each, to a height of four hundred cubits—the cubit of King Khusraw—its width the same. They are covered with Greek inscriptions, and within both of them are two passages to the highest part of each; there is, too, a remarkable vaulted passageway underground, excavated in the sand. Varying accounts have been given me about both structures, some saying that they are both talismans, others that they were the granaries of Joseph; others say no, rather, they are their burial grounds. I have read in the book of Ibn al-Faqīh that they are both bequeathed to the sand. It is said, moreover, that on both of them is written: "I built them both, and whoever claims power in his possession of them let him destroy them both; for destroying is easier than building." One of the kings purposed to destroy them both, but the revenue of Egypt did not suffice to do that, so he left them both. They are both smooth like big buildings, and may be seen from a distance of two or three days journey. One does not ascend them unless he is agile. Around about them both is a number of small similar structures, and this indicates that they are graves. Do you not notice about the kings of al-Daylam in al-Rayy, how they have, in imitation, put tall domes over their graves? They made them as strong and as high as they could, so that they would not be obliterated. There are even smaller than these lesser ones. Here also is an idol which some assert Satan used to take possession of and make to speak, with the result that he broke its nose and its lips.

At ʿAyn Shams are what look like two tall minarets. A single piece of stone is at the top of each one, pointed like a spearhead: they are called the obelisks. Here are also lesser objects of the same style. Concerning the two larger ones I have heard reports which intelligence will not accept. Moreover, I have read in the book of talismans that these two are talismans pertaining to the crocodiles, and this is conceivable; for do you not notice that the crocodiles in the district of al-Fustāt do not do any hurt, despite their size and great number? In al-Fustāt, at Qasr al-Shamʿ is an image of a deformed woman on whose head is a basin made of stone; it is said that she was a washerwoman for the family of the Pharaohs, but she harmed Moses and was deformed. On the main road to Upper Egypt are buildings called al-Barābī [the Temple Ruins] in which are numerous images. In them, and in the two pyramids are many ornaments and drawings. At Hulwān are remarkable caves, really dreadful, in which a person may easily lose his way. Within them is said to be a way to the Red Sea, smoothed as though the salt water flowed over it.

The lighthouse of Alexandria has its foundations firmly anchored in a small peninsula, and may be approached by a narrow road. It is firmly set in the rock, and the water rises on the lighthouse on the west side. The same is true of the fortress of the city, except that the lighthouse is on a peninsula on which are three hundred buildings, to some of which a mounted horseman may go; he may go to all of them using a password. The lighthouse is elevated above all the towns along the shore, and it is said that there used to be a mirror there in which could be seen every ship taking off from the shores of the entire sea. A custodian continuously attends to it every day and night, and as soon as a ship comes into his range of sight he notifies the commander, who dispatches the birds that go to the shore, that those there may be in a state of readiness. On one occasion the Romaean Dog [the Roman Emperor] sent a person who exercised guile and subtlety, so that he was appointed custodian of the lighthouse; then, it is said, he took the mirror away with him, but according to others, rather, that he broke it and threw it into the sea. In the book of talismans it is said that the lighthouse was built as a charm to prevent the water of the sea from covering the land of Egypt, so the Romaean Dog intrigued to destroy the top of it because of this, but he did not succeed. In al-Jifār is a talisman so that the sands will not cover the towns and the villages. It is supposed that the talismans are found only in Egypt and Syria, and are said to have been made by the prophets; however, I myself saw talismans in Fārs also.

The names of the **Coptic months** are: first the winter months: Tūt, in which occurs Nayrūz [New Year's Day], Babih, Hatōr, Kīhak, Tūba, Amshīr. The summer months: Baramhāt, Barmūda, Bashans, Baʾūna, Abīb, Misrā.

As for the **situation** of Egypt; the Romaean Sea is on its northern border, the Sea of China flows by two thirds of its eastern border, and these two thirds constitute five sections of the region: a section between the sea and the Mountain—this is dry; the second section is the mountain of al-Muqattam; the third section is al-Saʿīd, including the Nile and the territories on it. The fourth section is also a mountain, beyond which is the expanse containing al-Wāhāt (the Oases).

The length of Egypt from the Romaean Sea to al-Nūba (Nubia) is less than a month's journey. Its width in the south is a distance of eight stages, in the north, twelve stages. The distance along the inlet which is part of the Red Sea is four stages.

The **government** is in the hands of the house of the Fātimids, and the people live in justice and security, because he is a ruler powerful and rich, and his subjects live in prosperity. Here is administration and execution of the law; and everyone who hears the ruler obeys him, in full confidence, whether privately or publicly. The sermon at the noon service on Friday is addressed to the Amīr al-Muʾminīn, (The Commander of the Faithful) solely.

As for the **income** of Egypt—I have read in the *Book of Tribute* of Qudāma bin Jaʿfar to the effect that the income of Egypt from property is two million five hundred thousand *dīnārs*. I have read otherwise in the book of Ibn al-Faqīh, who at great length reports its income in the time of Pharaoh, then in the time of al-Hajjāj, then in the time of the dynasty of al-ʿAbbās, and he refers to it as a land tax. I enquired of an Egyptian in Bukhārā about the land tax, and he said that in Egypt there is no land tax, but that the *fallāh* declares his intention to use the land, whereupon he is granted its use by the ruler, and he cultivates it. When he has reaped, threshed and aggregated the grain, it is demarcated by piles, and left there. On this the treasurer and the secretary of the ruler go out and determine the amount of the crop to be paid as rent for the land; what remains is given to the *fallāh*. He said, moreover, that among them is a custom that should a person take from the ruler some additional land on contract, there is accordingly an increase for him in the land rent proportional to the amount he has taken. I said that in that case, then, no one held possession of the property on which he was. No, indeed, said he, except in the case of a person who had bought land from one to whom the ruler had apportioned it in former times, and had granted it when he, or his family needed the money for it: in such a case he offered it for sale to the public. I asked if this is why it is said that the land of Egypt is not owned because the people made a contract for it with Joseph, on whom be peace! He said that this is pure nonsense. "Do you not know," said he, "that Islām superseded everything that was before its time, or do you not know that Joseph—on whom be peace—restored to the people their property when Egypt regained its fertility. And one thing more, the people reached this settlement with the Muslims at the time of the conquest." Said I, "Why did they not make a settlement as they did with the people of Syria, since both countries were taken

p. 213 by force?" Said he, "Syria is a country where it rains every year and agriculture is not interrupted there, although at times it is fertile, and at times suffers from drought. But as for Egypt, its dependence is on the Nile; some years it does not flood as much as other years, some years it rises to fourteen or even sixteen cubits, sometimes even more than that. This matter of its flow constitutes a harsh disparity between the two situations; and if a regular land tax were imposed it would have to be collected from the man who is able to cultivate in any year, and the man who is not."

The **imposts** are heavy especially at Tinnīs and Dimyāt, and on the banks of the Nile. The Copts may not weave any at all of their superb cotton cloth known by the name of al-Shatawiyya [made in Shatā], unless they have the certificate stamped with the seal of the ruler; neither may they sell it except through brokers, to whom the transaction, by contract, is assigned. The deputy of the ruler records what is sold, in his register; it is then taken to someone who folds the cloth, then to someone who packs it in straw, then to someone who packs it in a basket, then to one who puts it in a wrapping—at every step a fee is charged. Moreover, at the gate to the docks another levy is exacted. Every dealer writes his sign on the basket, and the ships are inspected at sailing time.

At Tinnīs an impost of a *dīnār* is laid on a skin of oil, and a like amount on similar commodities. Moreover, on the bank of the Nile at al-Fustāt the taxes are heavy. On the shore at Tinnīs I saw a tax collector in his office, and it is said that the tax income at this place every day is a thousand *dīnārs*, with a like computation on the seashore in al-Saʿīd and on the coast at Alexandria. Moreover, at Alexandria there is a tax on ships from the west, and at al-Faramā on ships from Syria; at al-Qulzum there is an impost of a *dirham* on every shipload.

Addition/version MS. C.
The imposts here are heavy. One may not weave any cloth of the excellent Shatāwī variety, or any coloured cloth without having the prior approval for it stamped with the seal of the ruler, and it may not be traded except in the presence of the representative of the ruler. It is then taken to a depot to be rolled there, then to another place to be bundled in wicker, then to another place, there to be packed: to the officials at every one of these places a tax must be paid. Moreover, at the coast half a *dirham* is levied on every bundle, then at every harbour through which it is shipped, another tax is levied. At Tinnīs, on every skin of olive oil there is a levy of a *dīnār*, and there, one encounters very close inspection, and heavy exactions. Indeed, sometimes the very choicest of the goods being exported may be taken to the ruler, who purchases them at whatever price he pleases to give, even though such dealings are oppressive.

The **distances** in this region:
from al-Faramā to al-Baqqāra, one stage;
thence to al-Warrāda, one stage;

p. 214   thence to al-ʿArīsh, one stage;
thence to Rafh, one stage.

You go in the summer from al-Faramā to Jurjīr, one stage;
thence to Fāqūs, one stage;
and in the winter from al-Faramā to al-Rassad, one stage;
thence to Fāqūs, one stage.

You may go from al-Faramā by water to Tinnīs, one stage;
thence to Dimyāt, one stage;
thence to al-Mahalla al-Kabīra, one stage;
thence to Alexandria, two stages.

You may go from Dimyāt to Sardūs, one stage;
thence to al-Fustāt, one stage.

You may go from Bilbays to al-Mansaf, one stage;
thence to al-Qulzum, a like distance.

You may go from al-Faramā to Dayr al-Nasārā, which is on the coast, one stage;
thence to al-Mukhlasa one stage;
thence to al-ʿArīsh, one stage;
and from Bilbays to al-Fustāt, one stage.

You may go from Alexandria to al-Rāfaqa, one stage;
thence to Kūm Sharīk, one stage;
thence to Tarnūt, one stage;
thence to Dhāt al-Silāsil, one stage;
thence to al-Fustāt, one stage.

You may go from Alexandria to Būmīnah, one stage;
thence to Safā, one stage;
thence to Armasā, two post stages;
thence to Dhāt al-Humām, one stage.

You may go from Alexandria to al-Ghādhara, one stage;
thence to Fāqūs, one stage.

p. 215 You may go from al-Fustāt to Bilbays, one stage;
thence to al-Mansaf, one stage;
thence to al-Qulzum, one stage.

From al-Qulzum to Judda by sea is a journey of from twenty-five to sixty days, depending on the wind; it is a distance of three hundred *farsakhs*.

You may go from al-Jubb to al-Buwayb, one stage;
    thence to Manzil Ibn Bunduqa (Ibn Sadaqa), one stage;
    thence to ʿAjarūd, one stage;
    thence to al-Madīna, one stage;
    thence to al-Kursī, one stage;
    thence to al-Hafr, one stage;
    thence to Wayla, one stage.
From Aswān to ʿAydhāb is a safe road, but I will not describe it.

The Region of the Maghrib
(Northern Africa West of Egypt; Andalusia)

This is a splendid region, extensive and distinguished. It is possessed of many towns and villages, remarkable in its resources and abundance. It has important border towns with many fortresses; here too, are delightful gardens. Here, also, is a number of separated tracts—islands, as it were—as Andalusia, distinguished and marvelous, Tāhart, so pure and delightful, Tanja, that town so remote, and Sijilmāsa, the favorite and incomparable place; also Isqiliyya (Sicily), the profitable island, of which the inhabitants are continually engaged in the Holy Strife. Moreover, wealth here is on a solid base, and cities here comparable
p. 216 with al-Basra are many. The people seek what is good; the ruler is just, wise, and well respected. This region adjoins the sea, the very best of neighbours! The inhabitants are gracious towards everyone who traverses the region.

The cities of this region are concealed from view by olive trees, the ground covered with fig trees and vineyards; streams make their way through it, trees fill the lowland valleys. However, some of its areas are remote, much of it is desert, the roads are difficult and dangers many. Situated in a remote corner of the realm of Islām, part of it is intercepted from the rest by the sea. No one wants to go there, no one goes there, no one enquires of it, and no one speaks well of it. It has produced no scholar of renown, no celebrated ascetic, except, perhaps, for a very few. The people are louts, though blameless before God; they are misers, even though prosperous. Here is a pattern and representation of it. [Map IX]

We have considered the Maghrib and al-Andalus in the same manner as we have Haytal and Khurāsān, with the exception that we did not enter al-Andalus so as to be able to determine its territorial divisions. The first district as one comes from Egypt is Barqa; following that, Ifrīqiya, then Tāhart, then Sijilmāsa, then Fās, next al-Sūs al-Aqsā; the island of Sicily, which faces Ifrīqiya, then al-Andalus beyond the sea, in the territory of the Romaeans. Fās consists of two divisions, Tanja and al-Zāb. Barqa is the name of the district, and also of its principal seat. Among its towns are Dhāt al-Humām, Ramāda, Atrābulus, Ajdābiya, Sabra, Qābis, Ghāfiq.

Ifrīqiya has for its capital al-Qayrawān, and among its towns are: Sabra,
p. 217 Asfāqus, al-Mahdiyya, Sūsa, Tūnis, Banzard, Tabarqa, Marsā al-Kharaz, Būna, Bāja, Lurbus, Qarna, Marnīsa, Mas, Banjad, Marmājanna, Sabība, Qamūda, Qafsa, Qastīliya, Nafzāwa, Lāfis, Awdhana, Qalānus, Qabīsha, Rusfa, Banūnush, Lajam, Jazīrat Abī Sharīk, Bāghāy, Sūq Ibn Khalaf, Dūfāna, al-Masīla, Ashīr, Sūq Hamza, Jazīrat Bani Zaghannāya, Mattīja, Tanas, Dār (Hāz?), Sūq Ibrāhīm, al-Ghuzza, Qalʿat Burjuma, Bāghir, Yalal, Jabal Zālāgh, Asfāqus, Munastīr, Marsā al-Hajjāmīn, Banzart, Tabarqa, Hayyāja, Bāghir, Ghaybath, Qaryat al-Saqāliba,
p. 218 Lurbus, Marsā al-Hajar, Jamūnas al-Sābūn, Taras, Qastīliya, Nafta, Bantiyūs, Taqiyūs, Madīnat al-Qusūr, Miskiyāna, Bāghāy, Dūfāna, ʿAyn al-ʿAsāfīr, Dār

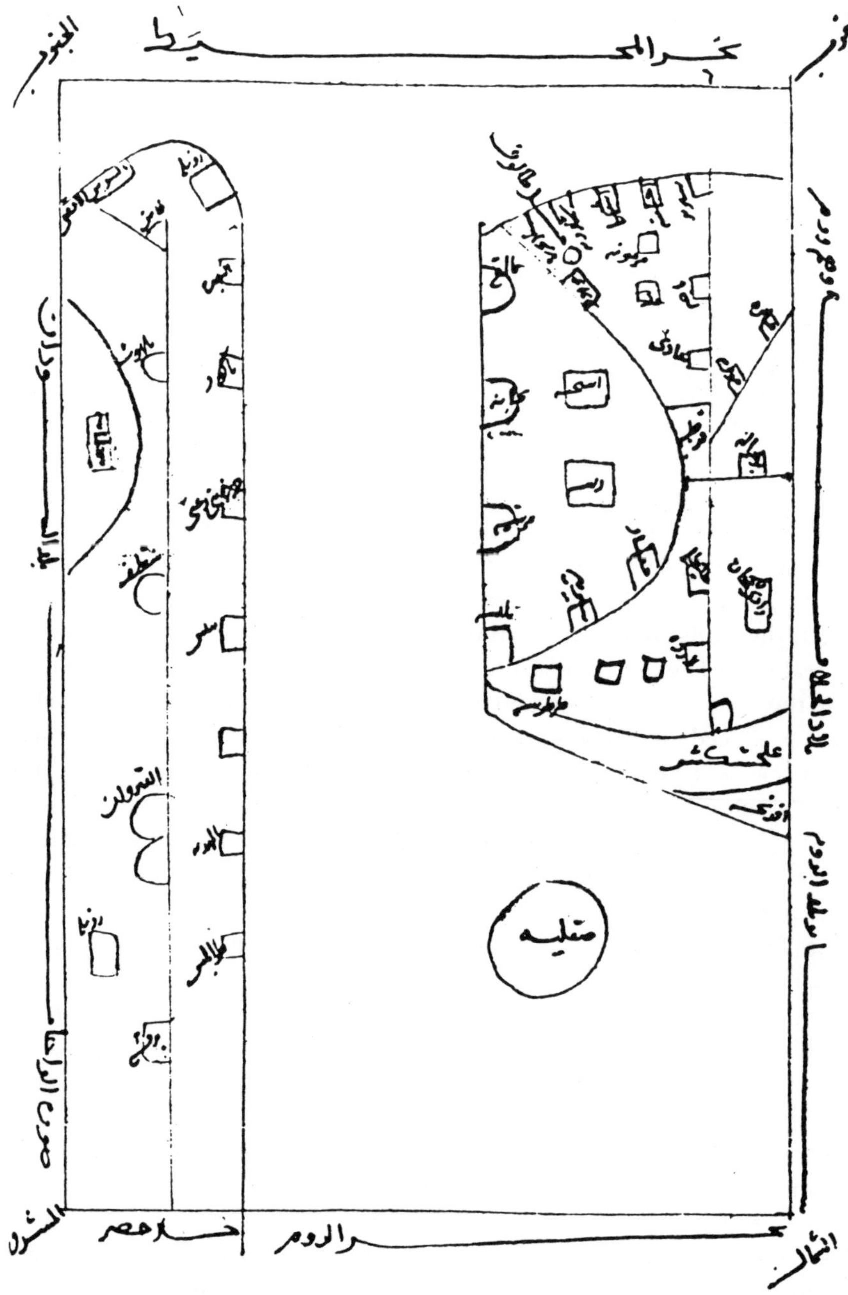

Map IX: Al-Maghrib (see p. 413).
From MS. Sprenger 5—Ahlwardt 6034 by kind permission of the Staatsbibliothek
Preussischer Kulturbesitz, Berlin, Orientabteilung.

Malūwwal, Tubna, Maqqara, Tījis, Madīnat al-Mahriyyīn, Tāmasnat, Dakkamā, Qaṣr al-Ifrīqī, Rakwā, al-Qustantīnīyya, Mīlā, Jījil, Tābarrīt, Satīf, Īkijā, Marsā al-Dajjāj, Ashīr.

As for the district of Tāhart—and this name is that of its chief city—it has among its towns: Yammama, Tāghlīsiya, Qalʿat Ibn al-Harb, Hazāra, al-Jaʿba, Ghadīr al-Durūʿ, Lamāya, Mindās, Sūq Ibn Habla, Matmāta, Jabal Tujān, Wahrān, Shalif, Tīr, al-Ghuzza, Sūq Ibrāhīm, Rahbāya, al-Batha, al-Zaytūna, Tamamā, Yaʿūd, al-Khadhrāʾ, Wārifan, Tanas, Qaṣr al-Fulūs, Bahriyya, Sūq K/arā, Manjasa, Ūzikī, Tabrīn, Sūq Ibn Mablūl, Rubā, Tāwīlt Abī Maghūl Tāmazzīt, another Tāwīlt (Laghwā), Fakkān.

Sijilmāsa is also the name of the chief seat of the district, and its towns are: Darʿa, Tādanqūst, Athar, Aylā, Wīlmīs, Hisn Ibn Sālih, al-Nahhāsīn, Hisn al-Sūdān, Hilāl, Imsala, Dār al-Amīr, Hisn Barāra, al-Khiyāmāt, Tāzrūt.

As for Fās, the offspring of the inhabitants are wastrels. Fās is the name of the chief seat, too, while the district is also named al-Sūs al-Adnā. The towns here are: al-Basra, Zalūl, al-Jāhid, Sūq al-Kutāmī, Wargha, Sabū, Sanhāja, Hawwāra, Tīzā, Matmāta, Kazannāya, Sala, Madīnat Banī Qarbās, Mazhāhiyya, Azīlā, Sabtā, Balad Ghumār, Qalʿat al-Nusūr, Nakūr, Balash, Marnīsa, Tābarīdā, Sāʿ, Miknāsa, Qalʿat Shamīt, Madāʾin, Burjan Ūzikī, Tayūnū, Maksīn, Amlīl, Amlāh Abi al-Hasan, Qastīna (Qastīliya?), Nafzāwa, Niqāwus, Biskara, Qabīsha, Madīnat Banī Zahhīq, Luwātat ʿAbd Allāh, Luwātat Barkiyya, Akdhār Ibn Shirāk, Madīnat Jabal Zālāgh.

The subdivision of this area of Tanja has these towns: Walīla, Madraka, Matrūka, Zaqqūr, Ghuzza, Ghumīra, al-Hājir, Tājarājara, al-Baydhāʾ, al-Khadhrāʾ.

Al-Zāb has as its capital al-Masīla, and towns: Maqqara, Tubna, Biskara, Bādis, Tahūdhā, Tawlaqā, Jamīlā, Bantiyūs, Adna, Ashīr.

As for al-Sūs al-Aqṣā: its capital is Tarfāna, and it has the towns Aghmāt Waylā [Aylān], [Āghmāt] Warīka, Tandalī, Māssa, and others.

The capital of Sicily is Balarm (Palermo); its chief towns are al-Khālisa, Atrābunush, Māzar, ʿAyn al-Mughattā, Qalʿat al-Ballūt, Jirjant, Buthīra, Saraqūsa, Lantīnī, Qatāniya, al-Yāj, Batarnū, Tabarmīn, Mīqush, Massīna, Rimta, Damannash, Jārās, Qalʿat al-Qawārib, Qalʿat al-Sirāt, Qalʿat Abī Thawr, Batarliya, Thirma, Būrqād, Qurliyūn, Qarīnash, Bartinīq, Akhyās, Balja, Bartanna.

Al-Andalus corresponds somewhat to Haytal in the area of al-Mashriq; however we did not travel through its domains so that we could enumerate its provinces, neither did we go through it so to define its territorial divisions. It is said to have a dimension of one thousand miles, and Ibn Khurradādhbih says: "Forty towns constitute al-Andalus," referring of course to those that are well known, because no one has anticipated us in detailing the districts and recording the capitals. Some of the cities he mentions are capitals, according to our classification. I enquired of one of the intelligent men from there about the rural districts surrounding Qurtuba (Cordoba) and that are linked with it, and the

p. 219

p. 220

p. 221

p. 222

towns of these districts. Said he: "We call a *rustāq* (rural area) *iqlīm* (a region); and there are thirteen *iqlīms* around Qurtuba with their cities," and he named Arjūna, Qastalla, Shawdhar, Mārtush, Qanbānush, Fajj Ibn Laqīt, Balāt Marwān, p. 223 Hisn Bulkūna, al-Shanīda, Wādī ʿAbd Allāh, Qarsīs, al-Māʾida, Jayyān; and as the suffix denotes, this last name indicates a district, its chief towns being: al-Jafr, Bayghū, Mārtush, Qant, Gharnāta, Mantīsha, Bayyāsa. The other well-known cities of al-Andalus are: Turtūsha, Balansiya, Mursiya, Bajjāna, p. 224 Māliqa, Jazirat Jabal Tāriq, Shadhūna, Ishbīliya, Ukhshunuba, Mariyya, Shantarīn, Bāja, Labla, Qarmūna, Mawrūr, Istija.

Barqa is an important capital, well built and prosperous. It has an abundance of fruit and other agricultural products, and honey; and life there is easy. This is a frontier town surrounded by mountains, which are well populated and farmed. It lies half a stage distant from the sea, situated in a basin, and the soil all around there is red. The inhabitants derive their drinking water from wells, and from what they retain of rainwater in cisterns. Barqa lies on the main road to Egypt. The people here are kindly towards strangers; of good and upright stock, they are less capricious than others.

Atrābulus (Tripoli) is a large maritime city, walled in stone and lime, having gates: of the Sea, the East, the North, and the West. The inhabitants have their drinking water from wells and rainwater. It is rich in fruits, pears, apples, dairy products, honey. Its fame is widespread.

Ajdābiya is a flourishing place, built of stone, on the sea-coast. The inhabitants derive their drinking water from the rains. The same may be said of Surt (Sirte); both these places are on a watercourse, and are surrounded by desert scrub.

Sabratha (Sabra), situated in the desert, is fortified, having palm trees and figs. The inhabitants have their drinking water from the rain; Qābis (Gabes) is smaller than Tripoli; here is a fast-flowing stream. Their buildings are of stone and burnt brick. Here is an abundance of palms, grapes, and apples. The town is walled, and with three gates; the hinterland is peopled by Berbers.

Ghāfiq is an extensive area with many villages: markets are held there on Friday. It is a maritime area and some people associate it with the region of Ifrīqiya.

Dhāt al-Humām is a city of recent foundation, and I learned from a person who had asked Abu al-ʿAbbās ibn al-Rāqī concerning it, that its buildings are one of the signs of the conquest of Egypt by the Fātimids.

Al-Qayrawān (Kayrouan) is the metropolis of its region [Ifrīqiya]; it is a delightful, expansive place, where the bread is very good, the meats excellent; it p. 225 produces fruits of every diverse kind. It adjoins plain, mountain, sea. It has great prosperity and learning, and remarkable lowness of price: for a *dirham*, one can buy five *manns* of meat or ten of figs, and you need not ask about its raisins, dates, grapes, and olive oil! It is the point of departure of travelers going west, and is the center of commerce for the two seas. One will not find an area having more towns, or more agreeable people than its inhabitants. There are none other than Hanafites and Mālikites here, and between them remarkable harmony—no discord, no factionalism. Without a doubt, they are instructed by the light of their God, accepting discomfort, and their hearts do not know revenge. This town is the glory of the Maghrib, the seat of power, and one of the pillars of the realm. It is more gracious than Naysābūr, longer than Damascus, more splendid than Isbahān.

Yet their water is inferior in quality, culture is scant, nor do you find elegance there. The water is stored in tanks. Imposts are levied on those who own shops, so they make their living in Sabra; hence the markets of the metropolis are abandoned. The populace is like a flock of stray sheep. They do not recite the *tarāwīḥ*: in fact, neither of the two sects [Hanafiyya and Shāfiʿiyya] has much influence there.

This city is a little less than three miles in either dimension, and is unwalled. The inhabitants keep their drinking water in large earthen vessels, and cisterns in which the rainwater is collected. Al-Muʿizz made a canal for them, which, coming from the mountains, fills the cisterns after going by his palace in Sabra. Their buildings are of clay and brick, and there are numerous large earthen vessels for olive oil. The congregational mosque is at a place called al-Simāt al-Kabīr, in the center of the markets, in the heart of the city. It is bigger than the congregational mosque of Ibn Taylūn, and with columns of marble, is paved with marble tiles. Its drain pipes are of lead, and it has the following entrances: Bāb al-Simāt (emporium), Bāb al-Sarrāfīn (cambists), Bāb al-Rahādina (flax merchants), Bāb al-Fudhūliyyīn (cloth merchants), Bāb al-Maʾdhana (minarets), Bāb al-Sabbāghīn (dyers), Bāb al-Hawwāriyyīn (clothes cleaners), Bāb Sūq al-Khamīs (Thursday market), Bāb al-Maydhāt (fountains for ablution); a special gate for the datesellers; also Bāb al-Lahhāmīn (butchers), and Sūq al-Rammāhīn (the spearmakers' market).

The main thoroughfares through the city are fifteen in number: Darb p. 226 al-Rabīʿ, Darb ʿAbd Allāh, Darb Tūnis, Darb Asram, Darb Aslam, Darb Sūq al-Ahad (Sunday market), Darb Nāfiʿ, Darb al-Hadhdhāʾiyyīn (shoemakers).

Sabra was built by the Fātimid [khalif al-Manṣūr Ismāʿīl, died in the year 341/953], immediately on his taking possession of this region; and its name is derived from the endurance [sabr] of his soldiers in war. It is rounded like a cup, and there is not another place like it. The ruler's palace is in the centre of the city, just as in Baghdad, and water runs through the middle of it. Very well populated, it has excellent markets within which stands the congregational mosque of the ruler. The width of the wall is twelve cubits, and it is separated from the buildings of the city, for between them and it is a space the width of a highway. The merchants go back and forth between the capital and Sabra, mounted on Egyptian asses. The gates of the town are: Bāb al-Futūh (triumphs); Bāb Zawīla; Bāb Wādī 'l-Qassārīn (valley of the fullers); they are all reinforced with iron. The walls are of burnt brick jointed with lime.

Asfāqus (Sfax) and Sūsa (Sousse) are both maritime towns, each encircled by walls of lime and stone. The inhabitants derive their drinking water from wells and cisterns.

Al-Mahdiyya is on the seacoast, surrounded by a wall of stone and lime. The drinking water here is from wells, and cisterns of rainwater. It is the granary of al-Qayrawān, the entrepôt of Sicily and of Egypt. It is a flourishing well-peopled place, and anyone wishing to see al-Qustantīniyya (Constantinople) need only go to al-Mahdiyya and not take the trouble to journey to the Romaean city: in fact it does resemble it, being built on a peninsula, so it may be approached by one access only, just like a trap.

Banzard (Bizerta) is a walled town, its buildings of stone; the mosque is in the centre of the town. A stream of salty water runs through there, entering from a lake close to the sea, and to which it returns; people cross it in skiffs.

Tabarqa is a maritime town dominated by a mountain. Its stronghold has been destroyed, and the people live on the outskirts. They derive their drinking water from wells. A salt stream runs through the town.

Marsā al-Kharaz, a town on a peninsula, is situated on the seacoast, and may be entered at one place only. Coral is gathered here, there being no other source of this substance, which originates in the sea here, only.

Būna (Bône) is a maritime walled town, possessing an iron mine. The inhabitants derive their drinking water from wells.

Bāja is situated between al-Qayrawān and the sea; it is rich in grains and agricultural products. In the middle of the town is a spring well that constantly flows.

p. 227 Lurbus is at the foot of Jabal Būragh; it has acreages of saffron. It is encircled by a wall of stone; the inhabitants derive their drinking water from wells. Around this town and around Bāja are markets and meeting places it would take too long to mention.

Qarna is so called from the name of a sweetwater stream that flows through it: it is encircled by a wall of stone.

Marnīsa is unwalled. The buildings are of clay, the drinking water obtained from wells. Many villages pertain to it in an extensive rural district.

Qamūda is an important country district, its chief town Jamūnas al-Sābūn. The inhabitants make their buildings of clay, and derive their drinking water from wells. The area is rich in figs, olives, almonds. It contains an important village named Khawr al-Kāf.

Marmājanna is a large place, in the administrative district of Tabassā. The drinking water of the inhabitants is from wells; there is an abundance of fruit.

Qalānus is a town in the rural district named Maknat Abī Mansūr: rich in figs, olives, and other agricultural products.

Qabīsha is a country district, its chief town, Tarnābasa (Taqerbāst?). There are many people of the tribe of Banu al-ʿAbbās here, and they have taken over the area. It produces excellent quinces, has an abundance of olives and figs. The inhabitants get their drinking water from wells.

Rusfa is a country district, the name of its chief city, Banūnush, which resembles al-Ramla. The inhabitants derive their drinking water from wells. Here are three hundred sixty olive presses; their buildings are of clay.

Jazīrat Abī Sharīk is in the sea. It comprises twelve rural districts; the name of its chief town is Manzil Bāshū. Unwalled; the buildings are of clay. The people draw their drinking water from wells, from which their farms are irrigated, just as at Shīrāz and Sarakhs.

Bāghāy is a large walled town at the foot of a mountain called Awrās (Aurès), whence the water flows to it. It has many gardens.

p. 228 Sūq Hamza is a town situated on the plain. The inhabitants construct their houses of clay, and derive their water from streams and springs.

[Marsa al-Dajjāj is a town situated on the seacoast. The inhabitants build in baked brick, and derive their drinking water from a stream and some springs— conjectural restoration by de Goeje to Arabic text].

Jazīrat Banī Zagannāya (Alger), on the seacoast, is walled; one sets out from here going to al-Andalus. Springs provide the drinking water.

Mattīja is situated in pasture land. The people have a supply of running water on which mills are constructed; a branch of the river enters the houses; numerous gardens.

Hayāja has the same name as its rural area, which is extensive; it produces a lot of wheat.

Al-Qustantīniyya (Constantine) is a pre-Islamic city two days journey from the metropolis.

Were it not for the risk of boredom, and the lengthening of my book, I should have described the remaining cities of Ifrīqiya and most of the chief towns of the districts of all the realm of Islām. However, as we are inclined to succinctness, we mention only what is indispensable. I know of no area that has more settlements than this, all well populated and first rate. We happen to mention some towns that are smaller than many villages in other regions, but which are widely known as towns. My scholarship is, of course, based on general usage. Do you not see that Mukhā, al-Jāmiʿayn, and al-Munīfa are indisputably towns, while Kafarsallām, Qasr al-Rīh, and Raʾs al-Tīn, though bigger than they, are incontestably villages. You should know that an area does not become illustrious by the number of its settlements, but rather by the importance of its rural districts. Consider, for example, the importance of Naysābūr and Bukhārā, despite the fewness of their towns, and the wretchedness of Zabīd and Hajar despite the multiplicity of the settlements of both those areas.

Tāhart has a principal seat of the same name; it is the Balkh of the Maghrib. Streams surround it, trees enclose it, and it disappears in the midst of its gardens; springs well up around about it. The region is important because of Tāhart: the stranger is refreshed here, and the intelligent traveler finds it agreeable. Some give it preference over Damascus—however, they err; or over Cordoba—but I do not think they are correct. It is a large city, prosperous, extensive, agreeable, with attractive markets, flowing water aplenty, good people; it is of ancient foundation, solidly built, and of truly remarkable appearance.

p. 229 However, when the Maghrib is compared to Syria, where in the realm of Islam is a city the like of Damascus! Similarly Cordoba has a famous name and is important.

Tāhart has two mosques built of stone and lime, occupying two thirds of the town, close to the market places. Of its main streets there are four well-known: Bāb Majjāna, Darb al-Maʿsūma, Darb Hārat al-Faqīr, Darb al-Basātīn. Near Tāhart is a town called [Wādī] al-Ruhā, in ruins.

Tanas is a walled town, situated on the sea coast; the drinking water of the inhabitants is taken from a river; similarly, Qaṣr al-Fulūs.

Tāhart al-Suflā (Lower) is in a large wādī; it has springs and gardens.

Fakkān is a walled town in a wādī with a flowing stream; it has gardens.

Yalal and Jabal Tūjān are the same as we have just described.

Wahrān (Oran) is a maritime town, walled, one takes off from here for al-Andalus, a passage of a day and a night.

Sabta (Ceuta) is situated on the Strait of Gibraltar; one may see the two lands from here, which is one of the best-known crossing points.

Jabal Zālāgh is a settlement on a high mountain which overlooks the district of Fās. Khalūf bin Ahmad al-Muʿtalī built it. As for the remaining towns, most of them are walled, and have gardens.

Fās consists of two important and extensive settlements, each one of them fortified. Flowing between the two is a rapid stream on which are gardens and mills. The Fātimids have taken possession of one part of it, the Umayyads the other. How many wars, and killings and triumphs have been there! The buildings in both sections are clay, the fortifications of brick. Here is to be found Qalʿat (the fortress of) Shamīt built by Ibn al-Būrī; another stands on the river, built by Ibn Ahmad. This area produces an abundance of agricultural products,

p. 230 figs, and olives. Yet, they are, as you see, in great distress from the wars. They are crude and ignorant people, scholars are few, but disturbances frequent.

Qastīliya is without doubt the counterpart of al-Basra in this world. A camel load of dates is to be had for two *dirhams*. The inhabitants avail themselves of a large stream which disappears among the palms. No need to ask about the multiplicity of its gardens! Much the same is at Nafzāwa. Both these places are at some distance from the sea.

Al-Basra used to be a large, flourishing, and important town; now reduced to ruins.

Niqāwus is a lovely attractive town with an abundance of water and walnuts, but it is cold.

Balad Ghumār is in a country district that takes three days to traverse its length or its width; its entire area encompasses many prosperous villages.

Qastīliya has an abundance of dates, just as we have said about Qābis (Gabes); a camel load may be had for two *dirhams*. The inhabitants have a large stream at their disposal.

Similarly Nafzāwa and Biskara are two places with palms and streams.

Niqāwus is cold; it is the district of walnuts and mountain fruits.

The residence of the Amīrs of Fās appointed by the Fāṭimids is at Jabal Zālāgh. The name of the quarter of Fās which they occupy is ʿIdwat al-Qarawī, that of the other, Madīnat al-Andalusī, which the Umayyads built, after crossing the sea and taking possession of Fās. All the other towns are prosperous.

Between Fās and Sāʿ is an important and pleasant town; it has abundant trees and flowing streams. It is in the rural area of Miknāsat al-Sāgha, but I do not remember its name.

p. 231   Tanja (Tangier) is an important area, delightful and flourishing, having prosperous towns both inland and on the coast.

Al-Zāb has as its chief town al-Masīla (Msila), and it is an area just like that which we have described. It is well-known in the region, but of course Tangier is more important.

Sijilmāsa is an important capital some distance from a river, which peters out to the south of the town. The town extends lengthwise towards the south. Surrounding it is a wall of clay, while in the center is a fortress called al-ʿAskar in which are situated the chief mosque and the palace of the Amīr. It has extremes of heat and cold, together, and the climate is quite healthy. Here is an abundance of dates, grapes, raisins, and fruits, grains, pomegranates, and a variety of other agricultural produce. It is an agreeable place for the many strangers who travel to it from every land; it is, moreover, an important frontier town. In its rural district are mines of gold and silver. The inhabitants are Sunnī; they are a very fine people, having among them scholars and intellectuals. The gates of the town are as follow: Bāb al-Qiblī, Bāb al-Gharbī, Bāb Ghadīr al-Jazzārīn (Gate of the Butchers' Creek), Bāb Mawqif Zanāta; and there are others besides these. The town is in the middle of the sands; the people have sources of water.

Darʿa has an extensive rural district, with a number of mosques. It is situated on a rapidly flowing river; the distance around the district is about a six-day journey.

ʿArīsh is a country district with a number of mosques; a number of other flourishing settlements are round about it, in the middle of the sands. There are silver mines at Tāzrart, and a gold mine between this district and the country of the Blacks; there is not in the world purer gold or a more extensive mine than this one. The roads to the area of Sijilmāsa are difficult because they cross desolate deserts of sand.

Balarm (Palermo) is the capital of Sicily; a maritime town situated on an island, it is bigger than al-Fusṭāṭ, but much more dispersed. The buildings, of stone and mortar, are red and white. Surrounding it are fountains and stands of rattan; a river named Wādī ʿAbbās irrigates it, and in the centre are mills. Fruits, agricultural products, and grapes are here in abundance. The sea-water laps the surrounding walls. This city has an interior city in which stands the chief mosque, while the markets are situated on the outskirts. Another walled settlement outside is named al-Khālisa, with four gates: Bāb Kutāma, Bāb al-Futūh (triumphs), Bāb al-Bunūd (troops), Bāb al-Sinā'a (maritime arsenal); here also is a Friday mosque, and markets.

p. 232

Atrābunush (Trapani) is a walled maritime town to the west; the drinking water is derived from a river.

'Ayn al-Mughattā and Māzar, two settlements, to the west.

Qal'at al-Ballūt is a fortified town at a high altitude; drinking water is from a spring that wells up there.

Jirjant is a walled maritime town; drinking water is from wells.

Buthīra is a walled maritime town to the west; surrounded with a protective wall giving it the appearance of a fortress.

Saraqūsa (Syracuse) consists of two adjoining settlements; endowed with a remarkable harbor; surrounded by a fosse in which the seawater flows.

Lantīnī, a walled town; situated on a river and close to the sea; the buildings are stone.

Qatāniya is a maritime town to the south; walled; also called Madīnat al-Fīla.

Al-Yāj (Acireale), walled, maritime, to the south; the drinking water is from a permanent stream.

Batarnū (Paterno) is to the east at the foot of "the mountain of streaming fire."

Tabarmīn (Taormina) is a maritime town to the east; it overlooks the land of the Romaeans (Italy) to the east. It has a fortress of stone, and is a seaport.

The other cities to the east, ten in number, are as we have described; however Qal'at al-Sirāt is at a high altitude.

Batarliya (Petralia), to the south, in the interior; walled. In the centre is a fortress within which is a church.

Bartinīq (Portinico) is not maritime. It produces much henna, similarly Akhyās; Balja is low-lying.

Siqiliyya (Sicily) is an island, extensive and important; the Muslims have no island more splendid, more prosperous, or with more cities. Its length is a distance of twelve days journey, its width four days. Between it and the country of the Romaeans is a strait in the direction of the rising sun, having a width of twelve days journey: this is al-Khalīj, numbered among the five seas.

p. 233

Qurtuba (Cordoba) is the capital of al-Andalus; I have heard some 'Uthmānī[?] remark that it is a more important town than Baghdād. Situated in a desert plain, a mountain overlooking it, it consists of an inner city (al-Madīna) and suburbs. The chief mosque is within the city, as are some of the markets; most of the markets, however, and the palace of the ruler are in the suburbs. In front of the town flows a large stream. The roofs are of tile: the mosque is of stone and mortar, with columns of marble; all around it are basins for the ablutions. Al-Madīna (the inner city) has five gates: Bāb al-Hadīd (iron), Bāb al-ʿAttārīn (perfumers), Bāb al-Qantara (arcade), Bāb al-Yahūd (Jews), Bāb ʿAmir. The evidence is clear, and opinions agree that it is an important metropolis, friendly and attractive, where one finds justice, wisdom, political sense, benignity, obvious prosperity, and religion.

The district of al-Andalus resembles Haytal in some characteristics. There is constant raiding, continual holy strife, and the people under arms. Here, too, is much learning, a strong ruler, some specialties, commercial activity, and considerable advantages.

A certain Andalusian told me that Cordoba consists of thirteen country districts.

Fifteen miles away is Arjūna, a walled town, without orchards and trees, being, rather, an area of grains. For drinking water the inhabitants have springs, while their farms are watered only by the rain.

Qastalla, thirteen miles from Arjūna, is in a plain; abundant in trees, olives, vineyards. The drinking water is derived from wells; and the people irrigate their gardens by employing norias.

Shawdhar, eighteen miles from Cordoba; situated on a plain. Here is a great abundance of olives; drinking water is from springs.

Mārtush, fifteen miles from Cordoba; it is situated in the mountains, having only vineyards. There are springs.

Qanbānush, fifteen miles away; on a plain. There are farms, most of them in an area called Qanbāniya; the drinking water is from wells.

Fajj Ibn Laqīt is twenty-five miles away; on a plain, having many cultivated fields. The drinking water is derived from wells.

Balāt Marwān is thirty miles away. It has a swift-flowing stream; on a plain, has some farms.

Buryāna has some farms; on a plain. The inhabitants derive their drinking
p. 234 water from wells. It includes a fortress built of stone, with suburbs around about. The Friday mosque is in the fortress, the marketplaces in the suburbs.

Hisn Bulkūna is rich in olives, trees, and springs. It is walled, with stone. The drinking water is derived from one spring, and some wells. It is forty miles from Cordoba.

Al-Shanīda is in the mountains. Vineyards, cultivated fields, figs, grapes in abundance. Drinking water is from springs and wells: two days journey from Cordoba, the overnight station being Fajj Ibn Laqīt.

Wādī ʿAbd Allāh, to the south, is forty miles from Cordoba; the overnight stop is Wādī al-Rummān. On a plain, possessing farms, streams, and some trees.

Qarsīs, sixty miles from Cordoba. On a plain; rich in figs, grapes, large olives; the drinking water is from springs.

Jayyān (Jaèn) is fifty miles from Cordoba. The name of its rural district is Awlaba (Awliya = Ulia). The town of Jayyān is on a mountain, and has a number of springs. Its fortress was destroyed even though it is defended by the mountains. It has twelve springs on three of which are mills which supply the provisions of al-Andalus; hence also is Cordoba provisioned. Jaèn produces an abundance of fruits. You may say all you wish about its delightfulness and charm, for it is the paradise of al-Andalus, according to what I have been told. The ending -ān of the name indicates that this is a district. The buildings are of stone. It becomes cold and winds blow frequently, even so, the district is sometimes hot. According to our classification Jayyān consists of a number of districts. The chief towns are: al-Jafr, in the mountains, about ten miles from Jayyān. This area, which has many streams and mills, abounds in trees, fruits, olives, grapes, and is situated in a wādī in which is a concentration of a variety of fruits.

p. 235

Bayghū (Priego), in the mountains. Here are valleys from which springs bubble forth and turn mills; an abundance of mulberry, olives, and figs.

Mārtush, a walled town on a mountain. The inhabitants derive their drinking water from springs; figs, olives, and vines in abundance.

Qānt, walled, situated on a plain; no orchards. The climate is healthy.

Gharnāta (Granada) is on a stream. Here is a *munya* thirteen miles long, belonging to the ruler, in it all kinds of excellent and remarkable fruit. The town is on a plain, and has many cultivated fields. I asked someone, "What is the *munya*?" Said he: "It is the pleasure ground of the ruler."

Mantīsha (Mentesa), a walled town on a stream; an abundance of olives and figs; on a plain.

Bayyāsa (Baeza), a walled town on a mountain; buildings of clay; drinking water from springs; many fig trees and vineyards.

I asked someone, "Has Cordoba any other rural districts and towns besides these?" He said, "No." Said I, "But Ishbīliya (Seville) and Bajjāna (Pechina)?" and I mentioned a number of other towns. Said he, "These are districts that pertain to regions, just as you refer to al-Qayrawān, and Tāhart, and Sijilmāsa." In al-Andalus they call a country district (*rustāq*) a region (*iqlīm*). But I consider these as districts (*kūra*) according to our classification, even though they are not more important than the districts of Haytal, and nor are they inferior to them. In fact, we may say that all our information has established that it is the same in the Maghrib (West) as in the Mashriq (Orient)—each one of these two consists of two separated sections; just as al-Mashriq comprises Khurāsān and Haytal, the Jayhūn separating the two, similarly al-Maghrib and al-Andalus are separated by the Romaean Sea (Mediterranean).

However, we have been unable to survey al-Andalus, so we left it all of a piece; we did, however, describe the district of Cordoba, because of the many informants who spoke to me about it, and gave me a very clear account of its character. I submitted my book to one of the shaykhs of al-Andalus, and said he: "On this basis al-Andalus should comprise eighteen districts," and he enumerated: Bajjāna (Pechina), Mālaqa (Malaga), Balansiya (Valencia), Tudmīr, Saraqūsa (Saragossa), Yābisa (Ibiza), Wādī 'l-Hijāra (Guadalajara), Tutīla (Tudela),

Washqa (Huesca), Madīnat Sālim (Medinaceli), Tulaytula (Toledo), Ishbīliya (Seville), Batalyawth (Badajoz), Bāja (Beja), Qurtuba (Cordoba), Shadhūna p. 236 (Sidonia), al-Jazīrat al-Khadhrāʾ (Algeciras). I asked another and he said that this information is correct; however, he added to the list: Libīra, and Ukhshunuba. It is possible that some of these names are names of districts, just on the analogy of Īlāq, Kush, and al-Saghāniyān. But God best knows the truth in this.

A Summary Account of Conditions in this Region

The Maghrib is an important region, great in area, and long, in which one may obtain most of the products found in the other regions, and at a low price. It is rich in palm trees and olives. Here are areas of heat, likewise zones of cold. Jews there are numerous. The climate is excellent, as is the water. As for the heat, one encounters it from Egypt as far as Sūs al-Aqsā, except in the mountain areas and the cold localities. The cold is predominant in al-Andalus. In this province are many lepers, eunuchs, stupid people, misers, few storytellers. The people are agreeable, liking knowledge and the learned; they are very busy with commerce, and with going from place to place.

As for the **religious schools**, there are three categories here: in al-Andalus the school of Mālik, and the reading system of Nāfiʿ prevail. The Muslims here declare: "We know nothing but the Book of God and the *Muwattaʾ* [*The Beaten Path*—a book of legal maxims taken from the Traditions, and the basis of Mālik's system of jurisprudence] of Mālik. Should they detect a Hanafite or a Shāfiʿite they expel him; but if they light upon a Muʿtazilite or a Shīʿa or anyone heterodox such as these, they may kill him.

In the remaining part of the Maghrib, as far as Egypt, the Muslims do not recognize the teaching of al-Shāfiʿī—on whom may God have mercy—acknowledging only Abū Hanīfa and Mālik—on whom may God have mercy. One day, as I was discussing a question with someone there, I quoted a saying of al-Shāfiʿī—on whom may God have mercy. Said he to me, "Hold your tongue! Who is al-Shāfiʿī? There are but two 'seas'—Abū Hanīfa for the people of the Orient, and Mālik for the people of the West. Shall we abandon both of these, and occupy ourselves with a 'trickling stream'?" I saw that the adherents of Mālik—on whom may God have mercy—hated al-Shāfiʿī, for, said they, "He received his instruction from Mālik, then went in opposition to him." As for myself, I have never seen two groups in better agreement and with less fanaticism than these [Hanafites and Mālikites]; and I heard them speaking, on p. 237 the authority of their elders, about that same matter, including a remarkable account to the effect that one year the man who sat as judge would be Hanafite, the next year Mālikite.

I asked, "How did it come to pass that the doctrine of Abū Hanīfa arrived among you, seeing that he was not on the path frequented by you?" Said they,

"When Wahb bin Wahb came here, having studied with Mālik—on whom may God have mercy—and with the knowledge of the law and of the religious sciences that he had, Asad bin ʿAbd Allāh disdained to be his pupil because of his own self-importance and egotism. So he, Asad, himself, left for Madīna with the intention of studying under the direction of Mālik, but he found him ailing. Asad having stayed with him a long time, Mālik said to him: 'Return to Ibn Wahb, for I entrusted my knowledge to him, to spare you the journey.' This was rather hard on Asad so he asked whether any equal to Malik was acknowledged. He was told that there was a young man at Kūfa named Muhammad bin al-Hasan, a disciple of Abū Hanīfa. Asad went to Muhammad, who devoted his attention to him more than to anyone else. Observing his understanding and eagerness, he instilled in him an exact knowledge of the law. When, then, he knew that he was able to stand on his own, and had acquired the knowledge he had wanted to, he allowed him to return to the Maghrib. When he arrived there the young people frequented him, and were enlightened on various aspects of the law that had confused them, subtleties that pleased them, and questions that had never even sounded on the ears of Ibn Wahb. Some of the people formed a study circle around him, and thus the teaching of Abū Hanīfa—on whom may God have mercy—spread in the Maghrib." Said I, "Why has it not spread in al-Andalus?" Said they, "It was no less current in al-Andalus than it is here. However, one day, representatives of the two schools exchanged their respective views in the presence of the ruler, who asked of them, 'Whence was Abū Hanīfa?' Said they, 'From al-Kufa.' 'And Mālik?' Said they: 'From al-Madīna.' Said he, 'The learned one from the town of the Hijra is sufficient for us,' and he expelled the adherents of Abū Hanīfa, saying, 'I do not wish that in my province there be two schools of law.'" I received this account from a number of the shaykhs of al-Andalus.

Addition/version MS. C.
I enquired about this account of a number of Andalusians, and they said that it is correct. For my part, I believe that the ruler was biased, because the Banū Umayya detest ʿAlī, and the viewpoint of Abū Hanīfa on ʿAlī. Moreover, they do not like the people of al-Kūfa, because they are Shīʿa.

The third group represents the doctrines of the Fātimids, and this consists of three subdivisions: the first, the points on which the Imāms have disagreed, p. 238 such as the *qunūt* in the morning prayer, the saying out loud of the *bismillāh*, saying the *witr* with one *rakaʿ* [bending of the torso in prayer, followed by two prostrations], and such matters. The second: a return to the practices of the early Muslims, such as saying the *iqāma* [the recitation of a part of the call to prayer] twice, which the Umayyads had restored to the saying it once; the wearing of white garments, the ʿAbbāsids having instated black. The third division: those practices which are proper to themselves and about which the Imāms do not disagree, even though they may not be known to be old practices, such as the "*hayya ʿalā*" during the call to prayer, making the first of the month the day on which the new moon is seen, saying the prayer of the eclipse of the moon with five *rakaʿs*, making two prostrations at each bowing. These are practices of the Shīʿa.

The Fātimids have literary works which they study, and I looked into their *Kitāb al-Daʿāʾim [Kitāb Daʿāʾim al-Islām—The Book of the Pillars of Islām* of al-Qādhī al-Nuʿmān ibn Abī ʿAbd Allāh]. It seems they agree with the Muʿtazilites in most of the principles of the law, and they profess the doctrines of the Ismāʿilites. They have a secret they do not teach nor communicate to anyone whatever, unless it is to one whom they trust, having taken an oath from him, and a solemn pledge. They have been called Bātiniyya, because they disregard the literal meaning of the *Qurʾān* in favor of hidden meanings and strange interpretations, and finical explanations. These *usūl* (principles) constitute the doctrines of the Idrīsids, who predominate in the district of al-Sūs al-Aqsā, and they are close to the principles of the Qaramites.

The people of the Maghrib and of the Mashriq view the doctrines of the Fātimids in three different ways: some acknowledge them and believe firmly in them; some have rejected them and refused to believe in them; the others look on them as merely divergences among the Muslim community.

Most of the inhabitants of Sicily are Hanafites.

I read in a book which some shaykh of the Karramites compiled in Naysābūr, that in the Maghrib his sect has seven hundred monasteries. But I can assert that it is not so, and that they do not have even one!

The system of reading the *Qurʾān* followed in the entire region is the reading of Nāfiʿ, solely.

Customs of the Region. In these six regions of the Arabs evidence is not taken except from an impartial witness. On one occasion when I was present at the signing of a marriage contract, Abu al-Tayyib Hamdān bade me sign my attestation, and I was congratulated for this. The inhabitants of the Maghrib carry the dead only by the head or the legs. They sit down after each prayer at
p. 239 night during Ramadhān. They do not skin the sheep in preparation for roasting. Very seldom do they enter the public baths without wraps.

It is the custom to follow the Egyptian fashion in the Maghrib, but it is seldom people wear the *taylasān*. They frequently fold the mantle in two and throw it over the back like a cloak. They wear dyed hoods; the Berbers wear a black burnoose. The country people wear tailored garments, the common people wear kerchiefs.

The merchants ride Egyptian asses and mules. All their copies of the *Qurʾān*, and their registers are written on parchment. The people of al-Andalus are the most skilled in copying; their script is rounded.

Some **trade** is carried on here. Wool cloth and garments are exported from Barqa; from Sicily the most excellent short garments. From Ifrīqiya, olive oil, pistachios, saffron, almonds, plums, satchels, leather mats, waterskins; from Fās, dates and all the other things we have mentioned. From al-Andalus, much cloth, and some remarkable products that are special to them.

Specialties. Among the specialties of this region is the coral extracted from the sea at a peninsula, the name of its town, Marsā al-Kharaz (La Calle); one goes to it by means of a narrow passageway as at al-Mahdiyya. From the sea, here, the pod grows up, and this constitutes the coral, which forms like mountains in the sea: there is no other source of it but here. People go out in skiffs to collect it, providing themselves with wooden crosses, around which they loosely tie some flax. To each cross they attach two ropes, of which two men take hold and throw the cross into the sea. The oarsmen cause the boat to rotate so that the cross clings to the coral, which they then pull in. One may extract from ten thousand to ten *dirhams* weight of coral. The coral is then polished in a special marketplace, and sold in bulk, at a low price; it has neither lustre nor colour before it is polished.

In Tutīla (Tudela), an abundance of sables. In al-Andalus, a leather used in the making of sword-handles. At a certain time of the year a goodly amount of ambergris is cast up from the Atlantic Ocean. A considerable amount of white ammonia is produced in Sicily. I heard that its production had been cut off, and that the Egyptians managed to do without it by using the soot from their public baths.

p. 240 **Weights and Measures**. The *ratl* of Baghdād was used in the entire region, except for that used in the weighing of pepper, this being lighter than that of Baghdād by ten *dirhams* weight; that of Baghdād is now used, however, in all the provinces under the Fātimids in the entire Maghrib.

As for **measures of capacity**: the *qafz* of al-Qayrawān is thirty-two *thumns* (eighths) and the *thumn* is six *mudd-s* of the *mudd* of the Prophet—God's peace and blessings be upon him. The *qafz* of al-Andalus is sixty *ratls*. The *rubʿ* (quarter) is eighteen *ratls*; the *fanīqa* is half a *qafiz*. The standard dry measure of the Fātimids is the *dawwār*, and this is lighter than the *wayba* of Egypt by a very little. The top of this measure is fitted tightly with an iron crossbeam, a vertical member of iron is erected from the bottom of the measure to meet the crossbeam above, which is rotated on the top of the measure (*wayba*), so that when the measure is filled the contents are smoothed evenly with the mouth of the *wayba*, and the measure is thus correct. Their *ratl* weights are made of lead, and stamped on each *ratl* is the name of the Commander of the Faithful. These weights are collected in one place from time to time, and ordered to be remoulded, each weight being stamped anew, if there are about ten of them to be processed.

The **coinage**: in all the provinces of this region, as far as the boundaries of the province of Damascus, the standard is the *dīnār*, which is lighter than the *mithqāl* by a *habba*, that is to say a grain of barley. The coin bears an inscription in the round.

There is also the small *rubᶜ*, (quarter of a *dīnār*); these two coins pass current by number, [rather than by weight]. The *dirham* also is short in legal weight. A half-*dirham* is called a *qīrāt*; there is also the quarter, the eighth part, and the sixteenth part which is called a *kharnūba*. All of these circulate by number [rather than by weight], but their use thus does not bring any reduction in price. The *sanja* (counterpoise weights) used are made of glass, and are stamped just as we described about the *ratls*.

The *ratl* of the city of Tunis is twelve *uqīya* (ounce), this latter being twelve *dirhams* (weight).

The **remarkable things** in this region are many. Among them is the Abū Qalamūn, a creature which scratches itself on the rocks on the seashore. It leaves some of its fur there, which has the softness of silk and the colour of gold. The people do not leave a thread of it behind, because it is very rare. It is gathered, and cloths woven from it; and in the course of a day it assumes various colours. The ruler has forbidden the export of it, though, of course, some is exported secretly. One garment made of it may fetch ten thousand *dīnārs*.

In Sicily is a mountain from which fire bubbles for four months, once every ten years; the rest of the time it emits smoke. Around the mountain the snow is compressed, except where the smoke comes out.

In the town of Īkijā are springs that flow at times of Prayer, and then cease to flow. Should a man go there who has killed someone unlawfully, the springs will not flow at all.

Now, should someone say to us that we have omitted mention of many remarkable things of this region, we should reply that we have omitted only what predecessors of ours have mentioned in their works. One of the excellences of our book is avoiding what others have mentioned; and the most objectionable feature of their books is that their methods are in every way opposite to ours. Do you not realize that if you read the book of al-Jayhānī, you will see that it contains all of the original work of Ibn Khurradādhbih, and that it is on this he built his work. Read the book of Ibn al-Faqīh, and it is exactly as if you were reading the book of al-Jāhiz and *al-Zīj al-Aᶜzam* (*The Great Ephemeris*). But read our book, and you find that it speaks for itself only, and, of its kind, somewhat like an orphan, is unique in its organization. In fact if I had felt myself at liberty not to have to put together this book of mine, I should not have troubled myself with it; but since God—may He be exalted—enabled me to travel to the remotest parts of the realm of Islām, showed me its conditions, and inspired me to classify it, it was obligatory that we complete the work for the benefit of all Muslims. Consider the saying of God—may He be exalted—: "Say: 'Journey in the land'" (*Qurʾān*, sūra 6, v. 11) and "Have they not traveled through the land so that they may behold ..." (*Qur'ān*, sūra 12, v. 109). In any case, in what we have set down is a lesson for the wise, and profits for the traveler.

As for the Country of the Blacks (*Ardh al-Sūdān*), it borders on this region [the Maghrib] and Egypt, from the south: it is a desolate, extensive, difficult country. The population is constituted of many races. In their mountains one finds those fruits that occur generally in the mountains of the realm of Islām, but most of the people there do not eat them. They have, however, other fruits, victuals, foodstuffs, and herbs not found with us. In trade among them, gold and silver are not used; however, the Qarmātiyyūn (Garamantes) use salt as means of exchange, and the Nubians and Abyssinians thus use cloth. The Nubians live beyond Egypt, the Baja beyond ʿAydhāb, and the Abyssinians beyond Zaylāʿ.

p. 242

The black eunuchs whom you encounter are of three classes: the class that is taken to Egypt, and these are the best kind; the class that is taken to ʿAdan—the Berber—and they are the worst kind. The third kind resemble the Abyssinians. Of white eunuchs there are two classes: the Saqāliba [Slavs], whose land is beyond Khwārazm; they are, however, taken to al-Andalus where they are castrated, then exported to Egypt. Then there are the Romaeans, who are exported to Syria and Aqūr; however, this source has been cut off because of the ravaging of our frontiers.

I asked a group of them about the process of castration, and I learned that the Romaeans castrate their youngsters intended for dedication to the church, and they confine them so that they do not preoccupy themselves with women, or suffer carnal desires. When the Muslims raid, they attack the churches and take the youngsters away from them.

Addition / version MS. C.
In the case of the Romaeans, they would remove the testicles, but leave the penis, and this they would do to their youngsters when they dedicated them to the church; when the Muslims would raid they would capture them from the church.

The Slavs are taken to a town beyond Pechina, where the people are Jews, and they castrate them. There was disagreement among my informants about how the castration was done. According to some of them, the penis and the scrotum are cut off at the same time. Others asserted that the scrotum is cut and the testicles removed, after which a stick is inserted under the penis which is then cut off at the base. I inquired of the eunuch ʿUrayb, a learned and truthful man, "Muʿallim (eunuch), tell me about eunuchs, seeing that the scholars are not in agreement about them. Abū Ḥanīfa asserts that they are able to have legitimate children, and are recognized as the fathers of the children their wives bear them: this is a matter that can be properly settled only by you." Said he, "Abū Ḥanīfa was correct—may God have mercy on him—and I will tell you how this is. You should know that when the youngsters are about to be castrated, the scrotum is cut open for the removal of the testicles. It may be that the youngster is frightened, so that one of his testicles ascends into his abdomen. If it is searched for and not found at the time, it will descend after the cut has healed. If it is the left testicle that remains, the eunuch can experience lust and have sperm; if it is the right one, he may grow a beard, as in the case of so-and-so, and so-and-so. Abū Hanīfa—may God have mercy on him—adhered to the saying of the Prophet—may God's peace and blessings be upon him— 'The child pertains to the conjugal bed,' for it might be that the eunuch would be one of those to whom a testicle remained."

I related this to Abū Saʿīd al-Jūrī in Naysābūr, and he said, "This is perfectly possible, for one of my testicles is small," and in fact, his beard was light and thin.

When the castration is done, a little pencil of lead is placed in the urinary opening; this is removed during urination, and [is replaced] until the wound heals, so that the hole will not close up.

Language. The language of the inhabitants of the Maghrib is Arabic, but it is hardly understandable, since it varies, as we have mentioned, from region to region. They have another language which is close to Romaean.

The further west one goes, the people are whiter, more blue-eyed, and have thicker beards ... [lacuna in MS.] ... their chief centre is the town of Satīf. It is the people here who prepared the way for ʿUbayd Allāh [the Fātimid Mahdī]. Most of the open country of this region is inhabited by Berbers, who are, however, most numerous in al-Sūs. They are a people like the people of Khwārazm: their language is incomprehensible, and their dispositions disagreeable, for they are mean and violent. I heard that one of them tightened his moneybelt around his middle, and went on the Pilgrimage, returning without having touched his money: then he married! The Berbers are the people who visit Jerusalem the least.

Their defects. In Ifrīqiya are two towns in which is sold the flesh of dogs hanging from butcher hooks; these are Qastīliya and Nafta, where the inhabitants are accused of putting dog meat in the *harīsa*. Along with that they are crude, vile-natured and coarse. One of them may be seen cooking some of it in the pot, then selling the meat or the *thurda* (broth).

The routes into the furthermost regions are difficult, running through sands and deserts.

The Governments. In al-Andalus, no ruler whatever is mentioned in the *khutba* [Friday sermon in the chief mosque] except the Umayyads. As for al-Sūs al-Aqsā, the first person who took it over was Idrīs bin ʿAbd Allāh bin Hasan bin Hasan bin ʿAlī ibn Abī Tālib, and this is how it happened. Idrīs escaped from the battle between the ʿAbbāsids and the Tālibites, at Fakhkh, during the khalifate of al-Hādī, and he proceeded to Egypt. Over the Post routes in Egypt at the time was Wādih, deputy of al-Mansūr, and, moreover, a Shīʿa. So Wādih conducted Idrīs on the Post route to al-Maghrib, and when he reached Tangiers the people there and round about deferred to him. When al-Rashīd succeeded to the khalifate and was informed of this, he beheaded Wādih and crucified him. He also secretly sent al-Shammākh al-Yamāmī, a deputy of al-Mahdī, as an agent against Idrīs, writing for him a letter of recommendation to Ibrāhīm bin al-Aghlab, his deputy over Ifrīqiya. Al-Shammākh continued on his way until he reached Zuwayla, where he announced that he was a physician, and one of the supporters of their cause [Idrīsid]. They trusted him and received him well. On one occasion Idrīs complained of a toothache, and in the evening al-Shammākh gave him a tooth remedy that was, however, poisoned, bidding him to treat his tooth with it the following morning; he then fled. When Idrīs treated his tooth with the poison, it killed him. Al-Shammākh was sought, but it was not possible to overtake him, and al-Rashīd appointed him director of the postal service in Egypt.

Addition/version MS. C.

These are they who are over the kingdom at the present time. The first of them was ʿUbayd Allāh. His missionaries and teachers, and those who supported him were the Banū Kutāma, and they made the conquests for him. The origin of the house is in Salamiyya, a city in the district of Hims. They are Bedouin, and a division of the Banū Bāhila. ʿUbayd Allāh was called al-Mahdī. After him came al-Hādī, then al-Muʿizz, and it is he who conquered Egypt; then al-ʿAzīz. When they were heading for Egypt with their armies, Abū Jaʿfar al-Tahawī, the jurisprudent of Egypt, rose up against them, and said he: "O you people! Go out against this tribe, for they are rebels, and holy strife against them is obligatory on you; for they are altering the Sunna of the Prophet, they are rending the religion asunder, and they are misleading the community." So the populace marched out against them as one solid troop; but the others routed them and threw them back, and gained a considerable amount of booty.

As for the **distances**:

from Barqa to al-Nadāma, one stage;
thence to Tākanast, one stage;
thence to al-Maghār, one stage;
thence to Halīmān, one stage;
thence to Makhīl, one stage;
thence to Jubb al-Maydaʿan, one stage;
thence to Jiyād al-Saghīr, one stage;
p. 245   thence to Hayy ʿAbd Allāh, one stage;
thence to Marj al-Shaykh, one stage;
thence to al-ʿAqaba, one stage;
thence to Kharā'ib Abī Halīma, one stage;
thence to Khirbat al-Qawm, one stage;
thence to Qasr al-Shammās one stage;

thence to Sikkat al-Hammām, one stage;
thence to Jubb al-ʿAwsaj, one stage;
thence to Kanāʾis al-Harīr (al-Hadīd), one stage;
thence to al-Tāhūna, one stage;
thence to Haniyyat al-Rūm, one stage;
thence to Dhāt al-Humām, one stage;
thence to Būmīnah, one stage;
thence to Alexandria, one stage.

From Tripoli to al-Masdūda, one stage;
thence to Aristā, one stage;
thence to al-Rāshidiyya, one stage;
thence to Qusūr Hassān, one stage;
thence to Maghmadāsh, one stage;
thence to Surt (Sirte), one stage;
thence to Qasr al-ʿIbādī, one stage;
thence to al-Yahūdiyyatāyn, one stage;
thence to Qasr al-ʿAtish, one stage;
thence to Sabkha Manhūsā, one stage;
thence to Baladrūb (Balbad), one stage;
thence to Barmast, one stage;
thence to Sulūq, one stage;
thence to Awbarān, one stage;
thence to Qasr al-Fīl (Qasr alʿAsal), one stage;
thence to Malītiya, one stage;
thence to Barqa, one stage.

p. 246 From Tripoli to Biʾr al-Jammālīn, one stage;
thence to Qasr al-Daraq, one stage;
thence to Bārjamt, one stage;
thence to al-Fawwāra, one stage;
thence to Qābis (Gabes), one stage;
thence to (Biʾr) al-Zaytūna, one stage;
thence to Katāna, one stage;
thence to al-Kabs, one stage;
thence to al-Qayrawān, one stage.

From there one crosses the desert areas as far as al-Sūs al-Adnā, a distance of two thousand one hundred fifty miles; to arrive at al-Sūs al-Aqsā requires a journey of twenty-three days. The width of the Romaean Sea at this point is eighteen miles.

One may go from al-Qayrawān a distance of seven stages to Qafsa (Jafsa), thence to Qastīliya, three stages; thence to Tāhart, a journey of fifteen days, passing through areas of sand, and some villages. One then travels among the

Berbers for three days on the way to Fās; then one travels through inhabited areas for eight stages, as far as al-Shaqūr; thence, a similar distance passing villages and some streams, as far as al-Basra. At this point, one has come to the limit of al-Sūs al-Adnā.

Should one wish to do so, one may travel from al-Qayrawān to Satīf, a distance of ten stages; thence to Tāhart, twenty; thence to Fās, fifty; thence to al-Sūs al-Aqsā, thirty.

From al-Qayrawān to Zawīla is a journey of one month. From al-Qayrawān to Sijilmāsa, over the desert, is thirty stages; through the settled areas, fifty.

From al-Qayrawān to Tūnis, three stages;
    thence to Tabarqa, ten stages;
    thence to Tanas, six stages;
    thence to Jazīrat Banī Zagannāya (Alger), five stages.

p. 247 From al-Qayrawān to Gabes, to Nafta, to Qarna, to Sabība, to Mādinat al-Qusūr, or to al-Mahdiyya, in every instance is two stages.

From al-Qayrawān to Lāfis, to al-Jazīra, to Ubba, to Marsā al-Kharaz, in every instance is three stages.

From al-Qayrawān to Qābis (Gabes) to Qasr al-Ifrīqī, to Majjāna, in every instance, five stages.

From Majjāna to Tabassa, to Bāghāy, to Dūfāna, to ʿAyn al-ʿAsāfir, to Dār Maluwwal, to Tubna, to Maqqara, or to al-Masīla, in every instance, one stage; and between every one of them and the next, in the order in which we have enumerated them, one stage.

From al-Masīla westward to Ashīr is a journey of three days;
    thence to Tāhart, five days;
    thence to Fakkān, five days;
    thence to Tilimsān (Tlemcen), two stages;
    thence to Jurāwa, two stages.

From Tilimsān to Sāʿ, two stages; [lacuna] ... similarly.
Masīla marks the extremity of Ifrīqiya.

From Tāhart to Nākūr, thirty stages;
    thence to Sijilmāsa, fifteen stages;
    from Fās to al-Basra, six stages;
    from Fās to Azīla, eight stages.

We have cut short and summarized somewhat enumeration of the distances between places in this part of the Maghrib, because they are long and many, and but few travelers pass through there.

From al-Qayrawān to Sūsa (Sousse), to Qalshāna, or to Tumājir, in every instance, one stage.

As for **distances in al-Andalus I** have verified that from Cordoba, which is the capital, to Ishbīliya (Seville) is a distance of three stages; thence southwards to Istija, one stage; from Cordoba to Tulaytula (Toledo), a journey of six days; and to Wādī 'l-Hijāra (Guadalajara), two stages.

From Cordoba to Miknāsa (Meknès) is a journey of four days; thence to al-Huwwāra, the same. Thence to Nafza, ten days; thence to Sammūra (Zamora) four days.

From Cordoba to Qūriya (Coria), twelve stages;
thence to Mārida, four days.

From Coria to Bāja, six days; and from Bāja to the last town of the district of Shantarīn (Santarem), seventeen days.

From Bāja to Fahs al-Ballūt, two days;
thence to Labla, fourteen days.

From Bāja to Qarmūna, four days, and this town, situated to the west, between Bāja and Seville, is on the route of Mārida (Merida).

p. 248 From Qarmūna to Seville, two stages; from Istija to Mawrūr (Moron de la Frontera), one stage; thence to Shadhūna, two days, or to Jabal Tāriq (Gibraltar), three days.

From Istija to Mālaqa (Malaga), seven days on the eastern route; or to Arjidūna, three stages.

From Istija to Bajjāna, six stages, or to Mursiya (Murcia), seven days; or to Valencia, twenty days,
thence to Turtūsha, twelve stages.

From Murcia to Bajjāna, six days;
thence to Malaga, ten days;
thence to Gibraltar, four days;

thence to Shadhūna, three days;
thence to Seville, four days.

As for this town of Seville, the people of the Maghrib have proverbs about it, because of its remoteness, just as the people of the Orient have about Farghānā. I do not know the first Isbīliya (Seville).

An Account of the Desert of the Bedouin

You should know that among the regions of the Arabs, excluding the Maghrib, there is a desert that has waters, streams, wells, springs, hills, sand dunes, villages and palm trees; there are few mountains, many Bedouin, frightening roads, and highways hard to find. The climate is excellent, the water bad. There is no lake therein, nor a river except al-Azraq; and no town except Taymāʾ. Some people consider it a part of the Peninsula of the Arabs, but of course it is not. Some people divide it up among the different regions, some consider it a part of Syria. We, however, have decided to treat of it separately, and give a clear description of it, because no one from any of the [other] thirteen regions going to Makka by land can get there except through this desert, so a knowledge of it is indispensable. Moreover, there are open roads there that are not generally known, and sources of water of which people are ignorant. Thus, in describing it there are advantages without number, and there is a benefit and a value that cannot be gainsaid.

As for myself, I have traveled in this desert numerous times, have surveyed its south, north, east, and west. I have searched for information on the routes, have asked about its water supplies, and have researched deeply so as to have a knowledge of it; thus I have arrived at information of its general conditions, and have become acquainted with most of its roads.

Here is a map of it, and in God is success. [Map X]

p. 249   We deem this desert to extend from Wayla to ʿAbbādān, then to Bālis in a curve, then to al-Raqqa, thence back to Wayla. We have distributed over it twelve routes, nine running the length of the desert, reaching to Makka, three going its width, reaching to Syria. There is also another road to Qurh, reaching Makka from al-Basra, then going on to Egypt. The first is the Route of Egypt; then the Route of al-Ramla; then the Route of al-Sharāt; then the Route of Tabūk; then the route of Wubayr; then the Route of Batn al-Sirr; then the Route of al-Rahba; then the Route of Hīt; then the Route of al-Kūfa; then the Route of al-Qādisiyya; then the Route of Wāsit; then the Route of Wādī 'l-Qurā; then the Route of al-Basra: these then are the highways, in order, and we describe them individually.

As for the Route of Egypt, one goes from al-Buwayb to Bunduqa (Manzil Ibn Sadaqa), one stage;

         thence to ʿAjrūd, one stage;
         thence to al-Madīna, one stage;
         thence to al-Kursī, one stage;
         thence to al-Hafar, one stage;
         thence to al-Manzil, one stage;
         thence to Wayla, one stage.

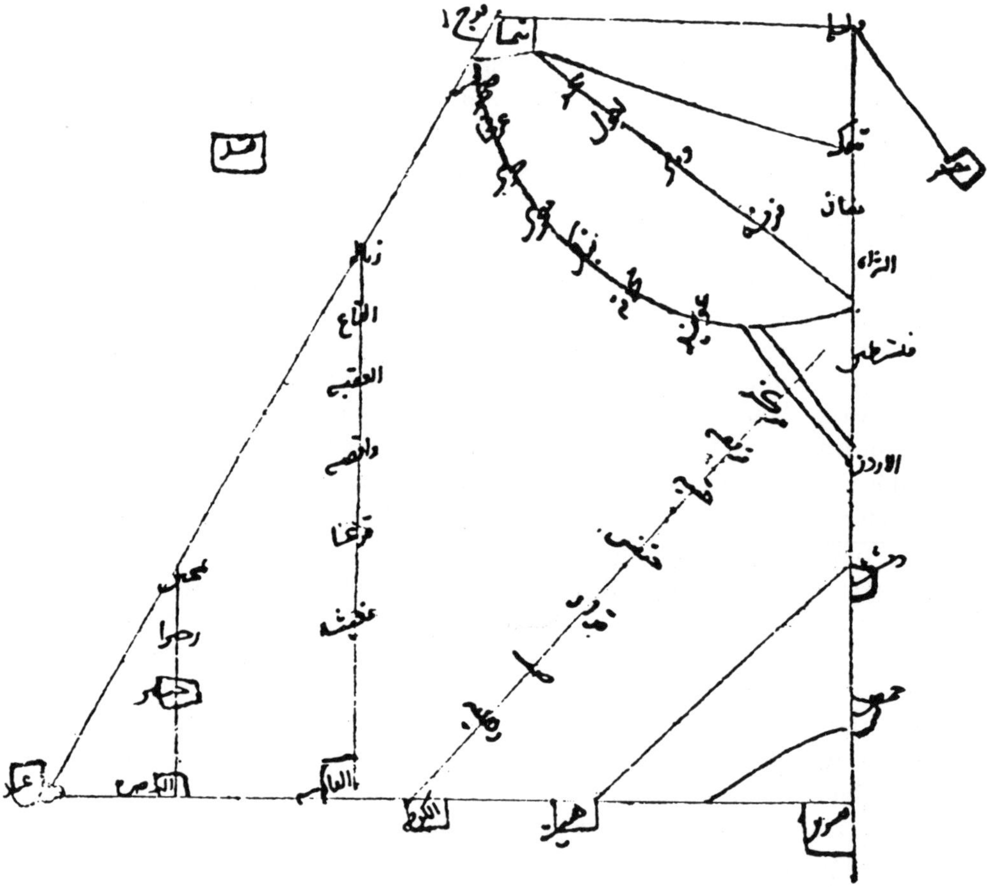

Map X: The Arabian Desert (see p. 414).
From MS. Sprenger 5—Ahlwardt 6034 by kind permission of the Staatsbibliothek
Preussischer Kulturbesitz, Berlin, Orientabteilung.

As for the Route of al-Ramla, one goes from al-Sukkariyya to al-Tulayl, two stages;

> then from al-Tulayl to al-Ghamr, two stages;
>
> thence to Wayla, two stages.

p. 250 As for the Route of al-Sharāt:
from Sughar to Wayla, four stages; and regarding these two [latter] routes, when they are in al-Shām, the passageway is through a desolate semidesert, so they go close to the edge of the desert we have mentioned.

As for the Route of Tabūk:
from ʿAmmān to Muʿān, a distance of two watering places [two days journey];

> thence to Tabūk, a similar distance;
>
> thence to Taymāʾ, four days;
>
> thence to Wādī ʾl-Qurā, four days.

As for the Route of Wubayr:

> from ʿAmmān to Wubayr, three days journey;
>
> thence to al-Ajwalī, four stages;
>
> thence to Thajir, two days;
>
> thence to Taymāʾ, three days.

As for the Route of Batn al-Sirr:

> from ʿAmmān to ʿAwnīd, two days;
>
> thence to al-Muhdatha, half a day;
>
> thence to al-Nabk, the same;
>
> thence to a source of water, one day;
>
> thence to al-Jarbā; one day;
>
> thence to ʿArfajā, one day and a half;
>
> thence to Mukhrī, three days;
>
> thence to Taymāʾ, four days.

These are the three routes leading to the destinations of Pilgrimage: there is the route of the Bedouin to Makka, and it was the post route for the Umayyad rulers when they were in Damascus; over it passed the troops of the two ʿUmars [Abū Bakr and ʿUmar bin al-Khattāb], the time of the conquest of Syria. These routes are close to each other, and safe, and are under the dominance of the Banū Kilāb, who conduct most of the Syrians assembling in ʿAmmān for the journey of the Pilgrimage. I have traveled over this road a number of times.

p. 251 As for the route of al-Qādisiyya:
from al-Qādisiyya to al-Mughītha, seventeen miles;

> thence to al-Qarʿāʾ, twenty-two miles;

thence to Wāqisa, twenty-four miles;
thence to al-ʿAqaba, twenty-nine miles;
thence to al-Qāʿ, twenty-four miles;
thence to Zubāla, twenty-four miles;
thence to al-Shuqūq, twenty-one miles;
thence to al-Bitān, twenty-nine miles;
thence to al-Thaʿlabiyya, twenty-nine miles;
thence to al-Khuzaymiyya, thirty-two miles;
thence to Ajfur, twenty-four miles;
thence to Fayd, thirty-six miles.

As for the route of Wāsit:
I did not travel along it; however, it meets the main road at al-Thaʿlabiyya.

As for the route of al-Basra:
from al-Basra to al-Hufayr, eighteen miles;
thence to al-Ruhayl, twenty-eight miles;
thence to al-Shajī, twenty-seven miles;
thence to Hafar Abī Mūsā, twenty-six miles;
thence to Māwiyya, thirty-two miles;
thence to Dhāt al-ʿUshar, twenty-nine miles;
thence to al-Yansūʿa, twenty-three miles;
thence to al-Sumayna, twenty-nine miles;
thence to al-Qaryatayn, twenty-two miles;
thence to al-Nibāj, twenty-three miles.

These are the routes of al-ʿIrāq going to Makka; also the nine routes leading to destinations of Pilgrimage going lengthwise in the desert.

As for the route of al-Kūfa:
from al-Kūfa to al-Ruhayma, twelve miles;
thence to al-Nahīt, two days;
thence to al-Qurāy, the same;
thence to al-Khanfas, one day;
thence to al-Hashya, the same;
thence to al-Ghurayfa, the same;
thence to Qurākir, the same;
thence to al-Azraq, the same;
thence to ʿAmmān, the same;
all of these, eleven short stages.

As for the route of Hīt: from Hīt to Damascus, ten days, and the same from
p. 252 al-Rahba. As for the route of Wādī 'l-Qurā, from al-Basra to Syria is a journey of approximately one month, and I did not travel over it.

As for the route of al-Rahba:
from al-Rahba to...[lacuna in MS.]

These are the three routes of Pilgrimage across the width of the desert, and there are smaller tracks that go out to Adhriᶜāt and elsewhere.

As for the route of Wādī 'l-Qurā, it is said to emerge at al-Munhab (al-Muntahab), beyond Fayd; and from al-Munhab to Wādī 'l-Qurā is a journey of five nights; to Taymāʾ, four nights; to Tabūk, seven nights; to Wādī Tayyiʾ, two nights.

From al-Basra to al-Kūfa on the fringe of this desert is ten difficult stages. Most of the stopping places we have mentioned are at a well or a creek.

This then is a description of this desert and its waters. You should know that it is an extensive desert with many Bedouin. In it grows a plant called the *fathth*, something like mustard. It grows wild, the people gather it and take it to the brook, soak it in water, causing it to open up so that the seed comes out: this they grind, bake, and eat. A common practice here is eating the flesh of the jerboa, and snakes. The people here are highwaymen, yet they give shelter to the stranger, and guide those who have gone astray; they also convoy caravans, and indeed, it is not possible for a person to travel this way without either a guard or some force. Sometimes you see them attack the Pilgrimage caravan, despite its strength, and they take the camels and the money.

On the boundary of this desert, you go from Wayla toward Madāʾin Qawm Lūt and you ascend to Maʾāb, then toward the border of ᶜAmmān and Adhriᶜāt, and the rural areas of Damascus, Tadmur, Silmiyya, and the area of Hims, on to Bālis. Then you return to the Euphrates, turning towards al-Raqqa, and al-Rahba, and al-Dālia, on to Hīt and al-Anbār; then toward al-Hīra and al-Qādisiyya, and the western end of al-Bataʾih (The Swamps), then toward the district of al-Basra on to ᶜAbbādān. There are some who add al-Sharāt to this desert; in any case, I have included its towns in it, and that seems quite correct.

In this desert there is no city except Taymāʾ; it is an ancient, extensive site, abounding in date palms, splendid gardens, abundant water, with remarkably good climate, and having an excellent spring which flows through an iron pipe to a pool, from which the water is distributed among the gardens. They have sweet water wells, also. The city is on a plain. However, much of it has been laid waste. The mosque is in the city, and the buildings are, generally, around the market. All the dates there are excellent. However, the people are greedy; there is no savant there anyone would consult, no judge there anyone would depend on. In fact their preacher there I saw was a vegetable vendor, their judge a shoemaker. Virulent fanaticism is rife in Taymāʾ, and the Dāwūdiyya put on armour during times of riot.

The stopping places between Egypt and Wayla are irrigated by *sāqias* (sakiehs, water scoops).

p. 253

Al-Ghamr has water and palm trees; close by is a sandy spot where if one digs an abundance of sweet water flows.

Wubayr has sweet wells; in a bright pleasant spot.

Al-Ajwalī, God has disgraced it! Anyone who drinks the water there swells up, and may even die.

Thajir: water here is not good, nor are there many streams.

Al-ʿAwnīd: two streams close to each other, both with bad water. It is surrounded by sand.

Al-Muhdatha: a canal of sweet water, lined with black stone.

Al-Nabk: two streams one of which is sweeter than the other; the road is between the two; palms. Some distance from it is a stream in a thicket, and a sweet water well, which does not flow very much. I forget the name of this place.

Al-Jarbā: here a stream or two, stinking water; it is in an overgrown area, with tamarisk.

ʿArfajā is in a nice pleasant spot, with two streams of sweet water.

Mukhrī, God has denounced it for its bad water, which loosens the bowels of men and camels; here are two streams in the black earth. The place derives its name from the diarrhea you suffer regardless of whether you drink of it, bake with it, or cook with it—it is all the same!

Al-Mughītha has been devastated; it has one well.

Al-Qarʿā' has a number of wells that are not of much use.

Wāqisa is a flourishing place with a fortress. It has sweet wells, and a large pool in which the water springs up.

At al-ʿAqaba are wells of which the surface is very far down, and buildings which have fallen into ruin.

Al-Qāʿ has been destroyed. It used to be an attractive, developed, well populated place. It has a well.

p. 254   Zubāla has a fortress, is flourishing. It has some splendid wells cut in the rock, and a number of small wells. Sometimes the Pilgrimage caravan deposits part of their stores there for safekeeping. Many Bedouin come here with their camels because of the pasturage and for other reasons. It provides repose for the pilgrims.

Al-Bitān: wells, now in disuse; the place is in ruins.

Al-Thaʿlabiyya is one third of the way; a flourishing place with many pools. Irrigation is by *sāqia*. Some people live in the fortress. The well has rather poor water.

Qabr al-ʿIbādī: at the entrance of this water place stands a large mound of stones. These are areas of sand. It is a quiet place.

At al-Khuzaymiyya are pools no longer serviceable, wells no longer used.

Fayd is a small town outside the desert, having two fortresses; baths are there, and a pool. The gates are of iron; here also monuments to ʿAdhud al-Dawla. Every kind of produce is to be found here, and the people on the Pilgrimage deposit some of their provisions there for safekeeping, for here are trustworthy people. It has springs, and wells, and ponds of middling water; some distance away is sweet water. This is without question one of the cities of al-Hijāz; but we arrived there via the route of al-Qādisiyya because of urgent necessity.

Addition/version MS. C: A SUMMARY ACCOUNT OF THIS REGION AND OF THE DESERT

You should know that this is an extensive desert, wherein are many Bedouin. Here are to be found no cultivated fields, no palm trees, except in the villages, and the village settlements here are sparse; sources of water here are also limited. In it grows a plant called the *fathth*, which sprouts up of its own accord; it contains a seed which resembles the mustard. The people gather it and take it to the brook, soak it in water, causing it to open up so that the pip comes out from that seed: this they grind, bake, and eat. It is in connection with this that al-Niqifūr (Nicephorus Phocas) said, when he took Tarasūs: "Go back to the people of the *fathth* and the jerboa, and return our land of Syria to us." A common practice here is the eating the flesh of the jerboa, and snakes. The people here are highwaymen, yet they give shelter to the stranger, and guide those who have gone astray; they also convoy caravans, and indeed, it is not possible for a person to travel this way without either a guard or some force. Sometimes you see them attack the Pilgrimage caravan, despite its strength, and their camels are taken away....

The people of al-ʿIrāq call all the land that is beyond the Euphrates River by the name of Syria, and it is with this understanding that Muhammad bin al-Hasan made the entry in his registers, in conformity with them, but there is no portion of Syria beyond the Euphrates except Qinnasrīn. Most of the scholars in our science agree that the portion of this desert that is beyond the Euphrates is the Peninsula of the Arabs, and both al-Zuhrī and Abū Zayd al-Balkhī concur in this, and it is with this understanding that they represented it in their maps of the regions.

Beyond Faya is a town called al-Munhab, a place with many palm trees and cultivated fields; also Wādī Tayyiʾ, and the mountain areas of both these places have palm trees, villages, and agricultural products, Fayd being situated between the two of them. The route from al-Basra to Syria passes by both of these towns; from al-Munhab to Taymāʾ, four nights; from al-Munhab to Wādī Tayyiʾ, a journey of two nights, thence to Tabūk, five nights.

So these then are the six regions of the Arabs, and their homelands; and in God—may He be exalted—is success!

p. 255 Now should some say to me, "You are a man who has devoted himself in his traveling to certainty and knowledge. You have become acquainted, moreover, with the routes over this desert and the watering places there. So what do you say about going on the Pilgrimage depending on God alone, and setting out without provisions?" The answer is that it is related Sufyān bin ʿAyyana that he said that two kinds of men there are who if they should ask your opinion you should strengthen their resolve, for they are asking you from a position of indecision; one is the bachelor who wants to marry, the other, the religious aspirant who asks about going on the Pilgrimage, without supplies. I was told about an ascetic in our own country during my time there who went out into this desert without provisions. After he had been out three days he was hungry, but, said he: "I came upon something soft, and behold, there were some flat cakes of bread with a mishmash of hot food wrapped up in them." For my part, I left a place in the afternoon, fasting, determined on performing the Pilgrimage without carrying provisions. When I reached ʿĀqir I said the evening prayer, turning towards the corner of the mosque to pray. I had not broken my fast any night until after the *witr* and saying the evening prayer. When the people had left the mosque, the muezzin came to me with bread and figs and a jar of water; you see I had decided not to carry either a pot or a cup with me, for I said that whoever provides the food will provide the water also. Well I had the very best supper there where I had never expected it. When I had said the noon prayers, p. 256 the following day, I rode off on the route to al-Sukkariyya; and when I had said the evening prayer a man brought me a loaf of bread of country style, and a jug of water, so I ate and drank.

On the following day I traveled until I reached the fork in the road, and there I gave what clothes I had on me to some passersby, taking from them a hair garment, shabby slippers, and a threadbare kerchief. I traveled on until the time of evening prayer, but I did not crave supper; eventually a fort came into view. I went to it, and on my entering the door, there was a man from Jerusalem, who embraced me and welcomed me. He told the people of the fort what my standing was, and different kinds of food and a blanket were brought to me. At dawn I slipped away from them and traveled until after the time of the evening prayer, when I came across a group from the Maghrib. They seized me, and called me a spy; but when I led them in the evening prayer they apologized to me and entertained me.

I went on, the following day, traveling until I reached al-Kusayfa, but not a single dwelling did I see there. However, there were five riders who took me and led me away against my will to a place of theirs, where they entertained me. When I realized I was receiving an invitation every night, and that God was restraining me on my journey, I set out for my own country, going on the Pilgrimage that year with food and a riding camel.

The first division is completed: following it is the second division, which treats of the regions of the non-Arab peoples, the first being the region of al-Mashriq.

AN ACCOUNT OF THE EIGHT REGIONS
OF THE NON-ARAB PEOPLES

IN THE NAME OF GOD THE MOST BENIGNANT, THE MERCIFUL

This is an account of the eight regions of the non-Arab peoples, and an exposition of conditions there, arranged according to the boundaries. The people of these regions are in the most comfortable circumstances, are the richest, most powerful, strongest, best natured; the most firmly grounded in knowledge, the most deep-rooted in religion. They delight in doing good works, and in deeds accounted in the record of God. Rivers flow through their regions, trees enclose their villages. We shall give a detailed account of their qualities, comment on the conditions in their regions; and we present in this chapter what is necessary by way of introduction.

We have learned from Abu al-Mandhar Hishām bin al-Sāʾib to the effect that when Qutayba bin Muslim [49/669 - 96/716] triumphed over Fayrūz bin Khusraw, he captured his daughter Shāhīn, and she had a basket with her; so he sent her to al-Hajjāj who took her to Walīd, and he opened the basket. And behold, within it, in the name of God, Shaper of the world, was a differentiation made by Qubādh bin Fayrūz [ruled 488-531 C.E.] of the parts of his realm, assessing the quality of the waters and of the soils, with the intent of building for himself a city wherein he would dwell. He found that the best places in the territory of his realm, after beginning with al-ʿIrāq, which is the most pleasant of regions, he found, I say, that the best were thirteen places, in number: al-Madāʾin, al-Sūs, Jundaysābūr, Tustar, Sābūr, Isfahan, al-Rayy, Balkh, Samarqand, Abīward, Māsabadhān, Mihrajānqudhaq, and Qarmāsīn.

He found the coldest places in his realm to be: Dabīl, Hamadhān, Qazwīn, Juwāniq, Nihāwand, Khwārazm, and Qālīqalā. He found the most pestilential places to be: al-Bandanījīn, Jurjān, Khwār al-Rayy, Kish, Bardhaʿa, and Zanjān.

He found the driest of his realm: Maysān, Dast Maysān, Bādarāyā, Bākusāyā, Māsabadhān, al-Rayy, and Isfahan.

He found the greediest among them: Khurāsān, Isfahan, Ardabīl, Bādarāyā, Bākusāyā, Istakhr, Shīrāz, and Fasā.

The most fertile: Armīnīya, Ādharbayjān, Jūr, Makrān, Māh al-Kūfa, Māh al-Basra, Arrajān, and Dawraq.

The most beautiful places: al-Madāʾin, Kalwādhā, Sābūr, Istakhr, Jannāba, al-Rayy, Qumm, Isfahan, and al-Nashawā.

The most intelligent among them, seven: ʿUkbarā, Qutrabbul, ʿAqarqūf, al-Rayy, Isfahan, Māsabadhān, and Mihrajānqudhaq.

The most despondent, the people of: Iskāfayn, Kaskar, ʿAbdas, Marw, and al-Rayy.

The most knowledgeable in arms: Hamadhān, Hulwān, Isfahān, Shahrazūr, Khwārazm, al-Shāsh, and Isbījāb.

The sources of the most palatable water, ten in number: Dijla, al-Furāt, Jayhūn, Jundaysābūr, Māsabadhān, Qazwīn, and the water respectively of Sūrā, Dhāt al-Matāmīr, and Fanjā.

The most cunning, eleven in number: Khurāsān, Isfahān, al-Rayy, Hamadhān, Armīniya, Ādharbayjān, Māsabadhān, Mihrajānqudhaq, Tustar, al-Madhār, and Artuwān.

The worst fruits: al-Madāʾin, Sābūr, Arrajān, al-Rayy, Nihāwand, Māsabadhān, and Hulwān.

The most shortsighted regarding consequences: al-Nawbandijān, Māsabadhān, Sīrāf, Rāmhurmuz, Armīniya, Ādharbayjān, and Istakhr.

The basest people, six in number: al-Nawbandijān, Bādarāyā, Bakasāyā, Wayhind, Nihāwand, and Isfahān.

He did not find between the Tigris and ʿAqabat Hamadhān a more pleasant place than Qarmāsīn; so he built there a city for himself, and the succession of the Khusraw built it up after him, from al-Madāʾin to al-ʿAqaba, as you see.

I found in a book in the library of ʿAdhud al-Dawla a chapter dealing with p. 259 the gardens of the realm, written in rhyme, and I have added to it the name of any place that should not be omitted, on account of the distinction of its reputation and its excellence; and so that this chapter will gather together the recreation grounds of the earth, and gratify the hearts of people. It was said in the book that the place on earth most favored with natural resources is al-Rayy, where al-Surr and al-Sarbān are located; the place with the finest reservoirs is Jurjān. The best known is Tabaristān. The best for the production of natural resources is Naysābūr, where Bushta(n)qān is placed. The best in antiquity and modernity: Jundaysābūr, where al-Ābān is situated; Marw, where are (the canals) Razīq and Mājān; the Ghūta of Damascus where flows the Zārbān. There are also Nasībīn, which has al-Hirmās, and Jerusalem with al-Buqʿa and Māmās. At al-Saymara are the two forts, and in Fārs, Shaʿb Bawwān; there is the river al-Ubulla, at which the eyes are caused to wonder, and do not have any doubt about the gardens of Sughd! There is Balkh with Barwān; Nihāwand, and the gardens of Isfahān. In al-Bahrayn are Qaysāriyya and ʿUmān; in al-Yaman, remarkable Sanʿāʾ. You need not ask about Jīruft in Kirmān, or about Bust, and Mūqān. The countryside of Bukhārā has great prestige, and we shall mention al-Shāsh, Fasā, Sābūr, and Hulwān. And the villages of al-Ramla without a river are illustrious for their olives and figs; we have mentioned to you too Tāhart and Jayyān; and stretching from al-Kūfa is the river, with date palms, and trees, for a distance of two post stages. This is our account of the gardens of the world as we see them.

You should know that most of the towns of the non-Arab peoples are named after their founders and builders, and we shall refer to this as opportunity offers, if God,—may He be exalted—so wills. The speech of the people of these eight regions is other than Arabic, some of it pure and fluent, some incomprehensible. All of the languages, however, are called "Persian", but that there are variations is evident; the variety is a problem, but we will explain that as occasion arises, if God—may He be exalted—so wills, and we will facilitate the understanding of it, as best we can. We will mention from the speech of every people some of the sounds, so that anyone hearing it, who is distant from there, should be able to identify its place of origin. And in God is success.

The Region of Al-Mashriq
(The Eastern Territories)

This is the most important of the regions, the most sublime. Here are the most scholars. It is the source of wealth, the abode of science; the solid support of Islām, and its mightiest fortress. Its sovereign is the most illustrious of sovereigns, its army the best of armies. The people are of great fortitude, correct in opinion. Their prestige is considerable, their resources extensive. They are renowned for their horses, their men, their conquests, their victories. They are a people such as were mentioned to ʿUmar that their dress is iron, their food, dried meat, their drink, ice. You see there very fine rural areas, beautiful villages, trees intertwined with one another, rivers flowing copiously. Blessings are evident there, fields extensive. In religious matters the people are correct, and justice abides, in a country ever firm in its victories, a realm God has made everlasting. Here the jurisprudents achieve the rank of kings; and people who were slaves here are kings elsewhere. It is the barrier to the Turk, the shield against al-Ghuzz [a Turkish tribe], a terror to the Romaeans, the glory of the Muslims. It is the wellspring of stability, the source of invigoration for the two holy places; here is the country situated on both sides of the river. Even though the Peninsula of the Arabs is more spacious than this area, yet the latter is much more developed, has more villages, wealth and business.

Abū Zayd has divided it into three regions: Khurāsān, Sijistān, Mā warāʾa al-Nahr ["the area on the other side of the river (Jayhūn)"]. We, for our part, however, make one region of it, consisting of two parts separated by the river Jayhūn, and we associate with each part the person who planned and built it. We have depicted and described each part by itself, because of the size of the region, the extent of building there, the number of its villages and towns. Now should someone ask, "Why do you not make each part a region by itself in accordance with accepted usage; or do you not know that they refer to ʿKhurāsān, and Mā warāʾa al-Nahr'?" I should reply that it is also accepted usage that from the boundary of Qūmis to Tarāz is called Khurāsān, or, moreover, do you not know that the dynasty of Sāmān are called the kings of Khurāsān, their residence being on this side, even though we do not call this side Khurāsān; so that what I have said enforces our argument. Again, should someone say, "Why did you include Sijistān in this region, thus disagreeing with the predecessors in this branch of knowledge?" I should say to him that it is also accepted usage that Sijistān is part of Khurāsān, or does he not know that the people of Sijistān give allegiance to the dynasty of Sāmān; moreover, if we were to make Sijistān a region, then we should make Khwārazm a region considering the progression of its development, the number of its towns, the variety of its speech, and the nature of its customs— but this is not feasible, and should not even be suggested.

If someone should ask why we made the region two parts, it should be said
p. 261 that it is just as al-Yaman is two parts, and al-Maghrib two sections: thus there
is precedent for it.

You should know that the two brothers Haytal and Khurāsān, two sons
of ʿĀlim bin Sām bin Nūh settled in this region, and this side of it is called
the side of the Haytal people.

The Province of Haytal (Right Bank of Jayhūn)

You should know that this province is the most fertile of the lands of God
—may He be exalted—its people are the most prosperous, have the greatest
knowledge of jurisprudence, have the most buildings, and the most avid desire
for knowledge. They are the most correct in religion, the most courageous,
the most obdurate, most persistent in striving in the way of God, yet the most
peaceful at heart, the most generous among mankind; they evince prosperity,
integrity, fairness, hospitality, respecting those who learn. In summary, Islām
there is extolled, rule is strong, justice is plain to be seen, the jurisprudent is
famed, the rich man is safe, the professional man is learned, the poor man still
can meet his needs. Rarely do they suffer drought. The mosques here are greater
in number than can be mentioned, areas more spacious than can be described;
even so we did our level best, to the limit of our capacity.

Addition/version MS. C.
From enemies they are secure. Pulpits (*i.e.* towns) in the area are many,
districts spacious. Here is the town al-Sughd, the precious, and Samarqand,
the splendid, and Khujanda, the remarkable. Here are schools, leaders of
the prayers, elders, honourable people, with good management, government,
conquests, valiant people, caravanserais, and horsemen. Here are grapes and
fruits, servitude and oppression, studies night and day. The people are always
under tutelage and guardianship, delighting in refinement, and researching
the Hadīth [the authoritative sayings and doings of the Prophet and his
Companions]; for it is the territory of the holy strife against the infidels, the
place of the troops defending the frontier; of the people who adopt the right
belief; no heretical doctrines are manifest, no conditions of injustice. Here
are precious minerals, many caravanserais, excellent waters, with security and
well-being. However, corruption has come in evidence there, and usury among
the people is notoriously widespread. Every villain has crossed over into there,
and I fear me that it will become like al-ʿIrāq or even worse, that al-Islām will
fold up its mantle there as the report has it, while around their ruler is a group
of superior people, the likes of al-Shaykh ʿAlī bin al-Hasan, and other persons
of distinction in the entourage.

The following is a representation of the form and features of the region.
[Map XI]

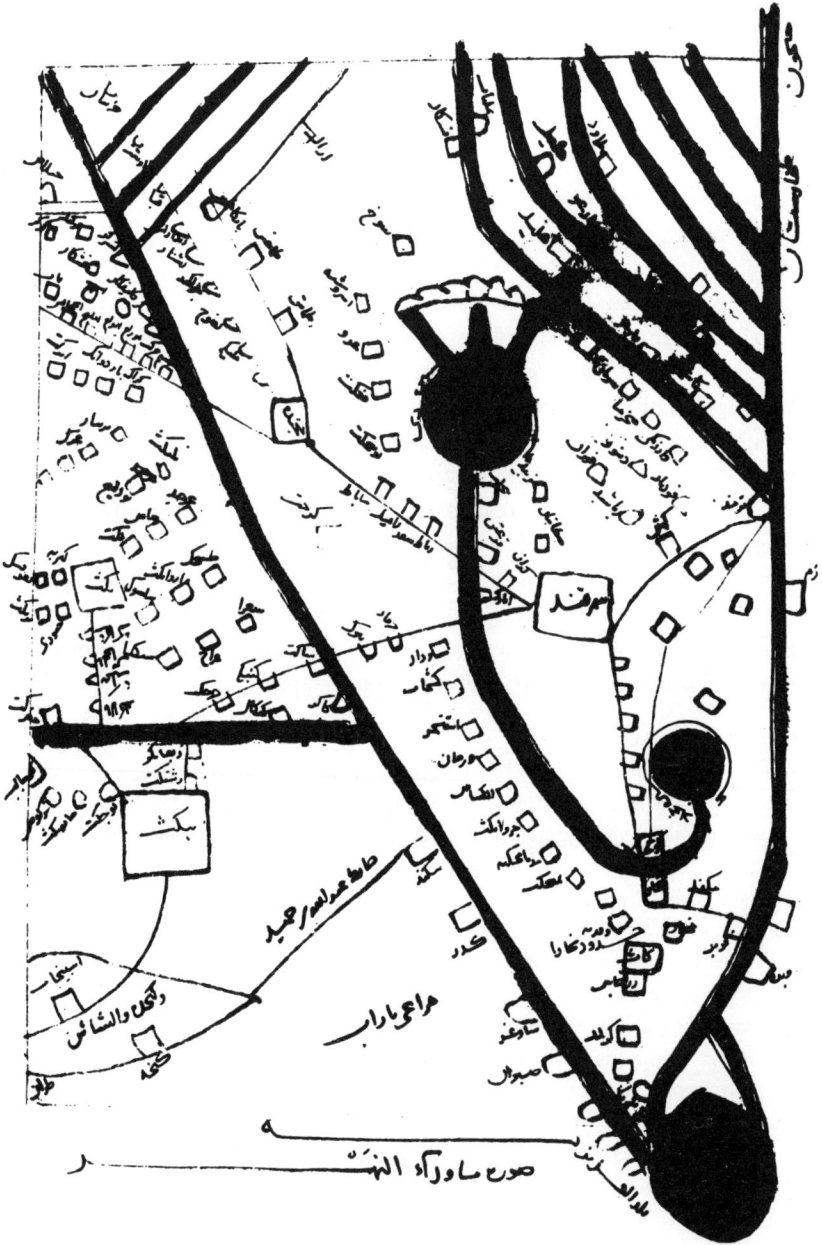

Map XI: Mā warāʾa al-Nahr (see p. 415).
From MS. Sprenger 5—Ahlwardt 6034 by kind permission of the Staatsbibliothek
Preussischer Kulturbesitz, Berlin, Orientabteilung.

We have divided this province into six districts and four cantons, the first of them towards the point where the sun rises, and the boundary with the Turks, being Farghānā, then Isbījāb, then al-Shāsh, then Ushrūsana, then al-Sughd, then Bukhārā; and regarding al-Sughd there is much to be said. The cantons are Īlāq, Kish, Nasaf, al-Saghāniyān.

As for Farghāna, it is an area in a corner of the region, on the east side, before you reach the downward slope. It is quite prosperous, and there are said to be forty mosques there. Its capital is Akhsīkath, and among its towns are al-Miyānrūdhiyya (Miyān Rūdhan), Nasrābadh, Manāra, Ranjad, Shikit, Zārakān, Khayralām, Bishabishān, Ushtīqān, Zarandarāmish, Ūzkand. Among the towns of Nasā are Ūsh, Qubā, Birink, Marghīnan, Rishtān, Wānkat, Kand. Among the towns of Wāghaz are Būkand, Kāsān, Bāb, Jārak, Usht, Tūbkār, Uwāl, Dakarkard, Nawqād, Muskān, Bīkan, Ishkhijān(?), Jidghil (Jadghal), Shāwadān. Isbījāb is at the boundary of the region, equable in climate. The capital has the same name, and among its towns are: Khūrlūgh, Jamshalāghū, Arsubānīkath (Usbānīkath), Bārāb, Shāwaghar, Sawrān, Turār Zarākh, Shaghlajān, Bālāj, Barūkat, Barūkh, Yakānkath, Adhakhkath, Dih Nūjīkat, Tarāz, Bāluwā, Jikil, Barskhān, Utlukh, Jamūkat, Shiljī, Kūl, al-Sūs, Takābkath, Dih Nawā, Kūlan, Mīrkī, Nūshkat, Laqrā, Jamūk, Urduwā, Nawīkath, Balāsaghūn, Labān, Shūy, Abāligh, Mādānkat, Barsiyān, Balgh, Jikarkān, Yagh, Yakāligh, Ruwānjam, Katāk, Shūr Jashmah, Dil Awās, Jarkard.

Al-Shāsh is beyond these two, its capital Binkath. Among its towns are Nukkath, Jīnānjakath, Nujākath, Binākath, Kharashkath, Gharjand, Ghannāj, Jabūzan [Jamūzan], Warduk, Kabarna, Namdawānak, Nūjkath, Ghazak, Anūdhkath, Bishkat, Barkūsh, Khātūnakath, Jabghūkath, Farankad, Kadāk, Nakālak, Bārskath, Ushtūrkath, al-Baykath, Kabāshkath, Ghannāj, Dih Kūrān, Tall Awsh, Ghuzkard, Zarānkath, Darwā, Faradkath, Ajakh.

Īlāq, its district and chief centre is Tūnkath. Among its towns are Shāwakath, Bānkhāsh, Nūkath, Bālāyān, Arbilakh, Namūdhlagh, Tukkath, Khumrak, Sīkath, Kuhsīm (Kūh-i-sīm), Adakhkath, Khās, Khujākath, Gharjand, Sāmsīrak, Biskath.

Ushrūsana adjoins this district. Its capital is Bunjikath, and among its towns are Arsubānīkath, Kurdakath, Ghazaq, Faghkath, Sābāt, Zāmīn, Dīzak, Nūjkath, Qatawān-Dizah, Kharaqāna, Khisht, Marsmanda. It has seventeen rural districts: Bashāghar, Mashā, Burghar, Waqr, Bānghām, Mīnak, Baskar (Baskan), Arsubānīkath, and al-Buttam which has no towns: for the others, the names correspond to those of their towns.

The capital of al-Sughd is Samarqand, which is also the metropolis of the region. It has twelve rural districts of which six are south of the river: Bunjikath, then Waraghsar, then Maymurgh, then Sanjirfaghan, then al-Dargham, then Awfar. Those to the north are as follows, the uppermost of them being Yārkath; then Būrnamadh, then Būzmājan, then Kabūdhanjakath, then Widhār, then al-Marzubān. In some of these are towns we shall ascribe to the rural areas;

remaining towns of the area are Riyūdad, Abghar, Ishtīkhan, Kushāniya, Dabūsiya, Karmīniya, Rabinjan, Qatawāna.

Bukhārā is a district not very extensive, nonetheless well developed and pleasant. A wall surrounds five of its towns. Its dimensions each way are twelve *farsakhs*, it has no untilled land, no village left fallow. The name of the capital is Numūjkath; among its towns are Baykand, al-Tawāwīs, Zandana, Bamijkath, Khujāda, Mughkān, Kharghānkath, Khudīmankan, ʿUrwān, Bakhsūn, Sīkath, Jarghar, Sīshakath, Aryāmīthan, Warakhshā, Wazarmīthan, Kamajkath, Fagharsīn, Kashafghan, Nawīdak, Warkā.

p. 267

p. 268

Associated with it is the district of Kish, with towns Nawqad Quraysh, Sūnaj, Iskīfghan; also Nasaf, with towns Bazda, Kasba; also al-Saghāniyān, with towns Dārzanjī, Bāsand, Bahām, Zīnwar, Būrāb, Rīkdasht, Bānbāb(?) (Bānyāb(?)), Shūmān, Hanbān, Dastajird. Bukhārā has sixteen thousand villages.

p. 269

There is some disagreement over these provinces and districts. Al-Jayhānī says in his book that al-Sughd is like the image of a man: his head is Bunjikath, his two legs, al-Kushāniya. His back is Awghar (Abghar), and the soles of his feet Kabūdhanjakath and Tarkasfā. His hands are Maymurgh and Būzmājan. He fixed its dimensions at thirty-six by forty-six *farsakhs*. He said that its finest mosque is that of Samarqand, then Kish, then Nasaf, then al-Kushāniya, and so on. Someone else has said that the capital of al-Sughd is Ishtīkhan, and he made it distinct from Samarqand.

Addition/version MS. C.

Some writers have associated Bukhārā with al-Sughd, and argue that the river from its source to its debouchure is given the name "The River of al-Sughd"; but if we wish to justify our own statement in the matter and give preponderance to it over others, our book would merely increase in length. We surely mention those other statements so that the reader of our book should know that we are not unaware of them. I have not originated anything except that it be based on science and experience; and indeed any man who has attained eminence in a science, and ranged far and wide in it, is permitted to use his own judgment, after exercising deliberation. Are you not aware that the Prophet—God's peace and blessings be upon him—when he sent Muʿādh to al-Yaman, permitted him to act according to his own judgment in matters to which he did not know a verse of the *Qurʾān* or a Sunna [a saying or doing of the Prophet] that referred to them, and this is also what the leading jurists did. So for our part, we did not draw a comparison in this science of ours except as they did in the science of the Sharīʿa [canonical law of Islām], and we have reached the conclusion that we consider Samarqand to be the metropolis of al-Sughd, and that we differentiate Bukhārā as one of its districts.

He also made Bukhārā a part of al-Sughd, arguing that the river from its source to Bukhārā is called the River of al-Sughd. This argument is wrong, however. Do you not know that the river of Jordan, in Palestine, is also called the Jordan

River, but no one claims that the valleys of Palestine are part of Jordan. When they mention the River al-Sughd this means only that it rises in al-Sughd, and irrigates the land there. In fact if we were to begin to argue about every opinion we express, and favour one argument over one that is equally sound it would merely lengthen our book. Our only aim in mentioning these other writings at all and explaining them is lest the reader of our book might think they were

p. 270 unknown to us. In fact Abū Zayd al-Balkhī in his book has a chapter which will spare people of discernment from arguing about this matter. He wanted in his work to confirm what he had mapped, but not the exact layout of the districts, for no one has preceded us in this detailing the districts of the regions; as he himself said, "There is no great benefit in the aggregation of these areas, putting one beside the other, and in differentiating among them nothing much is achieved, except merely to add the names of some towns and rivers there, and to facilitate exposition in presenting and mapping the area." And upon my life, he was right! This kind of argument neither invalidates nor confirms anything. Do you not know that leading scholars have presented their opinions, advancing on one point, then retreating; granting, as it were, then contradicting; allowing, then disallowing; permitting, then forbidding—and people have accepted this, and have been satisfied with it, and no intelligent person has denied them the right to do this. In fact the Prophet—God's peace and blessings be upon him—gave Mu'ādh authority to act on his opinions when he sent him to al-Yaman, and the Companions also acted in accordance with this. It is not anything remarkable, then, if we ourselves express some opinions in this science, or that we have our own frame of reference which we prefer.

Our preference is to make al-Sughd part of Samarqand and consider the towns of the former as towns of the latter; we appoint it, also, as the metropolis for this side of the territory, because it is older, more extensive, and has more rural districts. Should someone ask why we do not make Bukhārā the metropolis since here is the royal residence and the administrative offices of the region, we should say to him that the presence of the kings there does not necessarily mean that it is the metropolis, just because Bukhārā is a town favoured by the kings of the dynasty of Sāmān; in fact they went thither from Samarqand. Similarly it is not conceivable that we make Samarqand and Naysābūr, because of their importance, chief cities of the province, over Bukhārā; because for the reason you mentioned, it would be necessary to consider Naysābūr also a primary city over Bukhārā. Of course someone may ask if it is not the case that when the family of al-'Abbās took up quarters in Baghdād, that city became the metropolis of the region, and should the analogy not apply to Bukhārā; we should respond saying that the reply to this is easy. It is simply this: that the metropoles of al-'Irāq are of recent date, and under Islām one of them can replace the other. Do you not know that the metropolis used to be al-Kūfa; then it was al-Anbār, then Baghdād, then it became Sāmarrā, then Baghdād again?

Addition/version MS. C.

Al-ʿIrāq has but one capital. Do you not realize that it used to be al-Kūfa during the time of ʿAlī, it then again became al-Anbār at the time of al-Manṣūr, then again became Baghdād at the time of al-Manṣūr, then it became Sāmarrā at the time of al-Muʿtasim, thereafter returning to Baghdād.

p. 271 On the other hand the metropoles of the eastern provinces are long established, and one does not invalidate the other. If someone should say, "but did not Naysābūr supplant Tūs?" we reply that Tūs was not a metropolis ever, so could not be replaced as such, and it [Naysābūr] was merely added to it [Tūs], for a reason we shall mention. Then if someone should ask whether we did not abrogate the primacy of Tūs as Tūs did Marw, we should reply that we have been on our guard about this by our saying that under Islām any of them could replace another, hence Naysābūr superseded Marw only by the advent of Islām. Since the matter is so, you see that Bukhārā did not vacate Samarqand as metropolis, since we have not found a similar case in the basic principles of our science. Do you not know that because we do not find in the foundations of the jurisprudence that worship of God—may He be exalted—may be acceptable merely by one *rakaʿ*, hence we do not allow for the *witr* to be acceptable by only one unit? Moreover, if someone says, "Is it not true that al-Maʾmūn, and al-Rashīd before him, settled in Marw?" the answer is that they did not stop there with the intention of residing; this is perfectly clear.

Akhsīkath is the capital of Farghānā: a large, important town with trees all around it. The streams flow copiously there. It is a well developed, fertile area, and prices are low. It has an inner town penetrated by a number of canals which pour into reservoirs there. The town is well-built, of baked brick, gypsum, and lime. The mosque, and most of the buildings, are in the inner city. Extensive suburbs encompass a *quhandiz* and markets, and the circuit of the city is about one and one half times that of al-Ramla. Productive, though cold; the people here are rugged and ruddy.

Nasrābādh: a large town surrounded by trees—white willow and white poplar. A king built it for his son, Nasr, and named it for him.

Manāra: a small town; a stream flows by the portal of the mosque.

Ranjad has many cultivated fields; an attractive mosque stands in the shoemakers' district.

Shikit: a large town, producing walnuts aplenty, so that you may even purchase a thousand walnuts for a *dirham*. The mosque stands in the market.

Tishān: large and populous; the mosque is in the cotton cloth dealers' district.

Zārakān: medium sized; produces much rice. It is a pleasant place, with copiously flowing water. At the portal of the mosque is a pleasant garden with trees.

p. 272 Khayralām: a large town, with an attractive mosque in the markets.

Bishabishān: a large town; the mosque has a gate that enters the open area of the market.

Ushtīqān: a small town; the mosque is in the markets.

At the gate of Ūzkand is a stream through which one must wade, there being no bridge. A wall surrounds its suburbs. The town is well developed, having the markets, the mosque, and the *quhandiz*, with water flowing to all of them. It has four gates. I do not know in the towns of this area a *quhandiz* other than this.

Ūsh, with many streams nearby of excellent quality, is an extensive prosperous settlement. The mosque is in the center of the markets. The town lies close to the mountains, and is really well off, being very well watered. Here is a huge guardhouse, to which volunteer soldiers repair from all directions.

Qubā is more spacious, extensive, better, more pleasant, more remarkable than the capital, and perhaps by analogy it should be the capital; however, with us, general usage has precedence over analogy, from the use of which we then refrain. The town has an open place in the centre of it, the mosque standing in the markets. The scholars have said: "Farghānā is Qubā; everything else there is grass and water."

Birink: a small town; its mosque makes the town conspicuous from the direction of Samarqand.

Marghīnān: also a small town; the mosque, remote from the markets, has a stream at its portal.

Rishtān: a large town. The mosque has a portal that opens on to the markets, and another opening on to the public square; Wānkat is similar.

At Kand is a stream that flows in the middle of the markets.

In this district forty towns were counted for me.

Khujanda: a delightful town, not a better one than it on this side of the territory. A stream flows through the middle; it is close to the mountain. The town is situated at the very boundary of the district. Scholars have praised it, and poets have described it.

Isbījāb: an important capital, with suburbs. The city is well developed, having an inn for merchants, and a market for the cotton merchants. The mosque has four gates, a guardhouse at every gate: the Gate of Nūjakath, the Gate of Farrukhān, the Gate of Shākrāna, the Gate of Bukhārā. The guardhouses: Ribāt Nakhshabiyyīn; Ribāt al-Bukhāriyyīn; Ribāt al-Samarqandiyyīn; also Ribāt Qarātakīn (Qaratigin) — and here, too, is his grave, and a market he donated to *waqf*. The proceeds from the market amount to seven thousand *dirhams* a month, and bread with food to accompany it is distributed to the feeble. It is said that two thousand seven hundred stalls for animals are here, for this is a very important mercantile centre. This is an area of fighting, and around the outskirts is a fortification. Here also is a *quhandiz*, but in ruin. The people know of neither drought nor land tax, and among them fruit is extraordinarily cheap. It is a prosperous, good, delightful place, and the way of life is satisfying, even though there is continual clamour there. The people have integrity, but at heart they are crude. They are conceited about their traditions, and themselves, and you can feel this whether you do good or bad to them. The people of the country districts

p. 273

are better than the people of the capital, whom you see as lions at home, but as sheep when they are elsewhere.

Khūrlūgh: a medium sized town with a stream flowing through the markets; no fortification over it, no *quhandiz*, no rural hinterland.

Jamshalāghū: a large spacious town, with a permanent stream flowing through it. Many slaves have repaired thither; the mosque is some distance from the markets.

Arsubānīkath (Usbānīkath): an elegant, clean, fortified place. The mosque is in the town, the residential area in the suburbs.

Bārāb is the name of a rural area, not very extensive; the name of the biggest town is also Bārāb, and this is fairly large, having a population including about seventy thousand males. A fortress protects it in which the mosque stands, and some markets. The *quhandiz* and most of the markets are in the suburbs; in the fortress are some small shops.

Wasīj: a small town; a fortress stands over it; under a strong *amīr*. The mosque is in the market.

Kadar: a new town. Wars were going on when its mosque was being built. They are a strong people, the majority of them followers of the Hadīth (Prophetic tradition).

p. 274   Shāwaghar: a large town with an extensive rural district. A fortress stands over it; the mosque stands on the edge of the market. The town is far removed from the main road.

Sawrān: a large town with seven fortified walls one behind the other, the suburbs within them. The mosque is in the inner city. This town is the frontier against the Ghuzz (Oghuz) and Kīmāk [Turkish tribes].

Turār Zarākh: a town pertaining to a rural area beyond Sawrān, towards the Turks. It is a small fortified place with a *quhandiz*; Zarākh is a village in the rural district.

Shaghlajān: a large town on the frontier towards the Kīmāk. It is fortified, and is quite prosperous.

Bālāj: a small town the fortress of which has been destroyed. The mosque is in the market. From there we returned toward the capital.

Barūkat: a large town, with Bālāj a frontier post against the Turkoman, who have converted to Islām through fear. Its fortress has been destroyed.

Barūkh: a large old town, the mosque being in the market.

Yakānkath: a very fine important town, built by Kharākharāf; his guardhouse and his grave are there.

Adhakhkath: a large town with a fortress, within which is the mosque; and well developed suburbs within which are the markets; many guardhouses.

Dih Nūjīkat: a small town holding a market during the three months of spring; boned meat may be bought at four *manns* for a *dirham*. It used to be important, but when Ismāʿīl bin Ahmad conquered the area it was diminished. Even so it is well developed and fortified, having also a *quhandiz*.

Tarāz: an important fortified town with many gardens. The houses are there side by side. A trench surrounds the town, which has four gates, and well developed suburbs. A large stream flows by a portal of the *madīna*, beyond it a portion of the town over which the high road runs. The mosque is in the markets.

p. 275   Jikil: a small town within shouting distance of Tarāz. Over it stands a fortress; it has a *quhandiz*; the mosque is in the market.

Barskhān: a town about twice the distance of a shout, towards the east. It has a fortress, which has been destroyed; the mosque is in the markets.

Bahlū (Bāluwa) is bigger than Barsukhān; to the north of Jikil half a *farsakh*; has five rural districts associated with it, also a *quhandiz*; the mosque is in the markets.

Utlukh: an important town close, in extent, to the capital; with a fortress. The area consists mostly of gardens, and the rural area, for the most part, produces grapes. The mosque is in the town, the markets in the suburbs.

Jamūkat: large, with a fortress within which stands the mosque; the markets are in the suburbs.

Shiljī: a small town; many emigres here—some ten thousand said to be from Isfahan alone. It has a *quhandiz*, with the mosque outside it. The town is situated among the mountains. A stream flows through the courtyard of the mosque; nearby are seven villages.

Al-Sūs: a large town; Kūl is smaller than it; each one of the two has a fortress, and a stream.

Takābkath: a large town; one half of its people are heathen. These three are towns close to the mountains, sources of silver.

Kūlān: a fortified place, with a mosque. It has, however, declined. It is on the high road to Tarāz.

Mīrkī: medium sized in extent; fortified; with a *quhandiz*. The mosque was formerly a church. The *amīr*, ʿAmīd al-Dawla Fāʾiq, built a guardhouse outside the fortress.

Urduwā: a small town wherein resides the sovereign of the Turkoman; he still sends presents to the ruler of Isbījāb. A fortress stands over it and a trench full of water surrounds it. The residence of the king is in the *quhandiz*.

In Harrān most of the people are heathens, its ruler, however, is Muslim. It has fortifications in which is a *quhandiz*, where the *dihqān* [village head and tax collector] resides.

Walāsakūn (Balāsāghūn): a large, populous, prosperous town; the remaining towns here are fairly close to one another in size and population.

p. 276   Binkath: the capital of al-Shāsh, wide in extent; spacious residences, rare is the house without its garden, stable, and vineyard. In general terms, it may be described as a place where the good matches the bad, where the glory matches the faults; here is goodness, with discord; beauty of speech, with the vilest disorder; no matter how well developed you see it, you also see dilapidation there. In religion it is upright, but also in a state of confusion. The people are

Sunnī, but factional; they are a people of vigour and discord; they are an asset to the ruler, but they are of concern to him. The good people among them are excellent, the bad among them vile. They delight in knowledge, but are conceited in their sectarianism. They pass judgments on the evildoers, but their sentences are light. They are a pleasant people, but unfeeling; they are bold, at the same time stupid, combining generosity with bluntness. Though it is very cold here, fruits are plentiful; wages are low, but prices are low. The city measures about a *farsakh* in both dimensions; however, the gardens are as we have mentioned. There are suburbs in two areas of the town, at each place a fortress. The gates of the city are: Bāb Abi al-ʿAbbās; Bāb Kish; Bāb al-Janbad. The *quhandiz* is beyond the city, and has a portal that opens on the city, and a portal on to the suburbs. There are eight main roads [darb] in the inner suburbs: Darb Ribāt Ahmad; Darb al-Hadīd; Darb al-Amīr; Darb Farrukhān; Darb Sūrkadah; Darb Karmābaj; Darb Sikkat Khāqān; Darb Qasr al-Dihqān. Through the outer suburbs are seven main roads: Darb Farghakad; Darb Khāsakth; Darb Sandījā; Darb al-Hadīd; Darb Barkardajā; Darb Sakrak; Darb Dar Thaghrabādh. The mosque is beside the wall of the *quhandiz*, most of the markets being in the suburbs.

p. 277   Ushtūrkath is like Binkath in extent. Over it stands a fortress; a stream flows through the town; excellent inns.

Binākath is like Ushtūrkath; the people are troublemakers; no fortress; the mosque stands in the market.

Jīnānjakath has no fortress; the buildings are of wood and clay; the remaining towns are close to what we have described—they have streams flowing through them, and trees encircling them.

Tūnkath is on a bluff; large, populous, it is the capital of Īlāq. Its quarters are developed, and it is about half the size of Binkath. It has a *quhandiz*, an inner city, suburbs, the administrative buildings being in the *quhandiz*, the mosque outside it. In the inner city are some markets, the others being in the suburbs. A stream runs through the inner city; a good, prosperous place, with a powerful *dihqān*.

Bunjikath: the capital of Ushrūsana; extensive, fertile, and important. Water is abundant here, the population large; surrounded by gardens. The houses are attractive, as we mentioned about al-Shāsh, except that these people are purer of heart, and there is little confusion. It has an inner city, with two gates—the City Gate and the Upper Gate. The mosque is within the city, the *quhandiz* outside. The suburbs are extensive, having four roads: Darb Zāmīn; Darb Marsmanda; Darb Nūjakath; Darb Kahlabādh. Six streams flow through it, similar to the large river, which flows beside it. It is a superb and really delightful place.

Zāmīn: in two sections between them a stream with small bridges over it. The mosque is on the right on the road that leads to Samarqand; the markets are on both sides of the stream. The town is on the high road.

Sābāt: populous. Most of its markets are covered by low ceilings. A spring is here with a constant flow of water. Gardens surround the town, and a number of routes converge here.

p. 278 Marsmanda: an important place, with running water; without gardens; the cold is severe. It has markets. A populous town, the mosque is in the direction of the markets.

Khisht: situated among mountains; populous, with fertile villages, close to the silver mines. The remaining towns are close to what we have already described.

Samarqand is the capital of al-Sughd, the metropolis of the region—a splendid, important, ancient town, a brilliant and elegant metropolis; comfortable, with numerous slaves; abundant water from a deep river; buildings are strong, high, and solid. The adherents of the groups [Hanafites and Shāfiites] hold frequent assemblies. The mode of life is pleasant, routes lead to it, commodities are carried thither from every distant place. The sciences flourish there, and the learned man is honoured. Here is an abundance of horses, men, and wealth. Around here are important rural areas, delightful towns, trees, and rivers. Residents and merchants meet here. In the summer it is paradise, and the people are adherents of the Congregation and Sunna; here is kindness, charity, prudence, zeal. However, in the disposition of the people and the climate, is frigidity; roughness towards strangers, distress in wintertime. They riot against their leaders, and are boastful, vain, and quarrelsome. The young women are faultless, the youth, base.

The capital is situated on the river, in the middle of it an inner city with four gates: Bāb al-Sīn; Bāb Nawbahār; Bāb Bukhārā; Bāb Kish. There are eight roads through the suburbs: Darb Ghadāwad; Darb Isbask; Darb Sūkhashīn; Darb Afshīna; Darb Kūhak; Darb Warsanīn; Darb Riyūdad; Darb Farrukhshīd.

p. 279 Buildings are of clay and wood; and the most frequented place there is the Ra's al-Tāq (head of the arch). The mosque is in the inner city beside the *quhandiz*, most of the markets in the suburbs. A moat surrounds the inner city, the water carried to it by leaden pipes that are above the trench.

Bunjikath: a rural area; producing much fruit; fertile; surrounded by trees, walnut and other.

Waraghsar is the name of both a rural area and a town together; downstream from Bunjikath.

Maymurgh—not among all the rural districts is there one with more villages, trees, and natural products, than this. It used to be the residence of al-Ikhshīd, king of Samarqand, and his palace is there.

Sanjarfaghan: a small rural district with few villages; however, it is quite populous, the best of the rural districts in climate and fruit. Its length is about two stages.

Al-Dargham: the most fertile of the rural areas, with the most pasture and water. Its length is about one stage.

Awghar (Abghar): a rural area, most of it irrigated by rain. It has many villages; the people are livestock farmers; its length, about two stages. The farming returns in a good year are said to be worth those of all the rest of al-Sughd, or of two years production in Bukhārā.

Yārkath: the northernmost rural area, bordering Ushrūsana. The drinking water is from wells; much pasture irrigated by rain; the farms are naturally fertile.

Būrnamadh: a small district with few villages.

Būzmājan adjoins Yārkath; its chief town, Abārkath. It is the most extensive rural district of this area, also that with most villages. It measures a stage in each dimension.

Kabūdhanjakath—here the villages and the trees are continuous. Its chief town has the same name.

The chief town of Widhār has the same name; many farms; it consists of plain and hill, some naturally watered and some irrigated lands.

Al-Marzubān has no mosque.

Kushāniya and Ishtīkhan: two important towns—you need not ask about the fineness of these towns, their development, their natural production. They are in the province of al-Sughd, by all accounts. The length of the rural district of p. 280 Ishtīkhan is five stages, its width, one stage. The width of al-Kushāniya, about two stages; its length the same. Both these places are towards the north.

Addition / version MS. C.

... and this makes six rural districts. Both al-Jayhānī and Abū Zayd have gone beyond in the description of Samarqand and its districts, so as to spare us the necessity of reporting or re-iterating it; and if they had described the realm of al-Islām as they described al-Sughd it would have excused us from compiling this book. The remaining towns of this area are at the edge of the territory of al-Sughd, and you need not ask about their goodness, attractiveness, and spaciousness.

Numūjkath is the capital of Bukhārā. It resembles al-Fustāt in smelliness, in the blackness of its soil, and the extent of its markets. It resembles Damascus in its buildings, and its inner city; in the crowding of its houses, and the small lodging rooms with windows looking out over the street. Situated on a plain, it is growing every day. The inner city is very well developed, and has seven gates, plated in iron: Bāb Nūr; Bāb Hufra; Bāb al-Hadīd; Bāb al-Quhandiz; Bāb Banī Saʿd; Bāb Banī Asad; Bāb al-Madīna. Beyond the city is a *quhandiz*, of which the ruler has taken possession; it contains their treasury and the prison. The building has two gates—Bāb al-Sahla (the Gate of the Plain) and Bāb al-Jāmiʿ (the Gate of the Mosque). The mosque is in the city, and has a number of wide open areas in it, all of them clean. All its mosques are magnificent, its markets superb. The suburbs have ten roads: Darb al-Maydān; Darb Ibrāhīm; Darb Mardakshān; Darb Kilābādh; Darb Nawba(k)hār; Darb Samarqand; Darb Faghāskūn; Darb al-Rāmīthaniyya; Darb Hadsharūn; Darb Ghushaj. The development, however, has gone beyond even these. Inside the city are ten other p. 281 roads, now in disuse, where the city developed formerly; some of the names of these roads are now different. The residence of the king is on the plain, facing the *quhandiz*, the back of the house being towards the *Qibla*; and I have never seen in the realm of Islam a more beautiful, more admired door than that on the mosque; neither is there in this region a town more developed, with greater throngs of people living there. Blessed is he who goes there, it refreshes him who lives there, and there is kindness in him who resides there. The foods are wholesome, the baths excellent, the streets wide; the water is digestible, buildings elegant, and there is companionship in the eating houses and the inns. Fruit is plentiful. The topics brought before their councils are remarkable, and so the populace gains knowledge of the law, and refinement. Those who guard the nation for the cause of God are many; ignorant people are few. Here is the residence of the kings of the Muslims.

Addition/version MS. C.

... it is the centre of well-grounded scholars, no one preaches there unless he be a jurisprudent or an exegete. You do not see the tax collector of any group committing abuses under the justice of the ruler; and the people lead lives of ease and comfort in security and propriety.

However, the houses are cramped, conflagrations are common, it is stinking and flea-ridden. There are extremes of heat and cold, salty wells, polluted rivers, and noxious lavatories. The disposition of the people is repulsive, the houses are expensive. Dank bazaars, flagrant sodomy, this is the dunghill of the area, and the most depressed city of al-Mashriq. Thither have repaired people steeped in vice, who corrupted the way of life, disdained the communal meetings. Hirelings took over who dressed in silk and brocade, drinking from vessels of gold and silver, belittling the matters of religion.

Tawāwīs: an important place, a market is held every year. Its fortress has been destroyed, its mosque is remote from the town. Its marketplace is quite long; a prosperous place.

Zandana: towards the north; many villages around it; a fortress, within it the mosque; its suburbs are well developed.

Khujādā: a large town, over it a fortress within which is the mosque; an attractive, elegant place.

Mughkān has a fortress, handsome suburbs, an elegant mosque. A stream flows through it; many villages around.

Bamijkath is as we have described; and these five towns are inside the encircling wall.

Baykand is towards the Jayhūn River at the edge of the sandy desert; it has p. 282 but one gate. In the fortress is a busy market, and a mosque, of which the *mihrāb* is decorated with jewels. Below the town are suburbs, with a market having about a thousand stalls, some old, some new. This town has many excellences, among them the splendour of its mosque.

Afshana: towards the west; frequently raided; a busy attractive place.

Amdīzā: to the west of Baykand, on the edge of the desert; it has a fortress.

Ūshar: an extensive settlement with many gardens. It lies in the direction of the Turks; accounted a village.

Riyāmīthan (Aryāmīthan) is the old Bukhārā; a large town, its outskirts destroyed.

Barakhshā (Warakhshā): large, with a fortress; around it runs a trench filled with water.

Zarmīthan has a *quhandiz*, also a fortress; the mosque is in the middle of the city.

Wakhsūn (Bakhsūn): large, with a fortress and a *quhandiz*.

The remaining towns are much as we have described, and here also are large villages that do not lack the customs and the facilities of the cities, except in the matter of having a congregational mosque. They do not have the mosque, as the amīr lives in Bukhārā, and he is the one having access to the ruler. The one whose opinion is followed there is Abū Hanīfa, and, of course, among us [*i.e.*, followers of Abū Hanīfa] neither the *jum'a* [congregational prayer] nor the *tashrīf (taslīm)* [closing benediction] may be performed except in a metropolitan mosque, where the legal penalties could be administered. How hard the people of Baykand worked before they could build a mosque!

Kish is a large town consisting of an inner city and suburbs, and further development is connected with it beyond those. The inner city and its *quhandiz* are in ruin. The outer city is well developed, the administration buildings being outside the inner city. The mosque is in the ruined inner city, the markets in the suburbs. The buildings are of clay and timber, as in Bukhārā. This is a fertile area, and from here are brought the first fruits of the season. The inner city has four gates: Bāb al-Hadīd; Bāb 'Ubayd Allāh; Bāb al-Qassābīn (the gate of the butchers); Bāb al-Madīnat al-Dākhila (Inner). The outer city, two: Bāb al-Madīnat al-Khārija (Outer); Bāb Biraknān. There are two large streams here, Nahr al-Qassārīn (the stream of the fullers), and Nahr Asrūd, which flow near Bāb al-Madīna. This is a splendid city but for the fact that it is plague ridden.

Nasaf—they call it Nakhshab—is a delightful city; it has a *quhandiz* in ruins, populous suburbs. Situated on a plain, the river flows through it, the p. 283 administration building being on its bank near the end of the bridge. It has suburbs wherein stands the mosque, close to where the markets are. It has a profusion of superb grapes, fine fertile farms. A large place; however, water is scarce, and sometimes the river stops flowing. The people there are a rabble, among them the most vicious fanaticisms; they are a bad people, deserving to be arrested and punished.

Kasba is bigger than Nasaf, Bazda smaller.

Al-Saghāniyān is a district very well developed, with an abundance of agricultural produce; the capital city has this name also. The capital resembles al-Ramla, though the latter is somewhat better. The district is like Palestine except that the latter is more extensive. The drinking water is derived from rivers which flow into the Jayhūn River; however the tributaries are interrupted part of the year. The district abuts the area of Tirmidh, and has mountains and plains; on its borders are peoples called Kījī, and Kinjīna, who are Turks. The district contains sixteen thousand villages, and provides about ten thousand warriors with their provisions and riding animals, should foreigners attack the ruler.

The markets of the capital are elegantly covered. Here bread is cheap, meat plentiful, water abundant. The mosque is in the centre of the market; it is a fine building with walls of baked brick, without arches. In every house is running water. Trees encircle the city, and here are different kinds of birds which are hunted. In winter it is an excellent place, with an abundance of rain and snow, herbage so remarkable that the animals disappear in it! The people are Sunnī Muslims, loving the stranger and the upright; however, here are few learned men, and the place is devoid of jurisprudents.

Dārzanjī: a fine populous town, towards the Jayhūn River. Most of its people are wool makers, and they make clothing. The drinking water is derived from a river. The mosque stands in the midst of the markets. Another stream runs at the edge of the town.

p. 284

Bāsand, towards the mountains, a spacious town with many gardens; Sankarda is similar to it.

Al-Shūmān: one of the leading cities of the area; fine, populous.

Dastajird: a large town situated between two streams, tributaries of the Jayhūn River.

Quwādiyān resembles other districts on the Jayhūn River that we have mentioned in commenting on the districts; the remaining towns of al-Saghāniyān are fine populous places.

An Account of the Jayhūn River and the Settlements on it

This river, the Jayhūn, cuts through the region and flows into Buhayrat Khwārazm [Aral Sea]. Important districts lie along it, a number of towns stand on it. Several branches flow out from this river, and six streams flow into it. The districts are: al-Khuttal; Quwādiyān; Khwārazm; the towns are: Tirmid; Kālif; Nawīdah; Zamm; Firabr; Āmul. We shall describe the entirety before beginning our commentary on the districts of Khurāsān, because some people refer to these places as "Mā warā' al-Nahr", (the area beyond the river), and the remainder of Haytal as "Balad al-ʿAjam," (the country of the Persians), as far as the boundary with the Turks. On the other hand, some consider Khwārazm to be part of the territory of Haytal, even though the largest cities in this area are in Khurāsān. For our part, we are wary of such elaborations in these matters—but in God is success!

As for Khwārazm, this is a district on both banks of the Jayhūn River. Its greater capital is in Haytal, but there is another capital in Khurāsān. The people on both sides of the river differ in customs, language, disposition, and natural characteristics. This is an important area, expansive, with many cities extensively built up, somewhat after the manner of the cities of the Romaeans, of Sijistān, or of Kāzarūn. The rows of houses are continuous, as are the gardens; here are many grape presses, farms, trees. Fruits and other agricultural products are considerable articles of commerce. The people have understanding, knowledge, law, talent, refinement; and it was rarely I found anyone eminent in jurisprudence, culture, p. 285 and knowledge of the *Qurʾān* who did not have a student from Khwārazm— every student presenting himself and applying himself to his work. However, the people here suffer from obstinacy, and lack grace, elegance, gallantry, kindness. Their loaves of bread are short, their *farsakhs* long. God—may He be exalted—has favoured them with low prices, fertility, bestowing on them also correctness in reading, and understanding. They are a hospitable people, but gluttonous. They are powerful, strong in war, and have remarkable characteristics.

It is said that in olden times the king of al-Mashriq grew angry with four hundred men of his kingdom, especially at his court, and he ordered them to be taken to a place removed from civilization, so that they would be a hundred *farsakhs* removed; and this happened to be about the location of Kāth. After a considerable period of time he sent some people who would present him with a report on them; and when they arrived there, they found them alive, having built huts for themselves, and they saw them fishing for their sustenance; here also was plenty of firewood. When they returned to the king and told him about this said he, "What name do they call 'meat'?" Said they, "Khwār." "And firewood?" Said they, "Razm." Said the king, "I have caused them to settle in that area, so I name it Khwārazm." Moreover, he ordered four hundred Turkish maidens to be brought to them, so that to this day there remains among them resemblance to the Turks.

Now it had happened that when the king exiled them to Khwārazm he had directed a canal from the mainstream of the Jayhūn River thither for their daily needs; the mainstream flowed to a town beyond Nasā, named Balkhān. The prince of Balkhān arrived at the settlement of Khwārazm, once, and observed there a people of great fortitude; at any rate, the king of the Khwārazm caroused and dallied with him, and won over him in gambling. The condition had been that the prince would open the river for them a day and a night, and he fulfilled his promise. But when he released the water it overwhelmed everything around, and it was not possible to contain it again; so it has remained in its new course to this day. In fact they have dug canals from it and built towns on it. Balkhān was deserted, and I have heard some of the people of Nasā and Abīward mention that they go to Balkhān and bring back from there eggs aplenty, together with cattle and beasts of burden that have become feral.

I asked: "Why do your heads differ from those of other people?" Said they, "Our ancestors did three things by which they overcame the people of other nations. In the first place, they used to go on raids against the Turks, and, in fact, p. 286 were lenient with them. Now, some of them, themselves, looked like Turks, and they did not know but that eventually they would fall into the hands of [other] Muslims who would sell them into slavery. Accordingly they ordered that their women, on giving birth, should bind sacks of sand on the boys' heads on both sides, so that the head would flatten; by doing this they would avoid being enslaved, and anyone of them who was captured was returned to his district.

"The second thing they did was to convert the *dirham* into four separate parts, to prevent the merchants from taking the *dirhams* away from them. Indeed, to the present day, any silver that is brought in here is not allowed out." I have forgotten the third thing they did.

You should know that Khwārazm, measuring eighty *farsakhs* by eighty, in the region of al-Mashriq, resembles Sijilmāsa in al-Maghrib, the natural disposition of the people of Khwārazm being like that of the Berbers. Here the houses adjoin one another, the rivers flow copiously, here is an abundance of fish and sheep. Here is the entrepôt of the Ghuzz, and the Turks. The name of the largest capital here is Kāth; while among the cities in Haytal are: Ghardamān; Wāyikhān; Ardhakhīwa; Nawkafāgh; Kardar; Mazdākhqān; Jashīra; Sadūr; Zardūkh; Qaryat Barātakīn; Madkaminiyya.

p. 287 The name of the Khurasanian capital is al-Jurjāniyya; among its towns are: Nūzwār; Zamakhshar; Rūzawand; Wazārmand; Daskākhān Khās; Khushmīthan; Madamīthan; Khīwa; Kardarānkhās; Hazārasp; Jiqarband; Jāz; Darghān; Jīt; Jurjāniyyat al-Sughrā; another Jīt; Sadfar; Masāsān; Kārdār; Andarastan.

Kāth, which the people call Shahrastān, is riverine, about the size of Naysābūr; it lies on the east side of the river. A mosque stands in the midst of the markets, with columns of black stone the height of a man, above which are wooden pillars. The administrative offices are in the center of the town, there being also a *quhandiz* which the river had left in ruin. Streams flow through the town, which is indeed magnificent, having scholars, litterateurs, prosperity, agricultural products, commerce. The builders here are skillful, and the like of their reciters of the *Qurʾān* are not to be found in al-ʿIrāq. Here is perfection in p. 288 chanting, excellence in reciting, similarly in appearance and reputation. However, the river is constantly flooding it, so that they are all the time backing away from the bank. Kāth is dirtier than Ardabīl, for here are numerous channels along the streets into which they publicly defecate. They then collect the excrement in pits, to transport it to the arable land in buckets. It is not safe for the stranger to appear abroad until daybreak because of the extent of the excrement; but the natives walk in it and carry it on their feet into the communities. The people have a coarse nature, an ugly disposition; their food is bad, their city vile.

Ghardamān: a fortress stands over the town, a moat filled with water surrounds it, a bowshot in width. The town has two gates.

Wāyikhān: a fortress stands over it, a moat surrounds it; at the gates catapults are positioned.

Ardhakhīwa: on the edge of the wilderness, over it a fortress with one gate; close to a mountain.

Nawkafāgh: around it flows a channel from the Jayhūn River; it is towards the desert, and is fortified; Kardar is bigger and better fortified.

Mazdākhqān: large, around it twelve thousand villages; an extensive rural district.

Jashīra: large; a fortress stands over it.

Sadūr: on the bank of the Jayhūn, having a fortress and suburbs; the mosque is in the center of the town, in the fortress.

Zardūkh: large; with a fortress and suburbs.

Qaryat Barātakīn is a large settlement in the wilderness, close to the mountain from which building stone is derived. This town has a flourishing market wherein stands the mosque; the buildings are of an excellent workable clay. The remaining towns are flourishing and fortified; however the biggest of them is Mazdākhqān, which is close to al-Jurjānīyya in area. The town is surrounded by fortification on all sides.

Al-Jurjānīyya: the capital of the province of Khurāsān; on the Jayhūn River so that the water touches it on all sides; an effort was made every way they could to deflect it by the opposing of piles and boards, but it returned eastward. Then a remarkable thing happened: the structure turned the water towards the wilderness so that it reached to the village of Farātakīn (Barātakīn), and it flowed in just one direction; from it the people dug canals for their drinking water, flowing beside the gates of the town. The waters do not enter the town because of the constraints of the canals in which they flow. The town is growing bigger every day. At Bāb al-Hujjāj is a fortress which al-Maʾmūm built, on it a door than which there is none more remarkable in all of Khurāsān. His son, ʿAlī, built
p. 289 another fortress in front of it, outside the gate of which is a sandy area resembling the sandy area at Bukhārā; here cattle are sold. The town has altogether four gates.

Nūzwār: small, over it a fortress; with a trench. It has iron gates. The high road passes through the town, which has two gates, and a bridge that is raised every night. At the west gate of the city are public baths without compare in the region. The mosque stands in the midst of the markets, and is entirely roofed except for a small portion of it.

Zamakhshar: small, a fortress over it, and with a moat, a prison, and gates braced with iron. The bridges are drawn up every night; the high road passes through the town. The mosque is very fine, beside the market.

Rūzawand: medium in size, fortified, with a ditch; the main road cuts through it, also. The mosque is beside the marketplace. The drinking water is from a spring.

Khīwa: a town situated on the edge of the desert; spacious; on a branch of the river; there is a fine mosque here. Similarly situated are Kardarānkhās and Hazārasp, both of which have wooden gates, and a trench.

Jiqarband: like Khīwa, on a river; an abundance of trees and gardens. The market is large and thriving, the mosque beside it. The high road runs through the town.

Jāz: large; with fortress, a wide trench, and bridges. The inner city stretches from one entrance to another, some distance from which the high road runs and beside which stands the mosque.

Darghān is the biggest town in the area after al-Jurjānīyya. It has a beautiful mosque, without compare in the area, magnificently decorated with precious stones. Important, riverine, this town has five hundred celebrated vineyards, and the site of the vineyards stretches for two *farsakhs* along the shore; it produces raisins.

Jīt: large, with extensive rural areas merging with the wilderness. It is a frontier fortified town close to the lands of the Ghuzz [a Turkish tribe], and through here one enters their territory.

Quwādiyān: a small district on the Jayhūn River, bordering also on al-Saghāniyān; between these two and Khwārazm is a number of towns, but we introduce the districts before the towns, as our main intent of this book is to achieve clarity and elucidation rather than sequential arrangement. Not that anyone could reproach us in the matter of arrangement, except perhaps with regard to the districts, and even those we have striven to give in order, so that no p. 290 one would find a chance to criticize us in this matter, unless he is inadvertent. Now, a jurisprudent who had traveled all over Khurāsān read our book, and when he came to the districts of Mā warā' al-Nahr said he, "Ushrūsana is not between al-Shāsh and Samarqand." Said I to him, "If a man heads out from Samarqand bound for al-Shāsh does he not go by way of Zāmīn and Sābāt?" "Certainly," said he. "Well," said I, "both of those are among the towns of Ushrūsana, so my arrangement is correct. If he were to go by way of the capital then he had not taken our map into account."

Quwādiyān has three towns very well developed, penetrated by a branch of the river, which flows into the Jayhūn. This is a rather mountainous area, yet productive. The biggest town here is Bīz, itself not very extensive. The mosque stands in the center of the markets; a fortress stands over the town, with four portals.

Sakārā: close to the mountain, the mosque in midtown.

Awzaj: situated on the bank of the Jayhūn, a populous delightful place.

Būram: some distance away, spacious, in good condition. These towns are all on streams, are quite productive, and prices are low.

Al-Khuttal is an extensive district with many towns, some of which have been associated with Balkh, by some people—but this is an error; and since al-Khuttal is beyond the Jayhūn River [*i.e.*, north] we have with more propriety associated it with Haytal. Moreover, in this book we have treated separately the places that lie on the river from the other districts, so as to deal with them in one frame of reference. Al-Khuttal is more important than al-Saghāniyān, is more extensive in its layout, having bigger towns, and with more natural wealth. It is on the borders of the region towards al-Sind, and its capital is named Hulbuk. Among its towns are: Marand; Andījārāgh; Halāward; Lāwakand; Kārbank; Tamliyāt; Iskandara; Munk; Fārghar; Bīk.

Hulbuk is the capital of al-Khuttal, and here is the residence of the p. 291 ruler; smaller than al-Saghāniyān; the mosque in the center of the town. The drinking water is derived from a stream of middling water, and from some other sources.

Addition/version MS. C.
In this country are excellent horses, fruits, and agricultural products; the remaining cities are developed. In any case Halāward is larger than Hulbuk; Iskandara is on a mountain, and Munk is the largest of the towns of the district.

Marand: populous, well-developed.

Andījārāgh: a small town close to the Jayhūn River, the drinking water derived from streams that flow into the river.

Halāward: more important than Hulbuk; large; it produces an abundance of fruit, being very fertile.

Iskandara: on a mountain; highly developed.

Munk is the largest town of the district; the other towns are similar to those we have described.

Tirmidh is the most important city on the Jayhūn River; it is a fine well-kept town, and one of its quarters, with the markets in it, is paved with burnt brick. Water flows on both sides of the town, and vessels set out for it from every direction. It has a fortress and a *quhandiz*, the mosque being in the fortress, and the *quhandiz* outside it. The fortress has one gate, the city, three. There are suburbs to the city also, with fortified posts. Tirmidh is the most important city on the Upper Jayhūn.

Kālif, further west, is on the river. Here is a mosque in the guardhouse named after Dhu al-Qurnayn, and in Haytal, Ribāt Dhi al-Kifl faces it across the river. There is not on the Jayhūn River a site at which it is possible to build a town on both sides, after the manner of Baghdād. Wāsit is different from Kālif in that here the river is controlled and so does not have floods and deposits of sand.

Zamm: a large town on the bank of the river; the mosque in the midst of the markets, which are covered. The drinking water is derived from the Jayhūn River, and water is brought during harvesting time into the middle of the town.

Nawīdah: a small town on the Haytal side of the river; the mosque is in the middle of the town.

Firabr: a town on the Haytal side, about a *farsakh* distant from the river; a few villages around it. The taxes are low, the grapes excellent, water scarce. There is a *quhandiz* here, still in use, with excellent guardhouses. The mosque stands at the gate of the town toward Bukhārā. The *Musalla* is outside the gate; and here is a hospice built by Nasr bin Ahmad with accommodations for the wayfarers.

Āmul is developed, and all the towns of this region are developed. It abounds in agricultural produce, and is situated about a *farsakh* from the river, on the road to Khurāsān. Here are many villages, taxes are high, water plentiful. The p. 292 villages are in good condition though it is on the edge of the desert; the markets are shaded. The area is a source of the finest grapes. Its mosque is on a small hill; the wells are close to the surface.

An Account of the Crossing Points and of the Distributaries of the River (Jayhūn)

This river [Jayhūn; Oxus; Āmū Daryā] has several crossing points with which we are well acquainted; after inspecting and researching we identify twenty-five, apart from those of Khwārazm. The first of these from the side of al-Khuttal is Khuttalān; then Mīla; then Awzaj at the border of Quwādiyān; then al-Kūdā; then Tirmidh; then another below that, then another, then another; then Kālif; then Khārizmiyān; then Bukhāriyān; then Bunkāh Abī Wahab; then Bābakar (?) (Tūbakar?); then Karkūh, these latter two settlements being on opposite sides of the river; then al-Ribāt, and some close to here; then Khwārān; then Shīr; then Nawīdah, where the people of Samarqand cross; then Farhūna; then Barmādwā, which is a village belonging to the Bedouin; then another; then the main road of Khurāsān; then Firabr and Āmul; then Sakāwā; then Māhīkbarān. Then you meet the crossing points of Khwārazm—Darghān and Jiqarwand; then another; then Hazārasp; then Kāth; then the remaining crossing points until the lake is reached, among them those of al-Jurjān.

As for the effluents (canals) from the river, most of them are in Khwārazm. One of them, the Karīh, flows for five *farsakhs*; another, the Hazārasp, continues to widen until it has gone about the distance of a post stage; then beyond that it is not really confined to a channel until it has gone about a *farsakh* further. This canal irrigates the villages out towards the wilderness. Branching off, also is Nahr Kardarān-Khās, bigger than the Nahr Hazārasp, between the two a distance of two *farsakhs*. Next is Nahr Khīwah, also of considerable dimension, so that vessels ply on it. Next is Nahr Madrā over which vessels ply also; about half a *farsakh* from Nahr Khīwah. There is a like distance between Nahr Madrā; and Nahr Wadāk.

p. 293   Below the capital, and parallel to the main stream is Nahr Būwwah, and the waters from the two directions meet at the village of Andarastān. Vessels can travel on this to al-Jurjāniyya; then the barrier we have mentioned prevents further passage. From where the waters meet to the barrier is the distance of a post stage. Nahr Kurdar starts from below the capital about four *farsakhs*, from four points close to each other, eventually becoming one stream.

Branching off from the Jayhūn River, also, are streams that irrigate the rural district of Āmul. As for Firabr and the other towns which are on their banks, mention of them would merely lengthen the book. Moreover, we have not shown these streams on our map, there being so many of them.

The Territory of the Khurāsān side of the River

You should know that this region has excellences pertaining to this side of it, in most of which the side of Haytal shares. However, since this side was delimited first, was introduced to Islām first, and is nearer to the regions of the Arabs, it has been mentioned and known by its *nisba* [adjectival ending in "ī," *e.g.* "Khurāsānī"].

It is told of Ibn Qutayba that he said, "[The people of] Khurāsān are the people of the 'Call,' and the supporters of the state." When God brought Islām to them, they became Muslims with the greatest eagerness of all people, and were the quickest to do so, by the grace of God on them. They adopted Islām voluntarily and in multitudes, and made a lasting peace [with the Muslims] on behalf of their country. Hence their land taxes were light and their calamities few; nor was it necessary to take them into captivity. No blood was shed among them, despite their own capacity for fighting, their great numbers, and the strength of their power. And when God—may He be praised!—saw the conduct of the Umayyads, with their tyrannies and provocations against the family of His Prophet—on whom be peace—He sent against the Umayyads armies from the area of Khurāsān which He assembled from its provinces and put together from its districts. And they marched against them like the last darkness of the night. And what is expected from them when the *Mahdī* [Muslim messianic guide to appear before the last day] comes is more than that, for they are the people of the state, and of victory; and supporters of the truth when it appears.

It is reported that Muhammad bin ʿAbd Allāh said to his missioners: "The majority in al-Kūfa are Shīʿa, following ʿAlī; in al-Basra, they are ʿUthmānids, observing abstention [from conflict of Sunnī and Shīʿa]; while in al-Jazīra there are true Harūrites, Bedouins like heathens, and Muslims following the manners of Christians. Then there are the people of al-Shām (Syria), and they know only Muʿāwiya, and obedience to the Ummayads, with deeply seated enmity and profound ignorance. As for the people of Makka and al-Madīna, Abū Bakr and ʿUmar gained ascendancy over them.

p. 294

"But look at the people of Khurāsān! There, the numbers are great, perseverance is clear. There are the peaceful breasts, the hearts free of hatred. These people are not split up into sects nor divided into creeds. No vice degrades them. Rather they have an army of people with bodies and forms broadshouldered, broadbacked; their heads, and beards, and moustaches, and voices formidable. Their language is splendid, and from their mouths comes opposition to any wrong. In sum, I am indeed optimistic about the people of al-Mashriq, of the place of the rising of the lamp of the world, the light of mankind.

"And when God had put affairs in order, He put them in charge, with their successors, with a gentle rule, over the most capable, the most obedient to God, those with the finest morality among His subjects. He graced them with perfection, for they know not the vile."

I read in a book in the library of ʿAdhud al-Dawla that Khurāsān, in salubrity of air, goodness of water, healthiness of soil, perfection of fruit, skill of artisanship, in perfection of disposition, tallness of physique, beauty of countenance; in the swiftness of boats, the excellence of weapons; in its trade, science, probity, law, knowledge,—Khurāsān in all these is a shield against the Turks, who are the most powerful enemies, the most stubborn, and the most patient of their hardships, with the least interest in enjoying an easeful life.

Moreover, the people of Khurāsān are the most devoted to the law, the most steadfast in holding on to the truth. The Prophet—God's peace and blessings be upon him—said: "They will enable you to become victorious in the future, as followers of the faith, even as you enforced it on them in the past." By this he means that they will enable you to gain victory by the sword, in conformity with the religion of God; and the verification of this is to be found in the era of Abū Muslim.

You should know that the territory on this side of the river is indeed Khurāsān, and it is the more important of the two sides, since, [in comparison with Haytal], the larger metropolis is here, its people are more elegant, wiser, and more knowing about good and evil. They are, moreover, closer to the regions and the customs of the Arabs; their capital is more pleasant and better, and they have least cold in the weather, and in the disposition of the people. They are more honourable, have more righteous and intelligent people, and profound knowledge, and remarkable mental retention of the Qurʾān; they have wealth aplenty, and rightmindedness.

In Khurāsān is Marw, on which the world is founded, and Balkh, which is
p. 295 its pinnacle. Here also is Naysābūr, and do not forget the spaciousness of the area, the importance of its villages. However, vice has spread here, and the land tax is collected twice a year, so the people of the hamlets are in distress.

This is the map of it. [Map XII]

We have divided Khurāsān into nine districts and eight sections; and we have arranged them in this chapter according to their size, and according to the portrayal of their boundaries. The first of them from beside the Jayḥūn River is Balkh, but in extent Naysābūr is larger. Of the sections the greatest in extent is Būshanj; then Bādhghīs; then Gharjistān; then Marw al-Rūdh; then Tukhāristān; then Bāmiyān; then Kanj Rustāq; then Asfuzār. We have considered Tūs, and its two sister towns, storehouses of Naysābūr. Moreover we have considered Sarakhs as one of the places separate from the districts, because there is a problem here.

Balkh—this is also the name of the capital. Among its towns are Ushfūrqān,
p. 296 Salīm, Karkū, Jāh, Madhr, Barwāz. Among its sections are Tukhāristān, this being also the name of the capital; and some of its towns are: Walwālij, al-Tāliqān, Khulm, Gharbank, Siminjān, Iskalkand, Rūb, Baghlān al-Suflā, Baghlān al-ʿUlyā, Askīmasht, Rāwan, Ārhan, Andarāb, Khast, Sara-ʿAsim. Al-Bāmiyān has towns Basghūrfand, Sakāwand (Saqāwand), Lakhrāb. Balkh also has rural areas Badhakhshān, Banjahīr, Jārbāyah, Barwān. All these are important towns and extensive divisions.

Ghaznīn is an important district, and this is also the name of the capital. Among its towns are: Kardīs, Sakāwand (Saqāwand), Nawah, Bardan, Damrākhī,

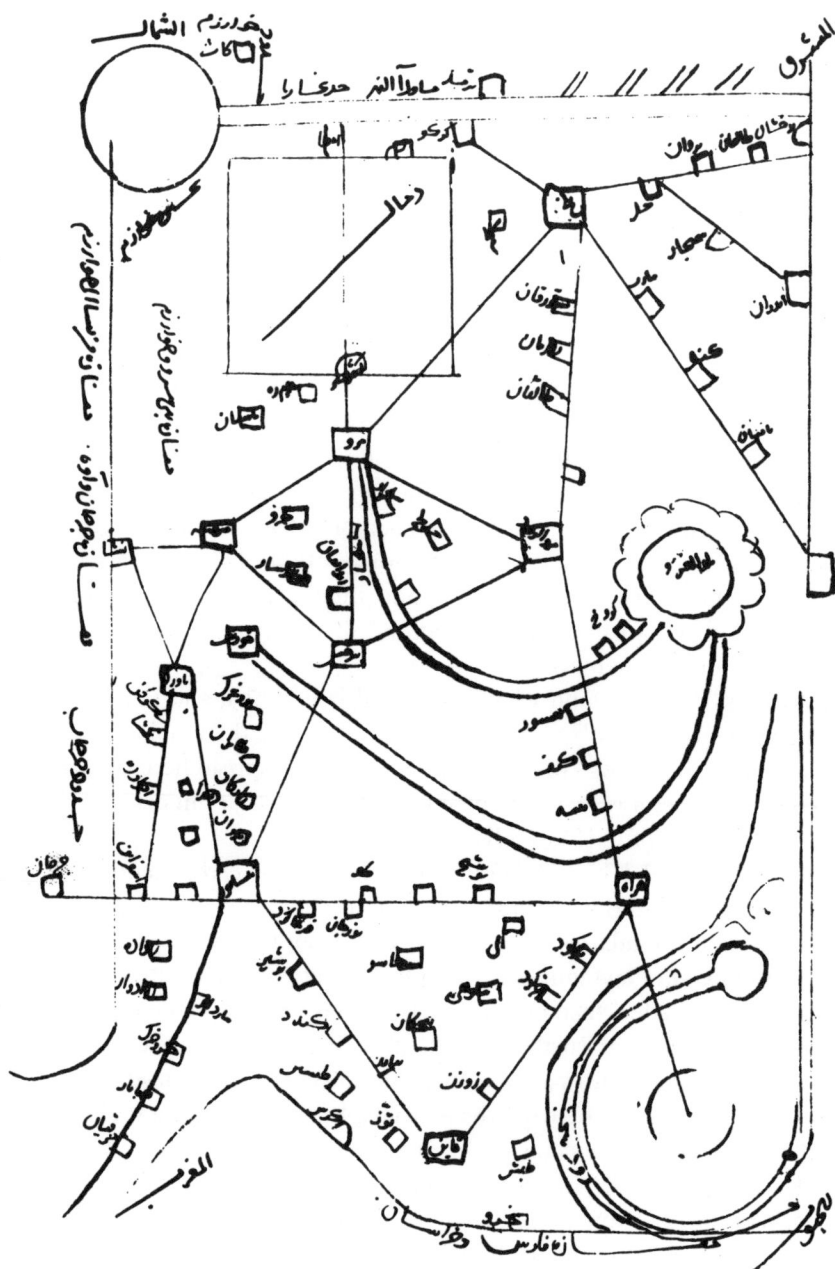

Map XII: Khurāsān (see p. 416).
From MS. Sprenger 5—Ahlwardt 6034 by kind permission of the Staatsbibliothek
Preussischer Kulturbesitz, Berlin, Orientabteilung.

Hashsh Bārah, Farmul, Sarhūn, Lajrā, Khwāst (-Ghurāb), Zāwah, Kāwīl,

p. 297 Kābul, Lamghān, Būdan, Lahūkar. The section of Wālishtān has six towns with mosques: Abshīn (Afshīn), Asbīdajah, Mastank, Shāl, Sakīra, Sīwah, and eleven hundred villages. The district has two thousand two hundred villages.

Bust—this is also the name of the capital; among its towns are: Jālaqān, Bān, Qarma, Būzād, Ardh (Balad) Dāwar, Sarwistān, Qaryat al-Jawz, Rakhūd, Bakrāwādh, Banjawāy, Kish, Rūdhān, Safanjāwī, Talqān (Tālaqān); and it has one thousand one hundred villages. Some of these towns are associated with Sijistān, but this is an error, and few make the distinction that we do. Abū Zayd attributed Ghaznīn and Bust to Sijistān; some people make both of them one district, naming it Kābulistān.

Sijistān is a district with continuous development, though the houses are separated from one another, there being few cities in the area; it has, however, many villages and is a source of date palms and snakes. The capital is Zaranj, and among the towns are: Kuwayn, Zanbūk, Farah, Darhind, Qarnīn, Kawārabwādh, Bāranwādh, Kizah, Sinj, Bāb al-Taʿām, Karwādikan, Nih, al-Tāq.

p. 298 Harāt is also the name of the capital; among its towns are: Karūkh, Awbah, Mālin, Khaysār, Astarabyān, Mārābādh. Of its sections Būshanj has four towns: Kharkard, Farkard (Faljard), Kūsūy, Karah. Bādghīs has eight towns: Dihistān, Kūghanābādh, Kūfā, Busht, Jadhāwā, Kābrūn, Kālwūn, Jabal al-Fidhdha. Kanj is a rural area, with three towns: Baban, Kīf, Baghshūr. In Asfuzār are four towns: Kuwāshān, Kuwārān, Kūshk, Adraskar.

Jūzjān(ān) is not an old district, being only annexed to the sections of Balkh; yet today it is one of the chief cities, and a district of the greatest importance, its ruler being a person of influence. There are not many towns here, because of the fewness of people; and they are a people of openhandedness, religion, knowledge, and understanding. The capital is al-Yahūdiyya, and among the towns are: Anbār, Barzūr, Fāryāb, Kalān, Shabūrqan (Ushfūrqan).

Marw al-Shāhijān is an ancient district, Dhu al-Qarnayn (Alexander the Great) having established it. It is recounted of Ibn ʿAbbas—and may God be merciful to them both—that he said, "What a wonderful city is Marw! Dhu al-Qarnayn built it, and al-ʿUzayr prayed there." Its streams flow into the pool from which there is no exit; however, an angel stands over it with drawn sword to ward off evil. According to Qatādā, in the words of God—may He be exalted—

p. 299 "warn the mother city and those who dwell around her"; (*Qurʾān*, sūra 6, v.92), said he, the mother city in al-Hijāz is Makka, and in Khurāsān it is Marw.

Moreover, he said that when Tahmūrath [a mythical king] began to build the *quhandiz* of the capital he set up a market which had everything one would need. And so it was that if a man would stay there in the evening when he was given his wages he would buy there the food and provisions and sustenance for his family, thus the *dirham* would return to the market. When the market was empty they would count the money, and behold it would amount to a thousand *dirhams*. It is a delightfully situated district, except that water is scarce, though the course of the river is constantly breaking out. The place where the water is most scarce is near the country domains of the ruler, and formerly they would not allow a ruler to buy a hamlet there. I heard some of them say, "A woman ejected al-Ma'mūn from our town." "How?" said I. Said my informant, "She came to him and said, 'You destroyed Marw, and Marw will not permit anyone to own its hamlets except the people.' So al-Ma'mūn ordered a retreat from the town."

Marw is also the name of the capital, and it is said that it was called Marw al-Shāhijān only because "al-shah" means "the king," and "al-jān" means "the spirit." Here is an abundance of dates and raisins; and the baths are very fine. The capital has the same name; and among the towns are: Kharaq, Hurmuzfarrah, Bāshān, Sanjān, Sawsqān, Sahba, Kīrank, Sink ʿAbbādī, Dandānaqān. Its sections are: Marw al-Rūdh, and its towns al-Tālaqān, Qasr Ahnaf, Hanīna (?), Lawkar.

As for Naysābur, people have disagreed about one of its names, Īrān-shahr. Some consider this to be the name of the entire district together with Jābulistān, including it in Sijistān and the area around it. Some have applied the name to this district; and some have applied it to the capital only. This last we accept, that the capital is Īrānshahr, by consensus; there is no need to prove this, since proof is incumbent only on anyone who asserts anything above and beyond this. The district is an extensive one with important rural areas, hamlets, and canals. It is

p. 300 said that Abū Bakr al-ʿAbadawī said, "I compared the waters of the Tigris with the waters of Naysābur, and they were both equal." The air is healthy here, you see no leper, and anyone here who consistently eats the fat of meat, goes to the baths, uses oil of violets, need not concern himself about the healthiness of the air.

It is told concerning Hammawīh that someone said to him, "If only you had established a hospital in Naysābur!" Said he, "My treasury is not rich enough for that." Said they, "How is that, seeing that you are commander of the army." Said he, "Because it needs to draw a wall around the entire city," meaning, by that, that all the people were in need of a hospital, because of their frivolity and lightheadedness.

The name of their capital is Īrānshahr; associated with it are four secondary metropolitan cities, twelve rural districts, three exporting towns, a castle, and an administrative seat. The secondary metropolitan centers are: al-Shāmāt, Rīwand, Māzul, Bushtafrūsh. The rural districts are: Busht, Bayhaq, Kuwayn, Jājarm, Isfarāʾīn, Ustuwā, Asfand, Jām, Bākharz, Khwāf, Zāwah, Rukhkhu. The administrative seat is Zūzan; the town with castle is Būzjān; the exporting towns are Tūs, Nasā, and Abīward. There are, in these rural districts we have mentioned, apart from the exporting towns, six thousand villages, like ʿAmawās; and there are two thousand one hundred mosques.

p. 301 The capital of Qūhistān is Qāyin; its towns are: Tūn, Junābid, Tabas al-ʿUnnāb, al-Raqqa, Khūr, Khwāst, Kurī, Tabas al-Tamr.

Addition/version MS. C.

As for Qūhistān, it is quite extensive, measuring probably eighty *farsakhs* by eighty, though the greater part of it consists of mountains and desert areas, inhospitable and treeless. Its capital is Qāyin, and among its cities are Tūn, Tabas al-ʿUnnāb, Tabas al-Tamr, Kurī, Khūr, Khawst, Yunābidh (Binābidh), al-Raqqa. Now, suppose someone says, "indeed whatever you have said is correct, and your classificatory presentation is perfect. However, you have added to Naysābūr three important districts, then you were not satisfied until you made them its granaries; so you are at variance with the customary knowledge which is reliable, and the basic consideration to which one must return." It should be said to him in reply, "you should know that Naysābūr is the most important area of al-Mashriq (the Orient), and is the parallel of Ifrīqiya in al-Maghrīb (the Occident), and you have seen what it has by way of towns and areas the attribution of which is undisputed. And we have agreed that Balkh and Harāt are primate cities linked with Naysābūr; we have, too, represented it as having districts more important than Tūs and its two sisters—for it is no surprise that we consider that Tūs does not stand entirely on its own so as to be considered a district, so it is necessary that it be added to a district; and there is no district more entitled to it than this one, from many aspects and reasons which are obvious. Hence, since the matter is so, and was not considered, except in the name when we called the district a granary, as far as Nasā and Abīward are concerned, they are both merely two unimportant districts without cities, and we have added them both to the most celebrated administrative district, and capital of the region, so that the administrative districts would be associated with one another in a coherent way, and the analogy extend so as to correspond with Ifrīqiya."

As for Balkh, we shall begin to describe it as Abu al-Qāsim al-ʿAkkī described it, considering that it was his city. Said he, "Balkh in the nature of its people, is beautiful and brave; superlative in character, intelligence, excellence of opinion, and height of capacity; in the grandeur of society, eagerness to administer lawful judgments, readiness to sacrifice for each other in time of need; in the beauty of the situation of the district, and its extensiveness; in the evenness of the conditions of its population; in the lowness of prices there. There is, moreover, the abundance of greenery, with the passage of streams through it; the envelopment by trees of its places of business and residences; its proximity to mountains and p. 302 valleys. Its civilized facilities are like those of Damascus in al-Shām (Syria). The credit for building Baghdād goes to the people of Khurāsān, because it was built for them. Then look at the magnificence of Balkh, the excellence of its situation, the width of its roads, the splendour of its streets, the multitudes of its rivers; the denseness of its woods, the purity of its water, the radiance of its palaces, the walls of its inner city, its Friday mosque. See the skillfulness of its artisanship, the importance of its location,—there is no place in the regions of the Persians to compare with it for beauty and wealth. From its yield a huge sum is taken every year for the treasury of the ruler, in excess of what is needed."

Balkh is situated on a plain, and from it to the closest mountains is four *farsakhs*. A wall surrounds it and there are suburbs. It is said that its name in the Persian books is "Balkh the brilliant."

Addition/version MS. C.

Balkh is an attractive metropolis, prosperous, agreeable; it is the garden of Khurāsān. Among the countries it may be compared to Tāhart, and matches Damascus of Syria. Streams cut through its streets, gardens and trees encircle it; its inhabitants have learning, renown, and spaciousness. It is the granary of *al-fiqh* [jurisprudence in Islam], the source of chivalry, the place of generosity, the abode of happiness, and of a population of refinement. Its houses are spacious, its markets beautiful, its fruits remarkable, its products low in price, its waters wholesomely light. Here are leading principalities, great Imāms, a great number of all different kinds of things, profitable articles of commerce, wealth abundant. In the regions of the non-Arabs there is no mosque to equal theirs; in the Orient, no territory to resemble theirs; it is the emporium of al-Sind, the glory of its side of the region. However, it is a boring place, far from the main roads; the routes thither are difficult, its riots are brutal, vices there are widespread. In area it is close to Bukhārā, saving that their houses are spacious, on the style of the houses of al-Dandānaqān; the walls are adorned with exterior decorations made of gypsum. The mosque stands in the midst of the markets, and one descends to it by steps: it is well-frequented, highly decorated with filigree of wood. The town is situated in the lowland, about one half of a stage from the mountains; it has an inner city, well developed, in which stands the mosque, also developed suburbs: it has seven gates—Bāb Nawbahār, Bāb Rahba, Bāb al-Hadīd, Bāb al-Hinduwān, Bāb al-Yahūd, Bāb Shast, Bāb Yahyā. There is a considerable stream here, a moat surrounds the inner city; all the buildings are of clay.... Al-Tayiqān is the largest city of Tukhāristān, stands close to the mountains, and has a stream, and gardens; it somewhat resembles Zabīd, and all the other towns are lesser than it—but you may say what you wish about the lowness of the prices of the agricultural products there! The remaining towns of Balkh, all of them, are good. Badhakhshān is a well-developed city with an extensive rural district; it is fertile, has vineyards and streams, and some mines are there. Banjahīr is situated in the mountains, has a stream and gardens, but no cultivated fields worth mention. Jārbāya resembles Sarakhs, or is somewhat larger; it is situated in the mountains, unfortified; has a large stream, but no gardens, rather, fruits are carried thither. The remaining towns are situated amidst streams, trees, and gardens.

p. 303   Khulm is the town of the Azd tribe. Small, yet its villages, rural district, and farms are many; the air is healthy, the breezes frequent.

Siminjān: bigger than Khulm; has one mosque. Here are fruits, valleys, hunting, cattle, also people of the Tamīm tribe.

Andarāba lies in forested valleys, and here are well-frequented markets.

Khast: delightful, wooded, fertile; there are Bedouin here.

Al-Tāliqān has a large market. Two streams, branches of the Jayhūn River, the Khuttalāb and the Barāb, flow through it. It is an exceedingly delightful and fertile place.

Iskalkand: small, yet delightful, yielding much agricultural produce.

Baghlān: there are two, the Lower and the Upper, and they are both among the gardens of Khurāsān. The mosque is in the Lower; the Upper is a large village in a wooded valley.

Shiyān: a town in the rural area of Askīmasht. Here is a remarkable spring, beside which stands the mosque of Qutayba bin Muslim.

Banjahīr, that is Jabal al-Fidhdha (the mountain of silver); here the *dirhams* are plentiful, rarely do you find debased or deficient coinage.

Farwān (Barwān): large, on the edge of the district; a well-attended mosque.

Badhakhshān borders on the land of the Turks above Tukhāristān. Here is the mine of the gem which resembles the sapphire, there being no other such mine anywhere. It is a first-rate outpost; and here is the remarkable fortress of Zubayda. Here is the source of lapis lazuli and quartz, of the bezoar stone, and asbestos. This latter is something like papyrus, and fire does not burn it. It is placed in oil and lighted, as the wick is lighted, but is not impaired. It may be taken out and thrown into a roaring fire for an hour and it returns to the state it was before. Table mats are woven from it, and when they are soiled and the people wish to clean them, they throw them into the baking oven, and they come out clean. Here also is a material which if taken into a dark room illuminates everything near it.

Al-Bāmiyān: an extensive section, with many products. Its capital is small.

p. 304 Ghaznīn, the capital, is not big, though roomy and prosperous. Prices are low, meats plentiful, fruits excellent and abundant. There are important towns here, and the way of life is good. This is one of the mercantile towns of Khurāsān, one of the entrepôts of al-Sind. Anyone who visits it frequently gains excellent health. Here are neither fleas nor scorpions, but rather a blessed company. However, the cold here is severe and there is much snow. Generally, their buildings are of wood, in which are set what is called *ghashak* [a small tile of sorts] resembling the tesselation of Egypt. This city is not famous. Its situation and atmosphere are dry, and its water is not pleasing. It is on a plain, and from it to the mountains is the distance of a *farsakh*. The town consists of two parts, and the citadel wherein resides the ruler is in the center of the inner city. The mosque is towards the south, and, with some of the markets, is in the city; the remaining markets and the houses are in the suburbs. The city has four portals: Bāb al-Bāmiyān, Bāb Sanbān, (?) Bāb Kardan, Bāb al-Sayr. The people are comfortable, well off. A river flows here, but there are no gardens.

Kābul has a populous suburb. The merchants meet in this town. It has a remarkable impregnable *quhandiz*. This is the land of the finest myrobalan, so prized by the people of India. The remaining towns are similar to those we have described, most of them being in the direction of al-Sind, according to what we have been told.

Bust is an important capital. The people are religious, manly, comfortable, well off, in an area of fertility. They are people of honour and elegance, acquainted with the Islamic traditions, and knowledgeable. Bust is situated between two rivers, and it is the community of the two fruits [of this world and the next]. The air is gentle, the towns delightful, the villages many, dates abundant, grapes aplenty; here also is the lotus tree, and sweet basil. I have heard Abū Mansūr, a jurist of Sijistān, say, "I have not seen a town so small in size that is more fertile, has more fruit, and blessings, than Bust." However, it is a pestilential place, outlying, of small area. It has a well-developed inner city, wherein stands the mosque; there are suburbs wherein are the markets. The drinking water is derived from the Hīrmīd (Hilmand) River, and from another river named Khardarūy, which meet a *farsakh* away. Over the Hīrmīd is a bridge of boats close to the place where the two rivers meet.

Half a *farsakh* away, in the direction of Ghaznīn, is a small city called
p. 305 al-ʿAskar [the army]; the ruler lives here. Banjawāy is close to the main road, fortified, with a handsome mosque; drinking water from a stream.

Bakrawādh: a large town; the mosque stands in the market; drinking water from a stream.

Dāwar: large, pleasant, at the border of al-Ghūr [Ghūristān]. It is an important frontier post with a well-organized garrison. From there to the border of al-Ghūr is one post stage. Some attribute this district to Sijistān, those of the school of Abū Zayd al-Balkhī, and very few separate its towns from Sijistān. Our opinion herein is correct, if God—may He be exalted—so wills.

Zaranj is the capital of Sijistān: it has a sturdy fortress, and is well built. There are snakes here. The people are clever, capable, intelligent, keenminded, having a knowledge of jurisprudence, good memory, subtlety, and brilliancy; they are possessed of polite learning, eloquence, skill, engineering, wisdom, being also people of commerce. There is good living here, lowness of prices, fruits. It is the Basra of Khurāsān, and you will not see a more elegant people in embellishments and building in the region. There is a remarkable fortress here, surrounded by a trench in which springs flow and into which the overflow of the canals runs. Here the food is clean, here are many elders, commerce is profitable, water abundant. However, snakes are abundant, the heat is oppressive; the date grown here is the *daql*; disorder is rife, there is constant turbulence among the people, with fanaticism between the two factions plain to be seen; you see those who are killed, and those who are fugitive. Everyone is differentiated there by a nickname; the children of fornication are there in swarms; they wear *ʿaqārib* (curls) but they themselves are *ʿaqārib* (scorpions). They slander one another in poems. In disposition they are disagreeable and cold; they wear their turbans folded as do the Khārijites, and most of them slander both in-laws of the Prophet. Their houses are narrow, the soil stinking, the community frightful—I do not wish to see anything like it. There is an inner city, which has a fortress and a moat; herein is the mosque with the jail opposite to it. The mosque is marvelously constructed, having two minarets, the old one, and another of brass built by Yaʿqūb ibn al-Layth. There is a fortified castle here also. The town is on

p. 306 a plain, has many gates and roads; half of it was built by Ardashīr, and half by Khusraw.

al-Tāq: small; abundant dates; with an extensive rural district.

Kuwayn has a strong large fortress; no pulpit is here, as they are Khārijites; similarly Zanbūk, and Fūfah.

Farah has two sections—one inhabited by the Khārijites, one by the Sunnī.

Darhind: large, close to the mountain; buildings are of stone, and there is a stream. All these towns except al-Tāq—for it is towards Harāt—are in the direction of Bust.

Qarnīn has a fortress. From here came Banu al-Layth al-Saffārūn (the brass founders), who went out and conquered Fārs and Khūzistān. It has a mosque, suburbs, a stream; it is small.

Bāranwādh has a fortress. A mosque is here, and no Khārijites. The area produces grain.

Sinj: close to the mountain; a mosque; the buildings are of stone.

Bāb al-Taʿām is an extensive section with important towns such as: Sūskan, Sakūkas, Malkān, Karsuwād, Barank, Adūrās, Kūtan, Diyārūd, Diyār; and it has other central towns. We have said that Sijistān is varied in its development as if it were one rural area, with few towns.

Wararank is an armed outpost against the Ghūr; here are guards and watchers and horses consecrated to the holy strife, and tools and equipment are brought there from all over.

As for the towns towards Fārs—there is Karwādikan, with a mosque; the buildings are of clay, the drinking water derived from the stream. It is not fortified. The mosque is in the centre of the town. The name of the rural district is Hūrsūna. Nih has a fortress, a mosque. The buildings are of clay, and most of the drinking water is from canals.

These four districts are in one line to the left [of the Jayhūn River], which is the west; at the beginning of the second zone from the side of the Jayhūn River is soft sand, as far as Marw, and Jūzjān(ān) is included in this zone. We shall start from Harāt, in accordance with our arrangement.

Harāt is an important capital, the garden of this side of the province. It p. 307 produces excellent grapes, superb fruits. It is a populous, well-developed area, with arable land, and continuous development; the villages are important. The people here have refinement, eloquence, charm, and knowledge. Various kinds of confections come from here, and the cloth made here is taken into regions near and remote. It is a fine, fortified place. However, its people are riotous, murder is a custom with them. Their preachers have no knowledge of the law, and no veneration; their language is vile, their vice disgraceful. Their bread does not satisfy, their turmoil does not cease. The inner city is well developed; there is a *quhandiz*, and in the suburbs a fortress. The gates of the suburbs face the gates of the inner city, and they correspond with the old names—Bāb Ziyād towards Naysābūr; Bāb Fīrūz; Bāb Sarāy [palace gate] towards Balkh; and Bāb Khushk towards the Ghūr area. The mosque is in the middle of the inner city among the markets; it is well attended. There is a remarkable stone bridge here. It is a populous district.

Karūkh: the biggest town of the district; well watered, and with gardens.

Awfah (Awbah): small; the mosque is in Mahalla Sabīdān; the buildings are of clay. Situated between two mountains, the width of its rural district is twenty *farsakhs*. The whole area occupied by gardens one beside the other, with flowing streams and populous villages.

Mālin: like Awfah; has gardens and water. The buildings are of clay.

Khaysār: a medium sized town; trees and water are in short supply; smaller than Mālin.

Astarabyān has flowing water and few gardens; most of it consists of farms; it is situated in the mountains.

Mārābādh: smaller than Mālin; there are many gardens, water is abundant; fertile, pleasant.

Būshanj is the most important section of Harāt, and is well-known in the region. However, we will be censured if we attribute it to Harāt, seeing that its ruler sometimes is a different one from that of Harāt; and it is said that its name is mentioned ahead of that of Harāt in the official registers, what is said about it being like what is said about Tūs. However, our guide whom we have followed is Abū Zayd, who was the most knowledgeable about the bureaucracy of Khurāsān, knowing the details of its areas better than anyone else.

Addition/version MS. C.

[He was the most learned in the bureaucracy of] the Orient, the division of its territories, and I noticed that he added it with its sister cities to Harāt; but if the addition of it to Harāt is correct, then our analogy is consistent with regard to the other districts of the realm of al-Islām.

It is about half the size of Harāt, situated on level ground, from the town p. 308 to the mountain being a distance of about two *farsakhs*. It has an abundance of water, lots of trees, and timber is exported from here to the other sections. It has a fortress, a moat, and three gates—Bāb ʿAlī; Bāb Harāt; and Bāb Quhistān.

The next biggest town is Kūsūy, about one third the size of Būshanj; gardens; the buildings are of clay.

Farkard (Faljard) has not many gardens; however the people are prosperous, have freely grazing livestock; running water.

Kharkard has streams, many gardens, but is small.

Bādhghīs—the largest of its towns is Dihistān, about half the size of Būshanj. The buildings are of clay; on a mountain, there is a deficiency of water. No gardens; and the farms are watered solely by rain; also tunnels underground. The residence of the ruler is in Kūghanābādh; Dihistān is more populous.

Jabal al-Fidhdha: on a mountain; its mines are in disuse.

Kūfā is in the steppe; it has no gardens or running water, its farms watered by rain alone; similarly Kūghanābādh, Jadhāwā, Kālwūn, Kābrūn,—these have neither gardens nor running water. The inhabitants derive their drinking water from rain and from wells; they grow vegetables and grain. These towns are on the road to Sarakhs.

Kanj Rustāq—its largest towns are: Baban, where the ruler resides, larger than Būshanj; Baghshūr, about the size of Būshanj in area; Kīf is about half that size, has an abundance of running water, gardens and many vineyards; the buildings of clay. Baghshūr is in the steppe, and the farms are watered by rain only, the drinking water is from wells. The land here is healthy, the climate temperate, the water light. It is on the road to Marw al-Rūdh.

Asfuzār—the largest of its towns is Kuwāshān; here are streams, and many gardens, vineyards; the buildings are of clay. The remaining towns are smaller p. 309 than it, all of them surrounded with trees, and having streams and parks.

Harāt has important areas and attractive localities, the mention of which would merely lengthen the book.

Addition/version MS. C.
You should know that Abū Hanīfa, the foremost Imām, and the jurisprudent of the community of the faithful, despite his pre-eminence and his knowledge of the law, was perplexed by three questions on which he had scruples, and of the responsibility for which he washed his hands. And there was one question on which he expressed misgivings, speaking slightingly of it and with circumspection, in order that God—may He be exalted—would let His creatures know that humans are feeble, and that above every possessor of knowledge is an Omniscient One. Now we, for our part, have classified this realm in detail, as you see, and God—glorious is His name—has disclosed to us, in this science, what He has not disclosed to any other than ourselves. He has, moreover, provided for us the means whereby we arrived at the furthermost extremities, and traveled over the lands; and He has put in order for us that knowledge for which we strove, so that we are able to gather and arrange it. We extended the analogy and applied it, with every discretion, carrying it from one stage to the next; however, we also were perplexed in the matter of three districts, and had our doubts in respect to one. As for those over which we were perplexed, Gharj al-Shār, and Marw al-Rūdh, and Sarakhs, we wavered and had our doubts, and excused ourselves in those sections; so we limited ourselves in our description of them, and did not add them to a metropolis, nor did we diverge from our analogy on their account. As for the doubtful one, that is Isfahān, we propound our position on it.

Gharj al-Shār—"al Gharj" means "the mountains," and "al-Shār" means "the king," so its meaning is "Mountains of the King;" the people call it Gharjistān, and to the present its kings are addressed by the title "al-Shār." It is an extensive section with many villages, and has ten mosques. The most important is Abshīn, wherein is the residence of the rulers, and their palaces are there. It has a fine mosque, and guardhouses; a river is here called the River of Marw al-Rūdh.

Shūrmīn is also among the cities of this area; and these two are close in size.

Balīkān also is among the towns here, situated in the mountains. Approaching this province are roads with iron gates, and it is not possible for anyone to enter except with permission. There is true justice here, respect and consideration are natural and instinctive; all things else done according to the custom of the two ʿUmars [Abū Bakr and ʿUmar bin al-Khattāb]. The manners here delight the eye, there are no oppressive rulers, nor do they create anything to change the facts. What is taken from the rich among them is given to the poor. Anyone who commits a crime is either pardoned or executed. Along with that, they are sound, virtuous people of the first clay. The Messenger of God—God's peace and blessings be upon him—spoke the truth when he said, "According to what you are, thus will you be ruled." We hesitated in assigning it because of these circumstances, and were not able to attach it to one of these districts around it, since it is itself independent, glorious in its ruler; neither could we make it a district, for this would controvert our rules followed in the case of Būshanj, and other towns like it. If someone should say, "It must be added to Balkh, because it is joined with its section in a certain respect, that is, in the end of the name; for do you not see that they say 'Gharjistān; just as "Tukhāristān," "al-Bāmiyān," "Barwān" are said?'" The answer to that is: "General usage, in our science, is more forceful than what you have said, because it is founded on matters of assurance. For example, God—may He be exalted—called the earth a carpet; now if a man swore that he would not sit on a carpet, and he were to sit on the earth he would not perjure himself, for this would not be in accord with the general usage."

Marw is known as Marw al-Shāhijān; a capital delightful, fine, elegant. It is brilliant, extensive, pleasant; there, foods are delicious, clean; the houses are well-built, tall; and because of their elegance, both sides of the town are like the decorated edges of a garment. Their scholars, of the highest intellect, are honoured. The two mosques are built of *bānāt* [a type of soft marble], without the use of wood and without colonnades. Every night groups of upright people meet in council; the preacher is a jurist, and follows the school of Abū Hanīfa; the schools have a daily allotment of food for each pupil. Their markets are fine—do you not see the rows of them winding around the Upper Mosque from every side? Here is the renowned region of abundance, here the courtyard of the noble ruler. Do not ask about the baths of Marw, nor of its *harīsa*; nor of its bread, its intellect, its strength, for they are well known. But do ask about their waters, their learning, manly qualities, for they are weak; and about their slyness, and their disorder—for I could write a book about them. The true account is desirable for itself, and I am not one of those who eats his bread by the exercise of his science; but I seek Paradise, and hope for the call to the blessed life. Marw is a notable town but its population is small, for it has gone to ruin except for a few houses; a third of the suburbs are laid waste as if it dated from antiquity.

Houses have decayed and the roofs have tumbled down. Vice is evident, their disorder well-known; their earnings are low, altogether insignificant. They are not generous, nor are their cooking pots clean. Their clay has no tenacity; and in summer the heat dries up everything. The bureaus of the land tax and of the police are in the mosque; their river is constantly overflowing its banks. They commonly put the sound of *zā’* [a letter] before the *yā’* [a letter] in the [word of] attribution [*e.g.* Balkhī, Balkhazī]. They are a people of mocking and laziness, as a man of understanding knows.

Addition/version MS. C.
Everyone in his cunning and mockery is subtle. However, it pours forth an abundance of agricultural produce, the pigeons in their flying to the dovecots try to outdistance one another, and excellent bread is readily available.

Marw is on a plain far from the mountains. The old central city is on a hill, in the middle of which is a place of prayer which used to be the Friday mosque formerly; there are many houses around it. At the gate of the suburbs are buildings and a small market, and in the suburbs are two mosques: one at the gate of the inner city, the other in the money exchange, and most of its congregation are followers of Abū Hanīfa. This latter mosque, and what is around it was built by Abū Muslim, the governor. The city has clean markets.

Addition/version MS. C.
Abū Muslim had brought it into desuetude because he cursed ʿAlī bin Abī Tālib—may God be pleased with him—on his pulpit; and he built another mosque amidst the suburbs, so the other was filled with refuse to the time of al-Maʾmūn; he ordered its restoration, Ashāb al-Hadīth (adherents to the Traditions) undertook that task, and they appropriated it. However, the call to prayer is uttered here twice.

My own impression is that the people only adorned themselves, and adopted ʿIrāqī habits because of the stopping-off of the khalif there, when the people
p. 312 of the country adopted from his mercenaries and followers the manners of al-ʿIrāq—but God knows best. Of all cities, it most resembles al-Ramla in Palestine. The inner city has four gates—Bāb al-Madīna beside the mosque; Bāb Sanjān in the other direction; Bāb Bālīn; Bāb Darmashkān, beside which stood the palace of al-Maʾmūn. The *quhandiz* is in the inner city; it is in ruins and difficult to get through, and may be entered only by the giving of a certain sign. The water channel enters the inner city and flows through all the suburbs. Here are well-tended reservoirs, on which are sluice gates, and canals run through parts of the town.

Kīrank is a large town, being on both sides of the river, a bridge between the two parts. Two branches of the main stream, with mills on both of them, cut through the town. The Friday mosque occupies a third of the town: beside it is a hostel, the minaret being between the two.

Sinj: populous; the mosque is on the edge of the market, a stream behind it. A garden is here, beside it a vineyard, belonging to the family of al-Musaffā.

Kharaq—its mosque is outside the market. The drinking water is from a branch of a canal which flows in the direction of the *Qibla* of the mosque.

Bāshān—its mosque is in the jewelry market. The drinking water is from a branch of the stream.

Dandānaqān: small, fortified, with one gate. The baths and the guardhouse are outside it, as in al-Juhfa, and it is a point in the defenses of Dihistān. The town has a fine situation, with a beautiful Friday mosque, and one place of prayer.

Sarakhs is a large populous well-known city, and if there were an army there we would have made it a district or a section; but I was hesitant about its circumstances, and the matter was problematical for me. I have read in one of the books called *The Division of the Districts of Khurāsān* that Sarakhs, Abīward, and Nasā are one district; but our procedure does not accept this statement, since p. 313 Nasā and Abīward are two important districts, each one having towns. Hence it is not permissible for us to consider them as provincial towns of Sarakhs, or to consider Sarakhs, either, a provincial town to those two. Al-Balādhurī says, "Khurāsān is in four quarters: the first is Īrānshahr, which is Naysābūr, with Qūhistān, Harāt, and Tūs; the second quarter is al-Marwān, Sarakhs, Nasā, Abīward, al-Tālaqān, and Khwārazm; the third quarter, al-Jūzjān(ān), Balkh, and al-Saghāniyān; and the fourth quarter, Mā warā᾽ al-Nahr." But this also contravenes our procedure, for our system of reference makes Sarakhs the treasury of Naysābūr. Even so, we have here set aside our model, for it seemed best to us to consider Sarakhs subjoined to Marw, seeing that it is with it in the same area, along with the closeness in customs, language, and distance between them. This is the country of grain and grazing livestock. Abu al-ʿAbbās al-Yazdādī asked me about Jerusalem. Said I, "It is like Sarakhs, except that Jerusalem is clean, beautiful, elegant." Sarakhs has an inner city, in which is the mosque with a small market. Most of the markets are in the suburbs. The drinking water is from wells, from which also is the irrigation of their farms. There is here a stream which flows intermittently.

Addition/version MS. C.

If Sarakhs had a number of towns in the rural districts mentioned, such as Tabarān and the like of it, we should have divided it into districts, and added to it Marw al-Rūdh, and Nasā, and Abīward, because it is intermediate to Khurāsān and al-Murabbaʿa al-Kubrā, and it is there, moreover, that all of the routes come together. Indeed I have heard Abū Ahmad al-Hishāmī declare: "Our community is hardly ever at a loss for anything, because the caravans from every direction come to a halt here." It is not possible for us, either, to include it among the military districts of Marw, seeing its preciousness and the importance of its institutions, because it is said of it that it seized for its ruler, Abu al-Hasan al-Faqīh, ten thousand small cattle and camels, and that to this he paid no attention, nor did he mention it to his courtiers before they had learned of it otherwise. It is, too, the source of succour for Naysābūr, and the river harbour of Khurāsān. I have calculated that every week as much grain passes through it as it transported from Egypt to the Red Sea. Now, these considerations bar it from being a citadel or a city—and indeed the territory does not lack either of these—and have made it impossible, in the case of Sarakhs, from one side, and have made it inescapable from another side; thus the matter is problematical, and has become like the question of the hermaphrodite, the difficulty that Abū Hanīfa encountered. It is a town of spacious markets, a stream runs right through it, and here, too, are wells of sweet water. It has an inner city that is somewhat disordered, and having in it the mosque and a number of shops. Suburbs surround the inner city on three sides, and beyond the fourth side is open country; beyond this, again, another city which had gone to ruin and is become a tell. The mosque is spacious and large, the roofed part built on pillars of baked brick; the courtyard is splendid. On one occasion, al-Shaykh Abu al-ʿAbbās al-Yazdādī asked me with what place Jerusalem might be compared. Said I, it is like Sarakhs, except that Jerusalem is populous, beautiful, and charming.

p. 314 Marw al-Rūdh is an important town with an extensive section; it is properly joined with Gharj al-Shār, being close to it and having been mapped in it. Do you not know that the postmasters enjoy the favour of al-Shār (the ruler) and are under his benefit and care.

Addition/version MS. C.
Marw al-Rūdh also is just as we have indicated in the maps, being interconnected with Gharj al-Shār, worthy of it, close to it, and planned after it. Do you see that the postmasters enjoy the favour of al-Shār, and are under his benefit and care? Moreover, it is distant from Marw al-Shāh, so it is not possible that it be added to it; nor is it to be added to Sarakhs, even though it is close to it. We have, too, restricted our description of it.

The capital bears the same name. The area has four other mosques. It is about two-thirds the size of Zabīd. The river cuts through its edge. It produces much agricultural products. The mosque is in the market, built on wooden pillars; the markets are shaded in the summer. Its towns are: Dizah, a large, fine town which the river cuts through, the mosque being in the market; Qasr Ahnaf—the river flows at its edge also, the mosque being in the market; Hanīna(?) and Lawkar(ā) are both well populated and extensive.

With regard to Marw al-Rūdh and Sarakhs there are problems and controversy, just as in the case of Gharj al-Shār, which we shall mention later, and which we shall classify as it should be. We have only brought Sarakhs in relation with Marw because it appeared advisable to us to do so, since Marw is the chief town in the regions of the non-Arabic speaking peoples, and is the more deserving of having the sections associated with it; and the association need not be disputed. And in God is success!

Īrānshahr is the metropolis of this side [of the province] and the capital of Naysābūr. It is an important town, a noble metropolis; I do not know any in the realm of Islām on a par with it. For it combines within it such characteristics and conformity of qualities as extent of area, spaciousness of site; pureness of water, healthiness of air, numerousness of scholars. It is a city of the venerable and the knowledgeable among the Imāms. Fruits are plentiful, delicious; meats excellent, cheap. The mode of living is pleasant, favourable; markets are extensive, houses spacious, hamlets superb, gardens delightful. The clay binds. Genius there is subtle, councils brilliant, schools elegant. There is gracefulness, suavity, honourable customs so choice; workmanship, skill, commerce, good expression, industriousness, chivalry, kindness, charity, cherishing of sacred things, friendship, all well known in distant realms, and renowned in the realm of Islām. It is the treasury of the two portions of the Orient, the entrepôt for east and west. Its goods are carried to distant places, its cloth has light and radiance, so the people of Egypt and al-ʿIrāq adorn themselves with it. Fruits are carried to it, and people travel to it to seek knowledge, and to trade. The port of Fārs, al-Sind, and Kirmān, the entrepôt of Khwārazm, al-Rayy, and Jurjān. The summer is good, ice is plentiful; winter is cozy, an abundance of grapes. The jurist does not lack refinement, nor is justice insufficient; nor is the day without a council of government. It is a metropolis of which the nobles diminish the leaders [of other places]; its scholars occupy the lofty positions; the [learned] Imāms can confuse [even] the scholars. Its quarters are more than those of other cities, and its extent more than other metropoles. Tell me what there is in the realm of Islām like it!

p. 315

I heard Abū ʿAli al-ʿAlawī say to Abū Saʿīd al-Jūrī: "You are an elder of the area; if it were separated from Naysābūr it would need [only] a drum, a flag, and a prince in residence." I was asked about it in Fārs and I said, "It has four and forty districts, some of them about half the size of Shīrāz, such as al-Hīra, al-Jūr, and Manīshak." It is more extensive than al-Fustāt, more populous than Baghdād, more complete than al-Basra, more important than al-Qayrawān, cleaner than Ardabīl, more developed than Hamadhān. There is no putridity here, no salt flats, no wearisomeness, no constraint of space. However, in its air is dryness, in its people dissension; in their language flaccidity, in their heads, lightness. There is no friendship, no magnificence, no places of prayer that are clean; streets filthy, hostels decaying, baths dirty, shops horrible, walls badly joined; misfortune has dogged it, and high prices have befallen it. Food and firewood are scarce; the mode of life and taxes are heavy. Dry land, and bare mountains. Their water is under the ground. Their dissension blinds the heart, and their fanaticism tears out the breast. Their *muhtasib* has no prestige, no rigour, their preacher no diffidence, no charm; nor on the days [of public prayer] is there a congregation in their mosque. Their Imām has no nobility, no refinement; their orator no candour, and no truth. Most of the people do not belong to the two groups [Hanafite and Shafiʿite]; the Shīʿa and the Karrāmites are both in opposition, hence the lot of the jurists is trouble and disgrace. And if the governor should be removed, then will there really be trouble, for disgrace will overwhelm it from both sides.

p. 316

The city measures about a *farsakh* each way. In the center of the inner city is a fortress, and around [the city] is a ditch; [the city] has four gates. There is a *quhandiz* beside it, the course of the ditch separating the two. The *quhandiz* has two gates, one of them towards the city, the other towards the suburbs. The roads leading to the metropolis exceed fifty in number, the most famous of them being Darb al-Jīq, Darb Khushnān, Darb Dard, Darb Manīshak, Darb al-Qibāb, Darb Fārs, Darb al-Khurūj, Darb Aswār Kārīz; before each of these gates stands a bridge that carries across the ditch. The mosque is in the suburbs below the city at the edge of the market, and it has six chambers. The *masjid al-minbar* [the raised portion of the mosque] was built partly by Abū Muslim, and this portion is on columns of wood; the remainder of it, built by ʿAmr bin al-Layth, is on rounded pillars of baked brick. Three porticoes go around the main hall of the mosque, and in the middle of this is the main building, decorated. The mosque has eleven gates, beside which are columns of variegated marble. The roof has three arches, the walls are decorated, and the roof ends in a point. You should know that it is an important metropolis, even though you do not see there a good market, a handsome hostel. There, whenever any Tom, Dick, or Harry screeches, the crowd follow him with their dreadful fanaticisms, and their behaviour is not at all pleasant.

Al-Shāmāt is an extensive quarter, having fine villages and many farms. The people there call it "Tak Āb," that is, "whither the water flows," since it is the lowest of the rural districts; all over the capital the water emerges and may be seen. There is no central city, fruit is not abundant, there being only farms.

Rīwand: a splendid, delightful quarter; many vineyards, excellent grapes, fine fruits; a quince is here the like of which is not to be seen. There is a town p. 317 here of the same name, most attractive, cut through by a stream; it has a mosque of baked brick, recently renovated.

Māzul is a delightful quarter with remarkable villages. From here comes the superb *ribās* currant. The village of Bushtaqān is here, of which ʿAmr bin al-Layth tried to buy a section—it has four sections, with the houses admidst the gardens, and streams cutting through them—but his treasuries were not sufficient, and what he had available was only the revenue of Naysābūr, and a thousand loads of goods. I have heard that they told him that in this village were trees, each one worth from ten *dinārs* to ten *dirhams*, "and we have sold you every one for a *dinār*."

Addition/version MS. C.
... but the value of his treasuries was insufficient; and I heard that when he entered into Naysābūr he had with him a thousand loads of *dirhams*. In it were *waqfs* (endowed lands), their extent about a *farsakh* square, which the ruler, ʿAmīd al-Dawla, had determined to annex to the capital.

Yushtafrūsh (Bushtafrūsh) is a quarter with many profitable things, including grapes; in fact in one day, at Bāb [gate] al-Jīq, there arrive ten thousand loads of grapes. I have heard Abū Saʿīd al-Jūrī say that there is a garden here in which is an apricot tree, the daily return of which is a *dīnār* from the beginning to the end of the apricot season. There is no inner city here, but a large village of the same name.

Addition/version MS. C.
The fourth secondary metropolitan centre lies towards the east; here are grapes in abundance. It does not have an inner city, but attached to it is a village bearing the same name; Kharq is bigger than it. I have heard that some of the dignitaries of Naysābūr dropped in to visit Abū ʿArūba, in al-Raqqa, and asked him about Naysābūr and its glorious qualities. Said he: "A village is here that is named Qaryat Kharq, from which is derived on every day without exception grapes to the value of a hundred thousand *dirhams*."

Busht is the most splendid of the twelve rural districts. It is a large district, having seven mosques. It is said that Abu al-Fadhl al-Balʿamī and Abu al-Fadhl bin Yaʿqūb attended the council of al-Amīr al-Saʿīd, and al-Balʿamī exaggerated in the praise of Marw. Said Ibn Yaʿqūb, "We do not deny the excellence of Marw, for it is, indeed, as you have mentioned. However, Naysābūr has twelve rural districts, among them Busht, and the income of three of its towns would equal the income of Marw." They looked into the matter, and lo, the matter was as he said. It is a rural district bringing together fruits, grains, the finest grapes. I have heard that there are olives and abundant figs; and from here the first fruits of the season are brought because the climate is temperate. The name of its chief town is Turthīth. It is a fine populous town, in it a mosque that is not inferior to the mosque of Damascus, being wealthier than it, handsome and well-kept. Beside the mosque is a market newly built, as are all the shops around it. A place of prayer has been added, built of baked brick and gypsum; at its door is a superb round water cistern, to which one goes down by stairs. The town is the port of Fārs and Isfahan, the storehouse of Khurāsān.

Kundur is smaller, fairly well like what we have just been mentioning, in its development and products. The remaining mosques are in a number of the villages.

Bayhaq is beside this rural district, and resembles it in agricultural products, fertility, and the fineness of the villages. The main road to al-Rayy cuts through it. There are two towns here—Sawzawār (Sālzawār) and Khusrūjird; they are well-developed, a *farsakh* between them. A village is here, cut in halves, each half on the main road. Here are splendid villages such as Jazīnān, and others like it. The people are refined, having produced a number of scholars and writers. Much cloth is produced here.

Kuwayn: an extensive rural area, with much produce. Fruits, grains, clothes are produced here. The road to Jurjān runs through it. The people are *ashāb hadīth* [followers of Tradition] and are refined. The name of the chief town is Azādhwār, highly developed, populous and quite productive.

p. 318

Jājarm: a small splendid rural district. It has a large, fortified town with the same name, and herein is a fine mosque. The district has about seventy villages. It is said that every rural district of the twelve, and every quarter of the area has three hundred sixty villages, with the exception of this one.

Isfarā'īn is a valuable rural district. It is a source of excellent grapes, here are farms, and cedars in abundance. The highroad to Jurjān cuts through here. Its chief town, of the same name, is developed, prosperous, not a town in the district more important than it. Here are good markets, and a number of specialties. The people here are also *ashāb hadīth*.

Ustuwā: a large rural district on the highroad to Nasā. In these rural districts
p. 319 there is not one more fertile, or more productive of grain than it; it is the chief source of provisions for Naysābūr. The land is watered by rain only. Much garlic is grown here, and a lot of clothing is produced. The name of its chief town is Khūjān, not very big, behind a mountain, far from the main road. The other rural districts are well developed.

Addition/version MS. C.
Ustuwā is an important town on the main road to Nasā: most of the fruits of the metropolis come from here. It is an area where grains and garlic are raised in abundance, and a source of many supplies; most of the land is watered by rainfall, and fruits here are few. Here are two towns, one of them Khūjan—not very large—in which stands a single market; the second, Dawīn, smaller than the other. Asfand is a small town producing little fruit. The main road to Marw cuts through it; it has no inner city. Zām is a large town, and Būzjān had been made its city, but we have made it a town. Bākharz is a district of grains and raisins; much cloth is made here, but the town is not thought much of. Its city, Mālin, is populous. Khwāf is a small district, producing much raisins and pomegranates. The name of its chief town is Salūmak. Zāwah is an area such as we have been describing: I do not know any town pertaining to it. Rukhkh, too, is small: the name of its chief town is Bīshak. The district of Tūs is a granary, important, extensive, and ancient. It is situated among the rural districts of Naysābūr, and considerable advantage accrues from it. Here are cultivated fields, rain-watered lands, fruits. The area has some particular characteristics, for here are mines, and dignitaries; but it is also the home of robbers, a hotbed of rebellion, mountains surround it, and the roads thither are difficult. Tābarān is its largest town. ...

Tābarān is the biggest of the cities of Tūs; over it stands a fortress. From a distance, it looked to me like Yathrib [Madīna]. There is a busy market here; venerable and distinguished people; there are profitable things and merchants. The mosque is in the markets, and Ibn 'Abd al-Razzāq embellished it. They have canals close to the surface, and wells. Produce is plentiful, prices are low; here firewood is plentiful; fruit is good. However, it is a filthy place, its outskirts in ruin; it is cold, the baths are bad, and they are the worst of people for trouble and strife.

Nūqān is smaller than Tābarān. The markets surround its mosque. There are people here skilled in moulding earthenware pots, and the like. They are a generous people, but their water is scant.

Junābid is smaller than Nūqān; it has seventy villages. The remaining towns are: Ustūrqān; Jarmaqān (Sarmaqān); Turūghbadh (Turūghūdh); Sarkū; p. 320 Rāyakān; Barnūkhkān.

Addition/version MS. C.
I have heard some of their dignitaries say, during the council meeting of Zarīf bin Ahmad al-Kātib in Nasā, that the people of Tūs were ahead in regard to both worlds, for in this world they anticipated in their conversion to Islām the districts of Khurāsān; as for the next world, God—may He be exalted—says: "On that day we shall call all men with their leaders" (*Qur'ān*, sūra 17, v.71)—and ʿAlī bin [Mūsā] al-Ridhā was, to his followers, the most excellent of the Imāms among them.

Nasā is an extensive district, delightful and fine: waters abundant, agricultural produce aplenty, trees intertwined. The fruit is good, the mosque elegant; bread is clean, the market paved. It has special qualities and excellences. There is but one doctrinal school there. Prices are always low. Here is jurisprudence, politeness, noble lineage, virtuous quality, power, vigour. It is the rare house that has no garden; here is flowing water, and large villages. Even so, every ignominy is here, for factionalism has ruined it; its villages contain Khwarazmians, who go beyond the meaning of the *Qur'ān*, and chant the call to prayer in a singsong; they have diverged from Islām. Here are ten roads, lost among the trees. There are two towns, Isfīnaqān and Jarmaqān, and two outposts, Afrāwa and Shāristāna. Afrāwa is an important guardhouse—here are brave men, a number of horses, and weapons. Three fortresses adjoin one another, and around one of them is a ditch; drinking water is from springs in the guardhouse. This is in the wilderness, the provisions are carried to there. They are a quarrelsome lot, and have destroyed community life.

Addition/version MS. C.
Close to it Abu al-Qāsim al-Mīkālī had built hospices, and endowed them with treasuries and *waqfs*. He selected, too, a number of villages whither he drew canals from the mountains; his grave is there. The hospice of Shahristān is inferior to the other, and the sands had overwhelmed it. Both of these places are fortified, have excellent treasuries, and a number of mosques.

p. 321 Abīward to me is more remarkable than Nasā; its market is busier, it is more prosperous, more fertile. The drinking water is from a stream. The mosque stands in the market; its fortress has gone to ruin. Its chief town is Mahana; its guardhouse Kūfan.

Addition/version MS. C.
Mahana is a small place, a fortress standing over it; and within it is a mosque

that has decayed. Kūfan is a caravanserai with a fortress standing over it. It has four gates, and its circuit, irregularly shaped, is said to measure a *farsakh*. In one corner of it is a hospice in which stands the great mosque; and within the mosque are a cistern and two pools; here too is a channel of water of rather middling quality. Zūzan, the center of habitation, is a large city situated about forty *farsakhs* from the capital. It is well developed, and is home to many weavers and makers of felt. Būzjān, the place of abode of the ruler, is a considerable city; some people assign it to the district of Jām, and do not mention the abode of the ruler; but what we have said is more correct.

Qāyin is the capital of Qūhistān; it is not agreeable or splendid, but small, cramped, lacking irrigation. The language is barbarous, the town dirty, means of subsistence slight. It has, however, a strong fortress, and its name is well-known in ʿUmān. Much cloth is brought from there, and groups of people walk thither. It is the export point of Khurāsān, the source of supply of Kirmān. The drinking water is from canals. The town has three gates.

Tabas al-Tamr (the date orchards) has a fortress; its market is small, its mosque delightful. Its drinking water is from cisterns to which open canals run. I saw good baths there.

Kurī is three *farsakhs* away towards the desert. It is smaller than [Tabas al-Tamr] in development.

Al-Raqqa: small, close to the desert; drinking water is from springs.

Tūn: a developed populated place, with many weavers. In both these towns are scholars and eminent people.

Khwāst has a fortress, is on the edge of the desert. It is bigger, but has fewer people than Tūn. Trees are few: drinking water is from springs.

Tabas al-ʿUnnāb (the jujube orchards) is called Tabas Masīnān; an abundance of jujubes.

Addition/version MS. C.
Qāyin is a city limited in area and water; it has little surplus or prosperity. Here stands a *quhandiz* (ancient fortress). The town is protected by a fortress and a moat, and has three gates - Bāb Kūran, Bāb Kalāwāj, Bāb Zuqāq Istaykhīr. The inhabitants derive their drinking water, for the most part, from underground channels. The people here are weavers. Their speech is uncivilized, their attire filthy; there is no generosity, no refinement. The villages here are dispersed, the steppes forbidding. Nevertheless in the area are many provincial towns, and remote districts. Its cities are well known, its reputation great, it is the goal of many. This city and Turthīth are the two river-ports of ʿUmān, the two entrepôts of Kirmān, the two treasuries of Khurāsān. Tūn is smaller than Qāyin; here are many weavers, and workers of wool. Over the town stands a fortress, in the middle of the town stands the mosque. The drinking-water of the inhabitants is from a channel, and this is visible in the mosque. Yunābidh has many villages, and extensive gardens. Khūr is a small town, the buildings here of clay; here stands no fortress, no gardens, and its supplies of water are scant. The town

stands on the edge of the desert. Tabas al-Tamr produces the dates called "Hijāzī" [a variety round and soft, somewhat flat to the taste]. A fortress stands over the town, which has a charming mosque. The drinking water here is from channels. Tabas al-ʿUnnāb, also called Tabas al-Masīnān produces an abundance of jujubes, though of inferior quality. Its fortress had been destroyed. I did not see in Qūhistān one permanently flowing stream or a wooded place other than Tabas [al- Tamr]; and wherever I went around there, about the distance of a post stage, it is all villages, and date palms, and water channels. Tabas Masīnān also is concealed amidst the jujube trees; and I did not see in the area a *quhandiz* except in Qāyin, and the mosque stood in it. Al-Raqqa is a small town; Khawst is at the foot of a mountain. This district is extensive but much covered with deserts and mountains; the whole area is cold except for Tabas and the villages.

p. 322

A Summary Account of Conditions in this Region

This is a **cold** region, except for Sijistān, Bust, and Tabas al-Tamr, for their climate is inclined to be hot like that of al-Shām (Syria); the climate of Balkh is like that of al-ʿIrāq; the climate of Marw like that of al-Shām. The cold of Khurāsān is less severe than the cold of Haytal. This entire region is generally dry, but the dryness also is not uniform there; and whenever the cold of a place in this region is severe, its heat is severe also. An exception is Samarqand which is fine in the summer, similarly Naysābūr where, however, the cold is less severe than at Samarqand. In this entire region the people sleep on the roofs when the weather is uncomfortably hot.

Someone told me that ʿAbd Allāh bin al-Mubārak came to see ʿAbd al-Razzāq in Sanʿāʾ, and enquired of him about the weather in Khurāsān. Said he, "We sleep three months in the houses, three months on the porches, three months on the roofs; then we repeat this arrangement." Said [the other], "Look, O Khurāsānī, in that case you are always on the move; but all my life, I sleep in this one place." It is the same with most of al-Shām, and part of Fārs, and part of Kirmān. For my part, I lived twenty years in Jerusalem, and I slept in the house. Gharj al-Shār is hot in the summer.

Here are many rivers and much fruit; no lake except in Khwārazm, a salt
p. 323 one; another one in Sijistān, and another in Bukhārā—both fresh water. Vessels travel only on the Jayhūn River and Nahr al-Shāsh.

This is the greatest of the provinces in knowledge and law, and preachers here are highly respected. The people have money aplenty. Many Jews are here, few Christians, some Magians. No lepers are here, they do not know leprosy. The sons of ʿAlī—may God be pleased with him—are held in highest honour, and you see no Hāshimite, unless he be a stranger.

As for their **sects**, they are proportionate, except that the Khawārij (Khārijites) are numerous in Sijistān and the districts of Harāt, Karūkh, and Astarabyān. The Muʿtazilites are evident in Naysābūr, but they do not predominate there, while the Shīʿa and the Karrāmites are very much in evidence. The majority of the people in the region are followers of Abū Hanīfa, except in the districts of al-Shāsh, Īlāq, Tūs, Nasā, Abīward, Tarāz, and Sanghāj; and the district of Bukhārā, Sinj, al-Dandānaqān, Isfarāʾīn, and Juwayn, all of these being Shāfiʿites, and the practice in these places is according to their respective schools. They also make themselves felt in Harāt, Sijistān, Sarakhs, and Marwayn, and there is no Qāḍhī except from the two groups [Hanafites and Shāfiʿites]. Moreover, the preachers of the places we have excepted [above], and of Naysābūr, also, are Shāfiʿites; this is so, also, of one of the two mosques of Marw, except that the *iqāma* there and in Naysābūr is made twice. The Karrāmites are much in evidence in Harāt, and Gharj al-Shār; they have retreats in Farghānā, al-Khuttal, and Jūzjān(ān). In Marw al-Rūdh there is a house of religious retreat, another in Samarqand. In the rural districts of Haytal are peoples called *Baydh al-Thiyāb* [the white-clad] whose teachings are close to atheism. Groups are here following the teaching of ʿAbd Allāh al-Sarakhsī, practicing asceticism, and closeness to God. Most of the people of Tirmidh are Jahmiyya [a sect]; the people of al-Raqqa are Shīʿa. The people of Kundur are Qadariyya [believers in predestination]; and the people of al-Shār pray at the two festivals [the Feast of Immolation, the Feast of Breaking the Ramadhān Fast] according to the doctrine of ʿAbd Allāh bin Masʿūd. The school of Abū Hanīfa constantly wavers between the two systems of reading, and they exclaim, "Allāhu Akbar" [God is Great] four times.

As for **commerce** here: in Naysābūr is produced white clothing of *al-haffiyya* and *al-baybāf* [methods of weaving]; also turbans of *al-shahijāniyya* [a type of expensive cloth], *al-haffiyya*; of *al-rākhtaj*, and of *al-tākhtaj* [types of expensive cloth]; veils; *bayna al-thawbayn* [a kind of garment]; *al-malāham* [a kind of garment] made of silk, and of plain cloth; also of *al-ʿattābī*, and *al-*saʿīdī, and p. 324 *al-zaraʾifi*, and *al-mushtī* [kinds of cloth]; bracelets; clothing of hair and of superior yarn; iron, and other things.

From Nasā and Abīward: silk, and clothes made of it; sesame, and its oil; clothes of *al-zanbafi* [a kind of cloth]. From Nasā clothes made of *al-banbuziyya* [kind of cloth]; fox fur; and clothing. From Tūs, superior earthenware pots; mats; and grain. From the rural districts of Naysābūr, much thick clothing. From Harāt, much cloth; silk brocade of inferior quality; taffeta; raisins like those of al-Tāʾif; a poor sort of dried grapes, both green and red, with essence and syrup of these; steel; pistachios; and most of the confections of Khurāsān. From Marw: *al-malāham* [a kind of garment]; veils of silk; silk; cotton; cattle; cheese; cotton seeds [or oil]; oil of sesame; and copper. From Sarakhs, grain and camels. From Sijistān, dates; woven baskets; ropes of bast; and mats.

In Qūhistān are produced white clothing resembling that of Naysābūr; rugs; fine dates. From Balkh come soap; sesame; rice; walnuts; almonds; raisins; dried grapes; clarified butter; honey of grapes dried in the sun; figs; pomegranates; vitriol; sulphur; lead; *asbark* [a yellow herb]; arsenic; incense; armour like that made in Jurjān; garments; oil and fats; and skins. From Gharj al-Shār: gold; felt;

fine carpets; saddle bags and the like; excellent horses; and mules. From Tirmidh: soap; asafetida. From Walwālij: sesame, and its oil; walnuts; almonds; pistachios; rice; chick-peas; coverlets; cheese; clarified butter; horns; fox pelts. From Bukhārā: fine clothing; dried dates; rugs; carpeting for inns; copper-coloured candelabra; hangings; horse girths woven in the prisons; cloth of [the type made in] al-Ashmūnayn; the tallow and hides of sheep; ointment. From Karmīniya, kerchiefs; from Dabūsiya and Widhār, *Widhāriyya* cloth, which is a cloth of plain colour, and I heard a ruler in Baghdād call it "the silk brocade of Khurāsān." From Rabinjan: shawls for the winter, of red felt; dried dates; round drinking cups of an alloy of silver and lead; hides; hempen ropes; sulphur.

p. 325   From Khwārazm: sable; squirrel; white weasel; fennec and its fur; fox; beaver; hare pelts variously coloured; goatskin; wax; arrows; cork; cowls [headgear]; fish glue; fishbones; castoreum oil [of beavers]; amber; [a skin called] *al-kaymakht*; honey; hazelnuts; falcons; swords; armour; *khalanj* wood; slaves from among the Slavs; sheep; cattle—all of these from the territory of the Bulghār. Also from Khwārazm: jujubes; raisins aplenty; *malāban* [a kind of confection]; sesame; garments; carpets; blankets; silk brocade of [a kind called] *bīshkish*; veils of [a cloth called] *malham*; locks; clothing of [a kind called] *aranj*; arrows that no one could use with the bow except the strongest men; cheese; whey; fish; boats hewn and smoothed; and the like from Tirmidh also.

From Samarqand are exported: silver-coloured cloths, and cloths called Samarqandī; large copper pans; excellent long-necked bottles; casks; stirrups; bits; girths. From Dīzak: felts the finest, and *aqbiya* [sing. *qabā³*—outer long-sleeved garment] of the felts. From Binākath: Turkistān garments. From al-Shāsh: saddles made of [a skin called] *al-kaymakht*, of excellent quality; quivers; casks; pelts purchased from the Turks, and dyed; shawls; dried dates; leather cloaks; cottonseed [oil]; very fine arrows; needles of inferior quality; and cotton and scissors are sold to the Turks. From Samarqand, also, silk brocade is sold to the Turks, and red cloths called *mumarjal*; *sīnīzī* [cloth made in Sīnīz or Shīnīz]; silk aplenty, and garments made of it; hazelnuts; walnuts. From Tūs: beautiful surcingles; good-quality garments. From Farghānā and Isbījāb: slaves from among the Turks; white cloths; engines of war; swords; copper; iron. From Tarāz: goatskins. From Shiljī: silver. From Turkistān to these places are exported horses, mules; and the like also from al-Khuttal.

There is nothing comparable to the silk brocade, embroidery, potters' clay, p. 326 truffles, *shahjān* cloth, needles, knives, and *ribās* (currants) of Naysābūr; nor to the *malāban* dates, *ishtarghāz* [seasoning plant], the great melons of Marw; and, according to anyone who has not been to al-Ramla, there is nothing in the world like their [Marw] bread, and there is certainly nothing to compare with it in the regions of the non-Arabic speaking peoples; nor do you see the like of their *harīsa*. The meat of Bukhārā is incomparable, as is a kind of melon called *al-sāf*; similarly the arrows of Khwārazm, the earthenware of al-Shāsh, the fine paper of Samarqand, the eggplant of Nasā, the grapes of Harāt.

Addition/version MS. C.

Boasting over respective countries arose between al-Ḥākim ʿAbd al-Ḥamīd and the dignitaries of al-Rayy, at the house of al-Ḥasan bin Buwayh. Said ʿAbd al-Ḥamīd: "God—may He be exalted—has allowed four things on which He did not put a value, and these four things are exported from Naysābūr to remote regions: stone, loam, water, and vegetation. Now the stone is the turquoise, and this is exported to the extreme areas of the world; the loam is an edible clay [Ṭīn Najāhī], and this is exported to Egypt and to the land of the Turks; the vegetation—these are the *rībās* (white currants), and are exported to the tables of kings; and the water—this is the salt that is exported to distant places for use in medicaments." And of course this last is the most powerful substance from which there is no danger.

There are many mines in this region. In Naysābūr, in the rural district of Rīwand, is a mine of turquoise. In the rural district of [lacuna in MS] is a mine of jet; in the rural district of Bayhaq is a marble quarry. In Ṭūs is earthenware clay, and in Zūzan an edible clay. In the rural district of [lacuna in MS] is found a clay used for seals and writing. At Barwān is a silver mine, also at Banjahīr and Shiljī—for here is a mountain that extends to Farghāna. Ammonia, silver, gold are obtained from Bārmān; soot from the district of Īlāq sublimated from the smoke of [smelting] silver—it is seldom one encounters it in unadulterated form. A spring of mercury bubbles near Qubā. This is not derived from a mine; Abū Yūsuf had thought that it was, then he was informed that it is as Abū Ḥanīfa had said. In Wāshjird is fine saffron, madder in Qūwādiyān. In this territory is naphtha and turquoise, of which the flow cannot be stopped; here also is pitch and asphalt.

Addition/version MS. C.

Here are many mines. From Naysābūr are derived turquoise, jet, marble; the people of Ṭūs make earthenware pots; from Badhakhshān come gems for rings. From Barwān and Banjahīr and Jabal as far as Farghāna and Shiljī stretch extensive mines rich in silver. From Īlāq comes ammonia, and here too are mines of gold and silver. Dhu al-fār, and that is the vapor of [smelting] silver, rises and is collected, and seldom one encounters it in unadulterated form. A spring of mercury bubbles near Qubā—this is not derived from a mine; Abū Yūsuf had thought that it was, then he was informed that it was a source such as Abū Ḥanīfa had said. In Wāshjird is saffron, in Quwādiyān madder; in Haytal occur naphtha, pitch, and asphalt.

p. 327 The **customs** in these areas differ from the customs of the regions of the Arabs, in most matters. For example the *Ṣāhib al-Raʾy* [upholder of one's subjective judgment in religious matters] and the *Ṣāhib al-Ḥadīth* [upholder of judgment made on the *Qurʾān* and Sunna—opposed to *Ṣāhib al-Raʾy*] carry the dead at burial time from in front of the *Qibla*; but not the Shīʿa, for they carry the body head foremost. One day I said to some people in Abīward: "You are a people who follow al-Shāfiʿī—may God be pleased with him—and you have the authority in

your lands to do as you like; so why do you not carry the dead head foremost?"
Said they, "We do not agree with the Shī'a, and we disagree with the Muslims."
The Imām does not turn his head to right and left at the prayers for the
Prophet—God's peace and blessings be upon him—he has preached.

Addition/version MS. C.
... except for al-Hākim Abū Sufyān in Sarakhs, for he was among those
who journeyed to Baghdād. I did not encounter in all the Eastern provinces a
single preacher except it be this al-Hākim, because they are all stupid, behaving
affectedly without eloquence, taking no pleasure in their chanting, which is far
from perfect—except in Naysābūr, for there the preachers are most accomplished.

The muezzins have a bench in front of the pulpit on which they call to prayer,
with chanting tunes. The preacher does not dress specially, neither does he wear
the *qabā'*, being attired only in the *'durrā'a*; he does not hasten away [after the
sermon]. In their mosques are large copper bowls set on stools; ice is put into
the water [in them] on Friday; and the people wash the slippers in winter and
summer. It is seldom they wear shoes. The preachers do not use a sermonbook.
In Marw, Sarakhs, and Bukhārā no one preaches except a jurist or a commentator.
In the rest of the region anyone who wishes to do so follows the school of Abū
Hanīfa; in these three places we have mentioned they preach from a book. In the
presence of important rulers a drum is played. Everyone testifies on every matter;
however, in every town is a number of attestors to the reliability of witnesses;
and should an opponent attack a witness the attestor is asked about him. No one
becomes sophisticated in this practice except a jurist or an important person.

Addition/version MS. C.
This is a region that makes the heart hard, and it is not like Syria or Yaman. Abu
al-Fadhl bin Nahāma informed me of the following tradition. He said that he
had it from Zubayr bin Muhammad, who had it from Ismā'īl bin 'Abd Allāh bin
Maymūn, who had it from Ismā'īl bin 'Abd al-Karīm, who had it from Ibrāhīm
bin 'Ukayl, who had it from his father, who had it from Wahb that he himself
heard Jābir bin 'Abd Allāh declare that he heard the Prophet—God's peace and
blessings be upon him—say that there is ruthlessness of heart and coarseness in
the people of the Orient, and those of Baghdād, but the law brought by the
Prophet is to be found among the people of Yaman.

p. 328 In Naysābūr are some attractive customs, among them the council of injustices,
held every first and fourth day of the week in the presence of the commander
of the army, or his deputy. Anyone who presents a case to the court is brought
before him, and is treated justly. Around [the commander] sit the judge, the
chief, the scholars, and the nobles. On the second and fifth day of every week
in Masjid Rajā' (the mosque of hope), a council of justice is held, the like
of which you do not see elsewhere in Islām. The notables of the town hold a
council in the early morning on Fridays, at which the readers gather and read
until the forenoon.

Addition/version MS. C.

The council of the *qādhī* (judge) is held every second and fifth days of every week in Masjid Rajā', and the council of injustices is held on the first and fourth days in the presence of the ruler or his minister. At the beginning of the councils in the mornings the Readers of the *Qur'ān* assemble there until midday, and read in turn.

They attire themselves in three ways: the jurists and the elders wear the *taylasān*, and no one tucks it under his chin except one who is considered stupid. They have a garment which they wear only in the winter; one puts it on, then puts the *taylasān* over the turban; over that he then puts the *durrā'a*; then from behind he loosens the edge of the *durrā'a* that is over the turban: I saw people in Tūs, and Abīward, and Harāt doing that. The people of Sijistān wind the turbans like crowns. In Mā warā' al-Nahr no one wears the *taylasān* except an elder; they just wear the *qabā'* open. In Marw the scholars of medium age wear the *taylasān* completely gathered on one shoulder, for a period of time; then when they wish to promote a jurist they bid him wear it in regular manner.

Addition/version MS. C.

The preeminent doctors of the law and the leading people wear the *taylasān* and turn the lower part of the turban under the chin; the leading merchants also wear the *taylasān*, but do not turn the lower part under the chin. Those of lower rank in either of these classes either do not wear the *taylasān*, or, if they do, they do not turn the lower part under the chin. One may dress, putting the *taylasān* over the turban, then putting on the *durrā'a*, then loosening the *taylasān* wrapped around the turban on to the collar of the *durrā'a*. Anyone who wishes to do so may ride a horse. No one wears the *taylasān* in Mā warā' al-Nahr, unless he be an important doctor of the law or a foreigner; they just wear the *qabā'*, because this side is in the area of the *jihād* [the holy strife enjoined on Muslims]. Most of the people of Bukhārā shrug their shoulders while they are conversing: I observed Abū Bakr al-Ismā'īlī doing so. The sleeves of the *qabā'* worn by the soldiers are narrow. It is the practice here to crack thongs in the air in the presence of the sovereign rulers. One does not enter the baths here unless wearing the *mi'zar* [wraparound apron, loincloth].

p. 329 Their supplies of **water** are extensive. At Naysābūr are tunnels running under the ground, cold in summer; one may descend to them by from four to seventy steps. Eventually the tunnels emerge in the villages and irrigate them. Some of these that emerge in the town flow around in the quarters of the town, as at al-Hīra, Balfāwā [?], and Bāb Ma'mar, and Qanāt Abī 'Amr al-Khaffāf, Qanāt Shād-yākh, Zuqāq al-Dāriyyīn, and Suwār Kārīz—in all of these places the canals flow at the surface. In some places sweetwater wells are found. A *farsakh* away in the village of Bushtaqān is a stream that turns seventy mills.

Addition/version MS. C.

The waters are widely distributed in Naysābūr. Here are conduits to which descent is made by flights of from three to seventy steps. It was told me of Abū Nasr al-ʿAbbādī, that he said that if the waters at Naysābūr were gathered together they would exceed those of the Tigris at Baghdād. The inhabitants have also a number of water channels that flow at the surface of the ground; also a stream about a *farsakh* distant on which seventy mills are situated. Some of their wells have sweet water.

Sijistān has a number of streams that irrigate the towns and the villages. Among them is the River Hīrmīd (Hilmand) which emerges from beyond the land of the Ghūr towards the south; it flows down to the town of Bust, then forms branches about a post stage from Zaranj. The Nahr al-Taʿām is drawn from it passing through the rural districts, until it reaches Nīshak. Next the Nahr Bāshtarūdh is drawn from it, which irrigates Bust. Then the river descends, irrigating a number of the villages as far as Kazak; there, a dam has been built which holds back the water so that it does not flow to the lake. In this district is the Nahr Farah which emerges from close to the country of the Ghūr, irrigating those areas; the rest of it flows into Lake al-Sanat [Zarah]. It forms a permanent sweetwater lake there in the direction of Kirmān; the length of this lake is more than twenty *farsakhs*, and its width a post stage [about thirty miles]. Much fish is taken from it; with hamlets and reeds on its edge it resembles al-Batāʾih (marshes) of al-ʿIrāq.

Addition/version MS. C.
Sijistān has a number of rivers, among them Nahr Hīrmīd (Hilmand) which emerges from beyond al-Ghūr, in the direction of Bust. It then forms branches, and irrigates the two districts. Here also is the Nahr Farah, which emerges from close to the country of the Ghūr, then flows to a lake towards Kirmān, on its way there irrigating a number of rural districts. This lake measures two stages in length by one stage wide, and contains a considerable population of fish.

The River Harāt emerges from below the country of the Ghūr, forming branches at the beginning of the district. A branch flows from it to the capital. The river flows through the country to the gardens, where there is a bridge, the like of which, as a marvel of construction, is not to be found in all Khurāsān. A Magian man built it, and wrote his name on it. In constructing it, the builders consumed a thousand sacks of salt. It is said that the ruler wished that his name be written on the bridge; some say that [the builder] became a Muslim, some say that he threw himself into the river. Near the capital seven canals branch out from it: Nahr Barkhuwī irrigating the rural district of Sandāsank; Nahr Bārisht irrigating the rural district of Kwāshan, and Siyāwashān, and Mālin, and Tīzān; Nahr Adhrījān irrigating the rural district of Sūsan, and Kūkan; Nahr Ghūsmān irrigating the rural district of Kark; Nahr Kank irrigating the rural district of Ghūban, and Karabkird; Nahr Sanfaghar irrigating the rural district of Sarakhs, at the border of Būshanj; Nahr Ānjīr irrigating the capital.

p. 330

Nahr al-Marwayn emerges from below the country of the Ghūr, flowing to Upper Marw, then turning towards Lower Marw. When it has passed there by about a stage, it reaches a deep ravine, which has been stopped up from both sides by a remarkable wooden dam. The water is impounded until it is level with the outlet, and it extends as far as Marw. A commander is in charge here with more jurisdiction than the commander of the garrison; under him are ten thousand hired men, and watchmen are there whose care is that the dam does not burst. You do not see anything better or more accurate than the apportionment of the water; and it is related of the man who apportions it that he said: "There is not an element of justice that I have not employed in apportioning the water, except where I could not help it." A post is erected, marked along its length, the width [between the marks] of a barleycorn. When the water rises so that its depth shown on the post reaches sixty barleycorns, there will be a good year, and the people rejoice. Just the same, when the measures reach [only] six barleycorns p. 331 there will be a year of drought. Their measurement station is a *farsakh* from the city, in a kind of pond, rounded. When the superintendent gauges the water, he sends the message at high speed specifically to the office of the river administration; then they send messengers to all the supervisors of the branch canals, and the water is distributed on the basis of the appraisal. At the place we mentioned first are four hundred divers who maintain the dam night and day, and if they need to enter the water when it is quite cold, they coat themselves with wax. With every man of them is a fixed amount of wood and a collection of spikes which they keep prepared daily for the time of need. While I was in Naysābūr, the dam burst, and the people watched the collapse; a considerable amount of property was lost.

Four canals from it enter the town—Nahr al-Zarq (Razīq) flows by the city gate from the direction of the suburbs; it enters the city and splits up into a few deep cisterns. From the second one, the Asʿadī, the people of the quarter of Bāb Sanjān and of Mīramāhān derive their drinking water. Nahr (canal) Hurmuzfarrah, from the direction of Sarakhs irrigates the extremity of the town, and the villages. It is Nahr al-Mājan that cuts through the town, penetrating the markets; then it goes out at the end of the town in a number of streams. While it is in the town it is crossed by a number of bridges connecting the streets. Here are cisterns, both covered and open, approached by steps, with sluice gates opened to them from the river, according to need; also sweet wells. If we were to include mention of the canals, and the places to drink, the book would lengthen and become boring.

Nahr al-Sughd (Zeravshan) ends at Bukhārā, entering the capital from Kalābādh (Kahlabādh). It used to flood, so a wide dam was built there, with timbers placed over it. Whenever, during the summer, the water was plentiful the people raised those planks one by one, in pace with the rising of the water, most of which, thus, flowed into the dam. Then, water flowed as far as Baykand. Were it not for this scheme the water would pour into the capital. This place is called Fāshūn. At the lower end of the city, also, is another sluice called Raʾs al-Waragh, similarly constructed. This stream flows through the town, penetrates the markets, and branches off into the streets. There are wide, uncovered cisterns in the town, on the edges of which structures of boards, with doors, have been erected, in which people wash. Sometimes the water of the stream overwhelms the overflow to Baykand, and the hamlets will be submerged in the summer.

p. 332 The year. I came there it flooded over many villages, so that people were impoverished. The elders went out to the dam, and the shaykh Abu al-ʿAbbās al-Yazdādī generously spent a large sum of money on it as a pious work. The water is really dirty, for a lot of excrement is thrown into it in the town. They say that the root of the name Bukhārā is *K-w-h Khūrān*; the "h" and the "w" were dropped to make it easier to pronounce, so it became *Kakhārā*. Then some substituted a "b" for the "k", to misrepresent it to people, so it became Bukhārā. I have heard one of the literati reciting:

> The *bāʾ* [b] of Bukhārā is *bāʾ* that merely makes the word bigger;
> and the *alif* [a] in the middle is of no avail to it;
> then nothing remains but "kharā" [excrement].

The river comes out of Samarqand; however, there are streams meeting it that come from the mountains from which waters flow to a lake beyond al-Saghāniyān. The Sughd River then flows to Raʾs al-Sakr [Waraghsar], and the canals of Samarqand branch off from it; a large canal flows around the city, another through it.

Addition/version MS. C.
The origin of Nahr al-Sughd is from the mountains, and its debouchure is at a lake that is beyond al-Saghāniyān; on its banks stand a considerable number of villages. Above Bukhārā, a dam has been constructed on it at a place called Fāshūn, and timbers placed over it: whenever during the summer the water was plentiful the people raised those timbers one by one, so most of the water flowed into the dam, and thus irrigated the villages in that area. Were it not for this scheme the capital would certainly be inundated. At the lower end of the city also is another dam similar to this; the water here is turbid, with much sediment, and said to contain various objects.

I do not know of bad water in this region except that of Kish and Nasā, and in the rural district of Tabas al-Tamr. There is no bad air here either except at Zamm, and there the people are yellow in colour. The air of Naysābūr and Samarqand is good, and [whoever breathes it] needs fat food; in fact the lives of the people of Naysābūr are lengthened by the healthiness of the air. Someone said that it was said to ʿAbd Allāh bin Tāhir, "Why did you choose Naysābūr over Marw?" Said he, "For three things: for I myself saw that its air was more healthy, its people more humble, and old aged people abounding there."

Addition/version MS. C.

There is no harmful climate here except that of Nasā and Zamm, and the country district of Tabas, and Kish: these are indeed plague-stricken places, and the people are yellow in colour. The air at Naysābūr and Samarqand is healthy and creates a need for fat food, entering the baths, and oil of violets. In any case, the lengthening of the lives of the people of Naysābūr is because of the climate. I have been informed that ʿAbd Allāh bin Tāhir said that he preferred Naysābūr over Marw for three reasons: its climate is better, its people more humble, and old aged people are many there.

p. 333 Among the **remarkable things**: at Naysābūr is a mountain the soil of which is black like ink; letters and so forth are written with it, and an impress is put on books with it. There are mountains at Haytal and Naysābūr from which the people cut the salt, just as rock is cut. Here also is a tree, and when the fruit of it is cut open a creature with wings comes out, and flies. Māʾ Māzul, Masjid Rajāʾ, and Tāhūna Ibn [lacuna in MS] and Īwān Abū Muslim. The windmills in Sijistān and Būshanj, and the fortress at Zaranj are among the marvels. At Sarakhs is a spot to which a bird ascends one day every year and throws itself down; the people collect many fragments of it. At Mazdūrān is a cave, no end to which is known.

Addition/version MS. C.

In the country district of Sarakhs is a place at which a bird arrives at a certain time of the year and casts itself down there; it does not come except at that time. At Mazdūrān is a cave which it is not possible for anyone to enter; there are stories told about it. At Sijistān and Būshanj are mills which the wind turns, and there are some remarkable features to the sands there. The fortress of Zaranj, the mill at Bar, and Māʾ Māzul are among the remarkable sights here.

Here are **shrines**: the grave of ʿAlī al-Ridhā is at Tūs; over it a stronghold has been built in which are houses and a market. Moreover, ʿAmīd al-Dawla Fāʾiq has built a prayer house over it, and there is no finer than it in Khurāsān. A *farsakh* from Sarakhs is the grave of the son of his paternal uncle, over which a shrine has been built. Two *farsakhs* from Marw is an outpost wherein is a small grave which people say is the grave of the head of Husayn the son of ʿAlī—may God be pleased with him. At Tabas is the grave of two of the Companions of the Prophet. On the bank of the River Jayhūn is Ribāt [outpost] of Dhu al-Qarnayn; opposite it to the east is Ribāt Dhu al-Kifl, and it is said that a chain used to be drawn across between the two.

At the edge of Nasā is the guardhouse of Afrāwa, and opposite Abīward is the guardhouse of Kūfan. Behind those Abu al-Qāsim al-Mikālī built two p. 334 guardhouses on which he spent much money. He brought thither equipment, and many machines. He endowed the two establishments with considerable bequests, tapped many sweet water wells in them, and established a number of villages; his grave is there. Between Naysābūr and Quhistān is Ribāt Suhayl, extensively appointed. A hot spring is here: some have said that the cold grew severe on the Companions of the Prophet—God's peace and blessings be upon him—and they prayed to God—may He be exalted—so that this spring emerged for them for their ablutions. A number of graves of the Companions are there. In Baykand is a mosque, well appointed. Ribāt al-Nūr is beyond Bukhārā; it has a fair every year; also Dast Qatawān.

The **languages** vary. The speech of the people of Naysābūr is grammatically correct, understandable. However, they insert the vowel *i* at the beginning of words, and they add *yā* [read *bā*], for instance *bēgu* and *bēshaw* ("he should become"). They also add *sīn*[s] unnecessarily as *bikhurdasti* ("you have eaten"), *bighuftasti, bikhuftasti* ("you have said"), and so on like that. In their speech is a flaccidity and indistinctness of utterance.

The people of Tūs and Nasā have better speech.

The speech of the people of Sijistān is drawled; they bring out the vehemence of it in their guttural pronunciation, and enunciate it aloud.

The speech of the people of Bust is better.

The speech of al-Marwayn [the two Marws] is unobjectionable, even though they drawl, lengthen, and stretch the ends of their words. Do you not notice that the people of Naysābūr say *ba-rayi-een*, and say *ba-taroon-een*, meaning "for the sake of", and that they have added a letter. Pay attention to this matter, and you will find it is quite common.

The language of Balkh is the finest of all; however, they have words in it that are disapproved of.

The language of Harāt is coarse. You notice them speaking and wagging their jaws, in an affected manner, drawling the words; then after all that, they utter the speech hesitantly and with a drawl. I heard one of the followers of al-Maˤdānī say, "One of the kings of Khurāsān ordered his ministers to assemble men one each from the five districts of Khurāsān, the principal districts. When they were assembled, the Sijistānī spoke, on which the minister said, 'This language is suitable for fighting.' Then he conversed with the Naysābūrī, and, said he, 'This language is suited for litigation.' Then he spoke with the person from Marw, and said, 'This language is suited for government ministry.' Then he spoke with the man from Balkh, and said, 'This language is fit for despatches.' Then when the man from Harāt spoke, said he, 'This language is fitted for the cesspool.'" These are the basic languages of Khurāsān, the others follow them, are derived from them, stem from them.

The language of Tūs and Nasā is close to that of Naysābūr; the language of Sarakhs and Abīward is close to the language of Marw. The language of Gharj al-Shār is between the languages of Harāt and Marw. The language of Jūzjān is between that of Marw and Balkh. The language of al-Bāmiyān and Tukhāristān is close to that of Balkh—however, they are both hard to understand. The language of Khwārazm is incomprehensible. There is repetition in the language of the people of Bukhārā; do you not notice how they say *yaki adrami* ("one drachma"), and "I saw *yaki mardi*" ("one man"), and so forth; one says, *atiytu adarami*, so you may have an idea by analogy how they speak. They frequently use the word *danisti* ("you know") in their speech, without any real reason. In any case this is the *darriyya*, the most chaste and prestigious dialect; and in fact language of this kind is called *darriyya* since it is the language in which the letters of the ruler are written, and in which reports are submitted to him. The derivation is from *dar* [door, gate, in the sense of palace], referring to the fact that it is the language that is spoken at the court. The people of Samarqand use a sound that is between the "kāf" [k] and the "qāf" [q]; they say [a sound that is between] *b-k-r-d-k-m* and *b-q-r-d-q-m*, and *b-k-f-t-k-m* and *b-q-f-t-q-m*, and so on. There is a stability in the language. The language of al-Shāsh is the best language of Haytal. The language of al-Sughd is unique to it and is approximated by the languages of the rural districts of Bukhārā, which are quite varied, but understood among them; p. 336 and I witnessed the venerable Imām, Muhammad Ibn al-Fadhl speaking in it often. There are few towns of those we mentioned but that they have, and their rural districts have, one more language.

There is variety in the **coloration** of the people: the fairest of them are the people of al-Shāsh and al-Farghānā, and the places in that area; then the people of Nasaf, and Tarāz, and Bārāb; and their women are incomparable. Then the people of Samarqand, then the people of Bukhārā, then the people of Marw—and that's it! The coloration of the people of Tabas al-Tamr resembles that of the people of al-Hijāz; similarly the people of Sijistān and Ghaznīn. The people of Khwārazm are white and ruddy; however they are distinguished by other characteristics.

There is **partisanship** between the western half of Naysābūr—it is the higher half, and pertains to Manīshak—and the other half, pertaining to al-Hīra: there is frightful bigotry against any other sect. And now it has arisen between the Shīʿa and the Karrāmiyya. There is fanaticism in Sijistān between al-Samakiyya, they being the followers of Abū Hanīfa—may God have mercy upon him—and al-Sadaqiyya, they being the followers of al-Shāfiʿī—may God be pleased with him. Blood is shed in these discords, so that the ruler intervenes. In Sarakhs the discord is between al-ʿArūsiyya, who are followers of Abū Hanīfa, and al-Ahaliyya, who are followers of al-Shāfiʿī; in Harāt, between al-ʿAmaliyya and al-Karrāmiyya; in Marw, between the city people and those of al-Sūq al-ʿAtīq (the old market); in Nasā, between the people of al-Khanah and those of the extremity of the market; in Abīward, between the Kurds and the extremity of the town. I heard a man say, "An owl has not drunk from the water without becoming a fanatic." In Balkh there is bigotry against any other sect, similarly Samarqand. Of all the towns there are few that are free from fanaticism.

p. 337 **Government**. In this entire region the dynasty of Sāmān is mentioned in the Friday sermon; and the land tax is paid to them, except by the *amīrs* of Sijistān, Khwārazm, Gharj al-Shār, Jūzjān, Bust, Ghaznīn, and al-Khuttal—they send gifts only, and their rulers avail themselves of the land taxes. The commander of the army is stationed in Naysābūr; Sijistān is under the control of the dynasty of ʿAmr bin al-Layth; Gharj is under control of al-Shār; Jūzjān is under control of the dynasty of Farīghūn; Ghaznīn and Bust are under the Turks.

Addition/version MS. C.

Jurisdictions here are many; however, the dynasty of Sāmān is mentioned in the Friday sermon, and gifts are given to them. Sijistān is under the control of the Banū Bānū, and Jūzjānān of Banū Farīghūn; Gharj is under control of al-Shār, Bust and Ghaznīn under control of the Turks; Khwārazm is under the control of two amīrs. The land taxes of these places are paid respectively to those whose rulership we have mentioned. These areas are the abode of justice and meritorious services in respect of the religion of Islām.

The first to govern this entire region was Ismāʿīl Ibn Ahmad in the year 287/900, when he set out for Bukhārā. Al-Muʿtadhad added to it Kirmān and Jurjān; al-Muktafī, in the year 90/709, added al-Rayy, and al-Jibāl as far as ʿAqabat Hulwān. When he died the people nicknamed him al-Mādhī (the vigorous one). His son Ahmad reigned after him; he was killed in Firabr, and they called him al-Shahīd (the martyr). After him his son Nasr reigned, and his chamberlain was Abū Jaʿfar Dhūghwā; the commander of his army was Hammawayh. His vizier was Abu al-Fadhl Ibn Yaʿqūb al-Naysābūrī, then Abu al-Fadhl al-Balʿamī, then Abū ʿAbd Allāh al-Jayhānī. When he died they called him al-Saʿīd (the auspicious). Then his son Nūh reigned, and his chamberlain was Rashīq al-Hindī, then Alftakīn (Alp Takīn); the commander of his army was Abū ʿAlī al-Saghānī, then Ibn Mālik, then Ibn Qarātakīn; his vizier was Abū Mansūr bin ʿUzayr, then al-Hākim al-Jalīl. When he died they named him al-Hamīd (the benign). He had assigned three of his sons to three of his eunuchs—ʿAbd al-Mālik to Najāh, Mansūr to Fāʾiq, and Nasr to Zarīf. Then they put ʿAbd al-Mālik on the throne, and his like has not been in the dynasty of Sāmān. His chamberlain was Alftakīn, then he appointed his slave as successor. The commander of his army was Ibn Mālik, then Alftakīn. He fell from his riding animal, died, and they named him al-Rashīd (the rightly guided). They enthroned his [of al-Hamīd] son Nasr for one day; then Fāʾiq assembled the p. 338 army, deposed him, and installed his patron, al-Mansūr. His chamberlain was Abū Mansūr Bāqrā [?], then Qalj. The commander of his army was Ibn ʿAbd al-Razzāq, then Abu al-Hasan Ibn Sīmjūr. His vizier was Amīrak Balʿamī, then al-ʿAtabī; then he restored al-Balʿamī, then he restored al-ʿAtabī. When he died they named him al-Sadīd (the correct). They enthroned his son Nūh, and his chamberlain was Tāsh; then Hū Anj. The commander of his army was Ibn Sīmjūr; then he put Tāsh in command of it; then he restored Abu al-Hasan

Ibn Sīmjūr. His vizier was Ibn al-Jayhānī; then Ibn al-ʿAtabī; then al-Mazinī; then al-Istakhrī; then ʿAbd Allāh bin ʿUzayr; then Abū ʿAlī Muhammad bin ʿĪsā al-Dāmghānī. They (the dynasty) are from a village in the districts of Samarqand called Sāmān, and their origin goes back to Bahram Jūr; and God has given them victory and power. They are among the best of kings in conduct and administration; the most sublime in the knowledge of God and the people of that knowledge. Among the sayings of the people: "If a tree were to revolt against the house of Sāmān, it would wither." Do you not see ʿAdhud al-Dawla, how he grew powerful and held sway; and the fullness of his power, the nobility of his situation! He was mentioned in the Friday sermon in all al-Yaman, which he overcame without a war—there was not a thing that crawled that was not entered in one of his books. Moreover, he sent a messenger, and was mentioned in the Friday sermon in al-Sind. He conquered ʿUman, and what he held he controlled. But when he opposed the dynasty of Sāmān and demanded Khurāsān, God destroyed him, and scattered his host; dispersed his armies, and put his enemies in possession of his kingdoms. May he perish who opposes the house of Sāmān!

Addition/version MS. C.

In the year 90/708, al-Muktafī entrusted to Ismāʿīl the governance of al-Rayy and al-Jibāl, the people of glorious deeds and virtues. I enquired of Zarīf what the king did at the time his army was defeated in Jurjān. He raised his hand, and said he: "O God! you still support my ancestors and secure their state; and now these Daylamites had invaded us and this tyrant oppressed us, and if they are more wicked than we, give us victory over them." And but little time elapsed before the death of ʿAdhud al-Dawla was disclosed. Thereafter, his brother died, as did the commander of their army, and God—may He be exalted—scattered their forces, dispersed their hosts, destroyed their offspring, except for any one of them that returned to the religion of al-Islām, and was reconciled.

p. 339 Among their [Sāmānids] **customs:** they exempt the doctors of the law from kissing the ground. They hold councils at night on the Fridays in the month of Ramadhān, for discussion in the presence of the ruler. He begins by asking a question; then those present speak on it. They incline towards the school of Abū Hanīfa. It is not their custom to be familiar with their subjects, but rather it is the vizier who takes care of affairs. So if they wish to promote a man they seat him with them at the diwan, as was done in the case of al-Shaykh Abu al-ʿAbbās al-Yazdādī. Sometimes they speak person to person with messengers on important matters, as they spoke to al-Shaykh Abū Sālih, when they sent him to the commander of the army, Abu al-Hasan. They always select the most expert legists in Bukhārā, and the most upright of them they elevate, and act on his opinion; they fulfill his requests, and appoint the deputies on his word: an instance is the elder, the venerable Imām, Muhammad bin al-Fadhl. In fact, the people eventually consider this the regular practice. They also point to whoever will succeed them; do you not observe their indicating al-Hākim al-Imām

Muhammad bin Yūsuf, because he is the wisest and most respected of the elders?

Addition/version MS. C.
But their court is not wanting in important notables and those whose judgments are influential; for example al-Shaykh Abu al-Hasan bin al-Fadhl, who, you would think, when he was instructing the ruler, had received some of his knowledge from beyond; or the likes of al-Shaykh Abū Ishāq al-Shuʿaybī, of good lineage, whose beneficence is evident to all people who have recourse to him. And I heard some of the notables say to Abū Nasr al-Harbī that there was not at the court a person more warm or more beneficial to the Muslims than al-Shaykh Abū Ishāq.

As for the **land-taxes**: On Farghānā, two hundred eighty thousand *muhammadiyya* [*dirhams*]; on al-Shāsh, one hundred eighty thousand *musayyibiyya* [*dirhams*]; on p. 340 Khujanda, by way of tithes, one hundred thousand *musayyibiyya*. On al-Sughd, and Kish, and Nasaf, and Ushrūsana, one thousand thousand, and thirty-nine thousand, and thirty-one *muhammadiyya dirhams*. The land tax of Isbījāb is four *dānaqs*, sent with a broom to the ruler every year with the gifts. The land tax of Bukhārā is one thousand thousand and one hundred thousand, and sixty-six thousand, eight hundred ninety-seven *ghitrīfiyya dirhams*. They were three brothers, Muhammad and Musayyib and Ghitrīf; they struck these *dirhams* which are black, used for small coinage. They are current only in Haytal, and are preferred over the white. The land tax of al-Saghāniyān is forty-eight thousand, five hundred twenty-nine *dirhams*; on Wakhkhān, forty thousand. On Khwārazm: four hundred twenty thousand, one hundred twenty of their *dirhams*, the *dirham* here equaling four and one half *dānaqs*. I found in a book that the basic land tax of Khurāsān is forty-four million, eight hundred thousand, nine hundred thirty *dirhams*, and thirteen *dirhams*; of beasts, twenty riding animals and two thousand sheep; of slaves one thousand and twelve head; of ore and sheets of iron, one thousand three hundred pieces. The imposts are light; but they are heavy on slaves at the bank of the Jayhūn River. One may not send a male slave across without a permit from the ruler; and with a permit one may take from seventy to a hundred. Similarly, in the case of women slaves without a permit if they are Turks, an impost is levied from twenty to thirty *dirhams* on each woman. On a camel it is two *dirhams*, and on the effects of the rider, one *dirham*. They send back ingots of silver to Bukhārā, and it is because of this that the inspection takes place. At the way stations the impost is from a *dirham* to half a *dirham*.

Addition/version MS. C.
The land tax there is light; however, it was doubled at the time of al-Amīr al-Hamīd for a project to which he gave his attention; so he asked for a loan of the land tax for a year, and it has remained in force to the present time. The land tax of Naysābūr is one million one hundred eight thousand six hundred *dirhams*; and on three of its treasuries one million six hundred twenty-four thousand

eight hundred forty-seven. The land tax of Sijistān is nine hundred forty-seven thousand *dirhams*; Qudāma mentions that the land tax of Sijistān is three million eight hundred eleven thousand, on Ghazna two thousand slaves valued at six hundred thousand *dirhams*, on Kābulistān one million five hundred thousand *dirhams*. The land tax on Balkh amounts to one hundred ninety-three thousand three hundred *dirhams*, on Khulm twelve thousand *dirhams*; on Tukhāristān and al-Bāmiyān one hundred fifty-six thousand four hundred thirty-two *dirhams*; on Jūzjān two hundred twenty thousand four hundred *dirhams*; on Marw al-Rūdh one million two hundred thirty-seven. The land tax on Marw al-Shāh is one million one hundred thirty-two thousand one hundred eighty-four *dirhams*; the land tax on Harāt and its districts, one million nine hundred thirty-five thousand four hundred twenty-one *dirhams*. The land tax on Quhistān is nine hundred eighty-seven thousand eight hundred eighty *dirhams*; the land tax on Sarakhs is ninety thousand, and the land tax of Khwārazm four hundred twenty thousand one hundred twenty Khwārazmī *dirhams*; on Tirmidh and Zamm sixty-seven thousand and forty-two *dirhams*. The land tax on Bukhārā is one million one hundred sixty-six thousand eight hundred seventy-seven *ghitrīfiyya dirhams*, and al-Saghāniyān fifty-nine thousand five hundred twenty-nine. The land tax on al-Sughd, Kish, Nasaf, and al-Buttam, is one million and thirty-nine thousand and thirty-one *muhammadiyya [dirhams]*; the land tax on al-Shāsh is one hundred eighty thousand *musayyibiyya dirhams*. The land tax on Farghānā is two hundred thirty thousand *muhammadiyya*; the annual tribute in tithing at Khujanda, one hundred thousand *musayyibiyya*. The land tax at Isbījāb is four *dānaqs* and a broom. The imposts in the region are light, the heaviest being those on the Jayhūn; indeed, there is no inspection here except, possibly, on a load of ingots [of precious metals]. A Turkish slave may not cross over except by permission, seventy *dirhams* being taken per head. The annual tribute from the mines of Naysābūr, from turquoise and other materials, amounts to seven hundred fifty-eight thousand seven hundred twenty *dirhams*.

p. 341 The **distances** in this region:

From Akhsīkath to Qubā, one stage;
   thence to A'ūsh, one stage;
   thence to Ūzkand, one stage;
   thence to al-ʿAqaba, one stage;
   thence to Tabāsh, one stage;
   thence to Barskhān al-Aʿlā (Upper), six stages;
   thence to the site of Bughrākhāqān, a like distance.

From Akhsīkath to Bāb, two post stages;
   thence to Turmughān, a half stage;
   thence to Jājistān, one stage;
   thence to Sāmghar, two post stages;
   thence to Khujanda, one stage.

From Isbījāb to Shāwāb, two post stages;
 thence to Badūkhkath (Barūjkath), a like distance;
 thence to Tamtāj, one stage;
p. 342 thence to Bārjākh, two post stages;
 thence to a way-station, one stage;
 thence to Shāwaghar, a half stage;
 and from Shāwaghar to Tarāz, two post stages.

From Isbījāb to Gharkard, two post stages;
 thence to Binkath, one stage;
 and you go from Binkath to Sutūrkath, one stage;
 thence to Binākath, two post-stages;
 thence to the river at al-Shāsh, two post stages;
 thence to Khāwas, one stage;
 thence to Zāmīn, one stage.

From Binkath al-Shāsh to Maʿdin al-Fidhdha, one stage;
 thence to Jājistān, one stage;
 thence to Turmughān, one stage.

From Binkath to Gharkard, one stage;
 thence to Isbījāb, two post stages.

From Zāmīn to Khāwas, one stage;
 from Zāmīn to Sābāt, two post stages;
 thence to Shāwakath, one stage;
 thence to Khujanda, one stage.

From Samarqand to Zarmān, one stage;
 thence to Rabinjan, one stage;
 thence to al-Dabūsiya, one stage;
 thence to Karmīniya, one stage;
 thence to al-Tawāwīs, one stage;
 thence to Dīmas, one stage;
 thence to Bukhārā, one stage.

From Samarqand to Zāmīn, one stage;
 thence to Khāwas, one stage;
 thence to Binākath, one stage;
 thence to Sutūkath (Ushtūrkath), one stage;
 thence to Binkath, one stage.

From Samarqand to Dirizdah, one stage;
 thence to Kish, one stage;

thence to Kandak, one stage;
thence to Bāb al-Hadīd, one stage;
thence to Qarna, one stage;
thence to Tirmidh, one stage.

p. 343 From Bukhārā to Baykand, one stage;
thence to Miyān Kāl, one stage;
thence to Firabr, one stage;
thence to Jayhūn, a half *farsakh*.

From Bukhārā to Jikm, one stage;
thence to Ribāt ʿAtīq, one stage;
thence to Jubb Saʿīd, one stage;
thence to Bazda, one stage;
thence to Ribāt Khwārān, one stage;
thence to Qaryat al-Bukhārīyyīn, one stage;
thence to Qaryat al-Khwārazmīyyīn, one stage;
thence to Balkhān, one stage;
thence to Kālif, one stage;
thence to Mahallat al-Qayyāsīn, one stage;
thence to Tirmidh, one stage.

From Bukhārā to Amzah, two post stages;
thence to Ribāt Tāsh, one stage;
thence to Shūrūkh, one stage;
thence to al-Raml, one stage;
thence to Ribāt Tughān, one stage;
thence to Ribāt Jikarband, one stage;
thence to Ribāt Hasan, one stage;
thence to Nābādghīn, one stage;
thence to the narrows of the river, one stage;
thence to Ribāt Māsh, one stage;
thence to Ribāt Sandah, one stage;
thence to Bagharqān, one stage;
thence to Shurākhān, one stage;
thence to Kāth, one stage.

From Kāth to Khās, one stage;
thence to Nūzkāt, two post stages;
thence to Wāyikhān, on the right bank, one stage;
thence to Nūbāgh, one stage;
thence to Mazdākhqān, in desert, two stages;
thence to Darsān, two post stages;

thence to Kardar, one stage;
thence to Juwayqān, two post stages;
thence to Qaryat Barātakīn, one stage;
thence to the lake, one stage.

p. 344 From Ribāt Māsh to Amīr, one stage;
thence to Bārāb Sār, two stages;
thence to Ardhakhīwa, one stage.

From Mazdākhqān to Wardarāgh, one stage;
thence to Kardar, one stage.

From Kāth to Ghardamān, one stage;
thence to Wāyikhān, two post stages;
thence to Ardhakhīwah, one post stage;
thence to Nawkabāgh (Nawkafāgh), one stage.

From Awzārmand to Daskākhān Khās, two post stages;
thence to Rakhushmīthan, one stage;
thence to Khīwa, one stage;
thence to Kardarānkhās, two post stages;
thence to Zardūkh, one post stage;
thence to Hazārasp, two post stages.

From Awzārmand (Wazārmand) to Rūzawand, one post-stage;
thence to Nūzwār, one stage;
thence to Zamakhshar, one stage,
and similarly to al-Jurjāniyya.

From Bukhārā to Nakhshab (Nasaf), in desert, thirty *farsakhs*, over which one
encounters a number of *ribāts*, thence to al-Saghāniyān, a full ten stages.

From al-Saghāniyān to Dārzanjī, or to Bāsand, or Bānbāb(?) (Bānyāb(?)), or
Sankardah, one stage in each case.

From al-Saghāniyān to Būrāb, two post stages;
from al-Saghāniyān to Bahām, or Ghashsh, or Zīnwar, three post stages in each
case.

From al-Saghāniyān to Hanbān, two stages;
p. 345 and from al-Saghāniyān to al-Khuttal,
thirty *farsakhs*; and from al-Saghāniyān to Samarqand, forty *farsakhs*.

p. 346 From Balkh to Khulm, two stages;
    thence to Warwālīz (Walwālij), a like distance;
    thence to al-Tāliqān, a like distance;
    thence to Badhakhshān, seven stages.

From Khulm to Siminjān, two stages;
    thence to Andarāba, five stages;
    thence to Kārbāyah (Jārbāyah), three stages;
    thence to Banjahīr, one stage;
    thence to Farwān (Barwān), two stages.

From Balkh to Baghlān, six stages;
    and from Samarqand to Baghlān, four stages.

From Balkh to Madhr, six stages;
    thence to Kāh (Jāh), one stage;
    thence to al-Bāmiyān, three stages;
    and from Balkh to Ushfūrqān, a like distance;
    thence to al-Fāryāb, a like distance;
    thence to al-Tāliqān, a like distance;

From Balkh to Shāwkard (Siyākird), one stage;
    thence to Tirmidh, one stage.

p. 347 From al-Yahūdiyya to al-Qāʿ (the Gulf), one stage;
    thence to Ushfūrqān, a like distance;
    thence to al-Sidra, one stage;
    thence to al-Dastajirdah, one stage;
    thence to Balkh, one half stage.

From al-Yahūdiyya to Qasr al-Amīr, one stage;
    thence to Fāryāb, one stage;
    thence to Karak, one stage;
    thence to al-Tālaqān, one stage.

From al-Yahūdiyya to Anbār, one stage;
    thence to a ribāt, one stage;
    thence to Balkh, one stage.

From Fāryāb to Āstāna, one stage;
    thence to Jūbīn wa-Malīn, one stage;
    thence to Andakhūy, one stage;
    thence to Ribāt Afrīghūn, one stage;

thence to Qanī Ghiyāth, one stage;
thence to Karkū, one stage.

From Marw to Fāz, one stage;
thence to Mahdiyy Abādh, one stage;
thence to Bahīrābādh, one stage;
thence to al-Qarīnayn, one stage;
thence to Asadābādh, one stage;
or thence to Hawzān, one stage;
thence to Qasr Ahnaf, two post stages;
thence to Araskan, one stage;
thence to al-Asrāb, one stage;
p. 348   thence to Kanjābādh, one stage;
thence to al-Tālaqān, one stage;
thence to Kashān, one stage;
thence to al-Yahūdiyya, one stage.

From Marw to Jarūjird, one stage;
thence to al-Dandānaqān, one stage;
thence to Talastāna, one stage;
thence to Ushturmaghak, one stage;
thence to Sarakhs, one stage.

From Marw to Kushmayhan, one stage;
thence to Ribāt al-Hadīd, one stage;
thence to Ribāt Nasrak, one stage;
thence to Jubb Hammād, one stage;
thence to Ribāt Bāris, one stage;
thence to Āmul, one stage;
thence to the Jayhūn, one *farsakh.*

From Abshīn to Ribāt Shūr, one stage;
thence to Ribāt Shār, one stage;
thence to Qaryat al-Qādhī, one stage;
thence to Shūrmīn, one stage;
thence to Qaryat al-Majūs, one stage;
thence to Khārah, one stage;
thence to Ribāt Miyānah, one stage;
thence to Karūkh, one stage;
thence to Harāt, one stage.

From Abshīn to Ribāt Kurzuwān, one stage;
thence to Marazk, one stage;

thence to Ribāt Rūdh, one stage;
thence to Marw al-Rūdh, one stage;
thence to Jisr Har, one stage;
thence to al-Tālaqān, one stage.

From Abshīn to Dizah, to Marw al-Rūdh, ten *farsakhs*.

p. 349 From Harāt to Asfuzār, three stages;
and to Mālin, or to Karūkh or to Bāshān, one stage in each case.

From Bāshān to Khaysār, one stage;
thence to Astarabyān, one stage;
thence to Mārābādh, one stage;
thence to Awfah (Awbah), one stage;
thence to Khasht, one stage;
you are then in al-Ghūr.

From Harāt to Baban, two stages;
thence to Kīf, one stage;
thence to Baghshūr, one stage.

From Ghaznīn to Ribāt al-Bārid, one stage;
thence to Asnākh, one stage;
thence to Hans, one stage;
thence to al-Bāmiyān, one stage.

From Ghaznīn to Kardīz, one stage;
thence to Awigh, one stage;
thence to Lajān, and here is a spring of water,
thence to Wayhind, in all, seventeen way stations; you are then in the country
of al-Sind and al-Hind.

From Bust to Ribāt Fīrūzqand, one stage;
thence to Mayghūn, one stage;
thence to Ribāt Kishshr, one stage;
thence to Banjawāy, one stage;
thence to Bakrābādh, one stage;
thence to Kharsād, one stage;
p. 350   thence to Ribāt Sarāb, one stage;
thence to Ribāt al-Awqal, one stage;
thence to Khinkil Abādh, one stage;
thence to Qaryat Gharm, one stage;
thence to Qaryat Khāst, one stage;

thence to Qaryat Jūma, one stage;
thence to Khāysār, one stage.

From Safanjāwī to a *ribāt*, one stage;
thence to Jankā, one stage;
thence to Ribāt al-Hajariyya, one stage;
thence to Banjawāy, one stage.

From Bust to Dāwar, four stages;
thence to al-Ghūr, one stage.

From Zaranj to Karkūyah, one stage;
thence to Bashtar, one stage;
thence to Juwayn, one stage;
thence to Bastak, one stage;
thence to Kanjar (Kankara), one stage;
thence to Sarshak, one stage;
thence to Wādī Farah, one stage;
thence to Farah, one stage;
thence to Darah, one stage;
thence to Kūstān, one stage;
thence to Jāshān, one stage;
thence to Qanāt Sarī, one stage;
thence to al-Jabal al-Aswad, one stage;
thence to Jāmān, one stage;
thence to Harāt, one stage.

From Zaranj to Zānbūq (Zanbūk), one stage;
thence to Sarūzan, one stage;
thence to Harūrā, one stage;
thence to Dahhak, one stage;
thence to Ribāt Karūdīn, one stage;
thence to Ribāt Quhistān, one stage;
thence to Ribāt 'Abd Allāh, one stage;
thence to Bust, one stage.

From Zaranj to Juzah (Kuzah), three stages;
thence to Farah, or to al-Qarnīn, two stages in each instance;
from Farah to Nih, one stage;
and from Zaranj to al-Tāq, one stage;
and from Zaranj to Kishsh, thirty *farsakhs*.

p. 351 From Qāyin to Tūn, one stage;
and from Qāyin to Bunābid, two stages;

thence to Kundur, a like distance;
thence to Turaythīth (Turthīth), two post stages.

From Yunābidh to Sankān (Sanjān), one stage;
thence to Jāyaman, one stage;
thence to Mālin Kuwākharz, one stage;
thence to Būzjān, two stages;
thence to al-Mallāha (saltworks), one stage;
thence to the castle, one stage.

From Naysābūr to Bīskand, one stage;
thence to Husaynābādh, one stage;
thence to Khusrūjird, one stage;
thence to al-Nūq (al-Būq), or to Yahyā Abādh, one stage;
thence to Mazīnān and Bahman Abādh, one stage;
thence to Asadābādh, one stage;
thence to Hafdar, one stage.

From Naysābūr to Qasr al-Rīh, one stage;
thence to al-Ramada, one stage;
thence to Sāhah, one stage;
thence to Mazdūrān, one stage;
thence to Ūkīna, one stage;
thence to Sarakhs, one stage.

From Qasr al-Rīh to Farhākird, one stage;
thence to Nūkdah, one stage;
thence to Mālāykird, one stage;
thence to Būzjān, one stage;
thence to Kalnā, one stage;
thence to al-Taq(?) [al-Tū?], one stage;
p. 352   thence to Amdah, one stage;
thence to Harāt, one stage.

From al-Qasr to al-Mallāha, one stage;
thence to Sankān, one stage;
thence to Yunābidh, two stages.

From Naysābūr to Kalkāw, one stage;
thence to al-Dārīn, one stage;
thence to Namkhkan, one stage;
and one who wants to get to Nasā should set out for Rīk, a distance of one
stage;

thence to Farukhān, one stage;
thence to Bardar, one stage;
thence to Baghdāw, one stage;
thence to Nasā, one stage.

One who wants to arrive at Abīward may travel to Dazāwand, one stage;
thence Huwayrān, one stage;
thence to Qalmīhan, one stage;
thence to Abīward, one stage:

from Qalmīhan to Kūfan is one stage;
from Kūfan to Abīward is one stage.

From Naysābūr to Baghīshan, one stage;
thence to al-Qaryat al-Hamrā', one stage;
thence to al-Mashad, one stage;
thence to Tābarān, two post stages.

From Naysābur to Nashdīghan, one stage;
thence to a *ribāt*, one stage;
thence to another, one stage;
thence to Turaythīth, one stage.

From Naysābūr to Rīwand, one stage;
thence to Mihrajān, two stages;
thence to Isfarā'īn, a like distance.

Here we have given a summary of the distances in this region.

The Region of Al-Daylam
(Lowlands and Highlands of Gīlān)

This is the region of silk and wool; here are skilled craftsmen. Its fruits are carried afar; its cloth is known in Egypt and al-ʿIrāq. Rains are abundant, prices are honest. A delightful metropolis, and the inhabitants have a delightful province. They honour the noble, have mercy on the weak, are eminent in the law, sublime in [knowledge of] the Prophetic tradition. Men in the fight; everyone of them is righteous. Their behaviour is good, they are upright people. Here is a deep river, sentinel cities. Excellent fish are here, fine villages, delicious fruits, all varieties of things. Abundant rice is here, figs, olives, citron, locust trees; there is jujube aplenty, fine grapes; spacious rural districts, fine cities, superb jute; a lofty name, abundant water, large revenue, very fine cloth.

However, we ascribe it to al-Daylam [the family of the Buyids] because their edifices are there, their dominion is there, and thence is their origin. For now they are a people who have taken possession of all the countries adjacent to them; and they comprise the leaders of Islām. The individual and the populace obey them. We did not find a name for this region that would embrace its districts, so we have ascribed it to them [the Buyids], and we have named it from them; so that we may describe in detail its districts, and publish the facts about it. It is not large, and its towns are not large. Were it not that the name of the mountain is correlative and complementary with that of the general area which extends to part of al-ʿIrāq, we should have assigned this region to the latter, making al-Rayy the metropolis thereof, and Qūmis one of its sections.

Here is a likeness and representation of it. [Map XIII]

We consider the region as five districts, the first of them, from the direction of Khurāsān, being Qūmis; then Jurjān; then Tabaristān; then al-Daylamān; then al-Khazar. The lake is centrally located in these districts, except for Qūmis, for it is high up in the mountains, medially situated between al-Rayy and Khurāsān, the district of Tabaristān separating the two districts from the lake.

Qūmis is an extensive, delightful district, and the fruits are good. It measures eighty by seventy *farsakhs*, most of it is mountains; towns are few, population is light, there is much grazing livestock, land tax is heavy, the climate is temperate. Its capital is al-Dāmghān; its towns: Simnān, Bistām, Zaghna, Biyār, Mughūn.

Jurjān is a district of plain and mountain, and were it not for the cold, palm trees would be grown there. Here are citrus, olives, jujube, figs. The rivers flow copiously, gardens are many. Here is an important rural district with an abundance of agricultural produce. The river is close by, the metropolis elegant, the name renowned, and the land tax heavy. The name of the capital, and it is the metropolis of the region, is Shahristān. Among its towns: Astarābādh, Aʿbaskūn, Alham, Ākhur, al-Ribāt.

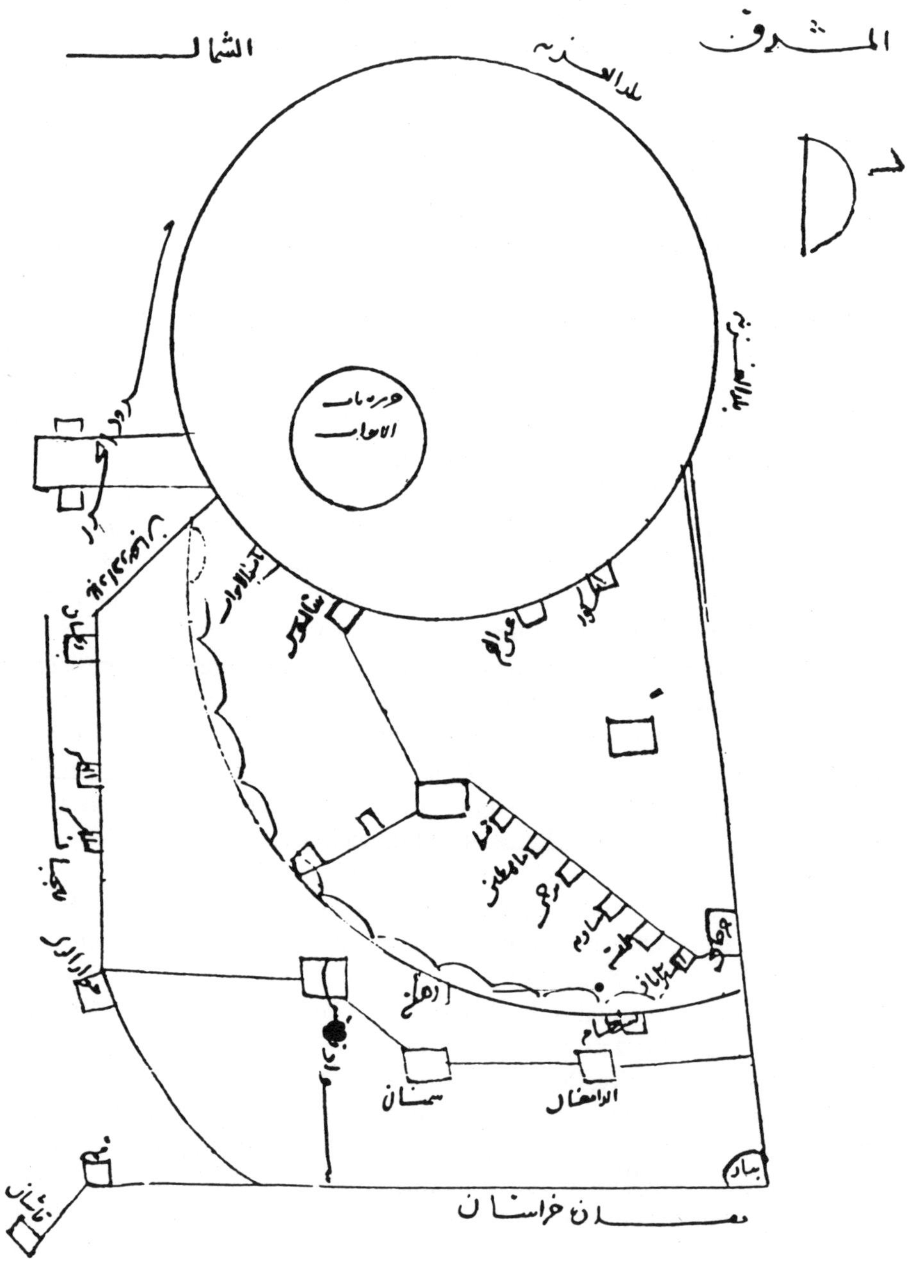

Map XIII: Tabar Daylam (see p. 417).
From MS. Sprenger 5—Ahlwardt 6034 by kind permission of the Staatsbibliothek
Preussischer Kulturbesitz, Berlin, Orientabteilung.

Tabaristān is a district on a plain, beside the lake; here also are mountains. Rain is abundant. It is a squalid, depressing, dirty, fleasome place. The bread is generally of rice; plenty of fish, garlic, and water fowl. Here are farms of flax and hemp. The capital is Āmul, among the towns: Sālus, Mīla, Māmatīr, Turunja p. 355 (Burjī), Sāriya, Tamīs(a), Harī, Būd, Nāmiya.

Al-Daylamān is a small district in the mountains. The towns have no elegance, no knowledge, no religion, but there is power, virility, and prestige. Here are remarkable customs, many villages. We have added al-Jīl to it, since most people can hardly differentiate between them. The capital of al-Daylam is Barwān; among its towns are: Wilāmir, Shakīraz, Tārum, Khashm. Al-Jīl has: Dūlāb, Baylamān, Shahr, Kuhan Rūdh.

Al-Khazar is an extensive district beyond the lake; a wretched, depressing place. It abounds in grazing animals, honey, and Jews. At its extremity is the rampart of Yājūj and Mājūj (Gog and Magog), on its borders the territories of the Romaeans. Two streams are here, most of its towns being on them; they flow into the lake. On its border from the direction of Jurjān is the mountain of Binqishlah. The capital is Itil; among its towns are: Bulghār, Samandar, Suwār, Baghand, Qayshawā, Khamlīj, Balanjar, al-Baydhāʾ.

Al-Dāmghān is a small capital in a gravelly area; its outskirts have been destroyed. The baths are dirty, the markets not good, and there are not many p. 356 superior people here. Even so, the climate is excellent, and the people are humble. A fortress stands over the town, with three gates—Bāb al-Rayy, Bāb Khurāsān, Bāb [lacuna in MSS]. There are two markets, a lower and an upper; and a small building as a *waqf* for the benefit of the caravanserai of Afrāwa and Dihistān, and for wayfarers. Not much return is derived from it, as those in charge do not increase the rental, as it was bequeathed to them. The mosque, which is in the alleys, is fine and well-kept. The water cisterns are like the cisterns of Marw.

Simnān is on the main road; here is a fine mosque situated in the market; water flows through the market, and tanks in turn are filled from it. Its population has decreased. Before it is the village of Simnānak, in the direction of al-Rayy: here is a much-frequented market.

Bistām has a small population, many gardens, fine fruits, a delightful rural district—it is exquisite. The mosque stands as if it were a fortress in the middle of the markets; the town has flowing water.

Mughūn: on the road to Khurāsān and Zaghna; a farming place, excellent fruit.

Biyār: a town with a fortress, and walls; here are farms and streams; vineyards and fruit. It is famed in the region and in the mountains; the populace has, in Khurāsān, business and wealth, along with religion, virility, and populousness; in culture they are the leaders, and the stars. The area produces camels, fats, sheep; and here is skill in building and in architecture. Here is chivalry, and philanthropy, and Islām; and godliness with it in private and public. The women are not seen in the town during the day; and neither songstresses nor drunkards are to be found here. No heresy is here that the two sects [Hanafites and Schāfiᶜites] notice; and no one, other than the Hanafites, has a jurist here or an ecclesiastical judge. Along with that, the people are renowned in all the lands; and I have personal knowledge, and have heard of their confections known as *afrūsha* [cake of flour, butter, and honey]. They are the most remarkable in their possessions, and their conversation; prosperous in money, and grazing livestock; famous for their going on the Pilgrimage, and for hospitality.

Nevertheless, they have faults and afflictions. There is no mosque there as in other places; the market and the houses are in the same area, and the sellers are
p. 357 women. The people do not render obedience to the ruler, and water is scarce in the soil and in the gardens. Water is distributed by waterclock, as is the custom at Arrajān; the most frightful enmity has arisen between the winegrowers and the revenue people, from al-Daylam to the Land of Āl-Sāmān. The millstones are below ground, and the water flows down; and its being in the desert is because there is no choice.

The town has two fortifications, between them, the houses. The great house of prayer is within the inner wall, which has one gate, and in the midst of which is a splendid fortress that has been neglected. The outer ring of defence has three gates which are iron-plated, the threshing floors inside the fortification. However, we examined its condition closely, as we do the capitals, because the stock of my mother's brother is from there; and any person from Qūmis that you see in Jerusalem, knows that he is from here! And they used to know my grandfather, Abu al-Tayyib al-Shawā, and they recalled that he traveled to al-Shām with eighteen men in the days of the Hamriyya [a sect].

Shahrastān is the metropolis of the region, the capital of Jurjān. Fruits, olive, pomegranates, are plentiful. Among the chief cities of the world it resembles al-Ramla of Palestine. It has glory, splendour, and energetic people with skill, humility, elegance, gentleness, goodness. The markets are fine, as are the places of prayer, the figs; superb are the watermelons, confections, eggplants; yet the bread is kneaded with oil of olives and fats. Here is the bitter orange, citron, jujube; there would be palms, but the cold would mar the dates. The fish are remarkable—they are like steers! It is a prosperous, noble town, with standing and prestige. Here are canals with bridges and arches. Here is the knowledge of God, religion, venerable people, riches. The people have adorned the mosque, and decorated the walls of the houses. The town is in two portions as are Fasā and Baghdād; and it is the custom to have a bench in front of the pulpit. Facing the house of the governor, and reaching to it, is a public square. The call to prayer is made in a chant, and with tunes. The preacher is a Hanafite; and the second call to prayer is made twice. Here is the river, and the rural district of Dihistān; and the town has disappeared in gardens, and trees, and sugarcane. And Khurramārūdh, do not forget, for forgetting is the most vexatious thing
p. 358 in science! Here are figs, medlars, pomegranates. There is no exclusion, or expulsion—nor payment of the price for these. The mountains are inhabited,

just as in Lebanon. The hostelries are charming, as is Masjid [place of prayer] Dīnār. This is all true—but now listen! This is a metropolis with withering heat, oppressiveness, flies; and noxious fleas to which we have given the name "bears"! Where the figs grow is mire, and the water is as bad as is possible; and anyone who settles there away from his own country, let him prepare his shroud, for herein is a scythe that mows down the bodies. On the Day of Sacrifice you see them in two groups at the head of the camel; and there is wounding, beating, confusion—the commotion and killing and raging do not separate them. An army is here from al-Daylam, another of Turks of Sāmān; there is the vilest factionalism on the part of the two sects [Hanafite and Shāfiʿite]; devastating partisanship, with even the inventing of a *Qurʾān*!

Nine roads lead to the town, the first of them Darb Sulaymān, then Darb al-Qūmisiyyīn, Darb al-Shāriʿ Hayyān, Darb Kanda, Darb al-Bādinjān, Darb al-Bārikāh; and before it Darb Khurāsān. This is what I have well established in the description of Jurjān.

Bakrābādh is associated with [Jurjān]—a river with arched bridges is between them: in itself it has the appearance of a populous town. Here are houses of prayer, with elders, nobles; the cemeteries are extensive. The town is across from the metropolis, on a bridged river. Another stream here runs crosswise through the town, called the Tayfūrī [Gurgan, Jurjān], cleaner and sweeter than the other. Here also are wells of sweet water.

Astarābādh has a better climate and healthier water than Jurjān. Most of the people are weavers of raw silk, and they are experts. Its fortress is in ruin, its ditch flooded. The mosque is in the market, with a stream close to its door.

Ābaskūn: on the lake; over it a fortress of baked brick. The mosque is in the market, the stream at the edge of the town. It is the port of Jurjān, the entrepôt of al-Rihāb.

Harī: on the lake; smaller than Ābaskūn, and with smaller population; a skinny people.

Ākhur: chief town of the rural district of Dihistān, on the right side of the road going towards the caravanserai [of Afrāwa]. Here is a minaret which may be seen from afar, amidst the villages. In all, there are twenty-four villages in Dihistān, and it is among the most important districts of Jurjān.

Al-Ribāt (the caravanserai) is on the edge of the desert. The ruler destroyed its fortress, which used to have three gates. It is populous and well-kept, good p. 359 houses of prayer, magnificent markets, delightful residences, fine foods. No congregational mosque here. The old prayerhouse here has wooden walls, is quite splendid, occupying the lowest portion of the guardhouse, in a place that resembles al-Dandānaqān. In the middle of that area is a prayerhouse with a minaret, pertaining to the adherents to the Traditions; the remaining prayer-houses belong to the followers of Abū Hanīfa—may God have mercy on him.

Āmul is the capital of Tabaristān: it is a town of fame and importance; here are admirable and beautiful clothes. It has the appurtenances of civilization, special characteristics, and a hospital; and they have, moreover, two congregational mosques. The old mosque, with the river and trees close by, lies on the edge of the markets; the other is near it. Each mosque is surrounded by porticoes. The river turns the mills, grinding fine. The countenances of the inhabitants are handsome, clean, and graceful; commerce is prosperous, weavers skilled. Its fame is great, the people are merchants; do not ask about the excellence of the fragrance, the fineness of the waists. Their outlook is sharp, with excellence of perception. Garlic makes it fragrant, rice is here in plenty, springs keep the rivers clear. Here is knowledge of God in abundance; nor does it lack a leader, or a person to examine and decide on religious questions.

However, their bread is of corn, their other foods repugnant, their faults many. Their bedbugs are astonishing, their depravity great. Their pouring rain lasts a long time; their heat is severe. Their houses are of grass, their habits despicable. Their wheaten bread inebriates, their waterfowl makes one sick. The fleas bite, the house leaks, the weather is harsh. The speech is fast, the town dirty, the market filthy, the summer rainy.

In Sālūs is a fortress of stone; the mosque beside it.

Sāriya is a populous place. The sciences are here; splendid cloths, and markets, and good manners. It is fortified, having also a moat and bridges. A magnificent orange tree is in the mosque; and there are porticoes round about it. Beside the stone bridge is a conspicuous fig tree: observe it carefully so that you may perceive its remarkable qualities and characteristics. I myself inspected it, and they are not frequently seen, as I hope to be saved!

p. 360   Barwān is the capital of al-Daylam: small, not prosperous or distinguished, no elegance or nobility here. No fine parks are here, no tall handsome houses. The markets are not extensive, not prosperous; the town is neither large nor attractive. There is no continuous development except in the enclosed villages. However, the people are remarkably patient, and a source of loyal soldiers. The place where the ruler lives is called Shahrastan. A well has been dug at the lowest part of the town, and here also are their wealth and their goods.

In Salārwand is a fortress called Samīrūm, on it lions, a sun and moon, of gold. The houses are adobe.

Khashm (Hawsam) is the town of the Dāʿi (missioner). The market is well-frequented, a mosque standing on the edge of the markets. The river flows beside the markets, with a splendid bridge over it; here also is the palace of the ruler. It is a small town, likewise Tārum.

Al-Tālaqān: a large, populous, splendid town, not another like it in the district. It should have been the place where the ruler lives, but I think they disliked the idea because the town is so remote. Here are learned and honourable people, with finesse.

Dūlāb is the capital of al-Jīl; the buildings here are of plaster and stone. The mosque is at the edge of the town: a good town with a fine market. In front of the mosque is a plain, beyond which is a point where the streams meet.

Kuhan Rūdh is close to the river. The buildings, some are of stone, some are wooden huts. The mosque is in the middle of the town.

Mūghkān (Mūqān): its population has diminished; the town produces little. The remaining towns of al-Jīl are on the littoral.

Itil is a large capital, on a river, flowing into the lake and also called the Itil [Volga River]. To it I add the name of the area on the bank of the river, towards Jurjān. Around it and in it are trees. There are many Muslims here. Their king was a Jew, who had customs and judges Muslim, Jewish, Christian; and p. 361 idol-worshippers. I heard that al-Maʾmum invaded them from al-Jurjāniyya, and overcame them, requiring the king to adopt Islām. Then I heard that an army from the Romaeans, called al-Rūs, invaded them and took possession of their country. A wall surrounds the town, the houses are spread out. It is like Jurjān, or bigger. Their buildings are pavilions of wood and felt, and wooden huts, except for a few that are of clay. The palace of the ruler is of baked brick: it has four portals, one in the direction of the river, and a person crosses to it by boat; another leads to the desert. It is a wretched, barren town, no prosperity, no fruits. Their bread is of corn, the accompaniment, fish.

Bulghār is in two sections. The buildings here are of wood and reeds. The night is short. The mosque stands in the market, and since they have become Muslims they have been going on raids themselves. The town is on the river Itil, closer to the lake than is the capital.

Suwār is on this river. The buildings here are wooden huts; many farms; bread is plentiful.

Khazar is on another river, towards al-Rihāb, and is on just one bank of the river. It is more extensive, more delightful than any we have mentioned. People used to remove from there to the shore of the lake; but now they have returned to the town. They have become Muslims, having been Jews.

Samandar is a large town on the lake between the River of al-Khazar and Bāb al-Abwāb. The dwellings are huts. Most of the people are Christians; they are a very humble people, loving the stranger. However, they are robbers. The town is more extensive than Khazar. They have gardens and many vineyards. Their buildings are of wood with reeds interwoven, the roofs fornicate. There are many mosques here.

The lake [Caspian Sea] is deep, dark, and dreary, and traveling on it is p. 362 harder than on the two seas. It provides nothing useful at all, other than the fish. The boats used here are large, nailed, and covered with pitch. No inhabited island stands in the lake. If a man wished to travel around it he could do so, because the rivers that flow into it are not big, except for Nahr al-Kurr and Nahr al-Malik [Samūr]. Some islands in the lake have thickets and swamps and beasts; here also is an island from which much aromatics is derived. The Rampart of Yājūj and Mājūj is beyond the lake, a distance of about two months' travel.

The Rampart of Dhu al-Qarnayn. I have read in the book of Ibn Khurradādhbih, and elsewhere, about the story of this rampart, and the accounts all agree. The account cited here and the chain of tradition are those of Ibn Khurradādhbih, because he was the minister of the khalif, and was more likely to have the knowledge of the library of the Amīr al-Mūʾminīn [Commander of the Faithful] entrusted to him. As he says: "Sallām the translator told me: ʿal-Wāthiq biʾllāh, when he saw in a dream as if the rampart, which Dhu al-Qarnayn (Alexander the Great) had built between us and Yājūj and Mājūj, was open, instructed me and said to me, "Inspect it and bring me a report of it." Al-Wāthiq had sent Muhammad bin Mūsā al-Khwārazmī, the astrologer, to Tarkhān, king of al-Khazar; so he gave me fifty men, also fifty thousand *dinārs*, and he gave me money for an indemnity of ten thousand *dirhams*. He bade me give to each one of the fifty, one thousand *dirhams*, with provisions for a year, and he gave me two hundred mules to carry the provisions and the water.

"We started out from Sāmarrā with a letter from al-Wāthiq to Ishāq bin Ismāʿīl, ruler of Armenia—he was in Tiflīs—to send us on our way. Ishāq wrote on our behalf to the ruler of al-Sarīr, and the ruler of al-Sarīr wrote to the king of al-Lān. Then the ruler of al-Lān wrote to the shāh of Faylān; then the shāh of Faylān wrote to Tarkhān, king of al-Khazar. We stayed with him a day and a night, so that he sent with us fifty guides.

"We traveled away from him for six and twenty days, until we arrived at a black malodorous place: however, before going in there we had been provided p. 363 with vinegar to sniff. We traveled there for twenty days until we arrived at some ruined towns, and we passed among them for seven and twenty days. So we asked about those towns, and were told they were those that Yājūj and Mājūj invaded and destroyed. We arrived at some fortresses close to the mountain in a ravine, in a gorge of which the rampart stands; and lo! in those fortresses were a people speaking Arabic and Persian. They were Muslims, who read the *Qurʾān*, and had mosques and libraries. They asked us whence we had come, and we informed them that we were messengers of the Amīr al-Muʾmini'n [Commander of the Faithful]. So they approached, wondering, and said, 'Amīr al-Mu'mim?' and we said, 'Yes.' Said they, 'Is he an elder or a young man?' Said we, 'A young man'. Said they, 'Where is he?' Said we, 'In al-ʿIrāq, in a city that is called Sāmarrā.' Said they, 'We have heard absolutely nothing about this person.'

"We arrived at the mountain, which is smooth; no vegetation on it; and the mountain is there cut by a valley one hundred fifty cubits wide. Here were two sidepillars built fast to the mountain on both sides of the valley, the width of each pillar, five and twenty cubits. Visible from below, they were ten cubits, outside the gate. It was all built of iron ingots covered with brass, to a thickness of fifty cubits. The lintel of the gate was of iron, its two ends resting on the pillars: its length, one hundred twenty cubits. It had been inserted into the pillars, in each one to an extent of ten cubits. It was five cubits wide. Over the lintel was a structure in that same ingot of iron covered with brass, extending to the top of the mountain, its height as far as the eye could see. Above that were balconies of iron, at the edge of each balcony two horns, bent, each one towards the other, and between the horns was a door of iron consisting of two leaves, closed; the width of each leaf was fifty cubits, its height fifty cubits, its thickness five cubits. The two pillars of both leaves were set in the lintel up to its full measure. On the door was a bolt seven cubits long, one fathom in girth, and the height of the bolt above the ground was five and twenty cubits. Above the bolt, at a distance of five cubits was a lock, of a greater length than the length of the bolt—the tongue of p. 364 each one was two cubits long—and on the lock hung a key. The length of the key was a cubit and a half, and it had twelve teeth, each tooth skillfully made, and bigger than could be taken from a mould. The key hung from a chain eight cubits long, in thickness, four spans; and the ring in which the chain was set was like the ring of a catapult. The threshold of the door was ten cubits thick, by one hundred cubits together with what was under the two pillars; [its thickness] was visible for five cubits. All these measurements are in units of the standard cubit.

"The superintendent of those forts rides out every Friday with ten horsemen, every horseman having an iron mallet, each one weighing fifty *manns* [*mann* = weight of two *ratls*]. They strike the bolt with those mallets, each man striking three times, so that whoever is behind the door will hear the sound and know that the guardians are there; and these will know that those have done no damage to the door. When our company struck the bolt they put their ears set to listen, and lo! the reverberation was there.

"Close to this place is a huge fort about ten *farsakhs* in each dimension; at the gate are two guardhouses, the width of each one, two hundred cubits. At the door of each of these two guardhouses are two trees, and between the guardhouses is a well of sweet water. In one of the guardhouses is the building equipment with which the rampart was built. Here were iron caldrons and ladles, four caldrons by each tripod, like the caldrons for soapmaking. The remainder of the iron ingots were there, stuck one to the other with rust.

"We asked there if they had seen anyone from Yājūj and Mājūj and they said they had once seen a number of them above the balconies; but a dark wind arose and cast them down on their own side, they said. And the height of a man of p. 365 them, as they saw with their own eyes, was a span and one half!

"Then the guides departed with us for the area of Khurāsān, and we emerged seven *farsakhs* beyond Samarqand. Those in charge of the fortresses had given us provisions, as much as we needed. Eventually we reached al-Wāthiq, and gave him the report.'" And this contradicts the report of anyone who should assert that the rampart is in al-Andalus.

A Summary Account of Conditions in this Region

This region is hot except for Qūmis; here is water and rain aplenty. It has no stream in which boats travel except in the area of al-Khazar. The worst water and climate is in Jurjān, rough and noxious. There are many *dhimmī*. The palm is not cultivated here.

The **sects** here are varied. Qūmis, most of the people of Jurjān, and some of those of Tabaristān are Hanafites, the remainder Hanbalites and Shāfiʿites. You do not see in Biyār followers of the Tradition, except Shāfiʿites. There are many Najjāriyya in Jurjān. The Karrāmites in Jurjān, Biyār and the mountains of Tabaristān have retreat houses. The Shīʿa are in evidence in Jurjān and Tabaristān.

Now should someone say: "Did you not say that in Biyār are no heretics; and then say that the Karrāmites are there," it would be said to him that the Karrāmites are a people of asceticism and piety, relying on the authority of Abū Hanīfa.

Now, anybody who appeals to the authority of Abū Hanīfa, or that of Mālik, or of al-Shāfiʿ, or to the People of the Tradition, without exaggerating in it, or being extreme on the side of Muʿāwiya, and also who did not liken God to and give Him attributes of created beings—he is not a heretic. And I am determined that I will not let my tongue wag about the people of Muhammad—God's peace and blessings be upon him—nor will I give witness against them as heretics as far as I find a way to avoid this. I am so inclined after hearing this beautiful and noble tradition: Muhammad bin Muhammad al-Dihistānī related to me, as did also Musāfir bin ʿAbd Allāh al-Istarābādhī, Muhammad bin ʿAlī al-Nahawī, ʿAlī ibn al-Hasan al-Sarakhsī, who had been informed by Yūsuf bin ʿAlī al-Faqīh al-Zāhid, who had been informed by Abu al-Walīd Ahmad bin Bistām al-Tālaqānī al-Faqīh al-Zāhid, who had been informed by Yūsuf bin ʿAlī al-Abbār al-Samarqandī, who had been informed by ʿAlī bin Ishāq al-Hanzalī, who had been informed by Bashar bin ʿImāra, who said that Misʿar bin Kidām had said: "I have known no person whatever who had an intelligence like the intelligence of Ibn Murra. A man came to him and said, 'God save you! I have

p. 366 come to you asking for guidance. I am a man who has joined all of these sects, and nothing admitted me to any sect of them unless the *Qurʾān* admitted me to it. And I was not ousted from a sect unless that the *Qurʾān* ousted me from it; so that I am left behind, and nothing is available to me.' Said ʿAmr bin Murra to him: 'Do you swear by Allāh, who is the only God, that you came for guidance?' Said [the other], 'I swear by Allāh, and there is no God except Him, that I have come seeking guidance.' Said ʿAmr, 'Very well! Have you noticed whether [the sects] disagreed in that Muhammad is the Messenger of God, and that what he brought from God is truth?' Said he, 'No.' Said ʿAmr: 'And did they disagree concerning the *Qurʾān*, that it is the book of God?' Said he, 'No.' Said ʿAmr: 'And did they disagree over the religion of God, that it is Islām?' Said he, 'No.' Said ʿAmr: 'And did they disagree over the Kaʿba, that it is the *Qibla*?' Said he, 'No.' Said ʿAmr: 'And did they disagree in the matter of prayers, that there are five?' Said he, 'No.' Said ʿAmr: 'And did they disagree about Ramadhān, that it is their month in which they fast?' Said he, 'No.' Said ʿAmr: 'And did they disagree in the matter of the Pilgrimage, that it is the house of God to which they make the Pilgrimage?' Said he, 'No.' Said ʿAmr: 'And did they disagree in the matter of the alms tax, that it is, from every two hundred, five *dirhams*?' Said he, 'No.' Said ʿAmr: 'And did they disagree in the washing away of ritual impurity, that it is obligatory?' Said he, 'No.' So ʿAmr referred to this, and more like it, and then recited: 'He it is who has sent down the Book to you, from which there are lucid verses that are the essence of the Book, while others are figurative.' (*Qurʾān*, sūra 3, verse 7). Said ʿAmr: 'And do you know what a lucid verse is?' Said he, 'No.' Said ʿAmr: 'The lucid verse is one on which there is agreement, and the figurative one, one on which there has been disagreement. Strengthen your intention in the lucid verses, and beware of searching the figurative.' Said the man, 'Praise be to God who has directed me to your presence; for I arise from before you, in very good condition!' And he invoked God's blessing on him and extolled him. Said ʿAmr: 'If the ruler were to invite the people of the book [Christians and Jews] to meet him, and they were to respond, and if he were to submit to them those matters that you have learned; then if he were to challenge you as he would challenge them, and he were to exchange with you on the matters he submitted to them, then make use of the foremost commandment! If someone should ask what the foremost commandment is, it is that on which our predecessors have agreed.'"

May God be merciful to the worshipper who ponders this story, and adheres to one of the four *madhāhib* that comprise the vast majority of people, and who restrains his tongue from cutting the Muslims to pieces, and from extravagance in the faith.

One day I attended the council of al-Qādhī al-Mukhtār, and he is the greatest Imām I have ever met, the most intelligent, the most religious of them. Mention was made there of the controversy among the people [of Muhammad], and the fanaticism of the people of the sects. So he pointed with his hand to the *Qibla* and said, "Who pray towards this *Qibla* are indeed our brothers, the Muslims." And I saw Abū Zayd al-Marūzī, and he was a religious Imām, saying the *witr* prayers with three units, and also following the school of Abū Hanīfa in a number of other matters. Moreover, I heard Abū al-Tayyib bin Ahmad say, "Every one of them considered the cases with independent judgment, and every one of them is considered correct."

p. 367   You should realize that this fanaticism you see, only the ignorant and exaggerators among the storytellers, and others, stir it up; but the [Prophet's] community is as I have told you.

The districts of al-Daylam are Shīʿa; most of the people of al-Jīl are Sunnī.

Most of the goods that come from this region are specialties. Qūmis produces white decorated cotton scarves, small and large; also plain ones, and cushions. Sometimes a scarf from there is worth two thousand *dirhams*. They also produce dresses, *taylasāns*, and fine wool clothing. The people of Jurjān produce silk veils that are sent to al-Yaman, also jujubes; they produce inferior brocade, figs and olives. From Tabaristān come dresses that are preferred over those of Fārs; *taylasāns*; and canvas clothing that is carried to distant places—much of it is sold in Makka. Some of it is cheap, some is expensive, and is called in the West, al-Makkiyya [Makkan]. They also produce bands of cloth. From Biyār come cloth, and much oil. They have a special competence here in the making of clay, so you do not see an important person, or a scholar, without skill in this art. Abu al-Ṭayyib al-Shawā, with his wealth and his dignity, you would always see him in his villages building a hut or raising a wall, likewise his sons and grandsons—they have the engineering and the skill in constructing a building without having studied specially for it. I have never seen finer construction than that of the houses of Biyār; for they have truly fashioned them with form, and increased their appurtenances of convenience.

The **waters** of this region: rivers flow down from the mountains; and there is the river of Jurjān—the Ṭayfūrī—and another. The river [lacuna in MS] [Asbīdrūdh?] is in al-Daylam, and many streams flow into it; it flows into the lake. The river Itil emerges from the direction of the dam, while the waters of al-Jīl flow down from the mountains of al-Daylam; and the waters of Ṭabaristān from the mountains, or from Khurramārūdh.

Places of interest here. Ribāṭ Dihistān which people from Khurāsān make a point of destination—it is splendid, exquisite. At a distance of a day's journey from Bisṭām is a place which people visit, for here are the pious associates of the mosque, [devoted to study and prayer]. Within sight of Bisṭām is the grave of Abū Yazīd; and in districts of al-Khazar are some distinguished guardhouses.

p. 368

Among the remarkable things is a small creature in Ṭabaristān, with one thousand legs; it is smaller than the locust, thinner than the worm; when it moves—well think of it as ripples appearing on clusters of grapes. There is another small animal, with two wings like the wings of a swallow; it is the size of a fox, and gnaws fruit. Here also are fish that look like a piece of sycamore; one day as I passed through the fish market in Jurjān, I saw a head the size of the head of a bull, and was told that it was the head of a fish. In the area of Jurjān is a well in which a tree appears every year, then disappears. One of the rulers tried to tie it with heavy chains, but it tore them and broke them, and disappeared.

The **languages** of Qūmis and Jurjān are close to each other. They use the hāʾ [h], saying hādih, and hākun—there is a certain charm to it. The language of Ṭabaristān is close to this, except that there is a rapidity about it. The language of al-Daylam, by contrast, is incomprehensible. In al-Jīl they use the khāʾ. The language of al-Khazar is forceful and incomprehensible.

The **features** of the people of Qūmis are attractive. The people of al-Daylam have handsome beards and faces; they are elegant. The people of Jurjān are skinny, the people of Tabaristān are good-looking and pure. Among the people of al-Khazar are similarities to the Slavs.

Most of the names of the people of Jurjān are Abū Sādiq, and Abu al-Rabīՙ; and Abū Naՙīm; for the people of Tabaristān it is Abū Hāmid.

Manners and customs. In Jurjān the preaching is by the jurists, and by the storytellers. People do not usually wear the *taylasān*. In al-Daylam, they have remarkable customs. They marry none but their own people; and one day I was in one of the hostelries when a young girl rushed past, a man with his sword unsheathed dashing after her, trying to kill her. I asked what she had done to merit her killing. Said my informant, "She married outside our people; and p. 369 killing anyone who does that is an obligation with us." On the occasion of a funeral, people uncover their heads and assemble; then the mourners and the bereaved wind themselves in raiment which they wrap around their heads and beards. They hold councils in the streets. Their markets are on high ground, and they assemble there with javelins in their hands, wearing cloaks made in Tabaristān. The learned men they call "teacher", and sometimes they got hold of me and said, "*Lauk muaՙllim*" [teacher], and "lauk" means "outstanding one." They are not accustomed to selling bread, and they despise begging; for the stranger need only go to their houses and help himself to food to satisfy his needs. Markets are held on Friday, on a stretch of level ground, and every village has its day in turn. When they finish, the men and women retreat to a secluded place where they wrestle with one another; a man sits there with a rope, and any one who wins he ties a knot for him. If a man likes a woman he goes with her, and her family accepts him with joy and welcoming, and they boast to one another over him since he is willing to accept their hospitality. They entertain him for three days, then the public crier makes an announcement, after he has been with her for a week in an isolated building. Meantime her people meet and plan. I asked Abū Nābita al-Ansārī; "Does he possess her before the contract?" Said he, "If they knew of such a thing they would kill him." Many times I attended the marriage ceremonies of the people of Biyār. The people gather after darkness, every man with a long-necked bottle of rosewater, and firing, which is lighted at the door of the bridegroom and bride. One of the elders delivers an eloquent speech, in which he makes requests of the couple; he then makes requests of the woman, and another person from the side of the bride answers p. 370 him in a speech, with a pleasant response—most of the speakers are well-bred people. They then make the contract, and the men with the jars begin to sprinkle the walls with them; whereupon each jarowner is given a dish of *āfrūsha*, and you never in all this world will see the like of their *āfrūsha*! I have heard that one of the kings summoned a man from there who excelled in making this pastry, and he made it with flour of their flour, some of their oil, and their syrup, and a woman made some, but it was not like what is made in Biyār. I saw a man who took some of it to Makka, brought it back, and it had not undergone any change.

I spent four months accepting their invitations and attending their weddings, and I never saw them enlarging on a menu of broth, then boned meat, then rice, then *āfrūsha* made with dates.

If snow falls there they turn the stream into the streets, so the waters clear away all the snow and wash the alleys. You do not see a woman during the day, they go out at night only, in black dress. A woman whose husband has died does not marry: if she does, the youngsters throw potsherds at her door.

The **water** of Jurjān is deadly to strangers. In Tabaristān is a fish noxious to man, and a bird the flesh of which is bad.

Al-Daylam [the Buyid dynasty] has the sovereignty; and war breaks out in Jurjān between them and the ruler of Khurāsān.

> *Addition/version* MS. C.
> Government: al-Daylam is under control of a people of two main families, the Sallārwand and the Bādharwand. As to the Sallārwand, they are from the direction of Ādharbayjān and they gained mastery over those areas; and the other family is here. In this region there is good administration, steadfastness, preparedness, spaciousness, peace. And for the people of al-Jīl, they obey only the sons of the Dāʿī [missioner] whose stock is from Saʿda: there are two dāʿīs, distinguished as "the First" and "the Second". As for the towns of al-Khazar, sometimes the ruler of al-Jurjāniyya conquered them; and as for Jurjān and Tabaristān, these provinces at times the house of al-Daylam ruled, and alternately, at times the armies of the king of al-Mashriq subdued them.

p. 371 The **land-tax** of Qūmis is one thousand thousand and one hundred thousand and ninety-six thousand *dirhams*. The land tax of Jurjān is ten thousand thousand and one hundred thousand and ninety-six thousand, eight hundred *dirhams*. The land tax of Biyār was six and twenty thousand *dirhams*; so a man went from there to Bukhārā, and built a house of very fine clay. Then he brought it on the necks of some men and set it before the prince, Nasr bin Ahmad, and he wondered at it. He said to him: "Ask what you want." Said he, "Return our land taxes to six thousand, and attach our administrative offices to Naysābūr;" and today it is one of the administrative districts of Naysābūr. Do you not notice that between it and Naysābūr is a village the land tax of which goes to Qūmis? Do you not notice that they call the people of Biyār "Qūmisites"?

There is factionalism in Jurjān, for between the school [of Abū Hanīfa] and the Bakrāwādhiyya there is murder over the head of the sacrificial camel. On the day of the Festival [sacrifice], between the followers of Hasan and the Karrāmites, frightful fighting, and the most amazing partisan strife break out.

The people of Tabaristān have three characteristics for which there are three bases: fragrance of breath from eating garlic, keenness and excellence of vision from eating vegetables, and fineness of waist from eating rice.

The **distances** in this region:
From al-Dāmghān to al-Haddāda, one stage;
    thence to Badash, one stage;
    thence to Murjān, one stage;
    thence to Hafdar, one stage;
    thence to Asadāwādh, one stage.

p. 372 From al-Dāmghān to Jarmjuwī, one stage;
    thence to Ribāt ʿIlyābādh, one stage;
    thence to Simnān, one stage;
    thence to Raʾs al-Kalb, one stage;
    thence to Qaryat al-Milh, one stage;
    thence to Khwār al-Rayy, one stage.

From al-Haddāda to Bistām, one stage;
    thence to Qarya. ..., one stage;
    thence to Zardābādh, one stage;
    thence to Khurramārūdh, one stage;
    thence to Juhayna, one stage;
    thence to Jurjān, one stage.

From Zardābādh ..., one stage;
    ... to Qarya ... one stage;
    thence to al-Qubāb, one stage;
    thence to Biyār to al-Hawdh, one stage;
    thence to Asadāwādh, one stage,
    and from there to Turthīth, thirty *farsakhs*.

From Biyār to al-Dāmghān, through the desert, twenty-five *farsakhs*.

From Jurjān to Dīnāzārā, one stage;
    thence to Amlūtā, one stage;
    thence to Ajagh, one stage;
    thence to Sibdāst, one stage;
    thence to Isfarāʿīn, one stage.

From there to Ābaskūn, or to Ribāt Hafs, or to Ribāat ʿAlī, one stage in every instance.

From Ribāt ʿAlī to Ribāt al-Amīr, one stage;
    thence to Bīlamak, one stage;
    thence to Ribāt Dihistān, one stage;
    and Ākhur is here.

From Āmul to Bulūr, one stage;
    thence to Ask, one stage;
    thence to Bāmhir (Nāmahand), one stage;
    thence to Barziyān, one stage;
    thence to al-Rayy, one stage.

From Āmul to Māmatīr, one stage;
    thence to Sāriya, one stage.

From Āmul to Turunjā (Burjī), one stage;
    thence to Raʾs al-Hadd, three stages.

From Sāriya to Abārast, one stage;
    thence to Abādan, one stage;
    thence to Tamīs(a), one stage;
    thence to Astarābādh, one stage;
    thence to Jurjān, two stages.

From Jurjān to al-Daylamān, twelve stages;
p. 373   thence to Ardabīl, a like distance.

From Ābaskūn to Astarābādh, one stage;
    thence to Sāriya, four stages.

From Āmul to Nātil, one stage;
    thence to Sālūs, one stage;
    thence to Kalār, one stage;
    thence to the mountains of al-Daylam, one stage.

From Sālūs to Isbīdrūdh, one stage;
    thence to Qaryat al-Rasad, one stage;
    thence to Khashm, one stage;
    thence to Baylamān, four stages;
    thence to al-Dūlāb, four stages;
    thence to Kuhan Rūdh, three stages;
    thence to Mūghkān, two stages;
    thence to [the river] al-Kurr, a like distance;
    thence to Hashtādhar, a like distance;
    thence to al-Shamākhiya, a like distance.

The Region of Al-Rihāb
(Ādharbayjān—Armenia)

Since this is an illustrious and delightful region, fruits and grapes have multiplied there, its towns among the most pleasant, as Kamūqān and Khilāt, and Tabrīz, which resemble al-ʿIrāq; prices have been low there, the trees intertwined, the streams flow through it; it contains mountains and honey, plains and provinces; in its wādīs are sheep, and since we did not find a general name for it that would embrace its districts, we have called it al-Rihāb [the spacious]. It is a region of Islam; within it are camels, and here the Romaeans blockade the Muslims. Sturdy wools are produced here, superb surcingles usually dyed crimson—I really fail in describing it. The price of a lamb is two *dirhams*, and the bread two loaves for a *dānaq*. The fruits cannot be counted nor weighed. Along with that it is an important frontier, an exalted region. Here were those who controlled the Aras River (al-Rass) below the mountains Huwayrith and Hārith [Ararat]. Here is a portion of al-Tā'if, it looks like Paradise! It is a glory to Islam, an area that invites invaders. Here is profitable commerce, ancient districts, copiously flowing rivers, delightful villages, admirable qualities, delicious fruits. The people are Sunnī Muslims, eloquent and prestigious. They have honeydew, madder,

p. 374 and jasmine, the excellent *qasbūya* fish, the sea, the lakes: the gateway and the guardhouses, the religion, the products. However, everyone in his sect is a fanatic, and along with that they are disagreeable. In their speech is dissimulation, and in them, conceit. The roads thither are difficult, and the Christians there have a majority. Here is a representation and an image of it. [Map XIV]

We consider this region as comprising three districts. The first one, from the direction of the lake, is al-Rān, then Armīniya, then Ādharbayjān.

Al-Rān constitutes about one-third of the region. It is like an island, between the lake and the River al-Rass. The River al-Malik cuts through its length. Its capital is Bardhaʿa, and among its towns are Tiflīs, al-Qalʿa, Khunān, Shamkūr, Janza, Bardīj, al-Shamākhiya, Shirwān, Bākūh, al-Shābarān, Bāb al-Abwāb, al-Abkhān (Abkhāz), Qabala, Shakkī, Malāzkird, Tablā.

Armīniya is an important district. It was set out by Armīnā bin Kanzar bin Yāfath bin Noah. From here come curtains, very fine fringed cloths, and many special items. Its capital is Dabīl, and among its towns are Bidlīs, Khilāt, Arjīsh, Barkarī, Khūy, Salamās, Urmiya, Dākharraqān, Marāgha, Ahr, Marand, Sanjān, Qālīqalā, Qandariya, Qalʿat Yūnus, Nūrīn.

p. 375 Ādharbayjān is a district laid out by Adhrabādh bin Biyūrāsaf bin al-Aswad bin Sām bin Noah—on whom be peace. Its capital, and it is the metropolis of the region, is Ardabīl. A mountain is here which has a dimension of one hundred forty *farsakhs*, all of it villages and farms. It is said that there are seventy languages spoken here. The agricultural products of Ardabīl are many. Most of the houses

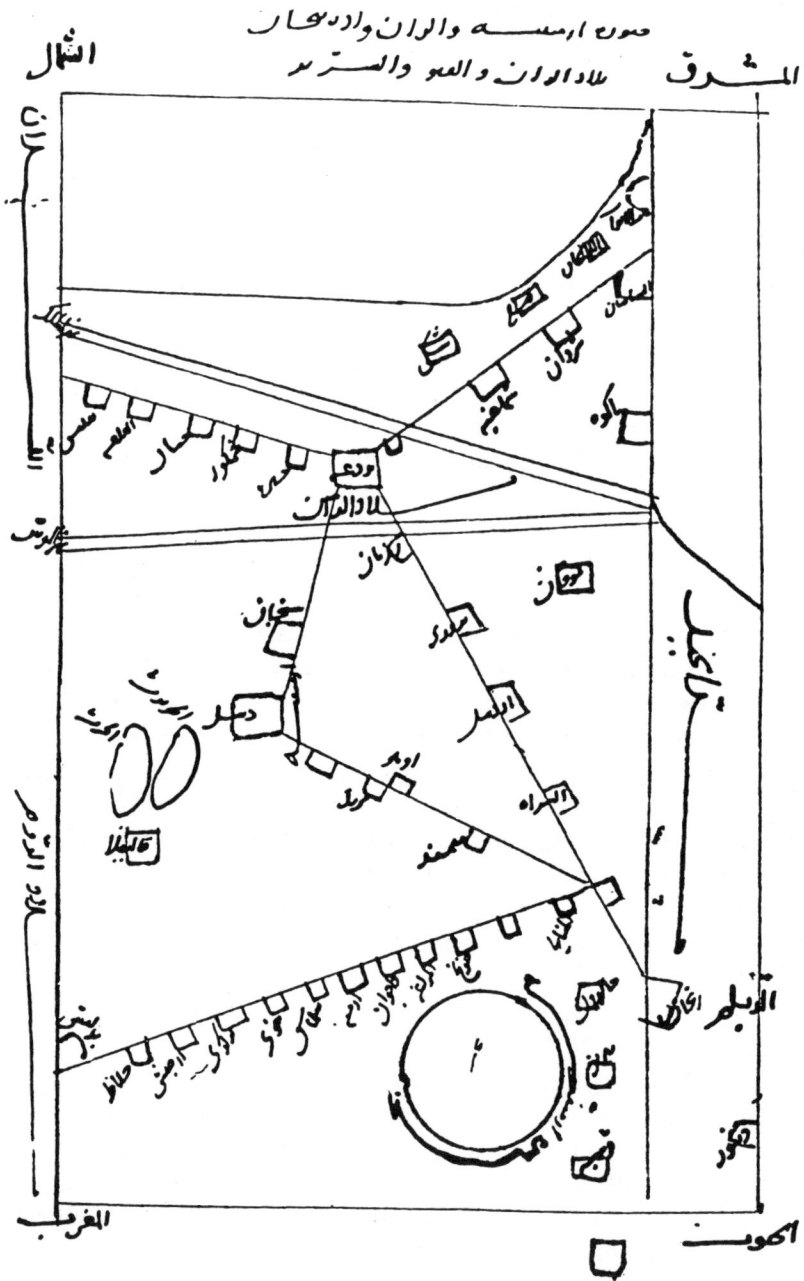

Map XIV: Ādharbayjān (see p. 418).
From MS. Sprenger 5—Ahlwardt 6034 by kind permission of the Staatsbibliothek
Preussischer Kulturbesitz, Berlin, Orientabteilung.

are under the ground. Among its towns are: Rasba, Tabrīz, Jābirwān, Khūnaj, al-Miyānij, al-Sarāt, Barwā, Warthān, Mūqān, Mīmadh, Barzand.

Should someone assert that Bidlīs pertains to the region of Aqūr and conclude that it was among the administrative areas of Banī Hamdān, I should reply that it is as the people of both regions have claimed it to be. We consider it part of this region because we have found a correspondence to the name, and that is "Tiflīs." In any case the administrative districts are not a proof in this matter. Do you not realize that Sayf al-Dawla had Qinnasrīn and al-Raqqa; but no one claimed that al-Raqqa pertained to al-Shām.

Bardhaʿa is the capital, large, quadrangular; on level ground, it has a fortress, and is affluent. Its markets are close together and shaded; the mosque is in the market. It is the Baghdād of this region. The houses are delightful, of burnt brick and plaster, good, handsome; there are fruits aplenty. Some of the pillars of the mosque are of plaster and baked brick, and some are of wood. A river flows through the town, and the River al-Kurr is about two *farsakhs* away. Streams flow fairly close to here. It is a pleasant town; however, its outskirts have been laid waste, its population thinned, and its fortress fallen into ruin.

Addition/version MS. C.
[The mosque] is built on tall pillars covered with gypsum; though some of them are made of wood of variegated grain. The town has a stream that runs by all the main thoroughfares, and flows in four directions. Good things are there aplenty and in superabundance, and a richness of excellent fruits. It is the Baghdād in its entirety of al-Rihāb. The dwellings are splendid, the yards of the houses spacious; low prices are constant, there is no heresy here. The River Kurr flows at a distance of a post stage from the city, which is itself situated between the two streams and the shimmering lake. What a pleasant, clean, and diversified place, were it not for a shortcoming; and if you wish to you may listen. Its outlying areas are in ruins such as Baylaʿa; its population has diminished, and the ruler is voracious. It is out-of-the-way, and unknown far away, and without much significance. Few are their jurisprudents who follow the school of Hanbal; the fortress has fallen into ruin, and the roads have disappeared. This is the description of the market of al-Rān of Bardhaʿa, a description candid and accepted; a gift to an eminent shaykh, and which I have thrown in for the sake of rhyming prose.

Tiflīs is a fortified town close to the mountains. The river al-Kurr flows p. 376 through it, so it consists of two parts with a bridge between. Its walls are built of stone, then timber laid on that.

Al-Qalaʿ (Qalaʿt Ibn Kandamān) is a town without a fort; on level ground not far from the mountain Lakzān.

Al-Shamākhiya: at the base of the mountain; the buildings are of stone and plaster; here are running water, orchards and parks.

Shirwān: a large town on level ground; the buildings are of stone. The mosque stands in the markets; a stream flows through the town.

Mūghkān is at the border. It used to be quite populous, but now its population is light. It is on the main road.

Bākūh: on the lake; one of the ports of the region.

Shābarān: without a fortress; most of the people are Christians from the boundary area.

Qabala: fortified; the river outside the town, the mosque some distance away, on a hill.

Shakkī: on level ground; most of the people Christians; the mosque in the market of the Muslims.

Warthān: on level ground, well developed; its market beyond the river, the mosque separated from it.

Baylaqān: small; its people are faultless. The sweetmeat produced here is famous.

Malāzkird: fortified; a number of mosques; many gardens; the mosque on the edge of the market.

Tablā is under the control of the Muslims; here are five hundred houses. Most of the people here are Christians; an attractive town.

Al-Abkhān (al-Abkhāz): delightful, and similarly the towns of this district. Qaryat Yūnus is the village of al-Dīrānī: Muslims here.

Bāb al-Abwāb (Darband) is on Bahr al-Khazar (the Caspian Sea). It is fortified by the wall which separates it from al-Khazar. It has three gates—Bāb al-Kabīr (the big gate), Bāb al-Saghīr (the small gate), and another towards the sea: this gate is closed and is never opened. There are a number of gates also towards the sea, and pre-dating Islām. The wall has been extended from the mountain, well into the lake, towers on it, wherein are houses of prayer, and sentinels. The mosque is in the middle of the markets, in it a spring of water. The buildings are of stone, the houses attractive. Running water is here.

p. 377   Dabīl is an important town with a fortress, well fortified. It has many products, its name is famous. Its wool is important, its river fluent; gardens surround it, and it has ancient suburbs, a strong fortress. Its markets are cruciform, its fertility amazing. The mosque is on a large hill, beside which is a church which the Kurds control; in it is a fortress. The buildings are of clay and stone. It has a number of gates, among them Bāb Kīdar (Kīrān), Bāb Tiflīs, Bāb Ānī. However, despite its distinction, the majority of the inhabitants are Christian, for its population has declined and its fortress gone to ruin.

Bidlīs: in a deep wādī in which two streams flow, meeting in the town. It has two sides to it: in it a fortress of stone, reddish like the sunset.

Akhlāt (Khilāt) is a town on the level ground; here are delightful gardens; over it a fortress of adobe. The mosque is in the markets; a stream flows through the town.

Salamās, very good; a fortress over it of adobe and stone. A copiously flowing stream is here. The mosque stands on the edge of the market. The Kurds have built a wall around it.

Urmiya: an attractive town; a citadel here; the town is populous. The mosque is in the clothmakers' market. The town has a stronghold, a stream.

Marāgha: splendid; has a fortress and a citadel; suburbs; the forts are of clay.

Marand: fortified; gardens surround it; here are populous suburbs; the mosque is in the markets.

Qandariya: a town which the Kurds established; a delightful mosque here.

Nūrīn is fortified; has a citadel. At the door of the mosque is a spring of water. Gardens are many; agreeable.

Qalaʿt Yūnus: the town of al-Dīrānī; here are Muslims.

Ardabīl is the capital of Ādharbayjān, and the metropolis of the region; a strong fortress stands over it. It is smaller than Dabīl. Its markets are cross shaped, being at the meeting of four roads, and the mosque is at the middle of the cross, on high ground behind the fortress. The suburbs are populous. Most of the buildings are of clay. There are many balconies, much fruit, and filth. Here is p. 378 running water, a standing mercenary army, abundance of agricultural produce, good baths. However they are a miserly, disagreeable populace, with few scholars. The town is horrible, stinking; one of the latrines of the world. They are a people of cunning and stupidity, never considering consequences; neither do they ever make allowances for sects other than their own. Their preacher is not a jurist, their leader not distinguished, their counselor not cultured, their physician not skillful.

Tabrīz—do you realize what Tabrīz is! It is gold, pure gold; powerful alchemy, impregnable town. It is preferred over the City of Peace [Baghdād], and the followers of Islām are proud of it. Streams flow through, the trees sway on its land. Do not ask about the low prices, the abundance of fruits. The mosque is in the middle of the town. There is no limit to its goodness!

Mūghān: a town which two rivers surround. Around it are delightful gardens, it is like Paradise in its spaciousness. With Tabrīz it makes up two parks, with al-Rihāb two glories of Islām. It is situated between Ardabīl and Jīlān; from it to Bardhaʿa is a distance of eight [farsakhs]. It has good worthwhile arable land; two streams flow there. The leading people are like pearls, like coral; they are generous and noble-hearted.

Barzand: small; the market of the Armenians, the port of the district; a good profitable place.

Miyāna: small; on level ground; many products.

Zanjān: at the boundary; it has fallen into ruin. There is a stream here, also the main road.

All the towns of this region are good, agricultural products are plentiful; here are low prices, fruits, meats, blessings and goodness.

A Summary Account of Conditions in this Region

This is a cold region, with much snow and rain, a certain degree of distastefulness, but the people are colder and more distasteful. They have big beards, their speech is not attractive. In Armīniya they speak Armenian, in al-Rān, Rānian; their Persian is understandable, and is close to Khurāsānian in sound.

Their **sects** are harmonious. However, the followers of the Tradition there are p. 379 Hanbalites; the majority in Dabīl are followers of Abū Hanīfa—may God have mercy upon him—and these are to be found in some towns, without being a majority. One day I was at the council of Abū ʿAmr al-Khuwaī listening to the Traditions, and he said, "Let us have a question." There was a companion with me, and we asked a question about a gift of property held in common, and we spoke on the matter for a long time until we wearied of it. Then a middle-aged man began to speak there, and spoke eloquently on the question. When the talking stopped I said: "How able you are! But you have exaggerated." And I pointed out what I disagreed with him on. Said he, "I do not belong to your school." Said I, "How is it your people do not give more attention to what you have alleged, since it is a question that has been quite difficult for us?" Said he, "What I have maintained is from the words of the judge Abū Nasr bin Sahl, the arbitrator of Khurāsān, for many times have I argued it with him." They do not expound scholastic theology nor do they take sides in such matters.

There was in Dabīl a cloister where the residents followed the lore of mysticism with the minimum of spirituality. One day I attended the council of Abū [lacuna in MSS.] from Ardabīl: it was packed with people standing and sitting, asking him questions about social interrelations. Said I, "What do you say—God preserve you!—about a man who had a conscience that guided him; suppose it were lost to him, where should he seek to recover it?" Said he, "Let him return to the original source where he obtained it, and let him have resort to that." Said I, "But circumstances have changed between him and the source." Said he, "Let him ask the original source to obtain it." "But," said I, "he no longer has any standing with the original source so that he could make a request." Said he, "He should knock at the door until it is opened to him, and he should shout in the darkness of the night until mercy is shown him."

The rivers that are well-known here are three: Nahr al-Rass, Nahr al-Malik, and Nahr al-Kurr which has the lightest water of them all. This last emerges from the mountain district at the borders of Janza and Shamkūr close to Tiflīs, then flows through the land of the heathens. Close to it in sweetness and lightness is Nahr al-Rass, which flows extending along the border of al-Rān. It comes out from Armīniya, flowing until it reaches Warthān, then it eventually flows beyond Mūqān, and flows into the [Caspian] sea. Nahr al-Malik comes out from the country of the Romaeans, beyond the district of al-Rān; it eventually flows into the sea. Only the Bahr al-Khazar [Caspian Sea] touches this region. In this p. 380 region are two lakes, one of them in Urmiya, its length about four days' journey, riding; it may be crossed by boat in a day and a night. The other is in Armīniya, and is known as Lake Arjīj [*recte* Arjīsh = Van].

The **commerce** here. Bardhaʿa produces much silk; Bāb al-Abwāb cotton cloth, slaves, saffron, the finest mules; Dabīl cloth and rugs of wool, cushions and the like, very fine surcingles. From Bardhaʿa also curtains; very fine mules are brought there, and in Bardhaʿa, on the first day of the week is a market called al-Kurkī. The people of the district, and of the areas around assemble there. In fact they say there Yawm al-Sabt [Saturday], Yawm al-Kurkī [instead of Yawm al-Ahad = Sunday], Yawm al-Ithnayn [Monday]. Silk and cloth are sold there. Nothing compares with their surcingles, their fringed quilts, their crimson [cloths] and such things, their dyes, the fruit called *al-zūqāl*, the *qasbūya* [fish] and a fish that is called *al-tarrīkh*. Here are figs, sheep, and acorns of the very finest quality.

Among the **remarkable things** of Bāb al-Abwāb is a fortification of the kind we mentioned for Tyre and Acre; it is guarded by a chain built into the rock with mortar and lead. In Tiflīs are baths such as we mentioned for Tabariyya (Tiberias), without heat. Jabal al-Hārith is high over the realm of al-Islām: no one can climb it. It is said to be, with Jabal al-Huwayrith, one of the mountains of al-Tā'if, and that on Nahr al-Rass were a thousand towns which are now underneath both of those mountains. In the mosque of Ardabīl is a large stone, which even if struck with bars of iron is not affected. It fell from the sky some distance from the town, and was then brought to the mosque. I heard Zarīf the eunuch say while we were traveling near Ardabīl, that lo! something was coming down from the sky like a huge shield, and it fell to the ground. There was a stone in it, and it could possibly be this; it is like the burnisher used by the dyers, with two thin edges. A post stage from Mūqān is a large fort called al-Hasra, above

p. 381 it houses and castles in which is much gold, pictures of birds and wild beasts. A number of rulers have tried to control it, but they were unable to get up to it. Three *farsakhs* from Dabīl is a white monastery of stone carved out like a capuche; inside is a picture of Maryam (Mary) on eight pillars between which are doors; by whichever door you enter you see the picture of Maryam. Nearby is a black rock the sweat of which is an oil wherewith people seek to be cured. Nearby is found the *qirmiz*, an insect that appears in the ground. The women come out and dig it up with a piece of copper they carry with them, and bake it in the oven. In the rural districts of Ardabīl the people plough with eight oxen and four drivers, one driver to each pair of oxen. I asked them if this is because of the hardness of the ground. They said no, but that it is because of the ice.

The *mann* of Ardabīl is one thousand two hundred; the *ratl* of Khūy is three hundred and their *mann* is six hundred, similarly in Urmiya; the *ratl* elsewhere is that of Baghdād. The *qafīz* of Marāgha and the *mudd* there is ten *manns*; the *kaylaja* is a sixth of a *qafīz*.

In Tabrīz it is among the customs of those in power to wear gold rings. In Lake Urmiya are mountains which are inhabited; the people there tie the legs of the youngsters with chains and ropes so that they do not roll down into the lake.

At Urmiya is a pass (ʿAqaba) on the road to Mosul; people have to go through on the necks of men even as animals are ridden, because of its difficulty.

The **distances** in this region:
From Bardhaʿa to Yūnān, or to Bardīj, or to Janza, or to Qalqātūs, one stage in every instance.

From Yūnān to al-Baylaqān, one stage;
    thence to Warthān, one stage;
    thence to Talakhāb, one stage;
    thence to Barzand, one stage;
    thence to Ardabīl, two stages.

From Bardīj to al-Shamākhiya, two stages;
    thence to Shirwān, three stages;
    thence to al-Abkhān (al-Abkhāz), two stages;
    thence to Jisr Samūr, two stages;
    thence to Bāb al-Abwāb, three stages.

p. 382 From Janza to Shamkūr, one stage;
    thence to Khunān, three stages;
    thence to Qalaʿt Ibn Kandamān, one stage;
    thence to Tiflīs, two stages.

From Qalqātūs to Matrīs, two stages;
    thence to Dumīs, two stages;
    thence to Kīlakūnī (Kaylakuwayn), two stages;
    thence you will be among the Armenians as far as Dabīl.

From Dabīl to Nashawā, four stages;
    thence to Khūy, three days journey;
    thence to Salamās, two stages;
    thence to Urmiya, one stage;
    thence to Kharraqān, two stages;
    thence to Marāgha, a like distance;
    thence to Ardabīl, four *farsakhs*.

From Marāgha to Qandariya, two stages;
    thence to a village, three stages;
    thence to Qalaʿt al-Hasan bin ʿAlī, one stage;
    thence to Shahrazūr, three *farsakhs*.

From Marāgha to Nūrīn, one stage
    thence to Marand....
    [lacuna in MS]

From Khūy to Qalaᶜt Yūnus, six stages;
    thence to Qaryat al-ᶜAsabiyyāt, one stage;
    thence to....
    [lacuna in MS]
    thence to Tiflīs, one stage;
    thence to Tablā, thence to Shakkī, thence to Lakzān, two stages in every instance;
    thence to al-Bāb [Bāb al-Abwāb], two stages.

From Marāgha to al-Kharraqān, two stages;
    thence to Tibrīz, one stage;
    thence to Marand, one stage.

From Ardabīl to al-Nīr (al-Bīr), one stage;
    thence to Sarāt, one stage;
    thence to Kūlsarah (Kūrsarah), one stage;
    thence to Marāgha, a like distance.

From Marāgha to Khurah Rūdh, one stage;
    thence to Mūsā Abādh, one stage;
    thence to Barza, two post stages;
    thence to Tiflīs, one post stage;
p. 383   thence to Jābirwān, one stage;
    thence to Narīz, two post stages;
    thence to Urmiya, one stage.

From Marand to al-Nashawā, two difficult stages;
    thence to Dabīl, two similar stages.

From Marāgha to Sāburkhāst, one stage;
    thence to Barza, one stage;
    thence to al-Baylaqān, one stage;
    thence to Sīsar, one stage;
    thence to Tall Wān, one stage;
    thence to al-Khabārjān (al-Jārabā(?)), one stage;
    thence to al-Dīnawar, one stage.

From Ardabīl to al-Miyānij, two stages;
    or to Qantarat Sabīdhrūdh, and from al-Qantara to al-Sarāt, one stage;

thence to Nawy, one stage;
thence to Zanjān, one stage.

From al-Miyānij to Khūnaj, one stage;
thence to Kūlsra, one stage;
thence to Marāgha, one stage;
and from Marāgha to Kharraqān, or to Urmiya, two stages in each instance;
thence to Salamās, a like distance;
thence to Khūy, one stage;
thence to Barkarī, five stages;
thence to Arjīsh, two stages;
thence to Akhlāt, or to Badlīs, three stages in each instance;
p. 384   and from Badlīs to Āmid, or to Mayyāfāriqīn, four stages in each instance.

From Marāgha to al-Dīnawar, sixty *farsakhs*;
and from Ardabīl to Tabrīz. ...[lacuna in MS]
thence to Barqūā.... [lacuna in MS]
thence to Malāzkird, three days travel;
thence to Arzan, six; thence to Āmid, four.

The Region of Al-Jibāl
("The Mountains": wide mountain area
WNW Īrān—ENE ʿIrāq)

The grass of this region is the saffron; the drink of its people, honey and milk.
Its trees, the walnut and the fig. It is a delightful recreation ground, fertile and
important. Here is glorious al-Rayy and Hamadhān, and the precious district of
Isbahān. Its superiority will appear to you when we describe its cities. We have
mentioned al-Dīnawar the elegant, imperial Karmān Shāhān; we have described
Nihāwand, and Qumm, and Qāshān. And we have described Dummāwand, and
Qarj, and Qasrān. No heat is here, no fleas, no flies; no snakes, no scorpions, no
worms. In summer it is a Paradise, a garden, an orchard; in winter there is wood
and charcoal free of charge. Its dried meat is carried to Khurāsān; its grapes
and apples last for a year; here is knowledge abundant, intelligence, skill and
proficiency. Even so, the cold is severe; you see their cheeks cracked in the winter.
Their arms and legs are always swarthy, their faces tawny, their noses running.
They are either extreme Hanbalites, exaggerated in their love of Muʿāwiya, or they
are fanatic Najjārites; the people who believe in the return of al-Hādī they call
heathens. And how often you witness the ground subside, and earthquakes! There
is injustice of authority, and disorder; constant going and coming. Anyone who
enters it to settle from above it or below it, you see him because of the cold and
the climate always kept busy. Understand what I say, then you will reason it. Look
out over al-ʿIrāq from the boundary of al-Saymara, for here are the mountains
that have been described and illustrated. On Isfahān I have a brilliant treatise, and
a jurist if he studies it will recognize it. So let me eliminate controversy and debate!

Addition/version MS. C.
... and on Khūzistān from the direction of al-Qantara (Qantara Anda) and here
are the mountains [al-Jibāl] that have been described and portrayed; here are the
events that have been celebrated and recorded, which Muhammad [ibn al-Hasan
al-Shaybānī] has set forth in his elegantly-written books. On Isfahān I have a
definitive treatise, explanatory, clear, and brilliant: a master of jurisprudence,
should he study it, will approve of it. So let me eliminate altercation and dispute
in matters of jurisprudence, analogy, and controversy.

Here is the map of it. [Map XV]

p. 385 We have made this region three districts and seven sections. We have
included Isfahān in the number, and have attached it to the edge of the map. We
have given a separate description of it and enlarged the features there, and the
excellent qualities we have mentioned.

The first district as you come from the direction of al-Rihāb is al-Rayy;
then Hamadhān, then Isfahān, then the sections of Qumm, Qāshān, al-Saymara,
Karaj, Māh al-Kūfa (Dīnawar), Māh al-Basra (Nihāwand), Shahrazūr.

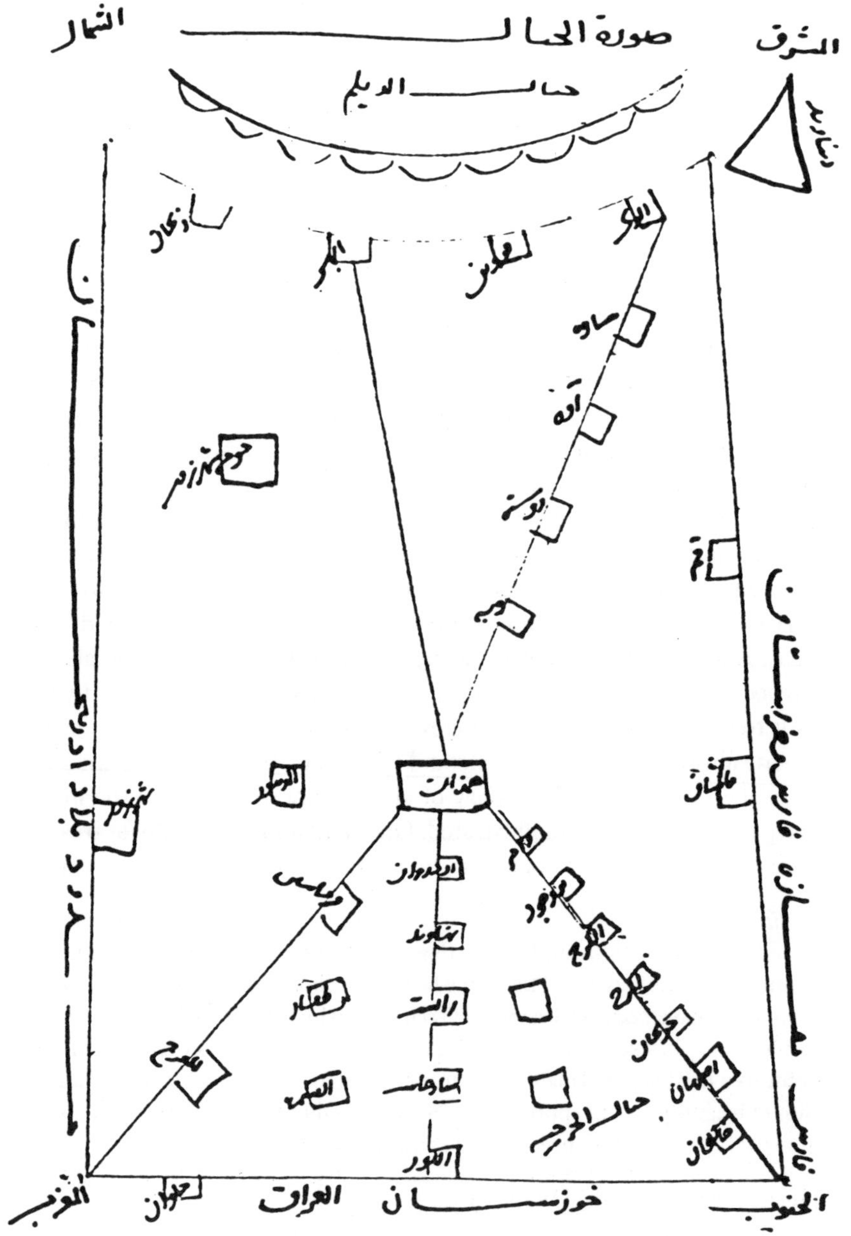

Map XV: Jibāl Al-Daylam (see p. 419).
From MS. Sprenger 5—Ahlwardt 6034 by kind permission of the Staatsbibliothek
Preussischer Kulturbesitz, Berlin, Orientabteilung.

Al-Rayy is a delightful district, with abundant water, splendid villages, fine fruits, extensive area, important rural districts. It was al-Rayy that ruined ʿUmar bin Saʿad, the troublemaker, so that he murdered Husayn, the son of ʿAlī; yet he selected the city despite damnation, so that one says that God humiliated him:

Must I leave the sovereignty of al-Rayy,
    and al-Rayy is my desire;
or must I return, censured
    in the killing of Husayn.
In killing him is the fire from which there is no escape;
    for the sovereignty of al-Rayy is the apple of my eye.

According to the annals, al-Rayy was a source of calamities and accordingly became damned: it is on a raging sea, its earth is damned, it refuses to accept the Truth. Hārūn al-Rashīd said, "The world is four abodes: Damascus, al-Raqqa, al-Rayy, and Samarqand." Rawā bin Baylān bin Isfahān mapped al-Rayy. It is also related that al-Rayy is one of the gates of the earth, and all mankind is drawn towards it. Said al-Asmaʿī: "Al-Rayy is the bride of the world, the road of the p. 386 earth." The climate is good, it is medial to Khurāsān, Jurjān, and al-ʿIrāq. For its capital I know no other name [than it]; among its towns are: Āwa, Sāwa, Qazwīn, Abhar, Shalanba, al-Khwār. Among the sections are: Qumm, Dummāwand, Sharazūr. Among the rural districts are: Qūsīn, Qasrān al-Dākhil, Qasrān al-Khārij, Surr, Bihzān, Qarj, Janā, Sīrā, Fīrūzarām.

Hamadhān is a district situated in the centre of the region. It has important towns, is of ancient record. Hamadhān bin al-Fallūj bin Sām bin Noah—peace be upon him—laid it out. It has been said that al-Jibāl is an army and Hamadhān its commander in chief. It has the sweetest water; its tracts are extensive, its rivers full, its trees intertwined, fruits are sweet, fighting is common; its rural district really filled me with astonishment. I read in some book that al-Rayy and Isfahān were not of the territory of the Bahlawiyyīn but only Hamadhān, Māsabadhān; and Mihrijānqudhaq, which is al-Saymara; and Māh al-Basra, which is Nihāwand; and Māh al-Kūfa, which is al-Dīnawar. Among the towns of Hamadhān are: Asadāwādh, Āwa, Būstah, Rāman, Wabh, Sīrāwand, Rūdhrāwar, Tazar; and sections: Māh al-Kūfa, Māh al-Basra, Māsabadhān.

The attribution of Isfahān, and places such as it, has an analogy in questions of the Sharīʿa in this way: it is to the water left after drinking by the mule and the ass, according to the schools of our shaykhs, the people of al-ʿIrāq, and they say that since both animals have a similarity from two different causes, and vary from two different points of view, one should be cautious in each instance, and each cause given its due weight. Do you not see that they both resemble the cat in that they live in houses: thus one is exempt from avoiding [as ritually impure] the water they leave after drinking. They also resemble the dog, in that the flesh of p. 387 both is forbidden; accordingly you have to consider the decision from each point of view. So it is in the case of Isfahān: since it resembles this region in language and customs, but is included within the borders of Fārs, so that the frontier rests right within the city, it is thus necessary that we attribute to it something from either side, giving it a distinctive position, a separate consideration. From this region its attribution is that it is mentioned and described as pertaining to it; that from Fārs is its layout and pattern. But suppose the following is adduced: "Why don't you make the question of Isfahān similar to that of the ears, as dealt with in the opinion of al-Shāfiʿī, when the dispute arose as to whether they are part of the head or part of the face? He made a third category for them, stipulated fresh water [for washing them], and a separate [ritual] cleaning of them. This is the position in which Isfahān is put when it is said to be partly of the region of Fārs, and partly of al-Jibāl, but must be distinguished from both of them, described by itself, and placed as a buffer between the two." The answer here is that this analogy is false, since you did not provide a common basis for the two analogues; for anyone who draws an analogy from a part of the whole, without having a common basis draws a false analogy. But suppose it is alleged that the common basis between them is that there is some specific factor in each side that pulls the city back and forth [between the two regions] in a decisive way; the answer to that is that the Prophet—God's peace and blessings be upon him—said: "The two ears pertain to the head," and so he relieved us of any doubt and misconception. For how could we make the matter fundamental in argument if we were in doubt about it! If it should be said that his saying that they pertain to the head means they are in the head, the answer is that the Messenger of God—God's peace and blessings be upon him—is exempt from saying anything idle, everyone knowing that they are in the head. All he wanted was to render a decision on the point in dispute, rather than making a statement on the location [of the ears]; for do you not realize that one does not allege that they are in the neck or in the shoulder. Moreover, even if this basic point were true, the analogy of Isfahān would not apply to it, for that would contradict the basic cause, giving rise, as it would, to fourteen regions and one *kūra* (district), the *kūra* standing without precedent. It is just as we have pointed out in the matter of the *witr*, where it is not permissible to fulfil this obligation with one unit of prayer alone, there being no precedent for this in the basic principles. If it should be asked, what this precedent is for the fourteen regions you have postulated, and among which you have distributed the realm of Islām, the answer is that the precedent is the setting up by the astrologers of the entire world into fourteen regions, seven inhabited, seven empty. Now if they had differentiated from them a portion, had distinguished a section from them, then the analogy with Isfahān would be correct. Suppose it were to be argued: "Why did you not make the case similar to that of the two ears, which are most certainly part of the head, thus saying that Isfahān is p. 388 definitely part of Fārs?" The answer here is that what is commonly accepted knowledge is basic, in our belief, and takes precedence over analogy even as we have said before; and it is commonly accepted that the city is in the region of al-Jibāl. Should some one say, "Well then, consider it part of al-Jibāl," the answer is that the demarcation and nomenclature [of places] by rulers, and their establishing of them, is also fundamental with us, and in our science. And the rulers are, in this matter, just as the Companions of the Prophet are in the matter of the Sharīʿa; then just as it is not for the jurisprudents to be at variance with the Companions in any matter on which they expressed an opinion, so it is not for us to contradict the rulers in what they have prescribed. Now, they have included Isfahān in the official records of Fārs, and have set the frontiers in it, but also in al-Rūdhān; thus these two have also become two fundamental considerations pulling Isfahān back and forth [from one region to the other] for this reason. Nor have we seen any reason why we should not bring it into relation with the aforementioned analogy.

> MS. B contains a reader's observation on al-Muqaddasī's discourse on Isfahān, as follows:
> The author did not hit upon anything in the depiction of Isfahān for the purpose of writing about it, and accordingly composed the questions and answers so that his book would not be deficient to the extent of saying at least something in respect of places such as that. May God shame him in as much as he has wasted our time in the reading of his irrelevancies that avail us nothing.

Addition/version MS. C.
One of the inhabitants of Isfahān had compiled an important book about the place, in which he mentioned its towns and villages, its revenue and its rulers: this work is to be found in Naysābūr, and in the library of ʿAdhud al-Dawla. Its capital is al-Yahūdiyya, and of its towns are al-Madīna, al-Bandajān, Sumayram, al-Zīz, al-Diz, Ardistān, Khūlajan.

Al-Yahūdiyya is the capital of Isfahān; it is large, developed, and populous; many agricultural products, a city of commerce. The wells are sweet, fruits delicious, climate excellent, water light, soil remarkable. It is a beautiful spot; wealthy merchants are here, skilled artisans. Cloth is exported to faraway places. The people are Sunnī Muslims, skilled and intelligent. Their mosque is always filled with congregations. No heat is here, no fleas, no vermin. It is said that when Bukht Nasar (Nebuchadnezzar) moved the children of Israel out from the Holy Land, they looked around the places of the earth, and saw no place except this that resembled their own land, so they settled there. However, it is a Paradise grazed by cattle; the people are barbarous in speech, no generosity, no kindness—under their turbans are pillows! In their business dealings is deceit; and they dry out their lungs in Hanbalite fanaticism. One of them may be seen in his clothes and sandals, and in his sleeve a loaf he is gnawing, or raisins he is nibbling.

It resembles Damascus. The buildings here are of clay—and what clay! Clay, I have never seen the like of it! Some of the markets are covered and some are p. 389 open. The mosque is in the markets. It is handsome, on rounded pillars, with a minaret on the side towards its *Qibla*, a height of seventy cubits, and entirely of clay, absolutely nothing else. The river flows through the town, but the people do not drink from it, for it has become polluted from the sewage dropped into it. The town has twelve gates.

Addition / version MS. C.

Al-Yahūdiyya is the capital of Isfahān, a populous town of many good things and glories. I have heard that the children of Israel, when Bukht Nasar [Nebuchadnezzar] moved them out from Jerusalem, traveled over the earth and did not find a place with a climate like that of Jerusalem and its excellence, other than this; accordingly, a considerable number of them settled there. For myself, I have not seen a mosque other than the mosque of Misr more crowded with congregations than their mosque, nor in the region a town more populous than their town, nor in the entire realm of al-Islām a soil the like of theirs. They are a people of the Sunna and Congregation, of refinement and eloquence. How many readers of the *Qurʾān*, litterateurs, jurisprudents, and intelligent people it has produced! There is fruit always available here, and prosperity everywhere in evidence. I used to buy the most excellent grapes there at the time of Nayrūz (New Year's Day) at a *dānaq* for one *mann* [a weight] of theirs, similarly for the most excellent apples. It is situated between Fārs, Khūzistān, al-Rayy, and Hamadhān; and the caravans are continually going to it from al-Basra and Khurāsān. It is a Paradise except for the grazing of swine there; the speech of the people is barbarous, their food dirty, their stream polluted. One of them may be seen in his attire and slippers and turban, in his pouch or sleeve a loaf he is gnawing, or raisins he is nibbling. They destroy business relationships. They dry out their lungs in their exaggerated fanaticism for Muʿāwiya.

The city is larger than Hamadhān, more developed than al-Rayy; it is situated on low ground some distance from the mountains. The mosque stands in the midst of the markets; the stream cuts through the town, but is polluted from the amount of filth tossed into it. The drinking water of the inhabitants is from sweet wells. The town has twelve gates. Most of their marketplaces are shaded, and not at all attractive.

Al-Madīna: is about two miles from al-Yahūdiyya; on high ground, with fortress, below it a large bridge; here is a mosque old and strong.

Al-Khālanjān: in the direction of Khūzistān; it is large, populous, producing much fruit.

Sumayram: at the foot of a mountain; an abundance of walnuts and fruits; here stands an exquisite modern mosque some distance from the markets; here is flowing water in the market and in the streets, coming down to them from a spring in the mountain on the way toward al-Yahūdiyya. A celebrated fortress is there with a spring of water; and the coffers of the kings are still in this fortress.

p. 390   Al-Zīz is a small town in the mountains, on the River Tāb. I bought bread there, eight *manns*, of their *mann*, for a *dirham*. Meat and walnuts and the other fruits there are cheap. A delightful mosque was built there in the year 367/977.

Addition / version MS. C.

The mosque here was built in the year three hundred sixty-eight [978 CE], while I was there. The town is situated in the mountains, on the river Tāb; the inhabitants have spring wells, also.

Ardistān: bigger than these towns, in the direction of the desert; the markets excellent; the town populous; a mosque; elders and jurists here. It is a town of the whiteness of flour, and from this it derives its name.

Qāshān is on the edge of the desert. Its name is famous and it is of ancient establishment. Around it are fine farms, and a number of canals. The people are skilled in the making of the long narrow-necked bottles. I saw tarragon there like myrtle, smooth; I have not seen its like. This town is one of the sources of excellent plums, and here are remarkable scorpions. I heard that when Abū Mūsā al-Ashʿarī failed to conquer the town, he brought thither some scorpions of Nasībīn that they had trapped in jars. He threw them inside the fortress, where they kept them busy and irritated them; so they surrendered the town.

Isfahān is an important district, and Qumm and Karaj pertained to it: however, one of the khalifs added them to al-Rayy and Hamadhān. The administrative offices of this district are still separate; mention of it has precedence because of its importance with the kings and the rulers.

Al-Rayy is an important town, delightful, distinguished; many glories and much fruit; the markets are spacious, the hostels attractive, the baths good, foods aplenty, little to hurt one, abundance of water, flourishing commerce. Learned people are the leaders, the public is intelligent, the women are good housekeepers; the stores are splendid. The weather is pleasing; it is an elegant, clean place. The people have beauty, intelligence, honour, refinement. Here are councils and schools; natural talents, handicrafts; granaries. There is generosity, and special attributes. The preacher is not wanting in jurisprudence, nor the leader in knowledge; the magistrate does not lack good repute nor the orator decorum. It is one of the glories of Islam, one of the chief cities of the countries. Here are elders, nobles, readers, Imāms, ascetics, conquerors, high purpose. Here is ice and snow aplenty. The barley beer is famous, the cloth renowned, the preachers are expert. The rural districts are important. Here is a library of remarkable books; the amazing "courtyard of the water melon;" delightful al-Rūdha. Here is a castle, and an inner city. The hostels are good, full of furnishings, pleasant, splendid.

One day we went to visit Abu al-ʿAbbās al-Yazdādī—Nāsir al-Dawla had given him a good place to live in Naysābūr—and said he: "I did not know that Naysābūr was as good as this; is al-Rayy similar to it?" Then everyone who was with him spoke. Said I, "God uphold the shaykh! Naysābūr is bigger, more populous, more prosperous; al-Rayy is more pleasant, more delightful, its water more abundant." In fact al-Rayy is beyond what we have described; however, its water causes diarrhea, its melons kill, its scholar is in error. Most of the animals they sacrifice are cows. There is little firewood, much discord. Their meats are

p. 391

hard, their hearts are hard, their congregation disagreeable. The Imāms at the mosque are at variance, one day for the Hanafites, one day for the Shāfi'ites. One of the poets has said:

> In al-Rayy the *dirham* has the value of a *dānaq*,
> the bread in its expensiveness has the eminence of the Creator;
> the meats hang as high there as the mountains.
> How many brigands and thieves are there!
> They steal everything from trifles to carnelians;
> there is no one you can safely be friendly with.
> He will swear by the Mount and by the Sun
> that he is in the right, but the reverse is true;
> but if he favours you especially, then he is a prime profligate.

It is a large town, about a *farsakh* each way; however, its outskirts have been destroyed. The mosque is on the edge of the inner city, beside the fortress, not behind it. The inner city is populous; the fortress is in ruins. The outer city is populous, without markets, the markets and the developments being in the suburbs. Streams flow through the town, and canals. The library is below al-Rūdha in a caravanserai; the water melon building is beside the mosque.

p. 392   Qazwīn: a large town with many vineyards; an inner city, a fortress in the suburbs. The drinking water is from wells, rain, and a stream. It is the frontier of the district, and one of the mines of jurisprudence and philosophy.

Hamadhān, the metropolis of the region, is a large, pleasant old town. The water is cold, many springs here; a beautiful mosque, and an old building. The people are given to flattery, loving the stranger. Gardens surround the town, and waters bubble up from it. It is good in summer, mild in winter. The mosque is in the market, and well-built; and their markets are in three rows. The inner city, in the centre, is in ruins, and the suburbs encircle it round about. Hamadhān is an attractive town; the bread there is cheap, the confectionery excellent, an abundance of meats. It has [other] special amenities, including a park. However, its cold is well-known, and the jealousy of the inhabitants is proverbial, their slyness disreputable, their exaggeration notorious. Here is thunder and lightning, snow and sleet. Said the poet:

> The fire in Hamadhān, its heat feels cold,
> and the cold in Hamadhān is a chronic malady.

p. 393
> Poverty is concealed in other towns,
> but the poverty in Hamadhān is not hidden.
> Said Kisrā, when he observed their problems,
> "There is Hamadhān; turn away from it, for that is Hell."

Today it has not so many buildings—al-Rayy is better, more populous, more developed than it; for its people have migrated, few are the scholars in it, while al-Rayy has taken away its prosperity. It is close to the mountain; their buildings are of clay. I read in a book that it was two post stages in both dimensions but that Bukht Nasar [Nebuchadnezzar] on his return from the conquest of Jerusalem, wanted to conquer it, but his general failed. So he wrote to him, "Map it for me;" and when he saw the map of it he gathered his sages and consulted them in the matter. Said they, "Block off their springs for a year, then release the water, and the city will drown." When the water did flow over the city it destroyed most of it, so he took possession of it; and to this day there are refuges and hiding places to be found there. The inner city is on an eminence.

Asadāwādh is a small town but well built; the market is busy; many agricultural products here, and honey. About a *farsakh* away is Īwān Kisrā [the Arch of Kisrā]; al-ʿAqaba is between it and Hamadhān. In this town there is running water; the mosque is in an alley, delightful and well attended.

Tazar: some distance from the main road; a palace of Kisrā here. Prices are low, especially for bread; the markets are covered.

Al-Rūdha and Būstah are sources of almonds; a *mann* of kernels for four *dānaqs*. A large stream here; situated among the mountains.

Qarmāsīn [(Kirmān Shāh(ān)] is a pleasant place, surrounded by gardens. The mosque is in the markets; a fine one. ʿAdhud al-Dawla built a beautiful residence there. The town is on the main road; its springs are famous.

Qasr al-Lusūs (Robbers' Castle) is a small town; a stone castle, upon pillars, is here. There have been some remarkable exploits here.

Nihāwand—that is Māh al-Basra—a large town with streams, good fruits; two mosques; saffron farms. The town is in two parts. The mosque, which is in the middle of the town, has no equal in building or beauty in the region.

A town near it is Rūdhrāwar, with saffron farms.

p. 394 Sīrāwand: a town at the foot of a mountain; the drinking water is from springs; many gardens and fruits.

Al-Dīnawar—is Māh al-Kūfa—is a fine town, well-built; elegant people. The markets are close together. The water is cold, and you will see no cleaner; for on the edges of the springs they have built drinking tubes of different kinds through which the water comes out—

Addition/version MS. C.
... siphon tubes through which the water is drawn out, similar to that called *muzammala* [insulated household vessel of cold water, perforated so persons may drink from it through straws] in al-ʿIrāq;

the town bubbles with springs. Gardens surround it; the mosque is some distance from the markets. Over the pulpit is a beautiful dome, and there is a *maqsūra* than which I have never seen finer, raised above the floor of the mosque.

Al-Saymara—it is Māsabadhān—is a large developed town, plenty of agricultural produce, a rural district beside it. It is among the mountains; quite an extensive province, on a difficult road.

Karaj Abī Dulaf is a town built on a height; the houses are not continuous; it has one mosque. The waters here are just as we said for al-Dīnawar; here too is another Karaj.

Addition/version MS. C.
It produces a great variety of fruits, palm trees, nuts. The buildings here are of plaster and stone, and streams flow among them. It is a good, pleasant place, but somewhat small; the town of al-Sīrawān here has cultivated fields and date palms. As for Karaj, the settlement is sparse, and it has one mosque. The waters here are just as we mentioned for al-Dīnawar, and it is ascribed to Abū Dulaf. Burj, lesser than it, is on the main road; behind it is an extensive district whither the route is difficult.

A Summary Account of Conditions in this Region

This is a cold region, with much snow and ice. It is light on the heart, for there is grace and elegance in the people, if you separate Isfahān from it. Jews are more prevalent than Christians here, with many Magians. Jurists and preachers here have respect and standing; and the area is famous for its agricultural products.

Addition/version MS. C.
Here there is no continuous hot weather, and no date palms, except at al-Saymara and at al-Sīrwān. In fact in of the regions of the realm of al-Islām the date palm is to be found, except for al-Rihāb; it does not occur, either, in the territories of the Romaeans. Abū ʿAbd Allāh Muhammad bin Ahmad al-Dabbās related to me the following tradition in Arrajān. He said that al-Qādhī al-Hasan bin ʿAbd al-Rahmān told him that he had it from ʿUqba bin Muhammad al-Basrī, who had it from Ahmad bin Abū ʿAbd Allāh al-Islamī, who had it from Abū Qutayba Muslim bin Qutayba al-Bāhalī, on the authority of Yūsuf, on the authority of al-Hārith al-Tāʾifī. Said he: I heard ʿĀmir al-Shaʿbī say that Qaysar wrote to ʿUmar bin al-Khattāb: "From Qaysar [Caesar], King of the Romaeans to ʿUmar bin al-Khattāb, greetings! My emissaries have informed me that you have a desiccated tree that does not have the ordinary characteristics of a tree, and which puts forth ears like those of an ass. It then bursts into the form of pearls, which then turn green like unto green emeralds, then redden so as to resemble the ruby. The parts then become succulent as food like *falūdhaj* [a sweet made of flour and honey]. It then dried so that it becomes a means of sustenance for a person who is settled, and a means of provision for a person traveling. Now if my emissaries have informed me correctly, this is surely one of the trees of paradise." So ʿUmar—may God be pleased with him—wrote in reply: "From ʿUmar to Qaysar, greetings! Indeed, your emissaries have informed you correctly, and it is the very tree that God—mighty and exalted be He—planted for Maryam [Mary] on the occasion she was in childbed with Jesus, so fear God, and do not ascribe divinity to Jesus unless it be from God."

p. 395   Various sects are here. In al-Rayy most are Hanafites, being Najjārites; except that in the rural districts of the metropolis they are Zaʿfarānites, believing in a created *Qurʾān.* I have heard one of the preachers of the ruler say: "The people of the countryside are my congregation in all matters, except in the matter of the creation of the *Qurʾān.*" I saw that Abū ʿAbd Allāh bin al-Zaʿfarānī had renounced the school of his fathers for the school of al-Najjār, and the people of the rural districts cleared him of any wrongdoing. In al-Rayy are many Hanbalites, and they are much in evidence, and the populace follows the jurists in the matter of the creation of the *Qurʾān.* The people of Qumm are extreme Shīʿa; they have given up assemblies and neglected the mosque; so that Rukn al-Dawla compelled them to take care of it and its needs.

The people of Hamadhān and its districts are followers of the Tradition, except in al-Dīnawar, where privately, and publicly, and openly they belong to the school of Sufyān al-Thawrī. In the mosque the *iqāma* is said twice: the people of Isfahān followed this manner in olden times.

They choose the system of reading of Abū ʿUbayd and Abū Hātim, the chanting of Abū ʿAmr and Ibn Kathīr.

Their **commerce** is flourishing. In al-Rayy they produce garments, and *munayyar* cloth, and cotton; large bowls, large needles, and combs. From Qazwīn, garments, leather sacks, arrows; from Qumm, chairs, bridles, saddles, cloth, and much saffron; from Hamadhān and its sections, cloth, saffron, tin, [or, alloy of silver and lead], fox skins, sable skins, boots, cheeses; from Surr fine *taylasāns*, handsome clothes.

p. 396

Among their **specialties**: the water melons and the plums of al-Rayy; the cloaks of Isfahān, its padlocks, salted meat and dairy products; the long-necked bottles of Qāshān, and its vegetables; the cheese of al-Dīnawar, the mint of Qazwīn, and its arrows.

There are **partisanships** in the matter of the creation of the *Qurʾān* in al-Rayy; and in Qazwīn also, between the Hanafites and the Shāfiʿites. In Hamadhān they do not follow any schools.

As for their **waters**: the wells of Isfahān are bad; the water of al-Rayy causes diarrhea. Anyone who drinks of the Qazwīn River, if he is a stranger, his toes fall off from both feet. The water of the Zanda Rūdh is healthy, the climate there remarkable. The fruits of al-Rayy are bad.

There are **remarkable things** here. Near Bīsutūn is a remarkable representation they assert is the steed of Kisrā. The river of Isfahān has a remarkable debouchment that only a bird can get near. In the rural district of Ruwaydasht are sands like mountains; the wind does not affect them nor do they bother the people. In the section of Qāshān is a fortress with a ditch around it, and around that the sand; the wind blows around there, but not a particle of the sand blows into

the ditch; and if sand is thrown into it, the wind blows immediately and takes it out. In the middle of the sands is a steppe about a *farsakh* in each direction, and the farms there are just as we have mentioned about the ditch. When lions encounter livestock in that steppe they do not even venture to harm them. In the sections of Qāshān is a mountain that exudes an exudation like sweat, but it is
p. 397   not, however, fluent; when the month of the day of Tīr [13th day of 4th month of Persian solar year] arrives, every year people flock there with receptacles, and the holder of the receptacle beats it with a stone, saying, "Water us with thy water, because of so-and-so," and each one of them collects enough for the occasion. In the sections of Qāshān are plants which are spread on the surface of the ground; they become glass, are white and shining, and are used in medicine. In the sections of Isfahān is a meadow in which are snakes between one and five cubits. In the rural districts of Quhistān are snakes with which youngsters play without their biting them. In the rural districts of al-Zārjānān is a village called Mātha; here is a small creature, in appearance like a dung beetle; it moves in the dark night, glows like a lamp; and you may observe that the place of the glow, by daylight, is green. In this section is a rock like granulated sugar, and if you strike one against another fire comes out. In Qāshān is water, which, after irrigating seeds, then turns to stone. In Quhistān is water, should anyone drink of it, and the leeches should stick in his throat, he will die right away. Here also is a cave from which water trickles, then turns to stone. A tree here grows very large, the leaves looking like spoons and fingers. In the rural district of al-Ghāmdān is a spring from which a fish emerges in the days of spring; then a black snake comes out of it, and when the two have come out, the water oozes away for a year. At the entrance of the mosque of al-Yahūdiyya is a tree said to resemble [wood from] al-Wāqwāq [Madagascar]. There are mines in the rural district of Quhistān, and in al-Taymara al-Sughrā and al-Taymara al-Kubrā, mines of silver and gold. In Quhistān is a source of bitumen; in Sāghand, excellent vitriol, somewhat like the Egyptian variety. The mountain of antimony [used in making kohl] is in the district of Isfahān.

The **mann** varies in size. The *mann* of al-Rayy is six hundred [grains], and their *ratl* is three hundred; the *mann* of the rest of the region is four hundred. Meat in al-Rayy is weighed by the *ratl*, pharmaceuticals are weighed by the *mann* of
p. 398   Khurāsān. The *mann* of the districts of Isfahān is three hundred, and the *mann* of al-Yahūdiyya is that used in Hamadhān.

The **measures** vary. The *jarīb* is twenty *qafiz* and six *akuff* (sg., *kaff*); the *jarīb* of Ardistān is seventeen *manns*; the *jarīb* of al-Yahūdiyya is thirteen of those used in Ardistān. The *counterpoise weights* used are those of Khurāsān; the weight used in al-Rayy increases in every hundred a *dirham* and a quarter. The weight of Tabaristān is heavier.

The people of al-Rayy alter their names. They say for *ʿAlī* and *Hasan* and *Ahmad*: "*ʿAlkā*, and *Haskā* and *Hamkā*." The people of Hamadhān say: "*Ahmadlā*, and *Muhammadlā*, and *ʿIshlā*;" in Sāwa they say "*Abu al-ʿAbbāsān, Hasnān, Jaʿfarān*." The most frequent agnomen of the people of Qumm is Abū Jaʿfar; of the people of Isfahān, Abū Muslim; of the people of Qazwīn, Abu al-Husayn.

The **languages** used here vary. In al-Rayy speakers use the *rāʾ* [r], saying "rādah," "rākin." The people of Hamadhān say "watum," "watū." In Qazwīn they use the *qāf* [q]; and most of them say for "al-jayyid" [good], "naj." The language of the people of Isfahān is barbarous—they drawl it. Among the languages of the non-Arabic speaking people there is none easier to use than the language of the people of al-Rayy.

The fairest in complexion are the people of al-Rayy; the others are swarthy.

Here are towering mountains, such as Bīsutūn, forbidding, smooth, not climbable; in it is a cave, within which is a flowing spring. Mount Damāwand is extremely forbidding; it may be seen from fifty *farsakhs* away, and I have heard it said that no one climbs it. The mountains of al-Khurramdīniyya are inaccessible—here are a sectarian people, without dissension among them. They do not wash themselves from ritual impurity, and I did not see in their villages a prayer house. There were some debates between them and me, and I said, "Do not the Muslims invade you, even though you believe this doctrine?" Said they, "Are we not monotheists?" Said I, "How is that, since you have repudiated the religious obligations of your God, and neglected the Sharīʿa?" Said they, "We pay the ruler a great deal of money every year."

p. 399

    I know of no sights here. However, here are some of the wonders of the Kisrās, and sites of the Pharaohs: for example Qasr (the palace of) Shīrīn, the palace of Khusraw, the palaces of Kisrā. Here is the canal which is raised in the rock, measuring about a *farsakh*, in which wine and milk used to flow, or some story to that effect.

Among their **faults** are what we set out in the summary of the region. In the people of Isfahān is stupidity, and exaggerated devotion to Muʿāwiya. A man was extolled to me for his asceticism and piety; so I set out to visit him, leaving the caravan behind me. I stayed that night with him, asking him questions. Eventually I said, "What do you say about the ruler?" Then he began cursing him and said that he had brought us a doctrine we did not know. Said I, "And what is that?" "He maintains that Muʿāwiya was not a worthy successor." Said I: "And what do you yourself say?" Said he, "I say, just as God said,—may He be great and exalted—'We make no distinction between any one of his messengers.' (*Qurʾān*, sūra 2, verse 285). Now Abū Bakr was a proper successor, and ʿUmar was a proper successor," and he went on until he named the four, then said he: "And Muᶜāwiya was a proper successor." Said I, "Do not say this. You see, the four were khalifs, and Muᶜāwiya was a monarch. And the Prophet—God's peace and blessings be upon him—said, 'The khalifate will come after me for thirty years. Then there will be a king.'" So he began to revile me, and started saying to the people, "This man is a Rāfidite [forsaker schismatic];" and if the caravan had not arrived they would have attacked me. They have several stories on this topic, and you notice them drying their lungs [shouting] and grieving over it.

The women are in charge of the baths. You see the turbans of the people, like pillows; they have dreadful dispositions, and abominable customs—AntiChrist will come out of their market!

The sovereignty there goes back to al-Daylam; and al-Rayy is among the most important of their dominions. The first man who overcame the region and took it away from the possession of the khalifs of the dynasty of Sāmān was al-Hasan bin Buwayh, who adopted the name Rukn al-Dawla; then his son, Buwayh who called himself Muᵓayyid al-Dawla; then his brother, ᶜAlī who called himself Fakhr al-Dawla—his commander-in-chief lives in al-Dāmghān. They p. 400 defeated the populace, taking their houses and their villages, and most of the people moved away from their tyranny. They are now more godly, and have a Persian administration, though some vicious customs. However, they do not deprive people of what is bequeathed them; and if they grant something they let it continue to the [person's] death. They have power and prestige, patience in war; they have backing, an extensive kingdom, a powerful state. They have been named in the Friday sermons in China and in al-Yaman; they have been a match for the kings at any time; and the king of the orient was unable to withstand them. And the khalifs of Bani al-ᶜAbbās are under their interdiction, and seven splendid regions are in their grasp.

The **imposts** in this region are neither many nor heavy except in Isfahān and its sections. Thirty *dirhams* are taken for every load entering al-Yahūdiyya.

The **land tax** of al-Rayy is ten thousand *dirhams*; the land tax of al-Dīnawar is three thousand thousand *dirhams*; the land tax of Qumm is two thousand thousand *dirhams*. Qazwīn, Abhar, and Zanjān a thousand thousand and six hundred thousand and twenty-eight thousand; al-Saymara, three thousand thousand and a hundred thousand; Qāshān, a thousand thousand; Damāwand, ten thousand thousand.

As for **distances** in this region:
From al-Rayy to Kīlīn, one stage;
    thence to Kays, one stage;
    thence to al-Khuwār, one stage.

From al-Rayy to Qustān, one stage;
    thence to Mushkūya, one stage;
    thence to Wabarūh(?), one stage;
    thence to Sāwa, one stage;
    thence to Sūnaqīn (Sūbaqīn), one stage;
    thence to al-Masdaqān, one stage;
p. 401   thence to al-Rūdha, one stage;
    thence to al-Dukkān, one stage.

From Hamadhān to Būzanajird, one stage;
    thence to Qaryat al-Jinn, one stage;
    thence to al-Dukkān, one stage.

From Hamadhān to Asadāwādh, one stage;
    thence to Qasr al-Lusūs, one stage;
    thence to Qantarat al-Nuʿmān, one stage;
    thence to Jabal Bīsutūn, one stage;
    thence to Qarmāsīn, one stage;
    thence to Qasr ʿAmr, two post stages;
    thence to al-Zubaydiyya, one stage;
    thence to Tazar, one-half stage;
    to al-Marj, a like distance;
    thence to Hulwān, one stage.

From Karj to Suwād Muqawwala, one stage;
    thence to Khūzan, one stage;
    thence to Barzānyān, one stage;
    thence to Āwa, one stage;
    thence to Qaryat Jarā, one stage;
    thence to Ribāt Jarā, one stage;
    thence to Warāmīn (Varāmīn), one stage;
    thence to Kaskāna, one stage;
    thence to al-Rayy, one stage.

From Karj to Wafrāwanda, one stage;
    thence to Dārqān, one stage;
    thence to Khurūdh, one stage;
    thence to Sāburkhuwās, one stage;
    thence to Karkawīsh, one stage;
    thence to the Khān (caravanserai), one stage;
    thence to Ruzmānān, one stage;
    thence to al-Lūr, one stage.

From Qasr al-Lusūs to Kīr Harās, one stage;
    thence to Nihāwand, two post stages.

p. 402 From Hamadhān to al-Daymar, one stage;
    thence to Rākāh, one stage;
    thence to Nihāwand, one stage.

From Nihāwand to Rākāh, one stage;
    thence to Khwārab, one stage;
    thence to al-Karaj, one stage.

From Hamadhān to Tāq Saʿīd, one stage;
    thence to Jūrāb, one stage.

From al-Karj to Jarānābādh, one stage;
    thence to Abtʿah, one stage;
    thence to Jurbādhaqān, one stage;
    thence to Qanwān, one stage;
    thence to Marj Wazhar, one stage;
    thence to al-Mārabīn (al-Sāramin), two post stages;
    thence to Izmīrān, two stages;
    thence to al-Yahūdiyya, one-half stage.

The Region of Khūzistān
(Littoral Lowlands of Īrān at Head of Arabian Gulf)

The soil of this region is copper, its plants are gold; here is an abundance of fruits, rice, sugarcane. Here are plums, grains, dates, superb citrus, pomegranates, grapes; a pleasant, good region. Its rivers are admirable; its cloth is silk brocade and poplin, and fine cloths of cotton and silk. It is a source of sugar, candy, superb confections, of honey, superb sugar syrup. Here is Tustar, whose name is known in the East and in the West; and al-ʿAskar which bestows distinction on the two realms; al-Ahwāz, famous in the East and in the West; Basinnā from where the curtains have the highest quality in the world. You do not see poplin like that of al-Sūs; and along with this, here are sources of naphtha and tar; farms of aromatic plants and birds. Then, it is situated between Fārs and al-ʿIrāq, right where the battles of al-Islām were fought, for there are the battlefields of the nation; also the grave of Daniel. It does not lack jurists and scholars; and not in the eight regions are there any with purer speech. Here are ingenious water wheels, remarkable mills; amazing achievements, numerous specialties, abundant waters. Its revenues used to support the khalif; and it has splendour and elegance. In the eight regions none other than it pleased me. Indeed there would not be

p. 403 a more splendid region, were it not for its people; nor finer capitals were it not for its metropolis; for the meaning of al-Ahwāz is "dunghill of the world," its people among the wicked of mankind. We shall mention about it every account that has been related, or proverb that has been coined. Ibn Masʿūd—may God be pleased with him—said, "I heard the Prophet—God's peace and blessings be upon him—say, 'Let no tribe marry with the Khūz, for their veins call for disobedience.'" Moreover, ʿAlī bin Abū Tālib—may God be pleased with him—said, "There is no one on the face of the earth more wicked than the Khūz, nor have they ever produced a prophet or a noble person." Said ʿUmar—may God be pleased with him: "If I live long enough I will certainly sell the Khūz, and will put their price in the treasury." And in another account, "Anyone whose neighbour is a Khūzī, and needs his price, let him sell him." A jurist was asked about a man who swore he would cook the worst bird with the worst firewood, and would feed it to the worst of mankind. Said he, "He must cook the Egyptian vulture with oleander wood, and feed it to a Khūzī." You do not find among them all that wealth, admirable commerce, valuable manufacturing, with the discrimination and management you find among others. When their youngsters grow up they send them into migration, making them experienced in travel and moneymaking, so they move around from country to country. They have no need of learning or refinement.

The Khūz are those who are higher up [the mountains] than al-Ahwāz, for most of the people of al-Ahwāz have moved from al-Basra and Fārs. One day I was walking with Abū Jaʿfar bin Mahsan in al-Ahwāz, when one of the marketeers began to argue with him, so said he: "You are the Khūz people, and you are no good." Said the marketeer: "The Khūz are the people above al-Ahwāz, such as those of al-ʿAskar and Jundaysābūr and al-Sūs; but we are ʿIrāqīs." I heard that the people of Basinnā, and Bayrūt, and the places in that area have tails between their foreparts and posteriors similar to fingers. Do you not notice that the people of al-ʿIrāq say to them in vilification, "Hey Khūzī, you with the tail!" And the man who was found among the Khwārij when they fought ʿAlī, the Commander of the Faithful—may God be pleased with him—was shown to him, and he said that he had a breast like the breast of a woman; this man was from the spot we have mentioned. You see them screaming for no reason; they are the

p. 404　people of hate and jealousy, and extremism in doctrine. May God forgive us, and them, but no offence in what I have said about their faults! For we do not wish to lift the curtain from them, nor to expose their failings; but we have merely clarified what was related about them, and attributed to the Prophet—God's peace and blessings be upon him—and his Companions.

Here is a map of what it looks like, correct to the best of our knowledge, and exercise of our science [Map XVI]. And of God we ask help and success; in Him we seek refuge, and of Him ask the right way.

Addition / version MS. C.

p. 404　And whenever one ʿIrāqī reviles another, he says to him, "begone, Khūzī". In them is barbarism and roughness, and but little chivalry; you find in them a stupidity so that they are of no service to the traveler, nor indeed is there any benefit in them for the settled populations. They scream that their water boils in the summer, their houses are scorched from the heat. They speak like fiends, and evident among them are the abodes of the unrighteous. You see them with those riches in abundance, handsome shops, and fine handicrafts. When their youths come into the prime of life they afflict them by traveling, exposing them to risks, and keeping them busy in making profits. They roam over the earth, but without learning or refinement, but of course they have no need for these, except perhaps for a very little. Most of the people are weavers. The pious among them are *Hubbiyya* [an anthropomorphist sect among the Sūfīs, who worship God, not through fear or in hope of reward, but solely through love]. The customs of the people are pre-Islamic, their heads are ugly, their dispositions vile. May God forgive us, and them, but we have not selected those faults of theirs we have portrayed except that we wanted thereby to present a clear illustration: it is certainly not done in calumniation, rather we have expressed what was transmitted from the Prophet—on whom be peace—and reported of the Companions.

You should know that this region was known formerly as al-Ahwāz, along with its seven districts; but now, the classification of some of those districts is in abeyance, some districts are in dispute, and about some our sources are contradictory. We have said that the situation of the kings, in our science, is like the situation of the Companions of the Prophet in the science of the Sharīʿa. For

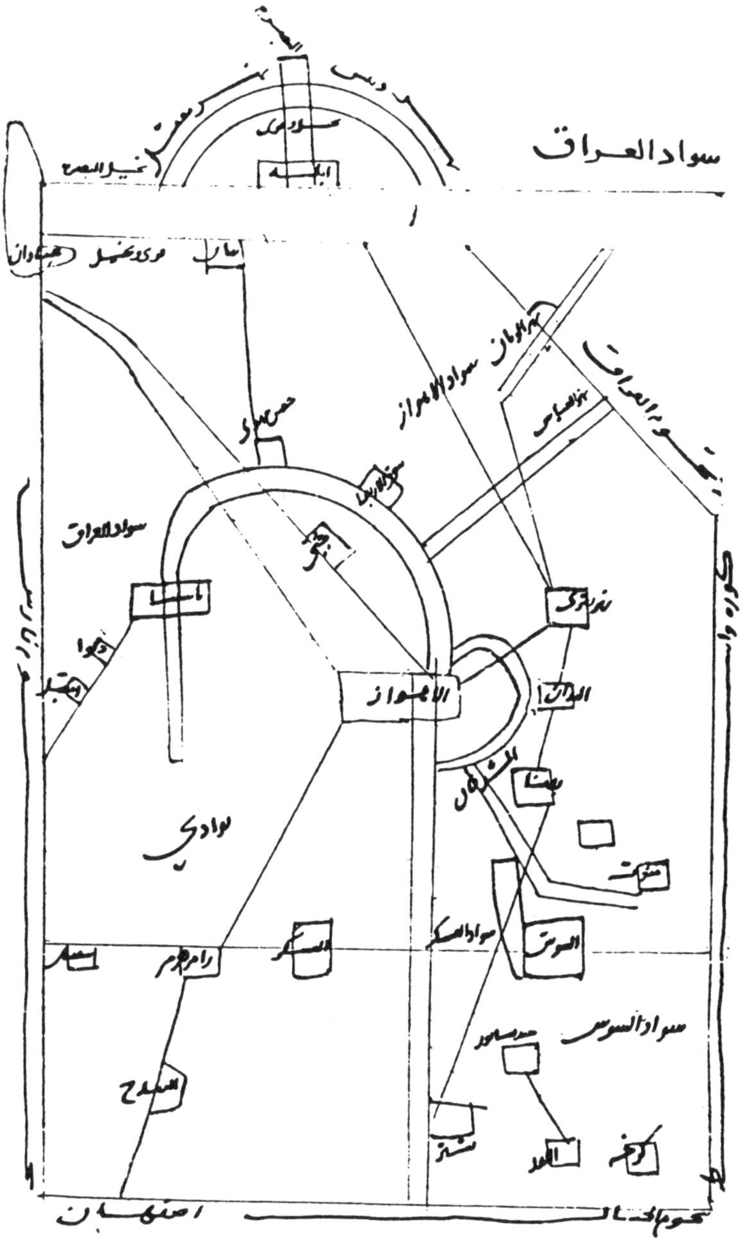

Map XVI: Khūzistān (see p. 420).
From MS. Sprenger 5—Ahlwardt 6034 by kind permission of the Staatsbibliothek
Preussischer Kulturbesitz, Berlin, Orientabteilung.

if one of them made a pronouncement to which there was no contradiction from among the Companions, his statement was accepted and became authoritative. Now ʿAdhud al-Dawla [324/936 - 372/983] was one of the most glorious kings of his time, for his marks and remarkable achievements are there in the realm of al-Islām—do you not see the cities which he built, and the canals which he dug, the names which he created, and the things he invented. Well, he used to refer to this region as 'the seven districts,' and that is commonly accepted; and this is what we follow since we found no contradiction to it.

The first of the districts as you come from the direction of al-Jibāl is al-Sūs, then Jundaysābūr, then Tustar, then ʿAskar Mukram, then al-Ahwāz, then Ramhurmuz, then al-Dawraq—these names are in common to the districts and the capitals. The districts have few towns and the boundaries of the region are close together.

p. 405　　Al-Sūs is a district on the frontier of al-ʿIrāq and the boundary of al-Jibāl; here are farms of rice, sugarcane, a considerable amount of sugar is extracted here. Among its towns are: Basinnā, Mattūt, Bayrūt, al-Bidhān, Qaryat al-Raml, Karkha.

Jundaysābūr is a district founded by Sābūr bin Fārs, and which he named after himself. It reaches the borders of al-Jibāl; a delightful district. It is said that it was the seat of the kings in ancient times. A considerable amount of sugar is extracted here. Among its towns are: al-Diz, al-Rūnāsh, Bāyūh, Qādhibīn, al-Lūr.

Tustar is a district with much fruit, grapes, citrus fruits, most of it being brought to al-Ahwāz and al-Basra. I did not notice any town there, after looking, and therefore we have adduced an objection in the account of it, saying that this is at variance with our canon to the effect that every capital must have towns, just as every general must have soldiers. Now if it should be said, "You have abrogated what you adduced, in the case of Sarakhs," then the answer is that Sarakhs is not referred to as a district, but this is referred to as a district. Names in this district refer to kings.

Al-ʿAskar is an important district, three rivers going around it and through it. The rural district of al-Mashruqān is here. Among its towns are Jūbak, Zaydān, Sūq al-Thalāthāʾ (Tuesday market), Hubk Dhū Qurtum, Burjān, Khān

p. 406　　Tawq. The market of al-ʿAskar is held on Friday. Khān Tawq has six villages named after the days of the week, there being a market for each day.

As for al-Ahwāz, when Sābūr built it he made it in two portions, one of which he named for God—may He be praised and exalted—and the other he named after himself; he then brought them both together under one name, and its name was Hurmuzdārāwashīr (Hurmuzd Ardashīr). Later his name was dropped and it remained Dārāwāshīr. Then the Arabs named it al-Ahwāz, and it is the district within which is included what was ravaged and abandoned of the old districts, which are Manādhir al-Kubrā, and Nahr Tīrā, both laid waste [226/841] by al-Mubarqaʿ. We crossed the district by the Rayyān canal, and I noticed its remarkable construction, learning that it connected the Tigris with the River Khūzistān [al-Ahwāz]. I said to the judge of al-Khūziyya, when I was with him one day in a boat: "What befell them?" Said he, "Al-Mubarqaˁ descended on it when he called on the Negroes and they responded to him, and they did to it what you see." He continued, "It was more splendid than al-Basra, and they say that to this day people dig up money that had been hoarded there, and dishes of brass, and other things." The towns of al-Ahwāz that I know are: Nahr Tīrā, Manādhir al-Kubrā, Manādhir al-Sughrā, Jūzdak, Bīrūh, Sūq al-Arbaˁāˀ (Wednesday market), Hisn Mahdī, Bāsiyān, Shūrāb, Bandam (Mandam), al-Dawraq, Sana, Jubbā. Al-Dawraq is a district that borders al-ˁIrāq at the angle. Among its towns are Āzar, Ajam, Bakhsābādh, al-Diz, Andabār, Mīrāqiyān, Mīrāthiyān.

Rāmhurmuz is a district that borders Fārs; delightful. The mountains are well-populated, and there is an abundance of date palms, olives, grain. None of it is plain, except a very small part, and there are no sugarcane farms here. The rivers of the region do not reach it, but they have a river away from the others. Among its towns are: Sanbīl, Īdhaj, Tīram, Bāzank, Lādh, Gharwa, Bābaj (Bāfaj), Kūzūk, all of them splendid and in the mountains.

Al-Sūs is a populous capital, a good city; the people desire to do good. There are excellent markets here, superb breads, and flowing waters which turn mills in the area. They have very fine baths, cheap confections, attractive villages, plenty prosperity, superb tilth, marvelous sugarcane; knowledge of God, the Qurˀān, the Tradition; literature, the way of the Prophet, and the decisions of the first khalifs. The mosque is perfect in every way, built on rounded pillars. However, they are Hanbalites, and in summer far from good, for then you see houses of prostitution at the doors of the mosque, in the open daylight; it is then you do not witness any reverence for their Readers or their elders, no standing for their preachers, no respect. They pass their time in dancing. Most of the people are Hubbiyya [a Sūfī sect]. The inner city is in ruin, and the people live in the suburbs. The city used to have a fortress on a superb elevated position; however, the armies of ˁUmar waged war on them intensively, and they demolished the defences. The grave of Daniel is in a stream beyond the city; and on the bank of the stream opposite the grave is a handsome prayer house. The grave is not known, except that it is the water; and there is a story about it.

Basinnā is small but populous; the men and women here weave howdah covers, and spin wool. Here is a stream which they call Dijla, with seven mills on it, built on boats. The mosque is handsome, at the portal of the city in the direction of the river; and the river is distant from the city a bowshot. Two solid fortresses stand here, a place of prayer for the Festival between them.

Bayrūt is large; here are many date palms, and people call it "little Basra." It is said that it was the capital of a district at one time. I saw it from a distance while traveling from al-Bidhān seeking Basinnā.

Karkha is a populous fine small town; its market is on Sunday. The drinking water is derived from a river. Over it stands a fortress, and there are orchards here.

The remaining towns are pleasant and populous. Rivers flow through the entire region.

Jundaysābūr was a capital populous and important, an ancient town, and was the metropolis of the region. Now, however, it has been overthrown, the Kurds have taken it over, and tyranny and vice have arisen there. However, it produces much sugar, and I have heard people say that most of the sugar of Khurāsān and al-Jibāl comes from there. The inhabitants are Sunnī Muslims. Here are two streams, *turuz* dates are in abundance, important villages, rice, farms, low prices, agricultural products. Here also are jurisprudents, prosperity.

p. 409

Al-Lūr is on the boundary with al-Jibāl, and it is said to have been added therefrom to this region. Here are *turuz* dates in abundance. The sugar here is not outstanding. I did not enter the other towns.

Tustar—there is not in the region a better, more fortified, more important town than this. The river flows around it, orchards and palm trees surround it. This is the source of every expert in the making of silk brocade and cotton. It has gathered within it every variety of thing, is the leading city, and has become famous throughout mankind. It is the city of which it was said that it is a Paradise in which the pigs graze. Do not even ask about its fruits and agricultural products, for to me they were a delight and a pleasure. You see the markets well attended, numerous specialties; people travel thither from the east and from the west. The people have cold water courses that flow underground. However, their mosque is insignificant, the heat here intense, the bridge long, and no access except by it. Many times the stranger loses his way in the markets. On the other side is little development. Their cemetery is in the middle of the town. The mosque is amid the markets among the cloth makers, and at the gate of the town is another cloth market. Near the bridge is a delightful spot in which the fullers are. Anyone who wants to go by boat to al-ʿAskar has to walk about a *farsakh*. Here are villages—but what sort of villages are they, without mosques!

Addition/version MS. C.
Their gardens are of citron and pomegranate the finest, grapes and pears of surpassing excellence, and dates; it is the garden of Khūzistān, the emporium of Fārs and Khurāsān. Brocade made here is taken to Egypt and Syria. Its inhabitants are well favoured, for here in summer cold water runs in channels under the ground. However, their mosque is insignificant, the heat here is severe, knowledge scant. The river surrounds it like a fosse. The bridge from the direction of Jundaysābūr is long and consists of boats, and from that side there is but little development. The mosque is in centre town near the market of the cloth makers; also, at the gate of the town is a cloth market. The town is surrounded by important villages, but they are without mosques.

Al-ʿAskar: al-Hujjāj bin Yūsuf had a young man named Mukram who settled with his army in this place and liked it. So people came thither and it was settled, and hence was called ʿAskar Mukram. It is a capital, cleaner than which

p. 410 you do not see one in the land of the non-Arabs. Fruit is good, markets delightful, plenty of produce; confections are cheap, breads excellent, and the inhabitants have their specialties. There is commerce; they are people of intelligence and understanding; most of them are scholars. You may see them learning in the prayer house up to twilight. However, they have made themselves odious to everyone by their skill in theology, and by their detachment have they offended all of al-Islām; hence preachers and public have rebuked them. There is a weakness here, and its cure is drunkenness; and scorpions kill with their poisons. Moreover the stranger here has no standing. I went in there the time of the morning prayer, and left it in the evening. It consists of two sides, the more populous being the side near al-ʿIrāq, and this also has the mosque and most of the markets. Connecting the two sides are two bridges of boats.

The remaining towns are on streams, and in them the *turuz* dates grow profusely, especially in al-Mashruqān—do you really realize what a place al-Mashruqān is! It is more fitting that Khān Tawq be included in the towns of al-Ahwāz.

Al-Ahwāz is the metropolis of the region; it is cramped, ugly, and nasty. The people have no religion, no element of humanity. The jurist is not a leader, nor is the preacher wise. The opportunity is never right, the heart never at ease. The stranger there is in confusion, depressed. And living is not a delight there either for the residents. There are bedbugs, fleas, great distress. In the night comes mildew, in the day the heat of the simoom. The inhabitants are constantly watching the north, fearing the south; they suffer scorpions, snakes and tepid water. A people of calamity; a metropolis of vice, poverty, depression. Fruits are brought there from distant places, flour is brought there from afar. Here is an arid place, sterile mountain, dirty market. The soil is briny; their reciter lacks
p. 411 polish, their mosque respect. Their country has no ruler, their jurists no council. They are a people of wrangling and fanaticism, of indecision and fickleness. You see the people of the town two factions, the followers of the Prophet two parties. However, it is the supply town for al-Basra, the entrepôt of Fārs and Isfahān; here are superb hostels, excellent breads, and other foods. Here are assembled the silks and the brocades, and thither are carried the goods, the wealth. Here is the supply house, the resources of the merchants, the thriving watering place for every passerby. Its reputation is great among the regions and the metropoles. Its winter is good, and so would the fall be, but for the flies; and so would be the spring, but for the fleas which are like wolves! Still, it is kindly, with clothing for the feeble. It is like al-Ramla, having two sides; however, the mosque and most of the markets are on the side towards Fārs, while the side towards al-ʿIrāq is an island, behind which is the main branch of the river, just as we mentioned about Fustāt in Egypt. Between the two sides is the bridge of Hinduwān, of baked brick, beside which is the handsome prayer house, overlooking the river. ʿAdhud al-Dawla had destroyed the bridge and rebuilt it magnificently with the prayer house, to have it named for himself; however the people refused to call it

anything but the bridge of Hinduwān. On the stream is a number of wheels which the water turns, and they are of a kind called *nā'ūra* [bucket type Persian wheel]. Here also the water flows in raised canals to reservoirs in the town. Some channels flow to the gardens. The main stream flows from beyond the island about shouting distance to a reservoir, remarkably built from the rock, and here it forms a pool. Here is remarkable roiling of water, and the reservoir holds back the flow, dividing it into three streams, which flow to the villages, and irrigate the farms; and they say that were it not for the reservoir al-Ahwāz would not be inhabited, nor would the rivers be of any use. On the reservoir are gates which are opened when the water rises: without them al-Ahwāz would be flooded. You hear the noise of the falling water, and it keeps you from sleeping, throughout most of the year. The rise occurs in the winter since it comes from the rains, and not from the snows. The river al-Mashruqān cuts through the lower part of the town, but it is dry most of the year. The water forms a lake in a place called al-Dawraq. Al-Ahwāz is well off with these rivers, and boats come and go and cross there just as at Baghdād. The streams branch off at the upper part of the town, and come together at the lower portion at a place called Kārshanān, whence the boats sail to al-Basra. There are some remarkable mills on the river.

p. 412

Sūq al-Arbaʿāʾ (Wednesday market) is on a branch of this river, in two parts, between them a wooden bridge under which boats pass. The side towards al-ʿIrāq is the more populous, and the mosque is there.

Hisn Mahdī is populous; all the streams of the region meet here, then flow into the sea. A fortress is here which Mahdī built. It is a port because of its proximity to the sea, and it has guard houses. The worshippers at the mosque assemble on the bank of the river. Here the roads also meet.

The other towns that are on the streams have an ebb and flow of the tides, have date palms and farms. The most populous part of al-Ahwāz is that towards Sūq al-Arbaʿā and what is included in that area.

Al-Dawraq is a populous capital in a remote part of the region away from al-ʿIrāq, and situated on a river. It has an extensive rural district. The market is large, and there are specialties and agricultural products. The site is attractive. It produces canvas. It is smaller than al-Sūs. The market is dispersed and the mosque is on the edge of it. The drinking water is derived from the river. The pilgrims of Fārs and Kirmān go there.

Mirāthiyān is in two sections; it has busy markets. In each section is a mosque.

Mīraqiyān has an extensive rural district. It is on a river reached by the ebb and flow of the tide. Here are many villages, and excellent lands.

Jubbā is an extensive district with populous villages; here are streams, and date palms. Abū ʿAlī, leader of the Muʿtazilites, came from here. Some have included ʿAbbādān in this district, whereas it is in al-ʿIrāq. Now if it were to be said, however, that we should include it in this region because of coincidence in language, and because there are similarities to it, in this region, in the rhyming

p. 413 [of names]—do you not notice that you say ʿAbbādān just as you say Bāsiyān,

Mīrāqiyān, al-Bidhān?-the answer to that is that the coincidence in language is not conclusive, since the masses of al-Basra are Persians, every one of them. And indeed the coincidences of these towns in the ending of their names also have parallels, in the towns near al-Basra, in this respect, for example Badrān, Rūmān, Shiqq ʿUthmān. If it should be said, "What we said before has greater probability for our argument than for yours, since the region itself conforms in this respect [of the rhyming of the ending], for do you not notice that you say 'Khūzistān'?" The answer is that this argument should hold true in all cases, and should apply to the other similar situations, so that we would say that Shāmān and Sulaymānān also pertain to Khūzistān. And if one were to swallow that notion then it would be said to him, "Then you do not controvert the one who says that ʿAbbādān pertains to the Peninsula of the Arabs, because it has parallels there, such as ʿUmān, Najrān, Samarān." Now, if it is not permissible for us to attribute it to the Peninsula in the light of that reason, you should know that it does not resemble the case of Bidlīs when we drew an analogy with Tiflīs, as we did not find in Aqūr a place with the same rhyme, but we found in al-Rihāb a number of [such] towns and villages.

Rāmhurmuz is a large capital, with flourishing markets, and an abundance of agricultural products. Here is a fine mosque, beside which are markets of the finest appearance, which ʿAdhud al-Dawla built; I have never seen more admirable than them in cleanliness and elegance. They have been decorated, ornamented, paved, and covered. Gates have been constructed on the markets and are locked every night; the cloth makers are here, the perfumers, the mat weavers. In the cloth market are excellent commercial hostels. The inhabitants derive their drinking water from a stream and wells, the water of the stream being available by turns to the farmers.

Addition/version MS. C.
[There are] wells, and outside the town streams, from which a channel enters, so that the water is available by turns to the farmers, just as at al-Basra and al-Rayy. There is a *waqf* here, and a continuous program of instruction for anyone who will study theology according to the school of the Muʿtazila; and there is a *shaykh* present under whose direction one studies.

Date palms and orchards surround the city. Here is a library like that in al-Basra, and in fact both institutions were entirely established by Ibn Sawwār. A fee is charged in both of them for anyone who resorts there, obligatory for reading and for copying. However, the library of al-Basra is bigger, more frequented, and has more books; in this one also there is always a teacher instructing in theology according to the school of the Muʿtazilites. The Oratory of the Festival is at the edge of the town among the houses. This is an attractive town; however, on summer nights they have need of nets, because of the great number of gnats. The population in the outskirts has diminished, and the ruler has taken possession of the villages.

I dropped in on the governor here, Abu al-Hasan bin Zakariyyāʾ, who
p. 414 had lived in Palestine for a long time. Said he, "I regret leaving that area, and
returning to a country so that I cannot see the delight of my eye, my native land."
And though he begged and besought to be given a part of his lands that were
taken from him, to cover his expenses, it would not be given to him. The roads
thither are difficult, and there are Bedouin all around; you notice their vile
natures and barbarous leaders.

Īdhaj is the most important town of the district; its ruler lives by himself.
Like Asadāwādh it is in the mountains; much snow falls there, and some is
carried to al-Ahwāz, and the districts around. The drinking water is from ʿAyn
Shaʿab Sulaymān (the well of the tribe of Solomon), the farms are watered by
rain; there is another source of water also. Water melons and other agricultural
products are here aplenty. The town occupies a low-lying site.

Kūzūk is also in the mountains; it has never ceased to provide grapes; here
is an abundance of violet and sweet basil. It is a good town.

Gharwa is among the well-known towns like the settlements we have
mentioned.

Lādh is also in the mountains, as are all the towns of this district, from one
point of view; from another point of view they are in a ravine.

A Summary Account of Conditions in this Region

This is a hot region, the waters are temperate, except the water of Jundaysābūr,
for, despite its salubrity it is hard. The climate of al-Sūs is unhealthy. However,
as one approaches the River Dijla [Tigris] on which Baghdād is, it is more
healthy. Date palms aplenty are here, no towering mountain, no soft sand
except between al-Bidhān and the River Tīrā. Snow does not fall here, nor
does the water freeze, except in the area of Rāmhurmuz. Rivers flow through
most of the region, and boats travel on all of them. There are few Christians,
and not many Jews or Magians. Preachers are here very much in evidence, but
p. 415 have little standing. Here also are ascetics, except in al-Ahwāz and in the guard
houses; also Sūfīs, except in al-ʿAskar. Their *Qibla* is not correct, especially that
of Basinnā, and when I returned from there to al-Basra my friends said to me
jestingly, "Repeat the prayers you said in Khūzistān, for they pray to another
Qibla."

The various **religious schools** here: most of the inhabitants of the region
are Muʿtazilites. Indeed, all the people of al-ʿAskar [are Muʿtazilite] as well as
most of the people of al-Ahwāz, Rāmhurmuz, al-Dawraq, also some of the
people of Jundaysābūr. As for al-Sūs and its districts, the people are Hanbalites
and Hubbiyya [a Sūfī sect]. Half of the people of al-Ahwāz are Shīʿa, and there
are many followers there of Abū Hanīfa, among them jurists and Imāms and
eminent people. In al-Ahwāz are also Mālikites.

When I entered al-Sūs I sought out the mosque, seeking a shaykh from whom I might hear some of the Traditions. Wearing a *jubba* [long outer garment open in front, with wide sleeves] of wool, copper in colour, and an apron of the style of al-Basra, I made my way to the Sūfī meeting. When I approached them they did not doubt that I was a Sūfī, and received me with welcome and greeting, sate me down amongst them, and began questioning me. They then sent a man who brought some food, but I refrained from eating as I had not associated with this sect before that time. So they began to wonder at my abstention, and my refraining from their practices. I wished then that I had had associated with this creed, and thus would have known their rituals and learned their truths. But I said to myself, "this is your opportunity, for this is a place in which you are unknown." Thereupon I opened up to them, and put off the mask of diffidence from my face; then sometimes I would converse with them, other times I would scream with them, then again I would read them the poems. And I used to go out with them to the cells, and attend their convocations, until, by God, they began to trust me, as did the people of the town to the extent I had never intended. I became famous there, visitors sought me out; clothing and purse were brought to me, and I took them and paid them for them completely on the spot, because I was rich; around my middle [with money belt] I had a lot of money. I attended a convocation every day—and what a convocation!—and they used to think that I was becoming ascetic. So people began to stroke by clothes [for a blessing], and proclaim an account of me, saying, "We have never, never, seen a *faqīr* [Sūfī mendicant] more deserving than this man." The result was that when I had learned their secrets, and found out what I wanted to from them, I fled them in the calm of the night. By morning I had put a long distance between us. Then when I was in al-Basra one day wearing my [Sūfī] clothing, my slave following behind me, a man of the Sūfīs saw me, and stopped and stared at me, apparently struck at the recognition. But I passed him as if I did not know him.

p. 416 Their **customs**: no one wears the *taylasān* except he be eminent. Most of them wear the *ridāʾ* [loose outer cloak], rectangular in shape. The populace wear scarves and wraps. They are a kindly people. When the Imām says the noon prayer in their mosques the people gather round him, and he finishes praying and says the invocation with them; it is the same in Shīrāz. Preachers there wear a *qabāʾ* and belt, in the manner of al-ʿIrāq. They do not jubilate [say "lā ilāha illāʾllāh"] after the Friday prayer. The preacher turns his head to right and to left, and lifts his voice in the invocation after the prayers, in the manner of Syria and Egypt. People enter the baths without trousers. They usually eat rice bread, and ride cattle. They commonly place large water jars in the streets and on the highways between towns, one about every *farsakh*, and sometimes the water must be brought to them from a distance. Their customs are close to those of al-ʿIrāq. They choose large stones for their rings, and the best pearls. In all the realm of Islām measures are not to be found truer than the measures of al-ʿAskar; then come those of al-Kūfa.

Commerce flourishes there, because all the sugar you see in the countries of the non-Arabs, and in al-ʿIrāq and al-Yaman, is from there. From Tustar are produced and exported fine silk brocade, howdah blankets, fine [cotton] cloths [like those of Marw], much fruit. From al-Sūs, much sugar, cloth, and silks.

Addition/version MS. C.
... and the finest cloth of cotton, and from al-Sūs comes a silk with which there is no cloth that can compare. They do not make turbans here, because al-Kūfa pours forth a steady stream of the best.

From al-ʿAskar silk veils, which are taken to Baghdād, very fine durable cloth, fabrics of hemp, scarves, and some of the other things the people of al-Ahwāz use. The curtains of Basinnā, and the howdah blankets of Qurqūb are famous. In the district of Wāsit curtains are made on which it is written that they were made of material from Basinnā, and thus are they represented; but they do not compare [with the original of Basinnā]. In al-Ahwāz wraps are made of silk; they are handsome and the women wear them. In Nahr Tīrā large shawls are made.

Here are **specialties** also. There is nothing like the pickles of Jundaysābūr, or the confections of the region, or the silk of al-Sūs—except in making turbans, as there is nothing to equal the *sakh* [a fine cloth] of al-Kūfa. One of the specialties
p. 417 also is the grape sugar. And the howdah blankets in Basinnā, the fine curtains, the excellent vegetables and aromatic melons of Tustar, the sugarcane of al-Sūs, the dates of Nahr Tīrā—all are of the highest quality.

There is **factionalism** in al-Ahwāz, and fighting occurs between the Marūshiyūn, who are Shīʿa, and the Fadhliyūn who are Sunnī; also between the people of al-Bidhān and Basinnā; between the people of Tustar and al-ʿAskar. Moreover, between the people of Tustar and al-Sūs there is partisanship on account of the coffin of Daniel—on whom be peace. Some said that when the grave of Daniel—on whom be peace—was uncovered, the remains were placed in a sarcophagus and carried around to places at which people prayed for water. So, they continued, the coffin was removed far from us here, and then was returned to Tustar, and the people kept it there. We sent them ten leaders as hostages against the time of our returning the coffin to them, [should they lend it to us]. But when they had obtained the coffin they dug this river, built this vault over it, and allowed the water to flow over it. They kept those hostages there; and from that time this intolerance has been between us, and because of this the prestige of our leaders has diminished to this day.

The *mann* used in the region in weighing meat and fish—except in al-Ahwāz—is four *ratls*; the *mann* for bread is the Makkan; in al-Ahwāz the *mann* of Baghdād is used for weighing everything. Their *coins*, as in the Orient, are of gold, using the *dānaqs*, every *dānaq* weighing eight and forty grains—of rice, that is. Every thousand *dirhams* weighed in Isfahān is less in Tustar by five and twenty; while the value of a thousand *dirhams* of Tustar exceeds that of al-Ahwāz by six *dirhams*. Every hundred *dīnārs* weighed in Qazwīn is greater in Tustar by five *dirhams* and four *dānaqs*. Every hundred *dirhams* weighed in Khurāsān is less in Khūzistān by two *dirhams*. They do not use the *qīrāt* [a weight].

The **dry measures** used are the *makkūk*, the *kurr*, the *makhtūm*, the *kaff*, and the *qafīz*. The *makkūk* of Jundaysābūr is three *manns* and one half, while the *kurr* is four hundred eighty. The *makhtūm* of al-Ahwāz is two *sāʿ*, the *sāʿ* being three *akuff*; the *qafīz* is seven *manns* of wheat, and their *kurr* is one thousand two hundred fifty *manns* of wheat, and that would be one thousand of barley.

p. 418

There is not in the non-Arab regions any purer **language** than that of the inhabitants here. They often blend their Persian with the Arabic, and they say, "Ayna kitāb waslā kun, wa ayna kār qutʿa kun," and even more attractive. You do not find them speaking in Persian without changing to Arabic; and when they speak in one of the two languages you would not realize they knew the other one well. In their speech is a jingle and an elongation at the end. When they say "listen" they say *bibakhshi* (excuse me); also for *kabād* they say *khaymāl*.

The heads of the people of Rāmhurmuz are wide and flat; they do not speak clearly, and their language is incomprehensible. Abu al-Hasan Mathar bin Muhammad from Rāmhurmuz told us that he had the following account from Mansūr bin Muhammad, who had it from Ishāq ibn Ahmad, who had it from Muhammad bin Khālid bin Ibrāhīm, who had it from Abū ʿAsma, who had it from Ismāʿīl bin Ziyād, who had it from Mālik al-Quttān, who had it from Khulayd, who had it from ʿImran al-Maqburī, who had it from Abū Hurayra. Said the Prophet—God's peace and blessings be upon him: "The worst speech before God is the Persian, the Khūzian is the language of the devils; the language of the people of hell is that of al-Bukhārā, and the language of the people of Paradise is the Arabic."

The **land-tax** of al-Ahwāz is thirty thousand thousand *dirhams*; the Perians used to apportion over the entire region a tax of fifty thousand thousand *dirhams*.

As for **distances** in this region:
From al-Sūs to Qurqūb, one stage;
    thence to al-Tīb, one stage.

From al-Sūs to Basinnā, two post stages;
    thence to al-Bidhān, a like distance.

From Jundaysābūr to al-Lūr, one stage;
    thence to al-Diz, two stages;

thence to Rāykān, one stage;
thence to Kul Bāykān, forty *farsakhs* of desert;
thence to Karaj Abī Dulaf, one stage.

From Tustar to Qaryat al-Raml, one stage;
thence to Basinnā, one stage.

p. 419 From al-ʿAskar to the fortress, one stage;
thence to the other fortress, one stage;
thence to Rāmhurmuz, one stage.

From al-ʿAskar to Tustar, or to al-Ahwāz, one stage each.

From Jundaysābūr to al-Sūs, or to Tustar, one stage each, and from Bayrūt to al-Sūs or al-Bidhān, one stage each.

From al-Ahwāz to Shūrāb, two post stages;
thence to Mandam (Bandam), one stage;
thence to Qasabat al-Dawraq, one stage.

From al-Ahwāz to Sūq al-Arbaʿāʾ, one stage;
thence to Hisn Mahdī, one stage;
thence to Fam al-ʿAdhudī, one stage;
at this point you are at the Dijla of al-ʿIrāq.

From Hisn al-Mahdī to Bayān, near a salt marsh, one stage.

You should know that the river of al-Ahwāz, and the Dijla (Tigris), flow into the Sea of China, and between them lies this salt marsh; so the people, in former times, used to travel by the river to the sea, then on their return would come in from the sea to the Dijla, thence to al-Ubulla, and here they would experience danger and discomfort. Then ʿAdhud al-Dawla cut a great canal from the river of al-Ahwāz to the Dijla, a length of four *farsakhs*, and the route traveled at present is by means of this.

From al-Ahwāz to Ajam, one stage;
thence to Āzar one stage;
thence to Rāmhurmuz, one stage.

From al-Ahwāz to al-Dawraq, one stage;
thence to a hostel, one stage;
thence to Basinnā, one stage;
thence to Qaryat al-Raml, one stage;

thence to Qurqūb, one stage.
There are two other routes here.

From al-Ahwāz to Nahr Tīrā, one stage;
    thence to Nahr al-ʿAbbās, one stage;
    thence to al-Khūziyya, one stage;
p. 420   then you travel by water to al-Ubulla, a distance of one stage.

From al-Ahwāz to al-Ishāqiyya, one stage;
    thence to al-Jisr al-Muhtaraq, one stage;
    thence to Hisn Mahdī, one stage.

From Nahr al-ʿAbbās to ʿAskar Abī Jaʿfar, one stage;
    then you cross to al-Ubulla, and this is the route over which animals travel.

From Rāmhurmuz to Sanbīl, two stages;
    thence to Arrajān, one stage.

From Rāmhurmuz to Tayram, one stage;
    thence to Gharwa, one stage;
    thence to Bāzink (Bāzīr), two post stages;
    thence to Īdhaj, one stage;
    thence to al-Diz, one stage;
    from al-Diz to [al] Dūlāb, one stage;
and from [al] Rām [Hurmuz] to al-Zutt, one stage.

From Rāmhurmuz to Nadah(?) [Badah(?)], one stage;
    thence to Jisr Jahannam, one stage.

The Region of Fārs (Southwest Īrān)

Of this region the soils are mines, the mountains wooded, the thorns are the Sarcocolla gum tree. From its goats is derived the renowned bezoar stone. Its supplies of bitumen are well-known. The eight regions [of the non-Arabs] are related to it. Here are date palms, citrus, olives, *ribās* [currants], cane, and artichoke; walnuts, almonds, locust. Here are made cloaks and silk fabrics; well-made rugs and cloths; admirable garments, draperies, cotton clothing looking like brocade; silk brocade and different kinds of garb. Here are the famous parks, the renowned capitals, fine cities such as Fasā and Shaʿab Bawwān; Sābūr and Nawbandijān; Dārābjird, splendid and renowned. And do not conceal the superiority of Sīrāf and Arrajān; nor in Istakhr the wonders and the buildings. Jūr has been great among cities for its blossoms and fruits; and Sābūr has closely resembled Sughd, and exceeded it in the production of olives, citrus and sugarcane; for here are trees, fruits, rivers.

p. 421

Fārs is a splendid region, excelling with an abundance of agricultural products, a fount of commerce. One day Abu al-Hasan al-Muʾammalī asked me how I found Fārs. Said I, "Of the regions I found it most resembling al-Shām (Syria), since it includes all kinds of fruits, and in it are places of heat, cold, and moderate temperatures. The mountains are forested, inhabited; there is honey, olives, blessings, the like of which I have never seen outside of al-Shām, except in Fārs. Nevertheless it is the seat of tyranny and corruption; scorpions abound, the language is barbarous, taxes heavy, some sections are hot, its cold areas bitter. The practices of the Magians are in the open there, and most of its villages have been appropriated."

Fārs the son of Tahmūrath settled it.

Here is a representation of its form and features. [Map XVII]

We have made Fārs six districts and three sections, the first, coming from the direction of Khūzistān being Arrajān, then Ardashīr Khurrah, and then Dārābjird, then Shīrāz, then Sābūr, then Istakhr; the sections are al-Rūdhān, Nīrīz, Khasū.

Arrajān is an important district with plain and mountain and coast; it has an abundance of date palms, figs, olives, with copious revenue and agricultural products. It is told of ʿAdhud al-Dawla that he said: "My aim is to have fame from al-ʿIrāq and income from Arrajān." Arrajān was the son of Qarqīsiyā bin Fārs; he grew angry with his father and left Aqūr, and this district was set up for him. I add to it some of the towns of Ardashīr Khurrah, and some others; and if the statement of the one who considered Rāmhurmuz as part of Fārs is to have force, then these should be added, even though now they have been added to Khūzistān. The capital of Arrajān has the same name; among its towns towards the sea are Qūstān, Dāryān, Mahrubān, Jannāba, Sinīz; and in the mountains Jūma, Hinduwān.

p. 422

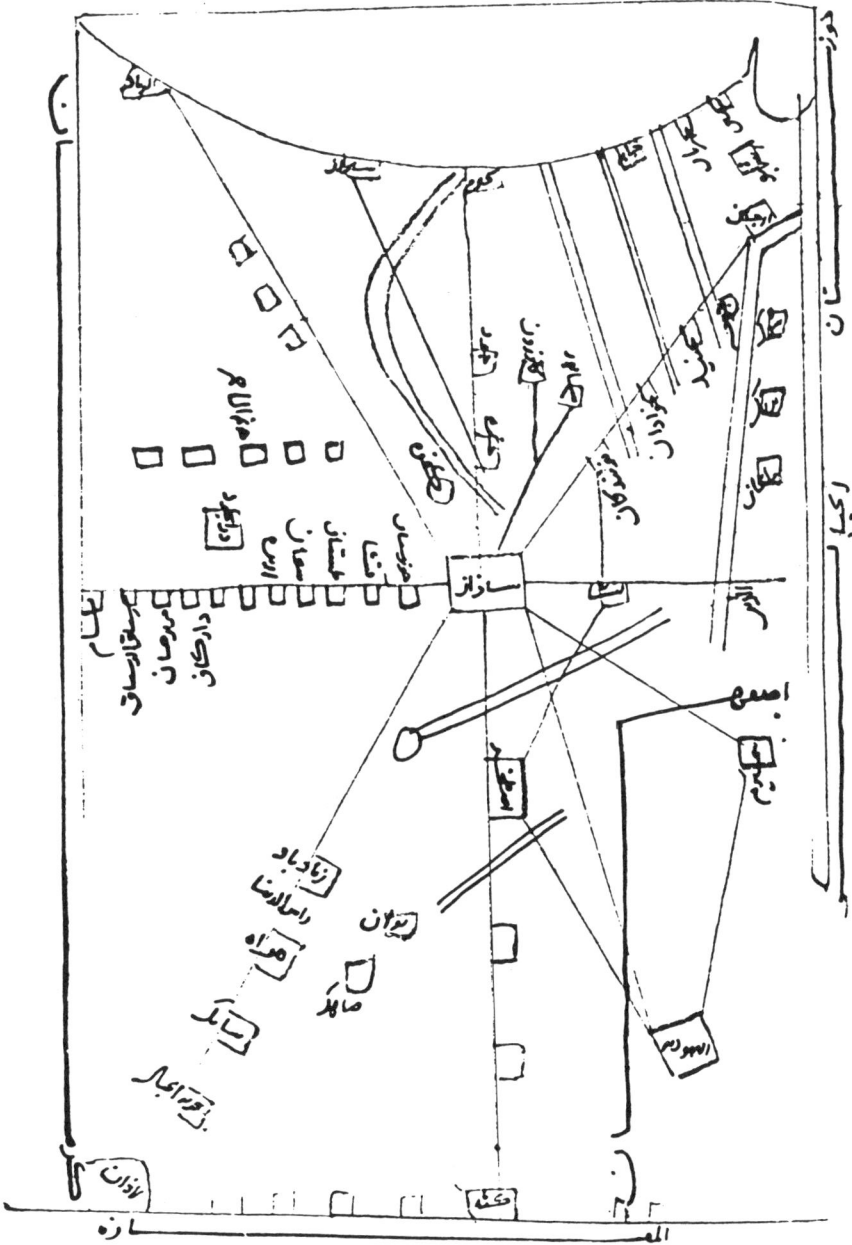

Map XVII: Fārs (see p. 421).
From MS. Sprenger 5—Ahlwardt 6034 by kind permission of the Staatsbibliothek
Preussischer Kulturbesitz, Berlin, Orientabteilung.

Ardashīr Khurrah is an ancient district which Nimrūdh bin Kanʿān planned; then Sīrāf bin Fārs built it. Most of it extends along the coast. The heat is severe, fruit scarce. The capital is Sīrāf, and among its towns are: Jūr, Maymand, Nāband, al-Sīmakān, Khabr, Khawaristān, al-Ghundijān, Kurān, Samīrān, Zīrabādh, Najīram, Nāband Dūn [lower], Sūrū, Raʾs Kishm.

Dārābjird is a splendid district which Dārābjird bin Fārs settled; formerly the metropolis, the kings used to stay here. Here are many mines, important specialties, excellent climate. The capital has the same name, and among the p. 423 cities are: Tabastān, al-Kurdibān, Kurram, Yazdikhwāst, al-Maskānāt, Zumm Shahriyār, Kadrū, Awjīn, Īk. It has a section, Nīrīz, with towns: Khayār, al-Murayzijān, al-Mādhawān; and the section Khasū, with towns: Rūbanj, Rustāq al-Rustāq, Furj, Tārum. Among the towns with important rural districts are: Juwaym Abī Ahmad, al-Isbahānāt, Sinān, Burk, Azbarāh.

Shīrāz was not formerly a district, just a city which Shīrāz bin Fārs built. However, the Muslims colonized it when they occupied the region, and the kings liked it and settled there, so it is now among the administrative centres. It is connected with Istakhr; but I have added many towns to it, and have made it a district, for here is the biggest metropolis; moreover, it has the sovereignty, and the administrative offices are there. Here are many mountains, and equable climate. The capital has the same name. Its towns are: al-Baydhāʾ, Fasā, al-Mass, p. 424 Kūl, Jūr, Kārazīn, Dasht Bārīn, Jamm, Jūbak, Jamakān, Kūrd, Bajja, Hazār, Abak.

Sābūr is a delightful district; and in every garden of it are to be found date palms, olives, citrus, locust, walnuts, almonds, figs, grapes, lotus, sugarcane, violet, jasmine; you see the rivers flowing, fruits within easy reach; villages spread out so that you walk *farsakhs* under the shade of the trees, just as in Sughd. And every *farsakh* there is a baker and a greengrocer. The district is close to the mountains; the name of its capital is Shahrastān. Among its towns are: Darīz, Kāzarūn, Khurrah, al-Nawbandijān, Kāriyān, Kundurān, Tawwaz, Zamm al-Akrād, Junbad [-Malaghān], Khasht.

Istakhr is the most extensive district; it has many towns, its name is great. Istakhr bin Fārs settled it, and among its towns are: Harāt, Maybud, Māʾīn, al-Fahraj, al-Hīra, Fārūq, Sarwistān, Usbānjān, Bawwān Kirmān, Shahr-Bātiq, p. 425 Ūrd, al-Rūn, Khurrama, Dih Ushturān, Tarkhanīshān, Sāhah (Sāhak), Shabābak.

Arrajān is a capital, very well built; many agricultural products; important towns; distinguished people; it has both snow and dates, lemons and grapes. It is a source of figs and olives, and in it are made the choicest syrup, and soap. It is the granary of Fārs and al-ʿIrāq, the emporium of Khūzistān and Isfahān. A copious stream cuts through the town; a handsome well-attended mosque is on the edge of the markets, having a tall, elegant minaret. The buildings here are of well-joined stone. The market of the cloth makers is here built like the market of Sijistān. The market has gates that are locked every night, the market, in orderly rows, being cruciform in shape. The gates are on four sides, one opposite the other, and you do not see a finer market there than the wheat market. It is a clean, nice place in the winter, sunk among the date palms and gardens. The wells are sweet, and no matter what you say, you could not describe the fruits and the fish, the snow and the dates. However, in summer it is hell itself, and the water of the river is salty from vintage time up to the rainy season. You do not see in the country women more coquettish than those here. The town has six gates-Darb al-Ahwāz; Darb Rīshahr; Darb Shīrāz; Darb al-Ruṣāfa; Darb al-Maydān; Darb al-Kayyālīn [supervisors of measures]. It was taken over by ʿUthmān bin Abi al-ʿĀṣā; the mosque was built by al-Ḥajjāj.

Jūma is a small town; the drinking water is derived from a stream. The name of the rural district is Balā Sābūr. Though mountainous it is delightful, resembling p. 426 the Ghūta of Damascus. It is said that Sābūr bin Fārs used to prefer this place over all the other places he established in Khurāsān and Khūzistān; it is there he died and was buried.

Al-Dayrjān is a town of the rural district of Rīshahr; it is of medium size, and spacious.

Bīrān is a town of Sanbīl; it pertained to Khūzistān formerly.

Hinduwān, towards the sea, is in two sections. The mosque and the market are towards Arrajān, the remaining buildings and the fish market being in the other section, towards the sea.

Dāryān has a busy market, an extensive rural district.

Sīnīz is half a *farsakh* from the sea, above Mahrūbān. It has a long market penetrated by an inlet on which boats ply. The mosque is distant from the market, the administration building opposite to it; there are many palaces.

Mahrūbān is on the sea, the mosque on the coast. Water here is scarce. This is the harbour of the district, the emporium of al-Baṣra. The markets are very fine, and well attended.

Jannāba also is on an inlet; its markets are in alleys. The mosque is in midtown. The drinking water is from briny wells, and ponds. Abū Saʿīd and Abū Tāhir al-Qarmatī came from here.

Sīrāf is the capital of Ardashīr Khurrah. At the time of its settlement its people preferred it to al-Baṣra because of the extent of its development, the beauty of its buildings, the elegance of its mosque, the charm of its markets, the affluence of its population, the extent of its reputation; it was at that time the point of access to China, after ʿUmān. It was, too, the entrepôt of Fārs and Khurāsān. In summary, I have not seen in the realm of Islām more remarkable buildings, or more handsome; they are built of teakwood and baked brick. They are towering houses, and one single house is bought for more than one hundred thousand *dirhams*. The population diminished when the Būyids were in power, for they left for the seashore, and established the capital ʿUmān. Then came the earthquake in the year 66 or 67 A.H. (685 or 686 C.E.), which jolted and shook it violently for seven days, so that the people fled to the sea; most of those houses were destroyed and tumbled down, and the event became a lesson for p. 427 anyone who should ponder it, a warning to anyone who will learn a lesson from it. I asked some of the people, "What did you do so that God took away His clemency from you?" Said they, "Fornication was rife among us, and usury spread among us." Said I, "And have you learned a lesson from what I see before me?" Said they, "No!" Something ignominious has been told me about their women; and I observed that the people of Fārs, because of the frequency of their whoring, coin sayings about them.

I was told that the people started building, and that the city was returning to what it had been; however, it is the gate of hell, with the intensity of the heat here. Water is brought thither from a distance, and they have a small canal of middling water. Their fruits are few. The town is situated between the mountain and the sea, and around about it is desolate land. However, not far away from it are date palms.

Zīrabādh is at the very boundary across from Kirmān. It is on the sea, with a stronghold than which I have never seen any more remarkable. The drinking water is from scant wells, and nothing better to drink is to be had here. Here is a gate which is the prerogative of the *amīr*. Whenever a well dries up they move to another.

Najīram is also on the coast, has two mosques. The vestibule of one of them was excavated from the rock, and beside it is a market, outside of the town. The drinking water here is from wells and ponds which are filled by the rain.

Karkam is populous; the mosque is on a small hill at the end of the market. One ascends to it by wooden steps.

Kāriyān is small, but its rural district is populous. Here is a temple of fire [Zoroastrian] to which the people attach great importance, and they carry fire from it to distant places.

Ra's Kishm is small; there is an extensive market with the mosque in it, to which you ascend by steps.

Sūrū is at the very boundary of Kirmān; coastal, and small. However, it began to develop because the exports of ʿUmān are carried there, and the caravans of Kirmān begin there. The people drink the water which comes from the mountains, and it collects in one place. When it stops they dig that place about five cubits, and sweet water emerges for them.

p. 428 Dārābjird is a delightful capital with a fortified inner city. Here are gardens, date palms, snow, and a number of different kinds of things. The markets are attractive, the climate equable; they have wells and canals. In the middle of the area is the Qubbat al-Mūmiyā' (dome of naphtha) and a hill on which the mosque stands. Some of the markets are in the inner city, the remainder in the suburbs. The city is one continuous settlement. The cloth market is like a hostel, with two gates; the inner city has four gates, and the houses are spread over a *farsakh*. On the Qubbat al-Mūmiyā' is an iron gate, and a man used to be appointed to take care of it. Then when the month of Mihramāh [seventh month of solar Persian year, beginning of autumn] came, the mayor, the judge, the postmaster, and the associate judge ascended; the keys were produced, the gate was opened. Thereupon a naked man would enter and collect whatever amount had oozed that year, and it would not amount to a *ratl*, according to what I heard from one of the associate judges. It would be put into a container, sealed, and sent with a number of the elders to Shīrāz. The spot would then be washed, and any of the material that would be seen on the man's hands—for it is only like paste in that water, the pure being found only in the treasuries of the kings.

Furj is not a large town; it has, however, a mosque and a bath incomparable in the region. It has many agricultural products. In the middle of the town is a fort on a small hill. Water is brought from some distance away.

Burk is in a depression, two *farsakhs* from the mountain. The mosque is beside the market, handsome and clean. The drinking water is derived from canals.

Juwaym Abī Ahmad is among the major cities. The width of its rural district is ten *farsakhs*, and the mountains enclose it. It is altogether covered with date palms and gardens. The drinking water is obtained from canals, and a small stream beside the market. Between the mosque and the market is a long alley. The mosque is handsome, stands on elevated ground, and one ascends to it by five steps; in the middle of it is a cistern which is filled by the rainwater, and each day the necessary amount is released from it. It is an elegant mosque.

Rustāq al-Rustāq is small, its market not large enough to merit mention. p. 429 However, its rural district is four *farsakhs* each way, all of it covered with gardens, waters, trees. The drinking water is from a river that flows thither.

Tārum is on the very border of Kirmān; the mosque is some distance from the market. The drinking water is obtained from the branch of a stream that flows thither. The area has gardens and date palms, and produces much honey.

Nīrīz is large; the mosque is beside the market; the drinking water is derived from canals; the rural district is twenty *farsakhs* each dimension.

I did not enter the remaining towns, but I was told that they are distinguished, agreeable, spaciously planned.

Shīrāz is the metropolis of the region; a filthy, cramped, newly founded town. The language here is crude, customs outlandish; there is no dependable leader, not even one wide street. The learned man is not refined, even the best people are sodomites. The merchants are licentious, the rulers tyrannous. People mill around in the markets, they are so narrow. Most of the people say one thing but do another. You may see them entering the baths naked without wraparounds, they bump their heads on the bay windows [because of narrowness of streets]. The Magians are not the only people who have no sense of shame: the wearer of the *taylasān* does not respect himself. I have seen wearers of the *taylasān* drunk, even beggars and Christians wearing it. The houses of prostitution are for everyone to see, the practices of the Magians are common. You cannot hear the sermon from the shouting of the beggars; in the cemeteries are the meeting places of the profligates. On the festivals of the unbelievers they decorate the markets. Heavy taxes have been laid on stores. The outsider may not enter unless he has a pass, the insider and the passerby are held prisoner. Living is difficult there, the land tax is doubled. They have not tasted the pleasantness of justice, nor walked the right path. Their farms are watered with leather buckets, so grapes and figs are dear; good bread you do not find. From the lowness of the balconies they are in trouble. It is not possible for two beasts of burden to go side by side in one market. They are a people of derision and hypocrisy. However, the climate is equable, comfortable in the summer and in the winter; the water is light if you drink from what flows. Moreover the water of the wells is sweet, and

p. 430 is close to the surface for irrigation. They are a people of prosperity and trade, with compassion for the strangers. They have specialties, handicrafts, intelligence, and subtlety; courtesy, charity, beauty. Scholars and notables merit praise; and there would be a valid chain of tradition were it not that the person taking dictation and the person giving it speak ungrammatical Arabic. There are many Sūfīs, and gatherings of readers. They assemble at dawn on Friday, and recite the entire *Qurʾān* with splendour and beauty. And a mosque, incomparable in the eight regions, is in glory on Friday; it is on pillars after the style of al-Masjid al-Aqsā. Here are the highest administrative offices; and for the people Naysābūr [nearby] is like a house of hospitality, a *shabistān*. Foods are clean, as is the *harīsa*, but roasted foods are not. It is famous for its dresses, cloaks, and hospital.

There are eight gates: Bāb Istakhr; Darb Tustar; Darb Bandāstānah; Darb Ghassān; Darb Silm; Darb Kuwār; Darb Mandar; Darb Mahandar. This city is like Damascus in extent, and in the narrowness of the houses; like al-Ramla the building is with stone; it is like Bukhārā in filth. The mosque is in the markets, at one side of it the clothiers' market, and the hospital at some distance from it: this has a splendid *waqf*, fine medicaments, skilled doctors. In Isfahān is another mosque more frequented than this. Bāb [gate] Istakhr is like the gates of Minā in Makka, and waters flow past it that are not clean; nor is the water of their wells light. The finest spot there is Bāb Istakhr and Bāb al-Jāmiʿ; the lightest of their waters is that of the canal that flows from Juwaym and enters through the palace of ʿAdhud al-Dawla. The most remote mountain from it is only a *farsakh* away, and the closest firewood to it is a post stage away. ʿAdhud al-Dawla had added an extensive, spacious quarter to it, with excellent markets, but it has been abandoned.

Addition/version MS. C.
Here are centres of administration, industries, specialties, scholars, mysticism, and elegant manners. Here is a distinguished mosque, well attended, with sessions of scholars, readers of the *Qurʾān*, meetings of communities every day. Here too is the palace of ʿAdhud al-Dawla, the like of which is not to be seen in the possession of any monarch; in it are gathered together everything from dates to snow. The buildings of the inhabitants are of stone after the manner of Palestine. The mosque is in the markets, built on rounded columns and vaulted arches, and it resembles the mosques of Syria. Here too is a hospital like that at Isfahān, in it equipment, physicians, attendants, food, the like of which I have

not seen in any country. The capital has eight gates: Darb Istakhr; Darb Sabaq; Darb Bandāstānah; Darb Ghassān; Darb Silm; Darb Kuwān; Darb Mandar; Darb Mahandar. The most extensive place there is Bāb Istakhr, resembling the gates of Minā at Makka; the finest place there is by the mosque. The lightest of their waters is that from the channel of Juwaym, which enters the palace of ʿAdhud al-Dawla. The most remote mountain from it is only a *farsakh* away, and the closest firewood is a post stage away. ʿAdhud al-Dawla had begun to extend the city, and developed two splendid quarters there, with their markets. Now, however, these have fallen into disuse, and the city at present resembles Bukhārā.

p. 431 Kurd Fannā Khusraw: Fannā Khusraw is ʿAdhud al-Dawla, and he planned a city about half a *farsakh* from Shīrāz, digging thither a large canal led from a distance of one stage away, spending an enormous sum of money on it; it is the one that flows at the lower end of his palace. Beside it he laid out a garden about a *farsakh* in width. He transferred to the city the woolworkers, the silkmakers, the brocade manufacturers, so that all *barrakān* [a fine cloth] is made there today. Do you not notice that the name of the town is written on the cloth? There the officers occupied beautiful houses and fine pieces of property. He established a yearly festival for them when they gathered there for pleasure and recreation. Now, however, the town has diminished after his death; it is going to ruin, and its market is in disuse.

As for Fasā-there is not in the region a people more delightful, upright, and good; no better fruits. There is a large inner city, in which is the market, built entirely of wood; the mosque is in the market, built of brick, bigger than the mosque of Shīrāz, and with two courtyards after the style of the mosque of the City of Peace [Baghdād]. Between the two courtyards runs a portico. You may say anything you like about the excellence of this town and its products; and
p. 432 there is much building with cypress wood here, such as you see in the country of the Romaeans.

Nasā, which people call al-Baydhāʾ, is a tidy, elegant, good town, in the other direction. There is a handsome mosque in it, and a shrine whither people repair.

Dasht Bārīn is a town which has no rural district, no gardens, no stream, no splendour. The people drink from scant water supplies.

Bajja is large, amidst the mountains; the buildings are of stone, the mosque in the market. The width of its rural district is two stages. Snow falls here.

Hazār is small, with an extensive rural district. The drinking water is derived from channels at the surface of the ground.

Kūl is populous; the mosque is among the [markets of the] clothiers and the butchers and the bakers. In the other direction is a public square. The drinking water is from a stream.

Jūr is a good, pleasant, attractive, spacious, elegant town; it is the source of roses and delightful specialties. Here is a solid, tall minaret. Along with that, it is a fortified town, in the middle of it a tall, well-kept citadel. Its rural district is about a short stage in length; its villages encircle it round about. The drinking water is derived from a stream, and from clean canals. It is truly a recreation ground, with its houses so well arranged; along with that it is renowned in the East and in the West for its spices. In Persian its name used to be "Kūr," which corresponds to the words, "the grave;" so when ʿAdhud al-Dawla went out there it used to be said, "the king is in *Kūr raft*," meaning that the king had gone to the grave. He disliked that, and changed its name to the better one it now is, calling it Bīrūzābādh (Fīrūzābād), meaning "for perfect government."

Shahrastān is the capital of Sābūr; it used to be a developed, well populated, fine city, but it has now fallen into disorder, its outskirts have been destroyed. However, it provides an abundance of produce, and is the source of a variety of specialties. It is a land of excellent citrus and essences, sugarcane, olives, grapes. Prices are low, there is a plenitude of dairy products. It is really a delightful place, with gardens, and copious springs. The houses of prayer are well kept, the baths are good, the hostels many. Here is asceticism and knowledge, snow, and every possible kind of fruit. Its gardens have been made fragrant with the scent of jasmine. Dates and figs are together there, as is to be found the remarkable carob. The buildings here are of stone and mortar. The mosque is outside the town amidst the gardens, handsome and delightful. The city has four gates: Bāb Hurmuz; Bāb Mihr; Bāb Bahrām; Bāb Shahr; around it is a trench. The river flows all around the capital, and is crossed by bridges. At the edge of the town is a fortress named Dunbulā, in front of it a house of prayer. In the middle of the town is another house of prayer, tiled, in which is a black stone; in the centre of it is a *mihrāb*, where, some say, the Prophet—God's peace and blessings be upon him—prayed. Here also is the prayer house of al-Khidhr, on whom be peace. Close to the fortress is a pre-Islamic jail, its walls of marble. The town is situated at the foot of a mountain, and it has two sections, both having gardens, trees, villages. Outside the town is a large bridge, which, while I was there, was closed. Here is a market the people call "al-ʿAtīq" (the ancient), but it is in disorder. The town has been ravaged, the population diminished, the people now being few in number. Kāzarūn has taken over its status; along with that, their water is disagreeable. Everyone there is pale and sick, and there is not an important scholar in it.

Darīz is a small town, with a fine market, and many linen weavers.

Kāzarūn is populous, large; it is the Damietta of the Persians, and that because the linen cloth made there with embroidery resembles the very fine linen of Shatā [in Egypt]. If this sort of cloth is made of cotton, it is made and sold here, except what is made in Tawwaz. Here on every side are castles, gardens, date palms, extending from the south to the north. There are substantial cambists in this city, a large busy market, agricultural products, fruits, buildings, trees, splendid houses. The mosque is on an eminence to which one must ascend. The markets and the merchants' establishments are below, for ʿAdhud al-Dawla raised a building there in which he assembled the cambists, and the income from it for the ruler, every day, is ten thousand *dirhams*. In the town the cambists have secure handsome mansions. The rural districts of Sijistān resemble this rural district—all of it farms, continuous fortifications, date palms. There is no sufficient stream here, only canals and wells.

Addition/version MS. C.
The marketplace is hot, palaces remarkable. Here ʿAdhud al-Dawla had built a great edifice with four gates, within it another structure in which these cloths were sold, and the income every day amounted to ten thousand *dirhams*. Most of the houses and the mosque are on an eminence to which one must ascend: the markets including the merchants' market are below. In the rural area here are cultivated fields of flax. There is no stream, just wells and some insufficient channels.

Khurrah, a celebrated town, is at the top of a mountain; an abundance of date palms. The river flows below the town. It is a source of dates and *nātif* [a sweetmeat].

Al-Nawbandijān is a pleasant town, renowned and important; and ʿAyān, the palace of Abū Tālib, adorns it. Here is the mosque, the waters, the garden; and twenty springs gush out at every place. Markets are large, busy, attractive; here are grapes, dates, bitter orange, pomegranates. Two *farsakhs* distant is Shaʿb Bawwān. As a stopping place the city is praised with a number of appellations. It is in a plain, but close to the mountains; and I observed that the people had added to the mosque, at its older section. However, their Imām is ignorant, their judges but two. This is what we know of Jadīda Bandijān, where the people do not give thought to whatever may be about to ensue.

p. 435 Khawrāwādhān is small, but populous and friendly. Living there is pleasant; do you not notice how it has embodied the two words for "ease" and "building"? A busy market is there, and the mosque is well frequented. Agricultural products and trees are here; and streams penetrate it, so that some of the stores are on them.

Junbad Mallaghān is a town in the midst of palms. It has a long market, and a delightful mosque to which one ascends by stairs; it is beside the market, and there are no other buildings around it. The drinking water is derived from canals, and in the town are cisterns. The town is at the boundary in a plain below the mountains. Mallaghān is a village, in ruin, at the edge of Arrajān.

Kundurān is large, in it a fortress wherein dwells the ruler. The drinking water is from rain water and from wells; the mosque is some distance from the market.

Tawwaz is small in size, great in name, because of the cloths that are made there of linen—do you not notice that they are called "Tawwazī"? Most of this kind of cloth is made in Kāzarūn but these are more skillfully and handsomely made. A large river flows beside the town, and between the mosque and the market is an alley. The town is situated far from the mountains.

Khasht is in the middle of the mountains; it has an extensive rural district. Its citadel is well known, its market well frequented. The drinking water is derived from a large stream.

Zamm al-Akrād has a rural district and a stream; it is among the mountains, with gardens, dates, fruits, agricultural products.

Istakhr is an ancient capital, mentioned in the writings, and renowned
p. 436 among mankind. Its name is great, important its record. The government offices were here originally; and even though it is the primary city at the present time, the population is light, the site is small. I have compared it to Makka, because it has two branches, and two mountains touch it. The mosque is in the markets, in the manner of the mosques of al-Shām (Syria); they are on rounded pillars, on the top of each pillar [the image of] a cow; and some say that in olden times this was a temple of fire [Zoroastrian]. The markets surround the mosque on three sides; the middle of the town is somewhat like a valley. Over Bāb Khurāsan is a remarkable arch, and a fine garden thereby: from that direction the river comes. The buildings here are of clay. The people have drinking spots near the river, and cisterns in the town; and there is not much water in the upper portion of the town. The waters here are not healthy, as they flow over rice farms. Here are lots of grains, pomegranates, agricultural products. Just the same, the people are stupid.

Harāt is a small town; the mosque is here; small stores, few houses. Most of the markets and the buildings are in the suburbs, and a large stream cuts through here. The city has one gate. Surrounding everything are fine gardens with excellent apples, olives, and other fruits. However, the water here is distasteful, and it is said that their women feel the rut when the sorb trees bloom, just as cats rut.

Jarmā is a large town with a busy market, the mosque close to it. The market
p. 437 has two gates. Their drinking water is from canals, easily seen at the surface of the ground.

Dih Ushturān is small, a village near it; here is a mosque with a tall minaret, standing in a small market. The stream flows under the town, and around it are pleasant gardens.

Bawwān is an extensive rural district, amidst the mountains; a stream cuts through it so it has two sections; no gardens.

Tarkhanīshān is small, the width of its rural district about a stage. The drinking water here is from a stream.

Kūrd is populous, source of walnuts, fruits; in the mountains. The drinking water here is from a stream.

Mihrajānawādh has an extensive rural district; the drinking water is from streams.

Māʾīn is on the main road to Isfahan; populous, has abundant fruit.

Sarwistān has the mosque in the middle of the town. It is mountainous; and the water canals here are visible [i.e., at the surface of the ground].

Sāhah (Sāhak) is small; they are a good people, with kindness for the stranger, and skill in copying the Qurʾān.

Kathah is on the edge of the desert; cold is severe, fruits few.

Khurrama has an extensive rural district; prices are low, there is a fortress. The drinking water here is from canals, and a stream flows underground.

Abarqūh is fortified; the buildings are close together: a large population, an excellent mosque.

Farʿā is close to Harāt; prices are low.

Karah is like Harāt; but I did not put in sequence the towns of this region.

Jarmaq is the most fertile of these towns, has the lowest prices, the most trees. It is on the desert main road.

Barm is on a plain, with a rural district irrigated from wells; it is fortified, having many castles.

Ūrd has a large fortress, populous suburbs. It is called "al-Har," and is counted among the towns of Isfahān.

p. 438   Al-Rūdhan belonged to the districts of Kirmān, and consisted of three towns—Unās, Adhkān, Abān. Unās remained on the very border, its inner city in Kirmān, so as to justify the boundaries of the two regions, and straighten the border. This region was drawn straight, and settled in these parts from this side, in Isfahān from the other side: most of the districts of Istakhr remained between them. Over the capital of al-Rūdhān is a fortress, guarded by eight gates: Bāb Unās; Bāb Bīrwa; Bāb Khawr Mardāwādh; Bāb Nasrīn; Bāb Mihmān; Bāb Shīrāz; Bāb Kaykhur; and the eighth, Bāb Māyafunā. When I saw it, it was closed. Here is a fine, delightful mosque to which one ascends by wide pebbled steps, and all their houses of prayer are elevated. There are many shoemakers and Muʿtazilites. Their baths are dirty. Here are fullers and weavers. Around the town are fine gardens. The cemeteries are on raised ground, with remarkable domes. Here is an abundance of dairy products, numerous canals, some of which enter the town. Here is a spring in the waters of which people seek to be cured. On the walls are battlements; no suburbs; a scant population. The sands surround it.

Addition/version MS. C.

The baths are in very poor condition. The gardens are pleasant, prices are low; and I have not seen in the territories of the non-Arabs more handsome burial grounds than theirs. Here too is a number of water channels. On the fortress of the town are battlements that extend all the way around. The town does not have suburbs, for the population diminished and the sands have blown to surround it. The villages resemble Sāwa. Here much cloth is made, in the style of that of Bamm, but it is not of good quality.

A Summary Account of Conditions in this Region

p. 439   *Addition/version* MS. C.

For my part, I settled in this region for about two years, and I entered it quite a number of times; I traveled over the areas in it of great heat and great cold, also the areas of moderate climate. I have, moreover, considered what Ibrāhīm bin Muhammad al-Fārisī and others have said about it. I have also asked questions about it of people experienced in the matter. It is not possible for me to examine thoroughly its characteristics, and to treat of all its conditions exhaustively, for fear the book would grow too long.

You should know that in Fārs are **cold** areas in which the trees do not bear fruit because of the severity of the cold, and agriculture does not flourish; for example al-Ūrd, al-Rūn, al-Ruhnān, and the surroundings of Istakhr. Then there are **hot** areas, in which sleep is not possible during the day, because of the intensity of the heat; for example Sīrāf and Arrajān, and the area between these two. There is moderateness between the two extremes, and in the territory there; for example, Shīrāz and its towns, and the surroundings of Sābūr. Snow is to be had in all the region, being brought from near and far. Most of it is in the mountains. Most of the region is forested, the agricultural land being scarce. Here is equable climate; delightful parks, strong citadels, many marvels, wondrous specialties, important mines, delicious fruits. There are more Magians here than Jews, and Christians are few. Lepers are rare; but I have never seen a town with more one-eyed people than Kāzarūn. Paralytics abound in Shīrāz.

There is much activity here on the part of the followers of the Tradition, and the followers of Abū Hanīfa—peace be upon him—are many. The Dāwūdites hold classes and councils; they are in the majority, taking over the judgeship and the administration. ʿAdhud al-Dawla used to consider that of the three sects the most jurists were Muʿtazilites. On the coasts are many Shīʿa.

Among their **customs:** when they say the afternoon prayer every day the scholars sit with the populace until evening, similarly after early morning prayer until forenoon. On Fridays they assemble elsewhere. Shīrāz had a superb mosque, and Sūfis here are numerous; they glorify God in their mosques after the Friday prayer, and they face the pulpit in the prayers for the Prophet—God's peace and blessings be upon him. The call to prayer is done in the presence of everyone by p. 440 all, together without chanting; and no one bears witness except a person of good repute. The populace wears black clothing; not wearing wool, but frequently wearing the *taylasān*; they also build up their turbans. In Shīrāz the wearers of the *taylasān* do not command respect, that going only to the wearers of the *durrāʿa*. As scholars are exalted in the Orient, the scribes are exalted here. Sellers of cooked meat have shops away by themselves.

The buildings here, when the stones are carefully laid, are good looking, even if the workmanship is poor. One day I sat with one of the builders—I mean in Shīrāz—while his fellow workers were chiseling with crude picks; the stones they were using were the thickness of brick, and when they had a smooth one they would set it up, draw a line on it, and cut along the line with the pick. Sometimes the stone would break, and when it broke evenly they would set it up on its edge.

So I said to them, "If you used wedges you would cut the stones square;" I described to them the method of building in Palestine, and discussed some questions in construction. Said the foreman to me, "You are an Egyptian." Said I, "No, rather a Palestinian." Said he, "I have heard that you people flute stones just as wood is fluted." Said I, "Yes indeed!" Said he, "Your stone is soft, and manageable for your workers." I noticed that they had some amazing achievements, and a dexterity and a proficiency that I never saw in the other regions; for example Raʾs al-Sikr, Jisr (bridge) Dakhwīdh, and Jisr Abī Tālib, built in this era: no builder in al-Shām or Aqūr would succeed in producing their like. Most of their mosques are on pillars. It is not possible to tarry in the inner rooms of the baths, because of the heat. I heard one of my father's—peace be on him—workers say that Abu al-Faraj al-Shīrāzī made the same blunder in the baths which he built in Jerusalem, by putting the fire under one of the inner chambers. However, it is not as he said. Rather, he saw that the practice of al-Shām in this matter differed from the practice of Fārs; he accordingly made some of the chambers according to the manner of his own region, and the remaining ones according to the manner of al-Shām. People seldom wear trousers [in the baths]. Sometimes women are in charge of the bathhouse. Rubble is thrown in one place only. The dead they carry head foremost, the men walking in front of the funeral, the women behind. In Khūzistān they walk on both sides, playing the pipe and the drum, at funerals, and in the cemeteries. Unknown completely in the non-Arab regions is the practice of going to the cemetery to read the *Qurʾān* right through; the people merely assemble for condolences for three days in the houses of prayer. They commonly wear shoes and sandals, with the wearing side p. 441 softened somewhat, since they are dry. They say the *tarāwīh* twice, letting the youth lead. They celebrate with the Magians the festival of Nayrūz [New Year's Day]; while entertainments and houses of prostitution are open and licensed in Shīrāz.

Addition/version MS. C.

In the region is a number of doctrinal schools, among them Hanafites, Shāfiʿites, Dāwūdites, Muʿtazilites, Hanbalites, and Shīʿa. You do not see Dāwūdites throughout the region, as most of them there fill the government offices; they hold their own assemblies, doctrinal sessions, and express formal legal opinions. However, the most prevalent usage follows the school of the adherents to Tradition, and the *iqāma* is recited separately, one person after another. Most of the Shīʿa are in Arrajān, and there is no one system of reading the *Qurʾān* which they prefer over others. Preachers here command no respect. Sufism is factious in Shīrāz. In the region are customs, some attractive, some repulsive. For example, late into the forenoon, in the mosque in Shīrāz, they assemble in study groups whether it be for study of the *fiqh* (jurisprudence), or for *dhikr* [invocation and praise of God], or for reading the *Qurʾān*. On *Yawm ʿArafa* [the day when the pilgrims visit Mount ʿArafāt near Makka], the attendants of the *Sharīf* (high born) among them attend the prayers, as do also the plebeians; and when they have said the afternoon prayers they disperse, ending the period between the two prayers in reading the *Qurʾān*, in praying, and in glorifying God. They do not chant the *adhān* (call to prayer) from the pulpit; they exclaim *Allāhu akbar* (God is most great) after the Friday prayer, just as is done in Syria; and they hold sessions, such as we have described, in the mosque, following the afternoon prayer, and that at sunset. Most of the buildings here are of stone. They do not mind showing themselves in wool and wearing black clothes clearly made from the wool. They screen the courtyard of the mosque at Shīrāz, just as at al-Basra and Misr. As for the repulsive practices here, the customs of the Magi are widespread among them, and houses of fornication in Shīrāz are very much in evidence; these are contracted for and frequented just as the public baths are. Good standing and honour are accorded to scribes and to the wearers of the *durrāʿa*. They carry the dead head foremost, the people except for the women, walking before the bier. People play the pipe and the drum at cemeteries and at funerals just as is done in Khūzistān. They go into the public baths here without trousers. Women superintend the bathhouses here, just as in Isfahān. I noticed beggarly fellows among shops in the markets, and drivers following their asses, and they were wearing the *taylasān*! It is here the attire of the weaver, the cupper, and the rustic.

Their **reckoning** is according to the months of the Persians, the first being Farwadīn [Farwardīn] Mah, then Ardibahisht, Khurdādh, Tīr Māh, Murdādh, Shahrīr [Shahrīwar], Mihr, Ābān, Ādhar, Day, Bahman, Asfandārmudh. For every day of the month on which there is official business there is a name, just as there is Ayyām al-Jumaʿ [Fridays] in the other regions. This begins Hurmuz,
p. 442 then Bahman, Ardibahisht, Shahrīr, Asfandārmudh, Khurdādh, Murdādh, Daybādhar, Ādhar, Ābān, Khawr Māh, Tīr, Jūsh, Daybamihr, Mihr, Sarūsh, Rashn, Farwadīn, Bahrām, Rām, Bād.

As for **commerce**: Arrajān produces very fine syrup, excellent soap; figs, olives; towels; Kandakiya cloths [coarse wool]; handling also Barbahār [precious Indian goods]. From Mahrūbān, fish, fruits, superb waterskins. From Sīnīz—cloths resembling embroidery; and sometimes linen is brought there from Egypt, though most of what is worked here at present is from what the people grow there themselves. From Sīrāf—towels, pearls, veils of linen, balances; and they handle Barbahār. From Dārābjird, everything of any value in cloth of top, inferior, and medium quality, also everything in the line of carpets; and mats like those of ʿAbbādān, finest carpets, needleworked curtains, many aromatic seeds, dates, syrup, finest jasmine. From Furj—cloths, rugs, curtains; fine syrup, aromatic seeds, linen. From Tārum—syrup, dates, waterskins, bottles, fine leather buckets, large fans. From Jahram—rugs, curtains, howdah rugs very well made. From Shīrāz—dresses of barrakān cloth—which is made no place else—and munayyar fabrics with which there is nothing to compare for durability, fineness, and beauty; superb cloaks; made here also is silk, and brocade, embroidery, and clothing. From Fasā—silk clothing exported to afar, very fine superb dresses, howdah blankets, rugs, towels; munayyar fabrics like those of Isfahān; variegated cloths; precious hangings; superior carpets; coverlets of silk dyed in safflower; tables; tents; scarves of Sharābiyya cloth, and other things.

p. 443   In Sābūr ten oils are produced—violet, water lily, narcissus, palm oil, lily of the valley, iris, myrtle, marjoram, citron, bitter orange. Here is produced also the bitter orange, with many other fruits, walnuts, olive oil, citron, sugarcane, and willow wood. The oils are sent to far away, the fruits to the metropolis. From Kāzarūn—embroidered cloths, the same from Tawwaz and Darīz and those areas, also *dabīq* [a cloth], and velvet scarves: these are carried to the far corners of the eight [non-Arab regions], and between these fabrics and those called *Shatawiyya* there is a great difference. From Jūr and Kūl, incomparable rose water, and much clothing. From Istakhr—rice and foodstuffs. From al-Rūdhan—cloths like those made in Bamm, and leather even better than that of Tripoli; also waterskins and sandals.

    There is absolutely nothing in Shīrāz to compare with the ʿUmarī plums, *barrakān* cloth and munayyar fabrics, and the syrup of Arrajān. Here is a tree like a thorn tree, and its fruit is Sarcocolla gum; and the same is in the areas around Sābūr, where fine boots also are made. From Dārābjird: dates; salt of naphtha, and of all colours. In the stream here is a boneless fish. In the mountains of Nīrīz there is Sarcocolla, also; from here, too, are derived whetstones, and magnesium stones. And in the districts of Shīrāz-sweet basil, its leaf like the leaf of lily of the valley, its inside like the narcissus; here too is a cucumber with a thorn like that of the porcupine. Saffron grows here, and mountain almond. In Fasā grows a very fine fig; also remarkable cypress, and a rare quince.

    Here are sources of bitumen in Dārābjird, and in Arrajān is also another source. In Nīrīz are iron mines, and a white clay with which youngsters write on their slates; also a black clay used for seals. Between Shīrāz and Sābūr much assafetida is found.

Addition/version MS. C.

From the mountains of Nīrīz, and the districts around Sābūr and Arrajān is derived the Sarcocolla, a thorn plant that spreads over the ground, the flower of the Sarcolla resembling that of wormwood.

    In Nīrīz are iron mines, and a white clay with which youngsters write on their slates, and with which people whitewash their houses; also assafetida in abundance. Saffron grows in the temperate areas of the region, and in Fasā, remarkable cypress trees. In Nīrīz corundum is found, also magnesia; at Jarmaq and at Barqūh, excellent vitriol.

p. 444   **Marvels** here: on the outskirts of Arrajān is a fire that burns at night and smokes during the day. Water emerges from wells in the mountains of Fasā, pouring from the mountain as from a teat; below is a hole in which gathers what benefits a person desiccated by the wind. Here are waters that if a man should drink, will purge him as a medicine would. Here also is a talisman, and when disease appears in an animal it is brought to that place, walking on the ground around it once. Then it sleeps on the ground, with its belly on the talisman, and very soon either dies or is cured. A *farsakh* from Istakhr is Malʿab (the stadium of) Sulaymān, to which one ascends by handsome stairs cut in the rock. Here are black pillars, and statues in niches, and remarkable constructions like the theatres of al-Shām. Below it is a spring of water, anyone drinking of it, it is said, goes away from it with a hangover lasting forty days. Between the pillars are the baths and the prayer house of Sulaymān. When a man sits in this stadium, the villages and the farms are all before him, as far as the eye can see.

ʿAdhud al-Dawla dammed the river which is between Shīrāz and Istakhr with a huge wall, setting the foundations in lead. The water formed a reservoir behind it, and rose. On both sides he built ten mill wheels, as we described in our account of Khūzistān, under each wheel a millstone, and this is still among the wonders of Fārs. Moreover, he built a town there, and carried the water by canals to irrigate three hundred villages.

> *Addition/version* MS. C.
> ... [also,] a Persian water-wheel (noria) to turn a mill, and on each side he cut scallops from which the water would fall down with full force on the lower parts of the waterwheels, and cause them to turn; and in those parts that turned were chambers that would be filled with water. Then when they turned they would spill out the water into a channel running to three hundred villages. He built at this place a splendid city, with excellent public baths and a handsome mosque.

In this rural district are apples, some sweet, some sour. At Sābūr is [the statue of] a servant made of black stone, garbed in a loincloth; something is written on his upper arm in Persian. It stands in the middle of the road, its waist nine spans, its height a fathom and a cubit.

A *farsakh* from al-Nawbandijān is a likeness of Sābūr, at the mouth of a cave; he is wearing a crown, and at the base are three leaves of green. The length p. 445 of the instep of his foot is thirteen spans, from his head to his feet, eleven cubits. Behind it stands an expanse of water without limit or outlet, and a violent wind emerges from there. At a *farsakh* from the gate Bāb Shahr [of Sābūr] is a cistern from which water issues, then splits into streams; it is pure and limpid as cold water. It is called Sarūshīr. In the village of ʿAbd al-Rahmān there is what resembles Biʾr Ayyūb (Job's Well) in Jerusalem.

> *Addition/version* MS. C.
> ... a well, some fathoms deep, dry as a rule throughout the year except for one period when water issues from it, irrigating the cultivated fields and turning the millwheels.

In Sābūr is a mountain on which is sculpted every king and satrap known to the Persians. In Mūrjān is a cave, water dripping from its roof. If one man enters, only enough trickles out to satisfy a man; should a thousand men go in, enough comes out to satisfy them.

In Jūr is a pool at the gate of the town; here are huge copper pots, and from the uppermost one of those pots flows a considerable amount of water. In Sāhik (al-Gharb) is a well which is bottomless; enough water bubbles out of it to turn a mill wheel, and irrigate that village. In al-Ghundijān is a stream between two mountains, and vapour comes out of it. No one can approach it, and if a bird passes over it it falls in and is consumed by fire. In the sea at Sīrāf is a place we passed by; some water dogs came down and jumped into the sea, holding waterskins. They then emerged, having filled them with sweet water. I questioned them on it and they said that a spring comes out at the bottom of the sea. Half a *farsakh* from Kāzarūn is a dome people said is the middle of the world. In the districts around Istakhr are hills asserted to be the ashes of the fire of Abraham—on whom be peace. Here also are remarkable bridges, some new, some pre-Islamic.

The **waters** of the area are copious, for here are numerous rivers. The River Tāb p. 446 emerges from the mountains of Isfahān, flows beside the boundary of the region to Arrajān. The main road is beside it, crossing it over arches many times.

Addition/version MS. C.
... [It flows] as far as Sīnīz, then turned at the boundary; over it is a number of stone bridges. This region has an abundance of stone bridges, among them Qantara (stone bridge) of Abū Tālib, stretching from one mountain to another, and Qantara ᵓAdhud al-Dawla, and this is a wonder!

The River Shīrīn, the River al-Shādhkān; the River Darkhīd; the River Khūbdhān; the River Ratīn; the River Ikhshīn; the River Sakkān; the River Jarsīk; the River al-Kurr; the River Farawāb; and the River Tīrza-these are the largest of the rivers.

There are five **lakes**—Lake al-Bakhtikān [Nīrīz] is about twenty *farsakhs* in length; it is salty, situated in the district of Istakhr. Lake Dasht Arzin in the district of Sābūr is ten *farsakhs* long; it is sweet water, dries up sometimes. Most of the fish for Shīrāz are from here. Lake Kāzarūn, ten *farsakhs* long, is salty. It has arms, and many fish are taken from it. Lake al-Jankān is about twelve *farsakhs* long; salt is derived from the edges of it, in the district of Ardashīr Khurra. Lake al-Bāfahūya, eight *farsakhs* long, is salty; papyrus and thickets grow in it. The Sea of China flows along the entire southern coast of the region.

Tribes of the Kurds here are thirty-three in number: al-Kirmāniyya; al-Rāmāniyya; Mudaththir; Hayy Muhammad Ibn Bashar; al-Thaᶜlabiyya (Baqīlī); al-Bundāmahriyya; Hayy Muhammad bin Ishāq; al-Sabāhiyya; al-Ishāqiyya; al-Adarkāniyya; al-Sahrakiyya; al-Tahmādahniyya; al-Zabādiyya; al-Shahrawiyya; al-Mahrakiyya; al-Bundāqiyya; al-Khusrawiyya; al-Zanjiyya;

al-Safariyya; al-Mubārakiyya; Istāmahriyya; al-Shāhūniyya; al-Furātiyya; al-Salmūniyya; al-Sīriyya; al-Azāddakhitiyya; al-Mutallabiyya; al-Mamāliyya; al-Shākāniyya; al-Jalīliyya [three names not included in al-Muqaddasī's list: Shahyarī; Barāzdakhtī; Kajtī]. They have five hundred tents.

The **citadels**. In Istakhr is a great citadel, the width of the main part of it p. 447 a *farsakh*. In it are water tanks. A commander is permanently there, as are merchants. A number of the kings' storehouses are there, and some pre-Islamic chattels. In Shīrāz is a citadel built by ʿAdhud al-Dawla. He spent a considerable amount of money on it, and in it dug a well at the base of the mountain. In Nasā, Kathah, Fasā, Qaryat al-Ās, Dārābjird, Junbad, Arrajān, Zīrabādh stand citadels, and some are by the sea. Ibrāhīm bin Muhammad al-Fārisī [al-Istakhrī] said that they would amount to five thousand citadels.

Addition/version MS. C.
In it are the treasures of the kings of Fārs from the pre-Islamic period. It is a difficult place to approach, well fortified, and with some ponds of water, and with the entrenched ruler who will not leave it. ʿAdhud al-Dawla built a fortress in Shīrāz on the top of a mountain, and dug therein a well, splitting the mountain until he reached water, spending a considerable amount of money on it. A fortress pertains to each one of the following: Kathah, al-Baydhāʾ, Fasā, Dārābjird, Junbad, Arrajān. Ibrāhīm al-Fārisī mentions five hundred fortresses, and three and thirty tribes of the Kurds.

The encampments here are five in number: the largest of them is *zumm* (the encampment of) Ahmad bin Sālih, known as al-Daywān; then that of Shahriyār, known as the encampment of al-Bāzinjān—these are they who are in the area of Isfahān, and some of the people of this encampment are nomads. Then there is that of Ahmad bin al-Hasan, known as the encampment of al-Kāriyān; it is the encampment of Ardashīrkhurrah.

The **situation** of Fārs: it is divided by a line from Arrajān to al-Nawbandijān to Kāzarūn to Khurrah, then along the borders of the coast to Kārazīn until it reaches al-Zamm; what lies to the south is hot, what lies toward the north is cold. In the hot areas lie: Arrajān, Nawbandijān, Sīnīz, Tawwaz, Khurrah, Dādhīn, Mūz, Kārzīn, Dasht al-Būsqān, Kīr, Kīzrīn, Abzar, Samīrān, Khumāyijān, p. 448 Khurmuq, Kurān, Sīrāf, Najīram, Hisn Ibn ʿUmāra, and areas in subjunction to these places. In the cold areas are situated: Istakhr, al-Baydhāʾ, Māʾīn, Īraj, Kām Fīrūz, Kūrd, Kallār, Sarwasīr (Sarwistān), al-Awsbanjān (Usbānjān), Ūrd, al-Rūn, Sirām, Bāzranj, Sardan, al-Khurrama, al-Hīra, al-Nīrīz, al-Maskānāt, al-Īj (Īk), al-Isbahānāt, Būrm (Barm), Ruhnān, Bawwān, Tarkhanīshān, al-Jūbarqān, Iqlīd, al-Jarmaq, Abarqūh, and there are other places similarly situated. The area of equable climate lies between those, being the district of Dārābjird, and Shīrāz, and Fasā, and what is included in this area, as far as Jūr and its territory.

The **imperfections**: the water of Arrajān is bad, as is the water of Dārābjird. The water of the wells of Shīrāz is afflictive. Most of the hot areas have a bad climate, and a changing of colours; there the healthiest places are Sīrāf, Arrajān, Jannāba, Sīnīz. The most moderate climate is that in the areas between the two extremes.

In Dasht Bārīn is a spring at which people seek cure from diseases; the water of the capital of Sābūr is afflictive.

This is a country of tyranny. I read in a book in the library of ʿAdhud al-Dawla that the people of Fārs are the most obedient of all people to the ruler; they are the most patient of tyranny; have the heaviest taxes; are the most obsequious in spirit. The people of Fārs have never known justice! But suppose one were to say, "Did not the Prophet—God's peace and blessings be upon him—praise them in saying that even if the faith were in the Pleiades, men from among the people of Fārs would attach themselves to it?" In reply it would be said that Khurāsān and Fārs were the same place as far as the Arabs were concerned, and when they produced any scholar at all the matter was mentioned far and wide. And see how many [scholars] Khurāsān has produced, such as Ibn al-Mubārak and Ibn Rāhwayh, and others like them in jurisprudence and the Traditions: and indeed to this day they do not lack eminent Imāms. On the other p. 449 hand, Fārs is entirely lacking in people of that stamp, they have written nothing dependable, no record in science that one can refer to. Do you not notice that Abū Khālid said, "Fārs is three thousand *farsakhs*," whereas this region is but one hundred twenty in each dimension? So you realize that he had Khurāsān and the places around it in mind.

Sovereignty there is in the hands of the Būyids. The first to dominate this area was ʿAlī bin Buwayh; but he had no children, so he adopted ʿAdhud al-Dawla, and he reigned after him. He was the son of his brother, and he built in Shīrāz an edifice the like of which I have not seen in the East or in the West. No ordinary person has entered it without being charmed by it, and no expert without coming to the conclusion that in it is the delight and excellence of Paradise. He had streams run through it, built domes over it; he surrounded it with gardens and trees, and excavated cisterns there. He assembled every convenience and contrivance there. I have heard the head of the custodians say that there are three hundred sixty compartments; and one hall in which was his place of assembly every day of the year, this hall being the lower portion of the building. In the upper part is the library, a compartment by itself. There is a manager, a librarian, and a supervisor from among the people of good repute in the town; and there was not a book written up to that time, of all the various sciences, but happened to be there. It consists of a long oblong gallery in a large hall, with rooms on every side. He attached to all the walls of the gallery and of the rooms bookcases six feet in height and three cubits long, made of wood, and decorated. On the bookcases are doors that open from above, and the books are arranged on shelves. For every subject there are bookcases, and catalogues in which are the names of the books; and no one has access to them except he be a person of distinction. I walked about in this building, all of it, below and above, and it had been completely equipped. And I saw at every seat what was needed there, both furniture and curtains. I noticed also the canvas awnings over which the water glides through tubes continuously from above, from conduits around it. I also observed the streamlets flowing uninterruptedly among the rooms and the living quarters. I really think he built it according to the accounts he heard of Paradise! However, he was so far from that realization that he undoubtedly went astray, and was burdened with his sins: even his house did not remain. He dwells in the grave, after having all the kingship and the trappings. He died [372/983] the worst manner of death, and God showed him misery. He became a stern lecture and a warning to us. One of the eunuchs recited some verses he said he heard from him near the time of his death. Now he had ruled the eight [non-Arab] regions and his name had been mentioned in the Friday sermon in al-Sind and al-Yaman. And he coveted the Orient, and opposed the ruler of the Maghrib.

p. 450   Monarchs feared him, and he made prisoner the emperor of the Romaeans. He knew a variety of sciences, and was experienced in astronomy. Said the poet:

> Enjoy the things of the world, for you will not remain forever;
> take from it what is pure in it, refrain from what is turbid.
> Do not put your hopes in destiny—I put my hopes in it!—
> and nothing was spared for me of my status; nor did it reserve any right for me.
> I voided the royal residence of every distinction:
> I dispersed them to the West, routed them to the East.
> And when I touched the star in my might and glory
> the necks of all mankind became enslaved to me.
> But death shot an arrow at me, and extinguished my firebrand;
> and here I am speedily cast into a grave.
> All my wealth availed me nought, nor did I find
> with the Hunter of Souls, in my perdition, aught of mercy;
> for I perverted my world and my religion insolently,
> and who is there, more than I, in his misery more damned.

Addition/version MS. C.

He gave himself the agnomen ʿAmīd al-Dawla; he did not have a son, and so adopted ʿAdhud al-Dawla, who ruled the region in succession; then his son, Abu al-Fawāris. ʿAdhud al-Dawla was one of the tyrants and one of those with ambition. He built a palace in Shīrāz the like of which I have not seen in the East or the West; and when Zarīf, the eunuch, entered Shīrāz an invitation was extended to him when he was in the garden. The palace was decorated and carpeted; he was brought in to make the rounds of it, and I was with him. No ordinary person has entered it without being charmed by it, and no intelligent person whose soul did not yearn for the castles of Paradise; I am of the opinion, indeed, that he built it after the pattern of what he heard of the abodes of Paradise. There is a lower part, and an upper part. A stream used to cut through to the lower part, turning a millstone, coming there from a post stage away: it enters the city he built, and passes among some of the compartments and galleries, flowing and turning. He had another channel brought to the upper level from a distance of two *farsakhs* away, and made the water to flow over the canvas roof terraces of the compartments so that it would continuously overspread them, and thus they would be always moist. Moreover, those compartments he coloured he did so in Chinese terra-cotta; of those he did not colour, some were of stone, some that were not carpeted were done in marble, some were gilded, some illustrated with drawings. He made of it three hundred sixty compartments, one for every day of the year, and no compartment resembled any other one in its construction, furnishings, draperies, or seating. He encompassed it round about with wondrous gardens in which were gathered together exotic fruits. The repository of the books was separate, and in charge of it a librarian, a supervisor, a keeper of the keys, and an overseer from among the people of good repute in the town; and there was not a single book published in a branch of the sciences that he did not gather together there. It consists of a long oblong gallery with rooms on every side. He had attached to the walls of the rooms bookcases six feet in height, three cubits long, and with shelves. On the bookcases are doors that come down from above, and the books are arranged on shelves. For every subject there is a bookcase, or bookcases, and catalogues in which are the names of the books. That gallery was carpeted with rugs of the most surpassing excellence from ʿAbbādān, and a screen fastened to the door. Doorkeepers were appointed over the entrance, and no one may enter unless he be distinguished.

Tyranny prevails in the region, and I read in a book in this library that the people of Fārs are the most abjectly servile in submissiveness to the ruler, and the most persevering under oppression, pay the heaviest land taxes, and are the most humble in spirit. In the book it said that the people of Fārs do not know any justice whatsoever. But suppose some one were to say: "Did not the Prophet—God's peace and blessings be upon him—praise them when he said: 'Even if the Faith were in the Pleiades, the men of the people of Fārs would attain to it.'"? It would be said in reply: "Khurāsān and Fārs were, in the notion of the Arabs, one and the same: do you not see that Abū Khālid said—'Fārs is three thousand *farsakhs*', whereas, in fact, this region is one hundred twenty in each dimension; so you realize that he meant to say Khurāsān. And upon my life, if both knowledge and the faith were in the Pleiades, the people of Khurāsān would cleave to it. And when did Fārs produce a learned man, or an ascetic, or a noble? May God preserve us from the **levies** of this region! The amīr Abu al-Fawāris used to assign to me every year three hundred *dirhams*. So I said to Abu al-Fadhl bin Nahāma: 'Will you find for me a rationale that would make this gift acceptable to me?' Said he: 'This is money that is the aggregate of imposts and revenue of villages over which he had gained the mastery.' Said I: 'Then I will certainly never accept it.'"

p. 451   The **land taxes** of this region vary. In Shīrāz on a *jarīb* [a measure of arable land] of wheat and of barley is an assessment of one hundred ninety *dirhams*; and of dates and of melon fields two hundred thirty-seven *dirhams*; on cotton, two hundred fifty-six *dirhams* and four *dānaqs* [one-sixth *dirham*]; on vineyards one thousand four hundred twenty-five *dirhams*. The large *jarīb* is seventy cubits, the "royal" cubit, that is, which equals nine *qabadhāt* [one *qabadha*, or fist = 12.5 cm]. The land tax in Kuwār is two-thirds of what we have mentioned; it was lowered by al-Rashīd. The land tax of Istakhr is less than the land tax of Shīrāz, on agriculture, by a little.

Rain irrigates only one-third of the region. And do not ask about the burden and the number of the imposts!

p. 452   A number of *ratls* are in use here. The *ratl* of Shīrāz is the big one equivalent to eight *ratls* of Baghdād; vinegar, milk, and such commodities are measured with it. Here also is used the Makkan *mann*. With the *ratl* of Baghdād is weighed meat and bread and the like. The *mann* of bread in Fasā is three hundred [*dirhams*], also of cotton, and of grain. Sugar, saffron, honey, henna, dye, pharmaceuticals are weighed by the *mann* of three hundred *dirhams*. Heavier than it is the *mann* used for dried meat, meat, iron and such, by five and twenty [*dirhams*]. The *mann* of Dārābjird, which is known by that name, used for everything except for pharmaceuticals; it is four hundred forty *dirhams*. Thread, bread, safflower, angora wool, and wool are four hundred eighty *dirhams*. The *mann* of Nīrīz in weighing everything except pharmaceuticals is three hundred twenty [*dirhams*], while the *mann* for thread is three hundred forty.

The **measures**: the *qafīz* of Fasā is six *manns*, a *mann* being three hundred *dirhams*, and is used with grain, and what almonds there are. For barley the *qafīz* is six *manns*; the *qafīz* for rice, chickpeas, lentils, eight *manns*. The *qafīz* of Nīrīz is three *ratls* of Baghdād, used with barley, raisins, seedless raisins, and durra; the *qafīz* of wheat is more than that. The *mann* of Arrajān is three *ratls*, except for sugar, and the big *qafīz* is ten *manns*. The *makkūk* is half the *qafīz*, and the
p. 453   *jarīb* is ten *qafīz*. On the assessed land is exacted for every palm tree one fourth of a *dirham*. The villages vary: in Sanbīl the tax is from three *dirhams* to half a *dirham*, in Arrajān from three *dirhams* to a *dirham*. For untilled assessed land the tax is twenty *dirhams*.

The **distances** in this region:
From Arrajān to Rīshahr, one stage;
    thence to Mahrubān, one stage.

From Arrajān to Bisābik(?), one stage;
    thence to Dihlīzān, one stage;
    thence to Khābarān, two post stages;

thence to Wādī 'l-Milh, one stage;
thence to Rāmhurmuz, two post stages.

From Arrajān to al-Zaytūn, two post stages;
thence to Habs, one stage;
thence to Bandaq, one stage;
thence to Junbad, two post stages, or one post stage by way of al-ʿAqaba
(ʿAqabat al-Fīl = the pass of the elephant);
thence to Zanak, two post stages;
thence to Dakhwīdh, one stage;
thence to Khwādhan (Khawrāwādhān), two post stages;
thence to al-Nawbandijān, the same.

From Arrajān to Kanīsat al-Majūs, one stage;
thence to Qarya (?), one stage;
thence to al-Zīz, one stage;
thence to al-ʿAyniyya, one stage;
thence to the river, one stage;
thence to Kharanda, one stage;
thence to Sumayram, one stage.

From Mahrūbān to Sīnīz, or to the river, one stage;
from the river to Arrajān, one stage;
from Sīnīz to Sanjāhān, one stage;
thence to Jannāba, one stage;
thence to Dasht Dāwūdī, one stage;
thence to Tawwaz, one stage;
thence to Khasht, one stage;
p. 454   thence to Nīmārāh, one stage, half of it difficult;
thence to Sābūr, a like distance.

From Sīrāf to Jamm, one stage;
thence to Barzara, one stage;
thence to Kīrand, one stage;
thence to Mah, one stage;
thence to Rāykān, one stage;
thence to Biyābshūrāb, one stage;
thence to Jūr, one stage.

From Sīrāf to ʿUmān, by sea, or to al-Basra, is a sailing distance of from five to
ten *farsakhs*;
thence to al-Bahrayn, seventy *farsakhs*, the width of the sea.

From Dārābjird to Khasū, one stage;
    thence to Karab, one stage;
    thence to Juwaym Abī Ahmad, one stage;
    thence to Kāriyān, one stage;
    thence to Bārāb, one stage;
    thence to Kurān, one stage;
    thence to Sīrāf, one stage.

From Dārābjird to Jarmuwā, one stage;
    thence to Rustāq al-Rustāq, one stage;
    thence to Burk, one stage;
    thence to Tārum, one stage.

p. 455 From Dārābjird to Jāh Zandāyā, one stage;
    thence to Taymāristān, one stage;
    thence to Fasā, one half stage.

From Shīrāz to Kafrah, one stage;
    thence to Kūl, one stage;
    thence to Būmhān, one stage;
    thence to Jūr, one stage.

From Shīrāz to Qaryat Juwaym, one stage;
    thence to Khullār, two post stages;
    thence to al-Kharrāra, a like distance;
    thence to Jarkān, one stage;
    thence to al-Nawbandijān, one stage;
    and here is Shaʿb Bawwān, which is one of the recreation grounds of the world.

From Shīrāz to Qaryat al-Rummān, one stage;
    thence to Sarwistān, one stage;
    thence to Kurram, one stage;
    thence to Fasā, one stage.

From Shīrāz to Dāryān, one stage;
    thence to Khurrama, one stage;
    thence to Kath, one stage;
    thence to Khayār, one stage;
    thence to Nīrīz, one stage;
    thence to Kadrū, one stage;
    thence to Ribāt Zarūdwā, one stage;
    thence to Nahr Man, one stage;
    thence to Hantah, one stage;

thence to Bīmand, one stage;
thence to al-Sīrjān, two post stages.

p. 456 From Shīrāz to Rakān, one stage;
thence to Ra's al-Sikr, one stage;
thence to Ziyādābādh, one stage;
thence to Jubb Amīr al-Mu'minīn, one stage;
thence to Ra's al-Dunyā, one stage.

From Shīrāz to Sāhah, one stage;
thence to Dasht Arzan, one stage—difficult, and here is ʿAqabat Bālān.

From Fasā to Kārazīn, one stage;
thence to Hurmuz, one stage;
and from Kārazīn to Khārzīn, one stage.

I do not know a metropolis that occupies the middle of its region except this one, and Hamadhān. Do you not see that from it [Shīrāz] to Kathah or to Tārum, or to Najīram or to the River Tāb is in every case sixty *farsakhs*; while from it to the four corners [of this region], to Sīnīz or to al-Rūdhān or to Sūrū, or to the frontier with Isfahān, is in every case eighty *farsakhs*. And around it are cities from which the distances to it are about equal. A man in Kāzarūn told me that someone fled the ruler and sped to Sābūr. Then he asked how far it is to Shīrāz, and they told him, eighteen *farsakhs*. Then he hurried to Kāzarūn and asked how far it is to Shīrāz, and they told him, eighteen *farsakhs*. He sped to Khurrah and asked how far it is to Shīrāz and they said, sixteen *farsakhs*. Then he sped to Jūr and enquired, and they said twenty *farsakhs*. From it to al-Baydhā' is one stage.

From Sābūr to Kāzarūn, one stage;
thence to Khurrah, one stage.

From Sābūr to al-Nawbandijān, one stage;
and from Sābūr to Karak, one stage;
p. 457 thence to Dasht Arzan, one stage.

From Kāzarūn to Qaryat al-Hatab, two post stages,
thence to Dasht Arzan, a like distance.

From Kāzarūn to Darīz, two post stages;
thence to Ra's al-ʿAqaba, a like distance;
thence to Tawwaz, a like distance;
thence to Qaryat(?), a like distance;
thence to Jannāba, a like distance;

From Istakhr to Ra's al-Sakr, two post stages;
>   and from Istakhr to al-Baydhā',
>   or to Qaryat al-Hammām (Kalūdhar), one stage;
>   and from Qaryat al-Hammām to Ziyādāwādh (Ziyādābādh), one post stage;
>   thence to Jubb Amīr al-Mu'minīn,
>   thence to Ra's al-Dunyā,
>   thence to Khawaristān, one stage;
>   thence to Harāt, one stage;
>   thence to Rādhān, one stage;
>   thence to Shabāwak (Shabābak), one stage;
>   thence to Riwār, one stage;
>   thence to Qaryat al-Jammāl, one stage;
>   thence to al-Rūdhān, one stage.

From Istakhr to Bīr, two post stages;
>   thence to Kahmanda, one stage;
>   thence to Qaryat Bīdh, a like distance;
>   thence to Abarqūh, one stage;
>   thence to Qaryat al-Asad, a like distance;
>   thence to al-Ūrd, one stage;
>   thence to Qala't al-Majūs, one stage;
>   thence to Kathah, one stage;
>   thence to Anjīrah, a like distance.

From al-Yahūdiyya to Khān Rash, one stage;
p. 458   thence to Qūmisa, one stage;
>   thence to Karū, one stage;
>   thence to Sumayram, one stage.

From al-Yahūdiyya to the caravanserai of Khān Linjān, one stage;
>   thence to Karū, one stage;
>   thence to Mās, one stage;
>   thence to Khān Rūshan, two post stages;
>   thence to Istakhrān, one stage;
>   thence to Qasr A'īn, one stage;
>   thence to Khuwiskān, one stage;
>   thence to Mā'īn, one stage;
>   thence to Āzār (Hazār) Sābūr, one stage;
>   thence to Shīrāz, one stage.
>   Should you so wish, you may take the route through the desert, from Qūmisa
>   to Ruzkān, one stage;
>   thence to Azkās, one stage;
>   thence to Sarwistān, one stage;

thence to Saramsah, one stage;
thence to Lāh Wikrah, one stage;
thence to Qaryat al-Khallāf, one stage;
thence to Kamāhank, one stage;
thence to Qaryat Ibn Bandār, one stage;
thence to Istakhr, one stage.

From Sumayram to Jaᶜfarābādh, one stage;
thence to al-Zāb, one stage;
thence to Kūrd and Kallār, one stage;
thence to Mihrajānāwādh, one stage;
thence to Ash Wabūrd, one stage;
thence to Nasā, two post stages;
thence to Shīrāz, one stage.

From al-Yahūdiyya to Khālanjān, one stage;
thence to Bārkān, one stage;
p. 459 thence to Isbīdh Dasht, a like distance;
thence to Jaᶜād Wajūrd, a like distance;
thence to the guardhouse, a like distance;
thence to Kūristān, one stage;
thence to Jisr Jahannam, one stage.

The Region of Kirmān (South Central Īrān)

This region resembles Fārs in pecularities, is like al-Basra in its customs, and approaches Khurāsān in its characteristics; this is because it borders the sea, and combines within it cold areas and hot, nuts and date palms; it has an abundance of dates and syrups, and fruits, and ripe dates. Here is Jīruft, about which sayings have been coined; and Manūqān to which there is so much traffic. And for the dates of Khabīs, people come to a halt. Here are level ground, mountains, sandstone, sands; flocks of grazing livestock, and camels. Here are remarkable special things, and workshops. Here is zinc that flows in pipes like cold water, and we have described this clearly in the account of Narmāsīr. The cloth of Bamm is famed in the East and in the West for beauty. Even so the people are humble, and not at all disagreeable. Kirmān is the storehouse of prosperity and luxury; its water is good, its climate moderate. Here is perfection of religion and decency; their speech is correct, in their intelligence is no lapse. Kirmān is distinguished; however, it is in an unbalanced condition. It is hot on the littoral, and the snakes there are long. They have no jurists, nor preachers, to expound the law publicly. Their bodies are skinny, resembling toothpicks! There is much wasteland here, and no river in which a vessel sails. Two states claim it, consider it domain for themselves. Hence, disorder is rife, and what fighting there is here!

p. 460

Here is a representation of its form and features; and in God is success, He has no partner. [Map XVIII]

This region consists of five provinces and districts, the first across from Fārs being Bardasīr, then Narmāsīr, then al-Sīrjān, then Bamm, then Jīruft.

Bardasīr is a district that lies close to the desert, and has both cold areas and hot. In their own language the people call it Kuwāshīr. Its capital has the same name, and among its towns are: Māhān, Kūghūn, Zarand, Janzarūdh, Kūh Binān, Qawāf, Unās, Zāwar, Khūnāwab, Ghubayrā, Kārishtān. Of the district of Khabīs the towns are: Nashk, Kashīd, Kūk, Kathrawā.

Narmāsīr also lies close to the desert in the direction of Sijistān; its capital has the same name, similarly al-Khams. Among its cities are Bāhar, Karak, Rīkān, Nasā.

Al-Sīrjān is in a central position among the provinces, though more towards Fārs. Its capital is the metropolis and among its cities are: Bīmand, al-Shāmāt, Wājib, Bazūrak, Khūr, Dasht Barīn.

p. 461

Bamm is also on the border of Fārs, and among its cities are: Dārzhīn, Tūshtān, Awārak, Mihrikird, Rāyin.

Jīruft is the most delightful district in the region, bordering on the Sea of China, and adjoining Makrān. All kinds of different things are here—the rivers flow abundantly, the fruit is excellent. It has many cities, among them: Bās, Jakīn, Manūqān, Darahqān, Jūy Sulaymān, Kūh Bārjān, Qūhistān, Mughūn, Jawāwan, Walāshjird, Rūdhkān, Darfānī.

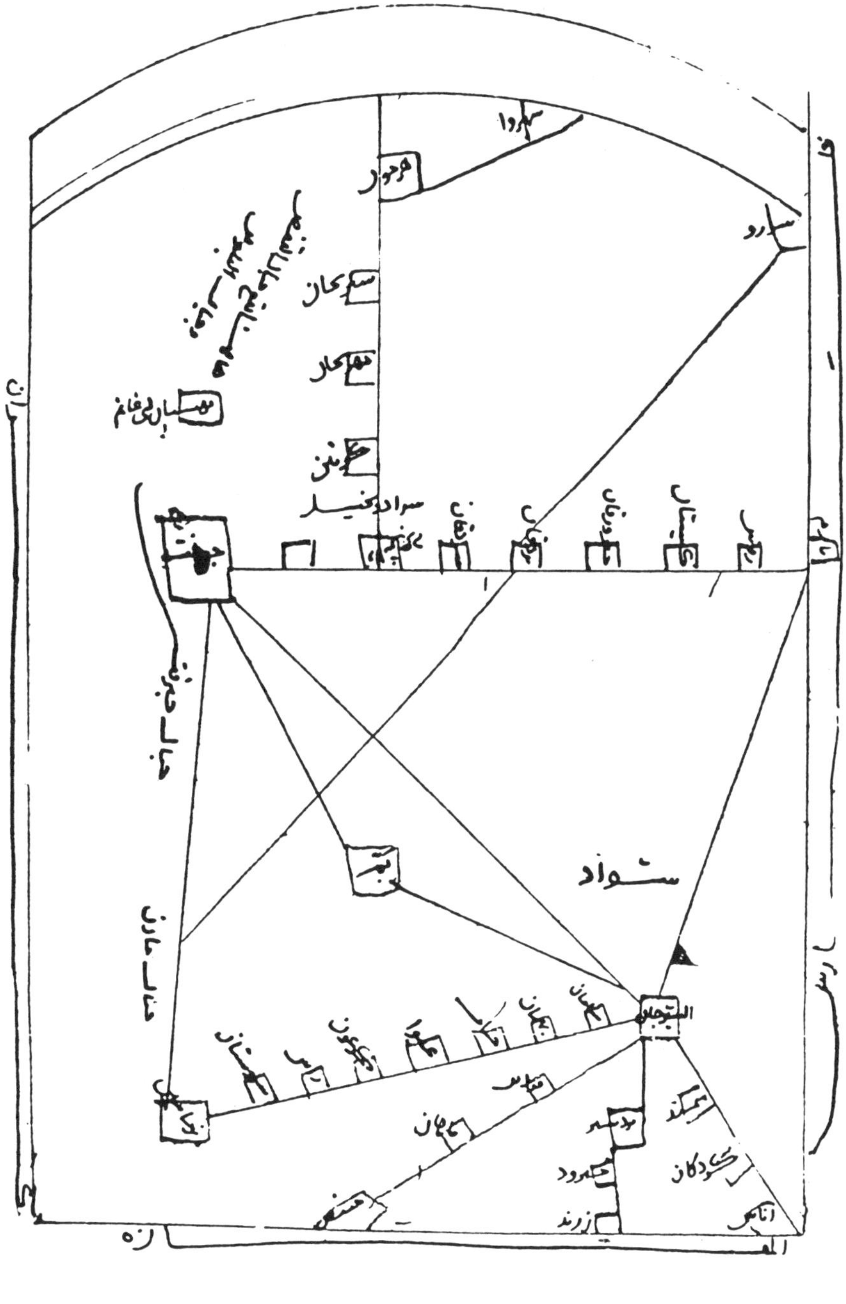

Map XVIII: Kirmān (see p. 422).
From MS. Sprenger 5—Ahlwardt 6034 by kind permission of the Staatsbibliothek
Preussischer Kulturbesitz, Berlin, Orientabteilung.

Bardasīr is the capital. It is not large, but it is fortified, and the government offices of the region are there at present, as is the army. Beside it is a large fort. Here are gardens; and a great and remarkable well was dug by Abū ʿAlī bin Ilyās, and it was he who selected this capital and lived here twenty years. There is a stronghold at the gate, and around the town is a moat with bridges over it. It has four gates: Bāb Māhān, Bāb Zarand, Bāb Khabīs, Bāb Mubārak. Most of the

p. 462 drinking water is from wells, and there is also a canal. In the middle of the town is another fort, and the mosque, a handsome one, is close to it. Gardens surround the town. The fortress is on high ground, and Ibn Ilyās used to go up there on mountainy horses accustomed to the climb, and he would sleep there every night. Canals surrounding the town irrigate the gardens here.

Māhān is a city of the Arabs. The mosque is in the middle of the town; the drinking water here is derived from a stream. In the middle of the town is a *quhandiz* with a single door, and a moat surrounds it. You travel a distance of one stage from the town to the citadel, situated among trees closely intertwined, and flowing waters.

The mosque of Kūghūn is in the centre of the town. The drinking water here is derived from a stream and canals.

Beside Zarand Ibn Ilyās built a fortress; it is a large town. The drinking water is from canals. The mosque is in the public square near the market.

Janzarūdh produces much fruit; the mosque is in the markets. There is a stream.

Unās is bigger than al-Rūdhān. It is situated right at the boundary, and is in ruin; some good copyists here. The mosque is in the middle of the market. The drinking water here is from canals. A fort stands in the middle of the town; and there are suburbs.

Kūh Binān: small, with two gates. Here are suburbs, with baths and hostels. The mosque is at the gate. Gardens surround it, and the mountains are close by. Its market is small. Knowledge there is slender, and the preacher is grievous to the spirit!

Zāwar is bigger than Kūh Bayān; there is a fortress. The town is at the boundary.

Khūnāwab is central to the region. The mosque stands amidst the markets. There are many farms, villages and sorb trees. Some of the irrigation here is by water wheels, and the mills here are turned by camels.

Qawāf and Bahāwadh have a distance of three *farsakhs* between them: they are in the cold region. Gardens are all over here; and both towns are populous and pleasant.

Thubayrā is a small town, with villages, in the cold area. The drinking water

p. 463 here is from a stream. In the middle of the town is a *quhandiz*; Ibn Ilyaīs had built a market outside the town. The mosque is in midtown.

Kāristān is cold; walnuts and farms abound. The drinking water is from a stream, from which five and twenty villages there drink.

Khabīs has a fortress, with four gates. The dates are excellent. The mosque is in midtown. The drinking water is derived from canals and a stream. Its towns are on the edge of the desert, and are quite populous. It is a source of dates, and silk; and the mulberry tree abounds.

Narmāsīr is a capital, important, large, and populous; it is an entrepôt and a source of supplies; hence it is much spoken of in this region. It is a source of supplies to which people travel, a precious place; a populous and remarkable town. Its palaces are handsome, elegant. Here are substantial merchants, an abundance of goods and camels: from here originate the caravans of Khurāsān, and thither are brought the goods of ʿUmān. Here are brought together the dates of Kirmān, and through it goes the Pilgrimage route from Sijistān. From it is exported valued Indian merchandise. Here are fine people, wealth and ease. However, the women are wanton, and the town is far removed from others. The ruler is not safe there, scoundrels are not punished. People there do not live long; there is no jurist to consider decisions, and no reader who is an Imām.

It is smaller than al-Sīrjān, has a fortress. The town has four gates: Bāb Bamm; Bāb Sūrkūn; Bāb al-Musallā; Bāb Kūshk. The mosque is in the middle of the markets, and is well attended; one ascends to it by ten steps. Built of burnt brick, it is a handsome mosque, with a minaret without compare in the region. Here stands a fort called Kūsh Warān; and at the Bamm gate are three forts named al-Akhawāt (the Sisters). Gardens and palm trees surround the town, and all kinds of fruits are assembled there. The drinking water is derived from canals; the baths here are not bad.

Rīkān has a fortress; the mosque is at the town gate. Palm trees and gardens abound.

Bāhar and Kark are two populous towns on the border of Sijistān; they both p. 464 have gardens and palm trees, a stream and canals. Both are attractive.

Nasā has gardens; is on a plain. The mosque is in the markets. The drinking water is from a stream. It is like Nābulus.

Al-Sīrjān is the metropolis of the region, the largest of the capitals, the foremost in knowledge and understanding, the best in its layout, splendour, and population. The people are prosperous, the markets extensive, the streets wide; the houses are beautiful. Here are gardens, flowing waters; the walls are lofty. It is a flourishing town, equable in climate. Plenty of money is here, abundance, special things, and manufacturing. Here stands a beautiful mosque, with a minaret. The town is large, fortified, more magnificent, more extensive than Shīrāz. The climate is moderate, the water pure, the food clean. All kinds of things are gathered there, with an abundance of agricultural products, low prices, knowledge, experience. However, most of the populace here are Muʿtazilites; and the city has few inhabitants: its towns are few. There are eight gates: Darb Hakīm; Darb Khārinjān (?); Darb Bamm; Darb Musallā; Darb al-Maydān; Darb Fudhayl; Darb Rūdhān; Darb Shaybān. The town has two markets, an old and a new, with the mosque between them, standing by itself. ʿAdhud al-Dawla built a remarkable minaret there, on top of it some very delicate contrivances, made of wood, some of which revolve. He built, too, over Bāb (Darb) Hakīm a fine house. The waters of the town are from two canals which ʿAmr and Tāhir, the two sons of Layth, constructed; they flow through the town, entering the houses of the people, spreading over their gardens. The buildings here are of clay. Most of their gardens are in the direction of Bamm.

Bīmand has a strong fortress, and iron gates. The mosque stands in the market. The drinking water is from canals.

p. 465 Al-Shāmāt has many gardens and vineyards. Its fruits are carried throughout the districts. The mosque is in the middle of the town.

Wājib is populous, has many gardens. The mosque is in the markets. The drinking water here is from canals; it has a very fine park.

Bazūrak has a large population, is at the foot of a mountain. It is surrounded by gardens, produces excellent fruit. The drinking water here is from canals.

Khūr is important, abounds in fruits. A stream flows through it, on its bank the mosque.

Dasht Barīn is an extensive rural district. Here is an abundance of dates, indigo, grains. I do not know if it has any towns.

Bahār is similar to Bamm, with buildings and date palms just as we have described.

Khannāb, from this side: some there are, however, who do not attach it to this district.

Bamm is a capital, important; fine, large. The inhabitants are a people of craftsmanship and skill. Its goods are sought after, its cloth renowned afar. In Islām it is renowned, and is the glory of the region. However, most of them are weavers, their waters are not sweet, nor is their climate good. It has a fortress. The city has four gates: Bāb Narmāsīr; Bāb Kūskān; Bāb Isbīkān; Bāb Kūjīn. In its midst is a citadel. The mosque and some of the markets are in the city, the remaining markets outside the walls. In the middle of the town is a stream that flows to the edge of the town, then cuts through the clothiers' market, enters the citadel, then goes out to the gardens. The buildings here are of very fine cohesive clay. Among their markets is the market of the Jurjān Bridge. Most of the drinking water here is from canals. Among the famous baths here is the bath of Zuqāq al-Bīdh (the Alley of the Willow). Jabal Kūd is a *farsakh* away. The mills here are on the water. Nearby is a large village in which most of the cloth is made.

Tūshtān has many gardens, produces excellent wheat. The drinking water here is from a stream and canals. It is a prosperous place, suited to agriculture.

Dārzhīn has a splendid mosque. The drinking water here is from a stream.

p. 466 Here are gardens, farms, and agricultural products; also a park.

Awārak and Mihrikird adjoin, between them a citadel which Ibn Ilyās built. The drinking water here is from a stream; the buildings are of clay.

Rāyin is small; the mosque is amidst the markets: many gardens. Much cloth is made there of the Bamm variety; it goes to the same market as the Bamm cloth.

Jīruft is the finest of the capitals, a source of fruits and produce. In it are assembled all varieties of things, here are parks and gardens. The markets, the baths are splendid, bread and meats are clean; the water melon is sweet. However, the heat is intense, and there are injurious things here. Along with that there are bedbugs and snakes; and but little knowledge or instruction. Over the town is a fortress. The town has four gates—Bāb Sābūr, Bāb Bamm, Bāb al-Sīrajān, Bāb al-Musallā (the gate of the oratory). The mosque stands at the edge of the town close to the Bamm gate, built of burnt brick and mortar, far removed from the markets. The inhabitants derive their drinking water from a stream that flows through the streets and the markets; it has a strong flow, turning twenty mill wheels. The town is bigger than Istakhr. The building is of clay on stone foundations. Snow is brought hither, and a stream flows in the mosque. The rural district is very fine indeed, assembling in its gardens date palms, walnuts; here are finest narcissus and bitter orange, and the breezes are filled with aroma from them both. This is a fine respectable city.

Hurmūz is a *farsakh* from the sea; the heat is intense. The mosque is in the markets. The drinking water is from canals of sweet water. The markets are on the main streets; the buildings here are of clay.

Bās and Jakīn are two towns a stage from the sea; smaller than Hurmūz. The mosque of each town is in the markets.

Manūqān is the Basra of Kirmān; from here come the provisions of Khurāsān of very fine cheap dates. Moreover it consists of two sections, between p. 467 them an extensive dry wādī; one side is Kūnīn, the other Zāmān. Midway between the two is a citadel and a mosque. From the two parts to the sea is a journey of two days, several days to Darahqān. It is glorious, and is like Mūqān in al-Riḥāb. Now, suppose someone were to say, "Whence did you learn that every city with name ending in '-ān' has some especial distinction?"; we should reply to him that it is known from the multiplicity of instances. There is proof for it also in the book of God—may He be exalted. Do you not see that a person may be named "Raḥīm"; so if you add the "alif" ["a"] and the "nūn" ["n"], the name becomes "Raḥmān," becoming a designation of God—may He be glorified and exalted! Do you not know also all running water is called "ḥamīm"? Then, when the "alif" ["a"] and the "nūn" ["n"] are attached to it the word becomes an attribute of Jahannam [hell]. Moreover "qiṭr" means "copper;" but when God—may He be exalted—wished to tell us that it is a punishment on the people of Jahannam, He attached the "alif" and the "nūn". ["qiṭrān," *i.e.*, "pitch, tar."]

Darahqān is surrounded by sand, and steppe, though in the vicinity of the sea. The drinking water here is from canals. Here are gardens, with palm trees. The mosque is in midtown.

Jūy Sulaymān is a medium sized town; the population is large, the rural district extensive. The drinking water is from a stream that cuts through the town. The mosque and *quhandiz* are in midtown.

Kūh Bārjān has many gardens, equable climate, many different kinds of things here. It has a *quhandiz*, and the mosque is in the town. The drinking water is derived from a stream and wells.

Qūhistān Abī Ghānim: the centre of town is hot; many date palms; the drinking water is from a stream that penetrates the town. The mosque is in midtown, and there is a *quhandiz*.

Mughūn has many gardens, and much bitter orange. The drinking water here is from canals. Here is one of the sources of indigo.

Jawāwan: small; the drinking water is from canals.

Walāshjird: over it a fortress, also a *quhandiz* called Kūsha. The drinking water here is from canals; it has gardens.

Rūdhkān: a populous town, with palm trees, gardens, and much bitter orange. The drinking water is from a stream and canals.

Of Darfānī, half pertains to the hot areas, half to the cold. It is on the main road. Here are different kinds of fruit; a fine attractive town.

Between al-Sīrjān and Bamm are: Rāʾīn, Dārzhīn, Māʾīn. Between Jīruft p. 468 and the desert are: Janzarūdh, Firzīn; and between Jīruft and al-Sīrjān are: Nājat, Khīr. Between al-Sīrjān and Fārs are: Kashīstān, Jayrūqān, Marzuqān, al-Sūraqān, Mughūn. I did not enter these places, nor did I meet any judicious person with whom I might consider their circumstances, and say to what [districts] they should be attributed.

Isbīdh, however, we consider to be like Taymāʾ.

A Summary Account of Conditions in this Region

The **hot** areas in this region exceed the cold areas, the middle being equable, like Fārs. Fārs is more extensive, more important, more populous; while this region has much wilderness, and inaccessible mountains. The area has a curved gulf at the sea coast, although al-Fārisī [Abū Ishāq Ibrāhīm bin Muhammad al-Fārisī al-Istakhrī] attributes the promontory here to Fārs, just like the sleeve of land near al-Rūdhān. The hot areas are equally hot with the hot areas of Fārs; the cold areas fall short of the cold areas of Fārs. Moreover, within the hot areas occur no cold spots, although sometimes you find a hot spot in the cold areas. The people are brown, tend to skinniness. They are submissive and blameless. The climate here is healthy, but I noticed some lepers.

p. 469 As for their **sects**: the majority are Shāfiʿites except for Jīruft, and here are but few jurisprudents. The followers of the Traditions have begun to gain the ascendancy, except in Hurmūz. Moreover, the preachers are mostly uneducated. One of their scholars was mentioned to me in Kūh Binān, so I sought out a prayer house in which their leader was, with a group of the elders. I asked them about him, so they sent a man to invite him, and then they began questioning me, eventually asking me if the people of Jerusalem prayed turning towards the

Kaʿba, and other puzzlements like that. Said I, "Does this scholar of yours hold sessions with you?" Said they, "Yes." Said I, "If he has not taught you even that much there is no point in my meeting him." I encountered another in Bamm and nothing whatever came out of his preaching. I did not find any first class people among them, or any discussions on which you could depend; much less are there literary people. The Khārijites are in evidence in Bamm, and the mosque is off by itself, containing their treasury.

Addition/version MS. C.
The sects. The overwhelming majority among their sects belong to the adherents to Tradition, except for Jīruft, where it is to the Hanafites; however the people of the Tradition clearly are increasing in the region, other than at Hurmūz. The followers of Abū Hanīfa also are numerous in the other districts; and you do not see many followers of other than the two sects, and Muʿatazilites, in Sīrjān. The majority in al-Rūdhbār, Qūhistān, al-Balūs, al-Manūjān profess to be Shīʿa.

The **customs** in this region: the people here are elegant in dress, resembling the people of Fārs in most of their fashions. They do not realize from their dates what their palm trees produce; and sometimes you find dates in places such as Manūqān, and other such as it, at one hundred *manns* for a *dirham*. It is the practice of the camel drivers to take the dates to Khurāsān on a fifty-fifty arrangement. Every year about one hundred thousand camels go there entering the place all of a sudden, and the ruler gives every camel driver a *dīnār*. Fornication and profligacy flourish at this time in Narmāsīr, and I heard one of the camel drivers say that there was a woman there with whom every camel driver down to the last man of them had fornicated on that trip.

Addition/version MS. C.
The **customs** in this region: The people here do not pick up from the ground the dates that fall, and sometimes you may find dates at one hundred *manns* for a *dirham*; moreover, even though production decreased those conditions still prevail. I heard some of them say that every year, between dates and costly Indian merchandise, about one hundred thousand loads are transported, the dates being on a fifty-fifty arrangement; sometimes they would enter the town at the same time. Someone said to me that when ʿAdhud al-Dawla entered the city the drovers came while he was there and he was awed by this. So he said: "Let us depart from a city that such masses of men can enter so suddenly; and if they leave, a *dīnār* will be given every camel driver, from the treasury of the ruler." Because of the presence of so many people Narmāsir developed considerably.

p. 470 **Commerce** is flourishing: dates are exported from here to Khurāsān, and indigo to Fārs, there being farms of this from the outskirts of Walāshjird to as far as Hurmūz. From Bamm are exported turbans, scarves, *taylasāns*, and fine cloths more choice than all of those of Marw; quite a quantity of this cloth is made in al-Sīrjān. Here too are made things also made in Qumm—some chairs, and the like, though not of quite so fine a quality. From the districts around Jīruft are raised much indigo, cumin; and the people make sweetmeats and sugar syrup for sale at a low price. The most common food of the people of this district consists of durra and dates.

The **specialties** of this region include tutty [zinc and its oxide], made up into small tubes, and indeed it is called "tubular"; the workers make up what resemble large fingers of pottery on which they pour the material, which then sticks to the fingers, staying in tubular form. I saw them gathering the ore in the mountains, and they had built a remarkable, long furnace there where they refined it just as iron is refined. I saw this only in the villages. You find no sweeter dates than the dates here, and they cannot be eaten raw, being used only for pastries. There is nothing to compare with the eight kinds of *sayhāni* dates of al-Madīna, the *burdī* date of al- Marwa, the *musqir* date of Wayla, the *musīn* date of 'Umān, the *ma'qilī* date of al-Basra, the *azād* date of al-Kūfa, the *inqilā* date of Sughar, and the *karmāshānī* (kūmāshānī?) date of this region.

The **mann** used here is that of Makka; the measures vary; the counterpoise used is the Khurasanian.

Here are **mines** of iron and silver.

Most of the **waters** used here are derived from canals. No large river runs in the region. The river of Jīruft has a strong flow; one hears its tremendous falling and roaring as it drags the stones along. It is not possible for anyone to get down to it.

> *Addition/version* MS. C.
> **Commerce** in this region: From the region dates are exported in great quantities, also syrup, and sweetmeats; from Narmāsīr, costly Indian merchandise; from Sīrjān, much cloth of the style made in Bamm, also chairs and the like; from Bamm itself, the most exquisite cloths, turbans, cloaks; from Jīruft, indigo, cumin, and other products. In the region are mines of iron and silver. It is, too, a source of sweetmeats and sugarcane. There is, too, stone that is collected from the mountains and is then refined just as iron is refined. They make up something resembling large fingers of pottery, on which they pour the material; this material is then pried from those fingers and is called "tubular", because it remains in the form of tubes. Most of the production of this that I saw was done in the villages. By far the commonest food in Jīruft is millet and dates.

The famous mountains in this region are the mountains of: al-Qufs, al-Balūs, al-Bāriz; and Silver Mine. The mountains of al-Qufs are to the north of the sea; p. 471 behind them the hot area of Jīruft, and al-Rūdhbār. To the east is al-Akhwāsh, and a wilderness lies between al-Qufs and Makrān. To the west are al-Balūs and the districts of Hurmūz;

Addition/version MS. C.

The Qufs, a people known also as al-Kūj, are the most iniquitous creatures of God—may He be exalted; they are the most malicious in disposition, the least honourable, the most remorseless at heart. They inhabit these mountains, and so did al-Balūs until ʿAdhud al-Dawla destroyed them; and we will give a thorough discussion of their condition, in our account of the Desert.

and here are said to be seven mountains, rich in date palms, fertility and farms, said to be virtually inaccessible. Most of the people there are skinny, tan in colour and perfect in features. They assert that they are Arabs, and we will make a thorough inquiry into their condition, in the wilderness, God willing. As for al-Balūs, ʿAdhud al-Dawla scattered them, taking them prisoner, and leading them into captivity; they had been quite strong, and al-Qufs used to fear them. They had grazing livestock and tents of hair, just like the Bedouin. The mountains of al-Bāriz are forested, and populated, as I have heard. They are also fairly inaccessible, but no one will be harmed among them, for they are newcomers to Islām; Yaʿqūb and ʿAmr, the two sons of al-Layth, invaded them. Here are iron and other mines. The Mountains of the Mines are those in which there is silver, their length being about two stages. In Kirmān are gorges, populated and forested, such as al-Darbānī (al-Darfānī), and others like it.

The **language** spoken here is understandable, being close to Khurasanian. Sometimes the language of the rural district is incomprehensible. The language of al-Qufs and of al-Balūs is not understandable, resembling that of al-Sind.

Addition/version MS. C.

As for their **coinage**: The Daylamites [Būyids] had struck *dirhams* like those called Qaṭārī, bought at thirty to the *dīnār*. It circulates in the seven regions [of the non-Arabs]. They have another very good *dirham* here, also, called the ʿAdalī.

The **site** of this region. Two-thirds of the region is hot, from Jīruft and the mountains of al-Qufs, and Dasht Bar(-īn) and Ruwīst, and the districts and villages included in this area. The towns of Bamm are within it also as far as the edge of the desert and the borders of Makrān. There is no cold area in what lies to the east beyond Jīruft and Bamm. To the west of Jīruft is a cold area, p. 472 and snow, between Jabal al-Fidhdha as far as Darbānī (Darfānī), until you look down over Jīruft.

Al-Mījān (Mīzān) is cold, and from here usually come the fruit and the snow for Jīruft. One-third of the region is cold area, from remote al-Sīrjān to the border of Fārs, then to the wilderness on this side. Kuwāshīr (Bardasīr) is included here; Khabīs, however, is in the hot area. This commentary of our report has possibly sometimes mentioned a cold area as being hot. East of the borders of Kirmān is the country of Makrān and its desert. The sea is beyond al-Balūs. To the west is the country of Fārs, to the north is the wilderness; the sea is to the south of it.

Āl Sāmān (Family of Sāmān) held the sovereignty over this region, and al Muʿtamid assigned it to Ismāʿīl, in the year 290/902 when he defeated ʿAmr bin al-Layth. Then Abū ʿAlī bin Ilyās rebelled and assumed control; these rulers used to be mentioned by name in the Friday sermons. Then ʿAlī bin Buwayh took possession of it and it remains to the Būyids to the present. However, every year they bring to the ruler of Khurāsān two hundred thousand *dīnārs*; nor did they take possession of the area without tremendous bloodshed and disruption of the population, most of the province being totally devastated. I read in a book in Fārs a tradition linked to the Prophet—God's peace and blessings be upon him: "I have a vision of the significance of the Daylamites in my community. They have protected their wealth, destroyed the mosques, raped the women, weakened Islām, eliminated prosperity, destroyed the armies, and no one will defeat them unless God orders. A man will emerge from the land of Khurāsān, fair of countenance, a horseman, white on his cheeks, on his chest a black mole; handsome of stature, of great seriousness, a learned philosopher, his name Nabiyyun, of the offspring of the Persians. Through his hands God will open al-Darwāzāt al-Sughrā [small gate of Khurāsān], and he will take possession of Khurāsān to al-Darwāzāt al-Kubrā [large gate of Khurāsān], and he will not put away his sword until not one remains who carries arms." It was said, "O Messenger of God, what will be after that?" Said he, "The ruler of Khurāsān will go out to the house of God, and he will be mentioned in the Friday sermon on the pulpits in Khurāsān, al-Zawrāʾ, the land of Fārs, al-ʿIrāq, and Makka, and al-Madīna." It was said, "O Messenger of God, what will be after that?" "A long period will ensue when people will become like lions; they will not perform their obligations, nor will they safeguard what is holy."

p. 473 The **land tax** of Kirmān is sixty thousand *dirhams*. The imposts at Shahrwā and Sūrū are lighter than the imposts of Sīrāf.

The **distances** in this region:
From Bardasīr to al-Sīrjān, two stages.

From Bardasīr to the edge of the wilderness to Janzarūdh, one stage;
    thence to Zarand, one stage;
    thence to the wilderness, one stage.

From Narmāsīr to al-Fahraj, one stage;
    and this is on the edge of the wilderness.

From Narmāsīr to Jūy Sulaymān, three stages;
    thence to Rīkān, one stage;
    thence to Mūkhkān, one stage;
    thence to al-Tīb, one stage;

thence to Marūghān, one stage;
thence to Bās, and Jakīn, one stage;
thence to Harūk, one stage;
thence to Qasr Mahdī, one stage;
thence to Hurmūz, one stage;
thence to al-Furdha [the gap], two post stages.

From al-Sīrjān to Kāhūn, two stages;
thence to Rustāq, one stage.

From al-Sīrjān to Bīmand, two post stages;
thence to Kardakān, one post stage;
thence to Unās, one stage;
thence to al-Rūdhān, two post stages.

From al-Sīrjān to al-Shāmāt, one stage;
thence to Bihār, one stage;
thence to Khannāb, one stage;
thence to Ghubayrā, one stage;
thence to Kūghūn, one *farsakh*;
thence to Rāʾīn, one stage;
thence to Sarwistān, one stage;
thence to Dārzhīn, one stage;
thence to Bamm, one stage.

From al-Sīrjān to Firzīn, two stages;
thence to Māhān, one stage;
thence to Khabīs, three stages.

From Bamm to Narmāsīr, one stage;
and from Bamm to Dārjīn, one stage;
thence to Hurmūz, one stage;
thence to Jīruft, one stage.

The Region of Al-Sind (Plain of Lower Indus)

This is the region of gold and of commerce, of medicaments and simples, of sweetmeats and resources, of rice, bananas, and wondrous things. Here are low prices, prosperity, palms and dates; justice, fairness, and administration. Here are specialties, profitable things and merchandise; profits, glorious qualities, commerce, manufactures. Here is an important metropolis, notable cities, capitals. Good health is here, and trustworthiness. The sea adjoins it, the river flows through it. It contains palms; and plains, agricultural lands not needing irrigation. Here is an elegant metropolis, a noble river, uncommon things. However, its non-Muslims are polytheists, scholars there are few; moreover, you cannot reach it except after the dangers of the land and the terrors of the sea, after hardships and mental stress. Here is a representation of its form and features. [Map XIX]

We have made this region five districts, and have added Makrān to it because it adjoins it, has an affinity with it; and so that the regions will be continuous with one another—but in God is success. The first area in front of Kirmān is Makrān [coastal province SE Īrān]; then Tuwārān, then al-Sind, then Wayhind, then Qannawj (Kannawj), then al-Multān; we have included al-Multān also for the reason we just mentioned.

For it is as if we had returned to the borders of Khurāsān, and completed our account of the regions of the non-Arabs, all of them; and we have excepted no Islamic country.

You should know that I have visited the frontiers of this region, have reached all its shores, and have seen and heard what I am about to recount. I asked many questions about the names of places here, and examined accounts of it; I have learned of its cities. Nevertheless, I do not vouch for the description of it as I vouch for that of the other regions. I describe only the metropoles, not going into an examination of any commentary that was related to me—it is sufficient to make a man a liar if he but relates everything he hears. And there is the saying of the Prophet—God's peace and blessings be upon him: "Merely getting a report does not compare with direct observation." Indeed, were it not for fear that this work of ours would be deficient, so that only the original Islamic lands would be in it, I should refrain from mention of this region altogether. The model and pattern have been made according to what I have derived from a person of understanding who has known this region, and has traveled over it. Most of the analogies I made in exemplifying the regions I did not use until I had checked with the judicious persons of that region, and had recourse to the people of understanding there; and I have derived much concerning this region from the work of Ibrāhīm bin Muhammad al-Fārisī [al-Istakhrī] whom we call al-Karkhī, on whom we have depended—but in God is our recourse.

As for Makrān, its capital is Bannajbūr, and among its towns are: Mashka, Kīj, Sarī, Shahr, Barbūr (Zhanzhūr), Khwāsh, Damindān, Jālak, Dazak, Dasht

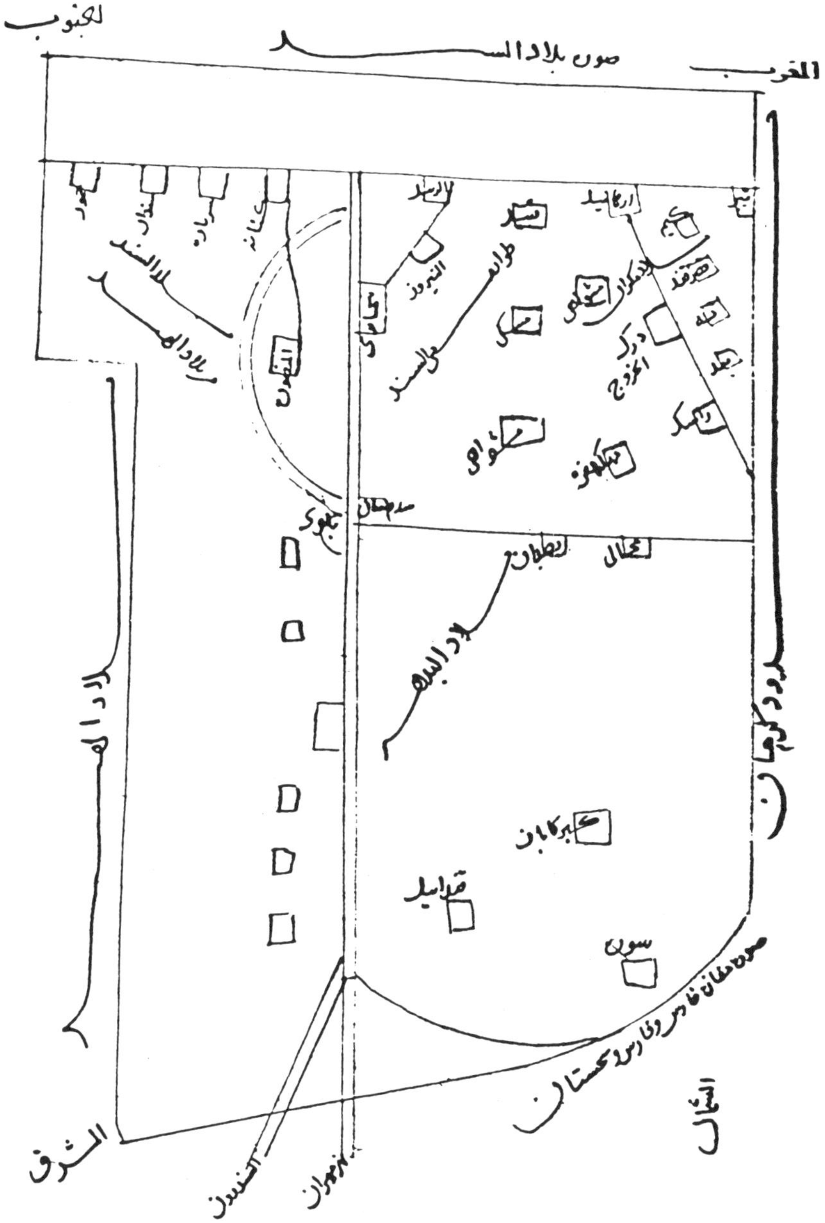

Map XIX: Al-Sind (see p. 423).
From MS. Sprenger 5—Ahlwardt 6034 by kind permission of the Staatsbibliothek
Preussischer Kulturbesitz, Berlin, Orientabteilung.

'Alī, al-Tīz; and the Persian [al-Istakhrī] mentions, Kabartūn, Rāsak—which he
p. 476 said is the town of exit—also Bih, Band, Qasr-Qand, Asfīqa, Fahal-Fahra, Qanbalā, Armābīl (Armā'īl). Among the foremost he mentions al-Tīz, Mashka, and Dizak, but he says nothing further about them.

As for Tuwārān, the capital is Quzdār, and among its towns are: Qandābīl, Bajathrad, Jathrad, Bakānān, Khūzī, Rustākuhan, Rustāq Rūdh, Mūrdān, Rustāq Māsakān, Kahrkūr. The Persian [al-Istakhrī] also mentions: Mahālī, Kīzkānān, Sūra [Shūra], Quzdār, and mentions no others.

As for al-Sind, its capital is al-Mansūra; and among its cities are: Daybul,
p. 477 Zandarīj, Kadār, Māyil, Tanbalī; and al-Istakhrī also mentions al-Nīrūn (Bīrūn), Qāllarī, Annarī, Ballarī, al-Maswāhī, al-Bahraj, Bāniya, Manjābarī (Manhātarī), Sadūsān, al-Rūr (Arūr), Sūbāra, Kīnās, Saymūr.

As for Wayhind, al-Istakhrī calls it al-Hind, saying that the cities of al-Hind are: Qāmuhul, Kanbāya, Sūbāra, Sandān, Saymūr, al-Multān, Jandarūr, Basmad; then said he, these are the cities of this country. I asked a man of knowledge and judgment who used to teach in Shīrāz and al-Ahwāz, and who used to relate narratives, who acknowledged that he was an ascetic, and who, moreover, had lived in those countries a long time—said I: "Describe to me those areas in a way that I can put into my book, and give such a good account of it so that I may, as it were, see them." Similarly, I asked another legist of the followers of Abu al-Haytham from Naysābūr, and he had traveled in those areas, and knew the conditions there. From what the two told me I verified that Wayhind is the capital, and among the cities are: Widhān, Bītar, Nūj, Lawār, Samān, Kūj.

p. 478 As for Qannawj (Kannawj), that is also the name of its capital; among its cities are: Qadār, Ābār, Kahāra, Bārd, Wujayn, Ūriha, Zahū, Har, Barhīrawā, but al-Istakhrī does not mention these at all.

As for al-Multān, that is also the name of its capital; among its cities are: Barār, Rāmādhān, Warwīn, Barūr.

Bannajbūr is the capital of Makrān, with a fortress built of clay, around which is a moat. It is situated among palm trees, and has two gates: Bāb Tūrān, Bāb al-Tīz. The drinking water here is derived from a river. The mosque is in the midst of the markets. They are a barbarous lot being Muslim in name only. Their language is Balūchī.

Al-Tīz is on the sea; it has an abundance of palms, excellent caravanserais, and a handsome mosque. The people are a middling lot, no science, no finesse; even so, it is a famous seaport.

Quzdār (Qusdār) is the capital of Tūrān. Situated in desert, it has two sections between which is a dry wādī without bridges. On one side is the palace of the ruler, also a fort. The other side is called Būdīn, in it the houses of the merchants, and the depots; this is the more spacious and cleaner part. The capital, though small, has much to offer, and caravans go there from Khurāsān, Fārs, Kirmān, and from the districts of al-Hind. The water there, however, is vile, and if someone should drink of it his stomach swells. Their ruler is just and unpretentious. The buildings of its towns are of clay. The drinking water is derived from underground canals—these are in the desert—except for Kathrad (Jathrad) and Kīzkanān—both of these have a stream; Kathrad has wells, also. The farm areas of both these towns have a healthy climate. All the towns are hot, except Kathrad—it is cold; in fact sometimes snow falls there, and the water freezes.

p. 479   Al-Mansūra is the capital of al-Sind, and is the metropolis of the region. It is somewhat like Damascus. The buildings here are of wood and clay, the mosque of stone and baked brick. The mosque is large like that of ʿUmān, built on pillars of teak. The town has four gates: Bāb al-Bahr, Bāb Tūrān, Bāb Sandān, Bāb al-Multān. A river encircles the area. The people are characterized by refinement and good character, and are favourable towards Islām. Many learned people are there, commerce is profitable; they are a people of intelligence, charm, knowledge and kindness. The climate is mild, the winter easy, the rains abundant. Many different kinds of things are assembled here, and some remarkable special things. Large buffaloes are here. The drinking water is derived from the Mihrān River (Indus). The mosque is amidst the markets. In manners the people here resemble those of al-ʿIrāq, having humbleness, and noble natures. However, the heat is great there, bedbugs are everywhere, and the people are phlegmatic. Most of them are infidels; their borders have been ravaged, and few noble people are left there.

    Daybul is on the sea, with about a hundred villages surrounding it; most of the people are infidels. The water beats against the walls of the town. It has an entirely merchant population, speaking both Sindī and Arabic. It is the port of the area, giving rise to a considerable income. There the Mihrān (Indus) flows into the sea, yet the mountains are within shouting distance. The market is right on the sea. Here are a people of elegance and fine dress.

    Tanbalī has a fortress; maritime; few Muslims here; the merchants are well-supplied.

    Wayhind is an important capital, bigger than al-Mansūra, possessing many superb gardens and situated on level ground. Here are flowing rivers, abundant rains. Many varieties of things are assembled here, with superb fruits, trees all around, evident prosperity, low prices. Three *manns* of honey cost a *dirham*, p. 480 and you need not ask about the cheapness of the bread and dairy products! The people are free of troubles and have rid themselves of infirmities. The trees grow thick all around here, including walnuts and almonds, with plenty of dates and bananas. The air, however, is humid, and the heat oppressive. The building here are of straw and wood, and sometimes fire breaks out in the cane buildings. The city is like Fasā and Sābūr, were it not for these problems.

    Qannawj (Kannawj) is a large capital with a central town and suburbs. Meats are abundant there, water flows freely, and gardens are all around about. The people are beautiful of countenance, the water is safe to drink. It is an extensive place, with profitable commerce. Everything is fresh there, and bananas are cheap. However, conflagrations are common, flour is scarce, their food being rice. The people wear loincloths. The buildings are wretched, the summers abominable. From the city to the mountains is four *farsakhs*. The mosque is in the suburbs. Meats are cheap. The river penetrates the town. The main food of the Muslims is wheat. There are scholars and important people here.

Qadār is a delightful place with an excellent climate; many gardens. The rulers of the capital go out there to summer, during the great heat, and the people of the other cities of the hot area do likewise. The drinking water is from streams and canals.

Al-Multān is like al-Mansūra, except that it is more populous. Though it has not much fruit yet prices are low: bread is thirty *manns* for a *dirham*, and you get three *manns* of sweetmeats for a *dirham*. The houses are handsome like those of Sīrāf, built of teakwood, and with a number of storeys. There is neither fornication nor drunkenness here; and anyone the people catch doing those things they kill, or imprison. They do not lie in their selling, nor lessen their measures, nor diminish their weights. They love the strangers. Most of them are Arabs. The drinking water here is from a copious stream. Produce is abundant there, commerce flourishing, prosperity evident; the rulers are just. You do not see a woman dressed up in the markets, nor would anyone speak to her publicly. The water is wholesome, living is pleasant and elegant. They are a fine people, speaking understandable Fārsi, practicing considerable commerce, and with p. 481 healthy bodies. However, the town is situated in a dirty salt pan, the houses are narrow, the air is hot and dry. The people are brown or black. And this is what I know of the description of the towns of this region.

A Summary Account of Conditions in this Region

This is a hot region, with palms, coconuts, bananas. Here are places with an equable climate. This is a community of much diversity, as for example at Wayhind, and the districts of al-Mansūra. The sea reaches the greater portion of it, but I do not know of any lake there. It has, however, a number of rivers. The non-Muslims here worship idols. Preachers here are not respected, nor do the people have any characteristics you would recount.

As for their **religious schools**—most of the Muslims here are Sunnī; and I saw the Qādhī Abū Muhammad al-Mansūrī, a Dāwūdite, acting as leader in his school. He provides instructions and composition there, and has produced a number of very good books. The people of al-Multān are Shī‘a; they say *hayya ‘ala al-salāt! hayya ‘ala al-falāh!* (Come to prayer! Come to salvation!) in the *adhān*, and they say the *iqāma* twice. The capitals do not lack jurists of the school of Abū Hanīfa—may God show him mercy; but there are neither Mālikites nor Mu‘tazilites there, nor are there Hanbalites; for the people are on the True Path. The schools there are praiseworthy, there is uprightness and decency, and God has kept them free of excess and fanaticism, confusion, and discord.

From Tuwārān are **exported** sweetmeats of the finest quality; from Māsakān and Sandān, much rice and cloth. In the rest of the region some mats are made, and the same sorts of things as are made in Qūhistān, and Khurāsān. A great amount of coconuts is exported, as are fine cloths. From al-Mansūra are exported expensive Indian sandals; also from here elephants, ivory, and other precious things, and effective medicaments.

The **mann** used in Tuwārān is that of Makka, likewise in al-Multān, al-Sind, and al-Hind.

p. 482 The **measures** used: that in Tuwārān is called the *kayjī*, and is the equivalent of forty *manns* of wheat; one may find between eight and four *kayjīs* for one *dirham*. The standard of measure in al-Multān is called *matal*, and equals twelve *manns* of wheat.

> *Addition/version* MS. C.
> The *mann* used in Tuwārān is that of Makka; and the name of the standard measure of al-Multān is *matal*, and it equals twelve *manns* of wheat, and their *mann* is that of Makka. The people of Tuwārān use the *kayjī*, the equivalent of forty-nine *manns* of wheat; one may find between eight and four *kayjīs* for one *dirham*.

The **dirhams** of al-Sind are called *qāharīyāt*, at five to the *dirham*. Also used in the *tātarā* which is the equivalent of a *dirham* and two thirds. The *dirhams* of al-Multān are the same as the *dirhams* of the Fātimids. The use of the *qāharīyāt* has spread here; that used in Ghaznīn resembles the *qurūdh* of Yaman; still the *qarawiyya* is the more important there.

> *Addition/version* MS. C.
> The **coinage** in this region: Their coins are the *dirhams* called *Qandahārī*, weighed at five to the *dirham*; also used is the *tātarā*, the equivalent of a *dirham* and two thirds. The *ratls* of al-Multān and the coins in circulation there are like those used by al-Maghribī [the Fātimids], and the *Qandahārī* is current there also.

The **specialties** in this region. Here is a fruit called a lemon, something like the apricot, and very sour. Another fruit, something like the plum, is called a mango, and is delicious. The *fālij* [large two humped camel] which you see in the Orient and Fārs covers the Bactrian female, being bigger than the male Bactrian. It has two humps, and is a first class animal. It is not used by anyone, indeed no one owns it, except kings; only it sires the Bactrian. Superb Indian sandals are made here also.

> *Addition/version* MS. C.
> The **customs** in this region: The people commonly let their hair grow quite long. They wear a garment called the *qurtaq*, and they pierce their ears in the manner of the people of al-Hind. They commonly wear a loincloth, except for

the merchants and people in high office; rarely do they go shod. The people of al-Multān do not commonly tuck their turbans under the chin. The people of Makrān are ignorant, brown in complexion, and their speech is like the sounds of birds.

The **people** of Makrān are stupid, brown in colour, wild of speech. They dress in a garment called *qarātiq*, wear their hair long, and pierce their ears, just as do the people of al-Hind; most of the areas of the region are just as we have reported.

The **Mihran River** (Indus) does not differ from the Nile at all, in point of the sweetness of the water, its rising, and the presence of crocodiles in it. Its source is from the district where appear some of the branches of the Jayhūn, before p. 483 al-Wakhsh. It appears in the area of al-Multān, then flows to the borders of al-Mansūra, and enters the sea at Daybul. Farms depend on its floods, just as we reported for Egypt. The river Sandarūd, about three stages distant from al-Multān, is large, and its water, sweet.

As for the **idols** in this region, there are two in Habrawā made of stone: no one approaches them. They have a power such that should a man try to lay his hand on one, it will be held back and will not reach the idol. They both appear as though made of gold and silver. It is said that if one expresses a wish in their presence, the request will be granted. Here is a spring of water, green like verdigris, colder than ice, and the stones in it will heal wounds. The eunuchs live on the profits of fornication, and many are the endowments from fornication here. Anyone who wishes to consecrate his daughter establishes a *waqf* there. The two statues are quite enchanting. I saw a Muslim man who said he had forsaken Islām to return to the worship of the idols, having been captivated by them; when he returned to Naysābūr he became Muslim again. The two idols really are miraculous! In importance after those two is the idol of al-Multān, and the whole district is devoted to it. It is sometimes called Faraj Bayt al-Dhahab (relief of the house of gold), because when the Muslims conquered al-Multān they were in poor circumstances, but they found enough gold there to enrich them. The temple of this idol is a palace built in the most flourishing part of the markets. In the middle of it is a handsome dome around which are the dwellings of the eunuchs. The idol is under the dome in the form of a man sitting cross-legged on a chair, made of plaster and brick, and he is dressed in pelts that look like those of the red squirrel; no part of him is seen except his p. 484 eyes, and these are jewels. On his head is a crown of gold. His arms are stretched out on his knees, and the fingers of his hands are folded as if he were counting four. The idols other than these are inferior to them.

The **vegetated** areas are Makrān, al-Rāhūq, al-Daybul, Armābīl (Armāʾīl), Qanbalā, these having the best climate. The grazing is extensive, with great numbers of cattle, though these live in filthy conditions. There are emporiums and ports. Sandān, Saymūr, and Kanbāya are fertile places; prices are low, and they are sources of rice and honey. Near the banks of the Mihrān are desert areas with many nomads. Most of the areas of Makrān are areas of desert, drought, and poverty. Here it is hot, open country, with one district called al-Khurūj (the exit), with its city Rāsak; another town called Kharzān. From the direction of Kirmān, the district of Mashka adjoins it, three stages wide; few palm trees are there, although there is some assortment of products. Most of Makrān, however, is desert. Where there is a cultivated area the climate is healthy. It has swamps like the swamps of al-ʿIrāq, deserts like those of the Kurds. Here are many Zutt (gypsies) living in reed huts, feeding on fish and waterfowl.

Al-Rāhūq and Kalwān are two rural areas adjoining and added to Makrān. Some consider al-Rāhūq as associated with al-Mansūra; in any case it produces little fruit. The biggest town in Makrān is al-Fannazbūr (Bannajbūr); in it are palms. Here is also al-Quzdār, fertile, with low prices; here are to be found grapes, and many different kinds of products, but no date palms.

As for the **situation** of this region: east of it is the Sea of Fārs, west of it, Kirmān, and the desert of Sijistān, with its provinces. To the north are the other countries of al-Hind, and to the south is the desert between Makrān and the mountains of al-Qufs, beyond which is the Sea of Fārs. However, the Sea of Fārs surrounds the eastern parts of these countries, and the southern parts beyond these deserts, since this sea reaches from Saymūr on the east to Tīz, the port of Makrān, then turns around this desert so that it curves around the territories of Kirmān and Fārs.

The towns in the area of Makrān are: al-Tīz, Kabartūn, Dazak, Rāsak, Bih, Band, Qasr-Qand, Asfiqa, Fahal-Fahra, Mashkā, Qanbalā, Armābīl (Armāʾīl).

Different forms of **government** are present in this region. There is an p. 485 independent ruler over Makrān: he is a humble, just man whose like you do not see. Over al-Mansūra, however, is a ruler from the Quraysh [tribe]. Here the Friday prayer is for the ʿAbbāsids, though it used to be for ʿAdhud al-Dawla; I saw their messenger who had come to his son while I was in Shīrāz. In al-Multān the prayer is for the Fātimids, and they neither dissolve nor make contracts except in that name, and their messengers are constantly going to Egypt with gifts. The present ruler is a powerful and a just man. The ascendancy in Qannawj (Kannawj) and in Wayhind is in the hands of unbelievers; the Muslims have an independent ruler of their own.

Addition / version MS. C.
[Al-Mansūra] was ruled by a people of the Quraysh, and the Friday prayer is for the house of al-ʿAbbās, though on the littoral it used to be for ʿAdhud al-Dawla; I saw their chief at the house of his son in Shīrāz, appealing for help for a youth who had rebelled against him. As for al-Makrān, it had a powerful ruler, but I

heard that at the present day the Friday prayer there is for al-Maghribī [the Fāṭimids]. At Kannawj most of the people are infidels, and the Muslims there also have an independent ruler; similarly at Wayhind. As for al-Multān, its ruler has given his allegiance to al-Maghribī, and the Friday prayer is in his name; moreover, communication never ceases between them, nor the exchange of gifts; neither do they appoint a governor without a directive from him.

Taxes. On a load entering Tuwārān an impost of six *dirhams* is levied; similarly on a load going out. On a slave is an impost of twelve *dirhams*, but only on his entry. On a load coming from al-Hind is a tax of twenty *dirhams*; on a load from al-Sind the tax is according to values of the quantities of imports. On a dyed leather the tax is a *dirham*. Every year the revenue there is a million *dirhams*, reckoned by the decimal system.

The **distances** in this region:
From Tīz Makrān to Kīs (Kīj), five stages;
    thence to Fannazbūr, two stages;
    thence to Dazak, three stages;
    thence to Rasak, a like distance;
    thence to Fahal-Fahra, a like distance;
    thence to Asfiqa, two stages;
    thence to Band, one stage;
    thence to Bih, one stage;
    thence to Qasr-Qand, one stage;
    thence to Armābīl, six stages;
    thence to Daybul, four stages.

From al-Tīz to Quzdār on the coast across the length of Makrān, twelve stages.

p. 486 From al-Mansūra to Daybul, six stages;
    from al-Mansūra to al-Multān, twenty stages;
    from al-Mansūra to the boundary of al-Budha, five stages;
    thence to al-Tīz, fifteen stages.

From al-Multān to Ghaznīn is a distance of eighty *farsakhs* through steppe and desert; a charge of one hundred fifty *dirhams* is levied on a load, apart from the money for safe passage. Sometimes the road is cut off by brigands for three months at a time.

From al-Multān to al-Mansūra, by way of villages and cultivated areas, forty *farsakhs*; and it is one hundred through the steppe, with little cultivation.

From al-Mansūra to Quzdār, eighty *farsakhs*;
    thence to Kankābān (Kandābān), a like distance;

thence to Sīwah, a like distance;
thence to the city of Walāshtān, a like distance;
thence to Sāghan, sixty *farsakhs*: in the midst of this town is a mosque;
thence to Ghazīn, one stage.

From Quzdār to Mashka, fifty *farsakhs*;
thence to Jālak, thirty *farsakhs*;
thence to Khwāsh, a like distance;
thence to Sarī Shahr, one *farsakhs*;
thence to Nahr (Jūy) Sulaymān, a like distance;
thence to Darhfā, fifty *farsakhs*;
and to Jīruft, a like distance.

From al-Multān to Bālis, ten stages;
thence to Qandābīl, four;
thence to Quzdār, five.

From Qandābīl to al-Mansūra, eight [stages];
or to al-Multān, fifteen, through desert areas;
and from al-Mansūra to Qāmuhul, eight stages;
thence to Kanbāya, four stages;
thence to Sūbāra, a like distance, and this town is about a *farsakh* from the
sea.

From Sandān to Saymūr, five stages;
thence to Sarandīb, fifteen stages.

From al-Multān to Basmad, two stages;
thence to al-Rūr (Arūr), three stages;
thence to Annarī, four stages;
thence to Qāllarī, two stages;
thence to al-Mansūra, one stage;
thence to Qamuhul, one stage.

The Desert that Lies Among these Regions

You should know that among the regions of the non-Arabs, except al-Riḥāb and Khūzistān, is a desert, oblong in shape, that is right in the middle of them. No river flows there, nor is there a lake; no rural areas, no towns. Very few people live there, but brigands are many! The roads are difficult, and areas of jurisdiction are not clear. The mountains are frightening, villages far apart from one another, places virtually impossible to get to. Roads are blocked off by robbers, springs are a trickle. However, the cisterns, with their protective domes on the roads through this desert, are frequent, and the distances between the cisterns short. In various places in the desert are salt marshes, sand dunes, some creeks, and some fearsome desolation. Most of it pertains to Khurāsān, some each to Kirmān, Fārs, al-Jibāl, al-Sind, and Sijistān; on this account there is much brigandage, since, when they are cut off in one jurisdiction they flee to another,

Addition/version MS. C.

... until ʿAḍhud al-Dawla carried out a military expedition against them, extirpated al-Balūs, ravished al-Qufs, taking eighty youths from them as hostages; and to the present time they are kept in prison in Shīrāz. They are sent back after a set time, and another eighty take their place; in this way the interests of the Daylamites are safeguarded from that direction; and the aggression occurs in the districts of Khurāsān...

and hide in the mountain of Karkas Kūh or Siyāh Kūh where they cannot be overcome, or even reached.

Addition/version MS. C.

Discussion of al-Qufs arose one day in the assembly of Abu al-Fadhl bin Nahāma in Shīrāz. He said that they displayed the courage of lions only because of the heedlessness of the ruler of Khurāsān in respect of them. Said I: "God support the shaykh! But you have the source of the spring and the fountainhead of the people [Qufs] under your control, and so the blame, then, is to lie on the ruler of Khurāsān?" On the contrary, the remarkable fact concerning the Daylamites is how they have left them in the midst of their territories, and have demarcated the boundaries of their communities as far as the desert.

No towns are here except Safīd, and this is on the border of Sijistān. But all around on the edges of the desert are well-known towns; pertaining to Kirmān are: Khabīs, Zāwar, Narmāsīr, Kūh Binān; to Fārs are: Yazd, Kathah, ʿUqda, Zarand; to Isfahan is: Ardistān; to al-Jilbāl are: Qumm, Qāshān, Dizah; to Quhistān are Tabas, Kurī, Qāyin, Khūr; and to al-Daylam is Biyār.

The desert is like the sea, and you may travel in it in any direction you wish, if you know your course. However, the roads we have shown on our map have become well-known and much used, because of the domed cisterns that are maintained there [Map XX]. And if we ... [lacuna in MS.] ... so that we were to

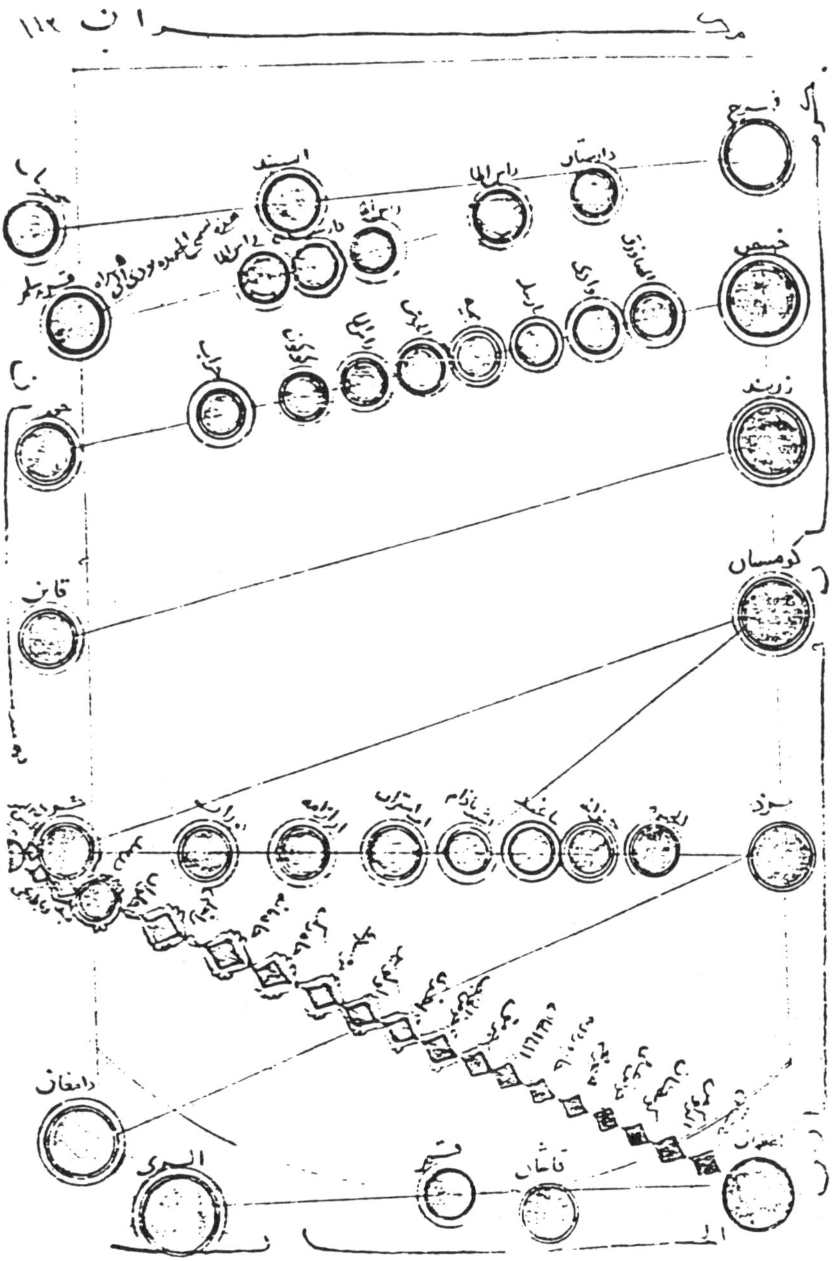

Map XX: The Persian Desert (see p. 424).
From Ayasofya, 2971 m. by kind permission of T.C. Basbakanlik, Kültür
Müstesarligi, Süleymaniye Kütüphanesi Müdürlügü, Istanbul, Turkey.

show all its roads and exits, the viewer would be amazed at that; for roads go out of it to Biyār and Khusrūjird and places no one pays any attention to. One time we left Tabas headed for Fārs, and we spent seventy days in the desert swerving from one area to another, one time getting on to the Kirmān road, another time coming close to Isfahān. In this way I saw so many of its roads and twistings that I could not count them. It is all mountainous, with a little sand, easy mountain passes, difficult saltpans, cold places, hot places, date palms, tillage. I saw that the easiest and most developed road is that of al-Rayy, the most difficult that of Fārs, the shortest that of Kirmān. However, they are all to be dreaded because of a people called al-Qufs,

Addition/version MS. C.
These Qufs inhabit the mountains in Kirmān, adjacent to the district of Jīruft in Naysābūr, and they move along from there as far as the desert, like locusts.

who descend on the roads from the mountains of Kirmān. They are an ignominious group with frightful faces, relentless hearts, strong and tough. They p. 489 spare no one; not being satisfied with just getting the money, they stone to death anyone they overcome,

Addition/version MS. C.
... so that they do not kill with a weapon every one of those they overwhelm, rather they pound their heads and thus they kill them; and every person they seize they slay.

just as you would kill snakes. You see them putting the head of a man on a rock, and beating it with a stone until it splits. I asked them about this practice, and they said it was so their swords would not be blunted. No one escapes from them except very rarely. They have hiding places in the mountains in which they can fortify themselves, and whenever they are cut off in one jurisdiction they flee to another. They fight with arrows, but they also have swords. The Balūs (Balūchī) were worse than they until ʿAdhud al-Dawla overcame them; he hit these others also. The ruler of Fārs always has a number of them as hostages—one group comes, and another group goes—so that if caravans have a bodyguard from the ruler of Fārs the brigands do not interfere with it. They are the most enduring of God's creatures in suffering hunger and thirst. Their food is just anything they can find, even the nuts of the lotus, on which they feed. They put their Islamic faith in abeyance, and are harsher on Muslims they capture than they are on Romaeans or Turks. When they capture a man they bid him run with them barefoot and half-starved for about twenty *farsakhs*. They have no wish for riding animals, nor do they practice riding, preferring to go on foot; occasionally they ride swift-footed asses.

A Muslim who had fallen into their hands told me the following. Said he, "They found with us some books and they asked among the prisoners for a man who could read them, and I said that I could. So they took me to their leader, and when I read the book he approached me and began asking me about some things

p. 490 in it. Said he, 'What do you say about our blocking off the roads and killing?' Said I, 'Anyone who does these things merits from God detestation, and most grievous punishments in the next world.' The other sighed deeply and toppled over onto the ground, his face turning yellow from the fear of God. Then he released me with a group of the people." I have heard a group of merchants say that, according to the robbers themselves, they take only ill-gotten money, and they consider what they take to be their right, and in fact an obligation on them.

The biggest and most forbidding of the **mountains** in the desert is Karkas Kūh [kūh = mountain], and to its area pertains the portion of this desert that is towards al-Rayy. It is not that it is so big, but rather that its ascent is very much interrupted, there being many steep inclines, turns, lurking-holes, and secret, out of the way hiding places. Near it, as we have said, is Siyāh Kūh: it is smaller than the other, but is, for all that, forbidding. The highway of al-Rayy lies between the two mountains, going near Qasr al-Jiss, and here is a low-lying area.

In the desert are some **remarkable sights**. About two *farsakhs* from Ra's al-Mā' toward Khurāsān are small black stones for a distance of about four *farsakhs*. Near Qabr (the grave of) al-Hājjī toward Barask are small pebbles some of which are white like camphor, some of a green color, like glass. Between Khurāsān and Kirmān are stone images of almonds, apples, lentils, vegetables, and a number of men. A remarkable castle is here in which are statues, wearing very fine necklaces; it is really amazing, and I have never seen anything like it.

Addition/version MS. C.
Near al-Jarmaq are some black mounds which people assert are the ashes of the fire of Abraham—on whom be peace! We have established that the well-known **routes** here are four in number, and they are the main roads; we mention, moreover, those of the secondary roads that should be mentioned. The first of the major routes is that of Isfahān, then the route of Fārs, then the route of Kirmān, then the route of al-Sind, all of which go out to the districts of Khurāsān, and al-Dāmghān, and al-Jibāl.

As for the route of Isfahān, it is to al-Rayy and to Naysābūr; the route of Fārs is to Naysābūr, and to Kūhistān, and to Dāmghān, with a number of secondary roads. The route of al-Sind is to Naysābūr and to Kūhistān, with a branch to Harāt. The route of Kirmān is to Khurāsān and to Sijistān, which is further away, but it goes to al-Sind only from Sijistān; and there is no exit from Sijistān to Fārs, except in Kirmān.

Distances on the route of al-Rayy:
From al-Rayy to Dizak, one stage;
    thence to Dayr al-Jiss, one stage;
    thence to Kāj, one stage;
    thence to Qumm, one stage;

thence to Qaryat al-Majūs, one stage;
thence to Qāshān, two stages;
thence to Hisn Badra, a like distance;
thence to Ribāt Ibn Rustam, one stage;
thence to Dānijī, one stage;
thence to al-Yahūdiyya, one stage.

Distances on the route of Naysābūr:
From Turthīth to Ribāt Zanjī, one stage;
thence to Bann, one stage;
thence to Darzīnak, one stage;
thence to Nūkhānī, one stage;
thence to Hulwān, one stage;
thence to another Bann, one stage;
thence to Jāh Rīk, one stage;
thence to Barmshīrak, one stage;
thence to Lūkīr, one stage;
thence to al-Akhrā, one stage;
thence to Hawdh al-Hājab, one stage;
thence to Jarmaq, one stage;
thence to al-Māʾ al-Harr, one stage;
thence to Khān Wardawayh, one stage;
thence to Hījarmakh, one stage;
thence to Hawdh ʿAlī, one stage;
thence to Kūshkān, one stage;
thence to al-Rakūnīn, one stage;
thence to Saksh, one stage;
thence to al-Yahūdiyya, one stage.

Another route:
From Turthīth to Bann, six stages;
thence to Bustādarān, one stage;
thence to Sarīsh, one stage;
thence to Rustāq Tabas (al-Tamr), one stage;
thence to Ribāt Kūrān, one stage;
thence to Arazama, one stage;
thence to al-Mahallabī, one post stage;
thence to Ribāt āb.Shuturān, one stage;
thence to Ribāt Busht Bādhām, one stage;
thence to Sāghand, one stage;
thence to Khazāna, one stage;
thence to Anjīrah, one stage.

Distances on the route of al-Dāmghān:
From al-Dāmghān to Wandah, forty *farsakhs*;
thence to Jarmaq, fifty *farsakhs*.

Distances on the route of Kūhistān:

From Kurī to Maʿzal, one stage;
 thence to āb Shūr, one stage;
 thence to Hawdh Hazār, one stage;
 thence to Jāh Bur (Bi'r Bur), one stage;
 thence to Ghamr Surkh, one stage;
 thence to Maʿzal, one stage;
 thence to Bīra, one stage;
 thence to Shūr Duwāzdah, one stage;
 thence to Darkūjuwā, one stage;
 thence to Zāwar, one stage;
 thence to Khabīs, one stage.

Another route:

From Kurī to Kūh Binān, sixty *farsakhs*; on this route are numerous domed wells and cisterns; at a distance of two stages from Kūh Binān is a spring of water.

Another route of Harāt:

From Harāt to Qaryat Silm, ten stages;
 thence to Raʾs al-Māʾ, four stages;
 thence to Dāristān, one stage;
 thence to Narmāsīr, one stage.

Distances on the route of Harāt:

From Qaryat Silm to Sabīd, five stages;
 thence to Narmāsīr, five stages, with some rather weak springs, and a few domed wells.

Distances on the route of Sijistān:

From Zaranj to Sabīd, a journey of five days; the new road is that from Harāt to Qaryat Silm.

Distances on the route of Khabīs:

From Khabīs to all-Darwāzak, one stage;
 thence to Shūr Rūdh, one stage;
 thence to Bārask, one stage;
 thence to Nīma, thence to al-Hawdh (the cistern), one stage;
 thence to Raʾs al-Māʾ, two stages;
 thence to Kūkūr, one stage;
 thence to Khawst, one stage.

As for the route of al-Sind, it goes to Kirmān and Sijistān; I did not travel over it, nor did I acquire a precise knowledge of it.

p. 491   As for a description of the way stations of which we began to give an account: Dayr al-Jiss has buildings of burnt brick, every brick like a huge piece of adobe. It is an extensive place, with all conveniences. It has iron gates, at one of which

p. 492   is a greengrocer who lives there. The water cisterns are outside it; rounded, the rain water collects in them. However, when I was there it seemed to me to be rather decayed. Kāj was a village on the plateau; it was destroyed, I believe by the Qufs, and its people fled. The roads branch off from there, one of which we have mentioned and in fact traversed, the other going to Qumm, a stage away,

p. 493   then another stage to Qaryat al-Majūs (the village of the Magians). Badra has a fortress and farms, and about fifty buildings.

At Ribāt ibn Rustam is running water which flows into a cistern within the *ribāt*. Dānījī is a large flourishing village. This is the most populated road through the desert, since it is on the borders of al-Jibāl. From Karkas Kūh to al-Dayr is four *farsakhs*, thence to Siyāh Kūh is five.

I did not travel over the road from Naysābūr to Isfahān; however, people tell me that it is very fine and well-traveled, though there are some difficult sands to be encountered. At Ribāt Kawrān is a fortress in which is a person who takes care of it; outside is a spring, salty, but the people drink of it anyway. At Arazāma (Arāzāma) are three wells, not adequate for large caravans. At al-Mahallabī is a weak spring; here is a ruined *ribāt*.

Ribāt āb Shuturān is a place to be feared; it is a place of refuge for al-Kūj (al-Qufs). Here is a canal of middling water which pours out into a pool. The *ribāt* is quite good here, in fact I have not seen a better one in all the countries of the non-Arabs. It is built of stone and gypsum after the manner of the strongholds of Syria, and has iron gates. It is a flourishing place, people being there to take care of it. Ibn Sīmjūr, commander of the army of the king of al-Mashriq built it.

> *Addition/version* MS. C.
> ... beautifully built in stone, fortified with iron doors. Nāsir al-Dawla Abu al-Hasan bin Sīmjūr built it, and within it a channel of water of middling quality, the main stream of which flows from the mountain, to pour into a pool at the gate of the guardhouse into which the water flows also. I have not seen a guardhouse superior to this one; however, it is a cause of terror, and a shelter for the Kūj, and there is a saying there to the effect that the Kūj are always in the guardhouse of Āb Shutūrān, for no sooner do they leave it than they are back again; and the people there are always on the alert.

Busht Bādhām is like a village, for you find everything there. It has extensive farms and flocks of sheep, a copiously flowing canal, and beauties unconcealed; here the traveler finds repose and supplies. Sāghand is a thriving populous village. Khazāna is a village with a fortress, and farms, both tillage and livestock raising; here are about two hundred people; gardens.

> *Addition/version* MS. C.
> Jarmaq is a village with date palms and buildings, beside it two other villages,

the name of one of them being Arāba, that of the other Biyāḍhaq. In these places are springs, cultivated fields, livestock, and altogether about two thousand inhabitants. From Busht Bādhām to Sāghand is a fortification in ruin, a distance of one stage; here are mulberry trees and areas surrounded by fruit trees, and but little cultivated. There the Qufs assemble and stand in readiness to block the roads, and they devise their plans of action. I met one man there who cultivated one of those areas I mentioned, and I asked if he did not feel afraid in this place. Said he: "You should know that I traveled to Naysābūr a number of years, and would be there about a month; and I would be dejected, and in fear of the people there until I would return here." Thence to a puddle of water, then another stage, possibly dry, thence to a rather weak spring, one stage, and here one spring fornicate with a small domed housing. Three *farsakhs* further on is a spring from a mountain, then to the end of the stage, to Mahābād, which pertains to Kirmān. These trails of the lesser roads are unimportant and difficult.

Al-Zāwar is a flourishing village, over it a fortress; a stream here that flows from p. 494 the border of Kirmān. At Darkūjuwā is a rather weak stream; the place is not well developed.

Shūr Duwāzdah is a *ribāṭ* which has gone to ruin. Here is a wādī in which are trees and palms, but no inhabitant: very dangerous. Dar Bardān is a desolate place; here are wells but no people; further on is a stopping place with a cistern filled by the rains: no one there either. Nāband is a *ribāṭ*, inhabited. Round about is a number of houses, and a stream that turns small mill wheels; it has tillage and date palms.

Addition/version MS. C.

Two *farsakhs* before it is a spring of water; here are small palm trees, and domed springs without any people around, and to the right of the stopping place, within shouting distance, stand a great number of palm trees, and grasslands, without buildings; here are the hiding places of al-Qufs.

Before Nāband are date palms, and a well dome, fallen into ruin.

At Biʾr Shak is a well of sweet water; uninhabited. Here is a number of well domes, side by side, and the cisterns are filled to capacity. Dāristān is a village with date palms, but by no means flourishing. Nīma is a *ribāṭ*; someone there takes care of it.

p. 495 At Qaryat Salm are buildings as far as the eye can see, but in ruin. There is not a spring there, not a cistern, not a person; it pertains to Kirmān. At Raʾs al-Māʾ is a spring that trickles into a cistern, and waters a farm. Kūkūr is a flourishing village pertaining to Quhistān. Bīra is a small village, with a number of people. At Maʿzal is a spring of water; you see no houses or development there. At Jāh Bur is a well, domed, as at Biʾr Shak, also a cistern. There is another Maʿzal, which has domes and a water cistern.

Asfīd is counted in the official records as a city of Sijistān, yet it is on the verge of this desert. In it are canals and many farms; it is flourishing and populous.

The foregoing is what is known about the famous stopping places in this desert on the roads we have mentioned. If we were to list the minor roads with the settlements and sources of water on them the book would be merely lengthened. Very few stages of the routes we have mentioned are without having domed cisterns. Every *farsakh* there is a cistern or a domed well, with structure to provide shelter during the rains. You find no *ribāts* in this desert besides those we mentioned; and there are no people other than those at Busht Bādhām; and apart from here, food and fodder are hard to get. Indeed you have to carry it; you need provisions for a journey of six days. The length, wherever you measure it, is sixty *farsakhs*, or so.

On the route of al-Rayy occurs a stream through which one must wade. A large stream, it flows down to Khūzistān, and one encounters it at a place that is extremely cold the entire year.

p. 496

[ENVOI]

This is what we know of the regions of the realm of Islām; what we have seen and heard and know to be sound, of the description of the countries. We ask God for pardon and forgiveness, for He is merciful and generous.

Addition/version MS. C.
... [In] that with which we occupied ourselves, and to which we devoted ourselves; there remained, however, cities we did not arrive at, but the number of them does not reach fifty.

And may God be merciful to His servant who looks into our book, and thinks well of it, or accepts it and approves it. Let him but pray for us with kind intent, and ask God sincerely that He not shower trouble on us, on the day when we will be asked about our deeds small and great, the little things and the important things; the day when excuses will be of no avail, and there will be no surmounting of difficulties. Neither the friend nor the bosom companion will be of help; only the one who comes to God with sincerity, and thus takes up this dread position, fearful of this momentous occasion: the day the prophets will fall on bended knees, and every connection and relationship will be severed.

Addition/version MS. C.
Let him but pray for us that we may escape on the day we are asked about the trifling things and the momentous; the day when wealth is of no avail, nor are children, no, nor bosom friend, nor parent, nor intimate; the day you will see every human being preoccupied with himself, with his head bowed, remorseful over that in which he was remiss in his former life; the day the parents will become white-haired with grief, and the fires of hell will be there in readiness, and the smoke rising up; the scales will be set up in place, the tongue will be mute, the Judge will pronounce a verdict. In that place everyone will receive retribution for his actions, and may rejoice in the good deeds of his life, and will

obtain there what he has already prepared for the day of his resurrection. May God render us, and the eminent shaykh, the magnificent and most excellent nobleman, among those who "shall have no fear, nor shall they grieve!" (*Qurʾān*, sūra 2, v. 38).

[*Hic Finitur* MS. B]

p. 497 Said the author in his farewell:
A book is like jewels, and like the spring time,
Like carnelians, and fertile gardens;
Thus, therein is an account of the earth in its entirety,
And in a special manner, hence is it called beautiful:
It mentions the regions of the countries and of all the earth,
And all the islands brilliant like the dawn;
The mountain passes of the countries, of ʿAdan and Shām,
And of Sūs al-Gharb, in a lofty account;
Its springs and streams in the deserts,
And the impassable mountains of the world,
And the fruits of the regions in addition to the palm trees,
With the strange occupations everywhere.
Some of it I saw myself, and explored
Until I was fatigued, from days of travel after nights;
Some of it I based on the authority of others, mentioning the ascription:
Derived from al-Shaʿbī or Wakīʿ.
I mentioned the magnificence of the various metropoles,
And all the cities brilliant like the dawn.
I distinguished among the seas by virtue of my knowledge
And experience, as the herdsman distinguishes the sheep in the flock;
And the languages of the peoples, nation by nation
And the dialects of the Arabs, from barbarous speech.
Also the merchandise of every region, and of the world,
The condition of the slaves, and the trading of them.
Here are examples of problems of every region,
And people dealing with them to the best of their capability.
So the reader can thus see the marvels of creation
And all the varied coloured ornamentation on the earth;
So that man knows truly the greatness of the Creator
And the magnificent work of the Almighty, the All-Hearing;
Hence he can worship Him as a true devotee in submission,
As an obedient servant of God.
p. 498 Thus may he propagate the works of the generous hands of the Merciful God everywhere,
He who manifests permanence to the preeminent of mankind;

Because spreading of the goodness grows up
Until it reaches the merciful God from the one who spreads it.
I have written with much thought in which I did my best,
Seeking eternal life on the dreadful day of judgment,
And forgiveness of my sins, by the kindness of my Lord;
And from hellfire, and grievous dismay.
So take wisdom, like pearls in its beauty,
O Abū Hasan, vizier of Ibn al-Rafiᶜ!
Sacred [Muqaddasa] it shines like the sparkle
Of sapphire, familiar to the most select.

It is finished; and praise be to God alone.

Addition/version MS. C.

p. 498   Said the copyist: I completed the copying of this work, praise be to God for
the gracious success He has granted, at the beginning of the blessed month of
Rajab [seventh month of the Muslim year] in the year 658/1259. Al-Hasan bin
Ahmad bin Mahmūd bin al-Kamāl edited it, praising God, worshipping Him,
and seeking His forgiveness.

APPENDIX:
ENGLISH KEYS TO THE ARABIC MAPS

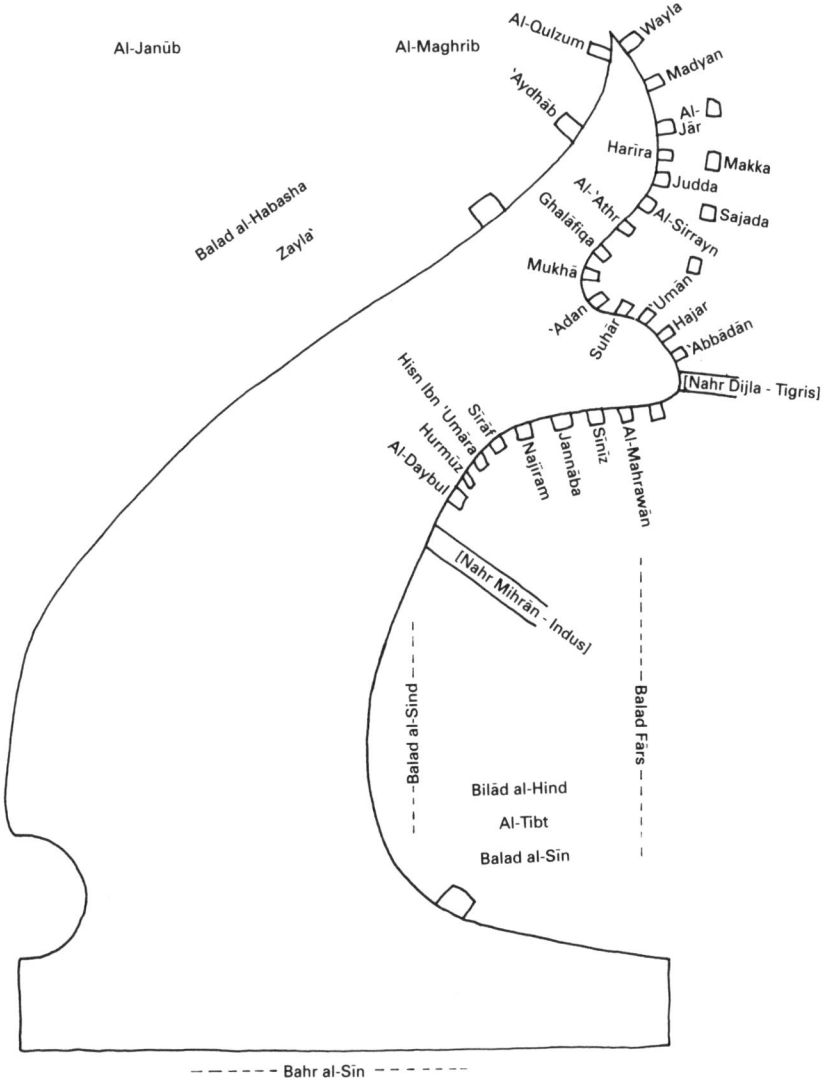

Map I: The Persian Sea (see p. 10).
From MS. Sprenger 5—Ahlwardt 6034 by kind permission of the Staatsbibliothek Preussischer Kulturbesitz, Berlin, Orientabteilung.

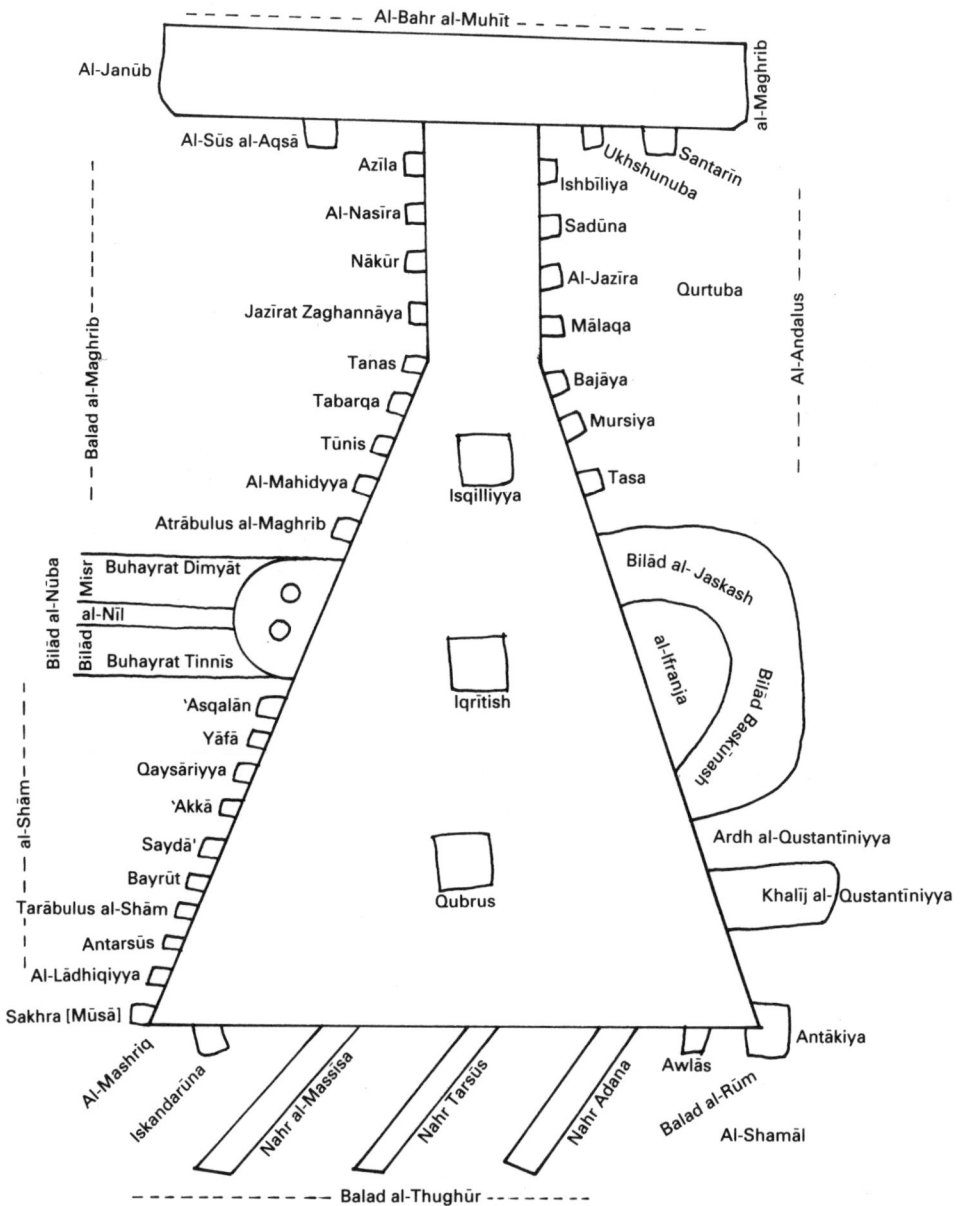

Map II: Bahr al-Rūm (see p. 14).
From MS. Sprenger 5—Ahlwardt 6034 by kind permission of the Staatsbibliothek Preussischer Kulturbesitz, Berlin, Orientabteilung.

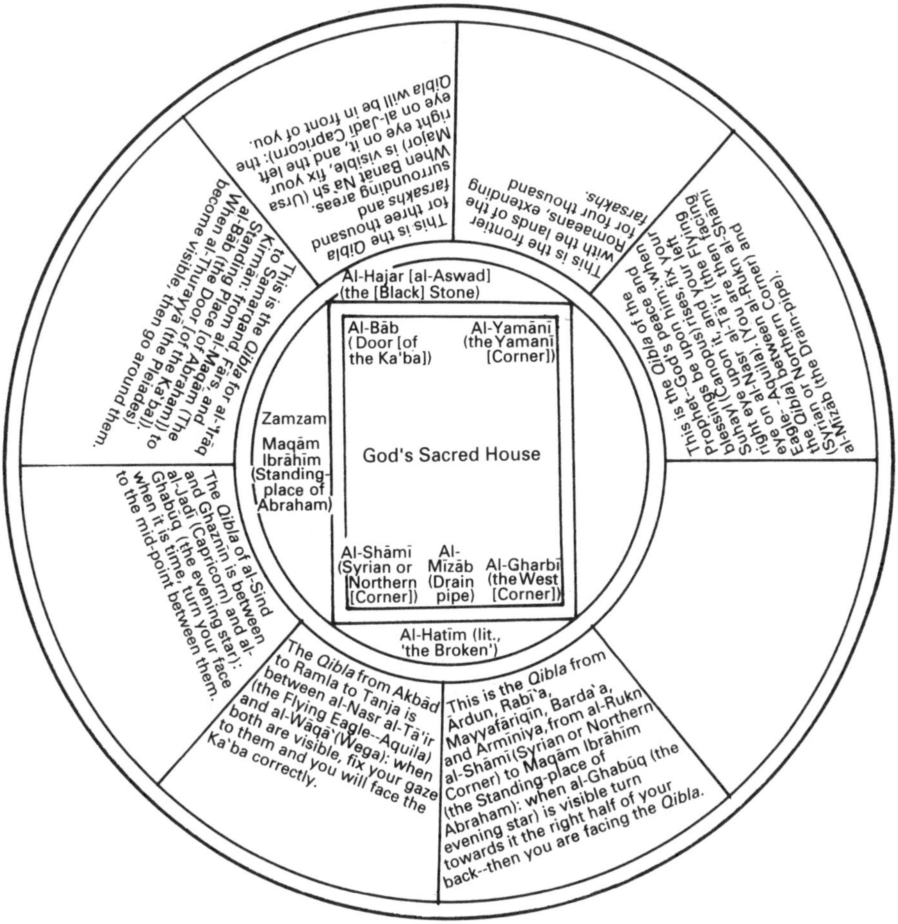

Qibla will be in front of you.
right eye on al-Jadi (Capricorn); the
Major) is visible, fix your left
When Banat Na'sh (Ursa
surrounding areas.
farsakhs and
for three thousand
This is the Qibla

This is the frontier
with the lands of the
Romaeans, extending
for four thousand
farsakhs.

This is the Qibla of the
Prophet—be upon him; your Flying
blessing (Canopus), and (the) facing
Suhayl, upon it, Ta'ir, then al-Shami
right eye on al-Nasr (You are) Rukn and
eye on Aquila(ween Corner) and
Eagle-Qibla(-Northern-pipe).
(Syrian (the Drain-pipe).
al-Mizab (the

Standing: from al-Fars, al-'Iraq
become visible, then go around them.
al-Thurayya (the Pleiades)
al-Bab (the Door [of Abraham (The
Kirmān, turqābuz (the Standing-
This is the Qibla for al-'Iraq
al-Jadi (Capricorn) and
Ghabuq (the evening star):
when it's time turn your face
to the mid-point between them.
The Qibla of al-Sind is between
and Ghaznin is between

Al-Hajar [al-Aswad]
(the [Black] Stone)

Al-Bab (Door [of the Ka'ba])	Al-Yamani (the Yamani [Corner])
Zamzam Maqam Ibrahim (Standing-place of Abraham)	God's Sacred House
Al-Shami (Syrian or Northern [Corner])	Al-Mizab (Drain pipe)	Al-Gharbi (the West [Corner])

Al-Hatim (lit., 'the Broken')

The Qibla from Akbad
to Ramla to Tanja is
between al-Nasr al-Ta'ir
(the Flying Eagle--Aquila)
and al-Waqa'(Wega): when
both are visible, fix your gaze
to them and you will face the
Ka'ba correctly.

This is the Qibla from
Ardun, Rabi'a,
Mayyafariqin, Barda'a,
and Arminiya, from al-Rukn
al-Shami (Syrian or Northern
Corner) to Maqam Ibrahim
(the Standing-place of
Abraham): when al-Ghabuq (the
evening star) is visible turn
towards it the right half of your
back--then you are facing the Qibla.

Map III: Al-Ka'ba (see p. 54).
(see p. 54)
From MS. Sprenger 5—Ahlwardt 6034 by kind permission of the Staatsbibliothek
Preussischer Kulturbesitz, Berlin, Orientabteilung.

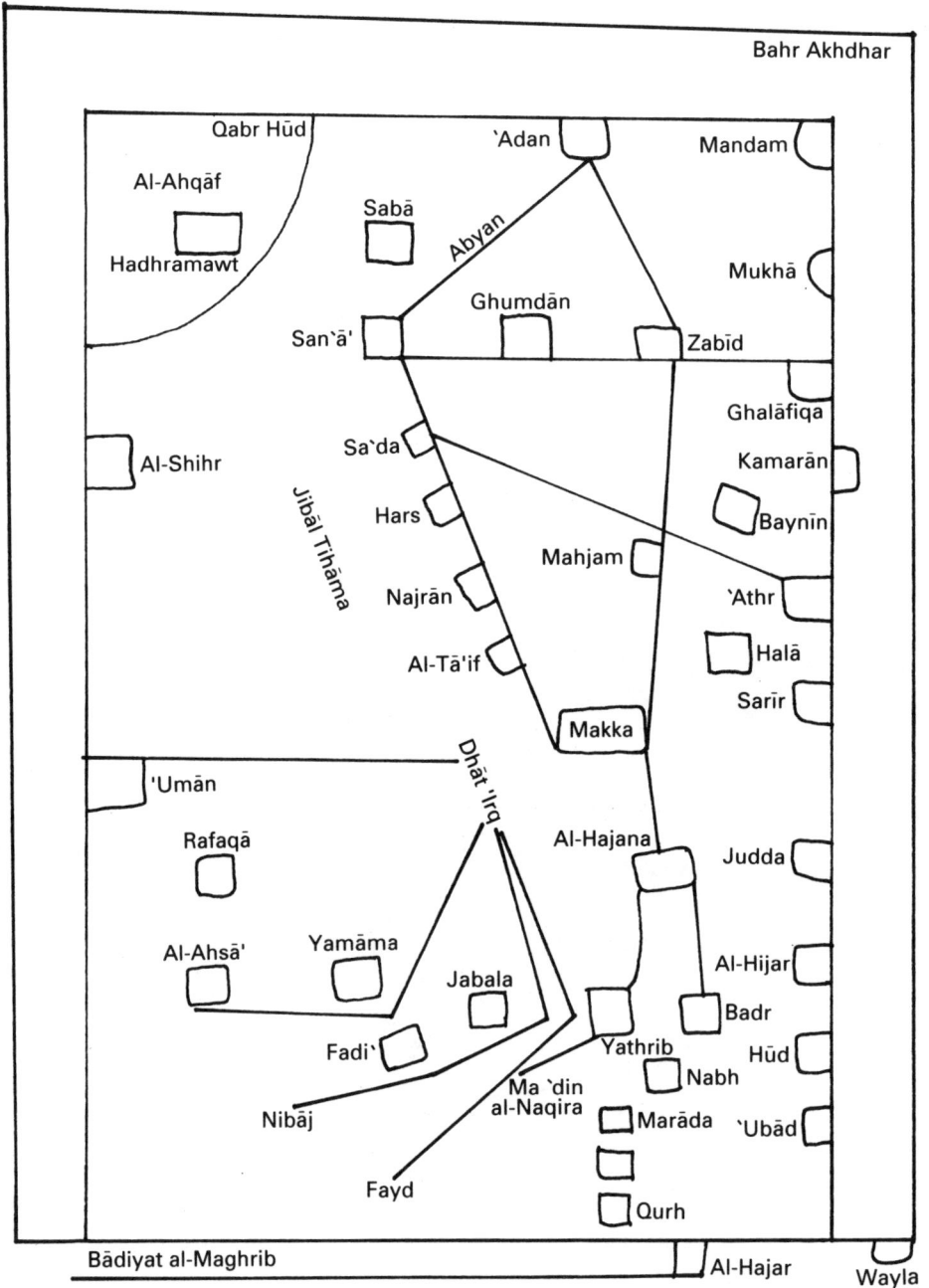

Map IV: Arabia (see p. 65).
From MS. Sprenger 5—Ahlwardt 6034 by kind permission of the Staatsbibliothek Preussischer Kulturbesitz, Berlin, Orientabteilung.

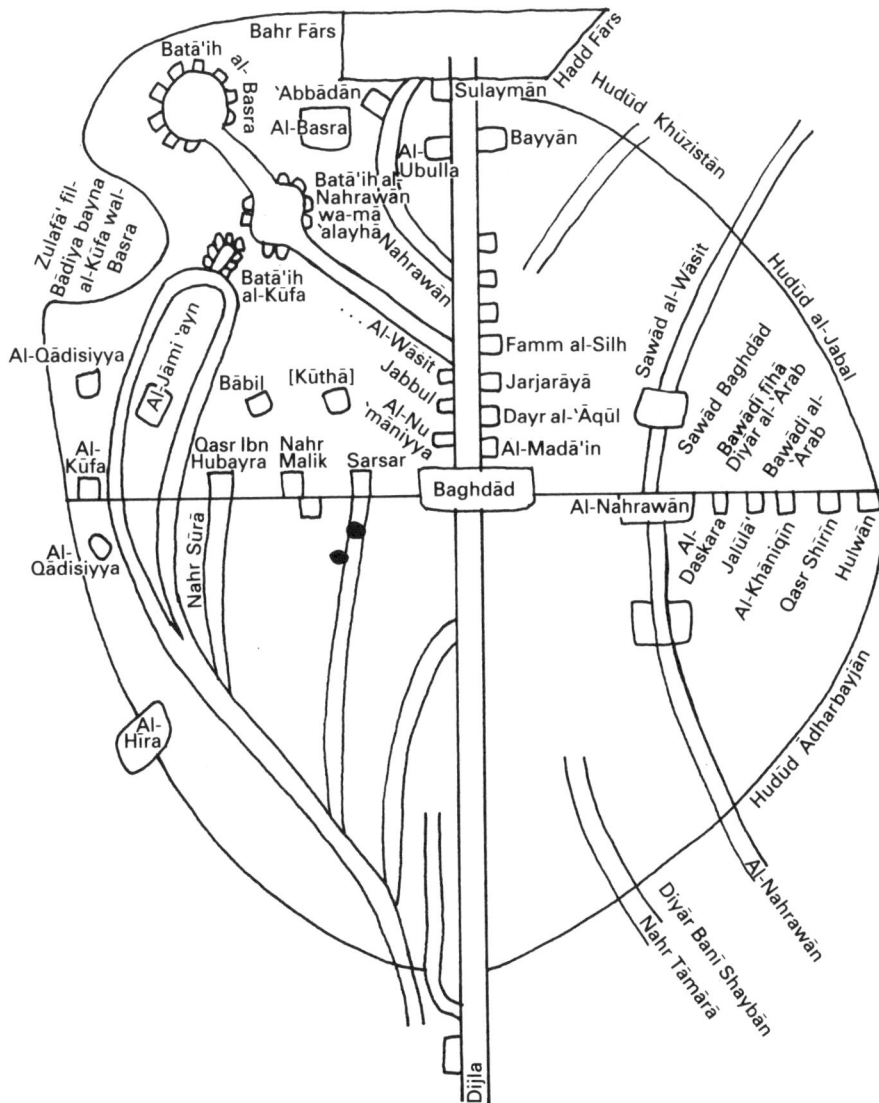

Map V: Al-ʿIraq (see p. 96).
From MS. Sprenger 5—Ahlwardt 6034 by kind permission of the Staatsbibliothek
Preussischer Kulturbesitz, Berlin, Orientabteilung.

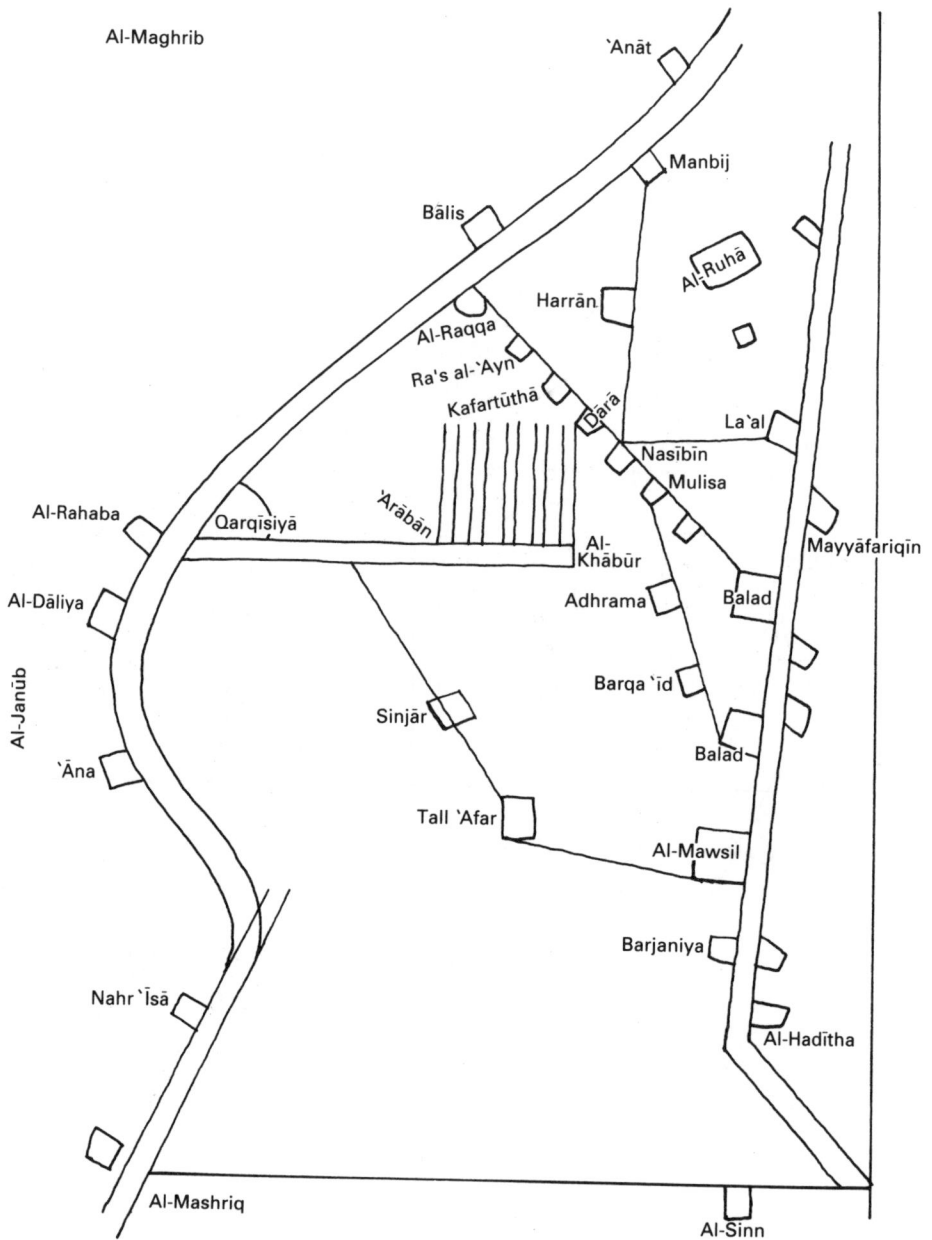

Map VI: Al-Jazīra (see p. 116).
From MS. Sprenger 5—Ahlwardt 6034 by kind permission of the Staatsbibliothek
Preussischer Kulturbesitz, Berlin, Orientabteilung.

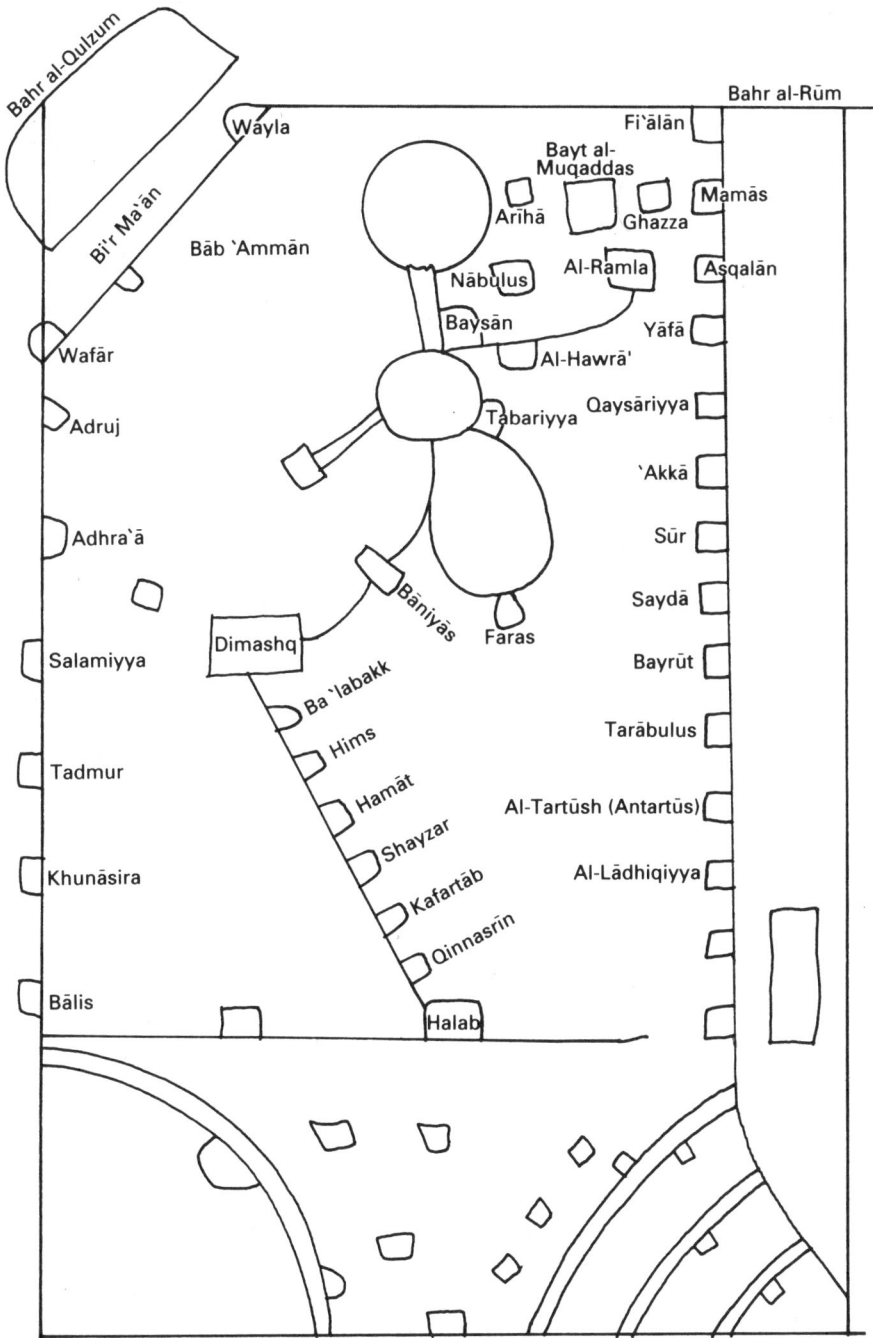

Map VII: Al-Shām (see p. 131).
From MS. Sprenger 5—Ahlwardt 6034 by kind permission of the Staatsbibliothek
Preussischer Kulturbesitz, Berlin, Orientabteilung.

Misr — — — — — — — — Al-Nūba — — — — Al-Nīl

Ardh al-Ma 'din

Uswān

Al-Wāhāt

Jabal al-Muqattam — · — · — · — ·

Al-Sa 'īd al-Ā'lā — · — · — ·

Balahiya

Al-Akhmīm

Jabal al-Wāhāt — · — · — · — ·

Al-Sa 'īd al-Ā 'lā — · — · — ·

Mafāza bayna Misr wa-Tīh — · — · — ·

Al-Bādiya

Ushmūnayn

Būshīr

Al-Fayyūm

Hudūd al-Maghrib — · — · — ·

Misr

Al-Qulzum

Al-Fustāt

Tūr Sīnā

Damīra

Al-Tīh

Wayrā

Rimāl al-Jifār

Buhayrat Tinnīs

Al-Rīf

Buhayrat Dimyāt

Tinnīs

Dimyāt

Al-Faramā

Al-Iskandariyya

— — — — — Bahr al-Rūm — — — — — — — — —

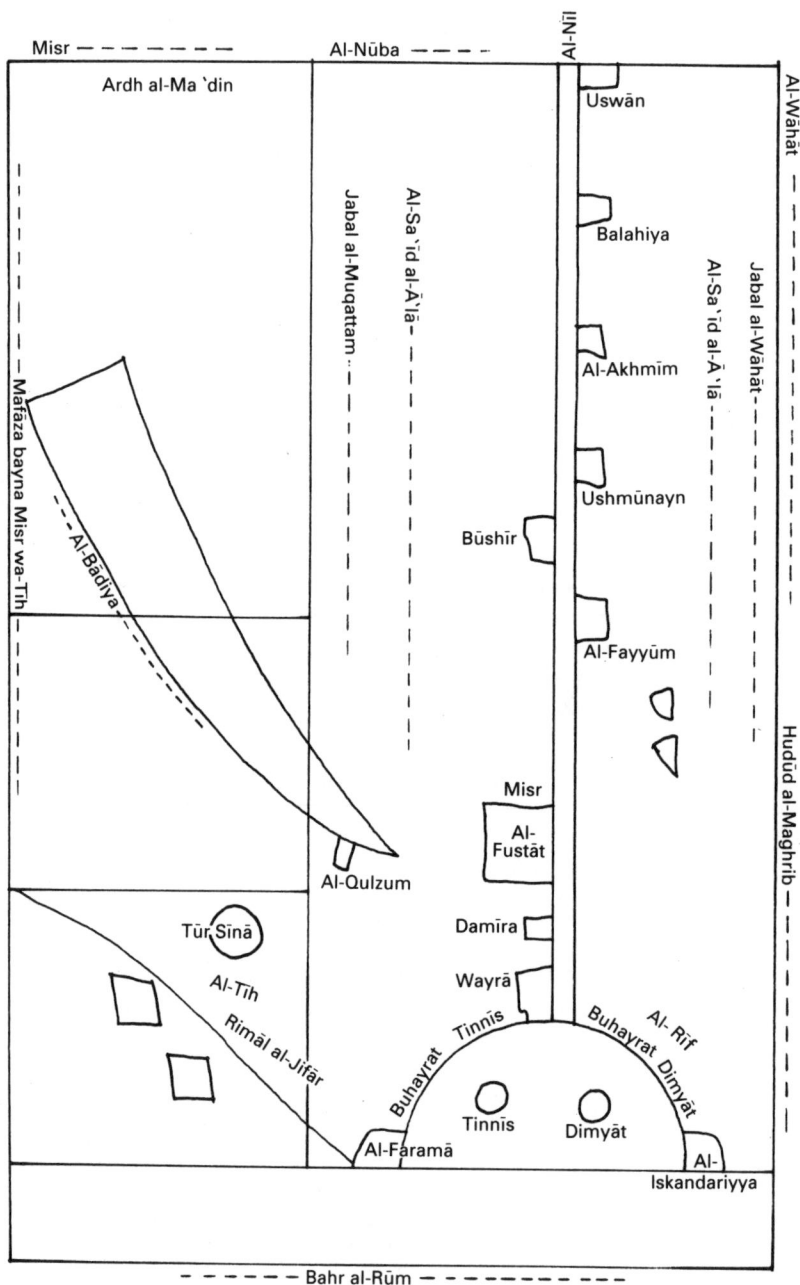

Map VIII: Misr (see p. 164).
From MS. Sprenger 5—Ahlwardt 6034 by kind permission of the Staatsbibliothek
Preussischer Kulturbesitz, Berlin, Orientabteilung.

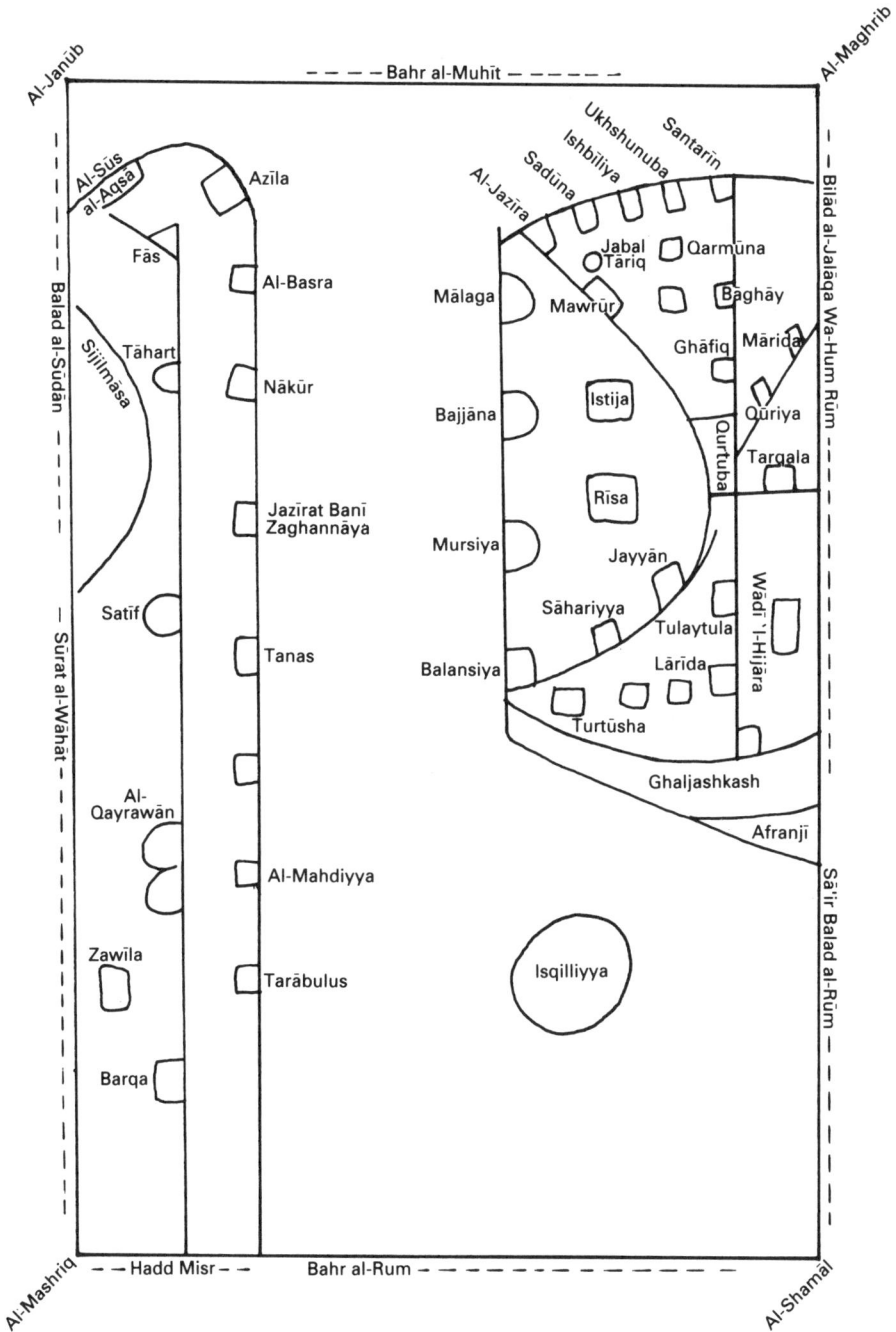

Map IX: Al-Maghrib (see p. 184).
From MS. Sprenger 5—Ahlwardt 6034 by kind permission of the Staatsbibliothek
Preussischer Kulturbesitz, Berlin, Orientabteilung.

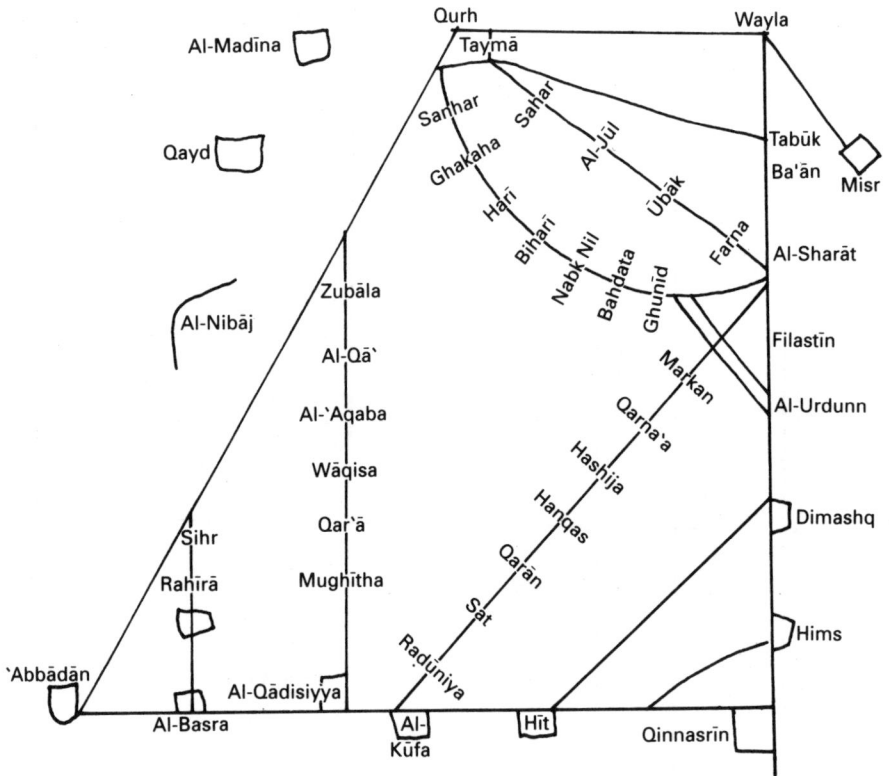

Map X: The Arabian Desert (see p. 208).
From MS. Sprenger 5—Ahlwardt 6034 by kind permission of the Staatsbibliothek
Preussischer Kulturbesitz, Berlin, Orientabteilung.

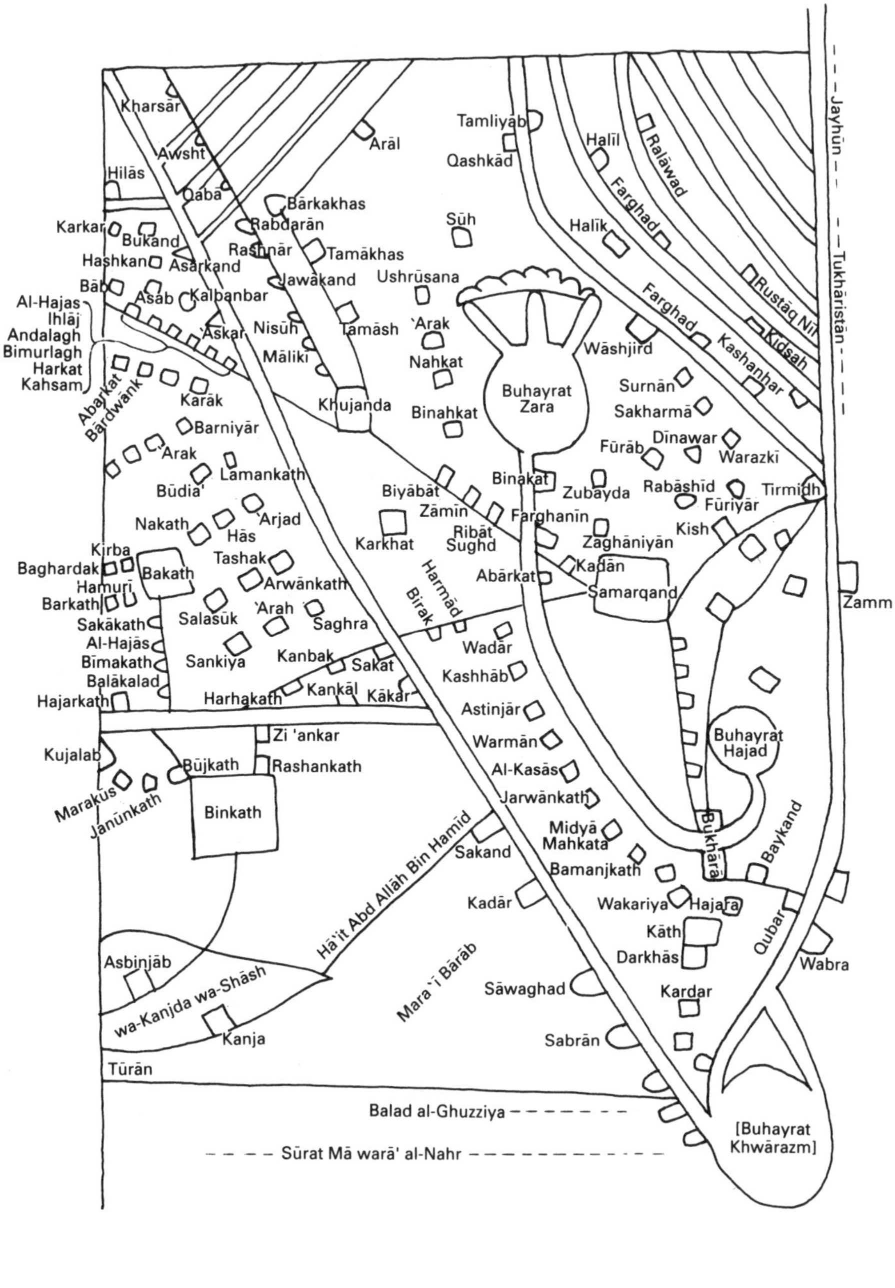

Map XI: Mā wara'a al-Nahr (see p. 220).
From MS. Sprenger 5—Ahlwardt 6034 by kind permission of the Staatsbibliothek Preussischer Kulturbesitz, Berlin, Orientabteilung.

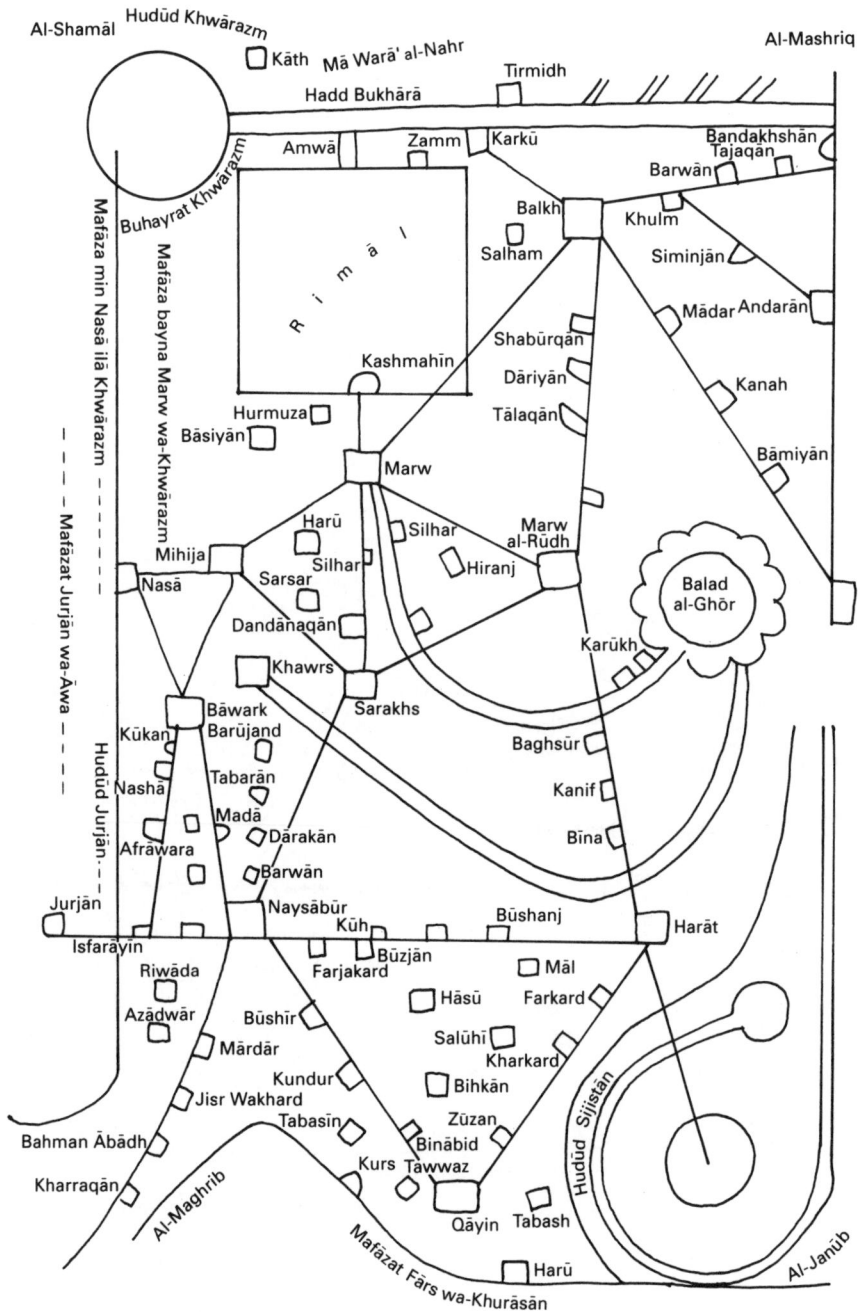

Map XII: Khurāsān (see p. 242).
From MS. Sprenger 5—Ahlwardt 6034 by kind permission of the Staatsbibliothek
Preussischer Kulturbesitz, Berlin, Orientabteilung.

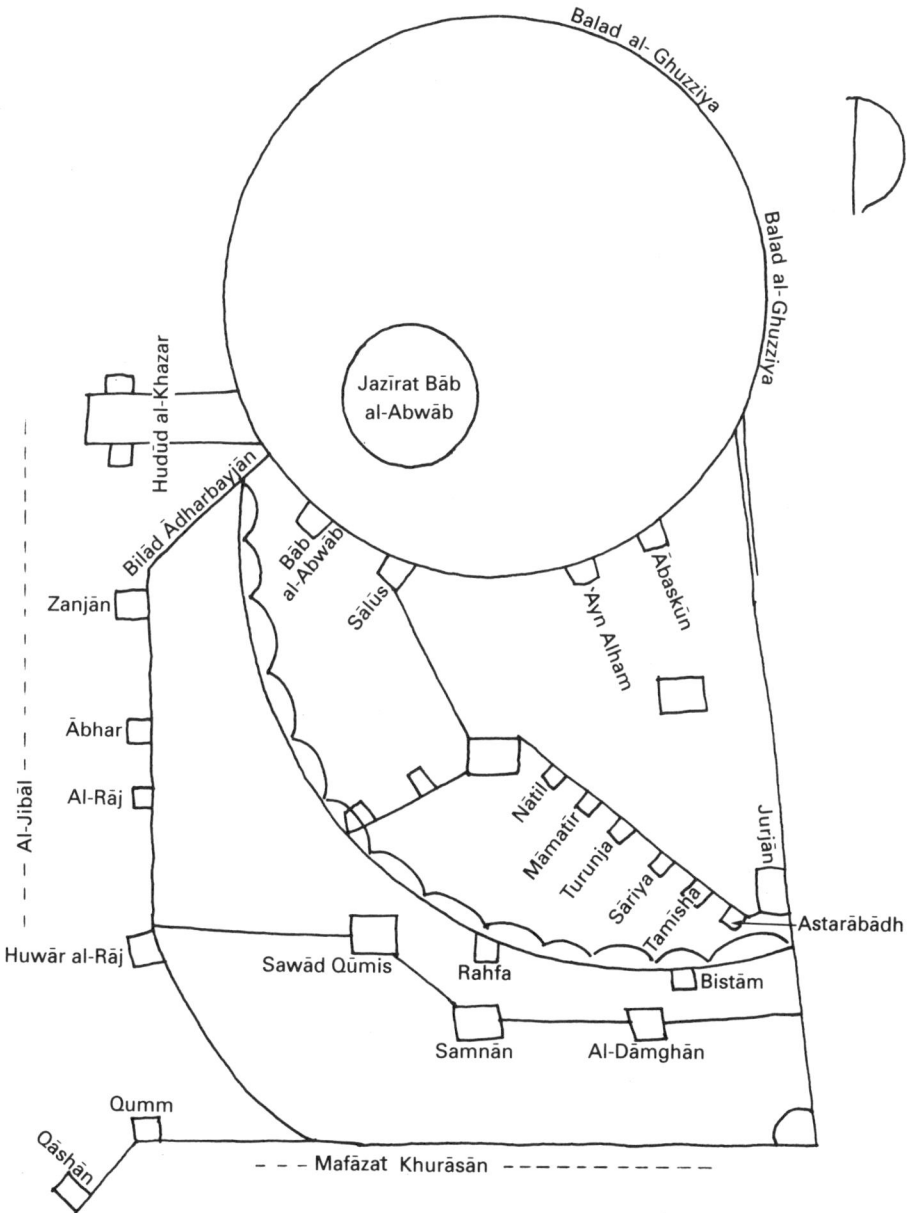

Map XIII: Tabar Daylam (see p. 288).
From MS. Sprenger 5—Ahlwardt 6034 by kind permission of the Staatsbibliothek Preussischer Kulturbesitz, Berlin, Orientabteilung.

Sūrat Armīniya wa'l-Rān wa-Ādharbayjān – – – –– – – – – – – – –

Bilād al-Rān wa'l-Qabq wa'l-Sarīr – – – – – – – – – – – – – – – –

Al-Shamāl– – – – –

Al-Mashriq

Al-Lān

Nahr al-Malik

Bāb al-Abwāb

Al-Lanjān

Al-Sābrawān

Qabala

Shakī

Shirwān

Al-Shamākhiya

Bākūh

Bahr [Al-Khazar]

Tiflīs

Al-Qal'a

Khunān

Shamkūr

Janza

Bardha'a

Bilād al-Rān

Nahr al-Rass

Mūqān

Warthān

Barzand

Sanjān

Ardabīl

[Jabal] Al-Hārith

Dabīl

Armīniya

Al-Sarāt

[Jabal] Al-Huwayrith

Marand

Maymand

Qālīqalā

Bilād al-Rūm

Al-Manaj

Al-Marāha

Al-Dahrāqān

Khūnj

Zanjān

Jaburqān

Bidlīs

Halāz

Arjīsh

Barkarī

Khūy

Salamas

Urmiya

Buhayrat Armīniya

Tabrīz

Al-Daylam

Dīnawar

Hadd al-Hind

Rasha

Al-Maghrib

Al-Janūb

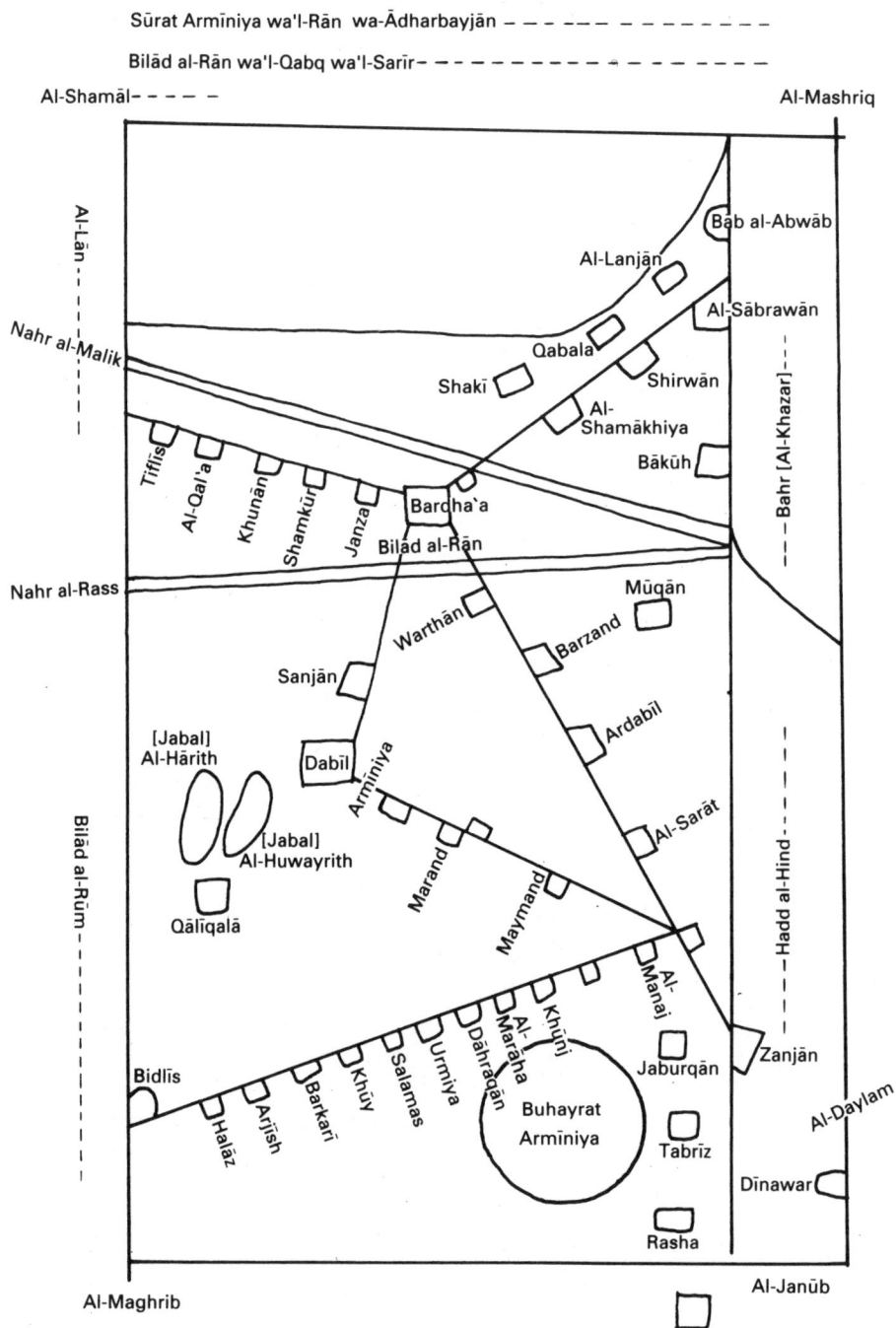

Map XIV: Ādharbayjān (see p. 304).

Al-Shamāl — — — — — Sūrat al-Jibāl — — — — — Al-Mashriq

— — — Jibāl al-Daylam — — — — —

Damāwand

Zanjān

Abhar

Qazwin

Al-Rayy

Sāwa

Āwa

Rōsana

Qumm

Waba

Hudūd Bilād Ādharbayjān

Mafāzat Fārs wa-Khurāsān

Hawmashahrazūr

Hamadhān

Rāmin

Qāshān

Al-Dīnawar

Barūjird

Shahrazūr

Rūdhrāwar

Al-Karaj

Qarmāsin

Niḥāwand

Al-Burj

Khawsjān

Tafār

Rāsht

Isbahān

Al-Marj

Al-Saymara

Sāburkhwās

Khālanjān

Jibāl al-Harjiya

Al-Lūr

Al-Maghrib

Fārs

Hulwān

Al-ʿIrāq

Khūzistān

Al-Janūb

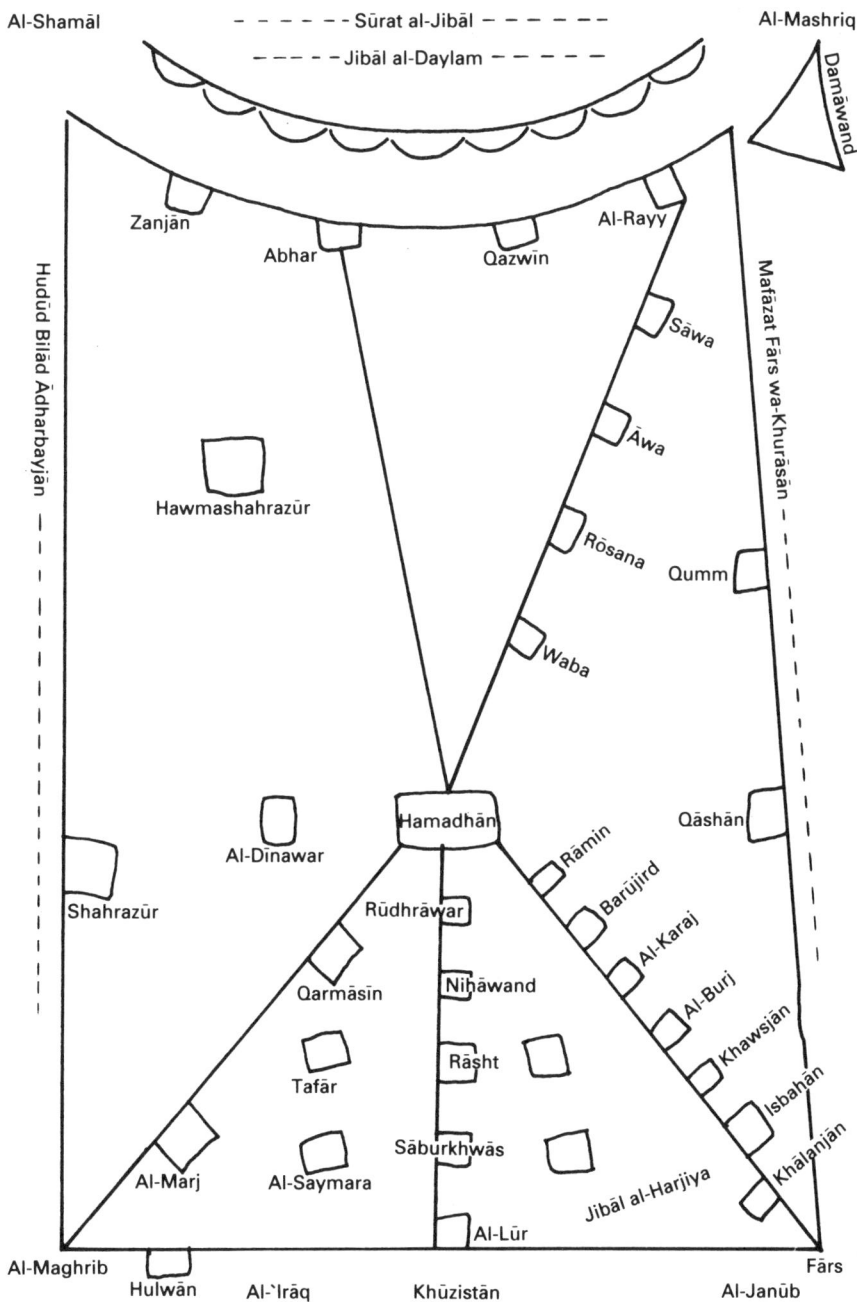

Map XV: Jibāl al-Daylam (see p. 314).
From MS. Sprenger 5—Ahlwardt 6034 by kind permission of the Staatsbibliothek
Preussischer Kulturbesitz, Berlin, Orientabteilung.

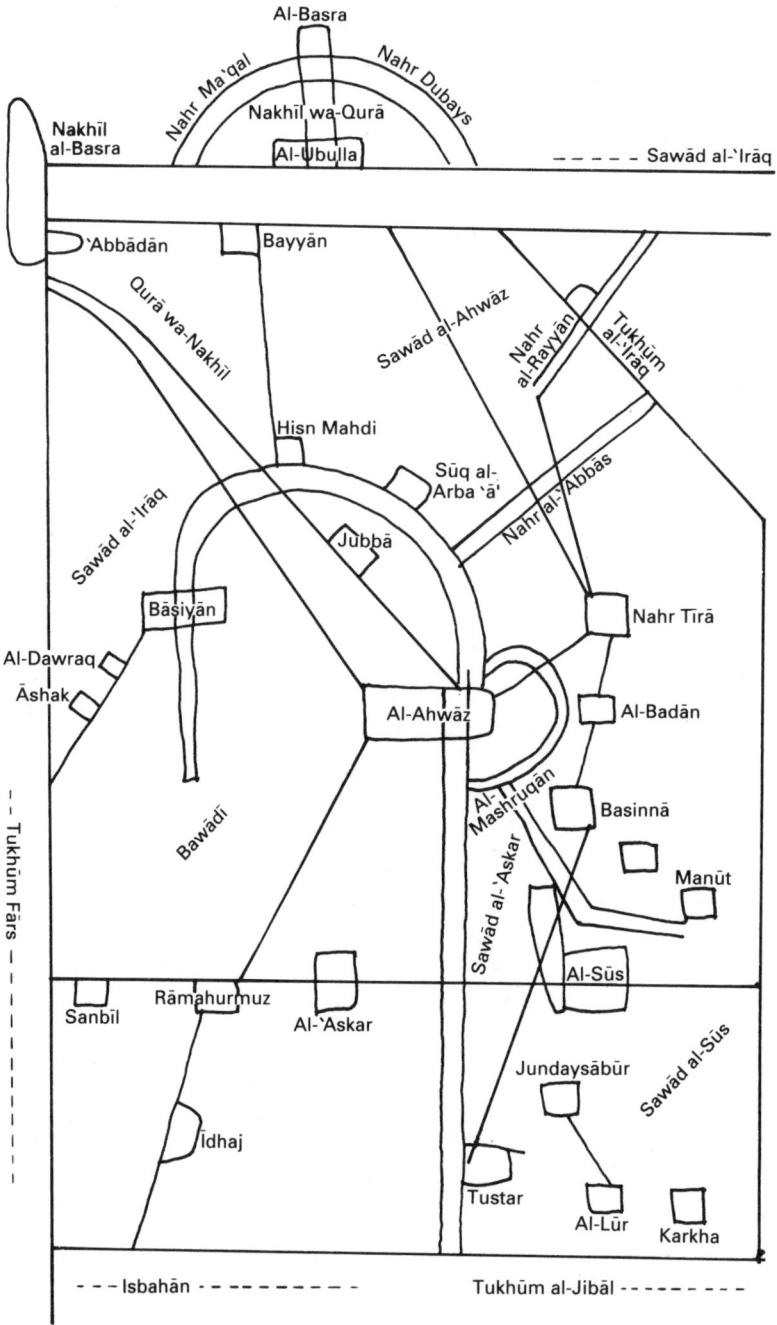

Map XVI: Khūzistān (see p. 331).
From MS. Sprenger 5—Ahlwardt 6034 by kind permission of the Staatsbibliothek
Preussischer Kulturbesitz, Berlin, Orientabteilung.

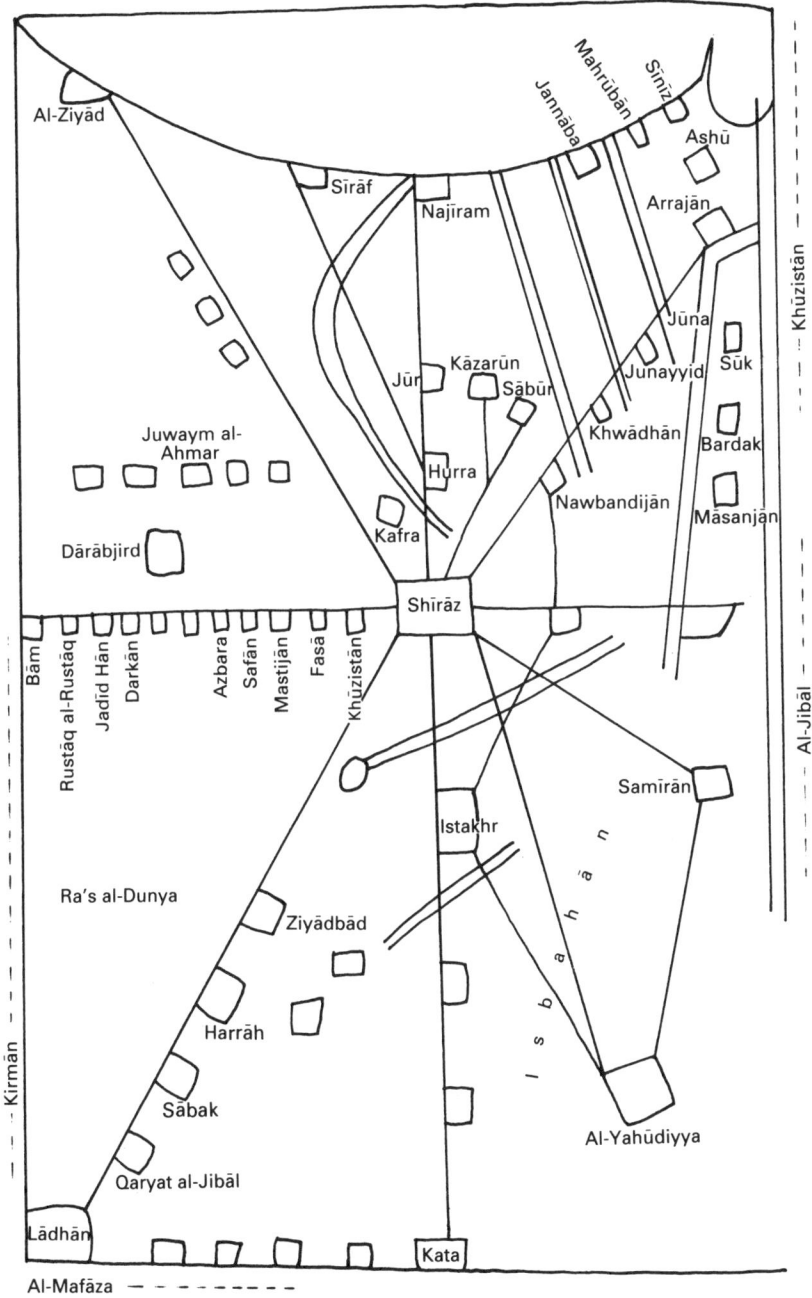

Map XVII: Fārs (see p. 345).
From MS. Sprenger 5—Ahlwardt 6034 by kind permission of the Staatsbibliothek Preussischer Kulturbesitz, Berlin, Orientabteilung.

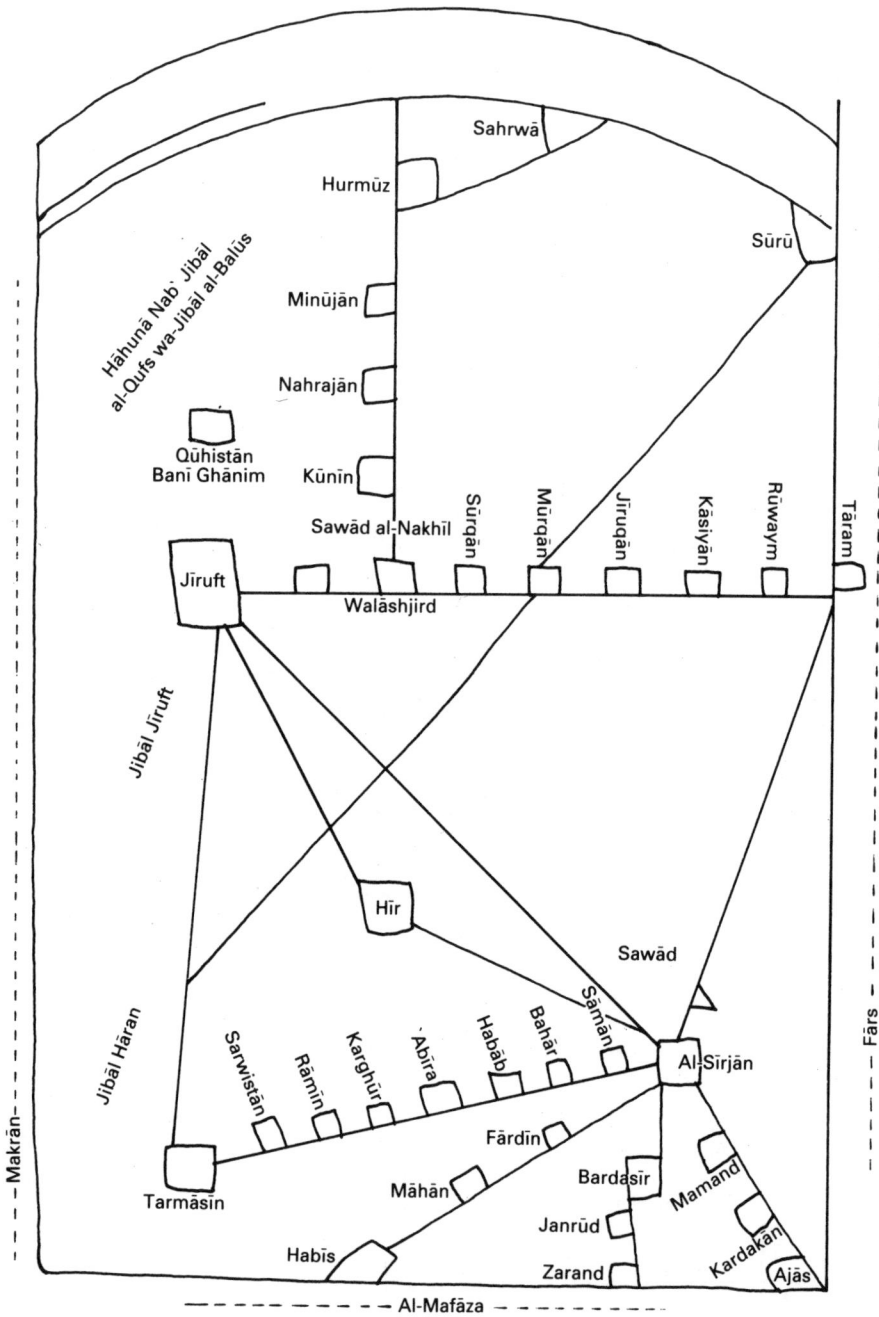

Map XVIII: Kirmān (see p. 373).
From MS. Sprenger 5—Ahlwardt 6034 by kind permission of the Staatsbibliothek
Preussischer Kulturbesitz, Berlin, Orientabteilung.

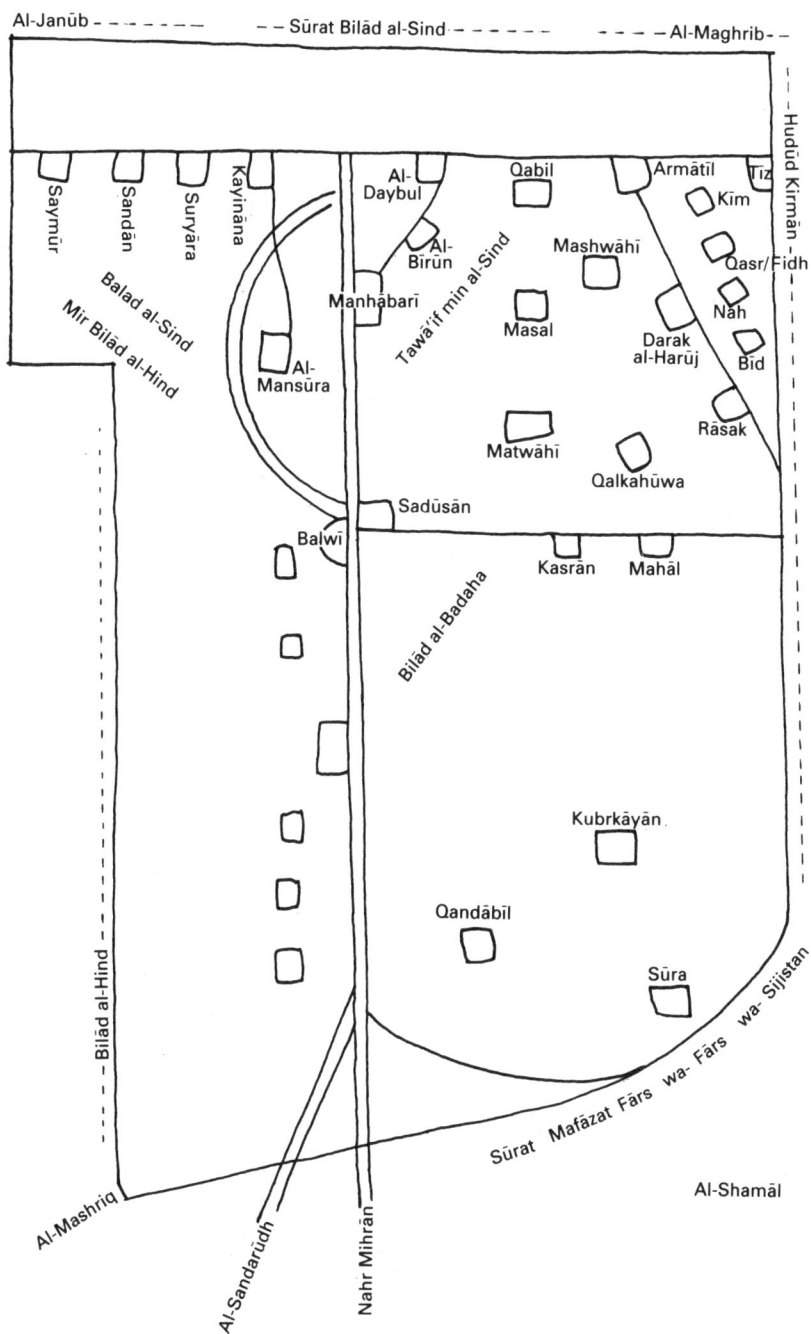

Map XIX: Al-Sind (see p. 385).
From MS. Sprenger 5—Ahlwardt 6034 by kind permission of the Staatsbibliothek
Preussischer Kulturbesitz, Berlin, Orientabteilung.

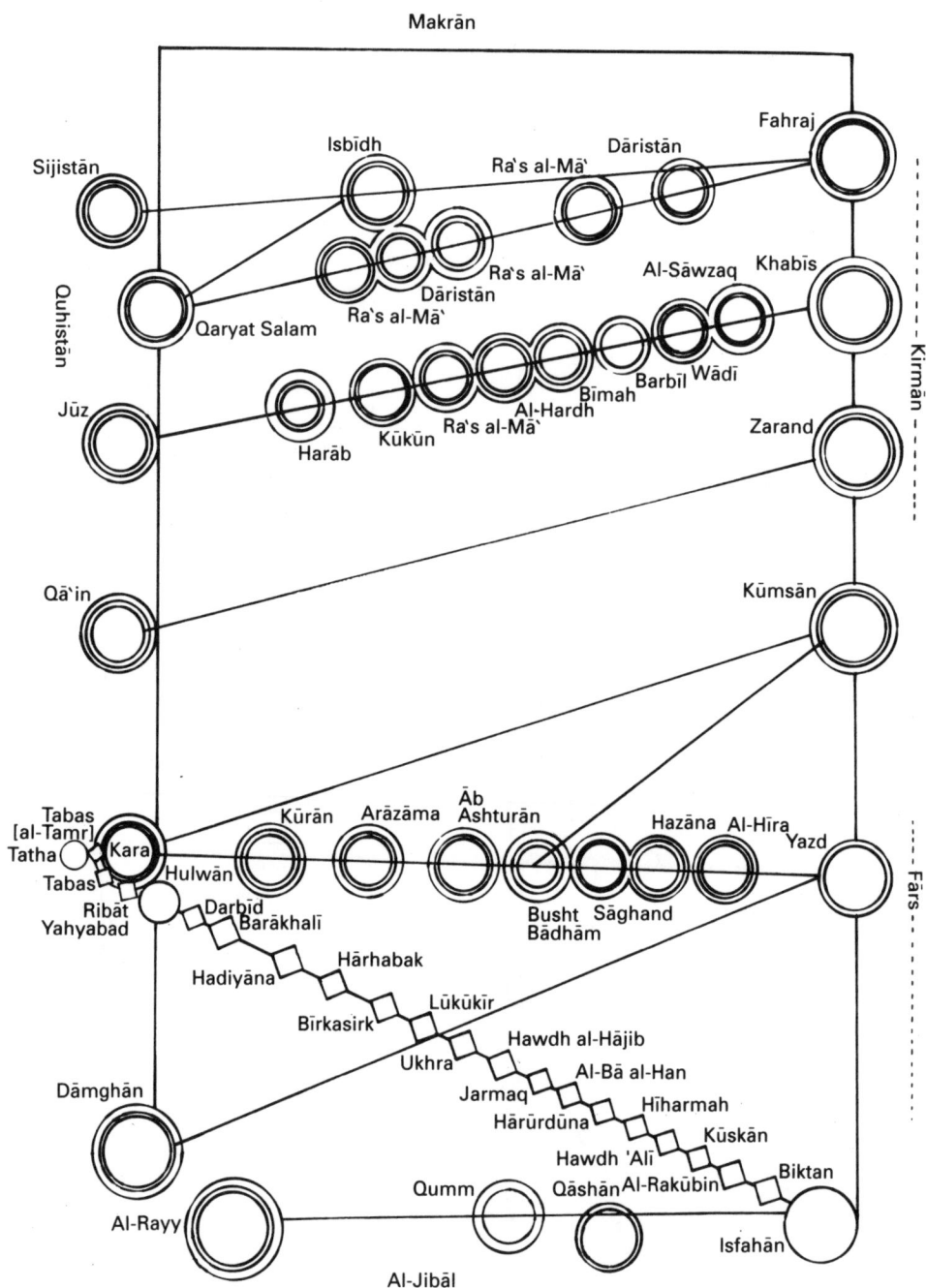

Map XX: The Persian Desert (see p. 395).
From Ayasofya, 2971 m. by kind permission of T.C.Basbakanlik, Kültür
Müstesarligi, Süleymaniye Kütüphanesi Müdürlügü, Istanbul, Turkey.

INDEX

A

adhān   82
afrūsha   290, 299
ahl al-hadīth   35
ansār   63
aqbiya [pl. of qabāʾ, q. v.]   264
ashāb hadīth i.q. ahl al-hadīth
ʿasīda   41

B

barīd   62
baysār   154

D

dāʿi   292
dānaq   85
dīnār   84
dirham; weight   84, 145, 152
dhimma   39
dihqān   227
durrāʿa   6

F

farāʾidh [pl. of farīdha q.v.]
farīdha   72
farsakh   2
fiqh   246

G

ghūta   137

H

hadīth   219
harīsa   37, 252
hayʿala   37

I

ihrām   70
imām   106
iqāma   196
izār   85

J

jarib   111, 366
jāmiʿ [pl. jawāmiʿ]   41

jihād   267
jubba   339

K

al-Khidhr   12
khutba   88, 201
kisāʾ   154

M

madhhab [pl. madhāhib]   34
mahdī   35, 240
mana   123
mann   295
maqān   67
maqsūra   73
marhala   89
mihrāb   44
minbar   23, 163
miʾzar (i. q. izār)   267
muadhdhin   106
muhtasib   85
mujtahid   35
musalla   70
mutʿa   37

N

nāʾūra   336
nayda   172
nīya   37

Q

qabāʾ   264
qibla   35, 128
qist   144
qubbayt   152
quhandiz   103
qunūt   37

R

rakaʿ   196
ridāʾ   339
rustāq   23

S

shariʿa   222

sikbāj   172
sunna [pl. sunan]   72, 222

T

takbīr, takbīra   37, 82
talbiya   71
tarāwīh [pl. of tarwīha]   85
tashrīq   38
taslīm, taslīma   37, 232
tawāf   66
tayammun   37
taylasān   6

U

ʿumra   70

W

wājib [pl. wājibāt]   72
waqf   128, 289
witr   37

CENTER FOR MUSLIM
CONTRIBUTION TO CIVILIZATION

The Center for Muslim Contribution to Civilization, a non-government,
non-profit making cultural organization, strives to lead Muslims and
non-Muslims alike to a better understanding of the Muslim contribution
to civilization and to a better knowledge of Islam.

Located in Doha, State of Qatar, the Center has the warm support of its patron,
the Emir of Qatar, H.H. Sheikh Hamad Bin Khalifa Al-Thani. Presenting
accurate translations of some of the best known works of the most eminent Muslim
savants, spanning the 800 years of the classical period of Islamic civilization
(c. 620 AD to c. 1500 AD), since its establishment in 1983 the Center has produced
nine volumes covering five major works in different fields of knowledge.

For further information on the work of the Center, all correspondence
should be directed to

The General Supervisor
Center for Muslim Contribution to Civilization
P.O. Box 327
Doha
State of Qatar
Arabian Gulf